Boris Pasternak

Pasternak by the sea, during a family vacation in Meriküla, a small resort town near Narva (Estonia), on the Baltic sea. Oil painting by Leonid Pasternak, 1910. *Pasternak Family Collection, Oxford, England.*

BORIS PASTERNAK

His Life and Art

By Guy de Mallac

Foreword by Rimvydas Šilbajoris

C.1

UNIVERSITY OF OKLAHOMA PRESS : NORMAN

By Guy de Mallac

Boris Pasternak (Paris, 1963; Turin, 1965)
Barthes (with Margaret Eberbach; Paris, 1971; Rome, 1973; Tokyo, 1974; São Paulo, 1977)
Boris Pasternak: His Life and Art (Norman, 1981)

Permission to quote excerpts from *Doctor Zhivago* and *I Remember* has been granted as follows:

From DOCTOR ZHIVAGO, by Boris Pasternak, translated by Max Hayward and Manya Harari, revised by Bernard Guilbert Guerney. Copyright © 1958 by William Collins & Co. Ltd. Copyright © 1958 by Pantheon Books, Inc. Reprinted by permission of Pantheon Books, a Division of Random House, Inc.

From I REMEMBER, by Boris Pasternak, translated by David Magarshack. Copyright © 1959 by Pantheon Books, Inc. Reprinted by permission of Pantheon Books, a Division of Random House, Inc.

Library of Congress Cataloging in Publication Data

Mallac, Guy de, 1936
    Boris Pasternak, his life and art.

    Bibliography: p. 405.
    Includes index.
    1. Pasternak, Boris Leonidovich, 1890–1960.
2. Authors, Russian—20th century—Biography.
I. Title.
PG3476.P27Z736   891.71'42 [B]   81-2616
                                             AACR2

Copyright © 1981 by the University of Oklahoma Press, Norman, Publishing Division of the University.
Manufactured in the U.S.A.
First edition.

for
all those
who have found inspiration
in Pasternak's achievement

and

for
Robert
who already loves
to weave his own stories

and

to
the memory of
Max Hayward

Contents

Foreword, by Rimvydas Šilbajoris   *Page* xi
Preface   xvi
Further Acknowledgments   xxiii
Note on Transliteration   xxv

Part One   More Than Crossing a Field:
   A Biography
1   Moscow Childhood: *Art, Mysticism,
    and Ecstasy*, 1890–1903   2
2   The Roots of Genius   18
3   The Adolescent as Musician,
    1903–1909   32
4   Between the Moskva and the Lahn:
    Philosopher in Moscow and Marburg,
    1909–1913   50
5   A Poet's Vocation, 1913–1917   74
6   The Poet After October,
    1917–1927   88
7   A Second Birth, 1928–1932   116
8   The Genre of Silence, 1933–1938   134
9   The War: A Liberation, 1939–1945   164
10   Toward *Doctor Zhivago*, 1945–1957   180
11   The Pasternak Affair, 1958–1959   220
12   The End and Its Aftermath, 1960–   258

Part Two   Pasternak's Historical
   Universe: *An Interpretation*   285
Introduction   287
13   Zhivago Versus Prometheus: *The
    Poetics of Nature*   288
14   The Voice of the Street: *The Poetics of
    History*   296
15   Individual Human Life: *A Personalist
    Philosophy*   310
16   Dissolving in All Others: *Community
    and Suprapersonal Values*   318
17   The Fire of Thy Hands: *The Religious
    Dimension*   326
18   The Poet as Critic: *Views on Art and
    Literature*   338

Appendices   357
1   Chronology of Pasternak's Life   358
2   Chronology of Pasternak's Works   374

Notes   376
Bibliography   405
Index   427

Illustrations

Pasternak by the sea, 1910	*Frontispiece*
Map showing Pasternak's birthplace in Moscow	*Page* 4
Trubnaia Square, Moscow	6
In old Moscow	6
Akulina Gavrilovna	7
Moscow School of Painting, Sculpture, and Architecture	8
Rainer Maria Rilke	12
Young Boris writing	13
Boris Pasternak with his family	15
Rosa Pasternak	22
Leonid Osipovich Pasternak	23
The poet's parents	25
Pasternak's sisters	27
Leonid Pasternak	28
Boris as an adolescent	34
Alexander Scriabin	35
Pasternak and his brother, Aleksandr	38
The Pasternak family	39
The family on vacation, 1907	43
Scriabin at the piano	44
Boris improvising at the piano	45
Score of Prélude	46
Leo Tolstoy	53
The University of Marburg	57
The University of Marburg	58
The Kalbstor, Marburg	59
Pasternak's university registration	60
The Schützenpfuhl Inn, Marburg	60
Pasternak's residence in Marburg	61
Frau Ort's house	61
View of Gisselbergerstrasse, Marburg	62
Hermann Cohen	63
Paul Natorp	64
Saint Elizabeth's Church, Marburg	66
Saint Elizabeth of Thuringia	67
Portrait of Pasternak, 1914–15	74
Plaque on house in Marburg	73
The children of Leonid and Rosa Pasternak	76
Pasternak in 1913	77
The family in 1916	78
The family, ca. 1913–16	79
Boris in the Urals, 1915	86
Pasternak in the 1920s	90
The family, ca. 1917–18	91
Pasternak, ca. 1918–20	93
Pasternak writing, 1919	94
Pasternak, early 1920s	102
Portrait of Pasternak by Iurii Annenkov	103
Pasternak, Maiakovskii, Brik, Shklovskii, and others	104
Pasternak, 1923	106
Pasternak, ca. 1925–26	110

Pasternak, Eisenstein, Maiakovskii, and Lili
   Brik, 1920s 112
Pasternak, photograph by Bogatyrev 113
Cover of *Second Birth* (1932) 118
Frontispiece in *A Tale* (1934) 120
Pasternak, April, 1930 123
Titsian and Nina Tabidze 125
Pasternak, 1933 140
Pasternak at the First Congress of Soviet
   Writers, 1934 143
Malraux, Meierkhold, and Pasternak 144
Pasternak, Rozhdestvenskii, and Petrovskii,
   1934 145
Lavrushinskii Lane, Moscow 155
Pond in Peredelkino 156
Pasternak in Christopol, early 1940s 166
Pasternak and Tregub at the front, 1943 175
Pasternak and his son Leonid 175
Pasternak in Peredelkino, late 1940s 176
Pasternak, his son Leonid, and Nina Tabidze 177
Pasternak at his desk in Peredelkino, 1947 177
Pasternak and Anna Akhmatova, ca. 1946–47 183
Olga Ivinskaia 185
Inscription from Pasternak to Ivinskaia 188
Ivinskaia 189
Ivinskaia beside the pond in Peredelkino 191
Pasternak with Ivinskaia and her daughter,
   Irina 191
Pasternak with Ivinskaia in Peredelkino 192
Pasternak in 1948 193
Russian Orthodox church in Peredelkino 197

Pasternak in Peredelkino, 1954 207
Pasternak, spring, 1956 210
Pasternak at his desk, 1958 222
Pasternak soon after the announcement of the
   Nobel Prize award 227
The poet in Peredelkino 228
Pasternak, 1958 229
Pasternak, 1958 230
Pasternak and his wife, Zinaida 231
Cartoon in *Krokodil*, 1958 234
Pasternak and Irina 243
Pasternak with Georges Nivat 245
Pasternak with Ivinskaia 245
Pasternak in front of the dacha in Peredelkino 247
Pasternak, 1958 251
Pasternak in his garden, 1959 253
Pasternak with Heinz Schewe at a performance
   of *Faust* 254
After the performance 254
Pasternak in Peredelkino 255
Certificate awarded to Pasternak by the
   American Academy of Arts and Letters 260
Pasternak working in the garden, 1958 261
Pasternak in his study 263
Pasternak's funeral, June 2, 1960 268
At the gravesite 268
At the gravesite 269
Pasternak's grave and monument 270
Pasternak's son Evgenii and his family 275
Bust of Pasternak 281
Pasternak in his garden in Peredelkino 284

When he had nearly crossed the distance of his life, Doctor Zhivago thought to himself of his friends Gordon and Dudorov: "The only live and radiant thing in you is that you lived at the same time as I and that you knew me." It may have been sad to see them as mediocrities, but this was not Zhivago's point. It was not a self-centered comparison between great people and small, but rather the contrary—the description of an individual consciousness aware of being engulfed by the meaning of life, radiant and shared by all. To have known Zhivago was to have received from him a gift of himself, best understood, perhaps, as the gift of recognition of that in our own selves which is great and hopeful about humanity. And since Zhivago is not, of course, an actual person but rather the author's creative word, no different in this respect from any other word in prose or poetry written by Pasternak, knowing Zhivago actually amounts to knowing the artist himself in the dimension of his achievement. It means to have received from him that gift of himself as an artist which, as Pasternak once put it, is his joy of life and which alone remains immortal.

The Russian readers have long known Pasternak as a poet, both in his original verse and in his many translations, notably of Shakespeare. His poems are a constant, living presence in the minds of many, providing a mode of inner response to the meaning of their country's life in history. During long years of military strife and peacetime domestic terror, many readers have come back again and again to the rapture for life; to the ardent, naïve vulnerability of love; and to the magic word-music in Pasternak's poems, reading them as the language of the human spirit describing its own revolutionary development underneath all the mechanical restructuring of society and reshaping of the earth—a revolution, as Guy de Mallac points out in the present book, toward "a spontaneity of the mind considering its liberty in the world."

Foreword
By
Rimvydas Šilbajoris

Pasternak's poetry also contributes to a pattern in the readers' minds—a model of the history of Russian culture at variance with the Marxist-Stalinist premises forced upon the Soviet public like potatoes in the time of Catherine the Great. This pattern consists of a free interplay of ideas, emotions, and perceptions among the best creative minds in Russia speaking for themselves in their own works and outside the limits of time. It is an ongoing conversation between Pasternak and Pushkin, Pushkin and Akhmatova, Pasternak and Blok, Pasternak and Mandelstam, and again Pasternak and Mayakovsky, and now the poets of the Leningrad underground, about the mystery of life and the mystery of death, about creativity and the creation of wonders.

Unfortunately, most Soviet readers still do not know the novel *Doctor Zhivago*, a work that Pasternak himself regarded as the centerpiece of his accomplishment as an artist. Instead of being allowed to judge for themselves whether this novel does indeed represent the inner essence of the Revolution and a testimony to the epoch more profound than Sholokhov's *The Silent Don* and certainly much superior to Aleksei Tolstoy's *Road to Calvary*, these readers have been enduring the indignity of simply being told that Pasternak's novel, his voice, is not the voice of the Revolution but a slander against it.

Western readers, on the other hand, have had *Doctor Zhivago* available to them for a long time now, and some still remember very clearly the scandalous events that surrounded the novel's first appearance, the shameful persecution of Pasternak (in a context that forced him to refuse his Nobel Prize), and his ultimate death with the wolves of the regime howling all around him. The tragic nature of this series of events and the great emotional involvement of both supporters and detractors of Pasternak have made it difficult for many readers in the West to think and write perceptively about the artistic merits of the novel and about Pasternak himself—who in the first place was certainly not a household name among Western readers at large before the publication of *Doctor Zhivago*. Gradually a number of intelligent and useful discussions did appear in journalistic criticism and in the academic press, but the average educated reader still does not have a sufficiently clear perspective on Pasternak, first, because he knows very little about Pasternak's poetry, and, second, because we have so far lacked a good, extensive biographical treatment of the poet.

De Mallac's book presents us with a reasoned, objective assessment of Pasternak's work and a lucid, affectionate story of his life. More than that—it also probes into the political, philosophical, and religious issues surrounding the events of the Russian Revolution in the light of Pasternak's own encounters with them, both personally and intellectually. A very welcome additional feature of the book is the succinct yet informative discussion of Pasternak's background and his family, underlining the talents of his father as a painter and those of his mother as a musician. The entire cultural ambience of the often brilliant intellectual and artistic circles of Russian society at the turn of the century is depicted here in a way that contributes a great deal to our understanding of the thoughts, aspirations, and illusions of people very much like them in the novel *Doctor Zhivago* itself.

The course of Pasternak's life appears in the book as a series of crucial decisions in response to oppressive outside events or ego-shattering discoveries about himself, both of which could make a person of lesser quality retreat to some refuge requiring the betrayal of his talent before himself and others. With Pasternak, however, every loss and blow of fate produced an ardent and life-affirming response in which the act of renunciation and sacrifice inspired a new vision of reality suffused with previously unseen poetic light. The decision to give up the piano because of his imperfect ear for music led Pasternak to listen carefully to the inspired reasoning of the Marburg philosopher Hermann Cohen; rejection in love revealed a world transformed with poetic truth; the vicissitudes of Stalin's terror plunged him deep into the translation of Shakespeare and Goethe, to give a contemporary Russian idiom to this universe of voices free from time and outrageous fortune; and the agony of his last days irradiated him with the light of sunny, enduring humanity. Every crucible thus became an experience akin to the act of artistic creation wherein, as Pasternak himself said, we cease to recognize reality, it appears to us under some new aspect, and, as we give this aspect a name—the result is art.

Pasternak spoke of these crucibles in his *Safe-Conduct* and *Sketch for an Autobiography* but in the manner of an artist involved in his own creative processes, without the benefit of the detached perspective of a thoughtful biographer. Guy de Mallac does give us such a perspective, and with it some new insights as well. Thus, in discussing the various turning points in Pasternak's life, he also reveals certain patterns of events and actions of people involved in them that throw an unexpected light on the role of some of the major figures in *Doctor Zhivago*. He establishes, for instance, that the writer Alexander Fadeev, a pillar of the Soviet literary establishment, and Pasternak's neighbor in Peredelkino, "functioned as Pasternak's protector and patron—much in the way in which Evgraf functioned toward Zhivago in Pasternak's novel, this very type of relationship being characteristic of the era." Similarly, Zhivago's outburst of creativity after Lara leaves him in Siberia is likened to the "creative self-renewal" induced by Pasternak's "stormy passion" for Ida Vysotskaia and by her rejection of him in Marburg. The intertwining lines in Pasternak's life and art are described here in a fashion reminiscent of the crossing of fates in Zhivago's poem "Winter Night," a work of creative imagination fulfilling itself together with the development of its author's own destiny. Such insight also helps us understand what Pasternak had in mind when he called his *Safe-Conduct* both an autobiography of himself and a biography of Rainer Maria Rilke; the creative spirit of one man was the life of another.

In the second part of his book the author points up certain dominant aspects of Pasternak's work as an artist, a critic, and a devout Christian thinker with roots in the Hebraic tradition. Pasternak is understood here as basically an anti-Promethean writer, one whose notion of human fulfillment through natural values clashes with the Promethean dream of the Soviet era, the dream of subduing nature instead of inscribing oneself in it, as Pasternak once said in praise of Chekhov, "on equal terms with clouds and trees." This opposition extends itself to human relationships not only in the context of nature but also in the context of the city, where the Soviet Revolution was born and eventually betrayed by the dogmatism of the regime. In this connection Guy de Mallac points out that *Doctor Zhivago* was not, as some had taken it to be, a short-sighted critique of the transitional vicissitudes of Soviet life in the twenties but was rather an indictment of the horrors of Stalinism that followed. From such a perspective Pasternak's emphasis on the importance of free subjectivity, on the meaningful function of an individual, also acquires an aspect of reaction against the abuses of Soviet social engineering. The individual freedom of the artist, his subjectivity, is also understood not as an isolating force but as a uniting one in a manner different from the Marxist view of the functioning of human community. To quote de Mallac: "If for Marx the only things that count are relationships arising from production . . . for Pasternak all that counts . . . is the relationship that arises from love." From this follows the understanding of the very meaning of life as a "dissolving of oneself in all others," indeed, "as if a gift."

One of the important aspects of Guy de Mallac's own gift to us is that it may help reestablish in our minds the relevance of Pasternak's thought and art to those ideas in our own time that seem to be accomplishing a spiritual revolution aimed at restricting the mechanized value systems of our civilization and at reconciling people with grass, birds, and all other living things for the sake of continued survival together on the spaceship *Earth*.

Boris Pasternak

Preface

Living a life is more than crossing a field.

> Pasternak, "Hamlet"[1]

Heeding your living trace,
Others will tread your path
Step by step.

> Pasternak, "It's Bad Taste to Be
> Famous," *When Skies Clear*[2]

Paradoxical and multifaceted, Boris Pasternak's personality eludes facile characterization. Who was the *true* Pasternak? The worshiper of Aleksandr Scriabin converted to Kant? The philosopher-turned-artist, the musician-turned-poet, the poet stammering with emotion and captivating his audience with his "scattered" speech as he recited his already famous verse? The generous and ardent friend and lover? The gentle maverick who unaccountably enjoyed Stalin's tolerance, if not admiration, and who mysteriously survived the purges of the 1930s? The self-effacing translator secluded in his dacha yet acclaimed for his *Hamlet* by countless Soviet playgoers? The middle-aged poet become the "grand old man" of Russian poetry, transfixing capacity crowds in postwar Moscow? The tragic victim of the "Pasternak affair" raging around his *Doctor Zhivago*? One critic has aptly observed that Pasternak's biography "may be regarded as a chain of metonymic jumps: from music to philosophy, from philosophy to poetry, from poetry to prose, frequenting this or that literary group, then breaking with it."[3]

Paradoxical too is the task of the biographer endeavoring to re-create Pasternak's life. For any such endeavor seems to contravene the feelings of the poet who on the one hand strove to "immerse himself in obscurity / and hide his footsteps in it" and on the other hand intimated that he had conveyed in his autobiographical writings everything there was to say about his life.[4]

These writings, however, confront the reader with many unsolved questions, prominent among which are the matter of Pasternak's complex relationship to Stalin and that of his attitude toward Christianity. Such a consideration has moved me to attempt a delineation of the main stages of the poet's rich existence, one that will, I trust, reveal for the reader new threads of a tapestry until now hidden in the shadows.

In many ways Pasternak occupies in his national and international literary age a place analogous to the one Goethe occupied in his age. Yet until now there has not appeared a portrait, drawn from the information that became available in the 1960s and 1970s, of the interrelated strands of life and art of a figure of this magnitude. This work aims at filling that gap—with some limitations, to be sure. What venture is free from any?

Almost every page of this book recounts some aspect of Pasternak's cultural and aesthetic universe—in particular his life-affirming philosophy—that inspired me to undertake the work and sustained me through its conception and progress over more than two decades. These aspects are discussed specifically in Part Two—an interpretative assessment of Pasternak's oeuvre.

During the first few years of my interest in Pasternak, in certain respects the concern for critical distance played a role secondary to my admiration for him and his work. In recent years, however, I have become increasingly aware that, while Pasternak was a being of flesh and blood—and to that extent alive, credible, and close to our all-too-human passions and weaknesses—the internal spiritual harmony he achieved was less than Goethean, or even less than Tolstoyan. I have not been overly pious, nor have I considered excluding or downplaying facts that may well jostle the undiscriminating admirer of Pasternak. Thus the reader will discover that Pasternak was intensely aware of his own strange lack of willpower. His impressionability was a necessary prerequisite for his aesthetic perception and his elaboration of art forms, and what he himself viewed as his excessive sensitivity and attachment to "places . . . trees . . . people" at times "took the place of work" and of any other sustained endeavor.[5]

In a similar vein some of those close to Pasternak in the Soviet Union may not like the revelation that, like a great many other Russian intellectuals on extended stay in Germany in the early 1920s, he probably gave serious consideration to remaining there as an émigré. And for all his nobility of soul, at times there appeared in him a strain of very worldly, almost petty vanity (which is here alluded to on occasion). Sometimes close to being a Brechtian hero, and suffering acutely—out of his deep sensitivity—from the diverse cultural, moral, and social ailments of his society and the modern world, Pasternak as I see him nonetheless emerges as a man of stauncher moral fiber than that of almost every one of his contemporaries among Soviet Russian intellectuals.

I believe that this book reveals why the most talented and sincere of the Soviet writers of the 1960s and 1970s have looked up to Boris Pasternak for inspiration. His novel *Doctor Zhivago* was the first important landmark in the post-Thaw* struggle of Soviet Russian writers for freedom of expression—a struggle that was to be continued in such other landmark events as the appearance in 1963 of Aleksandr Solzhenitsyn's novel *One Day in the Life of Ivan Denisovich*[6] and the trial in 1966 of Andrei Siniavskii and Iulii Daniel. Although, in the tradition of Pushkin and Chekhov, Pasternak refused to conceive of himself as a "master" with "precepts," it has nonetheless become increasingly clear that he has indeed had heirs and disciples on the Soviet literary scene—foremost among whom have been Andrei Voznesenskii, Bella Akhmadulina, Evgenii Evtushenko, and Iosif Brodskii (Joseph Brodsky). In Chapter 12, the concluding biographical chapter, I discuss the statement by one critic about the emergence in the 1960s of "a sensitive, a gifted, a Pasternakian intelligentsia." I believe that this book will make it possible for those readers who have heard primarily of the contemporary generation of Soviet writers to discover some of their cultural and aesthetic roots as well as the immediate background of today's Soviet literary scene.

My acquaintance with Pasternak's work began in the mid-1950s, well before the appearance of *Doctor Zhivago*, when I was an undergraduate student in France. Later I gave an informal talk to fellow students about the novel, which by the summer of 1958 had begun attracting the attention of readers in France. Some of the points I made then were an embryonic formulation of an interpretation that has gone through various stages of elaboration to become Chapter 14 of this book.

My small volume *Boris Pasternak*, published in Paris in 1963, happened to be the first book written about Pasternak in French—almost immediately to be followed by the distinguished publications of Michel Aucouturier and Jacqueline de Proyart.† During much of the past two decades I have maintained a continuing interest in Pasternak's work. The encouragement of the University of

---

*The process of liberalization that developed in the Soviet literary milieu in the wake of Stalin's death in 1953 came to be termed the Thaw.

†See Bibliography.

Oklahoma Press and of my friend Ivar Ivask has been a decisive factor that impelled me to pursue an investigation of Pasternak's life—about which I had already collected much material by the early 1970s.

My interest in Pasternak had been reflected in many endeavors from the early 1960s to obtain fuller biographical information about him. In 1960, I became acquainted, first, with his younger sister, Dr. Lydia Pasternak-Slater, and soon thereafter with his other sister, Dr. Josephine Pasternak, both of Oxford. Over many years they have made available to me much helpful information with the same generosity that they have shown to all other serious students of Pasternak.

During the visits I paid to Moscow in 1962 and 1963, I met several of Pasternak's relatives, including his brother, Aleksandr Leonidovich, and his family; Pasternak's widow, Zinaida Nikolaevna; and his son Leonid. Letters I received in the 1960s from his brother and his son Leonid helped me clarify various points of Pasternak's life. Pasternak's older son, Evgenii, subsequently supplied me with information and much valuable insight into a number of puzzling issues. For such assistance, to all of Pasternak's relatives, also including his niece, Dr. Ann Pasternak-Slater, of Oxford, I wish to express my heartfelt gratitude.

In an endeavor to obtain more specific data on various stages in Pasternak's life, I have sought out a number of individuals. In the 1960s, I was in contact with Princesses Olga and Vera Lvov (Lwoff), the daughters of Prince Aleksei Evgenevich Lvov (the director of the Moscow School of Painting, where Pasternak's father taught and lived with his family) and nieces of Prince Georgii Evgenevich Lvov (who was briefly head of the Provisional Government in 1917). From these two childhood—and lifelong—friends of Pasternak's sisters I obtained interesting information. I was also kindly granted the opportunity to consult Princess Vera Alekseevna's unpublished reminiscences about her childhood.

Through the kind offices of a fellow scholar of Slavic literature, Countess Jacqueline de Proyart, I obtained information from the by then elderly Ida Davidovna Vysotskaia-Feldzer, for whom Pasternak formed a youthful romantic passion (which he described in his autobiography *A Safe-Conduct*).* Another eyewitness of Pasternak's early childhood, during the family's connection with the Moscow School of Painting, was the noted artist and professor of sculpture Boris Daniilovich Korolëv, whom I questioned in Moscow about his recollections as a student of Pasternak's father. I obtained important information from Mme Z. I. Kanchalovskii, a good friend of Pasternak and his first wife, whom she saw frequently during the last few years of their marriage. Conference and correspondence with the late Sir Maurice Bowra, of Oxford University, yielded valuable specifics about the history of the nominations of Pasternak for the Nobel Prize. I also interviewed in great detail several eyewitnesses, both Western and Soviet-born, of Pasternak's funeral in May, 1960—a remarkable event if only in that it turned out to be the first cultural-political manifestation of the Soviet intelligentsia in the post-Stalin period, one that would be followed by other acts of civic courage by that intelligentsia.

*In this book quotations from Pasternak's works are cited with page numbers to the editions indicated in the Bibliography.

However controversial (in a few instances) their links with Pasternak from the viewpoint of many of the poet's relatives, friends, and admirers, I have interviewed a number of individuals who were in contact with Pasternak either for one-time visits or interviews or for continuing dialogue or association. Among these I must mention the late Arkadii Belinkov, Sir Isaiah Berlin, Henrik Birnbaum, Olga Carlisle, Ivo Fleischmann, David Floyd, George Katkov, Boris Daniilovich Korolëv, Iurii Vasilevich Krotkov, Ralph Matlaw, Nils Åke Nilsson, Georges Nivat, Hélène Peltier-Zamoyska, Jacqueline de Proyart, Angelo Maria Ripellino, Renate Schweitzer, and Fëdor Avgustovich Stepun. Over the years I have also had the opportunity to converse with various Soviet writers and obtain a sense of their impressions of their fellow writer. In addition, in the 1960s I was fortunate to be able to converse with Pasternak's friend of many decades Nina Aleksandrovna Tabidze. I corresponded with Heinz Schewe, who kindly supplied photographs (some of them published here for the first time) taken in the period when he was in very frequent and close contact with Pasternak. To all these individuals I would like to convey heartfelt thanks. In the 1960s, Pasternak's Italian publisher, the late Giangiacomo Feltrinelli, willingly granted me access to archival material (mostly an extensive collection of press clippings), and I want to acknowledge that courtesy.

The interested reader will find in the Bibliography particulars of other materials, some of them unpublished, upon which I have drawn. I had access to the letters (still unpublished) that Pasternak wrote to Hermann Bauer, of Marburg, and to Angelo-Maria Ripellino, of the University of Rome. The many other letters to and from Pasternak published in various works in the Soviet Union, the United States, England, France, Germany, and Czechoslovakia have added significantly to the corpus of letters I had at my disposal. I have had access to about three hundred of Pasternak's letters; a significant edition of his correspondence will no doubt see the light before long, and another era may thus produce a still more detailed treatment of the poet's life. The timorous view, however, still held by several, that the time is not yet ripe for a biographical portrayal of Pasternak had to be discarded. The richness of the insight that materials I have collected give into Pasternak's life and art led me to believe that it was time to make that insight available to others.

Earlier versions of some of the chapters have appeared in the following publications, whose kind permission to adapt the material is hereby acknowledged: Chapter 4, *The Russian Review*; Chapter 13, *World Literature Today* (formerly *Books Abroad*); Chapter 14, *Fiction and Drama in Eastern and Southeastern Europe: Evolution and Experiment in the Postwar Period*, ed. Henrik Birnbaum and Thomas Eekman, Columbus, Ohio: Slavica, 1980; Chapter 17, *The Russian Review*; and Chapter 18, different versions successively in *Problèmes soviétiques*, *Sowjetstudien*, and *Russian Literature Triquarterly*. Elements of Chapters 1 and 2 appeared as "A Russian Impressionist: Leonid Osipovich Pasternak, 1862–1945," in *California Slavic Studies*, vol. 10. An early version of what has become Part Two of this volume was submitted as a doctoral dissertation at Cornell University. In even more embryonic form, some of the contents of Chapter 17 were presented in Chapter 4 of my earlier *Boris Pasternak* (Paris: Editions Universitaires, 1963).

For specific advice and much help with various aspects of my work at different points over a great many years, I am grateful to Michael Henry Heim. Christopher J. Barnes was particularly generous in placing at my disposal much enlightening documentation and information, including materials obtained from the Pasternak family archives and other archives in Moscow; dialogue with him resulted in marked improvement of an earlier draft of the text. I owe a special debt to those who were brave enough to read very substantial portions of the manuscript and respond with detailed comments: Ronald Walter, whose moral support also helped; Victor Terras; Walter W. Arndt; and the late Max Hayward, who from the early 1960s encouraged my work on Pasternak.

I owe special thanks to Diane Ewing, Priscilla Heim, Pamela Skinner, and Carol Bass Pyle, who at different stages of my work were involved in research tasks and gave editorial advice. Mary Alice Kitti deserves credit for careful editing of the manuscript.

Aside from being an assiduous proofreader and helping in many other ways, my wife, Gail, cooked thousands of delicious meals while this book was in the making. To boost my morale, my son, Robert, very thoughtfully devised an elaborate chart that helped me keep track of progress on individual chapters.

Irvine, California   GUY DE MALLAC

Further Acknowledgments

This book owes much to the thoughtful help of a number of individuals, in addition to those already mentioned. Gleb Struve and Jacqueline de Proyart generously placed at my disposal much helpful information and materials. For their help in providing some of the information or documents that I needed or suggestions concerning individual sections of my text, I wish to acknowledge here my gratitude to Michel Aucouturier, Hermann Bauer, Natalie Belinkov, Malcolm H. Brown, Henry W. Ehrmann, George Emery, Victor Erlich, Lazar Fleishman, the late Victor S. Frank, George Gibian, Henry Gifford, Nikolai Gogoleff, Michael Green, Olga R. Hughes, Albert Kaspin, Jerome Katsell, Ivar Ivask, Vladimir Lefebvre, Vladimir Markov, Alexander Marston, Jay Martin, Czesław Miłosz, Anatole Nalpanis, Dale L. Plank, Jeremiah Schneiderman, Heinz Schewe, Ingeborg Schnack, Erika F. Sheikholeslami, Richard Sheldon, Rimvydas Šilbajoris, Gerald F. Smith, Lucy Vogel, and Josette Wittorski, as well as a number of colleagues from the School of Humanities in the University of California, Irvine.

Over the years a number of research assistants and other students at the University of California, Irvine, helped me with various aspects of my research, including Natalie Aristov, Marianne Armstrong, Catherine Bowers, Curtiss Buttke, George Cheron, Kathleen Clancy, Gary File, Monika Freeland, Serge Gregory, Carol Hamilton, Richard Kopcho, Darlene Lister, Priscilla Newton, Keith Rosten, Kathryn Sanford, Francis X. Sheehan, Gregory Smith, Jeanne Stearns, Sandra van Löben-Sels, Rochelle Wandzura, Maryjean Wetherell, and Gail White.

In recent years I relied on the helpful services of Yvonne Wilson, Richard Milligan, Diana Lane, and other staff members of the Library of the University of California, Irvine, for providing a considerable proportion of the bibliographical items necessary for my re-

Further Acknowledgments

search, to supplement what I obtained at various libraries in the United States and Europe. A great believer in the book, Bertha Marston provided resourceful advice and thoughtful help in countless ways that far transcended the regular duties of a departmental secretary. My gratitude also goes to Toba Wheeler, who typed an early draft of several chapters, and to GiGi Gast, who typed more than one version of the manuscript in its entirety.

The University of California at Irvine granted me an unpaid leave of absence in 1976 and also provided financial assistance (such as a grant from the School of Humanities Committee on Travel and Research, which paid part of my expenses for a research trip to Europe in 1972, and some aid from the Graduate Division Research Fund), for which I am most grateful.

Brief excerpts from the following books are reprinted by permission of Pantheon Books, a Division of Random House, Inc.:

Doctor Zhivago, by Boris Pasternak, translated by Max Hayward and Manya Harari, revised by Bernard Guilbert Guerney. Copyright © 1958 by William Collins & Co., Ltd. Copyright © 1958 by Pantheon Books, Inc.

I Remember, by Boris Pasternak, translated by David Magarshack. Copyright © 1959 by Pantheon Books, Inc.

Irvine, California   GUY DE MALLAC

The system of transliteration used is that of the Library of Congress, with the omission of diacritical signs. A few exceptions have been made in favor of forms of names that are more familiar to most readers, such as Dostoevsky (instead of Dostoevskii), Tolstoy (rather than Tolstoi), and Scriabin (instead of Skriabin). Also some of the original west European spellings of certain Russian names have been retained (Ehrenburg instead of Erenburg). Mandelstam (the rendering in Latin script preferred by the poet himself) is used instead of Mandelshtam. Russian tsars are referred to as Alexander and Nicholas (not Aleksandr and Nikolai). In addition, exceptions are made for several artists, whose names are given according to the spellings they used outside Russia (e.g., Koussevitzky and Kandinsky).

Part One

More Than Crossing a Field

A Biography

1

Moscow Childhood

Art, Mysticism, and Ecstasy

1890–1903

I was from early childhood inclined to mysticism and superstition and seized by a craving for the providential. . . . I suspected all sorts of mysteries and deceptions around me.

Pasternak, *Sketch for an Autobiography*[1]

To the dreamer, the midnight hound,
Moscow is dearest in the world.
He's at home, at the very fount
Of all that the age is to unfurl.[2]

Pasternak, "Vesna" ("Spring")

Moscow had belonged to Pasternak from the time of his birth.

Nadezhda Mandelstam, *Hope Against Hope*[3]

Boris Leonidovich Pasternak, the first child of Rosa (Roza) Isidorovna Kaufman and Leonid Osipovich Pasternak, was born in Moscow on Monday, February 10, 1890.* At the time the family lived in a red-brick building across from the Orthodox Seminary on Oruzheinyi Lane. In *Sketch for an Autobiography*,† Pasternak recalled his early-childhood walks along this street with his *niania* ("nanny"):

The district itself was rather disreputable. It included such slums as Tverskie and Yamskie Streets, the Truba, and the Tsvetnoi Lanes [the lanes adjacent to Tsvetnoi Boulevard]. Again and again I found myself dragged away by the hand. Some things were not good for me to know, others were not good for me to hear. But my nurses and nannies could not bear solitude, and then we found ourselves surrounded by a motley company.[4]

Everyday life, even in such modest surroundings, involved expenses that often could barely be met out of Leonid Osipovich's meager earnings as a young artist. Some challenging academic commissions became available, however. During the year of Pasternak's birth his father was invited to be the chief art editor of the first illustrated edition of Mikhail Lermontov's complete works. This edition, produced by the publisher Kushnerev, celebrated the fiftieth anniversary of the poet's death, and Leonid Osipovich invited the leading artists of the day, including Ilia Repin, Valentin Serov, Vasilii Polenov, and Mikhail Vrubel, to contribute to it. Two years after Pasternak's birth, in the autumn of 1892, his father, together with the well-known Repin, Vasilii Vereshchagin, and Aleksei Kivshenko, was invited to illustrate a serialized deluxe edition of *War and Peace*.[5]

Such commissions helped the artist care for a growing household.‡ With the birth of their second son in 1893, a new nanny, Akulina Gavrilovna, came to work for the Pasternaks. Those early years in Moscow were difficult ones for the family, even though Leonid Osipovich had become busily engaged as an illustrator, editor, and teacher. Awareness of the hard times is reflected in the lullaby that Akulina Gavrilovna composed and sang to Pasternak: "Sleep, my child; when you grow older, your papa won't have to paint any more, but will have hired hands [apprentices] instead."[6]

The Pasternaks' financial circumstances gradually improved as the artist earned increased recognition. In the spring of 1893, at the annual Itinerants' (Peredvizhniki) exhibition (in which Leonid Osipovich displayed one of his paintings), an associate introduced him to Lev Nikolaevich Tolstoy, a regular visitor to

---

*Or Wednesday, January 29, Old Style (Julian calendar). For the period until 1918 all dates are given here according to the Gregorian calendar.

†Pasternak's autobiographical work, completed in 1956 under the Russian title *Avtobiograficheskii ocherk*, was published in England as *An Essay in Autobiography* (London: Collins and Harvill, 1959), and in the United States as *I Remember: Sketch for An Autobiography* (New York: Pantheon Books, 1959; reprinted, 1960, by Meridian Books, New York). Throughout the text of this book it is referred to as *Sketch for An Autobiography*, while in the notes it is cited by the abbreviation *IR*. See Notes for a list of abbreviations used in this book.

Works by Pasternak are cited in the English translations listed in the Bibliography.

‡After the birth of Boris, the Pasternaks had three more children: Aleksandr (b. 1893), Josephine (Zhozefina, b. February, 1900), and Lydia (Lidiia, b. 1902). For details on their lives and pursuits, see Chapter 6.

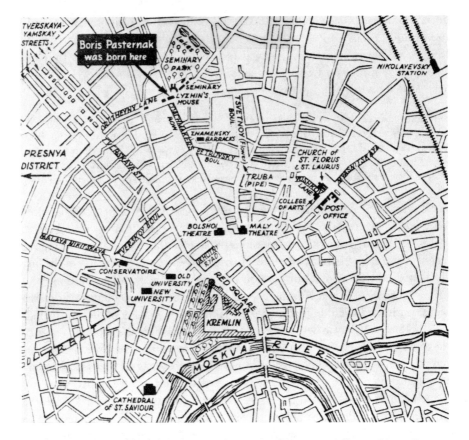

Map showing Pasternak's birthplace, in the center of Moscow. *Collins and Harvill Press.*

the Itinerants' exhibitions and a secret admirer of Pasternak's work.* Leonid Osipovich was then invited to call on Tolstoy at his residence on Khamovniki Street in Moscow. The Pasternaks became frequent visitors of the Tolstoys both in Moscow and at Iasnaia Poliana, Tolstoy's country estate. The friendship between the two families affected both the older and the younger members of each family, and, as Boris Leonidovich grew older, Tolstoy exerted an important literary and religious influence upon him.

When Pasternak was four years old, the family moved into a small apartment and studio at the Moscow School of Painting, Sculpture, and Architecture, after Leonid Pasternak was offered a professorship there.† Upon first being offered that position by Prince Aleksei Evgenevich Lvov (Lwoff), the school's new director

---

*The Itinerants (or Travelers or Wanderers) were members of the Society for Traveling Art Exhibitions, formed in 1870 and influential until the 1890s. Believing in depicting topics of contemporary interest and thereby denouncing inadequacies of the social order, they played a leading role in Russian art and fostered the concerns of a popular, democratic humanism.

†The Moscow School of Painting, Sculpture, and Architecture (hereafter referred to as the Moscow School of Painting) was affiliated with the Academy of Arts in St. Petersburg. It played an outstanding and progressive role in the history of Russian art, notably becoming a focal point for

(who was turning it into one of the most progressive art academies in Europe), Leonid Pasternak expressed both his delight in accepting and his fear that his being Jewish would stand in the way of the confirmation of the appointment by the trustee of the school, Grand Duke Sergei Aleksandrovich. The painter remarked:

I added that although I had been brought up in a Jewish family—admittedly religious but free from adherence to ritual—whose members, including myself, felt completely assimilated to our Russian surroundings, and although I believed in God but did not in practice belong to any religious denomination, I would never consider baptism as a means of facilitating my progress in life or raising my social status.[7]

Leonid Osipovich's appointment, "a thing unusual in those days, when civil servants had to belong to the Russian Orthodox church, or at least to profess another Christian creed," was approved, contrary to the artist's own expectations. The position carried an initial monthly salary of fifty rubles, later to be tripled.[8] Unexpected though the appointment had been, Leonid Osipovich soon felt completely at home at the school, where he and his family were to reside without interruption until 1911.

Of the family's new lodgings at 21 Miasnitskaia Street, Pasternak remembered that "the main building, which was old and beautiful, was remarkable in many ways." Miasnitskaia Street (renamed for Sergei Kirov in 1934) had in the nineteenth century become one of the main thoroughfares leading from the center of town to the three main railway stations. On the basis of what he saw when he was growing up, Pasternak later observed that around 1900 "Moscow was seized by the business fever of the great capital cities. . . . Brick giants, which seemed to grow imperceptibly, rose up to the very sky in all the streets." On Miasnitskaia and neighboring streets and lanes, however, most of the wooden or stone houses still had large gardens. Like those adjacent to it, the building where the Pasternaks lived was built in the eighteenth century for a noble family, but in the second half of the nineteenth century it became part of the central business district. Facing No. 21 was the Moscow Central Post Office, also an eighteenth-century building. On the school's spacious grounds were the main building (housing the classrooms) and three apartment houses for professors and servants. In the center was a well-planned garden with old trees and bushes; in the garden was a large workshop for manufacturing the plaster casts of sculptures and architectural ornaments used in lectures.[9] It was in this underground workshop—described by Pasternak in *Sketch for an Autobiography*—that the sculptures of Pavel Trubetskoi (such as his equestrian statue of Tolstoy) were molded.*

---

the development of realism in the second half of the nineteenth century. In 1918 it was renamed Vysshie khudozhestvenno-tekhnicheskie masterskie (Advanced Art Studios, also known by its acronym, Vkhutemas).

* A studio adjacent to Trubetstoi's was later to be occupied by Boris Korolëv, one-time student at the School of Painting under Leonid Pasternak, a participant in the students' demonstrations of 1905 at the side of Nikolai Bauman, a political exile, later a professor of sculpture in Moscow and a sculptor of a bust of Pasternak in the 1950s (Boris Korolëv, conversation of Fall, 1962 in Moscow with the author).

Trubnaia Square, in the Moscow neighborhood where Pasternak first lived (Irina Emelianova, Olga Ivinskaia's daughter, on the left). *Archives Georges Nivat.*

In old Moscow—a house whose appearance Pasternak very much liked (Irina Emelianova in the foreground). *Archives Georges Nivat.*

Akulina Gavrilovna, Boris's nurse. Pen etching by Leonid Pasternak, 1901. Collection of Josephine Pasternak, Oxford. *Photograph by Jeremy Moeran.*

Within the framework of a master plan to increase the school's revenue, a large exhibition hall was built in the winter of 1901 on the foundations of the work-shop. A consequence of this construction was that the wing of the building in which the Pasternaks lived had to be pulled down, and the inhabitants relocated. The Pasternak family was allotted a group of classrooms, recently transformed into a four-room apartment, on the top floor of the main building; most of the

The Moscow School of Painting, Sculpture, and Architecture, on Miasnitskaia Street, where Leonid Pasternak taught for twenty-five years. *Archives Georges Nivat.*

rooms were spacious, but since the building was circular at the angle of the rotunda, the Pasternaks' flat had one crescent-shaped unit—the bathroom and storeroom—which had huge dimensions and was always in complete darkness. The new exhibition hall, the first of its kind in Moscow, was regularly let for the Itinerants' exhibitions, which, together with similar art shows, brought in a substantial revenue. The Itinerants' exhibits were usually brought from St. Petersburg in the winter each year and stored in sheds opposite the back windows of the Pasternaks' apartment. Before Easter the caretakers would unpack the pictures and carry them across the yard to the hall. Pasternak described this yearly event:

Perching on the window sills, we watched them eagerly. It was in this way that there passed before our eyes the most celebrated canvases of Repin, Myasoyedov, Makovsky, Surikov, and Polenov, a good half of the reserves of paintings of our present-day picture galleries and State depositories.[10]

The properly "picturesque" atmosphere of the school obviously affected the child's development. Pasternak indicates that he was extremely sensitive to color and setting—to the "fairyland atmosphere" of the colorful Muscovite scenes that thrust themselves upon his perception: from the stuffed bears in the carriage establishments in Coachmakers' Yard near the school to the paintings by Vrubel and Serov hanging in the apartment of a family friend. Reviewing these early impressions, he tells us: "My sensations of infancy are made up of the elements of panic and ecstasy."[11] Fostered by Vrubel's hallucinatory canvases, this readiness for exaltation found strong stimulus in the sumptuous ceremonies of the Orthodox church, which the young boy began attending. His religious orientation was shaped decisively in early childhood, and his evolution toward Christianity was not unrelated to his exceedingly impressionable temperament.

The person who probably played the most important role in bringing young Pasternak, child of an assimilated Jewish family, to Christianity was his aged nanny, Akulina Gavrilovna. During the early years of his life she played for him a role similar to that performed by Maksim Gorky's old *babushka* ("grandmother") Kashirin or Aleksandr Pushkin's nanny Arina Rodionovna—that of educator of the child's sensibility through exposure to folk traditions and religious attitudes. There is no doubt about her strong influence on Pasternak both in his childhood, when she frequently took him to Orthodox services, and in his adolescence, when she talked to him about God (Pasternak mentions the Church of Saints Florus and Laurus, which stood in Iushkov Lane, adjoining the yard of the School of Painting, opposite the post office; perhaps it was to this church that Akulina Gavrilovna took him—or perhaps to the Church of Saint Euplos, which stood on the corner of Miasnitskaia and Markhlevskaia streets).* Pasternak himself describes Akulina Gavrilovna's impact on his spiritual makeup, as well as the power that Christianity was later to acquire over his life:

In my early childhood I was baptized by the nurse who looked after me, but because of restrictions upon the Jews and particularly in a family which was exempt from those restrictions and enjoyed a certain distinction as a result of its father's artistic achievements, the fact of my baptism was accompanied by various complications and remained semi-secret and private, thereby providing me with rare and exceptional inspiration rather than calm habit. But I believe this to be the source of my originality. During the years 1910–1912, when the main roots and foundation of that originality—together with my vision of things, of the world, of life—were taking shape, I lived most of my life in Christian thought.[12]

Although he found inspiration in Christian thought as a child and adolescent, for many decades circumstances did not permit him to attend church regularly or to participate openly in the life of the Orthodox church. But the church's sensuous pageantry, orchestrated with elaborate choirs, incense, and rich costumes (all of which, incidentally, was denounced by the austere philosopher of Iasnaia Poliana), had left its imprint on the sensitive youth. The religious awareness fostered by Pasternak's more sober parents was attuned to Tolstoy's moralistic, nondenominational faith.

The strength of the elder Pasternaks' friendship with the novelist was confirmed through their common sense of moral righteousness and similar interest in the arts, which during their encounters were often discussed and sometimes performed. One such encounter took place in November, 1894, when Tolstoy, accompanied by his daughters, attended a concert at the Pasternaks' given by Rosa Pasternak and two professors from the Moscow Conservatory, the violinist Ivan Grzhimali and the cellist Anatolii Brandukov. That occasion turned out to be memorable for Pasternak, who later conjured up the memories the child had pre-

---

*Pasternak's younger sister, Lydia, has confirmed that he was "frequently" taken to church by Akulina Gavrilovna. Lydia Pasternak Slates, conversation with the author, September, 1980.

served of the event that evening, when he saw Tolstoy and his friend Nikolai Ge, the painter,* for the first time:

I was awakened in the middle of [the concert] by a sweetly poignant pain, more violent than any I had ever experienced before. I cried out and burst into tears from fear and anguish. . . . The candles flickered, blinking like eyelashes, just as though the tobacco smoke had got into their eyes. They lit up brightly the polished red wood of the violin and cello. The grand piano loomed black. The frock coats of the men loomed black. The women emerged from dresses up to their shoulders, like birthday flowers out of flower baskets. . . .

. . . With [that night] my memory became active and my consciousness was set into motion. [From then I] believed in the existence of a higher heroic world, which must be served rapturously, though it might bring suffering. [13]

This is one of the instances of the combined working of "panic and ecstasy" that Pasternak remembered; in this instance bliss was reinforced by the poignancy attendant upon devotion to the "higher heroic world."

Another spectacle had a strong impact upon the impressionable child. In 1894, from the balcony of the school, young Pasternak and his family witnessed the funeral procession of Tsar Alexander III. The poet later described the scene:

[The crowd] pushed back to the very edge of the pavements by the drawn-up lines of soldiers, absorbed every sound as completely as water is absorbed by sand. Church bells began ringing slowly and dolefully. A sea of hands rose like a wave in the distance which rolled on and on, farther and farther. Moscow was taking off her hat and crossing herself. [14]

Two years later, from the same balcony, Boris Pasternak witnessed the coronation parades of the new tsar, Nicholas II. It is significant that the catalysts for mnemonic reactions in the young Pasternak tended to be experiences of sensuous displays laden with emotional import: parades, a funeral, a chamber concert, Vrubel's intriguing and somewhat frightening pictures. A very few years later another vivid imprint was left on him by the "tropical parade" of a circus. In the spring of 1901 the eleven-year-old Pasternak was taken to the Moscow circus, where he witnessed the parading of "a detachment of Dahomey horsewomen." [15] In *A Safe-Conduct* he described his impression of this spectacle, from which he derived his first physical sense of woman:

. . . for me the first awareness of woman was linked with a sense of naked ranks, of serried anguish, a tropical parade to the sound of a drum. . . . I became the slave of forms earlier than I should have done because, in these women, I had seen too early the form of slaves. [16]

This evocation echoes his earlier impressions on the shabby streets of Moscow, where the "hysterical wailings" he heard induced in him "a feeling of terrifying

---

*The distinguished elder Itinerant Nikolai Ge became very fond of young Boris, frequently seating him in his lap when he visited Leonid Osipovich's studio (Leonid Pasternak, *ZAP*, p. 143; (see page 376 for a list of abbreviations of works cited).

and breath-taking pity for woman."[17] Such was probably the beginning of the shattering effect of woman's state on the poet-to-be, who would view woman as an especially frail, vulnerable being, particularly worthy of sympathy—a feeling that reverberated in many of his works, from *A Tale* (1934) through *Doctor Zhivago* (1957) to the poem "Women in [My] Childhood" (1958).

These early impressions alternated with the enlightening glimpses of his father's professional pursuits, which were constantly focused on new, challenging tasks. Around that time, Leonid Osipovich executed many convincing, informal drawings and paintings of Tolstoy, his family, and life around Iasnaia Poliana; these portraits of the elderly writer were pronounced to be more successful than those of all other artists—not excluding Repin. A crucial development in Leonid Osipovich's career occurred in 1898, when Tolstoy commissioned him to illustrate *Resurrection*. On an October day in 1898, when Tolstoy's daughter Tatiana came to say that her father wanted him to illustrate a novella he was writing, Leonid Osipovich promptly took the night train to Iasnaia Poliana, where he spent a few days with Tolstoy going over the text and planning his task.[18] The text of that novella kept growing, finally to become *Resurrection*. Pasternak has left a vivid description of his father's work:

There was the risk that the illustrations of the original text would be at variance with the corrections subsequently introduced into it. But my father's sketches came from the same source whence the author obtained his observations, the courtroom, the transit prison, the country, the railway. It was the reservoir of living details, the identical realistic presentation of ideas, that saved him from the danger of digressing from the spirit of the original.[19]

The illustrator had to work intensively to meet the deadlines, since the Petersburg publisher, A. F. Marks, put great pressure on both artist and writer (Tolstoy himself was in a hurry to publish *Resurrection*, for the proceeds were to be devoted to helping the Dukhobors, a Christian sect, emigrate to Canada). At Iasnaia Poliana, Leonid Osipovich read the text of the novel during the day, discussed the illustrations with Tolstoy in the evening, and worked on the drawings in ink wash at night. In six weeks (first at Iasnaia Poliana, then back in Moscow) he finished thirty-three illustrations. When the assignment was completed, Leonid Osipovich fell ill from exhaustion.[20] In observing his father's working habits during this period, young Pasternak must have learned at least one lesson: the artist must work hard and conscientiously—at times even feverishly—to meet his commitments.

This was the period when both Tolstoy and Leonid Pasternak were visited by a guest from western Europe who was to become a good friend of the Pasternaks. In 1899 the young Austrian writer Rainer Maria Rilke had paid a visit to the Pasternaks' Moscow home. On May 31, 1900, the family, upon leaving Moscow from the Kursk Railway Station for their annual vacation in Odessa, met Rilke and his mistress, Lou Andreas-Salomé, the remarkable German-Russian woman of letters who had also been closely associated with Friedrich Nietzsche and would become so with Sigmund Freud. Pasternak's parents were delighted to see Rilke again. During the journey Rilke obtained helpful advice from Leonid Pasternak about visiting Iasnaia Poliana, the result being that he and his companion got off the train near Tula and went to call on Tolstoy. For Boris Leonidovich, this encounter with Rilke was the beginning of a spiritual dialogue that would be decisive for his creative life—indeed, he started his spiritual autobiography, *A Safe-Conduct*, with a description of the meeting of 1900 and dedicated the book "To the memory of Rainer Maria Rilke." Of this meeting with Rilke, Pasternak wrote:

Rainer Maria Rilke, ca. 1899–1900, during his visit to Moscow. Sketch by Leonid Pasternak. *Pasternak Family Collection.*

Young Boris writing.
Sketch by Leonid
Pasternak, July 20, 1898.
*Ashmolean Museum, Oxford
University.*

Although I knew the language perfectly, I had never heard it spoken as he spoke it. For this reason, there on the crowded platform, between two ringings of the bell, the foreign man seemed to me a silhouette amongst bodies, a fiction in the midst of the unfictitious.[21]

It was the manner in which Rilke used his native tongue, not his accent, that impressed the young Pasternak; specifically, the *creative* spirit of the man, expressed through his speech, generated for Boris Pasternak the "'higher reality,' the only 'real reality' which comes into being, . . . where the energy of the creative, artistic spirit has been at work shaping and molding the inchoate mass."[22] Rilke's volume of poetry *The Book of Hours* (*Das Stunden-Buch*)—in part the outcome of his Russian journey—was to reveal a God whose presence is felt on a romantic, mystical plane and is suggested by the inexhaustible flow of forceful images and rushing rhythms. The poet sent a copy of this book to Leonid Pasternak as a Christmas present in 1906.[23] It soon fell into the hands of Boris Leonidovich, making a great impression upon him.[24] Few meetings would be so crucial to Pasternak's poetical self, but such chance encounters on trains—poignant, emotionally enduring, even fateful—recurred in striking fashion throughout his life and work.

Exceptional encounters, such as those with Tolstoy, Ge, and Rilke were not, of course, the youngster's only pedagogical experiences. At first Pasternak was educated privately, his parents (most often his mother) and tutors attending to his studies. In a letter to his parents he later wrote, "All that I am, I owe to you: education and influence as well as intellectual patrimony."[25] Pasternak also spoke gratefully of his first teacher, Ekaterina Ivanovna Baratynskii, a writer of children's stories and translator of children's books from English: "She taught me reading and writing, elementary arithmetic and French, starting from the very beginning, that is, how to sit on a chair and how to hold a pen in my hand." Pasternak's familiarity with German began as he prepared to enter the German-speaking Petropavlovsk Grammar School in Moscow (it is not clear whether he did indeed enter the Petropavlovsk school; if he did, he could not have stayed more than a year, then transferring to the Moscow Fifth Gymnasium, a preparatory school). French and German seem to have been the only languages young Pasternak learned besides Russian; it is most likely that he did not speak Yiddish (no more than Mandelstam did). Russian he spoke with all the native charm of "a Muscovite born and bred," singing and mooing with his personal modulations, as noted by Nadezhda Mandelstam, who felt that his "born sense of music . . . gave his speech an orchestral quality."[26]

In 1901, Pasternak entered the second grade at the Moscow Fifth Gymnasium. As a result of the Vannovskii reform,* the curriculum provided for the study of the natural sciences (we know that botany fascinated Pasternak), while retaining the study of classical Greek (which he also took up) and Greek antiquity. The somewhat exclusive school with its unusual curriculum later counted among its pupils the poet Vladimir Maiakovskii, who was in the same class as Pasternak's brother, Aleksandr, and whom Boris Leonidovich then knew only by sight. Still another schoolmate, G. Kurlov, later gave a graphic and perceptive characterization of young Pasternak:

In everything . . . he possessed some kind of mixture of conscientiousness [*akkuratnost*] and carelessness; but more of the latter. For example, the parting in his thick, raven black hair was never straight. He was awkward in his movements, something that was especially noticeable in gym class, where we had a few very good gymnasts. He seldom took part in pranks, but always joined in with the group of pranksters if they were threatened by some kind of punishment.[27]

---

*In his modernization program, carried out in 1901–1902, the tsarist minister of education Pëtr Semënovich Vannovskii (1822–1904) bolstered the science curriculum at the secondary level, reducing the emphasis on classical languages.

Boris Pasternak in his school uniform with his father, mother, and brother, Aleksandr, early 1900s. His sister Lydia is in the nurse's arms. *Arthème Fayard.*

To his classmates Pasternak thus appeared markedly different, and somewhat estranged from many of their concerns. A combination of "carelessness," awkwardness, and aloofness (characteristic, incidentally, of the Baudelairean "Albatross" as symbol of the poet) was to remain typical of Pasternak in later years.*

The years of Pasternak's studious adolescence coincided not only with a general turn against positivism but also with the more specific beginnings of the Russian Symbolist movement, to which he began paying attention while he was still a schoolboy. The period 1890 to 1903 was heralded by Dmitrii Merezhkovskii's "decadent" manifesto, "On the Cause of the Decline and on the New Trends in Russian Literature." Soon afterward such early Symbolist poets as Konstantin

*In the poem "L'Albatros" (1859, later included in his collection *Les Fleurs du mal*) the French poet Charles Baudelaire (1821–67) presented a portrait of the albatross as a giant who soars on high on his large white wings but whose very size is a hindrance as he clumsily attempts to walk the deck of a ship and becomes an object of derision. For Baudelaire the albatross was an apt symbol for "the Poet," who tends to appear "comical" and out of place when, descending from his lofty sphere, he is "exiled" in everyday life.

Balmont and Valerii Briusov were published regularly in collections and in journals. Despite the differences in medium and emphasis, the Symbolists were united in their attacks on social preachment and realism and in their individualistic and romantic reevaluation of time-honored artistic concepts.

During the decade also were born an unusually imposing group of future literary masters: Ilia Ehrenburg (1891–1967), Osip Mandelstam (1891–1938), Konstantin Fedin (1892–1977), Vladimir Maiakovskii (1893–1930), Isaak Babel (1894–1941), Sergei Esenin (1895–1925), and Eduard Bagritskii (1895–1934). Crucial to Pasternak was the dialogue that he conducted with several of them, and the interaction of their respective fates is alluded to in this book. The world they were born into, while intensely vital and divisive on the literary front, was also one of recurrent economic crises and political repression, dissent, and assassination. Little attuned to such effervescence, Nicholas II (whom Iurii

Zhivago would view in a very unfavorable light)[28] held to the stale official policy of "Nationalism, Orthodoxy, and Autocracy"—a reactionary stance that only fed the flames of political and social revolt and exacerbated the critical and hostile attitudes of the intelligentsia. The intellectual effervescence rooted in those times was bound to engage and excite a precocious adolescent like Pasternak, who soon realized that the society he lived in was doomed to undergo radical upheavals.

On a more subjective plane, the childish dependence on "superstition and ecstasy" and faith in the providential fostered in Pasternak an enduring belief that major life decisions should hinge upon "signs from above" and that thus life is preordained. Such a belief was to be reflected in the adolescent and the young man as he came to grips with the delicate issues of intellectual and artistic commitment and the choice of a career.

2

The Roots of Genius

True greatness . . . is always a question of inheritance and filiation.

Marina Tsvetaeva, letter of 1927 [1]

Referring to his total absorption in poetry in the summer of 1913, Pasternak wrote that during that period, for the first time in his life, he "wrote poetry not as a rare exception, but often and continuously, as one paints or composes music." It is significant that, to describe his dedication to this art form, he compared it with the two artistic activities practiced in his home: painting (by his father) and music (by his mother). Later, in autobiographical statements, Pasternak emphasized his debt to his parents.

Alluding to Boris's talent, his friend the poet Marina Tsvetaeva* once commented: "True greatness never attributes itself to itself—in which it is doubtlessly right. This greatness is always a question of inheritance and filiation."[2] While no theory of heredity is postulated here, the pages that follow explore the filiation of genius through exposure to unique cultural sophistication.

It is impossible to overestimate the significance to Boris Pasternak of growing up in constant contact with his father's artistic pursuits. For three decades or so, as child, adolescent, and young man, Boris gazed at thousands of canvases and illustrations: strong vibrant oils, delicate pastels, and the sketches, etchings, and engravings of the most gifted Muscovite draftsman of his generation. Most important, Boris saw not only the finished works but the works in progress. He saw art as the product of a life, not merely in its finished singularity. It is therefore appropriate that this life of Pasternak include a discussion of his father's life and work.† Such an approach would have greatly pleased Pasternak himself, the greatest admirer of Leonid Osipovich's art.‡

Leonid Osipovich tells us in his memoirs that the Pasternak family counts among its ancestors Don Isaac ben-Iuda Abravanel (also spelled Abrabanel and Abarbanella, 1437–1508), a theologian and exegete sufficiently favored by Alfonso V of Portugal to be made minister of state to Ferdinand and Isabel, before he became minister in the employ of the Republic of Venice.[4] Little else is known of the Pasternak ancestors. Leonid Osipovich, who had seen a genealogy kept in the family (also referred to by Boris), reported that the Odessa Pasternaks descended from a Sephardic family that settled in southern Russia in the eighteenth century, rather than from Ashkenazy Jews of central or eastern Europe, which is the background of most Jewish families in Odessa.[5]

The son of Osip and Lea Pasternak, Leonid Osipovich was born in the Italianate harbor town of Odessa on April 4 (March 22, O.S.), 1862. In his memoirs he vividly recalled the sights, smells, and sounds of what he called "our legendary courtyard." His father, tending to innkeeping—one of the few positions open to Jews in the Pale of Settlement—rented out the courtyard to peasants spending the night in town. Teeming with topknotted peasants, petty landowners, rural merchants, carts, and animals, this remnant of Old Russia was terrifying to the young, impressionable Leonid.[6]

---

*Pasternak's relationship with Tsvetaeva is discussed in Chapters 6, 8, and 9.

†For a fuller treatment of Leonid Pasternak's life and work, see Guy de Mallac, "A Russian Impressionist: Leonid Osipovich Pasternak, 1862–1945," *California Slavic Studies* 10 (1977).

‡Pasternak dwells on his admiration for his father's work in letters he wrote to his parents in the 1930s (see Boris Pasternak, *Fifty Poems*, trans. Lydia Pasternak-Slater, Introduction, pp. 15–16).

When the boy was only seven, an aged house porter—to whom he later referred as "my first Lorenzo Medici"—commissioned him to draw pictures of borzois hunting rabbits to decorate the walls of his hut.[7] Later young Leonid Osipovich talked his mother into paying for informal "lessons" from various artistically inclined boarders. To pursue his vocation, however, Leonid Pasternak had to wage a long and unrelenting struggle against the prejudices typical of the extremely modest, unsophisticated, and unenlightened milieu to which his parents belonged. To them "daubing" ("*maliuvane*") held no significant guarantees for the future. Even his usually tender mother occasionally took extreme measures, such as burning the young artist's drawings in the stove, and, after he completed the classical gymnasium in 1881, exerted pressure on him to become a doctor or a lawyer.[8]

Leonid Osipovich began his search for a stable profession with the study of medicine in Moscow. In 1882, after an unnerving spell with dissection, he lost patience and applied for admission to the Moscow School of Painting, Sculpture, and Architecture. Although he lost the only opening to Countess Tatiana Lvovna Tolstoy, he would return there a few years later as an instructor. Leonid Osipovich then began studying law at the University of Odessa, from which he graduated in 1885. From 1883 to 1885 he studied at the Royal Academy of Art in Munich. There, while working under Ludwig Herterich and suffering many privations on a shoestring budget, he made the decision to devote himself exclusively to painting. Thus he was turning his back on the law studies that, in deference to parental concerns, he had pursued in absentia while in Munich and successfully completed in 1885.[9] In 1887 he returned to Moscow.

All Moscow was soon stirring with talk about this young artist's work, especially his widely exhibited sketches and portraits. The major patron of Russian art, Pavel Mikhailovich Tretiakov, bought several of Pasternak's more dramatic works. When Pasternak finished his first major canvas, *Letter from Home* (*Pismo s rodiny*, 1889), Tretiakov bought it straight from the easel for two thousand gold rubles. Soon Pasternak was unexpectedly invited to be the art director of the Moscow-based *Artist* (*Artist*), and was commissioned to create the set for Antonii Arenskii's opera *Raphael*.[10]

In 1894, Leonid Pasternak was accepted into the faculty of the School of Painting, Sculpture, and Architecture as an instructor in figure painting. This appointment (which he held for over a quarter of a century) provided him with a stable income and opportunity to work steadily. He formed such an attachment for the Moscow school that he later rejected offers of other positions. Such an opportunity arose in 1907, when, together with Valentin Serov, he was suggested by the school to the Petersburg Academy of Arts as a possible candidate to succeed Ilia Repin.[11] Shortly thereafter, during a visit to England, Edgar Vincent (later Baron d'Abernon of Esher and a trustee of both the National and the Tate galleries) tried to persuade Leonid to settle in London, assuring him that he would have a successful career in that country; however, once again he would not leave the school he so loved.[12]

During the period when he was first essaying his talent in Moscow, a major development had taken place in Leonid Osipovich's personal life. During a stay in Odessa in 1885, he had met Rosa Isidorovna Kaufman, a concert pianist who was teaching in the Conservatory of Music. He soon fell in love with her, and after his initial success in Moscow had reassured him about his own professional future, he married the brilliant young pianist on February 14, 1889.[13]

Rosa Isidorovna Kaufman* was born in Odessa on February 7, 1867, to a Jewish family of limited means.[14] Her father, a small-scale soda-water manufacturer, was well known locally as a chess player and mathematician, though he had had no formal schooling. Her mother, Berta, was practical-minded, with a predilection for music in general and an interest in singing in particular.

At the age of five Rosa began piano lessons with a local music instructor and gave her first public recital when she was eight (at that time many Odessa parents, especially Jewish ones, were exerting pressure to achieve on their musically talented offspring). Her second concert, in 1878, was attended by all the major music critics of Odessa, including the noted pianist and composer Ignatz Tedesco. Tedesco coached her for another public concert, which also took place in 1878 and included a Mozart concerto, a trio by Giovanni Pergolesi, a sonata by Alessandro Scarlatti, and several pieces by Frédéric Chopin.[15]

When she was thirteen, Rosa Isidorovna started on the first of many concert tours in southern Russia. She encountered enthusiastic audiences everywhere, but particularly in Kiev, one of Russia's most important musical centers. A major event in the young artist's life was her meeting with the famous composer and pianist Anton Grigorevich Rubinstein. Visiting Odessa in 1881, Rubinstein, skeptical about young prodigies, only reluctantly agreed to hear Rosa Isidorovna play. Captivated by her exceptional talent, Rubinstein himself conducted a concert in which the young artist reportedly performed Liszt's piano rendition of Beethoven's Fifth Symphony. Rubinstein persuaded her to give concerts in Moscow and St. Petersburg, introduced her into a friendship with his sister, Sofiia Grigorevna, and thereafter was a constant source of encouragement. That same year a concert tour took Rosa Isidorovna to Kiev, Poltava, Moscow, and finally St. Petersburg, where she accompanied the famous violinist Pablo Sarasate before an audience of several thousand. The tour was interrupted, however, when she caught a severe cold and then typhoid fever.

In October, 1882, Tedesco sent the young pianist on a series of concerts abroad, but again the concerts were interrupted, this time by the news of Tedesco's sudden death, which left Rosa in a state of shock. Nevertheless, the following year she undertook a highly successful concert tour throughout the major cities of Russia and Poland. Upon completion of this tour, following Rubinstein's advice, she went to Vienna, where she spent the next few years studying under the famous Polish pianist Theodor Leschetizky (whose other noteworthy pupils included Ignace Jan Paderewski, Artur Schnabel, and Benno Moiseiwitsch).

The Viennese received Rosa Isidorovna's concerts enthusiastically. One news-

---

*Her first name has variously been rendered as the more formal Rozaliia, Roza, and Rosa (she used the last form while in the West); her last name, as Kaufman, Kaufmann, and Koffmann.

Rosa Isidorovna Pasternak playing the piano. Sketch by Leonid Pasternak, 1914.

paper even ventured the opinion that in some of her interpretations she surpassed Liszt and Rubinstein.[16] When she returned to Odessa in the late 1880s, she was appointed advanced instructor at the conservatory.

For many years after her marriage to Leonid Osipovich, Rosa Isidorovna was to devote herself almost exclusively to family life and her husband's career. After the young couple settled in Moscow, she took upon herself a great number of tasks, from entertaining the many models who sat for her husband and planning and organizing exhibitions of his works to caring for the four children. To these combined ends, despite poor health, she applied all her energies and affections.

In the 1890s and 1900s musical evenings frequently took place at the Pasternaks', occasionally attended by the Tolstoys. Rosa Isidorovna often performed, and other musicians attended or participated (including Artur Nikish, Serge Koussevitzky, Scriabin, Josef Hofmann, Fëdor Chaliapin, and Jascha Heifetz, whose portraits Leonid Osipovich would sketch).[17]

If one is to believe the accounts given by her daughters—in which much more than token filial piety is evident—there was indeed a uniquely convincing quality to Rosa Pasternak's musical interpretations. Josephine Pasternak has said of the effect on her father of her mother's playing: "Like the rest of us, like audiences in her younger days, he [Leonid Osipovich] became overwhelmed by the manifestation of life's drama, of its irreconcilable duality of pain and joy, as one experienced an almost mystical identity of life and music when Mother played."[18] This quality may well have been the decisive element accounting for the mystical impact on her four-year-old son Boris of that chamber concert in November, 1894 (described in Chapter 1). As he grew up, "accustomed to the sound of the piano in the house"[19] and to such captivating performances, it was natural that young Boris (further stimulated by his mother's superlative interpretations of Scriabin's music) should decide on a musical career, dedicating himself to composition from 1903 to 1909. After he abandoned music for philosophical studies, it was once more his mother's musical talent that facilitated his pursuits. She saved a sum from fees for private music lessons and offered it to her older son with the advice to study abroad.[20]

In 1907, after a long interruption for family duties, Rosa Isidorovna resumed her concerts. What proved to be her final concert in Moscow was arranged by Serge Koussevitzky and took place in the Great Hall of the conservatory on November 11, 1911, when she performed the piano part in a Tchaikovsky trio.[21] Shortly thereafter, in 1912, she suffered a heart attack and took a cure abroad, in Bad Kissingen. She once more had to give up public performances.[22] In 1921, because of her heart condition, she again went to Germany, this time accompanied by her husband and two daughters.

Though Rosa Isidorovna never again performed in public, she continued to play privately, mostly in the evening, after she had attended to household duties and helped her husband. Josephine Pasternak recalls that in the 1930s, after a particularly stirring performance by his wife, Leonid Osipovich said in a voice of pure admiration: "I now realise that I ought not to have married you. It was my fault. You have sacrificed your genius to me and the family. Of us two, you are the

Leonid Osipovich Pasternak, self-portrait. Etching. *Alexander III (Pushkin) Museum, Moscow.*

greater artist."[23] Rosa Pasternak's selfless sacrifice of a brilliant career was not in vain, however. It fostered the growth of other remarkable talents in the family.

During the years following his marriage to Rosa Isidorovna, Leonid Pasternak's development as an artist took a unique path. From the 1890s on he exhibited with the Itinerants. Very soon afterward, however, he began painting typically impressionistic studies, much to the dismay of senior, orthodox Itinerants such as Konstantin Savitskii.[24] Under the influence of the French Impressionists and the German "Secessionists" of the 1890s, he early developed an exceptionally subtle sense of texture and an ability to record transient effects of light and movement while retaining firmness and vitality of color. Using the palette typical of Russian iconography, with its Oriental dusty blues and dark reds, as well as bolder colors, he developed into one of the most representative of Russian artists. Sir Maurice Bowra suggested that Pasternak's artistic goal was "to bring more light and color into painting, and to get away from the sombre tones and the glutinous quality of the preceding generation."[25] To reach that goal, even when he focused on movement and nuances of color in the background, he was always also concerned with the underlying structure. An extraordinary draftsman himself, whose artistic credo was bound up with his faith in the continuity of art, he believed that draftsmanship was the cornerstone of all art, and in this connection he quoted and analyzed statements by Michelangelo, Dominique Ingres, and Eugène Delacroix supporting this credo. The supreme mastery of Rembrandt's drawings and sketches served him as an inspiration and ideal. He insisted that draftsmanship constituted, as it were, the rudiments of artistic literacy.[26] If his first sketch did not catch the essential character of his subject, he felt that he had failed and must start again. This extraordinarily talented draftsman was obviously fascinated by the linear patterns afforded by subjects in a number of domestic poses (sitting, reading, sewing, or leaning over a table to write or to drink).

Leonid Pasternak introduced significant innovations on the Russian artistic scene as he resolutely broke with the subject-dominated, historical approach of the Itinerants and contributed significantly to the renaissance of Russian art at the turn of the century through his pioneering efforts in the graphic arts. Under his influence engraving, lithography, etching, and illustrating (all of which in his eyes constituted independent aspects of the fine arts) began a revival in the early 1890s in Moscow, where they had been sadly neglected. Good examples of this revival, through which the artist attracted the attention of connoisseurs, were his epoch-making illustrations for Tolstoy's *Resurrection*, as well as an altogether different kind of achievement: the illustrations for Mikhail Lermontov's *Masquerade* (*Maskarad*), which he did for the Lermontov jubilee edition of 1891.[27] His contourless, contrastless style of line drawing consists not of "lines" properly speaking but of combinations of extremely tenuous strokes and hachures. The Russian art critic A. A. Sidorov pointed out that such a technique came close to defeating the definition of modern graphics as practiced by Aubrey Beardsley and Konstantin Somov and stressed the merits of this original "impressionistic" and "tonal" variant. Sidorov went on to indicate that during the prerevolutionary period

The poet's parents: Leonid Osipovich Pasternak and Rosa Isidorovna Kaufman
Pasternak. Painting by Leonid Pasternak, 1927. *Pasternak Family Collection.*

Leonid Pasternak became perhaps the most typical representative of tonal and
chiaroscuro graphics among Moscow artists.[28] It should be mentioned, furthermore, that Pasternak deserves the credit for enriching the curriculum of the
Moscow School of Painting with a special graphics department and for endeavoring to establish a workshop where tempera, fresco, and pigment research could be
conducted.[29]

As an artist who experimented in remarkable ways with modes of conveying masses of light and air, he did not adapt to specifically post-Impressionist techniques; his method remained impervious to such trends as Cubism and was predominantly pre-Expressionist (with the reservation that his much bolder use of colors in his oil paintings of the 1920s possibly show the influence of contemporary trends in German painting). In this respect one sees a difference between his work and the more complex art of his friend Lovis Corinth (much of whose oeuvre is clearly impressionist, while some of his later achievements, characterized by extremely vivid, vibrant, and vigorous coloristic effects, definitely approach the style of Expressionism). Pasternak was unalterably opposed to nonfigurative art in its various forms and often condemned it, refusing to recognize the innovative aspects of Pablo Picasso's and Vasilii Kandinsky's work.[30] The tensions that occasionally developed between professors of the School of Painting, such as Serov and Pasternak, and students indicate a conflict of generations in terms of aesthetic conceptions.[31] Such conflicts were compounded by the politically motivated confrontations occurring between certain students and the school administrators, with Serov, Pasternak, Konstantin Korovin, and others sometimes caught in between.[32]

In spite of these divergences Leonid Osipovich should be credited with training a considerable number of notable artists in the solid pedagogy of his drawing classes. Prince S. A. Shcherbatov, among other students, praised him for systematically analyzing students' compositions and paintings by the masters, drawing upon his firsthand knowledge of the collections of western European museums, and discussing principles of art and achievements of great artists—in other words, for avoiding the "staleness" and "Moscow provincialism" typical of many art instructors of the time.[33]

Leonid Pasternak began by painting Russian scenes, widening his scope as he traveled abroad. He was noted for the wide range of his work (portraits, still lifes, interiors, genres, landscapes, illustrations, and others) and for his versatility of expression. Apart from the traditional media, he worked in a new technique of his own invention, a combination of tempera and pastel that enabled him to achieve a subtlety of expression he found otherwise unobtainable. To the intrinsic value of his portraits is added their documentary importance, for noted and distinguished men of arts and letters, science, and politics were among his sitters.* Bowra sees in all of Leonid Osipovich's portraits the same unerring sense of personality, the gift for presenting a man not through his superficial traits but through his inner character.[34] Leonid Pasternak was able to do this because he

---

*Including such prominent figures as, in Moscow, Vladimir Ilich Lenin, the statesman V. A. Maklakov, the learned Chief Rabbi of Moscow Jacob Mase, the poet Sh. An-Ski (author of *The Dybbuk*), Tchaikovsky, Prince Kropotkin, Gorky, Rilke, the writer Aleksei Remizov, the famous English *homme de théâtre* Edward Gordon Craig, Sergei Rachmaninoff, Tolstoy, Vladimir Soloviev, and the Belgian Symbolist poet Émile Verhaeren, and, in Berlin, Albert Einstein, Chancellor Gustav Stresemann, the Moscow philosophers Lev Shestov and Mikhail Gershenzon, the painters Max Liebermann and Lovis Corinth, the Jewish poets Chaim Nachman Bialik and Saul Chernichovsky, and the dramatist Gerhart Hauptmann. In addition, Leonid Osipovich did many sketches and portraits of his family, including his son Boris.

Pasternak's sisters, Lydiia (*left*)
and Josephine. Sketch by Leonid
Pasternak, November 20, 1918.
Ashmolean Museum.

brought a special touch of passion to his insight into human nature. He was uniquely perceptive in his depiction of youngsters; that appeared clear to Serov, who remarked that Pasternak had become a master in the art of capturing the essence of childhood.[35]

He brought to his paintings an unfailing sense of rhythm; a vibrating, animated quality; technical skill; and an overwhelming sense of integrity and purpose. He was equally felicitous in depicting youth and old age—his several portraits of Tolstoy are prime examples of his many-sided talent. One, suffused with warm yellow light, shows Tolstoy at ease with his family; another, a rough, brooding, weathered profile against a gray background, is suggestive of King Lear. The artist's watercolor *Tolstoy Reading* is both an essay in psychological portrayal and a study in contrast of color masses; it departs from the more subdued form of Impressionism practiced thus far by the artist in that it displays a less obvious concern for draftsmanship and a greater force in brushstrokes and color. Years later Boris Pasternak wrote his father:

I think that your best subjects were Tolstoy and Josephine [the artist's daughter]. How you drew them! Your drawings of Josephine were such that she grew up according to

Leonid Pasternak, self-portrait.
Ashmolean Museum.

them, following them in her life, developed through them more than through anything else.[36]

Aside from his work in pastel and oil, Pasternak's sketches in red pencil, chalk, and charcoal stand out conspicuously as his most abundant and successful achievements. The life expressed in the color of his oil paintings is conveyed through the lines of his sketches in charcoal or pencil—movement may originate with a chair or table, continue into a figure, and eventually reach into the background. Foreshadowing Boris Pasternak's critical-aesthetic formulation that stressed how he strove "to seize this whirling world as it was rushing headlong, and reproduce it,"* Leonid Osipovich's whole endeavor was to sketch nature *in movement*, and in his uniquely gifted way of accomplishing that through his mastery of the graphic media rests the originality of his achievement.[37]

The qualification of Pasternak as a "Russian Impressionist" may appear paradoxical—primarily because of the paradox inherent in the very concept of "Russian Impressionism." To start with, Impressionism came late to Russia; only after the turn of the century were French Impressionist paintings introduced there—thanks to the art patron Sergei Shchukin, who began purchasing them in 1897, and to the exhibitions organized after 1899 by the World of Art movement.[38] It

*See Chapter 18.

was not until the major Golden Fleece exhibition * of 1908 (twenty-two years after the eighth and last exhibition of the French Impressionists in Paris) that considerable numbers of Impressionist paintings were shown.[39] Although individual Russian painters, such as Serov, Pasternak, and Korovin, had become acquainted with French Impressionism during their stays in France before 1900, "Impressionist" was a term used very loosely in Russia—for example, to describe Kazimir Malevich's early works or Mikhail Larionov's work of the period 1902 to 1906.[40] Only in a derivative sense was there such a phenomenon as "Russian Impressionism." Thus Pasternak's belief in draftsmanship as the cornerstone of all art was the very opposite of Claude Monet's or Camille Pissarro's position, and the main thrust of French Impressionism does go against the tradition inherited from Ingres, whom Pasternak much admired. It is not surprising that among contemporary French artists Pasternak admired most Édouard Manet and Edgar Degas, the least "Impressionist" of the Impressionists.

No more than such other "Russian Impressionists" as Isaak Levitan, Korovin, or Serov did Pasternak have any direct impact on the Russian modernists who proclaimed their discoveries in the first quarter of the century. Like those artists of his generation, however, he fulfilled an essential function, representing a more or less "transitional" link between Itinerants and modernists and (clearly so in his case), in the demanding role of professor, providing rigorous training for two generations of artists. Although we believe today that, outside the realm of illustration and graphics, Pasternak's work was less innovative than that of such students of his as Konstantin Iuon, Ilia Mashkov, Kuzma Petrov-Vodkin, and especially Larionov, his achievement remains original and highly significant.

Leonid and Rosa Pasternak's move to Germany in 1921 turned out to have beneficial consequences for them, but at first it meant several lean years for the painter.† After a while, however, he began gaining recognition in Berlin, and a significant breakthrough was a one-man exhibition in the Galerie Hartberg in 1927. The pinnacle of his career was probably reached in 1932 with the publication of a monograph on his work by the noted art critic Max Osborn.

In spite of such recognition the Pasternaks left Germany in 1938, profoundly disturbed by an act ordered by the Nazi government: the impounding at the printer's and subsequent destruction of all copies of a new monograph devoted to the artist and containing illustrations by him and reproductions of his works.[41]

Because of this incident and their growing distaste for the darkening climate of Nazism, Leonid Osipovich and his wife planned to return to Moscow. First, however, they decided, upon their doctor's advice, to pay a visit to their married daughters, who were living in England, where they would have a chance to recover (Rosa Isidorovna's health had not improved, and her husband suffered from angina pectoris). There, on August 23, 1939, Rosa Isidorovna died suddenly at the house in which they were living in Streatham Hill, London. A week later

---

* Organized by the Symbolist monthly the *Golden Fleece* (published from 1906 to 1909).
† See Chapter 6.

World War II broke out, and Pasternak, with his two daughters and their families, moved to Oxford. Pasternak only slowly found consolation in his work, and owing to the war, age, and poor health, he led a very retiring life. Apart from his work, he spent his time with his children and grandchildren and in visits to the Ashmolean. Pressed by his daughters, he also wrote a series of reminiscences (he had earlier published a thoughtful monograph on Rembrandt, and also made notes and wrote reminiscences about various artists).[42] During his last years paucity of news from his sons and relatives in Russia disturbed him profoundly. The pacifist friend of Tolstoy suffered greatly from the reports of atrocities committed in the war. He continued to express the desire to return to the Soviet Union and spend the last years of his life as an art teacher there.[43] With an unfinished portrait of Lenin on his easel, he died in Oxford on May 31, 1945.

The cultural atmosphere of the household that the painter and the musician created together would have a profound impact on their son Boris. Because of Leonid Osipovich's position at the Moscow School of Painting, as well as his conspicuous success as one of the city's most prominent portrait painters, he and his family could develop contacts with some of the most exclusive artistic and social circles of the day. Without the very warm dialogue the painter conducted with such creative personalities as Rilke and Tolstoy, it is doubtful that his son would have been so decisively influenced by those writers' works. With Rilke, Leonid Pasternak maintained a cordial if irregular correspondence over a quarter of a century; the friendship was cemented during their several encounters in Russia in 1899 and 1900, as well as in a memorable encounter in Rome in 1904.[44] A friendly dialogue continued between the painter and the sage of Iasnaia Poliana over a seventeen-year period, from 1893 to 1910, the highlights of which were Leonid Pasternak's extended stays on the writer's estate in 1898, 1901, 1903, and 1909. At first intimidated by the association at close range with the towering figure of Russian letters, the artist was made to feel comfortable and then befriended by Tolstoy, who over the years shared his thoughts on many issues.* Rubinstein and Scriabin were representative of the musicians attracted to the Pasternak home by Rosa Isidorovna's art and drawn into the Pasternaks' circle of friends—further enhancing the already rich sophistication of their home.

This sophistication was matched by the pursuits of some of the Pasternaks' relatives. While we do not know much about the interests of Leonid Osipovich's sister Asia (who later lived in Petersburg) and of Rosa Isidorovna's brother Joseph, a doctor in Kasimov (in the Riazan region), Leonid Osipovich's first cousin Karl Pasternak, a rich Moscow merchant, was active as a philanthropist. Pasternak's first cousin Olga Freidenberg, of St. Petersburg, with whom he was to maintain a dialogue over decades, became a leading classical philologist and the first Soviet woman granted the doctoral degree.

*As the legacy of this dialogue the painter left a valuable memoir on Tolstoy—an 18,000-word narrative that breaks off at an account of the writer's funeral (see Leonid Pasternak, *ZAP*, pp. 169–212).

While primarily and authentically Russian, Pasternak's parents were also refined cosmopolitans who made many stays in Germany and Italy and for whom
communion with the mainsprings of western European culture was essential.* To
this orientation can be traced the three sojourns Boris Pasternak made in Germany, which provided the decisive enrichment of the artistic, intellectual, and
cultural soil out of which he grew.

Pasternak often acknowledged his debt to his parents. In a letter to them he
remarked, "When I was once asked for my biographical data, all I gave were data
on you two—is this not axiomatic?"[45]

While his relatives consider that Boris Pasternak was temperamentally closer
to his mother, they also grant that he had much in common with his father.† On
the plane of his art it is clear that he inherited from his father such traits as a
realistic bent, an objective observer's approach to nature, and careful draftsmanship. Soviet Commissar of Culture Anatolii Lunacharskii referred to Boris Pasternak in the 1920s as a "brilliant . . . poet-Impressionist," several critics have
given him a similar label, and even in the last years of his life he would view
himself as "a colorist." His father's impact on him went further, however. He
took to heart advice that Leonid Osipovich often gave him: "Be honest in your
art, and your enemies will be powerless against you." All his life Pasternak had
the strongest admiration for his father's achievement, as reflected in a letter he
wrote to Leonid Osipovich at age forty-four, recollecting what his father had
achieved upon reaching that age in 1906: "You were a real man . . . a Colossus,
and before this image, large and wide as the world, I am a complete nonentity and
in every respect still a boy as I was then [in 1906]." Against the background of
this almost overwhelming sense of the superiority of his father's merits, Pasternak
felt some dismay about what he viewed as the "incongruous smallness" of the
recognition the painter gained—a circumstance that taught him the hazards inherent in the artistic career.[46]

As time went by, however, Boris Pasternak developed a growing awareness of
the uniqueness of his talent and viewed with repugnance analyses aimed at reducing him to a mere convergence of cultural factors. Thus toward the end of his life
he wrote to his friend Boris Livanov with some irritation: "I hate it when you trace
my origins from refinement, from consciousness, from my father, from Pushkin,
from Levitan. Things that exist in their own absolute right have no need for a
pedigree."[47]

*See below, Chapters 3, 4, and 6.

†Pasternak always showed great deference to his father; thus he never addressed him by the
familiar *ty* ("thou") but used the more polite, formal *Vy*. Josephine Pasternak, conversation with
author, September, 1980.

3

The Adolescent as Musician

1903–1909

More than anything else in the world I loved music; more than anyone else in music—Scriabin.[1]

Pasternak, *A Safe-Conduct*

During the second decade of his life Pasternak nurtured strong interests in music, literature, and philosophy—while he also had a firsthand acquaintance with painting. His combining such interests (sometimes dramatically changing his preference among them) has come as a surprise to those unfamiliar with the cultural milieu to which he belonged. We should keep in mind that such pathfinders of modernism as Stéphane Mallarmé, Richard Wagner, and Scriabin were bent on breaking down the barriers between the arts, or bringing various art forms into a cosmically integrated drama, and that in the wake of such conceptions a shift from one art form to the other did not represent such a radical step as it would in a more rigid, less imaginative cultural context. It is characteristic that, when evoking the upsurge of modernistic art in the 1900s, Pasternak should list in the same breath of enthusiasm "the youthful art of Scriabin, Blok, Komissarzhevskaia, Belyi—advanced, gripping, original."[2] Encompassed by these names under a single rubric are such art forms as orchestral music, musical drama, the theater, the prose novel, the essay, and poetry. Of these artists Scriabin was the first who—through his controversial personality and creative endeavors—had a strong influence on Pasternak, from their meeting in 1903.

In the 1890s the music of Scriabin, a leading young composer, began reflecting the theories of Arthur Schopenhauer, Richard Wagner, and Friedrich Nietzsche, while attempting to solve the problems that engrossed Claude Debussy, Stravinsky, and Arnold Schönberg.

The sophistication of Scriabin's techniques of composition made him akin to those who followed "decadent" trends (as they were generally labeled) in other art forms. Such stylistic innovation and experimentation paralleled the most exciting endeavors in other aesthetic realms, such as the new techniques devised in literature by the Symbolists. Modernist experimentation in various art forms was a single topic for young Pasternak; he is reported to have begun a conversation about Sergei Prokofiev, gradually switching the subject to Guillaume Apollinaire, or to have begun discussing the painter Mikolajus Čiurlionis and veering to the subject of dissonance in music.[3] Toward the end of Scriabin's life, the Symbolists expressed strong faith in his genius, and Konstantin Balmont (who shared the composer's love of the sun and light) wrote an enraptured pamphlet entitled *Light and the Color Symphony of Scriabin*. Although Scriabin's works began reflecting more impressionistic, mystical, and revolutionary tendencies, he adopted and reformulated theoretical concerns into a new artistic credo: music as a vehicle of personality and a way of illumination. He was soon to acquire new friends and admirers in the Pasternaks.

In the late spring of 1903, Leonid Osipovich rented a dacha on the Obolenskoe estate, on the Briansk railroad line near Maloiaroslavets, about seventy miles southwest of Moscow.* Scriabin lived in the neighboring dacha, and there in the

---

*The Pasternak children were exposed to a number of interesting and varied localities during their vacations. Until 1901 the family spent summers in Odessa, visiting relatives in that region (where Leonid Osipovich painted several seashore scenes). After Obolenskoe the family spent the summer of 1904 in Voskresensk. During the period 1908–10 the Pasternaks spent their summer holidays in Raiki, near Moscow. In 1910 the family also visited the small resort town Meriküla, near Narva (Estonia), on the Baltic Sea.

country Pasternak discovered both nature and Scriabin. During that long summer Pasternak's emotional and intellectual development was furthered by exposure to both natural existence and artful creation, and this polarity between garden and drawing room is evident in the accounts we have of that period. His brother, Aleksandr, described that summer, the first summer the family spent not in the south but on the outskirts of Moscow, in "a place of exceptional beauty with hills and tremendously varied landscapes," within a rather unpopulated rural area:

> Almost from the first days of our stay at the dacha my brother and I would daily make new discoveries. Because of an assignment from school my brother would gather plants for a herbarium, which he rather methodically and exactingly filled up, making it very beautiful. . . . At times, this hunt for grasses and flowers took us to remote and unknown places. Then we felt a little like pathfinders, Leather-Stockings, trappers, or other Indians, following their practices of unobtrusiveness and secrecy. However, it was silly to observe secrecy, since all around us for a great distance there wasn't a soul at the time.[4]

In *A Safe-Conduct*, Pasternak speaks about his infatuation with botany, alluding to the period when "nature was revealed to the ten-year old, [when] in response to the five-petalled stare of a plant, botany became [the youth's] first passion."[5] In *Sketch for an Autobiography* he describes not only the natural beauty of Obolenskoe but also Scriabin's music, diffused throughout the underbrush:

> . . . just as the light and shade followed upon each other in the forest, [so] the *Divine Poem*, which was being composed on the piano in the country house next door, resounded and reverberated through it.

Boris Pasternak as an adolescent.
Ardis.

The composer-pianist
Alexander Scriabin, whom
the Pasternaks met in 1903
and who became a family
friend. Sketch by Leonid
Pasternak, 1909. *Scriabin
Museum, Moscow.*

Lord, what music it was! The symphony was continually crumbling and tumbling like
a city under artillery fire, and was all the time growing and being built up out of debris
and wreckage . . . breathing life and freshness. . . . there was nothing in the symphony
that was falsely profound or rhetorically dignified. . . . the tragic force of the composition in the process of creation put out its tongue triumphantly at everything that was
decrepit and generally acceptable and majestically obtuse, and was bold to the point of
frenzy, to the point of malice, playfully elemental, and free like a fallen angel.[6]

Nature and art met that summer in the long walks Pasternak took with his
father and Scriabin while listening to their earnest discussions "about life, about
art, about good and evil"; Leonid Osipovich strongly disagreed with Scriabin's
anti-Tolstoyan stance and Nietzschean advocacy of the Superman's amorality.[7]
Pasternak was "wild" about this genius, whose ideas and theories he did not fully
understand. His adoration for Scriabin—who was composing *The Divine Poem* at
the time—soon stimulated in the boy a passion for improvisation and composition that gave him a new orientation and dominated his life for the next six years.
Passion has blinders: in Pasternak's autobiographies there is no hint that he was
aware of Scriabin's complex feelings (including an aversion to public appearances)
induced by the tormented burst of creativity in Obolenskoe that gave birth to *The
Divine Poem*—a traumatic process about which the musician later reminisced bit-

terly.[8] Nor was the boy apparently in the least disconcerted by what contemporaries described as Scriabin's often nervous and high-strung manner, his capricious and flamboyant behavior. Decades were to go by before Pasternak reached some critical detachment about those aspects of the composer's makeup.

For Pasternak the stay in Obolenskoe was not an uninterrupted ecstatic contemplation of nature and art. It was punctuated by several accidents, including one in the autumn that delayed the family's return to Moscow. Boris Leonidovich fell from a horse and fractured his leg, which had to be put into a cast (the leg healed shorter than the other, and because of that he was later declared unfit for any military duties).[9]

After the family returned to Moscow, Pasternak began studying music theory and composition under the guidance of the theoretician and critic Iurii Dmitrievich Engel, a friend of Scriabin's, and under Reinhold Glière.* In December, 1903, during that first winter of Pasternak's music study, Scriabin came to say good-bye to the family before leaving for a long stay in Switzerland. Pasternak described in detail the gathering, as well as the agitation it aroused in him:

He played—this can't be put into words—had supper with us, talked philosophy, chatted simply and unaffectedly, and joked. All the time it seemed to me he was suffering an agony of boredom. The moment of leave-taking came, good wishings resounded, my own dropped like a clot of blood into the common heap of farewells. . . . The door banged; the key turned twice. . . . I raced . . . down the stairs and through Myasnitskaya Street in the night, to bring him back or at least set eyes on him once more. . . .
Of course, I did not catch up with him, and indeed scarcely thought I would.[10]

Within another few weeks, after complicated love intrigues in St. Petersburg (which reveal him in a light very different from that in which his young admirer saw him), Scriabin left Russia for Geneva, where he settled down for a period of productive creativity.[11]

Switzerland was crowded with Russians, and in the context of the earnest and spirited dialogue he soon developed with several of them, Scriabin devised such formulations as, "Real progress rests on artists alone"—a maxim clearly related to ideas that inform *Doctor Zhivago*. Some of his interlocutors he captivated with his dreamy eyes, which "reflected a universe of soul and melody"; others he fascinated by his references to Immanuel Kant and his deification of Will and Desire. His doctrine, hinging upon both the overwhelming importance of sensation (which he claimed should be experienced to the fullest) and a notion of *podëm* (a term to be rendered as *élan*, "lift," "upsurge of spirit," even "exaltation"), was developed through various media—his Geneva notebooks, many letters to friends and disciples, private harangues, poems, and program notes.[12] *Doctor Zhivago* provides us with not only echoes of individual aspects of Scriabin's views but also a unique fictional depiction of him as philosopher-seer. In this portrayal

---

*Reinhold Glier [Glière] later achieved immense success as a composer and was Prokofiev's teacher and the director of the Moscow Conservatory from 1920 to 1941. Glière's instruction of the youthful Prokofiev took place at about the same time as his association with Pasternak, during the period 1902–1904.

he appears reflected both in the ex-Tolstoyan Vedeniapin, Zhivago's uncle, who emerges from a long sojourn in Switzerland with a fresh spate of ideas, and in certain of Vedeniapin's interlocutors, whose theosophical constructions and pretentious symbolist cosmologies Vedeniapin gently ridicules.[13] The farfetched theories of these turn-of-the-century "cosmologists" derided in *Doctor Zhivago* bear strong resemblance to Scriabin's "doctrine," which has been characterized as "extraordinarily depersonalized, remote and withdrawn from the realities of the world."[14]

While Pasternak's infatuation with Scriabin followed its course in 1903 and 1904, literature and politics continued to develop their own spirited forms. The Russian Symbolist movement began shifting away from an interest in stylistic innovation and impressionism toward mysticism and religion and even social concerns. The Symbolists were no longer regarded as a renegade group, but were gaining popularity and the recognition given to legitimate literary leadership. The journal the *Golden Fleece* voiced some of the new concerns, counting among its contributors a number of modernist writers, painters, and musicians, including Scriabin.[15]

While he was aware of such developments on the literary scene, Pasternak also had other spheres of interest. He occasionally saw his uncle Aleksandr, the stationmaster of the St. Petersburg freight station of the Nikolaevskii railway line,* and through him developed contacts with employees of the Brest railway station in Moscow—people "from a different world" (to use a phrase in one of the chapter titles of *Doctor Zhivago*). It was a milieu that sharply contrasted with the upper bourgeoisie and artistic circles he knew. This "different world" he studied keenly, thanks to a unique insight into essentials and visual memory, conveying his observations to his friend Ida Vysotskaia, who later recognized his descriptions of this milieu of railroad workers as transposed in his novel.[16]

A particular visit to his uncle Aleksandr and aunt Klavdiia when he was fourteen or fifteen helped him make a fascinated discovery of the cultural sophistication of St. Petersburg. Pasternak described the vacation as follows:

> I travelled by myself to Petersburg for the Christmas vacation on a free ticket given me by my uncle . . . . For days on end I wandered about the streets of the immortal city, as though devouring with my feet and eyes a sort of magnificent stone book, and the evenings I spent at Komissarzhevskaia's theatre. I was intoxicated with the newest literature, raved about Andrei Belyi, Hamsun, Przybyszewski.[17]

The young adolescent's infatuation with St. Petersburg, which he perceived as a "stone *book*," foreshadowed the way in which he was later to "fall in love" with other remarkable architectural and scenic *texts* like Marburg and Venice. The precocious attraction linking him to literary "modernism" is also interesting to note. At that time the Polish writer Stanisław Przybyszewski was extremely well known in Russia, while Knut Hamsun was the object of a veritable cult among young intellectuals in Russia as elsewhere. The Norwegian novelist had pub-

---

*Aleksandr was the husband of Rosa Pasternak's sister, Klavdiia Isidorovna.

Pasternak and his brother, Aleksandr. Pastel on paper by Leonid Pasternak, 1905.
Ashmolean Museum.

lished the markedly Dostoevskian *Hunger* (*Sult*, 1890), the chaotically symbolist *Mysteries* (*Mysterier*, 1892), and *Pan* (1894), a volume pervaded with nature lyricism and winning its author wide acclaim in Russia. Like Hamsun's romantic lyricism, and like Bergsonism (which Pasternak was soon to discover at the University of Moscow), Przybyszewski's credo, reflecting the main trend of the "Young Poland" or "Moderna" movement, can be viewed as a reaction against nineteenth-century positivism. Thus was Pasternak exposed as an adolescent to a fairly broad spectrum of aesthetic schools: Decadence (Scriabin, the tragic-mystical and fatalistic aspects of Przybyszewski), Symbolism (Rilke, Andrei Belyi, Chekhov as performed by the avant-garde actress Vera Komissarzhevskaia), Naturalism (Hamsun).

The diversity and potential conflicts among literary styles and views were paralleled by tensions within the political arena. By 1904 the political movement toward "liberation" was as commonly accepted as the literary leadership of the Symbolists. There were tempestuous disputes and rifts among the many factions of Social Democrats, Social Revolutionaries, and Liberals (Kadets); however, only after the assassination of the minister of the interior, Wenzel von Plehve, and the defeat in the Russo-Japanese War was there any official attempt to confront unrest and criticism—if only by rather vague promises of constitutional reform.

The year 1905 was a landmark in the history of Russia, and its events deeply influenced Boris Pasternak and his generation. In January troops unexpectedly shot at demonstrators led by the priest Georgii Gapon in St. Petersburg and killed or wounded several hundred people. A few months later the crew of the battleship *Potemkin* mutinied, and in the following months thousands of political strikes occurred throughout the country. In October the tsar, unable to control the situation by force, issued a proclamation promising a constitution. On the following day Nikolai Bauman, who had participated in the student demonstrations, was killed by an officer of the secret police. Pasternak watched the demonstrations from the windows of the School of Painting and later recalled these episodes in his poem *The Year 1905* (written in the mid-1920s), which stressed that Bauman's courage would be an inspiration during the demonstrations that would follow.[18]

Throughout 1905 the School of Painting proved to be as important a center of revolutionary agitation as the university and the Technical School. Suspension of studies in February, 1905, "until further notice" in no way affected the constant stream of political gatherings and meetings, which continued in full swing.[19]

The October events were to bring more turmoil to the school. Things got out of hand when students took up arms and joined the demonstrators, actively seeking weapons and endeavoring to enlist the support of their professors. Young Pasternak himself (though only an onlooker, as far as we know) was whiplashed by one of the mounted Cossacks during the demonstrations. Finally, at the request of the school administration, the city authorities sent troops.[20] In the midst of the continuing panic Academician Leonid Pasternak remained staunch and was of great support to the director of the school as he tried to ensure the safety of faculty

Rosa Pasternak; Boris; his sisters, Lydia and Josephine; Rosa Pasternak's mother, Berta Kaufman; the nanny (*seated below*) and (*standing*) Aleksandr Pasternak. Photograph taken in 1905 at Safontevo, a summer resort near the monastery city Novyi Ierusalim, where the Pasternaks were spending the summer. *Pasternak Family Collection.*

and staff and play something of a conciliatory role with demonstrating students and the authorities.*

Boris Pasternak, who as an intent eyewitness followed the demonstrations then being organized against various institutions of higher education, later gave us a description of the defense efforts undertaken by the school (such as heaping cobblestones on the stair landings and connecting fire hydrants to repel looters). He added:

Demonstrators turned in to the school from the processions in the neighboring streets, held meetings in the Assembly Hall, took possession of rooms, went out on the balcony, and made speeches to those who stayed in the streets below.

Among my father's papers are some sketches he made at the time: a woman agitator, who was making a speech on the balcony, is being shot at by dragoons who swooped down on the crowd. She is wounded, but she goes on with her speech, catching hold of a column to prevent herself from falling.[21]

In December there were mutinies in the naval barracks at Kronstadt and Sebastopol, and in Moscow there was an armed insurrection. Again the School of Painting became the rallying point for students. Detachments of armed students and later of workers were formed there. To respond to the occupation of the school by demonstrators, the governor-general of Moscow issued an ultimatum: within the day the building must be cleared of demonstrators (and residents), or he would order it shelled. Boris Leonidovich's three-year-old sister, Lydia, ill with membranous pneumonia, was near death, and although the building had neither heat nor electricity, the Pasternaks remained. Leonid Osipovich appealed to one of his students who was in charge of a unit of armed demonstrators, and they soon vacated the school. The school was not shelled, but the commotion had been so disturbing that in late December, as soon as normal railway traffic was resumed and Lydia had begun to recover, the Pasternaks left for Berlin by way of Warsaw.[22]

Thus it was in a state of agitation that the Pasternak family met the new year in Berlin, where they were to spend the whole of 1906. At first they stayed at the hotel Am Knie, in the southwestern suburb Charlottenburg. This suburb, already popular with Russian émigrés, was a high-income residential area before World War I and later, in the early 1920s, became the focal point of a large Russian colony. The Russians living in Germany in the 1900s gained a heightened national consciousness because of their exposure to Western ideas and patterns of life; deserting the backwardness and the oppression at home, they "ended by idealizing in the abstract, past or future, a Russia whose present reality they had fled."[23] This kind of experience was not peculiar to the Russian intelligentsia; it was the lot of such representatives of modernism as T. S. Eliot, Ezra Pound, James Joyce, Samuel Beckett, Hermann Hesse, Paul Claudel, and Ilia Ehrenburg, for

*Concerning Leonid Pasternak's liberal stance at the time of the 1905 Revolution, see Guy de Mallac, "A Russian Impressionist: Leonid Osipovich Pasternak, 1862–1945," *California Slavic Studies* 10 (1977): 100. Leonid Pasternak's staunch support of Prince Lvov is indicated in the unpublished reminiscences of Princess Vera Alekseevna Lvov, his daughter, communicated to me in 1963.

whom exile became a privileged life-style (for such writers as Marina Tsvetaeva, however, exile proved a harrowing experience; far from enjoying a privileged life, they experienced material privation and failed to find a reading public in exile). Boris Pasternak joined the company of the fulfilled exiles as he began the first of three extended stays (whose duration added up to well over two years) he was to make in Germany between the ages of sixteen and thirty-three.

Focusing on his concrete perception of the West during this first visit, Pasternak later recalled the new sensations, the sights, and the sense of adventure it provided: "I soon got used to Berlin, loafed about its numberless streets and immense park, . . . tried to imitate the Berlin dialect, breathed a mixture of locomotive smoke, coal gas, and beer foam, listened to Wagner." "Berlin," he added, "was full of Russians." Among them he mentioned the composer Vladimir Ivanovich Rebikov (whose original, experimental music must have interested him). He also recalled that Gorky, who had recently been imprisoned in Russia, came to Berlin and visited the Pasternaks. Leonid Osipovich sketched his portrait, and Boris reported that Gorky's companion, the actress Andreeva, objected to the cheekbones in the drawing, which made Gorky's face look too angular.[24] This was Boris's first encounter with the famous writer, who was to become his protector and mentor. For Boris Leonidovich, exile thus meant continuous exposure to sophisticated, often experimental artists and art forms.

The winter of 1906 brought exceptionally severe frosts to Berlin, making it necessary for the Pasternaks to move to the better-insulated boardinghouse at 112 Kurfürstenstrasse run by a Fräulein Gebhardie. Pasternak and his brother Aleksandr were quartered in a small room above a greengrocer, also on Kurfürstenstrasse. Disturbing the peaceful atmosphere of their stay in Berlin, news came from Russia of the execution on March 6 on Berezan Island of Lieutenant Pëtr Petrovich Schmidt and the sailors he had led in the revolt at Sebastopol. The revolt became the subject of Pasternak's long poem *Lieutenant Schmidt* (1927).

The Pasternaks spent the summer of 1906 in Goehren, a small resort town on Ruegen Island, off the Baltic coast. Boris Leonidovich continued studying music; during the summer he took lessons in composition and music theory from Iulii Engel, who had come to Berlin in 1905. After the Pasternaks moved back to Berlin, they stayed at a different boardinghouse through the autumn and early winter of 1906, leaving for Moscow before the end of the winter.[25] During their absence the result of the 1905 Revolution had become clear. It was not a victory, since the liberal and revolutionary opposition was methodically punished and suppressed; after the first two dumas were dissolved, new electoral laws were implemented that would ensure a third duma favorable to the government.

Until 1907, however, when the new premier, Pëtr Arkadevich Stolypin, could enforce his policy of severe restrictions on the press, there was at least the intellectual advantage of a relaxation in censorship, and artistic publication and performance were in full flourish: three of Gorky's plays and Aleksandr Blok's allegorical lyrical drama *The Fair Booth* were performed, Leonid Andreev's Symbolist drama *Life of Man* and Gorky's novel *Mother* were written, and critical essays by Innokentii Annenskii and Anna Akhmatova's first poems were published. This was the time when Vladimir Maiakovskii, later the leader of the Futurists, came to live in Moscow. In 1908, at the age of fifteen, he enrolled at the Fifth Gymnasium, where he joined the class attended by Pasternak's brother, Aleksandr.*

After the return to Moscow, the seventeen-year-old Pasternak paid more and more attention to literary developments, while nearing the end of his secondary education. Music was still considered his calling, however, and he sometimes neglected academic studies for it. As he tells us:

> My future had been settled, my path in life correctly chosen. I was meant to be a musician, everything was forgiven me for the sake of music. . . . Even at school when, during the Greek and math lessons, I was caught trying to solve some fugue or counterpoint problem and, asked to answer a question from my place, stood like a fool and did not know what to say, my classmates did their best to shield me and my teachers forgave me everything. [26]

His schoolmate and friend G. Kurlov has also indicated that Pasternak was less than diligent:

> By the end of our studies at the gymnasium we were quite successful, progressing neck and neck, each of us fluctuating between third and sixth in our class. I'm sure, with some effort, he could have easily become second in the class. [27]

In spite of his uneven performance, Pasternak somehow ultimately redeemed himself academically: he received the gold medal upon graduating from the gymnasium in 1908. It was perhaps achieved through last-minute cramming—an approach that would not be out of character (to be seen in the ability he later demonstrated to pursue his philosophical studies intensively).

After working briefly as a tutor, Pasternak entered the University of Moscow School of Law—"because it was easy." He was already beginning to make contacts with literary circles. In *Sketch for an Autobiography* he tells us that new publishing houses were springing up, concerts of new music were taking place much more regularly, and there were more frequent art exhibitions, which were popular with the younger generation of Muscovites. All sorts of new artistic groups were forming. [28]

One of these groups was Serdarda, a band of about ten young poets, painters, and musicians, which Pasternak joined. Its appellation was (the poet tells us) "a name whose meaning no one knew. This word was said to have been heard one day on the Volga by a member of our circle, the poet and bass Arkadii Gurev." [29] In "a damp interlacing of ancient times, heredity and youthful promises," this group—"a drunken fellowship"—met in the "wooden Razguliai," a section of Moscow, in the apartment of the poet and painter Iulian Pavlovich Anisimov, whom Pasternak describes as "a highly talented man of excellent taste, an embodiment of poetry, but . . . only an amateur of great charm, not a character out of which a master of his craft is eventually produced." Members of Serdarda in-

---

*Maiakovskii soon left the gymnasium and joined an illegal cell of the Social Democratic (Bolshevik) party and was arrested for the first time during the destruction of the party's press. In contrast, during those years his classmate Aleksandr Pasternak was assiduously developing his skills as a violinist.

Two of Boris's school friends, Boris, Josephine, Rosa Isidorovna, Lydia, Leonid, and (*at the top of the steps*) the nanny. Photograph taken in 1907 at Raiki, a summer resort on the railroad line to Yaroslav, where the Pasternaks spent their vacations from 1907 to 1909. *Pasternak Family Collection.*

cluded Sergei Durylin, who persuaded Pasternak to give up music for literature and who (Pasternak tells us) "was able to find something worthy of attention in my first literary efforts"; the poet Arkadii Gurev, whose "powerful and soft voice . . . gave highly artistic renderings of the dramatic and vocal subtleties of whatever he happened to be singing" and whose poetry prefigured the candor and sincerity of Maiakovskii; Sergei Bobrov; A. I. Kozhebatkin, editor of the journal *Musagetes*;* and Sergei Makovskii,† founder and editor of *Apollon*.[30]

Pasternak made a significant contribution to the group when he introduced its members to the poetry of Rilke, after discovering in his father's library copies of *Early Poems* (*Mir zur Feier*) and *The Book of Hours* (*Das Stunden-Buch*) inscribed to Leonid Osipovich. A member of Serdarda later reported that the young man "could constantly be seen immersed in *Das Stunden-Buch*." Eager to share his excitement, the young man read Rilke's poetry to the group. Originally the Serdarda members viewed Pasternak as a musician rather than a *littérateur*—he tells us that he joined the group "on the strength of my standing as a musician and

---

*On *Musagetes*, see Chapter 5. Anisimov and Bobrov are also further discussed in that chapter.

†In his task as editor of the Petersburg literary journal *Apollon* (1909–17), Sergei Makovskii was assisted by Konstantin Mochulskii, Nikolai Gumilev, Mikhail Kuzmin, and the young Osip Mandelstam.

Scriabin at the piano during
a performance of his
Prometheus. Serge
Koussevitzky is
conducting. Pastel by
Leonid Pasternak, 1913.
*Collection of Mme
Koussevitzky.*

improvised on the piano a musical description of every new arrival at the beginning of the evening."[31]

The course of events would soon precipitate a dramatic decision for Pasternak
concerning his musical career. In early January, 1909, Scriabin arrived in Moscow
from Switzerland. With him he brought the completed version of *The Poem of
Ecstasy*. Four days after his arrival the Russian premiere of the tone poem took
place in St. Petersburg. Rehearsals for the Moscow premiere began the same
month.[32] Soon thereafter Scriabin paid a visit to the Pasternaks. Pasternak's
brother, Aleksandr, has given us his observations on the composer's return:

> He seemed to my parents and to my brother and me to be some other person, new, [or,]
> at least, renewed. There appeared in him new artistic and philosophical (theosophic)
> ideas, new views on the art of the future that had probably taken shape [in Switzerland]
> together with clear outlines of his future compositions. . . . Mother and I, often accom-
> panied by my brother, went to every rehearsal of *Ecstasy*, starting with the very first.[33]

It has been said that the dress rehearsal of *The Poem of Ecstasy* in Moscow looked
more like a public performance—while the fretful composer reacted intensely to
every movement in the piece. The *Poem* was performed in the Great Hall of the

Boris improvising at the
piano. Painting by Leonid
Pasternak, Molodi, 1913.
Pasternak Family Collection.
Photograph by Jeremy Moeran.

Moscow Conservatory on February 21, 1909, initiating a long "Scriabin Week."
The musical *Poem* was accompanied by unique program notes: a word poem of
over three hundred lines, which one critic later described as "foggy, turgid, prolix, diffuse, almost comically cosmic," but which does convey, for all its prolixity,
Scriabin's cult of art in a major key, of life as the great releaser.[34] The score itself
was characterized by the opulence of its orchestration (which included celesta,
organ, and bells). It was a decisive breakthrough; Scriabin had succeeded in fundamentally renewing his language and had taken a significant step in his progression toward atonal music.

Despite the elation with which the whole family met Scriabin's latest work,
during this period Pasternak made the radical decision to give up music. Although his peers and family were convinced of his musical vocation, and he had
already gained considerable success in the domain of composition, he had a "secret trouble" related to declining technical facility:

I could scarcely play the piano and could not even read music with any fluency. . . . This
discrepancy between the far from easy musical idea and its lagging technical support
transformed nature's gift, which could have served as a source of joy, into an object of

Score of Prélude (in G-sharp minor) by Boris Pasternak, dated December 8, 1906. *Pasternak Family Collection/Tempo* 121 (June, 1977): 20–25.

constant torment which in the end I could no longer endure. . . . At its root lay . . . an unpardonable adolescent arrogance, a half-educated person's nihilistic disregard of everything that appears to him to be easily attainable and accessible. I despised everything uncreative, any kind of hack work. . . . In *real* life, I thought, everything must be a miracle, everything must be predestined from above, nothing must be deliberately designed or planned, nothing must be done to follow one's own fancies.[35]

Besides lack of technical facility, Boris Leonidovich lacked perfect pitch (or pitch recognition). Though he was aware that many great composers shared this deficiency, he felt that it was "proof that [my] music was against the will of fate and heaven." Awareness of this flaw caused him exaggerated torment. Nonetheless Pasternak, with what he later described as "effrontery," went to Scriabin to play some of his own compositions for him. "His reception exceeded my expectations," wrote Pasternak. "Scriabin listened, encouraged, inspired, blessed."[36] Especially attracted by one particular phrase in Pasternak's music, Scriabin reproduced it on the piano—but in a different key. Pasternak, tormented by his own lack of perfect pitch, was horrified to find that very flaw in his idol and further disappointed by Scriabin's feeble justifications—the great composer being content to bring up such trite arguments as Wagner's and Tchaikovsky's similar failing and the "hundreds of piano tuners" endowed with perfect pitch.

After leaving Scriabin that night, Pasternak felt that "something was tearing and trying to get free. Something was weeping; something was exulting." He "plucked" music out of himself and "parted from it as one parts from something most precious."[37] He continued: "For some time I kept up my improvisations on the piano from force of habit that was gradually growing weaker and weaker. But later on I decided to take stronger measures to enforce my abstinence. I stopped touching the piano, gave up going to concerts, and avoided meetings with musicians."[38]

It was at this point that he began writing verse. During the transitional period Pasternak for a time seemed to be wavering between the two art forms, and in conversations with friends Leonid Osipovich would refer to the irresoluteness of his older son, pointing out that he kept "tossing" or "jumping" to and fro between the two vocations.[39] One of Pasternak's former classmates at the gymnasium recalled that "deep spiritual drama" marked by his farewell to music and new involvement with poetry: "It became evident that [Pasternak] did not have absolute pitch. He weathered this quite poorly and became sullen, shutting himself up, deciding to leave music entirely. This decision he carried through, ignoring the advice of his mother."[40] It seems clear that there was strong family opposition to Pasternak's decision. The whole household was accustomed to being moved by his spells of composing, while humming, sighing, and moaning; everyone in the family was sure he was sacrificing a brilliant career.[41]

Although at first Boris Leonidovich endeavored to "pluck music out" of himself, after the initial trauma wore off, he continued—in private life as well as in his poetry—to give evidence of his strong interest in music. It would have been difficult for him to do otherwise, in a domestic atmosphere so permeated with music: in addition to the mother with her rare talent, Aleksandr Leonidovich was a talented amateur violinist.* Those close to Boris indicate that "even in later years he would occasionally indulge in piano improvisation when alone."[42] He also greatly enjoyed the concerts performed (without a conductor) by the First Symphonic Ensemble in the period from 1910 to 1920; he regularly attended concerts in the 1930s, as well as various musical events in the 1940s (such as the rehearsal of Dmitri Shostakovich's Eighth Symphony) and in the 1950s (such as Leonard Bernstein's concert in Moscow, after which he met the conductor and developed a friendship with him by letter), and he counted among his friends a number of musicians, such as the pianists Mariia Iudina, Genrikh Gustavovich Neigauz, and Sviatoslav Richter.[43] In his correspondence and conversations he was often to express opinions, preferences, and judgments about musical matters, his essay on Chopin being his most highly developed piece of music criticism.†

While Pasternak abandoned music as a profession, his literary work was permeated by it. To quote from Christopher J. Barnes's well-documented and thoughtful analysis:

Pasternak's verse and prose abound in explicit reminders of his lasting knowledge and love of music. [There are] also innumerable mentions of musical works, personalities, etc., through Pasternak's poetry. . . . it is no doubt to Scriabin that Pasternak, and we,

---

*In a drawing in 1916, Leonid Pasternak depicted his son Aleksandr playing the violin with Rosa Isidorovna accompanying him on the piano.
†See Chapter 18.

are indebted for the poet's initial captivation by music, and for the development of his fine "composer's ear" which is traceable throughout the strongly "musical" poetry and prose.[44]

Scriabin's role in Pasternak's development cannot be overemphasized. Not only was he profoundly influential in bringing Pasternak to music, but he had a very real influence on Pasternak's musical style. Barnes noted, "A glance at any of Pasternak's pieces is sufficient to reveal a harmonic language and piano style strongly influenced by Scriabin," adding, however, "though in general derivative, Pasternak's writing shows a number of original harmonic features and a maturity surprising in one so young." These qualities are apparent in extant musical compositions by Pasternak, such as his Prélude in G-sharp minor (1906).*

In later years, while acknowledging that as a child he had "idolized" Scriabin, Pasternak was able to gain some objectivity about his erstwhile idol and what he termed "this share or this touch of egocentrism, not to say of Nietzscheanism, which characterized Scriabin." Nonetheless, Pasternak's portrayal of Scriabin in his autobiographies is a highly expressive and eloquent tribute to the enchantment woven over him by the composer. Faubion Bowers was to note, "Of the reams of documentation adoring Scriabin, none surpasses Boris Pasternak."[45]

Pasternak's musical training, pursued until he completed the full course of studies in composition, had an important consequence: its sheer discipline kept him on a strict nonverbal diet. When he abandoned the medium of music for expression through verse, the long-repressed verbal medium imposed itself with irresistible power. He tells us: "My fifteen-year abstinence from words, which I had sacrificed to sounds, doomed me to originality as a certain kind of maiming forces a person into performing acrobatics."[46] To judge only in terms of the quality of Pasternak's later commitment to his art, the considerable investment of endeavor and creative energy in one art form yielded a rich return when the artist essayed another.

Later, with an eight-year perspective, Pasternak was to view his farewell to music as an act of revolt against himself, as a "suicidal" gesture, "a direct act of amputation" whereby he had cut off "the most vital part of his existence" and "killed in himself the main thing." He saw that such an error "could not be set straight" and had to live with occasional insistent visitations of a "burning need for a *composer's biography*." But the die was cast in favor of the verbal medium.[47] Pasternak's beginnings in the new medium were timid and even secretive, however; both his sister Josephine and one of his classmates indicated that he did not read, show, or mention these first verse endeavors of his "literary minority," considering them as "unfortunate weaknesses."[48]

---

*Barnes says that the prelude contains "the characteristic Scriabinesque melody supported by rapid pulsing chords (familiar from the close of Scriabin's fourth sonata); nervous but self-assertive left-hand octaves vying with an independent melody in the treble (cf. the second movement of Scriabin's third sonata, or the étude op. 8, no. 9); melodic climax achieved by several successive repetitions of the thematic fragment at rising pitch (cf. Scriabin's étude in D# minor, op. 8, no. 12)." Christopher J. Barnes, "Letter to the Editor: Scriabin and Pasternak," *Musical Times* (London), January, 1972, p. 268.

4

Between the Moskva and the Lahn

Philosopher in Moscow and Marburg

1909–1913

A sturdy fellow, whose mind and muscle have been steeled in intellectual grapplings with the Kantian "sum-total" of existence, who has gone through the Marburg school of robust slaps in the face by German idealism, who has crawled in the guise of lubricator under the wrecked "special express" of the great European culture—he [Pasternak] is well suited to the role of verbal engineer on the main railway of Russian poetry.

Nikolai Aseev[1]

Both while he was officially pursuing a calling as a musician and after he transferred his interests to philosophy, Pasternak's literary interests gradually became
more variegated and intense—though generally within the scope of Symbolism.
Pasternak was personally acquainted with several leaders of this movement in
Russia. Konstantin Loks, a fellow *littérateur* and student friend, was the first to
consider Pasternak's essays akin to the poetry of the Symbolist Annenskii, an
opinion later shared by various critics, including Dmitrii Sviatopolk-Mirskii.*
The latter, however, hastened to point out the differences between the two poets:
"Annenskii was decadent and morbid to the core; Pasternak is quite free from all
morbidity—his poetry is bracing and all in the major key."

During those years Pasternak would occasionally meet with the Symbolist poet
and sage Viacheslav Ivanov, for whom the mythmaking function of art pertained
to "Dionysian" frenzy, ecstasy, or tragedy (which he identified with Christianity).
In 1911, Ivanov published his collection of poetry under the Latin title *Cor Ardens*
(*Burning* [*Ardent*] *Heart*), which demonstrated his usual richness of allusion to
mythology and ancient religions; this is very probably the volume that we are
told he presented to Pasternak "with a moving inscription."

Referring to that period of his literary adolescence, Pasternak later observed,
"The depth and charm of Belyi and Blok could not but be revealed to me." Andrei
Belyi he described as "a first-class poet and author of the particularly striking
Symphonies in Prose and of the novels *The Silver Dove* and *Petersburg*, which created
an upheaval in the pre-Revolutionary taste of his contemporaries and gave rise to
the first Soviet prose."[2]

Pasternak remembered first reading Aleksandr Blok's poems after spending a
year in Berlin, around 1906. The impact they made on him was so distinct that he
sought to re-create it in his second autobiography half a century later. There he
defined the realm of literature of the time as one of "unnoticed artificiality" in
which famous people produced "abstractions, reiterations, and ratiocinations."
Pasternak claimed that against that background Blok created "the impression of a
revolution," because "he [knew] something and [wanted] to say it" with "his solitary, unspoilt, childlike word."[3] For Pasternak, Blok's poetry was to remain a
model of "melodic authenticity,"[4] and, like others of his generation, he was
drawn to the great Symbolist's poetry for its exquisite naturalness, its true-to-life
quality: "It seemed as though the page were covered not with verses about wind
and puddles, street lamps and stars, but the street lamps and the puddles themselves were spreading their wind-blown ripples on the surface of the journal."[5]

Pasternak considered Blok (who was just ten years his senior) a genius and
praised his quality of "impetuosity, his roving intentness, the rapidity of his observations."[6] Especially for Pasternak, Blok's style represented the spirit of the
age. His powerful influence on the younger generation in revolutionary Russia
permeates *Doctor Zhivago*: young Zhivago relates that the "young people in both
capitals were mad about Blok," and the extent of Zhivago's admiration for Blok is
revealed when he says that Blok reflects "the Christmas spirit in all domains of

*Referred to here by his full name; he was later better known in the West as D. S. Mirsky.

Russian life"; subsequently Iurii Zhivago's poem "Star of the Nativity" is to become a tribute to the poet. Like Blok, the generation of students Zhivago represented—"followers of Blok"—welcomed the 1905 Revolution, the "idealized intellectuals' revolution of 1905" so unlike "the soldiers' revolution led by those professional revolutionaries, the Bolsheviks." The ending of *Doctor Zhivago* is an interpretation of one of Blok's lines—"We, the children of Russia's terrible years"—in the perspective of the country's subsequent history.[7] Indeed, it seems that Pasternak was attempting to do in his age what Blok had tried to do before him.

Pasternak would meet his revered *maître* in person in May, 1921, during Blok's last visit to Moscow, where he gave readings of his poetry; in that conversation Blok said that "he had heard many good things" about the younger poet. Blok died in Petersburg three months later.[8] Even decades afterward a visitor to Pasternak's dacha in Peredelkino came away with the impression that Pasternak still professed membership in a veritable cult of Blok—whom he referred to as "the Russian Dante."[9] This cult was reflected in the practice of Pasternak, who has been termed "the true successor to Blok in Russian poetry."[10]

Pasternak tells us that he was especially attracted to the Blok "of the second volume of the Alkonost edition," and he lists some of the poems that most affected him.[11] To judge by those poems, what he seems to admire is the constancy of Blok's original poetic vision, even throughout the Symbolist's growing disenchantment with the ideals that had inspired the "Poems About the Beautiful Lady." That was the period (1905–1908) when Blok was most eclectic and experimental. Because of his unconventionality in both form and context he was attacked by his fellow Symbolists, who saw a weakening of poetic power in his descent from the metaphysical heights of his early poetry to the commonplace and seamy realities of Petersburg. While flaunting his disillusionment and deriding his earlier ideals, Blok longed for the innocence, faith, and rhythm of the past. His duality is expressed in many of his poems—especially those singled out by Pasternak. The Blok that Boris Leonidovich admired is the poet of the city, who captured its mood of hopelessness and doom, of pretense and *poshlost*,* and depicted it as a soulless entity that transformed people into walking corpses, automatons mechanically performing their role of living. This duality of perception is what distinguishes Blok from the other Symbolists; although the poems reflect his pessimism and even despair, they are not entirely black. They bespeak his longing for another reality, and that longing elevates him above the boredom and vulgarity of daily existence and offers him his only hope of recapturing, if only in part, the music, the harmony of the universe to which his ear was once attuned. This hope is embodied in his formula relating to such a "recapture" of the "mystical" values "in everyday things" (*mistitsism v povsednevnosti*).[12] Pasternak, in his emulation of Blok, maintained the optimism the latter lost after *The Twelve*.

---

*To convey in English the flavor of this untranslatable Russian substantive, Vladimir Nabokov has suggested such epithets as "cheap, sham, common, smutty, pink-and-blue, high falutin', in bad taste, . . . inferior, sorry, trashy, scurvy, tawdry, gimcrack" (Vladimir Nabokov, *Nikolai Gogol*, New York: New Directions, 1961, p. 64).

Leo Tolstoy, who befriended
Leonid Pasternak. Etching by
Leonid Pasternak, 1906. *Tolstoy
Museum, Moscow.*

If for Pasternak's generation the discovery of Blok meant the opening of a window on the future, the death of Tolstoy in November, 1910, at the small railway
station in the hamlet of Astapovo marked the end of an era. Leonid Osipovich was
immediately summoned to make a drawing of the dead man, and Pasternak
joined him as he left by night train for Astapovo. Pasternak heard Countess
Tolstoy address his father with recriminations about various matters, behavior
that struck him as petty and inappropriate to an event of such cosmic dimensions.
He left us a description of the funeral procession:

> To the chanting of a requiem, the students and the young people carried the coffin
> across the little yard and the garden of the stationmaster's house to the railway platform
> and put it in the freight car {to Iasnaia Poliana}. . . .
> It seemed natural, somehow, that Tolstoy was at peace and that he should have found
> peace by the wayside like a pilgrim.[13]

The impact on Pasternak of the death of the sage of Iasnaia Poliana was considerable, in spite of the seeming irreconcilability between Tolstoy's world view and
other philosophies—for example, Scriabin's quasi-Nietzschean lore—that held
sway over the young man (Pasternak himself was aware that this juxtaposition of
influences might appear contradictory).[14]

While the death of Tolstoy meant the turning of a page, in the same year also occurred the deaths of two figures who, in their respective spheres, had heralded important trends within modernism and made some impact on Pasternak. They were the actress Vera Komissarzhevskaia, to whose avant-garde Petersburg theater Pasternak had paid many visits, and the painter Mikhail Vrubel, several of whose works had deeply affected him as a child.

A new era was beginning, some of whose representatives—the "angry young men" of the Futurist movement—were soon (in 1912) to advocate throwing Tolstoy and other "classics" overboard "from the steamship of Modernity."[15] In February, 1909, Filippo Tommaso Marinetti had published the original manifesto of European Futurism in *Le Figaro*. Marinetti was the founder of this modern-day iconoclasm, an independent variety of which was acclimated to the Russian scene between 1910 and 1912 by Velimir Khlebnikov, Maiakovskii, and a few fellow poets. While Pasternak was exclusively engaged in intellectual and artistic pursuits, Maiakovskii, during his last year at the gymnasium from which Pasternak had just graduated, became involved in underground political activities (notably helping convicts escape from prison)—practical-political bravado that resulted in his second arrest a few months after the theoretical bravado of Marinetti's manifesto. Soon thereafter Maiakovskii was expelled from the Stroganov Art School. In August, 1911, he transferred to the Moscow School of Painting, where he joined the ranks of a small group of unruly and brash innovators. One of these innovators was Mikhail Larionov, who had forsaken the benches of the school—where he was chiefly known as a troublemaker—because he felt that he had nothing more to learn from the overly "traditional" instructors. By 1910 he was exhibiting the first nonfigurative canvases in Russia. These paintings, and those of Nataliia Goncharova, Pasternak mentioned as landmarks of the artistic life of the time.[16] Alongside Larionov's new theory, "Rayonnism," and Futurism, still another modernist movement, "Acmeism," was emerging—with two of whose practitioners, Osip Mandelstam and Anna Akhmatova, Pasternak was to maintain a thoughtful, if sporadic, dialogue over the years.*

During the time these new trends were developing, the Pasternaks moved to another district of Moscow. In the summer of 1911, Leonid Osipovich—together with Aleksandr (who had just completed his studies at the gymnasium) and his daughters—left Moscow to vacation on the Black Sea near Odessa. Pasternak and his mother stayed in Moscow to attend to the details of moving from their apartment on Miasnitskaia to new quarters at No. 14 Volkhonka Street, Apartment No. 9.† The second-floor apartment, provided by the School of Fine Arts, was furnished in traditional rather than contemporary taste[17] and was to be Pasternak's chief Moscow residence until 1934. It was in a two-story house, next door to the Museum of Fine Arts, near the south end of the street. The house was directly

---

*In opposition to the deepening mysticism and intangible references of images in Symbolist poetry, Acmeism arose, characterized as modern Neoclassicism, dedicated to the pursuit of "beautiful clarity," greater realism, simplicity, precision, logic, and concreteness.

†Volkhonka Street, which begins at the southwest corner of the Kremlin and runs parallel to the Moskva River, is fairly close to Mokhovaia Street, where the University of Moscow (now known as the "Old University") was situated.

opposite the late-nineteenth-century gold dome of the Church of Christ the Savior (Khram Khrista Spasitelia), an architectural landmark of Moscow. The church's shining cupola, which surveyed the whole of the district, was probably the inspiration for the cupola around which, with Futurist desultoriness, the poet was to suggest "throwing a fresh towel."[18]

The move to Volkhonka Street meant that Pasternak was living almost next door to the classrooms of the University of Moscow, which he had begun attending a couple of years before. From 1909 to 1912 Pasternak's involvement with literature remained an avocation while he was enrolled in other disciplines. After barely a semester at law school, on Scriabin's advice, he changed to the Historico-Philological Faculty (or School of Arts and Letters) to study philosophy. His earlier schoolmate G. Kurlov,* who had become a fellow student, tells us: "For all appearances, both he and I were not especially conscientious about attending our lectures, and seldom met at the university. This I remember already happening in our first year during the lectures by V. O. Kliuchevskii."[19]

Whether or not he missed many of Kliuchevskii's lectures, Pasternak had other occasions to hear the famous historian. He tells us of entertaining the professor while he sat as a model for his father.[20] Another classmate depicts Pasternak's "image" among fellow students: "I remember . . . Pasternak's masklike, dark, taut, African face. Pasternak's behavior was full of reserve—he would arrive for lectures, and he would leave. He had a life of his own, into which he admitted no one." Pasternak is contrasted to another student, portrayed by the author of these reminiscences as frankly cordial, maintaining ties with the university and spending much time in the school library.[21]

Retiring or not, Pasternak did immerse himself in the study of philosophy. According to his own later account, the ideas of Henri Bergson were claiming the largest following among students at the University of Moscow; by 1913, *L'Évolution créatrice* and six other significant works by the French philosopher had appeared in Russia. Next came Husserlianism and the Göttingen school, supported most militantly in word and print by the young lecturer Gustav Shpet. Pasternak took sides in such doctrinal debates to the extent of composing a lampoon against an enemy of both the Marburg and the Göttingen schools, the advocate of logical psychologism Theodor Lipps.[22] Pasternak moved closer to the Marburg school, whose three mentors, Plato, Hermann Cohen, Paul Natorp, soon shifted Hegel from the center of his attention. This movement occurred under the influence of certain philosophers at the university, such as S. N. Trubetskoi, the rector, who wrote extensively on the Marburg school and sent his best students there to complete their education. Two peculiarities of his newfound system Pasternak found most attractive: the resolute independence with which the Marburg school "dug everything over to the very foundations," turning to the primary sources in the

---

*Ida Davidovna Vysotskaia tells us that Kurlov (son of a lawyer and a future lawyer himself) appears in *Doctor Zhivago* as the character Koka Kornakov, described in the novel as a "young law school student, . . . son of an assistant public prosecutor," and a ballroom enthusiast like Kurlov (*Doctor Zhivago*, p. 81; Jacqueline de Proyart, "Une amitié d'enfance," *Boris Pasternak, 1890–1960: Colloque de Cerisy-la-Salle [11–14 septembre 1975]*, p. 2).

history of knowledge and its "scrupulous and exacting" historicism—stressing
both a thorough acquaintance with the particulars of history and the unity and
homogeneity underlying the historical structure of knowledge.[23]

Marburg might have remained for the young philosophy student but a
nebulous idea had it not been for an unexpected development. Although she had
given up a brilliant career as a pianist to care for her family, his mother had continued teaching piano, which made it possible for her to lay by money to be used
for Pasternak's studies. In April, 1912, she called him and explained that by col-
lecting her earnings and economizing on the housekeeping she had saved two
hundred rubles,* which she was giving to him "with advice to travel abroad."
Pasternak has recorded his reaction to that present: "Neither my joy nor the complete unexpectedness of the gift can be described, nor how undeserved it was. No
small amount of strumming on the piano had had to be endured to make up such
a sum."[24]

The young philosopher knew immediately what he wanted to do. While attending Moscow University, he had met a young man named Dmitrii Samarin,
the most outspoken of the Moscow followers of the Marburg school† (he reminded Boris Leonidovich of Tolstoy's Nekhliudov). One cold February evening
at the Café Grec on Tverskoi Boulevard, Samarin had described Marburg to him
and another fellow student, evoking the city's antiquity and poetic atmosphere so
beautifully that the impressionable Pasternak, who had already deeply pondered
the historical and intellectual significance of Marburg, had fallen under the spell
of Samarin's vision. He now told his mother that he would spend the money on
studies at the University of Marburg.[25]

It was not uncommon for young Russians like Pasternak to be attracted to the
German universities, for to them Germany had come to signify not only Europe
but "culture" at large; however, whereas many highly politicized Russian-Jewish
students based their decision to study in Germany on social and political considerations,‡ Pasternak made a personal intellectual choice. Young Russians had
been particularly attracted to Marburg ever since the famous scholar and scientist
Mikhail Vasilevich Lomonosov had studied there in the eighteenth century. In
going to Marburg, young Pasternak was overwhelmingly conscious of making a

---

*A sum then worth about one hundred dollars.

†Dmitrii Samarin was a scion of a famous Russian aristocratic family who counted among its
notable members the agronomist Ivan Ivanovich (1774–1847) and Iurii Fëdorovich (1819–76), the
Slavophile publicist and politician who took an active part in preparations for the emancipation of
the serfs in 1861. Pasternak wrote of Dmitrii: "Philosophy, dialectics, and a knowledge of Hegel
were in his blood. He had inherited it" (*I Remember: Sketch for an Autobiography*, p. 75). In the 1920s a
close relative of Dmitrii Samarin returned to Moscow from Siberia (where he had been sent during
the Civil War), covered with lice and afflicted with the aftereffects of starvation. Shortly thereafter
he died of typhus near Moscow. He very probably served as one of the prototypes for Iurii Zhivago in
the final episode of his life.

‡In 1905 there were 360 Russian students at the University of Berlin, 261 of whom were Russian
Jews. The Germans watched this trend with rising dismay, and, as one historian writes, "The fear of
an influx of revolutionary Jewish students from the East never quite disappeared from the German
mind after 1905" (Robert C. Williams, *Culture in Exile: Russian Émigrés in Germany, 1881–1941*,
p. 24).

The University of Marburg as it looked before World War I.

pilgrimage in the footsteps of Lomonosov, whose image as a pathfinder in Marburg he found inspiring. The philosopher Christian Wolff, in particular, had then attracted many Russian students; after his departure in 1740, the flow of Russians to Marburg had lessened. At the beginning of the twentieth century, however, Marburg once more attracted students from Russia, this time because of Cohen and the Marburg Neo-Kantian school. Within the precincts of the University of Moscow, Cohen had a staunch supporter, B. A. Vogt, who regularly directed Moscow students to study under the master on the banks of the Lahn.[26]

Marburg's intellectual atmosphere was as much a product of its ghosts as of its present-day scholars. Under the sponsorship of Landgraf Philip the Magnanimous, Martin Luther and other theologians had met there during the Marburg Colloquium on Religion in the sixteenth century, and the Brentano-Savigny Circle had flourished there in the 1800s. Other notables of the modern age included Jacob and Wilhelm Grimm, as well as Eduard Zeller, the renowned historian of philosophy, and, at the turn of the century, the Neo-Kantians Natorp and Cohen; Rudolf Otto, who did pioneering conceptual work defining the notion of the holy; and Rudolf Stammler, a prominent scholar in the philosophy of law. In the 1920s the philosopher Martin Heidegger was to teach in Marburg, where he wrote and published his landmark treatise *Being and Time* (*Sein und Zeit*). By

The University of Marburg.
On the ground floor of this
building (erected in
1874–78) was the
philosophy seminar room.

1958, Marburg would boast eleven Nobel Prize winners (including Pasternak) among its alumni and faculty. There were two contrasting elements in the blend of the Marburg experience, the intellectuals' cafés and the lecture rooms, and these elements commingled with the town's ancient tradition of learning. One could not live there without a sustaining sense of deep and sturdy intellectual roots.[27]

Anticipating these benefits, Pasternak left Moscow in early May and enrolled for the Marburg summer semester on May 9, at a time when the "Alma Mater Philippina" counted slightly over two thousand students (the population of the town was about twenty-six thousand). He found the town to be everything Samarin had promised. Situated in the heart of Hesse, Marburg stood on the slopes of a hill, reaching down to the banks of the quiet Lahn River. Many of its inhabitants still wore the colorful regional costume. The town was picturesque in pre-

Pasternak was delighted by a number of enchanting vistas in Marburg, such as this view through the Kalbstor, the only medieval city gate still standing. *Bildarchiv Foto Marburg.*

cisely the ways that a German university town should be picturesque: shadowed and dominated by a castle on the hilltop above it, its skyline broken by the twin towers of a Gothic church, its streets narrow, twisting, and changeful with sudden vistas, many tiny gardens, and gabled wooden houses. These traditional sights coexisted with a more boisterous tradition of *Burschenherrlichkeit* (frolicsome, often bibulous student merriment), apparent in the jovial atmosphere of the bustling taverns. There the Marburg students went to drink, sing, and argue. Pasternak recalled frequenting the café patronized by philosophers (which can thus be identified as the hillside Café Vetter, with its terrace commanding a view of the valley). The pubs were warm and cheerful, but Pasternak was also fond of going to the cool, dark nave of Elisabethkirche to admire statues and altars.

Of all the descriptions of Marburg by university alumni and visitors, Pasternak's impressions in *A Safe-Conduct* are perhaps the most vivid, articulate, and original. His cultural and emotional experiences during his one summer there were so intense and, he must have sensed, so crucial to his future that he absorbed Marburg life with vivid consciousness and later conveyed it in his spiritual autobiography.

Pasternak's university registration, filled out on May 9, 1912, with a notation that he checked out on August 3. His home address is given as No. 14 Volkhonka Street, Moscow. *Hessischen Staatsarchiv, Marburg.*

The Schützenpfuhl Inn by the Lahn, where Pasternak first stayed in Marburg and which he later described in a letter as a "Hauff's robbers' inn." *Initiativgruppe "Marburger Stadtbild."*

Pasternak depicted the town's physical appearance as the "sullen hill with the small ancient town," the streets clinging "to steep slopes like Gothic dwarfs," and the lighting up of Marburg, "operatically, on the top of the hill." He described Barfüsserstrasse (which led toward Gisselbergerstrasse—or the road to Giessen—where he lived): "Flying downhill, the street grew more and more twisty and narrow the nearer it came to the university. In one of the house-fronts, baked in the cinders of the centuries like a potato, was a glass door. It opened into a corridor that led out on one of the precipitous northern slopes."[28]

Boris Leonidovich spent several hours of his first day and perhaps his first night in Marburg at the Schützenpfuhl Inn. Decades later he recalled that "the inn-keeper was a grumpy and stout man, apparently a drunkard, who spoke a juicy popular dialect, mysterious like music. Have I really not described this house which reminded one of a Hauff's Robbers' Inn?"[29]

After staying briefly at the inn (merely alluded to in *A Safe-Conduct* as "the medieval hostelry"), Pasternak moved into a nearby apartment on the second floor of the guesthouse at No. 15 Gisselbergerstrasse. This apartment is still intact, and its balcony looks as "miserable" and ramshackle as it does in Pasternak's description. His landlady, Frau Elise Ort ("the widow of a civil servant," as Pasternak describes her—actually, of a veterinarian) and her daughter, were afflicted with goiters, and both, he says, "kept catching my glance, that was furtively directed to their collars." The goiters reminded Pasternak of "children's balloons that are gathered into an ear-like point at one end and tightly tied," and he feared they guessed his thoughts.[30]

Pasternak was enrolled in three classes: logic, taught by Paul Natorp; Hermann Cohen's course on ethics; and Nicolai Hartmann's series of lectures on modern philosophy, focusing on Gottfried Wilhelm von Leibniz.[31] Natorp, whose "great white beard" and quick delivery the poet later vividly recaptured, was the

Pasternak's residence in Marburg from May to August, 1912: Frau Elise Ort's house (at No. 15 Gisselbergerstrasse), in which he rented a room. *Klaus Laaser, Marburg.*

The back of Frau Ort's house. Pasternak had a room on the third floor, whose "ramshackle balcony" looked out on the fields he described in "Marburg." *Klaus Laaser, Marburg.*

author of *Plato's Theory of Idea* and other noteworthy studies in logic and psychology.[32] His ideas were taken up with great seriousness by his Russian student, who soon penned an essay "About the Object and Method of Psychology," a critical discussion of Natorp's book of the same name, published that year. This paper, which was to be one of a series of essays on the topic "Symbolism and Immortality," contains an adumbration of Pasternak's later notion of feeling as a force in the physical and psychic spheres, as has been pointed out in a recent study.[33]

It was specifically to study under Hermann Cohen that Pasternak had gone to Marburg. Cohen, a university luminary, taught there from 1876 to 1912 and became the leader of the Marburg Neo-Kantian school. His famous *System of Logic* comprised *Logic of Pure Knowledge* (1902), *Ethic of Pure Will* (1904), and *Aesthetic of Pure Senses* (1912). For the Marburg school, life and thought were based on laws, just as science was, and the world was seen as a coherent, orderly system or systematic unfolding of events. Intuition and irrationality did not exist; sensation was not "known" but was an object for study; religion was no more than a system of morality, and God an ethical ideal to be imitated on earth. On the whole, the Marburgers were more faithful to Kant than the other Neo-Kantian schools were, but they diverged in that they did not confine their interest to the individual but went so far as to seek a fusion of Marxist philosophy with Kantianism.[34]

Sharing Pasternak's youthful feeling about Cohen, another foreign student,

View of Gisselbergerstrasse from Frau Ort's house. *Klaus Laaser, Marburg.*

Hermann Cohen,
Pasternak's philosophy
professor. Pasternak is on
the left. Sketch made by
Leonid Pasternak during his
visit to Marburg, early
summer, 1912. *Pasternak
Family Collection.*

José Ortega y Gasset,* considered Marburg to be the place where he was converted to philosophy, claiming that to Marburg and to Cohen he owed "at least
half of my hopes and almost all of my discipline."[35] As Ortega was to observe,
Cohen's great achievement was that he "renovated the impulse towards system,
which is the essence of philosophical inspiration"[36] (three of Cohen's students,
Ernst Cassirer, Hartmann, and Ortega, were among the most thorough and systematic thinkers of their time).

No less than Ortega, Pasternak would later believe that the Marburg experience had been highly positive, and would acknowledge his debt to Cohen, who to
him was "a genius." Pasternak depicted Cohen in a lively, perceptive way, presenting him as a "shock-headed bespectacled old man" who would

raise his head and step backward as he told of the Greek conception of immortality, and
would sweep his arm through the air in the direction of the Marburg fire station as he

*Ortega y Gasset studied under Cohen in 1907 and again in 1911.

Paul Natorp, another of
Pasternak's neo-Kantian mentors
in Marburg. Sketch by Karl
Doerbecker. *Universitätsmuseum,*
Marburg.

interpreted the image of the Elysian fields. Already I knew how on some other occasion, stealthily creeping up on pre-Kantian metaphysics, he would croon away, pretending to woo it, then suddenly utter a raucous bark and give it a terrible scolding with quotations from Hume.[37]

While Pasternak wrote of his master with humorous appreciation, another Russian disciple of Cohen's, the Symbolist Andrei Belyi, wrote of the philosopher in an anecdotal and sarcastic vein:

> The Marburgian Professor Cohen,
> Creator of dry methodologies!
> . . . .
> He twists his finger carelessly,
> And twisting like bison horns
>
> The hair falls over his marmoreal brow
> Into his steely azure eyes.
>
> He speaks, casts spells,
> In a torrent of sunlit dust;
> And with *The Critique* blesses
> As a monk does with a Bible.[38]

Like Kant, Cohen (as can be seen from his *System of Philosophy*) divided philosophy into three realms: logic, ethics, and aesthetics. While remaining anti-

Zionist and nonsectarian, over the years Cohen was increasingly attracted to Judaism,* but his interest in religion was confined to its function as an ethical system. Mysticism (and this in the town of Saint Elizabeth) was not admitted as a subcategory of religion. God embodied one idea, and that was truth. To regard God as being endowed with life or personality was to step out of Cohen's rationalistic *Weltanschauung*. The philosopher staunchly abided by his renovated version of Kantianism—and wanted no compromise with other schools holding sway at the time. To Bergson in particular he was vehemently opposed, accusing him of propagating a cheap nonphilosophy by using "publicity and propaganda."

Although he did not absorb all of Cohen's theories, Pasternak was influenced by the philosopher's monotheism and high ethical standards. He not only preserved his memories of the ancient university town and his newly polished German (to the end of his life his most fluent foreign language) but also retained the marks of the dichotomies pervading the Kantian philosophical system.† When one is assessing the influence that Pasternak claims Cohen had on him, it is reasonable to surmise that some of the master's concern with spiritual values rubbed off on the disciple (Cohen was already actively involved in conceiving and formulating some of his statements on Judaism, such as his essay *German Ethos and Jewish Ethos* [*Deutschtum und Judentum*, 1915], the principles of which he had certainly evolved by 1912). What Pasternak obviously inherited from Cohen, however (as evidenced later by his own religious philosophy), was the high-minded, conciliatory, generous attitude that pervades the German philosopher's essays and statements, rather than any specific concern for Judaic traditions and values as such.‡

Of all the experiences that were to have an impact on Pasternak in Marburg, however, the most powerful was that of rejected love. It was that experience that tore him from Cohen and philosophy and transformed him into a poet.

For about eight years Boris Leonidovich had been acquainted with the two daughters of the wealthy and worldly Moscow merchant D. V. Vysotskii, who lived in the same neighborhood where he had grown up (Miasnitskaia Street). For generations the family had imported tea from Eastern countries. Vysotskii was a patron of the arts who cultivated some of the Mir iskusstva (World of Art) artists, including Leonid Pasternak, who painted his portrait. Pasternak had tutored the Vysotskiis' older daughter, Ida Davidovna, a refined girl who was slightly younger than he.[39] Ida Davidovna later said that Pasternak and she "practically were reared together"[40] (it would appear to be an instance of Baudelaire's *vert paradis des amours enfantines*). Boris tried to impart to her his enthusiasm for such

---

*As has been pointed out, "It is the historic merit of Cohen to have refuted Spinoza's presentation of Judaism as a political legislation without universal religious significance, a view which Kant adopted from Spinoza. Cohen took up the challenge and vigorously renewed the Jewish claim to spiritual leadership" (Alexander Altmann, "Judaism and World Philosophy," in Louis Finkelstein, ed., *The Jews: Their History, Culture, and Religion*, 3d ed., 2:992–93. Cohen devoted sixty-eight papers and articles to various aspects of Judaism.

†These and other dualisms in his thought are discussed in Chapter 18, where some of Pasternak's categories are compared with aspects of the Kantian system.

‡For further discussion of Judaism, see Chapter 17.

View of Saint Elizabeth's
Church, Marburg, from the
east. *Bildarchiv Foto
Marburg.*

subjects as Greek, for which he had developed a (transient) passion. In retrospect he wrote, "My feeling toward [Ida Davidovna] was not new; and I had known about it since I was fourteen. She was a charming, pretty girl, excellently brought up."[41] The old French governess (who blended with the Vysotskiis' Swiss nanny to become Mademoiselle Fleury in *Doctor Zhivago*),[42] chaperoned the tutorials and, when they went on until too late in the evening, would tell the young tutor: "Boria, ukhodi, pora spat" ("Off with you, Boris, it's time to go to bed").[43] Pasternak was to observe later:

[The governess] knew better than I did that the geometry I was bringing into the house for her favourite at such unearthly hours was more Abélardian than Euclidian. . . . In her presence my feelings could remain inviolate. . . . I was eighteen years old. In any case, temperament and upbringing prevented me giving rein to my feelings, nor would I have had the boldness to do so.[44]

As adolescents Pasternak and Vysotskaia held long conversations lamenting the *poshlost* pervading contemporary society, especially in prevailing attitudes toward sexuality. Such conversations were to find their reflection in *Doctor Zhivago* in the "endless discussions" that the adolescents Iura Zhivago and Tonia Gromeko have about the *poshlost* of sex[45] (it should be borne in mind that this was the period when Andreev's and Mikhail Leonid Artsybashev's luridly erotic fiction enjoyed great vogue in Russia; perhaps Pasternak and Vysotskaia in their discus-

In Saint Elizabeth's Church, statue (ca. 1470) of Saint Elizabeth of Thuringia, whose legend Pasternak found touching and discussed in *A Safe-Conduct*. *Bildarchiv Foto Marburg.*

sions regarded such a phenomenon as the "vulgarization of voluptuousness" which Nietzsche's Zarathustra had viewed as an imminent danger).

In 1912, Ida Davidovna spent several months in Cambridge, enrolled at the university. There she discovered English poetry, her enthusiasm for which she tried to convey to Boris Leonidovich in voluminous letters. While spending the summer of that year in Belgium, she and her sister had occasion to travel to Germany. Upon arriving in Marburg to visit Pasternak, she presented him with an edition of Shakespeare's works and impressed upon him the need to study English to read the poet's works (to that tender advocacy can be traced the emergence of a rare talent—that of one of Russia's most sensitive translators of Shakespeare). In *A Safe-Conduct* Pasternak described his special elation during the sisters' three-day stay in town: "The three days I spent constantly in their company were as unlike my usual life as festivals are unlike workdays. I was endlessly telling them something or other, and was intoxicated by their laughter and the signs of understanding from people who happened to be with us."

On the morning of the sisters' departure, the young man, highly distraught, declared his love for Ida Davidovna and asked her to marry him: "There was nothing new in this at all except for my insistence upon it. She got up from her chair and backed away from the explicitness of my agitation which seemed to be advancing upon her. As she reached the wall she suddenly remembered that there existed a means of putting a stop to all this at one blow—and refused me." This rejection made Pasternak break into sobs while he exclaimed, "How beautiful you are!" The sad fact of which he was not (or not yet fully) aware was that Ida Davidovna's parents, alarmed by the young man's "lack of firm prospects," had prevailed on her to turn him down.[46]

His excitement undiminished by denial, Pasternak followed the two young women to the station and impetuously leaped onto the Frankfurt Express with them, to release the good-byes still choked up in him. They bought his ticket, and he had a "fairy-tale holiday" riding to Berlin with them. Once there, he was abandoned, and in a mood of great despondency he returned to Marburg: "My thirst for a final farewell, one that would be utterly and wholly devastating, had remained unquenched."[47] Later Vysotskaia was to concede the truthfulness of Pasternak's account of that day's events, events that she described as highly "romantic."[48]

The intensity of this youthful experience affected Boris Leonidovich so strongly that he soon made another decision: he would not marry a woman; he would divorce a profession. Even the dinner invitation he received from Cohen, a summons that symbolized acceptance into a career as a philosopher, did not alter his resolve. Early the next morning he left Marburg for Frankfurt, thus giving up the Sunday dinner and with it, in effect, philosophy. He intended henceforth to devote his time to poetry, converted for life by the emotions he had experienced on the streets of Marburg. Upon his return to Marburg there was a final, dramatic encounter with Cohen on a meandering footpath, marked by an awkward, half-hearted explanation by Pasternak that left both of them unsatisfied.[49] It should be stressed that Pasternak was saying "no" to a philosophical career, not to Cohen's system of ideas, which continued to claim his sympathy, if not his commitment. From Pasternak's description one may deduce that the encounter took place in Heu-Gässchen, a lane that still winds its shady way downhill past Marburg's Old Cemetery. A remark made by Pasternak suggests that he stayed in town long enough to hear the final official address that Cohen—according to university records—delivered on July 4, his seventieth birthday.[50] This occasion, coincident with the philosopher's retirement, was marked by various festivities at the university and articles in the national press. It was probably not the last Cohen saw of his favorite Russian student.* Pasternak formally took leave of the university on August 3, setting off shortly thereafter for a brief tour of Italy before returning to Moscow.

The impact of Vysotskaia's refusal opened Pasternak's eyes to the "fresh laconicism of life," and, impelled by this new, poetic perception of the world, he began writing poetry.[51] A passage of the famous poem "Marburg" (begun at that time to record the experience)[52] shows that the involvement with Vysotskaia was a *learning* experience, an existential exercise in knowledge, and as such necessarily had to eliminate and replace philosophy. In the poem, addressing the girl, he wrote:

> V tot den, vsiu tebia, ot grebenok do nog,
> Kak tragik v provintsii dramu Shekspirovu,
> Nosil ia s soboiu i znal nazubok,
> Shatalsia po gorodu i repetiroval.[53]
>
> [That day, from combs to feet,
> Like a provincial actor his Shakespeare,
> I carried you with me, and had you down pat,
> Wandered about the city and said my lines.]

Maiakovskii was always impressed by that particularly effective stanza, liked to recite it, and once called it "Pasternak's sublime quatrain."[54] It is embedded in a complex poem in which an essential personage is Marburg itself (characterized here—among other notations—by the historic houses where Martin Luther and the brothers Grimm had lived). The drama enacted in Marburg's presence originates in a refusal (Vysotskaia saying no to the young man), which triggers an epiphany in the philosopher, for whom suddenly "every detail came alive" and emerged with apparently final meaning of its own. Vysotskaia's refusal in turn triggers a refusal by Pasternak—his saying no to the invitation from Cohen, no to philosophy: "A refusal / Is fuller than a farewell."[55] The newly perceived Marburg landscape does its work on the erstwhile philosopher through the agency of insomnia (literal and figurative), and as a result he apprehends things poetically. Vysotskaia—whom the young man "learned" like a grammar—has taught him

---

*We may speculate that Pasternak and his father (who in recent years had reinforced his sympathies for the cause of Judaic culture) most likely were in touch with Cohen, then attached to the Academy of Judaic Studies in Berlin, when he visited Moscow in May, 1914, during a tour of lectures on Judaic ethics (cf. M. Z. Ben-Ishaj, "With the Pasternaks in Moscow," *Ha-doar* [New York] 12 (December, 1958); excerpted in the *Rassegna mensile di Israel* [Rome], February, 1959). See also Chapter 17.

that a different system of categories can replace Kant's and that henceforth the poetic vision will provide him with a new system.

Pasternak's farewell to philosophy was graphically illustrated by his physical desertion of Marburg—his leap onto the train to follow Vysotskaia to Berlin. As the impact of the girl's refusal began wearing off, Pasternak discovered that his passion for her had driven philosophy out of his soul and that still a new passion, poetry, could occupy the space that had thus been freed. The events in Marburg reveal that Pasternak was as much as ever a compulsive believer in signs and miracles, impulsively moved to act on that belief.

After Pasternak's return to Moscow, Vysotskaia's farewell proved not to be final; he continued to see her from time to time. One evening in 1914 he brought to her Renaissance-style salon Vladimir Maiakovskii, who, clad in his usual eccentric garb, recited his verse (for which Pasternak had conceived a passion). It was clear, however, that Pasternak's feeling for Vysotskaia was waning. Ida Davidovna believed that the final parting took place between the time of her betrothal in February, 1917, and marriage in December of that year to a banker from Kiev, Emmanuel Feldzer (with whom in 1918 she went to Siberia, and from there to western Europe). This break, she believed, released Pasternak's spiritual energies, and was related to the feeling of cosmic freedom that pervades his collection of verse *My Sister, Life* (written in 1917).[56] By then the personal transvaluation that had taken place in Marburg was sealed. A tender sentiment remained between them ever after, however. During the visits he was to pay to Berlin in 1922–23 and to Paris in 1935, Pasternak would see Ida Davidovna, and between the two visits she was the postal intermediary for some of the correspondence between him and Rilke.[57]

According to a pattern that Pasternak was later to depict in *Doctor Zhivago*[58] (the outburst of creativity that takes hold of Zhivago as a result of the separation from Lara), creative self-renewal is directly induced by a stormy passion; this pattern was to be repeated in Pasternak's life in 1930–32, when the self-renewal he described in the appropriately titled volume *Second Birth* was the direct outcome of an emotional upheaval. Pasternak's encounter at Marburg with philosophy and poetry—dramatically depicted in "Marburg"—was truly the experience of a man at a crossroads; it has been correctly pointed out that this poem is about the meeting of "existential opposites,"[59] the meeting of the Middle Ages and the contemporary world, of reason and love. The creative solution of the conflict between these opposites provided the basis for Pasternak's development.

The experience in Marburg fostered in him ceaseless devotion to his new poetic vocation. From July, 1912, during his last weeks in Marburg, he was "completely taken up" with poetry, which he wrote "day and night, at every opportunity."[60] As with Rilke (with whom Pasternak had such striking affinities on more than one plane) a total commitment to poetry as a way of life was accompanied by a fairly casual approach to the need to earn a living. Thus an attitude far removed from the established, bourgeois conception of a career is to be seen in the letter Pasternak wrote a friend before leaving Marburg: "I shall look for some position as secretary or correspondent in some commercial business or other. . . . I can picture to myself some mélange like the following for the future: private lessons, secretarial or correspondence work, and literary fancywork."[61]

Pasternak paid one more visit to Marburg, in February, 1923, when he found both the city and Germany "cold and starving," in the throes of the postwar depression. By then Cohen was dead, and Pasternak's goitrous elderly landlady (still alive, to his surprise) and her daughter were sitting and sewing in their usual places.[62] Decades later, when Pasternak resumed contacts with Marburg by mail, he learned that surviving members of the Ort family fondly remembered his gracious presentation to them of a large walnut cake on that bleak winter day.[63]

Many years after his last visit to Germany, Pasternak spoke of *A Safe-Conduct* in this way: "When I wrote these memoirs, I wanted to rebuild the stony city which I once gratefully inhabited, rebuild it with the force of my gratitude."[64] Several of his Russian contemporaries, who perceived in him the "Göttingenesque soul" of a dreamer who looked very much like a German university student, were aware of his debt to Marburg.[65] It is clear that, more than any other period in Pasternak's life, the rich few months he spent in Marburg in 1912 were dense with developments that were to shape the rest of his life. The intellectual, emotional, and cultural experiences he underwent at that time were crucial to his future growth.

The Marburg episode also reveals for the first time certain dimensions in Pasternak the young adult that will remain characteristic of him for the rest of his life: a highly impressionable temperament and a passionate nature, prone to impulsive actions. According to the categories of the so-called Groningen school of characterology (formulated by Gerardus Heymans and Enno Dirk Wiersma, whose work was continued in France after World War II by René Le Senne, Gaston Berger, and André Le Gall), Pasternak would be classified as a *secondaire* (a subject in whom the past reverberates strongly)—as opposed to a *primaire* (a subject who lives in the present, relatively unaffected by the past), and would be somewhere between a *sentimental* (defined as "Emotif, non-Actif, Secondaire") and a *passionné* ("Emotif, Actif, Secondaire").[66] On the other hand, in terms of traditional Jungian categories, Pasternak would appear to be an "irrational" type—and an intuitive rather than a "sensation" type. According to Jung, predominance of introverted intuition produces such types as both "the mystical dreamer and seer" and "the fantastical crank and artist," while intensification of intuition often results in "extraordinary aloofness of the individual from tangible reality" and a completely enigmatic nature—enigmatic even to the subject's immediate circle—traits that certainly were present to some extent in Pasternak.[67] The relevance of such categories seems obvious when we are dealing with one in whom sensitivity and memory (even memory of early childhood) were highly developed, at the expense of will (Pasternak's markedly weak willpower was perceived and discussed by the poet himself, who observed that there must be "a great deal of the feminine, of the passive" in his character—alongside an active and industrious attitude).[68]

The stay in Marburg reinforced the impact of his first stay in Germany as an adolescent and fixed in him the deep personal significance of German culture. His friend Marina Tsvetaeva was quick to notice that it was their Germanic roots in common—going back "deep in their childhood"—that brought Pasternak and her together.[69] Like her, he had a strong affinity for German literature, music, and landscape. In Tsvetaeva, it has been said, this affinity was "the exterior expression of the spiritual qualities which she felt were part of her innermost core and which were expressible and describable only in German—*Übermass* ('excess') and *Schwärmerei* ('enthusiasm,' 'rapture')"[70]—and the same holds true to a significant extent of Pasternak.

Pasternak's sojourn in western Europe was crowned by a hurried excursion to Italy. Now a penurious student, he had scraped together just enough for this luxury. At the beginning of August, 1912, Pasternak left Marburg, traveled through Basel and Milan (where he marveled at the Duomo during a brief stopover), and paid admiring visits to Venice and Florence. Then his funds ran out, which precluded a pilgrimage to Rome, and, like other penniless students in such a plight, he had to repair to the parental nest—now relocated in Marina di Pisa* for the summer—to obtain money for the return journey to Moscow.[71]

Italy, which had beckoned so many Russian writers since the days of the Romantics Zhukovskii, Gogol, and Viazemskii and which was a privileged source of inspiration to such contemporaries as Blok, Merezhkovskii, and Mandelstam, also spoke eloquently to Pasternak. In Italy he continued his searchings—this time trying to define his origins and aspirations through communion with the mainspring of western cultural and artistic tradition (his *démarche* thus being much the same as Blok's quest in the spring of 1909 for the message of inspiration in Italy's culture).[72] Pasternak later explained:

The chief thing that everyone carried away from an encounter with Italian art is a sensation of the tangible unity of our culture, whatever he may have seen this in, and whatever name he may give it. . . .
Italy crystallised for me what we breathe in unconsciously from the cradle.

What Pasternak discovered in Venice is that culture is characterized by unity and continuity: "I understood that the history of culture is a chain of equations in images, which link in pairs the next unknown thing with something already known."[73] New and original art does not spring forth from nowhere but has its foundations in the admired work of predecessors. It is this continuity of culture, discovered in Venice, that Pasternak would try to maintain in all his work,† including his autobiographies.

Back in Moscow, Pasternak enrolled at the university for the 1912–13 academic year, to prepare for his final examinations. He finished his studies with the help of

---

*From this resort town Leonid Osipovich made many day excursions to Pisa, Florence, Perugia, Siena, and Assisi (Leonid Pasternak, *ZAP*, p. 75). It is very likely that his older son accompanied him on some of these excursions.

†As Olga Hughes pointed out: "The idea of the continuity of art appears in a more generalized form in *Doctor Zhivago*. In his Varykino journal Zhivago defines the forces at the source of progress in the sciences and in art as rejection and attraction, respectively. Science moves ahead by rejecting mistakes and disproving false theories of predecessors; in art, the example of the predecessors serves as a catalyst for the art of the followers" (*The Poetic World of Boris Pasternak*, p. 56).

books and lecture notes provided by a young research student named Mansurov, a relative and friend of Nikolai Trubetskoi (nephew of the rector) and of Pasternak's friend Samarin (all three of whom Pasternak had first met at the Fifth Gymnasium). After taking his state examinations (presumably in June or July, 1913), Pasternak spent the summer of 1913 with his parents on an estate in Molodi. During that summer he wrote his first book of poetry.[74]

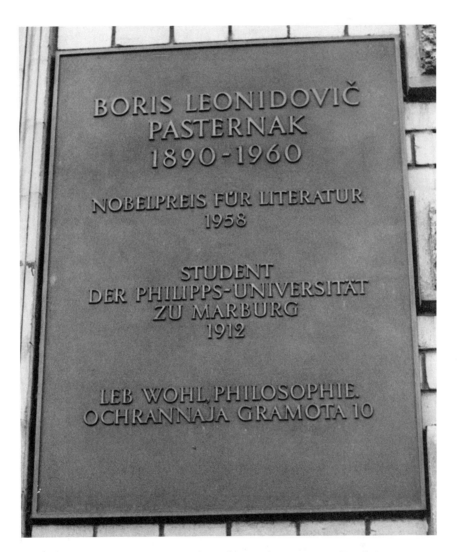

Plaque on the house where Pasternak lived in Marburg: No. 15 Gisselbergerstrasse, with inscription: "Boris Leonidovich Pasternak, 1890–1960. Nobel Prize for Literature, 1958. Student at the University of Marburg, 1912. 'Goodbye, philosophy' (*A Safe-Conduct*)." *Photograph courtesy of Ivar and Astrid Ivask.*

5

A Poet's Vocation

1913–1917

Boris Pasternak: Large eyes, puffy lips, a proud and dreamy look, a tall stature, a harmonious gait, and a beautiful and resonant voice. On the streets, not knowing who he was, passers-by—in particular women—would instinctively stare at him.

Iurii Annenkov[1]

Gravure portrait of Pasternak, 1914–15, by E. S. Kruglikovaia. Printed in the journal *Pechat i revolutsiia*, September, 1923.

Leonid Osipovich and his family spent their summers from 1913 to 1917 on an eighteenth-century estate in Molodi, near the Stolbovaia railway station on the Moscow–Kursk line, thirty-eight miles from Moscow. The Pasternaks occupied a full floor of the mansion, which overlooked picturesque grounds. Its well-proportioned, high-ceilinged rooms reminded the painter of rooms in Italian Renaissance villas and furnished him with the opportunity and inspiration to do a large-scale painting, the execution of which he viewed as a decisive development in his career (this painting, *Silver Anniversary*, of 1914, portrayed in life scale the artist's four children offering their respects on the occasion of the parents' wedding anniversary that year: Boris Leonidovich is first in line, reading a madrigal, while his sisters carry flowers).

During the whole of the summer of 1913 in Molodi, Pasternak, ensconced in the bower formed over a stream by the tangled branches of a half-broken birch tree, devoted all of his attention to poetry. He had brought with him a volume of Fëdor Tiutchev's verse, and for the first time in his life he wrote poetry, "not as a rare exception, but often and continuously, as one paints or composes music."[2] With philosophy now behind him Pasternak was able to give himself with some continuity to his new medium. From this summer emerged his first collection of verse, *Twin in the Clouds* (*Bliznets v tuchakh*). The poet later said that his choice of title betrayed "quite stupid pretentiousness" in that it echoed the "cosmological ingenuities which were characteristic of the book titles of the symbolists and the names of their publishing houses."[3] The collection appeared in print early in 1914 and included two poems describing his western European experience of 1912, "Venice" and "The Railway Station."

Pasternak spent the droughty summer and the fall of 1914 near Aleksin, on the Oka River estate of the Symbolist poet Jurgis Baltrušaitis, whose son he tutored while translating Heinrich von Kleist's *The Broken Jug* (*Der Zerbrochene Krug*) for the Moscow Chamber Theater. This assignment put Pasternak in contact with a number of writers and artists, such as Konstantin Balmont and Viacheslav Ivanov, in the entourage of Baltrušaitis.* Later in the fall, while he was still tutoring (now in the household of a wealthy German businessman, Moritz Philipp), Pasternak met the former governess of his childhood friends the Vysotskiis—a young Englishwoman who taught him her language and inspired the character Arild in *A Tale* (*Povest*, 1934).[4]

During the two subsequent summers the poet made only fleeting visits to Molodi; most of the time he stayed in Moscow. There he sustained himself almost exclusively on milk and bread and, elated by creativity, played dangerous games with insomnia, "transforming night into day." These continued games were to have a severe effect on his health in the next two decades.[5]

During these years his parents' Moscow apartment continued to be Pasternak's pied-à-terre. Occasionally he absented himself for tutoring assignments and on

---

*Jurgis Baltrušaitis, a noted translator of Ibsen, Wilde, and Strindberg, was close to leading figures in the theatrical world—Komissarzhevskaia, Gordon Craig, and Vsevolod Meierkhold. During the summer of 1914 he wrote several poems marked by a concern with the soul and spiritual assessment of individual fate (Jurgis Baltrušaitis, *Liliia i serp*, pp. 66–75).

The children of Leonid and Rosa Pasternak. Left to right: Boris, Josephine, Lydia, and
Aleksandr presenting gifts to their parents on the occasion of their silver wedding
anniversary. Painting by Leonid Pasternak, 1914. *Tretiakov Gallery, Moscow.*

journeys, such as his extended visits to the Urals during the winters of 1915 and
1916. During the second winter, while in Vsevolodo-Vilva, a village north of
Perm, Pasternak received a copy of Maiakovskii's recently published *Simple as
Mooing* (*Prostoe kak mychanie*). Maiakovskii asked him to review it for *Centrifuge*,
but not until a year later did Pasternak compose an enthusiastic article (which did
not appear because the journal soon ceased publication).[6]

By the winter of 1916–17, Pasternak had moved to the Quiet Mountains
(Tikhie Gory) area on the Kama River. There he managed the draft board at the
Ushkov Chemical Plant and exempted from military service entire districts of
people attached to factories engaged in defense operations.[7] While in the Urals,
Pasternak became acquainted with a young woman who at the time meant a great
deal to him and who very possibly inspired several of his female characters: the

adolescents anguished by the discovery of their femininity—Lara, of *Doctor Zhivago*, and Zhenia Liuvers, of *"The Childhood of Liuvers"* ("Detstvo Liuvers"), the only remaining fragment of a novel of the 1920s—and Zhenia Istomina, of "A District Behind the Lines" (published in 1938, an excerpt from a novel of the 1930s). The two Zhenias portrayed by Pasternak share with the later Lara her radiant goodness and femininity. It is of course not unlikely that these characters were also to some extent inspired by Evgeniia (Zhenia) Vladimirovna Lourié, whom Pasternak would meet in 1921 and who would soon thereafter become his wife.[8]

During his second winter in the Urals, Pasternak worked on a book of poetry that would have formed a link between *Over the Barriers* (composed in 1914–16) and *My Sister, Life* (composed primarily during the summer of 1917), but the notebook containing the poems was lost. When in March, 1917, news of the revolution in Petrograd reached the Ushkov factories, Pasternak undertook the return trip to Moscow in a horse-drawn covered cart with runners; he made a stop at the

Pasternak in 1913, when he was completing his philosophy studies at the University of Moscow. *Pasternak Family Collection.*

Left to right: Josephine, Aleksandr, Lydia, Boris, Rosa, and Leonid, Molodi, 1916.
Pasternak Family Collection.

Izhevsk ordinance works, traveling the rest of the journey with a Socialist Revolutionary chemical engineer, Boris Zbarskii.* That summer he joined the family in Molodi and continued writing poetry. The family also spent parts of the summers of 1917 and 1918 in Korsinkino, near Moscow, on the estate of their friend the well-known Moscow publisher A. Stybel.[9]

Such were the main events of Pasternak's life during this period, in the course of which he graduated from amateur versifier to poet whose achievements were acclaimed in both Moscow and Petrograd. Let us now retrace his intellectual steps during those years.

More than any other single influence, the poems of Rainer Maria Rilke provided a lasting stimulus throughout Pasternak's career. He recalled being arrested by "the urgency of what [the poems] had to say, the absoluteness, the gravity, the direct purposefulness of their language."[10] Even before the publication of his own earliest poems in the journal *Lirika* in 1913, Pasternak was translating Rilke's verse.[11] Discussing these translations, made in 1911–13, Christopher J.

---

*Zbarskii later participated in the embalming of Lenin's body. Pasternak continued their acquaintance and in 1916 dedicated poems to Zbarskii's wife (*STIKHP*, p. 629).

Barnes concluded that such free occurrence of fragments translated from Rilke interspersed among Pasternak's own earliest poetry suggests Rilke's importance as stimulus for the young poet's first creative endeavors.[12] Going further, Michel Aucouturier postulated very plausibly that it was "after reading Rilke that Pasternak for the first time felt the temptation to write."[13]

Rilke's significance for Pasternak extended to aesthetic prose as well. Points of convergence between Rilke's *Notebooks of Malte Laurids Brigge* (1910; Russian translation, 1913) and Pasternak's *A Safe-Conduct* (1931) have been discussed by Angela Livingstone. She has suggested similarities in the focus on perception of objects, the importance of the motif of visage (or personality: *Gesicht, litso*), and such themes as pity for woman, death, and the force generated by unrequited love.[14] At the same time, as Barnes noted, "The exuberance of Pasternak's impressionist imagery and the Futurist 'storm and stress' in many [of his poems] tended to obscure more fundamental similarities."[15]

As Pasternak developed his creative talents, the one-sided admiration he had for Rilke's verse was eventually replaced by a more complex relationship—a mutual admiration. In 1925, Rilke wrote Leonid Pasternak ". . . the youthful renown of your son Boris has reached me from more than one quarter," calling Pasternak's poems "very *beautiful* ones."[16] The following year Pasternak responded by writing his first letter to the German poet—an electrified utterance, in which he owned, "I am indebted to you for the very basis of my character and the very

Left to right: Pasternak's maternal grandmother, Berta Kaufman; Rosa Pasternak; Lydia; Josephine; Aleksandr; and Leonid, Molodi, ca. 1913–16. *Pasternak Family Collection.*

mode of my spiritual being." Pasternak later claimed that Rilke's recognition and the short ensuing dialogue (Rilke died later that year) enabled him to complete his work on the long poem *The Year 1905*.[17]

Describing Rilke's impact on Pasternak as "ultimately a spur to individual and original creativity," Barnes suggested that this influence did not cease after the 1930s, though from then on Pasternak rarely spoke or wrote of Rilke. He traced Rilke's continued significance through the clear emergence in *Doctor Zhivago* of Rilke's religious themes and imagery, while stressing that "it is mainly the Rilke of *Das Stunden-Buch, Das Buch der Bilder, Die Neuen Gedichte* and *Das Marien-Leben* who is represented and embodied [in the verse of Iurii Zhivago]."[18] Pasternak once spoke of his novel as moving largely in the "world of Malte Laurids Brigge."*[19] Thus the spell of Rilke endured. In a letter of 1959, Pasternak observed that he had "only recently" freed himself from Rilke's influence and yet felt that generally he had done little but "translate or diversify" Rilke's motifs and "swim in his waters."[20]

Pasternak's contribution in acquainting the Russian public with Rilke was considerable. In 1907–1908 he read *Early Poems* (*Mir zur Feier*) to the writers and artists of Serdarda. Later he introduced Iulian Anisimov to *Das Stunden-Buch* (very probably lending him his family's autographed copy), which Anisimov translated as *Kniga chasov* (*The Book of Hours*, 1913). In addition to translating several poems from *The Book of Pictures* (*Das Buch der Bilder*) in 1911–13, Pasternak later published other translations from Rilke in Soviet journals† and in *Sketch for an Autobiography* again endeavored to acquaint the Soviet public with Rilke's work through a discussion of two poems he made available in his renderings.

Somewhat improbable appears the path that Pasternak followed from eager sympathy for Rilke's spiritual refinement to a fairly close relationship with the vulgar, brash Russian Futurists. Yet the continuity between the two trends should not be overlooked; springing from the declining Symbolist movement, Russian Futurism opposed it yet essentially continued the revolution of poetic form begun by the Symbolists. The Futurists declared literary war on all conventions, cultural and aesthetic. They debunked the classics, insisting that language must be a writer's first concern and calling for its revitalization. Their tenets that all words may freely intermingle and that all subjects, even colloquialisms, may become "poetic" were central to Pasternak's aesthetic.

During these years Pasternak participated in three literary groups: the Musagetes, Lirika, and Centrifuge. Something must be said about his involvement in each. He tells us that in 1912–13 around the Musagetes publishing house‡ "there

---

*A reference to the spiritual universe of the protagonist of Rilke's *The Notebooks of Malte Laurids Brigge* (1910).

†Pasternak's renderings of "Requiem für Wolk Graf von Kalckreuth" ("Requiem for Count Wolf von Kalckreuth") and "Requiem für eine Freundin" ("Requiem for a Lady Friend") appeared in *Zvezda*, no. 8 (1929), and *Novyi mir*, nos. 8–9 (1929), respectively. Draft translations that Pasternak made in 1911–13 of "Der Schutzengel" ("The Guardian Angel"), "Die Engel" ("The Angels"), "Die Stille" ("Stillness"), and "Der Knabe" ("The Boy") were published posthumously (1969).

‡Musagetes (Greek for "leader of the Muses"; in Russian, Musaget) is a periphrastic name for Apollo. The publishing house brought out the literary journal of the same name.

was formed something in the nature of an academy," under whose auspices various experts lectured to individual "circles" (*kruzhki*) on such subjects as poetic rhythm, the history of the German romantic movement, Russian lyric poetry, the aesthetics of Goethe and Wagner, Baudelaire and the French Symbolists, and pre-Socratic philosophy.[21] A former Musagetes lecturer reminisced that the main theme of all discussions was "the crisis of European culture."[22] The prime mover of the academy, Andrei Belyi, met with a circle to conduct extremely minute and technical investigations, based on various statistical and computational methods, of the rhythmic figures and variations of Russian classical iambic verse. Those lectures Pasternak did not attend, unable to overcome a repugnance based on his belief that "the music of the word is not an acoustic phenomenon and does not consist of the euphony of vowels and consonants, taken by themselves, but of the relationship between the meaning and the sound of the words."[23]

Pasternak participated mainly in two circles: Lev Ellis's group for the study of problems of aesthetic culture and symbolism in art and the philosophical circle led by Fëdor Stepun, a disciple of the Neo-Kantian Heinrich Rickert.

On February 10, 1913, Pasternak delivered to a meeting of Ellis's circle a paper entitled "Symbolism and Immortality." If one discounts his readings of Rilke, this was his first public lecture.* A release announced that the closed meeting would take place at the studio (on Bolshaia Presnia) of Konstantin Krakht, a jurist turned sculptor.[24] The paper dwelled on an immortal subjectivity that allows man to participate in the history of human existence, a topic broached later in a similar vein in *Doctor Zhivago* as Iura Zhivago's bedside tirade to Anna Ivanovna Gromeko.[25] According to this earliest elaboration of Pasternak's views, generic immortal subjectivity is that portion of the soul which is the

sphere of action and the main subject of art. . . . Though the artist [is] of course mortal like the rest of mankind, the joy of living experienced by him [is] immortal, and . . . other people a century later [may] through his works be able to experience something approaching the personal and vital form of his original sensations.[26]

One commentator, L. Fleishman, has argued that the notion of the impersonality of subjectivity, or of subjectivity without a subject (which permeates Pasternak's poetry), is clearly linked with the Husserlian system.† Indeed, it is undeniable that the appearance in 1910 in Petersburg of a Russian version of Husserl's *Logische Untersuchungen* (*Logical Investigations*) did not go unnoticed by Russian intellectuals and that Pasternak was exposed to the Husserlianism pro-

---

*Pasternak wrote that he read this paper in the fall of 1910, at the time of Tolstoy's death; his son Evgenii pointed out his error (*IR*, pp. 63–64; E. B. Pasternak, editorial note to the Soviet edition of Pasternak's *Sketch for an Autobiography, Liudi i polozheniia: Avtobiograficheskii ocherk, Novyi mir* 1 [1967]; 219).

†Although he has a tendency to overdramatize Pasternak's intellectual promenades (e.g., arguing about a "shift" in the poet's allegiance from Marburg-Cohen to Göttingen-Husserl), Fleishman gives an interesting interpretation of Pasternak's "phenomenological" poetic vision (L. Fleishman, "K kharakteristike rannego Pasternaka," *Russkaia literatura* 12 [1975]: 82–88). Another critic has characterized Pasternak as a "phenomenological poet," as opposed to Maiakovskii as the "historical poet" (V. A. Shoshin, *Poet i mir {o tvorcheskoi individualnosti v sovetskoi poezii}*, Moscow, Leningrad: Nauka, 1966, pp. 122–24).

pounded by Gustav Gustavovich Shpet both at the University of Moscow and at a Musagetes circle.[27]

Early in 1913, Pasternak joined a new group of young, largely German-oriented poets, whose active promoters were Sergei Pavlovich Bobrov, Nikolai Nikolaevich Aseev, and Anisimov. The group, Lirika, had split off from Musagetes without severing all ties with it.

In addition to metrics and theory of poetry, Bobrov had a special interest in typography and made possible the functioning of the small cooperative publishing enterprise—also called Lirika—that brought out works by Aseev, Pasternak, and himself in 1913–14.[28] It is testimony of their friendship that Pasternak in 1913 dedicated to Bobrov his poem "Lyrical Expanse." Bobrov in his turn professed great admiration for Pasternak's verse of the period. Bobrov was, however, a literary *agent provocateur* of sorts, who created imbroglios and feuds among his acquaintances. Thus Pasternak tells us that Bobrov sought to watch over his "Futurist purity" and protect him "from harmful influences" ("by these he meant the sympathy shown by older people") and estranged Anisimov and Viacheslav Ivanov from Pasternak.[29] Bobrov also insisted that Pasternak protest vigorously to Gorky's journal, the *Contemporary*, about editorial changes made in Pasternak's translation of Kleist's *The Broken Jug*. Pasternak wrote a brash letter "full of studied and ignorant arrogance" (his own words) dated May 8, 1915, and later discovered that the "unknown hand" that had improved his manuscript "beyond recognition" was Gorky's. Eventually Pasternak made profuse apologies to the older writer. For years he was overcome by embarrassment at the memory of this incident.[30]

Pasternak and Aseev met through Bobrov and by 1913 were on friendly terms.* They dedicated several poems to each other until the 1920s, and from Pasternak's effusive inscription on Aseev's copy of *My Sister, Life* it appears that they came to think of each other as "brothers."[31] The years 1913 and 1914 were the period of the most intensive mutual artistic interaction between the two poets, though they maintained contact throughout the years (thus in 1917, when Pasternak was living in the Arbat district of Moscow, Aseev would appear "at any moment" to pursue the dialogue temporarily interrupted by his service at the front and Pasternak's stays in the Urals).[32]

Aseev later remarked, "Pasternak won me over by every trait: his appearance, his verse, his music."[33] In November, 1913, Aseev conveyed his admiration in the warm preface he wrote to *Twin in the Clouds*, declaring Pasternak to be an "original lyricist of modern Russian poetry" and his work a worthy heir to the great Symbolist "Armada." At least one Soviet critic clearly identified Pasternak as an important influence on Aseev's poetry.[34] During the 1920s, Aseev actively defended Pasternak's idiosyncratic art from more ideologically oriented critics of the day (the ranks of LEF and New LEF).† In a memorable essay Aseev remarked

---

*As a poet Aseev moved away from his more Western early literary manner, closer to the Slavic-oriented verbal experimenter Velimir Khlebnikov and to the magnetic Maiakovskii. His poetry of this period began reflecting his predilection for the Russian heritage and "the motherland," specifically in his abundant use of exotic and stylized Slavic and Old Russian forms.

†For a discussion of LEF and New LEF, see Chapter 6.

that Pasternak practiced a literature "meant to be studied" (as opposed to a litera-ture just "meant to be read") and claimed that there should be room for both kinds. Aseev's attitude toward Pasternak remained friendly in the 1930s, though it acquired a somewhat patronizing and reproachful coloration (displayed, for ex-ample, at a meeting of Moscow writers in March, 1936), reflecting his growing ideological incomprehension of Pasternak (it could well be that, in the context of Stalinism, Aseev, losing his nerve, was simply behaving in the way the regime expected him to).[35]

Pasternak declared that, in the period from 1913 to 1917, of all the young poets of his generation only Aseev (and Marina Tsvetaeva) possessed an already mature manner and mastery. It was through his study of Aseev's evolving style that Pas-ternak discovered Khlebnikov (indeed, in Aseev's work Pasternak was attracted to typically Khlebnikovian traits: "revived archaism and dialect usage combined with crisp alliterative structures and a songlike manner"). Pasternak praised Aseev's "disheveled, vivid imagination, [his] ability to transform triviality into music, [his] sensitivity and . . . guile of a genuine artistic nature."[36] The gener-osity with which Pasternak would lavish such praise on the mediocre Aseev—like his exaggerated admiration of Maiakovskii—suggests that in his judgments of close associates sentimental factors outweighed sober critical appraisal. Pas-ternak, however, sadly recognized what he called "the tragedy of Aseev": his betrayal of his talent through closer and closer association with Maiakovskii's clique in the 1920s and his demise before "the keenly felt political demands of the time."[37]

In the spring of 1914, Lirika was officially dissolved, and many of its followers regrouped under the banner of the new Futurist group Centrifuge (T'sentrifuga). This group—chiefly Bobrov, Pasternak, and Aseev—also ran its own publishing enterprise, under whose imprint Pasternak published almost exclusively until 1917. Centrifuge was a benign form of the Futurist disease, as opposed to the more vociferous Hylaea (from 1914, Cubofuturism), whose main representatives were Maiakovskii, Aleksei Kruchenykh, Benedikt Livshits, and the Burliuk brothers, David and Nikolai. Centrifuge's first significant publication was a col-lective book, *Brachiopod* (*Rukonog*), which contained a polemical document by Pasternak provocatively entitled "The Wasserman Test." Even Pasternak afi-cionados would not claim that this treatise—with its ambitious theoretical stance and disquisitions about the unfortunate democratization of poetry—was anything but diffuse and prolix. That would not be true, however, of Pasternak's second manifesto, "The Black Goblet," published in the 1916 volume *Second Cen-trifuge Miscellany*.*

Pasternak often met with a select circle of friends who shared literary interests. Among them were the Siniakov sisters—Mariia, Zinaida, and Kseniia (or Ok-sana)†—whose Moscow and Kharkov dwellings served as Futurist salons and with whom Pasternak, Aseev, and Khlebnikov were in love at different times. There was also that "Futurist Jesuit of the word" (as Maiakovskii called him) Al-

---

*See Chapter 18.
†Oksana Siniakov, who married Aseev, furnished the title for his collection *Oksana* (1916).

exei Eliseevich Kruchenykh, a former high school art teacher who became "one of the most controversial of Russian futurists and probably the most radical innovator among them."[38] Kruchenykh maintained friendly contacts with Pasternak over the years and often attended Pasternak's readings after World War II.[39]

Then there was Khlebnikov. Both a poet and a highly creative theoretician, he sought to revitalize poetic speech with his original vocabulary, based on his own complex, highly elaborated Slavic "folk" etymologies, which were little more than stimulating anthropological fantasies. His most famous theoretical contribution pertained to *zaum*, an artificially concocted non-sense language which was used in varying degrees by Russian Futurists.* The Formalist critic Viktor Shklovskii affirmed: "From V. Khlebnikov proceeded the poets Maiakovskii, Aseev, Pasternak," and in the 1960s, Ehrenburg would reminisce: "Maiakovskii, Pasternak, and Aseev have told me that without Khlebnikov they would not exist."[40] Although Pasternak was later to express reservations about Khlebnikov's parahistorical poetry, he continued until about 1918 as a member of Khlebnikov's Society of 317 (rechristened Society of Presidents of the Globe) and later as an active member of the Society of Khlebnikov's Friends, during its 1928–32 existence. A Soviet critic unsympathetic to both Khlebnikov and Pasternak suggested "an impressionistic fortuitousness of poetic associations" as a trait common to them.[41] While the poetic filiation of Khlebnikov and Pasternak has not yet been fully explored, their use of rhyme, consonant sound, uncommon vocabulary, and disaffected imagery is similar. It has been suggested that Pasternak was the Futurist Khlebnikov's true successor in experimental work with Russian poetic speech.[42]

Pasternak was in closest interaction with another member of this circle. At the end of May, 1914, a clash between two Futurist factions in an Arbat café brought Pasternak and Maiakovskii face to face for the first time (although Pasternak had known the latter by sight from the halls of the Fifth Gymnasium). Pasternak was already familiar with Maiakovskii's poems (those that would appear in his collection *Simple as Mooing*) and had decided that he liked them very much. Before him now in the coffeehouse sat their author, "a handsome youth of gloomy aspect with the bass voice of a deacon and the fist of a pugilist, inexhaustibly, deadly witty." The next day they met again by chance, and Maiakovskii recited from his tragedy *Vladimir Maiakovskii*, which had premiered on December 2, 1913, at Petersburg's Luna Park. Pasternak wrote: "I listened with held breath, my heart overwhelmed, oblivious." This early impression was later elaborated in a statement by Iurii Zhivago: ". . . he's a Dostoevsky character writing lyrical poems—one of his young rebels, the 'Raw Youth' or Hippolyte or Raskolnikov. What all-devouring poetic energy!" Late in his life Pasternak recalled that "against the background of buffoonery that was so characteristic of those days" the seriousness

---

* *Zaum* has variously been rendered in English as "transrational," "transsense," "transmental," and "metalogical" language, and in Nabokovian as "submental grunt." In his introduction to Kruchenykh's *Kalendar* (1926), Pasternak considered "transrational" poetry as poetry without reference, or pure and palpable sound that can evoke new referents (Boris Pasternak, *Works*, 3:15), whereas Khlebnikov's conception did not suppose a meaningless language.

of Maiakovskii's poetry—so heavy, so menacing, and so plaintive—was quite unusual."[43]

During the ensuing winter (1914–15) Pasternak and Maiakovskii often attended gatherings in the home of Zinaida Siniakov-Mamontov, where, during intervals of cooking *kotlety** on the first Primus stove Pasternak had ever seen, Maiakovskii would declaim *Vladimir Maiakovskii* or *The Cloud in Trousers*. Pasternak later observed, "By then I was accustomed to seeing in him the greatest poet of our generation."[44]

A serious artistic problem arose, however, from this interaction. In his autobiographies Pasternak tells us that, as he got to know Maiakovskii's poetry better, he encountered unexpected similarities in their respective techniques, notably in the structure of images and in the use of rhyme. What Pasternak viewed as a phenomenon of *convergence* or *coincidence*, however, appears to the literary historian as Maiakovskii's *influence* on Pasternak. Maiakovskii should receive full credit for discovering the genius of the Russian "semantic rhyme." Yet these explanations are not mutually exclusive, and together they help cast light on a complex artistic process. From Barnes's study of this process the following picture emerges. From 1914 until early 1916, Pasternak successfully imitated Maiakovskii; some of the resulting poems appeared in *Over the Barriers* (1917). By mid- or late 1916 the imitative period was over, and Pasternak was experimenting with a new approach in longer narrative poems.[45] Moreover, Pasternak ascribes the "nonromantic" elements in *Over the Barriers* to a conscious effort to renounce Maiakovskii's influence as he suppressed in himself elements he shared with his fellow poet, such as the "heroic tone" and the "desire for effects." By the time of his return to Moscow from the Urals in 1917, Pasternak had cut loose from Maiakovskii. The obvious literary influence had been overcome through qualitative growth, demonstrated in the full maturity and originality of *My Sister, Life*. The poet felt that this volume was "immensely bigger" than both himself and the poetic conceptions surrounding him.[46]

These artistic pursuits, as well as life in Russia and Europe of that decade, were disrupted by cataclysmic events. World War I erupted the very year the Futurists deployed a major offensive on the literary front—a wide-ranging tour of Russia during which they hoped to stir and perhaps win over the public by eliciting interest, disapproval, or *épatement* ("stunning the bourgeois"). News of the declaration of war reached Pasternak on Baltrušaitis's estate at the end of the torrid month of July, 1914. Summoned to Moscow, he was declared exempt from all military service because of the injury that had resulted from the fall from a horse in childhood. Returning briefly to Baltrušaitis's estate, he observed the first mobilizations of the tsarist army.[47]

Back in Moscow shortly thereafter, Pasternak assumed duties in the household of Moritz Philipp, whose son Walter he tutored intermittently until 1916. Late in the summer Philipp's residence and office, at the same location, were looted in a government-sanctioned anti-German riot, and in the turmoil Pasternak's books

---

*Meat patties prepared in the traditional Russian way.

Boris, aged twenty-five, in the
Urals, 1915. *Archives Jacqueline de
Proyart/Gallimard.*

and manuscripts were destroyed.* This incident prompted him to observe that he
never had been sorry for the loss even of successful works: "In life it is more necessary to lose than to gain. A seed will only germinate if it dies."[48] Pasternak moved
to a rented apartment with the Philipp family.

At about this time Leonid Pasternak was asked to create a poster for the war
victims' relief fund; he accepted eagerly and depicted a dramatic wounded soldier. The painting became extremely popular, and was reproduced in various
forms in hundreds of thousands of copies.† Initially Pasternak shared his father's
upsurge of patriotism, fully attuned to Maiakovskii's enthusiasm for the war (be
it said that, one year earlier, during his Moscow visit, Filippo Tommaso Mari-

---

* *In Sketch for an Autobiography* (pp. 80–81), Pasternak indicates that this incident occurred during the riot in the summer of 1914; however, it is possible that it took place rather during the anti-
German demonstrations in Moscow in June, 1915.

† The tsar, however, criticized the poster on the grounds that it aroused pity rather than admiration for bravery. Four years later the same poster was used as antiwar propaganda by the Soviet
government (Leonid Pasternak, *ZAP*, p. 84).

netti, the founder of Futurism, had pronounced war a salutary and vivifying hygiene). There are indications that Pasternak's attitude soon became more complex, however. His friend Annenkov recalled that their intimate circle was opposed both to the war and to such chauvinistic demonstrations as the ransacking of the German embassy in Petersburg. Pasternak's stance, Annenkov added, was that one should "close one's eyes to the war" in order to forget that "bad dream."[49] Indeed, in 1914, Pasternak did write the poem "Bad Dream," in which he described, with some details of military action, the "blizzard" raging over the country (this poem is very probably an elaboration of a nightmare about the impending cataclysm that Pasternak had in Marburg in 1912—a truly astonishing premonition).[50]

Pasternak did not enlist. Even if it had not been for his physical disability, educated Russian Jews had little chance of obtaining commissions (his fellow Futurist Livshits remarked: "A Jew, especially one equipped with a university diploma, appeared to every division of the armed forces as a bugbear, as the suspected bearer of revolutionary contagion, whom it was better, out of elementary caution, not to allow near a barracks").[51] Disillusionment soon set in when he found out about the bloody, dismal frontline reality and was dissuaded from joining the war, as he tells us in *A Safe-Conduct*: "Shestov's son, a handsome lieutenant, entreated me by all that was holy to give the idea up. . . . Shortly after this he perished, in the first battle following his return to position from that leave."[52]

Although the war naturally upset the course of literary activities in Russia, we should not be led to believe that it completely halted the pursuits of the literati. Konstantin Paustovskii, a witness of those days, evoked the intellectual effervescence, unaffected by frontline operations, that characterized the period:

The auditorium of the Polytechnical Museum was crowded with people when the Futurists put on a show with Igor-Severyanin. Rabindranath Tagore had captured people's minds. The Moscow Art Theater was desperately looking for a new Hamlet. Literary circles continued to exist in Moscow, and writers in these circles talked very little about the war. Religious philosophy, the search for God, symbolism, the challenge to a rebirth of Hellenic philosophy—these went right on, along with progressive revolutionary thinking, and competed with each other for men's minds.[53]

While he participated in this life, Pasternak's service in the Urals in 1915–17 made him feel that he was making some contribution to the war effort. From there he wrote home expressing dismay at what he termed "the abyss which is opening up between the cheap politics of the day and what is just around the corner." The former he qualified as "the prevailing darkness"; the latter he connected with "the new era" that he felt would soon begin, replacing the absurd with the meaningful.[54] Back in Moscow in March, 1917, he would live through that "new era" in Russia's turmoil.

Seated at his desk that spring, Pasternak, muffled in woolen sweaters and wearing Russian felt boots (*valenki*), continued composing poetry, with occasional interruptions to rearrange logs meticulously in the Dutch stove. While writing, he would smoke (as revealed in a sketch by his father) or drink many glasses of strong tea.[55]

6

The Poet After October

1917 – 1927

There is in his face something of the Arab and his horse: an alertness, an attentiveness, a full readiness to gallop away at any moment . . . a pronounced, also horselike, wild and shy slant of the eyes. . . . Thus he imparts the impression that he is always listening to something, with an uninterrupted attention, only to burst suddenly and prematurely into word, as if a rock or an oak tree had spoken. His speech . . . resembles the interruption of a primeval silence.

Marina Tsvetaeva[1]

"Together with people—roads, trees, and stars held meetings and made eloquent speeches." Such was the poet's perception of the revolutionary events, particularly of "that remarkable summer of 1917" in the interval between the two revolutionary episodes.[2] It was his sincere endeavor to apprehend the era's political turmoil, albeit in a peculiar mode of cosmic awareness. That vision was embodied in *My Sister, Life*, subtitled *Summer 1917*.*

This title has obvious Franciscan connotations, and Pasternak certainly shares with the bard of Assisi a conception of life as an enchanting force, yet as familiar as a close relative. It seems most probable that Pasternak derived some inspiration from *I Fioretti*, a Russian translation of which (*Tsvetochki*) had been published in 1913 by Centrifuge. If anything, Pasternak's enthusiasm is even more breathless than that of Saint Francis. The poet later owned to Nadezhda Mandelstam that the writing of *My Sister, Life* was the only instance in his life when "the miracle of a book in the making" had occurred.[3] The miraculous nature of this process had undoubtedly to do with the poet's endeavor to bring his writing "as near as possible to extemporisation." He tells us, "In 1917 and 1918 I wrote down only what by the character of the language or by the turn of the phrase seemed to escape me entirely of its own accord, involuntary and indivisible, unexpectedly beyond dispute."[4]

The results of such a method were utterly striking in their freshness. While the fifty poems in this cycle were composed under a single lyrical impulse, they unfold a diversity of topics. The setting ranges from restricted and intimate like a Mallarméan garden (with the expectable grass, lilacs, gardenias, dripping leaves and branches, siskin, goldfinch, swing) to the wide, empty spaces of the Russian steppe, made more immediate through the evocation of its peculiar vegetation in such localities as Saratov, Balashov, and Romanovka. Here the stock-in-trade of Russian lyric poetry has undergone an explosive renovation; the poems are invaded by such down-to-earth objects as silkworms, corks, aprons, mignonettes, calico, nitrogen, and sunflower seeds. Cultural and literary references are frequent: the narrator mentions Byron, Poe, Lermontov, and Kipling as familiar interlocutors or references. The unifying focuses are the love story that unfolds during that one summer and the constant upsurge of a life-force present primarily in the form of the water element—vivifying downpours, spoutings, and drippings. The landscape and its objects metonymically describe the narrator, who is strangely absent as agent from most of these poems.[5]

The volume established Pasternak as one of the masters of contemporary verse and with *Themes and Variations* (*Temy i variatsii*, 1923) sufficed to make him one of the two or three most original and significant poets of his generation. The credo for life and art that he affirmed in *My Sister, Life* was not altered later.[6] The book was met with wild enthusiasm by the more sophisticated of the younger poetry lovers. Nadezhda Mandelstam viewed it as "a book of knowledge about the world, of thanksgiving and joy." Marina Tsvetaeva claimed that the book was a high point of her stay in Berlin in 1922, saying that for ten days she "lived by this

---

*Additional aspects of Pasternak's reaction to the revolutionary era are discussed in Chapter 14.

book—as on the high crest of a wave." She forthwith penned a vibrant review, "A Downpour of Light," from the viewpoint of a critic whose "speciality" was Life, as she informed her readers. Mandelstam saw in the poems "a collection of marvelous breathing exercises: each time the powerful breathing apparatus is adjusted differently." He also proclaimed that not since the Romantic Konstantin Batiushkov had "such a new and mature harmony sounded in Russian poetry," and he hailed Pasternak as the "founder of a new mode, a new system of Russian poetry." With this achievement, as the émigré critic Dmitrii Sviatopolk-Mirskii put it, Pasternak "gradually became the universal master and exemplar, . . . and very few poets escaped his influence." For many years Pasternak, in Nadezhda Mandelstam's words, "held undisputed sway over all other poets."[7]

During the period when he was composing *My Sister, Life*, Pasternak was searching for the ideal pied-à-terre in Moscow. Part of 1917 he spent on his own in furnished rooms, first on Lebiazhii Lane, then on Gagarin Lane. Finally, during the winter, he lived in a room overlooking the roofs and trees of the Arbat, on Sivtsev Vrazhek, a street lined with two- and three-story stone houses and

Pasternak in the 1920s. *Ardis.*

Leonid, Rosa, Lydia, Josephine (*in front*), Mme Stybel, Boris, ca. 1917–18, on the estate of the publisher Stybel, in Korzinkino, near Moscow. *Pasternak Family Collection.*

haunted by the childhood memories of Aleksandr Herzen and Pëtr Kropotkin. This room he rented from a certain D. M. R. (a journalist on the staff of *Russkie novosti*), whom he described as "a bearded newspaperman of extreme absentmindedness and kindly nature."[8] In his turn the landlord, when asked to describe his boarder, once laughingly called Pasternak eccentric and unsociable.[9] At the end of the winter the poet returned to live in his parents' apartment on Volkhonka, which remained his residence until the mid-1930s. From that base he set forth to participate in the changing literary and social scene in Russia in the aftermath of the Revolution.

This was the time when many of the intellectuals who remained in Russia, whether or not they felt close to the Communists, worked in various public administrations. For example, Tsvetaeva served as filing clerk in the People's Commissariat of Nationalities—an experience that made her deeply miserable.[10] At a more responsible level Blok started working in 1918 at the Commission for the

Publication of the Classics, as well as for the theater division of the People's Commissariat for Education, or Narkompros. Pasternak was employed, also at Narkompros, from March to November of the same year, not as a librarian, as has sometimes been stated (although his desk was in the Narkompros library), but as a press screener, culling news items and reporting on foreign periodicals and newspapers.[11] Pasternak's employment there was probably not unrelated to the fact that the head of Narkompros, Anatolii Lunacharskii, was on friendly terms with Leonid Osipovich.

This job—referred to in the semiautobiographical introduction to *Spektorskii* (1931)—afforded Pasternak an excellent opportunity to become acquainted with literary life in the West at a time when regular access to the foreign press was almost impossible for the average Russian intellectual. Here he first became acquainted with the work of Marcel Proust and Erich Maria Remarque. After quitting Narkompros, Pasternak was never again to take service in an administration. In 1924–25, however, he reported that he was living "extremely modestly, not to say in poverty," and during that period tried his hand at various occupations, such as poorly paid bibliographic work on Lenin. He also applied for a position in an office dealing with statistics (a prospect that did not materialize) and considered an assignment as an editor that would have lasted the whole winter of 1925.[12]

Except for a very few poems, the composing of *My Sister, Life* and *Themes and Variations* had been completed by 1917–18. A period of about four years then set in during which the poet wrote only "circumstantial poetry" (that is, in response to commissions) and stopped doing, in his own words, "serious artistic work"— working on poetry that would become part of a cycle or a book. For a few years he devoted most of his time to writing prose. Officially his vocation was still considered to be poetry, however, and on such grounds in 1919 he joined the poetry section of the newly formed Moscow Professional Union of Writers. When completing the application for that section, however, he paradoxically declared that during the past two years he had been writing mainly prose, a novel and three short stories.[13]

Pasternak's first essays in prose date back to at least 1915. His desire to try his hand at a major fictional work probably also developed early, and had in any case crystallized by the spring of 1918, when he told Tsvetaeva: "I want to write a big [*bolshoi*] novel: with love, with a heroine—like Balzac."[14] In 1917–18 he wrote the draft of such a novel, which sometime thereafter was lost. Its first chapter appeared in revised form in 1923 as the short story "The Childhood of Liuvers."

That *Doctor Zhivago* was forty years in the making is attested by similarities in theme, structure, and content between the novel and some published as well as unpublished extant early prose pieces.* A typical example is a short piece entitled "Without Love" ("Bezliube"), first published in 1918 in two issues of the small

---

*We know for a fact that Pasternak destroyed certain drafts. For example, he tried to destroy the manuscript of his story "History of a Counter-Octave" ("Istoriia odnoi kontroktavy") by asking his son Evgenii to feed it to his stove (his son demurred, and the story was published posthumously in 1974).

Pasternak, ca. 1918–20. *Ardis*.

and short-lived Social Revolutionary newspaper *Liberty of Labor*.[15] This piece is a precursor of *Doctor Zhivago*, sharing themes, events, characterizations, and names with the later novel. The central conception of the novel is foreshadowed in "Without Love" in the contrasting attitudes held toward the Revolution and its supporters by the story characters Kovalevskii and Goltsev. The latter, indeed, is a prototype of Iurii Zhivago. Furthermore, the short story hints at a role that, when developed in *Doctor Zhivago*, becomes Lara. This early fragment mentions three names that are included in the novel—Gimazetdin, Galliula, and Mekhanosin—and also depicts Chistopol in the Ural Mountains (an area familiar

Pasternak writing. Sketch by
Leonid Pasternak, 1919. *Tate*
Gallery, London.

to Pasternak from 1915). As Max Hayward has pointed out, the tramcar accident
in "Without Love" foreshadows "three important events in the novel: the death of
the hero's father, the interruption of a concert because of an accident to one of the
performers, and the death of Zhivago himself." [16] "Without Love" thus makes it
clear that the revolutionary events had a significant artistic impact on Pasternak,
though decades were to pass before he could bring to completion the full-scale
fictional depiction of the events he conceived.

But such early fictions went unnoticed, whereas the appearance in 1925 of Pasternak's volume *Stories* (*Rasskazy*) brought him wide recognition as a prose writer.
The book comprised four stories, written and published individually in various
publications between 1915 and 1924. The Tuscan atmosphere of "Apelles' Mark"
(written in 1915) reminds us of Pasternak's visit to Pisa three years earlier; it is a
lively mixture of anecdote and allegory, although the author is not fully successful
in conveying what appears to be his deeper meaning: a statement on the signature
of the artist and artistic reality. The narrator of "Letters from Tula" (written in
1918) is a young poet, tormented by his awareness of art as an exacting vocation,
who writes from Tula (which he views as "the realm of conscience" insofar as it
stands for the principles of Tolstoy, who lived nearby), suggesting that authenticity in art is over and above mere faithfulness to realistic method. In "Aerial
Ways" (written in 1924) we have the first depiction by Pasternak of Communism
and its atmosphere ("the sky of the Third International"), specifically of the iron-
hearted morality of the high official Polivanov, an interesting precursor of *Doctor*

Zhivago's Strelnikov, who places an ideological cause above pity or other human concerns.[17]

The most remarkable of these four stories, "The Childhood of Liuvers" (written in 1918, published in 1923), is concerned with fourteen-year-old Zhenia Liuvers and her adolescent encounter with the outside world and discovery of womanhood. These experiences are told through the unfolding of a fine web of "sensations existing on the frontier between elementary, 'purely physiological' sensations and more complex 'mental' motions—sensations from things, rooms, trees, light and smell, sensations of the atmosphere of a house, a street, a spring corridor."[18] Shortly after its appearance the poet Mikhail Kuzmin commented on "Liuvers" as "the freshest Russian prose of the past three or four years" and said that it reminded him of the novels of Goethe and the early Tolstoy. Gorky thought the story "brilliant" and wrote a substantial foreword to an English translation by Baroness Moura Budberg, which in 1926–27 was being prepared for publication.* From his exile in Sorrento the dean of Russian letters wrote Pasternak urging him to write more prose, adding that "Liuvers" provided evidence that he could "write remarkable books." In Paris a prominent Russian émigré critic, Dmitrii Sviatopolk-Mirskii, also praised Pasternak's striking achievement in prose. These and other such commentaries on the *Stories* were the first evidence of serious critical attention to Pasternak's prose.[19]

These prose works represented Pasternak's response to the revolutionary events and the postrevolutionary scene, and should be considered in the context of a whole gamut of attitudes that Russian writers had toward the Revolution. Many of them so thoroughly disapproved of the new regime that they left the country, among them such acquaintances of Pasternak as the poet Vladislav Khodasevich, the former editor of *Apollon* Sergei Makovskii, and the Symbolist poet Viacheslav Ivanov. Over the years the political stance of Pasternak's mentor Gorky fluctuated: after the February Revolution he set up a Menshevik group called New Life, and in a series of articles entitled "Untimely Thoughts" (1917–18) sharply criticized the Bolsheviks. In 1921, at the "suggestion" of the authorities, Gorky left the Soviet Union, and many years were to go by before he would be reconciled with the Soviet regime. Anna Akhmatova's former husband, the poet Nikolai Gumilev, first served the Provisional Government, but in 1921 was accused of conspiracy with the Whites and shot. Shortly after the October Revolution, Blok wrote his famous poem *The Twelve*, which depicted Christ walking at the head of a squad of twelve Red guards. It was hailed by many as a striking pro-Soviet work, though Pasternak's erstwhile associate Bobrov denounced it as "a bitter bit of nothing." Soon Blok's growing disillusionment about the new regime was reflected in his statement on the anniversary of Pushkin's death: "Peace and freedom are taken away. . . . life has lost its meaning." Blok, who had been "a god" to Pasternak, died a few months after that statement, in August, 1921.

---

*This edition, which was to be published by Robert McBride in New York, never materialized (*Literaturnoe nasledstvo* 70 [Moscow: Nauka, 1963], pp. 308–10). In 1959, Baroness Moura (Mariia Ignatevna) Budberg visited and interviewed Pasternak in Moscow (Olga Ivinskaya, *CAPT* 49–50).

We can reasonably surmise that Pasternak felt close to a movement styled the Serapion Brothers (an appellation coined after Hoffmann's character). In 1921 the brotherhood—which included the prose writers Veniamin Kaverin, Konstantin Fedin, Mikhail Zoshchenko, and Vsevolod Ivanov and the poet Nikolai Tikhonov—issued a manifesto that proscribed utilitarianism and propagandistic purposes in writing, while proclaiming the individual writer's right to "paint his hut his own color"[20] (by the time he became Pasternak's next-door neighbor in the Writers' Village in Peredelkino, Fedin had changed his stance and had become one of the most conformist of Soviet writers).

Other writers moved more quickly toward an acknowledgment of the new regime. Acceptance of the Revolution was voiced by writers as diverse as Maksimilian Voloshin, Belyi, and Maiakovskii, while Briusov's new poetry glorified typically Soviet values like unremitting labor and pride in proletarian accomplishment. Ilia Ehrenburg (who in 1917 went to greet Pasternak at Briusov's instigation and introduced him to Tsvetaeva's work) published a volume of poetry, *Meditations* (1921) that indicated an acceptance of the Bolshevik Revolution. The acquaintance of Pasternak and Ehrenburg was to be pursued for decades in many encounters (in Moscow, Berlin, and Paris) and was marked by sincere mutual esteem. Pasternak described Ehrenburg as a "clever writer, active and unreserved and with a cast of mind so different from mine."[21] In total independence of the ideology of the day, Ehrenburg often spoke warmly and generously of Pasternak, first in the 1920s, in his *Portraits of the Russian Poets*, and then in the 1960s, when he was courageous enough to break the conspiracy of silence still preserved around Pasternak's name.

Many events facilitated intellectual dialogue during these years. First, there were Moscow's sometimes short-lived literary cafés and cellars, such as Pittoresk, Bom (with its red-velvet seats), the Futurists' Café, the Imagists' Café,* Pegasus's Stall, Domino, and the proletarian writers' café, The Smithy. In the evenings "Futurist," "Imagist," "Constructivist," or simply "poetic" soirées were held in these institutions, during which poets declaimed their works to oftencrowded motley audiences: intellectuals, frivolous ladies, blackmarketeers, officers, self-styled young "Futurists." Sometimes poetry readings were held in private residences. In January, 1918, Pasternak attended such an event, which had been announced as a "meeting of two generations of poets," at the apartment of the poet A. Amari (pseudonym of M. O. Tsetlin). Among members of the older generation Konstantin Balmont (who read some of his sonnets) and such acquaintances as Baltrušaitis, Viacheslav Ivanov, and Belyi joined the younger poets Ehrenburg, David Burliuk, Vasilii Kamenskii, Tsvetaeva, and Aleksei Tolstoy in acknowledging the significant talent of Maiakovskii, who read his poem "Man."[22]

Sometimes these programs featured Pasternak's poetry. For example, in March, 1921, one of the regular literary Wednesdays of the Press House was de-

---

*Imagism, or Imaginism (*imazhinizm*), a poetic movement organized in Russia in 1919, stressed the use of imagery, particularly of the metaphor, as the true basis of poetry.

voted to the reading (by the actress Vera Alekseeva-Meshieva) and discussion (by Maiakovskii, among others) of Pasternak's latest unpublished poems.[23] Only very seldom did the poet recite in a one-man show. As early as 1919 he expressed reluctance to read his poetry before mass audiences (such as those in the main auditorium of the Polytechnic Museum, where Maiakovskii and other Futurists liked to perform), "in view of the monstrous situations through which public appearances run nowadays." At the same time he indicated that he would gladly read "among writers and poets enjoying my respect."[24] When he was on the platform, Pasternak was the perfect antithesis to the stentorian Maiakovskii: "Modest, timid, endeavoring to remain in the shadows, Pasternak admitted neither noise nor publicity about himself and his works." While he recited, his manner also contrasted with Maiakovskii's: "No declamatory play, no architectonics based on modulation, nothing of the charm that derives from an enveloping and musical scansion."[25]

Pasternak was conspicuously absent from a particularly boisterous poetry evening held at the Polytechnic Museum in the early 1920s under the chairmanship of Briusov. During the evening Pasternak's poetry was subjected to heavy fire from several vociferous participants. On that occasion Briusov, with the masterful persuasiveness of a skillful debater, saved the situation by defending Pasternak's poem "The Mirror" (admittedly recondite for young Komsomols* uninitiated in modernist aesthetics) and arguing convincingly that this poetry was not meant for the "lazy reader" but for the attentive and serious reader adept at delving into the meanings of poems.[26]

Typical of the more intimate—and more creatively oriented—gatherings that Pasternak enjoyed was the session held at an apartment in May, 1919, during which the poet, in the company of Maiakovskii, Roman Jakobson, and Khlebnikov, consumed much tea spiked with rum while participating in a virtuoso exercise in versification: the composing of quatrains based on rhymes assigned by some of those present.[27]

Of all the writers with whom Pasternak developed a dialogue during this period, Tsvetaeva became the most significant presence on his intellectual and spiritual horizon. Their acquaintance began early in 1918, at the instigation of Ehrenburg, who tried—unsuccessfully at first—to instill in them an interest in each other's work. Tsvetaeva later listed the five occasions on which Pasternak and she met during the four-year period before her departure from Russia in mid-1922—occasions during which no spark of admiration or love flared, though mutual esteem was established.[28] They began to recognize how much they had in common, apart from love for poetry: each had a father who had achieved prominent status in the academic world, a mother-musician who had been Anton Rubinstein's protégée, and a deep love for Germany's rich culture and philosophy.

The *coup de foudre* occurred in the spring of 1922, when Pasternak bought a copy of Tsvetaeva's *Versts* and "was instantly won over by the great lyrical power of the form of her poetry, which stemmed from personal experience."[29] At the

*Members of the Communist youth organization.

same time that *Versts* became "a revelation" to Pasternak, an ecstatic Tsvetaeva discovered Pasternak's *My Sister, Life* (until her recent arrival in Berlin she had been unable to see the significance of his poetry). Pasternak then wrote her about his enthusiasm for her art, initiating an intense friendship by mail. As Tsvetaeva's biographer has observed, this correspondence was "a continuous inspiration and comfort" to her.[30] The whole history of Tsvetaeva's subsequent relationship with Pasternak is in keeping with her well-known propensity for forming passionate in absentia friendships.

The dialogue between the two artists was mainly on the plane of creative endeavor. They exchanged manuscripts and critical comments and dedicated many poems to each other, notably eighteen poems by Tsvetaeva during the period 1923–25, including the folk epic *The Swain* (1924) and the cycle "Twosome" (1924); and Pasternak's *Lieutenant Schmidt* (1926) and "To Marina Tsvetaeva" (1928).* Throughout this exchange their debts to each other's art grew. On the one hand, Pasternak acknowledged Tsvetaeva's early mastery, later commenting on her exceptional force and assurance and original style within the context of a generation of young and technically somewhat immature poets (among whom he included himself). As Tsvetaeva's talent developed, he particularly admired her long poems "Poem of a Mountain," "Poem of the End," and "The Pied Piper" (1924).[31] On the other hand, Tsvetaeva's avowed intention in publishing her article "A Downpour of Light" (1922), devoted to *My Sister, Life*, was to vouch for Pasternak's quality to the Western world.[32] Within the context of this warm dialogue it was natural for Pasternak to give thought to Tsvetaeva's spiritual and material welfare. Thus he begged Rilke to send her copies of his *Duino Elegies* (*Duineser Elegien*) and *Sonnets to Orpheus* (*Sonnette an Orpheus*)—a request that initiated the dialogue between Rilke and Tsvetaeva. In 1927 he went out of his way to try to engineer his fellow poet's return to her native soil, stressing to Gorky her "huge talent" and her "unhappy, unbearably twisted fate" (Gorky's response, based on a gingerly appraisal of the political and literary factors involved, amounted to a refusal to take an interest in her fate, and on October 27, 1927, Pasternak wrote Gorky a hasty letter that led to a temporary break between them).[33] The dialogue between Pasternak and Tsvetaeva was reflected in Pasternak's novel in verse *Spektorskii* (1931), in a similar intercourse between two characters, the *émigré* poetess Mariia Ilina and the poet-protagonist, both creative artists who are out of tune with their environment, much like Pasternak and Tsvetaeva by the end of the 1920s.[34]

In both her letters and her poems addressed to Pasternak, Tsvetaeva presented their relationship with strong, emotional, even passionate overtones. In the poems Pasternak is present in the form of natural phenomena, and their encounters are described in the vocabulary of lovers' trysts.[35] Because of her fascination for her fellow poet, she wanted to discover and penetrate his everyday existence (she wrote to him: "Describe the everyday life [*byt*] in whose context you live and

---

*To Tsvetaeva's sister Anastasiia, who conveyed messages between Gorky and him, Pasternak dedicated his long poem "High Malady" ("Vysokaia bolezn") (1924).

write, Moscow, the air, yourself in space. This is important to me"); the world of his childhood, to which she felt attracted and to which she wanted to revert (in certain of her letters she and Pasternak are conceived of as children playing together); and the people he associated with—(in 1922–23 she told a common acquaintance in Berlin that she would like to know what Pasternak's bride was like, what he did there, who his friends were).[36] To another friend she wrote in 1923: "Pasternak is something sacred to me, all my hope; at one moment, the sky beyond the edge of the earth; at another, what has not yet been; and then, what is to be." A few months before, she had written the poet, "Now, you are my life."[37] And when a son was born to Tsvetaeva in 1925, she almost predictably declared that she wanted to name him Boris "in honor of my favorite contemporary, Boris Pasternak," though at her husband's insistence she finally agreed to another name.[38]

There was, however, more to life than intellectual dialogue and exalted friendships. The economic crisis of the 1920s placed a heavy burden on the Pasternak family. Leonid Osipovich's portrait commissions dwindled, and he found it increasingly difficult to manage the household on his moderate salary from the School of Painting. His older son took on some of the responsibility for the family's support. In June, 1920, Pasternak wrote a sarcastic petition to the Literature Department of Narkompros, declaring himself to be nearly starving and itemizing his qualifications for a subsidy with the following comment:

The list consists mainly of translations done to order [in one year] for the publishing house World Literature and for the Theater Department of Narkompros. . . . Numerically, the total amounts to 12,000 (twelve thousand) lines of poetry. That constitutes a level of intensity, a form and condition of involuntary labor whereby its vehicle and agent . . . gradually abandons the province of art, then of independent craft as well. Finally, forced by circumstances, he sees himself subjected to an impossible professional involuntary servitude that . . . given the inevitable social inertia, cannot be lifted.[39]

Such was Pasternak's first encounter with the seamier side of the writer's craft.

Soon the need to earn an adequate living became more urgent. In the fall of 1921 he met at a party a fellow artist from Petrograd, the painter Evgeniia Vladimirovna Lourié, fell madly in love with her, and married her in the spring of 1922. Evgeniia Vladimirovna was a small woman with blue eyes and brown hair. Her husband later described her beautiful Renaissance profile, so reminiscent of a portrait by Ghirlandajo that "one wanted to bathe in her face"; but he pointed out that since "she always needed this illumination in order to be beautiful, she had to have happiness in order to be liked"—whence her inability to cope with life's distresses.[40] It has been remarked that, in contrast to Pasternak, who was a very mobile person, his wife was a languid beauty who liked to sit around the house. Born into a traditional Jewish intellectual family, she had received a well-rounded education and spoke French fluently.[41]

Pasternak and his bride soon went to Germany for what was officially described as a "health cure" (one of the few acceptable purposes that could be listed on an application for a foreign passport).[42] They sailed for Berlin on August 15, 1922;

the scene was recorded in the poem "Sailing Away," complete with Baltic land-scape, birchbark, and a swooping seagull.[43]

Pasternak had two reasons for making the visit to Germany, which was to last nine months. One was to introduce his bride to his family—all of whom except his brother, Aleksandr, had moved to Berlin the year before. The other was a quest for the literary and intellectual sophistication that the German capital promised. Also, compared with Moscow, which was still plagued by many shortages, life in Berlin (for all its limitations) was considered, at least until 1922, to be more pleasant. Writing Pasternak from Berlin in that year, Tsvetaeva had listed additional advantages that it offered: elbow room (*prostory*) and anonymity.[44]

The year 1921 had marked the end of Leonid Osipovich's thirty-two-year stay in Moscow and his long professorship at the School of Painting. Because of Rosa Isidorovna's deteriorating heart condition and his own need for medical care for an eye ailment, he and his wife and their daughters had obtained permission to leave for Berlin through the intercession of Anatolii Lunacharskii. Even more compelling was the destitution from which the family was suffering. Moreover, one can reasonably assume that during the period 1918–21 Leonid Pasternak's position at the School of Painting, now restructured as Vkhutemas, could only have been uncomfortable. The atmosphere was pervaded by the revolutionary aesthetics of Kazimir Malevich, Vladimir Tatlin, Anton Pevsner, and Vasilii Kandinsky, which he thoroughly disliked. In the art world it was a time of great turmoil, and even Marc Chagall was ousted by Malevich from the Vitebsk Art School on the grounds that his work was old-fashioned and irrelevant. There is, however, no reason to believe that Leonid Pasternak was in political disagreement with the Soviet regime; his eagerness to portray Lenin and his subsequent good relations with the Soviets bespeak his sympathy with the new government. The Pasternaks retained their Soviet passports.

Life in Berlin was not easy for the painter and his family. It took many years for Leonid Osipovich to develop the necessary contacts with galleries and art connoisseurs. His younger daughter, Lydia, began studying chemistry, while her sister, Josephine, read philosophy at the university. Both ultimately obtained doctorates.* The new home the parents established continued to attract the family after Pasternak's visit. Aleksandr Leonidovich stayed in Germany from August, 1924, until November, 1925, to continue his architecture studies. The painter developed misgivings about what he termed "existential compromises" (that is, the concern for a family), believing that they had an adverse effect on an artist's development; he even broached the subject to his younger son.[45] The latter, however, disregarded his father's advice to remain a bachelor for a while and returned to Russia to marry Irina Nikolaevna Viliam-Vilmont (sister of the philologist

---

*Shortly before the Revolution, Lydia Leonidovna had expressed a strong desire to study medicine but had been dissuaded by her parents because of a typhus epidemic. After switching to chemistry, she worked for a time in the 1930s at the Institute for Advanced Research in psychiatry in Munich. Both she and her older sister later published poetry.

Nikolai, who had been a university friend of Boris Pasternak's).[46] Aleksandr Leonidovich's decision to return to Russia appears to have been based on a personal preference, since staying in Germany would have been an entirely feasible course of action.*

Having joined the family circle in exile, Pasternak and his wife were at liberty to explore the lively and amazingly variegated scene of postwar Berlin with its significant new Russian component. Until the 1920s the Russian colony had been made up mostly of monarchists and political refugees (in 1919, Russians were arriving at the rate of 1,000 a month). Most of the Russian émigré artists and intellectuals came in 1921–23. With them came army officers, bureaucrats, financiers, politicians, and members of the old court society. With well over 100,000 Russians living in the city at the peak of the emigration, Berlin was often referred to as "Russia's second capital" and Kufürstendamm as Nepskii prospekt (a pun on the name of the well-known main artery of Petrograd, Nevskii prospekt) and "the Nevskii Perspective" (the pun refers to NEP, the New Economic Policy inaugurated by Lenin in 1921). Berlin also became the main cultural center for East European Jewry in the 1920s.[47]

The Russian colony was scattered over the southwestern suburb Charlottenburg, an affluent residential area before World War I, as well as Wilmersdorf suburb, especially the district around Pragerplatz. The postwar shabbiness of that middle-class area was carefully hidden. Russians who lacked funds were aided by the YMCA, the German government, and the Red Cross. A great many of them, aristocrats and others, worked as waiters, droshky drivers (*Droschkenkutscher*), or taxi drivers. Their grief or joy reverberated along with the strains of balalaika music in vodka-dispensing bars also run by Russians.

The attraction that postwar Berlin held for intellectuals in particular was due to several factors: easy entrance visas, the cordial reception of the Germans, a large reading public, and publishing opportunities.[48] By 1900, Germany had become the world's largest publisher of books, and by the 1920s, Berlin had become almost a paradise for intellectuals. Until the early twenties the only publishing outlet available to Russian writers not of the monarchist camp was the newspaper *Golos Rossii*, whose contributors shared a platform of war-weariness. But from the

---

*Although he disregarded his father's advice and married, Aleksandr Pasternak made good progress in his career. In the 1920s he became one of the members of the Association of Contemporary Architects (sometimes referred to by its Russian acronym, OSA), which was to become the most prominent architectural organization of the period. This Moscow-based Constructivist group advocated the use of new techniques (which kept abreast of achievements by Charles-Édouard Le Corbusier and other leading Western architects), and a communal socialist approach to the economic aspects and challenges of architecture. Aleksandr Pasternak worked closely with the renowned theoretician and practicing architect Moisei Iakovlevich Ginzburg, one of the founders of the association and a prominent housing and urban planner in Moscow and the Crimea. Under Ginsburg's direction Aleksandr Pasternak joined a team that concentrated on the development of a living unit "for the future," a complex of communal residential quarters linked by covered passages—a prototype of which was successfully built on Gogol (Gogolevskii) Boulevard in Moscow. In that complex Pasternak obtained an apartment in which he has lived with his family for the past few decades, and where I visited him. Cf. O. A. Shvidkovsky, ed., *Building in the USSR, 1917–1932* (New York: Praeger, 1971), pp. 22–23, 90–96, 98.

end of 1921 to the spring of 1923, Berlin was flooded with Russian publishing operations, which found conditions there far better than they were in Russia, where paper was still very scarce. Berlin publishers sold their books locally and also in the Soviet Union.

Perhaps the most colorful figure of the Russian publishing world in exile was Zinovii Grzhebin, who, after settling in Berlin in 1920, founded the most important émigré publishing house. Before leaving Russia, Grzhebin had bought manuscripts "hysterically" and now was publishing books by the hundreds: ". . . books as such. Books for their own sake. Books to assert the name of his publishing house." Under the imprint of that man, who had an "appetite for the creation of things," Pasternak's *My Sister, Life* appeared late in 1922.[49] Another prominent publishing house was Helikon, which brought out Pasternak's volume of poetry *Themes and Variations* in 1923 and also published Ehrenburg's masterpiece *The Adventures of Julio Jurenito* (1922), a zesty neopicaresque novel that was the vehicle for incisive political and social satire and gained immediate acclaim. Other notable Berlin publications included Shklovskii's brilliant *Zoo, or Letters Not About Love* (1923) and Ehrenburg's *Portraits of Russian Poets*, which con-

Pasternak, early 1920s. The frontispiece in one of his early collections of poetry.

Cubistic portrait of Pasternak by
Iurii Annenkov, 1921.

tained a vibrant appraisal of Pasternak. It should not be assumed that only
extreme-right or permanent émigrés were publishing their works in Berlin:
Maiakovskii, who was in the German capital from mid-October to late November, 1922, signed a contract with the publishing house Nakanune for *The Selected
Maiakovskii*.[50]

Flocks of displaced Russian intellectuals,* including Pasternak and several
publishers, frequented the cafés and *Weinstuben* in the large Russian quarter.
These places were important centers of Russian intellectual life. Often four or five
separate literary gatherings or poetry readings were going on simultaneously on a
given evening. Ehrenburg described the Café Landgraf, a favorite meeting place:
"[It] reminded one of Noah's Ark, where the clean and the unclean met peaceably;
it was called [by Russian patrons] the House of Arts and was just an ordinary
German café where Russian writers gathered on Fridays." Ehrenburg recalled

---

*Among others who resided in Berlin were prose writers Gorky and Boris Zaitsev; poets Pavel
Antokolskii and Nikolai Otsup; critics and scholars Viktor Shklovskii, Pëtr Bogatyrev, and Pavel
Muratov; and artists Chagall, Ivan Puni (Jean Pougny), Aleksandr Arkhipenko, Naum Gabo, and
El Lissitzky.

Standing, from the left: Vladimir Maiakovskii, Osip Brik, Pasternak, Viktor Shlovskii (others unidentified); *seated, from the left*: Elsa Triolet, Lili Brik, and Evgeniia, Pasternak's first wife (others unidentified), mid-1920s.

that in the House of Arts such writers as Pasternak, Aleksei Remizov, Aleksei Tolstoy, Boris Pilniak, Sergei Esenin, Tsvetaeva, Maiakovskii, Belyi, Vladislav Khodasevich, and Igor-Severianin recited their prose or poetry.[51]

Along with these sessions Berlin was the setting of more dignified assemblies of Russian intellectuals. In 1921, Belyi and others founded a local branch of Petrograd's Free Philosophical Association, and in 1922 the émigrés founded the Russian Religious-Philosophical Academy, which offered a full schedule of public lectures. Nikolai Berdiaev spoke on religious philosophy; Fëdor Stepun (whom Pasternak remembered from his Musagetes days), on romanticism; Iulii Aikhenvald, on Russian intellectual history; Nikolai Arsenev, on early Christianity; Ivan Ilin, on the philosophy of art; Lev Karsavin, on the Middle Ages; and Semën Frank, on Greek philosophy. These intellectual discussions revolved around the value systems that had helped bring on World War I, as well as the religious and historical significance of recent world events.[52]

Pasternak was present at many of these lectures. He also spent a great deal of the fall of 1922 in the company of Ehrenburg, Shklovskii, Belyi, Zaitsev, Maiakovskii, and Khodasevich at the various establishments most favored by the Russian intellectuals, such as—in addition to the Café Landgraf—the Café Leon and the Prager Diele on Pragerplatz, debating both the literary activities of the day and the eternal metaphysical issues dear to Russians. He attended both theatrical performances, such as Arthur Schnitzler's pantomime *Pierrette's Veil* on September 26, and also various poetry readings.[53]

Some of the sessions were given over to Pasternak, who read from his verse. While returning home after one such reading, Belyi and Khodasevich complained loudly about the difficulty of Pasternak's verse and about its limited interest once the difficulties had been overcome. The Futurist element in Pasternak remained unpalatable to those nurtured on a Symbolist aesthetic. In spite of these criticisms, however, Pasternak continued his dialogue with poets of various aesthetic creeds. He also saw other acquaintances, such as his former love, Ida Davidovna Vysotskaia (now Mme Feldzer), whom he visited two or three times.[54]

Despite the company of such friends and of his beautiful young wife, and despite exposure to the sophistication of both Russian and German Berlin (with each of which he felt quite at home), Pasternak was uneasy during the first few months of 1923. Shklovskii described aspects of this uneasiness in his striking portrait of Pasternak in *Zoo*. Describing the poet's elliptical speech ("hurling a dense throng of words this way and that, while the most important thing remained unsaid"), Shklovskii alluded to Tsvetaeva's well-known likening of her fellow poet to both an Arab and his horse and elaborated: "Pasternak is always straining in some direction, but without hysteria: he pulls like a strong and fiery horse. He trots, but he wants to gallop, throwing his legs far forward." This perception of the poet is supplemented by an analysis of his dynamic character:

Pasternak was feeling the propulsion of history. He feels movement; his poems are remarkable for their propulsion: the lines bend; they do not align themselves like steel bars; they collide like the cars of a suddenly braked train. Good poems. A happy man. He will never be embittered. He will surely be happy and cherished to the end of his life.[55]

For Shklovskii this sense of propulsion was at the root of Pasternak's uneasiness in Russian Berlin, among whose inhabitants he felt "an absence of propulsion" and a lack of "destiny." The prospect of settling down in the Russian colony—that "enclave of waiters and singers within a conquered nation"[56]—could not have been alluring.

The vitality of Russian intellectual life in Berlin reached its zenith in 1922–23 and then began to decline under the impact of widespread political unrest and soaring inflation. The bleakness of Germany's fate saddened Pasternak. He had difficulty recognizing Marburg when, accompanied by his wife, he paid it a two-day visit in February, 1923. He later commented: "Germany was cold and starving, deceived about nothing and deceiving no one, her hand stretched out to the

Pasternak, 1923. Drawing
by Leonid Pasternak, early
March, 1923. *Tretiakov
Gallery, Moscow.*

age like a beggar (a gesture not her own at all), and the entire country on
crutches." The country's plight shook him so profoundly that (as he later confessed) it took him "a daily bottle of brandy and Charles Dickens to forget it."[57]

Shklovskii and Belyi ultimately found exile intolerable and returned home in
the 1920s; Aleksei Tolstoy, converted to the Change of Landmarks ideology,* left
in 1923; others like Tsvetaeva and Gorky remained in exile a few more years be-

---

*The Change of Landmarks (*Smena vekh*) movement, based first in Paris, then (in 1922–24) in
Berlin, was composed of a number of intellectuals who advocated acceptance of the Bolshevik re-
gime, acknowledgment of its leaders as the de facto rulers of Russia, and ideological dialogue with
Moscow.

fore being lured home; and the Khodaseviches and others sought a shelter else-where in the West.

In early March, 1923, Tsvetaeva (who had been in Prague since mid-1922) heard for the first time about Pasternak's imminent return to the Soviet Union. She wrote him, "If I had known that you would be leaving so soon . . .," explaining that she could not arrange a trip to Berlin on such short notice. Thus he would depart without having met her during his German sojourn.[58] Even such a close friend as Tsvetaeva did not then know why Pasternak was going back, obviously having assumed that he would stay in Berlin.[59] Pasternak's return to Moscow is mentioned by one memoirist in the context of other "returns" (those of Mikhail Gerschenzon, Belyi, Shklovskii, and Aleksei Tolstoy) that were based on a most difficult choice, at a time when others, such as Pavel Muratov and the Khodaseviches, decided (often after long vacillation) to stay in western Europe.[60] Decades later Pasternak remarked that his liking for Berlin had been tempered by a feeling that a writer could exist only in his own linguistic surroundings,[61] an observation suggesting that his continued functioning as a Russian writer was the decisive consideration in his return, though other considerations favored staying. We are left with the clear impression that, like a great number of other Russian intellectuals in Berlin, Pasternak was torn between the two courses of action: return to the Soviet Union or stay permanently in the West. It could not have been an easy decision.

On March 12, Leonid Osipovich painted a portrait of his older son—probably not suspecting that it was the last one and that he would never see his son again.[62] On March 18, the younger Pasternak and his wife left Berlin for Moscow. In their minds the departure bore no mark of finality; the poet apparently intended to visit Germany again. Perhaps partly to console Tsvetaeva about the meeting that had not taken place, he suggested that they meet in Weimar two years from then.[63]

Pasternak took back from Berlin his book of poetry, *Themes and Variations*, which had been issued in a lilac cover during his stay there. The volume is composed of six cycles of poems, the most striking of which are (1) "Themes and Variations," which revolves around allusions to Pushkin and his poetry, stressing the motif of the unity of the creative artistic force with the stormy elements and illustrating the extent to which a poetic piece can be influenced by music, in terms of both structure and devices; (2) "Illness," which associated the poet (the sick man) with the Revolution, personified through natural phenomena; and (3) "The Break," an evocation of the poet's final quarrel with his mistress, particularly masterful in its emotional tension and rhythmical force—which elicited superlative praise from critics as diverse as Aseev,[64] Dmitrii Sviatopolk-Mirskii, and Tsvetaeva. *Themes and Variations* solidified Pasternak's reputation as a great poet, established with *My Sister, Life*; Sviatopolk-Mirskii felt that *Themes and Variations* "though not always on the same level" as *My Sister, Life* nonetheless at times achieved "even greater things." Tsvetaeva viewed such a striking achievement as a signal that Pasternak should now write "a big thing."[65]

On September 23, 1923, a few months after the Pasternaks' return to Moscow, their son, Evgenii, was born. As he grew, Evgenii began to resemble his father closely in his movements, voice, speech, and features, while giving the impression of a more withdrawn personality (one acquaintance later described him as having the same "craggy features" as his father, with similar "sensitive, soft, thoughtful eyes" looking out over prominent cheekbones).[66] It is most likely that the verse for children that Pasternak published in the second half of the 1920s was written primarily for his young son. On that occasion he joined in the Russian tradition in which significant writers practiced the genre of children's literature.[*] Of the two children's poems that the poet published as separate booklets, *The Carrousel* (1925) and *The Menagerie* (1929), the latter is the more unconventional. In it the narrator underscores humorous descriptions of animals with sadder comments on the effects of captivity on them: the lioness, "relentlessly the floorboards pacing / Is driven by her very raging / When brushing at the iron caging." A panther and a cheetah are sent into the same frenzy by their small enclosures— rather like repressed human beings (the influence of Rilke's poem "Der Panther," with which Pasternak was most certainly familiar, is obvious). Thus strong negative undercurrents run beneath the humorous surface, and besides being a delightful simple snapshot, *The Menagerie* reveals a more sophisticated dimension not always typical of children's literature.

After his return to Moscow, Pasternak continued adapting to the changing literary scene of the mid-1920s, upon which political events and processes had their impact. Thus, when in January, 1924, Lenin died (leaving the reins of government in the hands of Leon Trotsky, Joseph Stalin, Aleksei Rykov, Lev Kamenev, and Grigorii Zinovev), Maiakovskii composed his celebrated long poem *Vladimir Ilich Lenin*, while Pasternak published *High Malady* (*Vysokaia bolezn*), also a long poem, which concluded with a description of Lenin's speech at the Ninth Congress of the Soviets in 1921. The focus in *High Malady* is the poet's place in a changing society, against the background of historical events. The Revolution is depicted as an elemental fury sweeping aside and leaving behind "The idealist-intellectual / Who printed and wrote placards / About the joy of his decline." In earlier days the intelligentsia had worked for the Revolution; since then, however, they had lost contact with the masses and had become alienated from them to the point that they could do nothing but "step down from the stage."[67] Conveying Pasternak's personal experience, the narrator relates how, endeavoring to dispel his doubts and hesitations, he betakes himself to the Congress of Soviets, where the impressive appearance of Lenin succeeds in restoring some of his faith.

Although Maiakovskii had reservations about some passages in the poem, which he thought were too obscure and inaccessible, nonetheless he loved other passages so much that he learned them by heart and would sometimes recite them. The image of Pasternak as an archdifficult, enigmatic poet was steadily

---

[*]During the 1920s especially, this extremely popular genre was practiced by such writers as Aleksei Tolstoy, Samuíl Marshak, Mikhail Zoshchenko, and Mandelstam as an escape from "serious" literature, where, being ideologically suspect, they ran a risk of being taken to task.

gaining credence in those years. In 1925 the artistic team Kukriniksy published a caricature of him entitled "The Sphinx," which showed him as a sphinx in tie and jacket perched on the speaker's stand at the Writers' Union. In two unpublished texts of the mid-1920s, Lunacharskii, while conceding that Pasternak had great talent, qualified him as "foggy, strange, . . . unintelligible in the extreme, and unsuited to our epoch."[68]

In those years various literary groups and orientations claimed the allegiance of the writers. Each group had its own approach to the depiction of problems of the day. Gorky, Zamiatin, Kornei Chukovskii, and others collaborated in editing the ideologically flexible journal the *Russian Contemporary* (*Russkii Sovremennik*), which in 1924 printed poems by Pasternak, as well as works by Aseev, Leonov, Aleksei Tolstoy, and Fedin. Pasternak's works were also published by the liberal *New World* (*Novyi mir*), founded in 1925 in a period of political and literary ferment. The journal *Red Virgin Soil* (*Krasnaia nov*) was publishing both Komsomol and nonpartisan writers, while in 1925 *On Guard* (*Na postu*), the organ of the Moscow Association of Proletarian Writers, began bitterly attacking non-Communist writers, specifically those Trotsky dubbed "fellow travelers" (*poputchiki*). *On Guard* took its cue from a resolution of the First All-Union Conference of Proletarian Writers, dated January, 1925, which declared the works of the fellow travelers to be essentially "directed against the proletarian revolution." This trend was reinforced by a July, 1925, resolution of the Central Committee of the Communist party, which admonished writers: "It is necessary to deal more decisively and boldly with the prejudices of gentility in literature, . . . and to work out a proper form understandable to the millions."[69] While that resolution was relatively liberal, it represented one of the earliest stages of the gradual process whereby writers were driven to follow the literary trends recommended by the party.

The conflicts and misgivings that plagued intellectuals during the postrevolutionary era are clearly reflected in their literature. Some of the novels written in the 1920s display an originality of approach (soon to be banned from Soviet letters) in treating the issues that Pasternak would later take up in *Doctor Zhivago*. Zamiatin's antiutopian novel *We* (which later inspired works by Aldous Huxley, H. G. Wells, and George Orwell) took critical distance in relation to the Soviet Brave New World, and was read avidly in manuscript in literary circles in Petrograd and Moscow in 1924. Mikhail Bulgakov's *White Guard* (1924) told the story of a family that fights on the side of the White Army, is caught in the blizzard of the Revolution, and is torn between two camps before gradually discovering the meaning of the Revolution. Fedin's *Cities and Years* (1924) described the reaction of an intellectual to the Revolution; the critics maintained that Fedin shared the misgivings of his heroes. In his terse and striking novel *Envy* (1927), perhaps the finest literary work of the decade, Iurii Olesha demonstrated as much independence of mind in treating the complexities and peculiarities of Soviet society as Pasternak was to display later in *Doctor Zhivago* (though the grain of Olesha's prose is more subtle). The year 1927 also saw the appearance in book

Pasternak, ca. 1925–26.
Pasternak Family Collection.

form of Aleksandr Fadeev's popular novel *The Rout*, which described Red guerrillas in Siberia during the Civil War and the hero's scorn, evidently shared by the author, for what he views as the boring rhetoric of intellectuals (as the neighbor and frequent interlocutor of Pasternak during two decades in Peredelkino, Fadeev would have ample chance to argue the case for a literature oriented to the party's needs, in disregard of the intellectuals' own aspirations and principles).

Although Pasternak fundamentally always "lacked the talent to be insincere," he was trying to respond to the demands that the era, with a greater or lesser degree of direct pressure, was making on writers to adjust in terms of topic, style, and tone. One such effort met with great success. A significant date in his artistic career was the appearance in 1927 of his volume of poetry *The Year 1905*, comprising the two long poems "The Year 1905" and "Lieutenant Schmidt" (which had shortly before appeared separately in journals).[70] The time was ripe for literary treatments of revolutionary and patriotic themes; 1926 had already produced Eduard Bagritskii's magnum opus, *The Lay of Opanas* (portraying the Civil War in the Ukraine), and Aseev's *The Twenty-six* (dealing with the Baku commissars executed in 1918), and 1927—the tenth anniversary of the October Revolution—saw the appearance of several more such monuments, including Aseev's "Semën Proskakov" and Maiakovskii's "Khorosho!" These last two works were praised highly, as was Pasternak's *The Year 1905*, in an article of November 30, 1927, in the Leningrad *Krasnaia gazeta*. *The Year 1905* went through four editions and remains that part of Pasternak's achievement which is most often mentioned and praised by Soviet critics and anthologized in the Soviet Union. In a letter to Gorky, Pasternak described the genesis of the poem (along with an assessment of Gorky's role in the Revolution):

I don't know what would have remained for me of the Revolution, and where would be her *truth* if Russian history had not had you. But for you—in the flesh and in your full individuality—and save for you as an immense generic personification, her fibs and shallowness become directly exposed. . . . Having—along with everyone else—breathed these ten years her unavoidable falseness, I had gradually come to think of liberation. For this it was necessary to select the revolutionary theme in a historical perspective, as a chapter among chapters, as an event among events, and raise it to the power of a tangible and live, nonsectarian pan-Russian [reality]. I have pursued this goal in the book I have sent you [*The Year 1905*].[71]

In this volume Pasternak for the first time dealt squarely with the convergence of poetry and history, giving evidence that he shared with Tsvetaeva a notion of "the paradoxical phenomenon of the timelessness of art and its irrevocable connection with its time."[72] The first poem, "The Year 1905," is composed of six episodes, which present us with a number of vivid scenes, amounting—somewhat impressionistically—to a poetic chronicle of the events of that year. The following vignettes successively unfold the distant background of 1905 (the deeds of the late-nineteenth-century intelligentsia), the Moscow scene drawn from the author's childhood recollections, and various groups in their roles in revolutionary events: peasants, workers confronting the Cossacks, *Potemkin* sailors mutinying, students rebelling in Moscow. An accelerated five-foot anapestic meter sometimes suggests the excitement and tension of the times. As opposed to the first poem, the somewhat less successful "Lieutenant Schmidt" deals with only one episode of the Revolution—the mutiny of the Black Sea fleet under Schmidt. Many aspects of the poem are memorable: the conflict between Schmidt's love for his mistress and his sense of mission, which provides psychological texture; his protest against the whole cycle of rebellion and repression (not just within the tsarist regime) and against the state as idol; his act of self-sacrifice.

The volume won Pasternak wide acclaim. Maiakovskii, in a lecture on "How to Write Poetry," delivered at the Polytechnical Museum in September, 1926, dwelled at some length on Pasternak's achievement and in particular on his treatment of the *Potemkin* episode. In *Red Virgin Soil* the Pereval* critic A. Lezhnev welcomed the new social orientation of Pasternak's poetry, and in December, 1927, he published in *Pravda* a detailed, enthusiastic review. Tsvetaeva expressed strong admiration for her friend's new achievement, indicating that, beyond its

---

*The literary group Pereval (the Pass—as in "mountain pass") was organized in 1924 when a group of Communist writers belonging to the Young Guard (Molodaia Gvardiia) seceded from the October (Oktiabr) group. Pereval's goal was to merge the proletarian writers and fellow travelers. Its literary declaration of February, 1927, called for a reassertion of the humanistic traditions of Russian and western European literature and stressed the need for "intuition" and "sincerity."

social-revolutionary theme, the work had technical merit (she was not enthusiastic about the figure of Schmidt himself, viewing the character as a mere "member of the intelligentsia" like, say, Chekhov—a negative comparison, on her scale of values). The émigré poet Nikolai Otsup pointed out that, while Pasternak had become "clearer" and more accessible in these poems, the results were more "ordinary" than the unique achievements of his previous three volumes; he concluded by paradoxically suggesting that Pasternak *not* try to get rid of the "shortcomings" in *My Sister, Life*.[73]

The success of *The Year 1905* had two significant consequences for its author. First, he came to play a role of literary guide and mentor, which he discussed in a letter to Gorky: "You cannot imagine how I am snowed under by letters and manuscripts from the provinces and have almost no chance to work; I sacrifice . . . my own work to weak grown-ups in need of a nanny who turn to me for want of one."[74] From Pasternak's letters to her Tsvetaeva also formed the impression that he was bothered by crowds of people—poets who, not knowing how to write, came to him for advice. She commented to the poet's father, "This is not the reverse side, but the *face* of glory," and advised Pasternak to be strict with people who tried to rob him of his valuable time.[75] Second, the several editions of the volume brought an improvement in Pasternak's financial circumstances. In 1927

Pasternak and Sergei
Eisenstein (*standing*);
Vladimir Maiakovskii and
Lili Brik (*seated*), 1920s.
*Archives Jacqueline de
Proyart/Gallimard.*

Pasternak. Photograph
taken by Pasternak's friend
Konstantin Bogatyrev.
Ardis.

he could say that there was "no longer any trace of [financial] difficulties" and attributed the improvement to *The Year 1905*. The book's success even made it possible for him to help others now and then.[76]

The Year 1905 did not bring Pasternak any closer to "left-wing" literary groups, however. His relationship with the Neofuturist LEF* was sharply deteriorating. Throughout the decade following the Revolution, Pasternak maintained ties with Futurism; in 1921 he was listed by the Moscow Association of Futurists

---

*LEF (an acronym for Left Front of Art), created in late 1922, was composed of former Futurists (such as Aseev, Kruchenykh, Maiakovskii, and Kamenskii), theoreticians who discussed and defended their work (notably N. Chuzhak, Osip Brik, Boris Kushner, and Boris Arvatov), and Constructivist artists (like Aleksandr Rodchenko).

(MAF) as one of its contributors, and in May, 1923, he published his poem "May Day" (written "to order"—at Maiakovskii's request), in the second issue of the new journal *Lef*, where it was juxtaposed with first-of-May poems by such Futurists as Aseev, Vasily Kamenskii, Aleksei Kruchenykh, and Maiakovskii.[77] From the start LEF's program emphasized "purposeful" (that is, "agitation") art* and poetry conceived as a "useful craft" and opposed any return to conservative realism or (in its initial days at least) to any cult of the "classics." As Edward J. Brown has said, it led the fight against "the already advanced petrification of political life into fixed hierarchical forms and the revival of materialistic incentives and petty-bourgeois economic and social 'virtues.'"[78] It championed such activities as the "building of life" and the "production of things." Predictably enough, aspects of this platform grew increasingly distasteful to Pasternak. He maintained ties with the movement only out of friendship for Maiakovskii. In the mid-1920s the critic Lezhnev pointed out discerningly that Pasternak's link with the Futurist "school" was shaky and that as an innovator he did not exhibit the school's sharp, polemical angles.[79] LEF welcomed Pasternak, however, and its first theoretical declaration listed him as a key participant whose special achievement was "the application of a dynamic syntax to the revolutionary objective."[80] During most of the 1920s, Maiakovskii considered Pasternak one of the "inner circle" of Futurists and then of the Neofuturist Lefovites. He frequently explicated Pasternak's poetry in public, recommended it to Lunacharskii for publication, defended it when it came under fire, propagated it at poetry readings and conferences at home and abroad (for example, in New York in 1925 and in Prague in 1927). In the spring of 1927 he listed in a polemical context "Lieutenant Schmidt," just completed, as "an achievement of LEF," stating, "Now . . . Pasternak has completed a revolutionary work, 'Schmidt,' from which we must learn."[81] About that time the critic Konstantin Loks,† though an opponent of LEF, could not but recognize the innovative significance of Maiakovskii and Pasternak, whom he discussed jointly, declaring: "Maiakovskii and Pasternak have accomplished an achievement in the realm of the structure of the poetic image and poetic expression that may already be taken out of its context and defined as the common property of the age."[82]

The polemics that LEF conducted in 1927 with the journals of the Russian Association of Proletarian Writers, as well as with V. P. Polonskii, the editor of *Novyi mir*, triggered Pasternak's decision to part with the movement. In May and June, 1927, crossing the Rubicon, he broke with LEF. He wrote Polonskii a detailed letter saying that his departure from LEF was "for good," in spite of his personal "love" and "appreciation" for Maiakovskii. In the letter Pasternak quoted from the draft of an apologia that he intended to address to Maiakovskii (but never dispatched); the draft referred to Maiakovskii as "a cornerstone" and "an axiom," while denouncing the "stupidity" of LEF's theoretical posture and labeling its very existence "a logical puzzle." Pasternak concluded his epistle to

---

* "Agitation" art (sometimes "agitational art"—a neologism to translate the Russian *agitatsionnyi*) was art pertaining to *agitatsiia*, active participation in propaganda, and the "political education" of the people in the interests of the Communist party.

† Konstantin Loks had been a friend of Pasternak's from their student days.

Polonskii by remarking: "This break is not easy for me. They don't want to understand me, and more than that, they want to misunderstand me. I shall be more lonely than before."[83] A fellow Lefovite has given us some idea of how Pasternak's departure from the movement struck Maiakovskii, indicating that LEF's enemies "wanted to split it so as to get at Maiakovskii. . . . They started on Pasternak. For a long time, Maiakovskii had loved Pasternak. Pasternak broke away. 'They've snatched one,' said Maiakovskii."[84] It is clear that Pasternak's departure, which did wound Maiakovskii, was a significant step in the deterioration of the relationship between the two poets, a subject that will be discussed below.

Since writing *My Sister, Life*, Pasternak had had misgivings about his "belonging" to the Futurist movement. His departure marked the end of his connection with any literary group or school. From now on he would work as an independent, if often isolated, artist, in pursuit of aims he would define for himself.

7

A Second Birth

1928–1932

Exegi Monumentum

To Boris Pasternak

And what if storm should burst in spite this day,
And all the gathered thunders blunder on our head,
And all the floods we read in fables foam
From secret clouds like Time's avenging ghosts .

George Reavey[1]

Between 1928 and 1932, Pasternak's life underwent upheavals that were to become the background and the source of the poetry in his collection *Second Birth* (1932). Yet he continued work on what in 1928 he termed an "autobiographical phenomenology of sorts,"[2] that is, the text—closely connected with the genesis of *Second Birth*—that was to become *A Safe-Conduct* (1929–31).

By that time Pasternak was gaining full recognition. In 1928 the well-known émigré critic Dmitrii Sviatopolk-Mirskii published a sensitive, admiring study entitled *Boris Pasternak's* The Year 1905. Ilia Ehrenburg said in 1930 that he considered "The Childhood of Liuvers" one of the ten most important prose works written in the Soviet Union and went on to explain: "It was Pasternak who laid the true foundation of Soviet art, and this is the reason why his creative strength has caused such bitter controversy in the past, and still does today."[3] Controversy did recur during those years, focusing mainly on the "difficult" texture of Pasternak's verse, which made reading it an arduous exercise for many. This fact was acknowledged by a critic in the ranks of the Russian Association of Proletarian Writers (RAPP) who, however, concluded that, in spite of the concentrated labor involved in reading the poet, "the conquest of difficulty sooner or later turns out to be highly profitable, for though Pasternak is miserly of elucidation, he is astoundingly rich in images, thoughts, emotions and sensations which give knowledge of the world."[4]

These merits became widely acknowledged. In 1928, Shklovskii pointed out that Pasternak's work of the past fifteen years had become part of the "public domain" and that he was influencing novice poets, such as Nikolai Ushakov and Nikolai Dementev, who emulated Pasternak's laconic syntax and richness of vocabulary.[5] Such a sharp critic as Kornelii Zelinskii conceded that Pasternak was exerting an influence on "many proletarian poets."[6] Echoes of Pasternak have also been detected in Nikolai Tikhonov's book of satirical poetry *In Search of a Hero* (1927). Positive reaction to Pasternak was widespread in the late 1920s, when letters from Gorky, Sviatopolk-Mirskii, and the Eurasians* began pouring into the poet's mailbox, "unexpectedly warm, undeserved, exaggerated," in their praise of *The Year 1905*.[7] During these years the party theorist N. I. Bukharin continued to be a staunch admirer of Pasternak's poetic talent. In a statement composed in 1926–27, Gorky made the following comments on Pasternak's achievement:

Boris Pasternak is a poet who has thoroughly deserved the epithet "most original." His verses, always *sui generis* in terms of rhythm, with unexpected and willful rhymes, are distinguished—according to the statements of certain critics—"by their surcharge, their oversaturation with images." . . . He is already considered a "master" [*"maître"*]; he has enough power to influence other poets. . . . As a person he is, like all true artists, absolutely independent; he is "a man who was born and will die with a countenance all his own."[8]

---

*The Eurasians were a group of thinkers active in the 1920s and early 1930s, including historian G. Vernadskii, economist P. N. Savitskii, philologist N. S. Trubetskoi, and literary critic Sviatopolk-Mirskii. These émigrés emphasized the Asian elements in Russian culture.

БОРИС ПАСТЕРНАК

ВТОРОЕ РОЖДЕНИЕ

Cover of *Second Birth* (1932).

The poet's fame began to spread abroad as well. In the 1930s he came to be highly regarded in Polish literary circles.[9] Within that chorus of praise, however, negative voices soon emerged, such as that of V. Pertsov, critic and fanatical supporter of Maiakovskii, who railed at what he termed a veritable "Pasternak cult" and blamed Ehrenburg as one of its initiators, criticizing him for giving the impression in his novels that Komsomols read Pasternak.[10]

Stimulated by the positive comments, the poet managed to progress well with his literary work in spite of various ailments that afflicted him during these years—ranging from torn shoulder ligaments complicated by hemorrhage, as well as a bad case of influenza (in late 1927 and early 1928), to recurring and very painful pyorrhea, which more than once (as in March, 1929) resulted in a swollen cheek[11] (these ailments in the cheeks and jaw were not isolated instances; all his life Pasternak had dental problems).[12]

Having more or less recovered from the latest of these problems, Pasternak spent the summer of 1930 in Irpen, a small, picturesque resort town near Kiev, about which he wrote enthusiastically to a friend: "I felt strongly like not returning to Moscow, and if I had had, as Maiakovskii says . . . the appetite to live, . . . I would have stayed there. . . . Kievan friends, about whom I'll tell you some time, were enticing us [to stay] there."[13] This circle of unusually thoughtful and talented friends included the noted philosophy professor Valentin

Asmus; his wife, Irina Sergeevna, a poetry lover and Pasternak fan; a Kiev critic named Perlin and his family; the Kiev-born pianist Vladimir Horowitz, already a celebrity in the West, and his sister Giniia; and the distinguished pianist and piano professor Genrikh Neigauz and his wife, Zinaida Nikolaevna, a portly brunette of half-Italian descent. Pasternak soon became the idol of this company, most of whom went to Moscow to live within the next few years.[14] He later indicated that the stimulating and carefree atmosphere of that friendly milieu made it possible for him to complete his long poem *Spektorskii*, which had become "like a book, with a beginning and an end."[15]

In 1929, Pasternak had made a report on his work in progress:

> [I am] at work on three connected works, which, when completed, will be part of my four-volume collected works (but as yet there has been no publisher's agreement for this latter): *Spektorskii* . . .; *Povesti*; completion of *A Safe-Conduct*, left aside after a first third was written last winter ["a philosophical thing of autobiographical content"]. . . . I worry about my ability to meet publishers' schedules.[16]

On his workbench *A Safe-Conduct* was shedding the first draft's essayistic envelope and turning into an autobiography.[17] By 1931 his work on two of the three major projects was completed, and the final, revised versions of *Spektorskii* and *A Safe-Conduct* appeared that year in book form.

Soon after completing *Spektorskii*, Pasternak gave readings of this "novel in verse" to various audiences, such as a gathering at the club of the Federation of Associations of Soviet Writers in Rostov House and public assemblies on the premises of the State Publishing House of Belles-Lettres (in March, 1931). While showing aesthetic appreciation for the surface of the poem, listeners were not fully won over by its structure and content.[18] Unlike *Lieutenant Schmidt*, this new work of Pasternak's centers on a weak hero, Sergei Spektorskii. Certain notations in the introduction (describing the narrator's work as press screener in the Narkompros library after the Revolution) suggest closeness between the author's own experience and the events in the work. The author's lyrical "I" reappears at various times during the narrative (sometimes merging with the voice of Spektorskii), indicating that Pasternak shared some of the estrangement from contemporary society that characterized Spektorskii, a hero representative of the intelligentsia as depicted by Aleksandr Blok (in some specifics the plot is reminiscent of the poem "The Brothers," by the nineteenth-century poet Iakov Polonskii). Spektorskii stands out in sharp contrast to his sister, who reproaches him for his aloofness and singles out as a fault his "detachment from his generation."[19] Like such famous heroes of Russian fiction as Ivan Turgenev's Rudin, Spektorskii fails to engage in socially meaningful activities. At the same time, like Eugene Onegin, Rudin, and Ivan Goncharov's Oblomov, he is unsuccessful as a lover; with neither Olga Bukhteev, the proud daughter of a *narodnik*,* nor Maria Ilina, a Russian émigré poet seemingly patterned after Tsvetaeva, are his relationships

---

*A "populist," a member of the ideological and political movement that emerged in the Russian radical intelligentsia in the 1860s.

Drawing of the early 1930s, used
as a frontispiece in Pasternak's
A Tale (1934).

conclusive. Although the poem contains a number of delightful lyrical scenes, as
an endeavor to go beyond lyricism and attain an epic dimension, it is a failure.

Very soon, in an article published in *Pravda*, the critic Aleksei Selivanovskii
leveled an attack against Pasternak, deriding "the haze of allusions and subjective
images" in which the poem flounders. Selivanovskii was displeased with Pasternak's theme—the debacle of the traditional intelligentsia, lost in its refined atmosphere. Using a metaphor borrowed from military strategy, in a fashion typical of the new rhetoric of the artillerists active "on the literary front," the critic
expressed the opinion that the only course of action appropriate for Pasternak was
"ideological rearmament." On the other hand, while labeling the poem a failure,
Anna Akhmatova was to identify its chief weakness as inadequate psychological
portrayal, while claiming that typically Pasternakian poetry had been successful
when dealing primarily with nature ("thunderstorms, forests, chaos").[20]

A later critic claimed that the very type of hero represented by Spektorskii was
imposed on Pasternak by the "metonymic vision" that he employed in the work.
Investigating the relation between *Spektorskii* and Pasternak's prose work *A Tale*
(a relation hinted at by the author himself), Michel Aucouturier argued convincingly that those two works, taken together, still remain incomplete because
they represent only the "beginnings of Pasternak the novelist," a novelist still
unsure of himself.[21]

An event traumatic for Pasternak, as well as for others in the Soviet literary world, was Maiakovskii's suicide in 1930. In January of that year Maiakovskii's play *The Bathhouse*, which sharply satirized Soviet bureaucracy, was premiered in Leningrad and was received badly by the press.[22] By April 10 its continued poor reception had made the playwright extremely gloomy, as various acquaintances reported.[23] This setback, combined with the recent lukewarm and sometimes even hostile reaction of Soviet proletarian audiences to his poetry readings, convinced him that his lifework was a failure. Four days later, on April 14, Maiakovskii shot himself. On his desk was a note addressed "To everyone," asking the government to take care of his family, and including the entreaty "Liliia, love me," as well as a verse epilogue that said in part, "Now Life and I are quits."* Such was the end of a greatly talented poet, who had been "a living human face" and then had become alienated, Pasternak felt, through adherence to "something lofty, but deadening and pitiless."[24]

Of that day Pasternak wrote in *A Safe-Conduct*: "Between eleven and twelve the undulating circles generated by the shot were still rippling outward. The news rocked telephones, covered faces with pallor, sent people rushing to . . . the house."[25] Pasternak's book, almost one-third of which is taken up with his fellow poet, ends with Maiakovskii's death. The friendship that grew between Pasternak and Maiakovskii was at once stormy, emotional, and strangely distant (they never said the familiar "thou" [*ty*] to each other).[26] From his first meeting with Maiakovskii in 1914 at a polemical meeting of two hostile Futuristic groups, the other poet seemed to Pasternak "a miracle," forcing everyone to turn in his direction.[27] Pasternak's two separate accounts of their friendship are markedly different. The first account, to be found in *A Safe-Conduct*, was written in 1931, soon after Maiakovskii's death, and is long and detailed, warm and filled with a sense of great loss. The second, a shorter, ten-page statement in *Sketch for an Autobiography*, is cool and in places accusatory and censorious. Someone who had been a close friend of both Maiakovskii and Pasternak found the latter statement "unkind, cold, and . . . inaccurate." To that friend Pasternak seemed embarrassed and guilty that he had spoken "badly" of Maiakovskii in his new autobiography.[28] Another friend, Ehrenburg, has given us an observer's summation of the relationship between the two poets:

We used to say as a joke that Maiakovskii had a "spare voice" for women. It was this spare voice, extraordinarily gentle and affectionate, which in my hearing he used to only one man. That man was Pasternak. I remember a Pasternak evening at the Press Club in March 1921. . . . During the discussion that followed someone ventured to "point out some shortcomings" as the phrase goes. Thereupon Maiakovskii rose to his full height and began to extol Pasternak's poetry at the top of his voice: he defended it with all the passion of love.[29]

A common friend of the two poets was later to describe how Maiakovskii's eyes would change and he would look rejuvenated while listening to the reading of

---

*Liliia Iurevna [Lili] Brik, Maiakovskii's great love, was the wife of his friend the critic Osip Brik.

Pasternak's verse in the 1920s.[30] Something in the leader of Russian Futurism strongly attracted Pasternak, brought him close to Maiakovskii, who was, in Pasternak's view, a "man with an almost animal craving for truth."[31] Before and during the Revolution, Pasternak saw that "the time and the sharing of common influences" bound him to Maiakovskii.[32] While discovering the coincidences in their respective achievements, Pasternak had a strong liking for "the beauty and the felicity" of the other poet's speech.[33]

That feeling of admiration was mutual. According to Lili Brik, in Maiakovskii's eyes Pasternak was an "enticing, slightly enigmatic" poet. He knew much of Pasternak's poetry by heart and loved to recite some of it, certain lines "almost daily."[34] Throughout most of the 1920s, Maiakovskii defended Pasternak from attack and surrounded him with thoughtful attention, and in an official pronouncement he singled out Pasternak's "work on sentence construction and his elaboration of a new syntax" as features that were attractive to LEF.[35] Pasternak was one of the two poets to whom Maiakovskii ever ascribed genius (the other was Khlebnikov).[36] Although Maiakovskii was sensitive to the formal aspects of Pasternak's poetry, however, one may wonder whether he appreciated its "metaphysical" and emotional qualities.

For all its warmth the dialogue between the poets had stormy moments. On one occasion, already disillusioned by Maiakovskii's "uncreative" *150,000,000*, Pasternak listened to him recite parts of his *War and the Universe*. Again unimpressed, Pasternak remarked straight out "how marvelous it would be if he [Maiakovskii] could now publicly send it all [Futurism] to the devil."[37] A failure by Maiakovskii was considered by Pasternak to be a failure "in some way" of his own. In such a close relationship, Ehrenburg points out, their quarrels were "frequent and tempestuous":

> After one of their differences, Maiakovskii and Pasternak met again in Berlin [and went through a passionate reconciliation]. I spent the whole day with them; we went to a café, then we dined and later sat in a café again. Pasternak read his poems. In the evening Maiakovskii gave a reading of *The Backbone Flute* at the Arts Club; he recited with his face turned toward Pasternak.[38]

Some time thereafter, in 1923, when penning a verse inscription in a copy of *My Sister, Life* for Maiakovskii, Pasternak bemoaned the negative turn of his friend's talent; without doubting Maiakovskii's sincerity, he lamented poetry's loss at the expense of propaganda.[39] In 1926, Pasternak was still a frequent visitor at Maiakovskii's apartment on Gendrikov Lane.[40]

The final break with Maiakovskii occurred in 1927. Pasternak had long felt alienated by aspects of Maiakovskii's poetic modus operandi—what he viewed as his "propagandist zeal, the worming of himself and his friends by force into the public's consciousness, his idea that a poem could be written by several hands, by an association of craftsmen, and his complete subordination to the demand for topical subjects."[41] That was the primary reason for Pasternak's departure from LEF in 1927. Pasternak was not the only poet to criticize Maiakovskii's new orientation; Mandelstam and another fellow poet, Anna Akhmatova, joined him in

Pasternak, April, 1930. In *Istoriia
russkoi sovetskoi literatury v chetyrekh
tomakh, 1917–1965* (Moscow,
1968).

regarding "with shame and distaste" Maiakovskii's daily labor at the production of "agitation" verse on any topic assigned to him.[42] Maiakovskii's works of the late 1920s (except "the immortal document *At the Top of My Voice*") became "inaccessible" to Pasternak, and he was to "remain indifferent to those clumsily rhymed sermons, that cultivated insipidity, those commonplaces and platitudes, set forth so artificially, so confusedly, and so devoid of humor."[43]

Pasternak made efforts at reconciliation. In December, 1929, he went to a party organized by Maiakovskii's friends at the poet's apartment, only to be turned away by his host, who addressed him coldly, hinting that a reconciliation was not "as simple an operation as sewing a torn button back on."[44] Lili Brik later told Pasternak that she felt that if he had been close to Maiakovskii during the last, tormenting few months the poet would not have committed suicide.[45]

Recalling his presence in Maiakovskii's living room after the tragedy, Pasternak wrote, "I burst into floods of tears, just as I had long been wanting to."[46] A witness has described the scene: "I saw a high-cheekboned, dark-lipped mulatto face all glistening with tears, which seemed to overshadow everything else. I recognized Pasternak. His hands were moving mechanically as though he wanted to tear open his breast, crush the frame of his chest."[47]

Pasternak recorded the thoughts he had when going home that day: "Suddenly, down below, under the window, I imagined his life, now utterly in the past."[48] Yet it was the life of a man who was so *present* to Pasternak that he remarked: "I carried the whole of him away from the boulevard . . . into my own life."[49]

Strangely enough, this traumatic experience unquestionably had a cathartic effect on Pasternak, releasing his creative energies. It should be borne in mind that, paradoxically, the poets Maiakovskii and Pasternak stood close to one another at the same time that they represented antipodes of Russian poetry. On the one hand, Aleksandr Gladkov, a contemporary, stressed that, in the experience of that generation, Pasternak's poetry was never in opposition to Maiakovskii's but rather complemented, deepened, and broadened it. On the other hand, as early as 1927 the critic Lezhnev pointed out the polarity between them within the framework of Futurism:

Maiakovskii, is . . . the leader, the herald, even the theorist of the school. In this respect he differs radically from Pasternak. We have before us . . . two types of poet different in principle. The age, according to its demands, sometimes places one, then sometimes the other in the literary spotlight. When the era of the breakdown of art (an era that demands pointed, negating, declarative, and theorizing innovation) pushes Futurism and its standard-bearer, Maiakovskii, to the fore, Pasternak is left in the shade.[50]

Commenting on that statement at a debate organized by LEF, Maiakovskii added: "When the age pushes forward Pasternak, Maiakovskii is left in the shade."[51] And over two decades later, the Pasternak-Maiakovskii polarity was to be reflected in the Zhivago-Strelnikov axis in Pasternak's novel, where Zhivago says of Strelnikov: "He is a doomed man. I believe that he'll come to a bad end. He will atone for the evil he has done."[52] At the time, however, Maiakovskii's death served as a liberating event—as depicted in *A Safe-Conduct*—that made it possible for his fellow poet to write *Second Birth*.

The other factor that had a direct, specific creative impact on Pasternak, impelling him to write *Second Birth*, was the upheaval taking place in his domestic life. In the summer of 1929 and for a while thereafter, although Pasternak continued to be seen with his wife, Evgeniia Vladimirovna, their close acquaintances already knew that they had decided to separate because of divergences and grievances on both sides. Once Evgeniia Vladimirovna even went to a Moscow party official to complain that the poet was "a bad family man." When summoned by the official for a scolding, Pasternak meekly listened and readily agreed to mend his ways.[53] It appears that part of the conflict between Pasternak and Evgeniia Vladimirovna (who was very close to Judaism) had to do with allegiance to Judaic values. Also, Pasternak, who had no patience with amateurism, probably considered his wife's painting as nothing more than an idle way of killing time. Apparently Evgeniia Vladimirovna felt oversecure in her belief that she was "irreplaceable," and must have been taken aback when Pasternak initiated the decision to separate.[54] As his estrangement from his wife grew, Pasternak drew closer to his friend Zinaida Nikolaevna Neigauz, whom he had met in Irpen (and who was not Jewish and was Russian Orthodox). After the return of the Pasternak and Neigauz

Two of Pasternak's close
friends, the Georgian poet
Titsian Tabidze and his
wife, Nina, in Tiflis, 1933.
Einaudi.

families from Irpen in September, 1930, the poet and Zinaida Nikolaevna had
become increasingly attracted to each other. One day later in the fall he declared
his love for her. Shortly thereafter he had a frank discussion with his friend
Neigauz. The rift between Neigauz and his wife widened, though there were attempts at reconciliation that were tormenting to Pasternak.[55] At some point during 1930, Zinaida Nikolaevna finally left Neigauz and went to live with Pasternak, while Evgeniia Vladimirovna parted from the poet, keeping their son,
Evgenii.[56] A few months before the break with his wife, during the winter of
1929–30, Pasternak had befriended the Georgian poet Paolo Iashvili and his wife
and had been their host in his home. Now Iashvili offered "a place of refuge" (his
home in Tbilisi) to Pasternak and Zinaida.[57] The two were without a roof over
their heads (Evgeniia Vladimirovna apparently continued occupying the apartment on Volkhonka Street, at least for a while).[58]

Late in 1930, Pasternak left with Zinaida Nikolaevna for the Iashvilis' house in
the Caucasus. The couple also visited the Tabidzes on Griboedov Street in Tbilisi,

and were met with warm hospitality. To many Russians, Georgia, "with its abundance of sunshine, its strong emotions, its love of beauty and the inborn grace of its princes and peasants alike,"[59] was a place of enchantment and inspiration. Pasternak's love affair with the Caucasus—which in effect became his second home during those years—perpetuated the fascination that, since the days of Pushkin and Lermontov, Georgia had exerted on Russian writers.* For Pasternak, Georgia was a symbol of the synthesis of opposites: man and the elements, the present and the past, the revolutionary upheaval that art constitutes and the continuity needed for artistic creation.

During the winter of 1930–31, Pasternak began translating Georgian poetry into Russian, an activity that in years to come was to occupy a central place in his literary life. Another inspiration is revealed in some of his own poetry, written while he was in Georgia with Zinaida Nikolaevna. There he sang the special charm emanating from his new companion:

> Liubit inykh tiazhelyi krest,
> A ty prekrasna bez izvilin,
> I prelesti tvoei sekret
> Razgadke zhizni ravnosilen.[60]

> [To love most women is a heavy cross,
> But you're graceful and straightforward,
> And the secret of your charm is
> As deep as life's enigma.]

Back in Moscow in the spring of 1931 after six months in Georgia, Pasternak and Zinaida Nikolaevna moved from apartment to apartment.[61] Pasternak soon divorced Evgeniia Vladimirovna, leaving with her their son. In 1934 he married Zinaida Nikolaevna,[62] who had two sons from her first marriage. She was to bear one son to Pasternak, Leonid (Lenia). Once the trauma of the early 1930s was over, the Pasternaks remained on friendly terms with Neigauz. Stanislaus (Stasik) Neigauz and Andrian (Adik) Neigauz, Zinaida Nikolaevna's sons, later went to live with the Pasternaks.[63]

Marina Tsvetaeva made the following comments about the developments in her friend's life:

I learned . . . that Boris Pasternak has parted with his wife—because he loves another. But the other is married, etc. I fear for Boris. In Russia poets die as in an epidemic—a whole list of deaths in ten years! A catastrophe is unavoidable: first, the husband; second, Boris has a wife and son; third, she is beautiful (Boris will be jealous); fourth, and chiefly, Boris *is incapable of a happy* love. For him to love means to be tortured.[64]

Ida Davidovna later commented that she felt Evgeniia Vladimirovna, with her "unbalanced" artist's temperament, had not been a beneficent influence on Pas-

---

*After the Revolution the Georgia-born Maiakovskii made three stays in Tbilisi. Among other Russian writers of the period who visited the area and drew inspiration from contacts with Georgian writers were Belyi, Esenin, Mandelstam, and Ehrenburg.

ternak, whereas Zinaida Nikolaevna made the poet happy. Ida Davidovna, who had refused Pasternak years before, felt that she would not have made him happy either.[65] As it turned out, Zinaida Nikolaevna's role was undoubtedly effective if not always ideal: she stood by Pasternak's side during the last three decades of his life.

Zinaida Nikolaevna was born into the Eremeev family, a well-educated and enlightened Russian Orthodox family of Saint Petersburg. As a schoolgirl of fifteen she experienced her first great love, an ill-starred and traumatic affair with a cousin, a dashing young officer named Melitinskii.* After the Revolution her parents left the Russian capital for Elizavetgrad in the Ukraine, where Zinaida Nikolaevna studied music. Within a few years she married her piano professor, Neigauz, spending the first years of her married life in Kiev and suffering from hunger and cold like many other inhabitants of that city. With her smooth, dark hair, dark-brown eyes, and bright, feminine face, Zinaida Nikolaevna was noted for her sparkling wit, clarity of soul, pride, optimism, and (in the words of a friend) "a purely Russian tendency toward self-sacrifice."[66] With her ability to be cordial and hospitable,[67] however, went an uncommunicative manner and a blunt matter-of-factness that would eventually become distasteful to the poet. For now, however, Pasternak was overwhelmed by her charm and by a certain telluric stability in her, about which he had this comment: "She is in far less need of anything on earth than she herself is necessary to the earth, for she is femininity itself," while he also noted her fearlessness in adversity.[68]

When they were in Irpen in the summer of 1930, Zinaida Nikolaevna confessed that she neither liked nor understood Pasternak's poetry, upon which he laughingly remarked that from then on he would write only for her.[69] Whether or not she understood better his new verse of the 1930s, she did play a vital role in ministering to his talent, as is reflected in the letters he wrote her at the time: "You are the sister of my talent. You give me the feeling of the uniqueness of my existence. . . . You are the wing that protects me. . . . You are that which I loved and saw, and what will happen to me."[70] In another letter Pasternak told her: "When you are not there, I cannot bring myself to undertake anything; I don't feel like taking care of any matter; I don't feel like working." In these letters Pasternak made it clear that he considered her presence indispensable to his functioning as an artist.[71]

For quite a while Pasternak and Zinaida Nikolaevna led a financially precarious life. During the summer of 1932 they seized on one of the new opportunities that the regime was granting to writers (who were now recognized as a guild) and made a trip for "creative purposes" (*tvorcheskaia komandirovka*) sponsored by the new Union of Soviet Writers. The union offered the poet a chance to "immerse

---

*This episode made a deep impression on Pasternak when Zinaida first told him about it in September, 1930. Aspects of the story appear in Lara's relationship with Komarovskii in *Doctor Zhivago*. (This much transpires from Zinaida Nikolaevna's later statement to Iurii Krotkov. Cf. Iurii Krotkov, *KROT 1*, p. 64. Despite Krotkov's long-standing role as an agent of the KGB, he appears to be a reliable source for many details of life in the Pasternak household. For more about Krotkov, see Chapter 12.)

himself" in the life of the masses and "find inspiration" in this new material. Accepting the invitation meant the resolution of a delicate housing problem: the apartment on Volkhonka Street, which he was occupying with Zinaida Nikolaevna and her children, had to be vacated for Evgeniia Vladimirovna (who with her son had been staying in Berlin—presumably with Pasternak's parents—but was now coming back to live in the apartment). The housing shortage in Moscow was acute, and Pasternak jumped at the opportunity to leave the city.[72]

He chose a construction site near Lake Shartash in the Urals, and Zinaida Nikolaevna and her children joined him on the trip. They were feted on their arrival in Sverdlovsk and at first installed in the best room of the hotel. Then the Ural Regional Committee of the party assigned Pasternak a government dacha on Lake Shartash. From the cottage they enjoyed a view of an enchanting landscape: "a forest stretching for a hundred miles, pines and birches, the mica-like surface of the water, the clouds, the graves of the old churchyard, the familiar Northern gamut of impressions."[73] The construction works Pasternak dismissed as "gregarious standardization, organized mediocrity" (statements in *Doctor Zhivago* were to echo this evaluation of certain contemporary endeavors).[*] The development in the Urals he compared with the construction of St. Petersburg on the banks of the Neva.[74]

The family ate at a cafeteria to which "specialists" involved in the construction works were admitted, and which turned out to be the opulently provided dining rooms of the officers of the local Cheka (Soviet political police). Around the cafeteria roamed hungry people in rags, begging for bread with outstretched hands until they were driven away by the security guards. The contrast between the abundant fare at the specialists' tables and the lot of these starving people became too much for Pasternak to bear (once a peasant woman to whom he had given some black bread he had saved from his meal forced a ten-ruble note into his hands, and he had to run after her to return the money). He was losing his appetite, becoming ill, not sleeping at night—so strong was the impact on him of this jarring contrast. One day he told Zinaida Nikolaevna that he had to return to Moscow immediately. She has reported that the stay at Lake Shartash revealed to her for the first time that Pasternak was far from being an egocentric completely engrossed in his poetry but that, inspired by Christian values, he had a deep-seated love for mankind and reacted acutely to the unhappiness of other human beings. The poet's reaction is strongly reminiscent of an earlier outburst of his, at a sumptuous supper at the house of Aleksei Bach, vice-president of the Academy of Sciences, in January, 1930. Pasternak had exploded in protest at the contrast between that lavishness and the plight of "those starving in the Ukraine, on the banks of the Volga, assailing trains to beg for a piece of bread."[75] An ironic aspect of that episode is that, as a young leftist intellectual and member of the revolutionary Populist movement (Narodnaia volia), Bach had published a pamphlet,

---

[*]A number of passages that would later appear in *Doctor Zhivago*—such as the Siberian scenes— were written while Pasternak was staying near Lake Shartash (Georges Nivat, "Pasternak dans l'Oural en 1932," *Boris Pasternak, 1890–1960: Colloque de Cerisy-la-Salle (11-14 septembre 1975*, p. 522).

based on lectures he had given vigorously criticizing the tsarist government for the widespread starvation in Russia.

Back in Moscow, Pasternak wrote a frank report on his "mission" to the board of the Writers' Union. When *Pravda* asked him to write something about his stay, he replied, "How would you want me to write about that desolation?" Never again was he to go on an official trip "for creative renewal" sponsored by the Union of Writers.[76]

Pasternak soon thereafter learned of a tragedy that not only made headlines but aroused much quiet speculation. In November, 1932, after a heated argument with her husband at a friend's house, Stalin's wife, Allilueva, died—probably having committed suicide. In *Literaturnaia gazeta* on November 17 appeared a letter of condolence to Stalin signed by thirty-three prominent writers, including Fadeev, Pilniak, and Shklovskii. Pasternak declined to sign the cliché-ridden statement and instead penned his own message, which was printed as a postscript to the letter: "I share the feelings of my comrades. On the evening before, I found myself thinking profoundly and persistently about Stalin for the first time from the point of view of an artist. In the morning I read the news. I was shaken exactly as though I had been present, as though I had lived through it and seen everything."[77]

Such a statement must have conveyed to the Georgian Stalin an image (readily acceptable to an Oriental mind) of Pasternak as poet-seer, one endowed with special powers of insight—in this case, into a shattering domestic drama. Thus was the basis laid for the respect Stalin felt for Pasternak. Pasternak's comments, however, could also be construed as an ingratiating gesture toward an all-powerful dictator—making it easier to understand how certain ambiguous statements he made to and about Stalin* later lay on the poet's conscience.[78]

Such were the main events of Pasternak's life during these years. More indisputably than any of the poet's previous works, *Second Birth* and *A Safe-Conduct* reflected his personal experience—the exhilarating, harrowing moments of his recent rebirth, with its emotional and political dimensions. As Zelinskii was quick to notice upon the appearance of *Second Birth*, Pasternak's poetry in this volume was "full of the hieroglyphs of his biography" and attained a special quality of "inner wholeness, bought at the price of biography."[79]

The concept of rebirth was first brought up by Pasternak in *A Safe-Conduct*, where, meditating on the death of Maiakovskii, he spoke of the latter's confrontation with a new, incomprehensible, and unsympathetic city, in which Maiakovskii lost his former security, experiencing "the vulnerability of this new birth."[80] In this context Pasternak contrasted "second birth" with "death" as mutually exclusive options. The implication seems to have arisen within the poet's extraordinary idolization of Maiakovskii that, with the latter's death, the responsibility for carrying on the deeper purpose of Russian poetry had shifted to his own shoulders. Pasternak thus inherited from Maiakovskii the confrontation with the alternative—second birth or death.

*See Chapter 8.

This development occurred at a time when most Soviet writers were being forced to confront the problem of fundamentally altering their world view and their style if they wished to survive as artists. In its strategy of persuasion the Communist regime was certainly making the most of a fundamental necessity of life—the need to adapt to survive—to bring the spirit to heel. Not all artists found it easy to make such adaptation. Thus, in his speech to the First Congress of Soviet Writers in 1934, Iuri Olesha conveyed the excruciating feelings he underwent as he found himself incapable of writing until he had "established a common ground" with the new Soviet man, the young socialist generation.[81] For Pasternak, as we have seen, the trip to Lake Shartash ended in dismal failure. On the other hand, in the summer of 1930 the prose writer Veniamin Kaverin joined one of the brigades of writers sent to a gigantic wheat farm in Kirghiz territory, in the southern steppes, and in 1931 he published the result of this successful "creative mission": his volume *Prologue*, subtitled *Travel Stories*.[82] Ehrenburg, Kataev, Pilniak, and others also had "successful" missions. *Second Birth* marked Pasternak's most significant effort since *The Year 1905* to follow the strategy of ideological adaptation, while conveying the rebirth in his personal life.

Both Zelinskii, a leading Soviet critic, and the émigré A. Boehm (the inspirer of a "Pasternak circle" that met in Prague in the late 1920s and 1930s) concurred in their appraisal that Pasternak's new book of poetry was a major achievement.[83] Boehm acknowledged in its author "a major [*krupnyi*] poet, indisputably the most significant poet now alive." While Zelinskii remarked that *Second Birth* was "above all a book marked by simplicity," Boehm listed some of the characteristics of the poet's new economy of material and directness of expression: simplification of his earlier complex syntax, more compact and intelligible lines, less reliance on formal, technical display.* Both agreed that in much of this poetry one could witness a revival of certain strains of Russian romantic verse, obvious in the nature poetry, whether in the passages on the luxuriant, exotic wildlife and vegetation in the Caucasus or in those on the quietly picturesque charm of Irpen. Akhmatova, however, was to criticize the volume for being "an effort at being comprehensible," indicating that she felt that "The Childhood of Liuvers" and *A Safe-Conduct* were more credible.[84]

Along with nature, two other themes are present in *Second Birth*: love and the poet's concern with civic consciousness. The collection contains some of Pasternak's most memorable love poems; even Zelinskii, prone to point out the volume's ideological shortcomings, could not but concede that certain of the poems would "always remain in Russian poetry . . . as masterpieces of intimate lyric poetry."[85] Though at least one of the love poems, "Don't fret, don't cry, don't pine . . ." ("Ne volnuisia, ne plach, ne trudi . . .") is addressed to Evgeniia Vladimirovna, most are to Zinaida Nikolaevna, and certain lines reflect the poet's concerns for femininity and the oppression of women. Discussing the different addresses of the poetry, at a time when her friendly ties with Pasternak had become

*While most critics—and Pasternak himself—have emphasized the differences in the various stages of his poetic development, one can discern an underlying invariance (as yet insufficiently analyzed) in his style.

closer, Akhmatova was to observe: "Perhaps I dislike this book because Zina [Zinaida Nikolaevna] is present in it"; she went on to comment that *Second Birth* was "a bridegroom's poetry—the poetry of a bridegroom beside himself. . . . And what unpleasant verses are addressed to his former wife. . . . He makes excuses to one woman, and runs to the other with a flower for her corsage."[86]

Pasternak's new perception of his vocation is expressed most memorably in the short poem "Oh, had I known that it happens so . . ." ("O, znal by ia, chto tak byvaet . . ."), in which he looks back on his youthful indulgence in poetic virtuosity, comparing it with his present awareness of the craft's tragic obligations.[87] The poet is now the vehicle not just of art and vitality but also of history and fate. The gush of liquid that recurs throughout his work is now not the waterspout of spring showers but blood—the poet is required no longer merely to turn on a tap but to stake his life. This new interpretation of the poet's role no doubt owes much to the tragic fates of Maiakovskii (the subject of a separate poem, "Death of a Poet")[88] and Esenin. In this collection the poet is invited to sense the reality of the new ideology, of that "faraway [realm] of socialism," which is somehow presented as "close at hand" and yet assured of victory only in a dim future. This theme is presented in a major key in the introductory philosophical poem, "Waves."[89] In that famous piece (whose appearance is recalled by one memoirist as an event almost as significant as that of Olesha's *Envy*),[90] the poet states his intention of including "everything"—his past experiences, his present ideals and aspirations, his place as a poet in Soviet Russia. Such an all-embracing, secure, and near-triumphant vision is a new element in Pasternak's poetry.

In the long run, Pasternak's exercise in ideological tightrope walking in this collection—an attempt to balance his ideals with the more noble of the aspirations professed by the regime—displeased readers in diverse camps. On the one hand, the Marxist Zelinskii, scrutinizing the "civic poetry" in the volume, found undue stress on "intimism." He criticized the poet's "social egocentrism"—an attitude fostered, he thought, by an elitist bourgeois upbringing—and was indignant at the poet's excusing of abuses of the Soviet era by means of a comparison with excesses committed under Peter the Great.[91] On the other hand, for many readers in eastern Europe, *Second Birth* created the impression that, reconciling himself to socialism, Pasternak was placing his moral credit behind the regime's ideology; that action they later interpreted as a deceit of sorts.[92] Czesław Miłosz spoke of his own tendency to accuse Pasternak of "programmatic helplessness in the face of the world, of a carefully cultivated irrational attitude."[93] It is probably unfair to reproach the author of *Second Birth* for making a courageous effort to establish a point of convergence for his aspirations and the new society's principles. While it is true that the effort does not amount to a unified ideological system, could it be expected of any poet of that period that he should forthwith achieve a unified vision of such a complex reality?

Alongside *Second Birth* was the other monument to Pasternak's creative renewal of those years, *A Safe-Conduct.* The poet's first autobiography, and a breviary for Pasternak connoisseurs, the work was first published serially during the period 1929–31.[94] When it appeared in book form in 1931, the ten-thousand-

copy edition was immediately sold out. Simultaneously the volume was attacked—labeled "idealist" and considered so subversive that it was soon banned.
According to one report, copies were removed from libraries within a few weeks
after its appearance. A second edition, planned in 1933, never materialized; the
text was not considered appropriate to the emerging platform of socialist
realism.[95]

Pasternak wrote that *A Safe-Conduct* had been conceived as "something midway between an article and artistic prose, dealing with the way in which, in [the
poet's] life, life was transformed into art, and why."[96] Again, like Mandelstam,
the poet was developing his craft in a crucible of prose, melting earlier poetic
ideas into new, reexamined images. Appearing at this stage in Pasternak's life, *A
Safe-Conduct* served a vital function for its author. Drained emotionally and creatively, Pasternak felt a need for self-definition; by assessing his past, he might
somehow clarify or justify his future as a poet. The style of this text is strikingly
metaphoric and metonymic, in stark contrast to *Sketch for an Autobiography*, Pasternak's concise, simple account of almost thirty years later, in which he deplored
what he termed the "unnecessary mannerisms" that (he claimed) "spoiled" the
earlier book (this later denunciation by Pasternak is to be understood within the
context of his shift in the 1940s toward an aesthetic of greater simplicity).[97]

A Safe-Conduct is a selective autobiography. Perhaps to the reader's surprise, we
learn little of Pasternak's family life, and there are gaps in time between some of
the incidents described. For example, he omits the years 1903 to 1909 (the period
of Scriabin's absence from Russia), while compressing the time of his acquaintance with Maiakovskii (from 1914 to 1930) into a seemingly short span of time.
But the people and events he does describe are those that had a major impact on
the direction of his life. Indeed, Pasternak's emphasis is not on himself but on
whatever it was that made him who he was.

The poet begins by recounting his meeting, at age ten, with Rilke.[98] The appearance of Rilke at the opening of his autobiography is a foreshadowing of Pasternak's eventual decision to make poetry his lifework. As previously indicated,
Rilke was for many years Pasternak's chief source of inspiration, and his poetry
the main prototype for the Russian poet's work. Pasternak described the unique
relationship between the two artists:

> The poet deliberately gives the whole of his life such a steep incline that it cannot exist in
> the vertical line of biography, where we expect to meet it. It cannot be found under his
> own name and has to be sought under those of others, in the biographical columns of
> those who follow him. . . . I am not presenting my reminiscences to the memory of
> Rilke. On the contrary, I myself received them from him as a gift.[99]

Even the organization of the book stresses Rilke's significance; as Pasternak goes
from idol to idol in search of a true hero, Rilke's name recurs. After describing the
meeting with Scriabin, Pasternak discusses the composer as the first major influence in his life. There follows the dramatic story of his love affair with music.
Soon after his break with that art, Pasternak recounts, he discovered a volume of
Rilke's poetry in his father's bookcase.[100] This discovery signals, both realistically

and symbolically, that poetry will eventually capture the young man. But for the time, Pasternak tells us, he suppressed his interest in poetry and turned instead to philosophy, which he expected would help him achieve cultural and intellectual wholeness.

Pasternak devoted about one-third of *A Safe-Conduct* to Marburg. This section of the autobiography is perhaps the most important, for here the reader discerns the impulses that will ultimately drive the author toward poetry. He goes deeply into the intellectual motivations, from both past and present, of his interest in Marburg.

Pasternak's description of Marburg is detailed and highly figurative. He describes the streets, which "clung to the steep slopes like Gothic dwarfs," and the roofs of the houses, which "resembled a flock of doves, bewitched in mid air as they swooped." [101] These unexpected, mystical images, coupled with the legend of Elizabeth of Hungary, lend a supernatural feeling to the text. Indeed, Pasternak seems to have placed particular importance on signs and their interpretations. One feels that he was undertaking an elated, frenzied search—guided by signs—to realize transcendent values. He had hoped that Marburg, where others had realized these values, would provide some sort of answer for him, and he did find valid cultural models in Saint Elizabeth (the supernatural standing for transcendent values) and Mikhail Lomonosov (a trailblazer). Closer in time, Hermann Cohen and philosophy represented one answer to his continuing quest for a hero and an object of worship. Pasternak's realization—coinciding with the failure of his first courtship—that his interest in philosophy was misguided led him to abandon that pursuit and devote himself wholeheartedly to the writing of poetry.

Futurism was the next stage in Pasternak's quest, when Maiakovskii became the object of his worship. [102] The poet was for a time so overwhelmed with admiration for Maiakovskii's achievement that he contemplated abandoning literature—a testimony to his flexibility and continued willingness to reorient himself—as well as to his desire to do only that in which he could be original. Maiakovskii's death provided the catalyst that enabled Pasternak to review his own creative life. To continue on, renewed, the poet finally abandoned his quest for a hero and concentrated on realizing himself through his own creativity and originality. Both *A Safe-Conduct* and *Second Birth* are evidence of that creativity. In *A Safe-Conduct*, Pasternak depicts the genesis of poetry in his life: it was born from the intertwining in his memory of the various orders of experience he describes in the book. [103]

It has been rightly asserted that sections of *A Safe-Conduct*—notably the passages about the narrator's childhood and love for Ida Vysotskaia and about Scriabin, Rilke, and Maiakovskii—compare with the best of Russian prose. [104] This aesthetic form admirably serves the book's raison d'être: in it Pasternak gives us a forceful assessment of the origins of his poetic creativity, as well as a justification for its continuation.

8

The Genre of Silence

1933–1938

Vsë tonet v fariseistve.
[All is drowning in pharisaism.]

Boris Pasternak, "Hamlet"[1]

Pasternak was a man of unusual inner constitution, endowed with a phenomenal inner hearing and a fantastic keenness and sensitivity. For decades he led the isolated life of an Olympian, not participating in politics and not belonging to a single literary group. In 1936 he could, with his own peculiar poetical light-headedness and childlike confidence, join the chorus of enthusiastic comments on Stalin's constitution and its author. But at times, without reasoning, he instinctively manifested political courage, because he could not act otherwise.

Nina Skorbina[2]

The art of translation has had a strange, dual fate in Russia. On the one hand, there have been the translators of genius, like [Vasilii] Zhukovskii, one of the greatest poets of the Golden Age, who was almost exclusively a translator, or Pasternak, whose versions of Shakespeare are works of original genius. . . . On the other hand, translation has acquired a bad smell as a sort of intellectual Siberia to which writers whose own work is politically suspect are banished.

Clarence Brown[3]

During this period—the decade the purges were beginning—the atmosphere became stifling for poets and writers. Mandelstam entered the decade already burdened with heavy Soviet censure, and before its end he had died in a Siberian camp. In those dark days Pasternak made a courageous choice: to practice what Babel, at the 1934 Writers' Congress, called "the genre of silence." For nearly a quarter of a century he practiced it with great dignity. With the exception of his translations and two slim collections of wartime poetry (1943 and 1945), no new book by Pasternak was published between *A Tale* (1934) and the appearance outside the Soviet Union of *Doctor Zhivago* (1957).

In spite of his decision to remain silent, Pasternak continued to be intensely active intellectually, and inasmuch as the circumstances of the decade clearly discouraged the expression of personal thought, he turned to translation. When in 1933 he started working with Georgian poetry, he laid the foundation for a dedicated and fruitful career as translator. Secluded first in his Moscow apartment, then (from 1936 on) in his dacha in Peredelkino, or (during part of World War II) in an evacuated writers' colony in the Urals, Pasternak also devoted himself to English poetry (certain sonnets and seven plays by Shakespeare and the poems of Walter Raleigh, Ben Jonson, Keats, Byron, and Shelley); German poetry (both parts of Goethe's *Faust*, Schiller's *Maria Stuart*, Hans Sachs, von Kleist, Rilke, and Johannes Becher); such Romantics as the Pole Juliusz Słowacki, the Hungarian Sándor Petőfi, and the Ukrainian Taras Shevchenko; the French Symbolist Paul Verlaine; and contemporaries like the Czech Surrealist Vitězslav Nezval and Rafael Alberti and Óndra Lysohorský. By the end of his life he had published well over two thousand pages of poetic translations—approximately one-half of his entire literary output.[4]

Although in 1920 one of his first attempts at literary translation, a rendition of Goethe's unfinished epic *The Mysteries* (*Die Geheimnisse*, 1784–85), drew rather sharp criticism from Blok,[5] a quarter of a century later Pasternak had achieved considerable mastery. Certain of his translations, in particular, those of Shakespeare's plays and sonnets, have come to be recognized in their own right as works of original genius. Such theorists of literary translation as Kornei Chukovskii and Efim Etkind consider Pasternak's achievements in "literary translation" (*khudozhestvennyi perevod*) on the same plane as the work of M. L. Lozinskii and Samuil Marshak.[6] Lozinskii and Pasternak are singled out by the critic Iu. Levin as most conspicuously successful in creating a "Soviet Shakespeare."[7] More than one critic has mentioned Pasternak's name in the same breath with that of Vasilii Zhukovskii, the pre-Romantic whose translations of the *Odyssey* and of German and English pre-Romantics and Romantics have secured him a unique place in the Russian literary pantheon.[8] Recognition of Pasternak's deserts in this field has grown steadily in the Soviet Union among experts writing both in the scholarly series *Masterstvo perevoda* and in the staunchly conservative journal *Zvezda*, one of whom referred to him as "the most cultured of our poet-translators" (obviously a sincere acknowledgment, close though it may sound to a left-handed compliment).[9]

Pasternak undertook his translation of Georgian poetry fired with enthusiasm after hearing it interpreted for him during his first visit to Tbilisi in 1931. He took his work seriously and constantly badgered his Georgian friends for the literal versions from which he fashioned his literary renderings.* In addition, he soon came to appreciate the work as a means of earning a living. Nonetheless, his attitude toward this professional activity soon became ambiguous. On the one hand, as he indicated to friends, translation work gave him "immense pleasure and satisfaction,"[10] and he made an enthusiastic speech at the First All-Union Soviet Convention of Translators in January, 1936.[11] On the other hand, he soon realized that the considerable investment in time and creative energy it exacted from him depleted his resources for his own work. He told a friend in the late 1930s that he did translation work only when he needed money badly.[12] In the 1930s and 1940s he discovered that other literary work did not provide a solid "financial basis" (*neprochno*).[13] Moreover, he was not always free to chose what he wished to work on because his own wishes did not always coincide with the needs of state publishing houses. He complained that the more serious and significant the work to be translated, the fewer chances it had of providing adequate remuneration. He remarked, "Shakespeare yields nothing," while his work on the Georgian poets would bring in an income stretching over one to one and a half years.† When all was said, however, he found that he could translate "in a more rationalistic and sedate spirit" than he could compose his own verse. Translation provided a welcome release from his own creative work.[14]

Pasternak's conception of translation must be patched together from several statements in his letters and a few critical essays. Most revealingly, he told a correspondent:

I completely reject contemporary views on translation. The works of Lozinskii, [Anna] Radlova, Marshak, and Chukovskii are alien to me and seem to me artificial, shallow, and soulless. I share the viewpoint of the past century, when translation was seen as a literary task which, because of its lofty conception, left no room for an involvement in philology.[15]

Let us overlook whatever bias this characterization of his contemporaries may contain[16] and examine the unique focus that Pasternak advocated. He indicated that he turned "from the translation of words and metaphors to the translation of thoughts and scenes."[17] Elsewhere he commented that, rather than hoping to find a minute rendering of all the individual Cervantesian stylistic flourishes in a newly published translation of *Don Quixote*, he was more concerned that the deeper content of the work was conveyed.[18] And Pasternak himself certainly avoided attention to details to the detriment of the whole (a defect that at times mars Lozinskii's achievement).[19] Whereas in the Briusov-Lozinskii tradition the essential was extreme "objectivity," maximum care for historical accuracy, local

---

*Composing a literary translation on the basis of Russian *podstrochniki* (cribs, or line-by-line literal translations provided by a linguistic informant) has been standard practice for Russian poet-translators since the days of Zhukovskii (especially when they are translating from languages other than French, German, and English).

†Such a statement in no way implies that Pasternak had little regard for the poetry of the Georgians. The popularity of Georgian poetry at the time may be attributed in part to Stalin's Georgian origin.

color, and stylistic characteristics of the period—all concerns that magnified the *distance* between the text and the contemporary Russian reader—Pasternak believed in attempting an imaginative act of sympathetic and creative reconstitution that would make the author of the original appear *as a contemporary*.[20] Here Pasternak harked back not only to the Romantic notion of *Nachdichtung* (practicing on a monumental scale with his *Hamlet* and *Faust* what Lermontov, say, was doing in a more fragmentary way)[21] but also to the eighteenth-century spirit of supreme freedom in which Voltaire gave his contemporaries a highly idiosyncratic re-creation of *Hamlet*. At times Pasternak's translations are so free that one may wonder whether his achievement belongs to the genre of translation proper or to that of a free and original poetic creation inspired by the primary work; the latter interpretation has been upheld by certain Soviet critics.[22]

The crowning success of Pasternak's method of poetic translation was his ability to make Shakespeare speak a markedly colloquial twentieth-century Russian. This, to be true, he achieved through resolutely jettisoning many of the original's euphuisms, conventional turns, or occasional declamatory strains, in order forcefully to bring out individual characterizations. In so doing, Pasternak evolved his own keynote, using lexical, phraseological, and syntactical devices to create the simple, colloquial speech he had chosen.[23] As a result, his rendering of Shakespeare's Sonnet 73, for example, "is quite removed from Shakespeare and very close to Pasternak," as one critic has pointed out.[24] On the other hand, the general effect of Pasternak's translations of Shakespeare is, in Henry Gifford's words, "to thin out the original, so that it becomes an autumn wood with fewer leaves and with the outlines showing more clearly." Critics agree that Pasternak, Lozinskii, and Marshak are the most distinguished Shakespeare translators of the Soviet period, and among them Pasternak stands out as probably the most original. His tendency to present Shakespeare as a contemporary no doubt did much to change the Soviet attitude toward the ideological characterization of Shakespeare.* His notion that Shakespeare was a "prophet" of a new age (our own) is arch-Romantic and echoes the way Victor Hugo viewed the Bard.[25]

Before his involvement in the translation of western European classics, Pasternak had started devoting time to Georgian poetry. The fascination that Georgian literature held for him in the 1930s was due to the convergence of several factors: his discovery of an enchanting land, in terms of its exotic vegetation and its artistic and architectural heritage; his feeling that for various historical and geographical reasons it had preserved a unique blend of authentic values and attitudes;† the warm friendship with the hospitable families of three Georgian poets,

---

*Whereas in the 1931 edition of the *Shorter Soviet Encyclopedia* Shakespeare was presented as an "ideologist of the aristocracy," by the time of his four-hundredth anniversary in 1964 he had been fully "rehabilitated" and even hailed as somewhat of a forerunner of socialist realism (cf. *Pravda*, April 24, 1964).

†This is reflected in Pasternak's remark to Iashvili: "[What you have in Georgia] has become a rarity in the whole world. For (even leaving aside its fairy-tale originality) [Georgia] . . . is a country that most astonishingly never experienced a hiatus in its existence, a country that has remained tied to the earth even to this day, not having been carried away into a sphere of abstraction" (Pasternak, letter of July 30, 1932, to Paolo Iashvili, *LGF*, p. 40).

Titian Tabidze, Paolo Iashvili, and G. N. Leonidze, and consequently his view of
Georgia as his "second home."[26] In the modern Georgian literary idiom he most
appreciated the fiery strain, the natural and authentic rhetorical vein, the fantasy,
the stylistic reflections of a quaint past and its beliefs, and the subtle formulas
inherited from proverbs.[27] These feelings of sympathy are reflected in the extent
and significance of his role in translating Georgian poetry: he soon emerged as the
Russian translator most active in this field, earning the warm friendship of the
Georgian public. While visiting Georgia in November, 1933, with a delegation
of Soviet writers, he undertook, in conjunction with Nikolai Tikhonov, a vast
program of translations of Georgian poetry, which were soon to appear in both
Moscow and Tbilisi.

A critic writing in *Znamia* in 1935 singled out Pasternak's exceptional talent in
bringing to life in a fresh and creative Russian idiom a number of Georgian masterpieces that until then, in dull and inadequate translations, had gone unnoticed
by the Russian public.[28] Over the years Pasternak translated lyrics by such contemporary poets as Titian Tabidze, Iashvili, Leonidze, Valerian Gaprindashvili,
Nikoloz Mitsishvili, and Simon Chikovani; the long narrative poem *The Snake
Eater*, by the pre-Revolutionary Vazha-Pshavela; and works by the Romantic
Nikoloz Baratashvili. Essaying the method that he would later apply to Shakespeare, Pasternak was successful in making the "Russian Baratashvili" sound like
a live and close contemporary.[29] The appearance in 1935 of the collection of
his translation of *Georgian Lyric Poets* was greeted in *Literaturnaia gazeta* with
a warmly appreciative article by his long-term admirer Dmitrii Sviatopolk-
Mirskii, who defended the poet from the reproach that he had "Pasternakized" in
the extreme the works he translated and developed the notion of the "conge-
niality" with which Pasternak approached his authors.[30]

Such intensive and prolonged interpretation of rich poetic voices other than his
own had a far-reaching effect on Pasternak. It provided him with a spiritual refuge and kept him in touch with great masters at a time when Soviet intellectuals
were being aesthetically starved. Shakespeare was especially important to him.
He confided to a friend that in the Elizabethan he found an "inner freedom" inconceivable to his contemporaries.[31] Working so closely with Shakespeare reinforced and crystallized the strong fascination he had had in his youth when reading the English poet.* Pasternak felt strongly about the privileged access to his
original, by which, "with a tangible certainty . . . not given to the biographer or
the scholar, the translator becomes aware of the personality of Shakespeare and of
his genius."[32] In addition, the discipline of translation took Pasternak "further
away from modernism and impelled him to examine again the problems of com-

---

*The presence of Shakespeare makes itself felt directly in such early poems as "Shakespeare"
(1919) and "English Lessons" (1922, a programmatic poem of sorts) and through the influence of
Shakespearean historical drama in such "chronicles" as *The Year 1905* (1927) and the posthumous
The Blind Beauty (*Slepaia krasavitsa*, 1969). A contemporary who often heard Pasternak converse
said that the poet conveyed the impression that he was truly shaken or gripped (*oburevaem*) by Shakespeare (L. Ozerov, "Zametki Pasternaka o Shekspire," *Masterstvo perevoda: Sbornik shestoi*, Moscow:
Sovetskii pisatel, 1968), p. 112.

munication in poetry."[33] It also brought him closer to the directness and simplicity necessary for communication with a large audience. Furthermore, the poet in many ways tried to do in translation what he could not do in his original poems—"tell the truth about his own life, discuss problems of his generation, engage in polemics with the authorities."[34]

Nonetheless, translation did not consume all of Pasternak's creative energy. The last fictional volume to appear before his long silence was *A Tale* (*Povest*, 1934). This text, of about 16,500 words, breaks with the autobiographical mode of Pasternak's earlier works sufficiently to enter the realm of fiction. To be sure, he still includes a number of autobiographical details: the initial setting, a small town in the Urals; a flashback to the torrid summer of 1914; and the protagonist, Sergei (Serezha) Spektorskii, who spends that summer as a tutor in a well-to-do family, has an inconclusive love affair with the young Danish woman staying with the family, and is driven into the arms of another, the young prostitute Sashka, out of both sensuousness and compassion (Serezha connects this attraction with a generalized pity for the fate of woman, which echoes the feeling that Pasternak had had since adolescence).* The properly fictional structure adds complexity to this framework. The title has a double meaning: it refers both to Pasternak's text and to the story within the story—the "tale" that Serezha, an aspiring writer, is endeavoring to compose. The hero of this inner composition, a writer christened Y3, is consumed by the dream that also haunts Serezha—and Pasternak himself—the rescue of woman from the humiliation and misery with which she is afflicted. This the artist (Y3/Serezha) proposes to do through the redemptive value of his art and his life.

Certain details in *A Tale* prefigure *Doctor Zhivago*. Serezha's sister is married to an official, Pasha (Pavel), in a small town in the Urals; the complex structure of the hero's dual relationship to Anna and Sashka suggests Zhivago's dual allegiance to Tonia and Lara; Y3 is "a very Christ of passivity," a trait consonant with Zhivago. This and other evidence suggests that, like other prose fragments written by Pasternak in 1937–39, *A Tale* was a sketch for the long novel that he had begun, renewing his endeavor of over a decade earlier. It is not inconceivable that one of the stimuli prompting him to resume this lifelong project was the suggestion made by a participant in an April, 1932, "creative evening" of writers devoted to his work: "Compose a novel about our epoch; freshen it with our great reality." To that end Pasternak devoted much time on and off, between 1934 and 1939, progressing toward what would become *Doctor Zhivago*. During part of that time Pasternak used "The Diary of Zhivult" ("Zapiski Zhivulta") as a working title for his text (Zhivult would soon turn into Zhivago). These fragments cover the period 1902 to 1905 and, taken together, represent an early draft of the first few chapters of *Doctor Zhivago*. In this *"Ur"-Zhivago* we witness the early life

---

*That the young Pasternak—no less than the young Tolstoy—was at times not above calling on ladies of easy virtue will be documented by some later, less bashful biographer. Readers of *A Tale* will recall that the thoughtful feelings accompanying such visits turn them into anything but heartless episodes.

Pasternak, portrait by A.
Iar-Kravchenko, 1933.
Private collection.

of the hero, Zhivult (who had been temporarily renamed Patrikii), a ten-year-old orphan from Kazan who comes to live with Aleksandr Aleksandrovich Gromeko, a professor of natural history; his wife, Anna Gubertovna; and their daughter, Antonina (Tonia). Patrikii grows up, plays, and studies with Tonia, and many episodes are close to life in the Gromeko household as depicted in *Doctor Zhivago*. In another excerpt the hero lives with his wife, Tonia, and son, Shura, in the wartime atmosphere of the town of Iuriatin in the Urals and visits Evgeniia Istomina, née Liuvers, the daughter of a foreign-born bankrupt lawyer from Perm and wife of the physics and mathematics teacher of the Iuriatin secondary school.[35] Interspersed in sections of the narrative are obvious autobiographical traits, such as the hero Patrikii's suffering from a prolonged, year-long chronic insomnia (as Pasternak himself did in 1934–35).[36]

Underlying this major venture into prose was Pasternak's intention to compose an important fresco depicting chapters of Russia's history and his generation's contribution to it. Thus he told the Mandelstams—"every time" he met them—that he was writing a prose work "about [them] all."[37] In 1934 he also confessed to the poet Nezval: "It was a time [the period following the October Revolution] when things were bad, very bad for me. I want to write about this. In a quite simple manner . . . I intend to write a book in prose about how bad things were for me, a book quite simple and realistic. You understand, sometimes a man must force himself to stand on his head."[38]

By 1937, Pasternak said that he had not yet made a final decision about the title but described the book as a three-part novel, with the first part dealing with the childhood of the protagonists.[39] Somewhat earlier he had indicated to his sister Josephine that the book would be a partial payment of what he felt he owed to his wife, Zinaida Nikolaevna, that it would be "about her": "I will write a novel. . . . A novel about that girl. . . . Beautiful, misguided. A veiled beauty in the private rooms of night restaurants. . . . Her cousin, a guardsman, would take her there. She, of course, could not help it. She was so young, so unspeakably attractive."[40] In a letter to his father Pasternak discussed the aesthetic and ideological conversion that he claimed motivated him to write the work:

Well, though late, I too have at last seen the light. Nothing I have written so far is of any significance. That world has ceased and I have nothing to show to this new one. . . . But luckily I am alive, my eyes are open, and hurriedly I am trying to transform myself into a writer of a Dickensian kind, and later—if I have enough strength to do it—into a poet in the manner of Pushkin. Do not imagine that I dream of comparing myself with them! I am naming them simply to give you an idea of my inner change. In other words I have become a particle of my time and state, and their interests have become my own.[41]

In a later communication to his parents he continued to discuss the novel, further elaborating on his new style, which he felt was close to that of Chekhov and Tolstoy:

Do you remember my *Tale?* That was by comparison a decadent work. This new work is growing into something big, by much more modest but also more lasting means. I mentioned *A Tale* because what few qualities it did possess were all of an inner order. The same plastic authenticity is working here too, but with all its strength, and as I said, in a simple, more transparent form. I keep thinking of Chekhov, and the few to whom I have shown parts of it are reminded of Tolstoy.[42]

But the general disease afflicting the age brought Pasternak to an aesthetic stalemate and a standstill on his work. He wrote at this time: ". . . some kind of period in general literary life and in my own personally has come to an end. Mine came to an end even earlier; I could not cope with my prose, I fell sick mentally, I did translations."[43] We shall soon discuss the disease that struck his generation.

While in the mid-1930s Pasternak had almost ceased writing poetry, many editions of his poetry were published and reissued until 1936, with the result that tens of thousands of readers had free access to them.* This indicates that he did not yet find himself in any kind of disfavor (at a time when others, such as Mandelstam, had already fallen in disgrace). His significance as a poet was both recognized abroad—by 1935 he had been translated into five foreign languages—and still frequently acknowledged at home. Thus the *Literary Encyclopedia* appearing in 1934 contained a fundamentally sensitive article, whose author, Aleksei Selivanovskii, attempted to demonstrate Pasternak's "internal poetic affinity for music" and, despite some reservations, generously granted that he was a major talent. In 1935, Dmitrii Sviatopolk-Mirskii, writing in *Literaturnaia gazeta*, called Pasternak "the greatest Russian poet."[44] The same year Aleksei Surkov, who on ideological counts had many reservations about the type of literature Pasternak stood for, classified him nonetheless as a "master," as opposed to a "virtuoso."[45] Though in principle hostile to any "Soviet" poet, the leading Russian émigré critic Georgii Adamovich also praised the musicality and authenticity of Pasternak's lyre and acknowledged that he was being idolized (*ego liubiat i "obozhaiut"*) by both Soviet and émigré readers.[46] Another indication of Pasternak's high status in the literary scene was that in 1934 he was invited by Gorky to be one of the editors of the significant new literary series Biblioteka poeta (the Poet's Library), which printed the works of major modern poets.

While during that decade Pasternak's poetry often elicited positive and sympathetic reactions, and while he occasionally published shorter units of his long prose work in progress, he had not yet successfully defined in his own eyes his creative identity. Thus he exclaimed in a letter: "How I'd have liked to know, but in all truth, who I am and what I am!" As he pointed out, Zinaida Nikolaevna believed that it was a matter of his channeling his creative abilities into specific tasks: "She thinks, with all the personal interest of a great friend, that I am a good-for-nothing loafer and expresses doubts about our future life together if I do not at last sit down and do some work once more." To Pasternak the need to achieve such concentration appeared less appropriate and relevant to his true self than his propensity "to become attached to places and to certain times of the day, to trees, to people, to the history of souls." Of this tendency, which he felt was "the only definite thing" about his character, he said: "[It] is so powerful in me that it takes the place of work and seems to be my profession. . . . To become attached somehow not like a man, but stupidly is the only thing that . . . I know and can do."[47] To his extreme impressionability with regard to Georgia, Shakespeare, and the tribulations of his friends in the 1930s we are indebted for the ability of the mature artist to elaborate aesthetically powerful forms.

In the mid-1930s Pasternak's literary activities were disrupted by necessary participation in a number of professional meetings, an activity he came to dislike

---

*These editions were *Selected Verse* (*Izbrannye stikhi*, 1933), *Small Book of Poetry for Children* (*Knizhka dlia detei*, 1933), *Poems* (*The Year 1905, Lieutenant Schmidt*, and *Spektorskii*, 1933), *Poetry in One Volume* (*Stikhotvoreniia v odnom tome*; the first edition of 1933 was followed by a second of 20,000 copies in 1935 and a third in 1936), a second edition of *Second Birth* (1934), and *Selected Verse* (*Izbrannye stikhotvoreniia*, 1934).

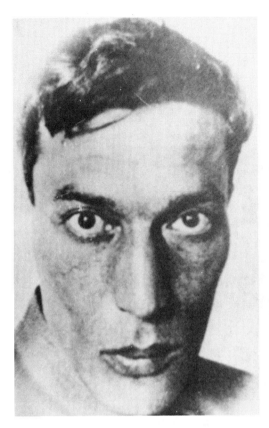

Pasternak at the First Congress of
Soviet Writers, held in Moscow in
1934. *Arthème Fayard.*

more and more, and by serious health problems. The first Congress of the Union
of Soviet Writers, which opened in Moscow on August 17, 1934, proved to be of
significance to Pasternak's literary career because of the special recognition that
his place in modern Russian poetry received during the proceedings. The congress, which lasted for fifteen days, met in the Hall of Columns; it was estimated
that a total of about 25,000 Muscovites attended the sessions.[48] Organized because Stalin felt that Soviet writers were insufficiently enthusiastic in proclaiming
socialism, it was to provide a convenient platform from which to assert the new
doctrine of "socialist realism," coined to suit the conjuncture.

The participants in the congress were the seven hundred members of the Union
of Writers, as well as about thirty specially invited left-wing writers from various
foreign countries. Conspicuous among the sizable Czechoslovak delegation was
its foremost poet, Vítězslav Nezval, a Surrealist and a Soviet sympathizer, who
was soon on good terms with Pasternak (Nezval later said that Pasternak was the
only Russian poet who used the word "love" in their conversations).[49] Also present were the Bavarian anarchist Oskar Maria Graf, the German revolutionary
Ernst Toller, the French Surrealist-turned-proletarian Louis Aragon, Klaus
Mann, and Gustav Regler (a member of the German Communist party). Instead

At the 1934 congress (*right*), with the French novelist André Malraux (*left*) and the
dramatist Vsevolod Meierkhold. *Arthème Fayard.*

of maintaining the genteel reserve expected of foreign guests, André Malraux
launched a furious attack against the simplistically crude formula for socialist
realism, as well as against the slogan "Writers Are Engineers of the Soul," which
Stalin had coined for the Congress.[50]

After the political keynote address by Andrei Zhdanov, the secretary of the
Central Committee, Maksim Gorky, the dean of Soviet letters and head of the
Union of Writers, presided over the proceedings. Gorky, probably under severe
pressure, was no longer willing to oppose the regime; *White Sea Canal*, published
by him that year, extolled all aspects of Stalinization.* He opened the debates
with a forty-page address, which he took about three hours to deliver, often with a
thundering tone. In that speech, marked by prolixity and banality, the old writer
defended the positions of atheistic materialism and attacked "capitalistic" literature under its various guises.[51]

It is not surprising that after such a note was struck Pasternak found himself
the target of some criticism on the floor. The proletarian poet Aleksandr Bezy-

*The collection Belomorsko-Baltiiskii kanal *imeni Stalina*, edited by Gorky and others, is discussed in vol. 2 of Aleksandr Solzhenitsyn's *The Gulag Archipelago*.

menskii expressed the wish that Pasternak "direct his glance to broader expanses."[52] The staunch Communist poet Aleksei Surkov similarly stated that Pasternak was too limited by a narrow lyrical platform and not enough involved with
Soviet themes: ". . . the immense talent of B. L. Pasternak will never fully reveal
itself until he has attached himself fully to the gigantic, rich, and radiant subject
matter [offered by] the Revolution; and he will become a great poet only when he
has organically absorbed the Revolution into himself."[53] On August 29, Pasternak in effect responded to the main point underlying Surkov's remarks ("You need
to come closer to today's world") by stating his own view on the dangers besetting
the artist in the new Soviet society, with its incipient tendency toward the bu-
reaucratization of inspiration:

The party tells us to remain close to the masses. As for myself, I have never acquired the
right to speak in the language of the Party. I would say only this: never surrender your
personality, and this is a statement which the Party can never reject. The people and the
state surround us with their warm affection, and so there is always the danger that we
shall be transformed into high literary functionaries. Therefore let us keep our distance,
but gently, so that we may remain faithful to the springs of poetry in the name of our
great love for our country and for the men who are its principal adornments, in the name
of the love which remains fruitful and full of attachment to the world of reality.[54]

While Pasternak spoke up at the congress to defend the values for which he
stood, forceful voices were also heard on his behalf. The most significant of these
was Nikolai Bukharin, who in his speech lavished praise on Pasternak as "one of

With the poet Vs. Rozhdestvenskii and the critic D. V. Petrovskii around the time of
the First Congress of Soviet Writers in 1934. *Pasternak Family Collection.*

the most important masters of poetry of our time." This qualification came in the context of a polemical argument. Recommending the use of "fewer brass instruments" and less pompous language, Bukharin criticized the aesthetic of contemporary poets he termed "Wagnerians" (Bezymenskii being listed as an example), and, by implication, the initiator of that aesthetic, Maiakovskii. Bukharin held out instead as an ideal the more lyrical strains of Pasternak's work.[55] This direct blow to Maiakovskii was viewed as a threat by those most directly interested in defending his poetic legacy and image as "committed" poet—his close associates Lili (Liliia) and Osip Brik—and after the congress the Briks began "lobbying" at the highest levels until Stalin released as his own the formula suggested to him by Brik: "Maiakovskii was and remains the best and most talented poet of our Soviet epoch."[56] Pasternak later wrote that in a personal letter he thanked Stalin for this oracle, which protected him from the "inflation" of his own role subsequent to Bukharin's speech.[57] It was in character for Pasternak to resent the publicity brought on by Bukharin's praise.

Another participant in the congress praised Pasternak's creative endeavors. Responding to accusations that the three most talented Soviet writers of the period, Babel, Olesha, and Pasternak, had been too slow in producing new books, Ehrenburg explained that a writer's output should not be judged by the standards applicable to construction work and that it was simply a fact that some writers worked more slowly than others. The matter of pace, he said, was neither a vice nor a virtue but an attribute of the individual writer; it was therefore absurd to condemn Pasternak for slowness.[58]

For all the intense and sometimes solemn speeches of the congress, the image that one participant, Ehrenburg, retained in his memory was that of "a great and marvelous festival," an "extraordinary kind of carnival."[59] Such an impression was fostered by the frequent colorful episodes during visits of delegations from all walks of life, professional groups, and parts of the Soviet Union. One incident during such a visit—that of the Moscow metro builders—illuminates Pasternak's character:

Pasternak sat on the platform beaming all the time. When the metro builders' delegation arrived he jumped up to take a heavy tool from one of the girls; she laughed, and the entire audience laughed with her. As for Pasternak, he tried to explain his gesture in the speech he made: "And when an unconscious impulse made me try to take off the shoulder of the metro worker a heavy tool, whose name I don't know, how could the comrade on the platform who ridiculed my intellectual's sensibility know that at that moment this metro worker was in some immediate sense my sister, and I wanted to help her as someone close and familiar to me."[60]

The superficially comic incident (the poet unsuccessfully attempting to wrench from the young girl a tool that she firmly refuses to surrender) at a deeper level reveals Pasternak's aristocratic sensibility, which prompts him to chivalrous behavior which is out of context in this markedly proletarian atmosphere; his lack of familiarity with realia of the new society (he would probably have been much less efficient than the girl in handling the cumbersome industrial tool); and his naïve unawareness of the purely *theatrical* nature of this parade, which would have struck him as false had he understood it better (only in ~~the~~ *real* situation of a worker having to carry the tool for a functional purpose would it have made sense to help her).

Although at Fadeev's suggestion Pasternak was elected (on September 1) to the board of the Writers' Union, he was disheartened about the achievements of the congress. Its political aftermath did not help improve his low spirits. He left the congress before its end, on August 30, to go off to the Odoevo rest home. His health was deteriorating seriously. In his *Sketch for an Autobiography* he tells us that for a whole year, from about mid-1934, he suffered from insomnia—no longer the somewhat metaphoric or poetic state he had on occasion referred to by that label from as early as 1912, but prolonged, chronic, and acute insomnia. The condition became so serious ("feeling ill and on the point of a breakdown from insomnia lasting for almost a year")[61] that he had to be treated in a sanatorium near Moscow. At the time he mentioned to a friend that the doctor had diagnosed nervous debility.[62]

One day in June, 1935, while Pasternak was still in the sanatorium, the telephone rang, and he was told, "You are going abroad"—to attend the International Congress of Writers for the Defense of Culture that had just convened in Paris. As reported by his sister Josephine, the conversation took the following turn: "[Pasternak:] 'I am not [going] . . . how could I, I am unable to walk even in the streets of Moscow, I am ill!' With his peculiar vehemence, with the stubbornness of a sick person, he refused to move away from the sanatorium even though he knew that the decision to send him to Paris had been taken in the Kremlin."[63]

At that point the caller—reportedly a Stalin aide speaking from the Kremlin—asked him: "'But if you were a soldier and received an order, how would you act?' [Pasternak:] 'I would fulfil the order.' 'Consider this an order from Comrade Stalin.'"[64] Pasternak's sister continued:

In the end he had to give in, and his last excuse that he had nothing to put on was brushed aside by an official who took him to various shops in Moscow, and in a hurry bought him a hat, a couple of shirts, a suit off the peg which did not quite fit, and so on. "And now," Boris finished, "I have to go to this Congress—but I am unable to speak, how can I in this state, appear on a platform?" Why did they wish him to take part at the Congress whose meetings had already started?[65]

Referring to that episode, Pasternak confided to a friend, "I did not dare not to leave, Stalin's secretary came to me, I—became frightened."[66]

Since Pasternak's health did not allow him to fly, he and Babel, who did not want Pasternak to travel by himself, went by train. During their stopover in Berlin, Pasternak saw some of his relatives, whom he had hurriedly notified of his arrival. When they received the news, his parents were not well, and so his sister Josephine and her husband alone made the trip from Munich (where they were visiting) to meet him. Josephine Pasternak was deeply concerned about her brother's condition, and later remarked:

Everything was overshadowed by the strangeness of his bearing. He behaved as if only a few weeks, not twelve years, had separated us. Every now and again he burst into tears. And he had one wish only: to sleep! One could see he was in a state of acute depression. . . . He was complaining about insomnia which must have tortured him for the last few months.[67]

The Berlin stopover was only a few hours long. Pasternak spent the first three hours sleeping, and only later did he sit down with his sister and brother-in-law in a restaurant to talk. The conversation centered mostly on Pasternak's illness, but he found time to tell his relatives about Zinaida Nikolaevna and some of his current literary projects.[68] Then the two delegates to the Congress hurried on to Paris.

For the hierarchy of the Union of Writers in Moscow, the inclusion of Babel and Pasternak in the delegation was an afterthought; originally they had not wanted to include them. It was only after the Soviet delegation arrived in Paris that Mikhail Koltsov and Ehrenburg, who acted as liaison between the Soviet writers and the congress organizers, became aware that the two masters, though invited, were absent. Koltsov and Ehrenburg, as well as others from the secretariat of the congress, reflected that the absence of two such conspicuous talents would not best serve Soviet interests; from the Soviet embassy they cabled Bukharin, the editor of *Izvestiia*, with a pressing request that the two be sent immediately.[69] The large Soviet delegation already included Aleksei Koltsov (the *Pravda* correspondent); Ehrenburg (a Parisian of long standing who had recently espoused the Soviet regime, becoming the *Izvestiia* correspondent); novelists Fëdor Panfërov, Aleksei Tolstoy, and Vsevolod Ivanov; poet Nikolai Tikhonov; "Proletarian" novelist Anna Karavaeva, playwrights Vladimir Kirshon and Ivan Mikitenko; Byelorussian poet and writer Iakub Kolas; and Iranian poet (later dean of Soviet Tadjik literature) Abolgasem Lakhuti.

The idea for the International Congress for the Defense of Culture—sometimes referred to as the Anti-Fascist Congress—had originated in anti-Fascist and leftist writers' circles in France. At the head of the movement stood Henri Barbusse, André Gide, and André Malraux—the latter two harboring strong pro-Soviet sympathies. It was clear to many onlookers that the congress was "a Communist initiative"; to fellow organizers Malraux and Jean-Richard Bloch (also a Communist sympathizer), Ehrenburg explained frankly that the aim of the congress was to organize (*noyauter*) intellectuals with a view to action. During the proceedings Gide proclaimed, amid much sensation, his allegiance to Communism—or to his own very liberal and idealistic Communism.[70] Alongside hardcore Communists, however,—such as the Americans Waldo Frank and Michael Gold—and ardent socialists, participants counted such "unattached" liberals as the French critic Julien Benda and the English novelists E. M. Forster and Aldous Huxley.*

---

*The presiding committee of the Association for the Defense of Culture, elected by the congress, included Gide, Heinrich Mann, Sinclair Lewis, and Barbusse. The French delegation included, in addition to those already mentioned, Louis Aragon, Romain Rolland, the philosopher

The congress met from June 21 to 25, 1935, in the huge, ugly Palais de la Mutualité. It was this building that Babel and Pasternak, tired from the long train journey, entered on the fourth and next-to-last day of the proceedings, after many important issues had already been discussed. Before their arrival, however, the Russian poet's name had been mentioned on several occasions: in their speeches several Russian delegates cited Pasternak as an example of diversity within Soviet literature. This was, strategically speaking, very opportune, in order not to make Soviet literature appear too monolithically "proletarian," one of its obvious shortcomings in the eyes of many foreign literati. Thus, after discussing the satirical and humorous attributes of Maiakovskii and the simple emotional and nature-loving images of Bagritskii, Tikhonov (whose "fierce geniality" was noted by an eyewitness) told the congress: "Boris Pasternak presents us with the complex world of psychological expanses. [What a] sincere striving to perceive and combine in the world at once the multiplicity of intersecting poetical movements."[71] Tikhonov's assessment of Pasternak drew an ovation, according to Ehrenburg's report in *Izvestiia*: "When Tikhonov came to his evaluation of Pasternak's poetry, the hall rose, and with lengthy applause, greeted the poet [Pasternak] who had shown, throughout his entire life, that great mastery and great conscience were not incompatible."[72] In his speech, entitled "Socialist Realism," Panfërov bestowed left-handed praise on Pasternak when he included him as one of that "excellent pleiad of writers whose books are well known not only in our country but in the entire world." Ehrenburg referred to Pasternak twice in his address, both times in connection with the working class and the "different breath, different rhythm, different will" they experienced through Pasternak's poetry.[73]

Much expectation had thus built up by the time Pasternak actually came to the rostrum. The first draft of his address had been chiefly about his illness, and Ehrenburg recalls that it "took a lot of persuasion to get him to say a few words about poetry."[74] When on the fifth and last day of the congress Malraux introduced him as "one of the greatest poets of our epoch" and he stood before the gathering in the main hall of the Mutualité, there was a long ovation. Speaking in Russian, Pasternak began his speech hesitatingly and with a slight stammer—which earned him the nickname "Divine Stutterer." By then he had made up his mind and declared: "I should like to speak here of poetry and not of sickness." He went on to say:

Poetry will always remain that celebrated light, above all the Alps, which is scattered about in the grass, underfoot, so that it is only necessary to bend down in order to catch sight of it and pluck it up from the earth; it will always be too simple to be discussed at meetings; it will forever remain the organic function of the joy of a human being filled to overflowing with the blessed gift of rational speech—and in such a way, the happier man is on this earth, the easier it will be for him to be an artist.[75]

Alain (Émile Auguste Chartier), the art historian Élie Faure, and the novelist Victor Margueritte. Germany was represented by Heinrich Mann, Bertolt Brecht, Gustav Regler, Anna Seghers, Ernst Toller, and Johannes Becher.

In his article on the last session Ehrenburg recounted: "André Malraux translated Pasternak's speech and then read his poem ('So one begins, about two years old . . .'). The gathering responded with a long ovation."[76] Malraux himself later reminisced with emotion about Pasternak reciting his poems "before the subdued students" in the auditorium.[77]

Pasternak was not one to stay on the congress platform long. His great friend Tsvetaeva looked him up during the proceedings, and they were seen conversing and reciting poetry to each other in the corridors of the Palais de la Mutualité while the debates were still in progress.[78] Thereafter he visited her home in Meudon, where he met her husband, son, and daughter for the first time. He discussed with her what kind of dress he should buy for his wife, whom he described to her as "a beauty."[79] Tsvetaeva's admiration for Pasternak as an artist had continued to grow with the publication of Pasternak's collected poetry in 1933; she had devoted two articles to him* and on occasion had defended him against attacks by Russian émigré writers, who by and large viewed Pasternak as "belonging to the Soviets" and therefore incapable of fine poetry.[80] Pasternak found time to accompany Tsvetaeva to the small resort town Saint-Gilles-sur-Vie, on the Atlantic, where they discussed Tsvetaeva's plan to return to the Soviet Union, about which Pasternak expressed serious reservations (he feared for her well-being and for her chances of survival).[81] It appears that Pasternak left Paris without taking formal leave of Tsvetaeva, whether out of a desire "not to hurt" her (Tsvetaeva's interpretation)[82] or out of weakness or an inability to face some issue that had arisen within the context of their dialogue (most likely, the rather too exacting and passionate nature of the dialogue Tsvetaeva wanted). The omission left a bitter taste in Tsvetaeva's mouth; she told a friend of the "nonmeeting" with Pasternak and in a long letter to the poet complained on a sour-sweet note and urged him to be less egocentric ("Think less about yourself"). It is clear that the naïve Tsvetaeva completely failed both to see that Pasternak was on the brink of a nervous breakdown and to understand the workings of the Stalinist regime and the overwhelming predicaments in which it placed its citizens; thus she found it incomprehensible that Pasternak had yielded to pressures from the Kremlin to go to Paris and that he did not make a special trip through Germany to see his mother before returning to the Soviet Union (as a matter of fact, Pasternak did not visit his parents "because of a stupid sense of false pride," as he put it later; he did not want them to see him in such a pitiful, dejected state).[83]

During his brief Paris sojourn Pasternak stayed at the Madison Hotel, 143 Boulevard Saint-Germain.[84] From that pied-à-terre he could conveniently make many visits and excursions within the French capital, about which he commented: "This is not like a city, this is more like a landscape." Having reached by telephone Ida Davidovna Vysotskaia-Feldzer, he joined her for a long walk. They managed to elude a certain "Mr. B.," whose job was to tread Pasternak's steps,

---

*The articles, "Epic and Lyrical Poetry of Contemporary Russia" and "Poets with History and Poets Without History," were enthusiastic, as idiosyncratic as most of her other criticism, and of limited value as analytical reasoning (cf. Karlinsky, *Marina Cvetaeva: Her Life and Art*, p. 276).

and visited the Sorbonne. Pasternak appeared to her to be "in a terrible state," as if going through a nightmare. He kept repeating, "You can't imagine, you can't understand."[85] Pasternak asked another old friend (now a Parisian), Iurii Annenkov, to show him Rilke's residence on rue Campagne Première. There he recited Maiakovskii's verse describing the Hotel Istria on that street, where Maiakovskii had stayed. To Annenkov he commented on the "gray, mourning" tones of Notre Dame and the "impetuousness" of the Champs-Élysées. At least once he sat in the famous meetinghouse of Paris intellectuals, the Café la Rotonde, where he had a long conversation on diverse topics with Ehrenburg and Annenkov.[86] To his wife Pasternak wrote a long letter describing both Paris and his exceptionally high spirits.[87] This great elation may well have been a symptom of an overwrought psyche, or some deeper psychological disturbance.

The Soviet writers were generally content with the achievements of the congress, among which was the appointment of twelve of them, including Pasternak, to the newly created Board of the International Association for the Defense of Culture.[88] Parting with their fellow writers, the Soviet delegation members started home on a ship that made a brief stopover in England. Participation in the Congress had been taxing for Pasternak, and his nerves were shattered.

Once in Leningrad, most of the writers boarded a train to Moscow. When Zinaida Nikolaevna came to the Leningrad station in Moscow to meet her husband, he was not there. The head of the delegation, Sergei Shcherbakov, told her that Pasternak suffered from "some psychic ailment" and had had to be hospitalized in Leningrad. Soon he was transferred from the hospital to the Leningrad apartment of an aunt, Anna (Asia) Osipovna Pasternak.* Hastening there, Zinaida Nikolaevna spent several days at Pasternak's side; by then he had reached a state of acute nervous depression. Her constant care and affection, as well as medical treatment, helped restore him to health. Zinaida Nikolaevna has owned that Pasternak's proneness to depression did not disappear with time, although it never manifested itself again with such severity as in the summer of 1935. She had learned the lesson, however, and thereafter Pasternak rarely undertook a journey without her.[89]

During the latter part of the summer of 1935, Pasternak convalesced in various rest houses—but even there, instead of experiencing greater peace of mind, he was (as he wrote a friend) going out of his mind "from worry and loneliness." His recovery was slow but hastened by his decision to foster the process as much as was in his power. In October he wrote, "I am still far from well, but I have made up my mind to pay no attention to my heart, my liver, my sleep, or my nerves."[90]

Pasternak was rested and in better health when the time came for him to attend another professional meeting, the Third Plenary Session of the Board of the Union of Writers, which met in Minsk in February, 1936. Zinaida Nikolaevna attended the proceedings, and was at her husband's side during the numerous banquets which graced the official program.[91] During the debates, Pasternak's

---

*This aunt, Leonid Pasternak's younger sister, was to die during the Siege of Leningrad (Aleksandr Pasternak, Notes to Leonid Pasternak, *ZAP*, p. 263).

eminent place in Soviet literature was again confirmed. True, Surkov lamented his "subjective-idealistic" ideology, and pointed out the "timidity" and "inconsistency" of the poet's recent efforts to bring his art "closer to reality"; nonetheless, even he acknowledged that Pasternak was "a poet in the full strength of his mastery and creative abilities."[92] Praise or mention (even when partly negative) of Pasternak at the congress was so frequent that the poet felt obliged to remark that such constant attention was excessive.[93]

Pasternak's address at that meeting was characterized by an independence of thought that was rarely heard at conferences. It is true that, alluding to "our socialist realism," the poet implied that with goodwill he was sharing the aesthetic platform of most of his fellow writers. He boldly took issue, however, with appeals that had been made at the meeting for writers to be "diligent." He protested that poetry could not be written to order and would not take shape merely with conscientious labor. He outlined his own aesthetic desiderata: great boldness (*smelost*) of the imagination in the exercise of creative freedom, something that he claimed no "directives" from the board of the Writers' Union could provide. The "storm of prolonged applause" that, according to official records, greeted his speech proves that Soviet writers still welcomed such appeals to genuineness. Pasternak also vented mixed feelings when, echoing a note sounded by Olesha at the Writers' Congress of 1934, he explained that he would be going through a transitional period, while endeavoring to adapt to the new society and that as a result the quality of his writing would for a time be inferior (*ia budu pisat plokho*).[94]

The meeting exacerbated Pasternak's long-standing distaste for what he had termed the "rostrum-orientedness" (*estradnost*) of most writers and for the publicity surrounding writers-turned-officials of the new Soviet society. At the time even Bukharin's flattering recognition of his significance at the 1934 congress prompted Pasternak to observe in November, 1935: "Since the recent Writers' Conference in Moscow I have had the feeling that people are "inflating" me (that is, factitiously exaggerating my importance) for their own purposes and quite underhandedly, without asking for my approval. And there is nothing on earth I try to avoid more than noise, sensationalism and so-called newsprint fame."[95] He had been displeased by the polemics surrounding his name in the Soviet press in the wake of the Paris Writers' Congress of 1935.* The "grand" style of the meeting in Minsk proved distasteful to him, especially the numerous and lavish banquets that punctuated the writers' journey from Moscow to Minsk and the schedule of the meeting. Echoing some of the feelings he had voiced at Lake Shartash in 1932 when confronted with the prodigal entertainment of cadres, Pasternak remarked to his wife, "It's not worth spending so much money, food, fruit, wine for

---

*The Soviet press generally tried to underplay the enthusiastic welcome given Pasternak at the Writers' Congress in Paris, sometimes interpreting it merely as a friendly gesture toward the Soviet Union. Ehrenburg was drawn into complicated polemics with a journalist of *Komsomolskaia pravda*, who seemed willfully to misinterpret his eulogistic account of the impression the poet had made at the congress ("Za prostotu i narodnost," *Literaturnaia gazeta*, February 16, 1936; Ilia Ehrenburg, *Memoirs: 1921–1941* (Cleveland: World Publishing Co., 1962), p. 305).

such a purpose; it would be better to give this to those who're starving."[96] In the same vein Pasternak in his speech criticized the "banquet-oriented" conception of the profession (*banketno-pisatelskaia praktika*), which he claimed made writers lose touch with the tradition of Tolstoy and Gorky.[97] During the debates he had been criticized by the poet Bezymenskii for not going on tours to read his poetry; he responded sharply, holding out in contempt the "cheap brilliance" of platform appearances, and pointing out that he much preferred embarking only on the journeys attempted by Pushkin and Tiutchev, who confined their travels to their verse.[98] In addition to shunning platform publicity, in 1937, Pasternak appeared to a friend, playwright Aleksandr Afinogenov, to be singularly unconcerned with the success of his works.[99] It is clear that Pasternak had espoused Rilke's view of fame as "the sum of all the misunderstandings that gather about a new name." Pasternak must have been influenced by Rilke's "Requiem for a Lady Friend" ("Requiem für eine Freundin"), which he translated in 1929 and in which the artist is shown consciously to shun fame and its limelight.[100] Much of Pasternak's poetry is more fit for the drawing room than for the rostrum.

Within a few months of the congress in Minsk the Pasternaks had settled down in a permanent abode in Moscow—apartment No. 72 in the twelve-story apartment house of the Union of Writers (Dom pisatelei), at 17/19 Lavrushinskii Lane, off Tverskoi Boulevard in central Moscow (according to some indications, as early as 1934 the Pasternaks had left the apartment on Volkhonka to move to the House of Writers).* That year too Pasternak was assigned a dacha in the Writers' Village, which had been carved out of the former Samarin estate in Peredelkino. Between 1936 and 1941 the family spent only summers in Peredelkino, but from 1941 to 1943 Pasternak lived at the dacha for many months at a time.[101] The writers' settlement is adjacent to the small village of Peredelkino, about twenty-five kilometers southwest of Moscow—a twenty-five-minute ride by suburban electric train since World War II. There the Pasternaks were given a two-story brown-frame house at the end of a long, narrow lane, against a landscape strewn with occasional grazing goats and almost choked with firs and white birch trees. Nearby flows a small picturesque river, the Setun, along whose rush-grown banks Pasternak took long strolls. The poet became fond of Peredelkino's silvery birches and of the weeping willows of the nearby Lake Izmalkovo; his neighbor Kornei Chukovskii has identified individual poems obviously inspired by these landscapes.[102] The house in Peredelkino soon turned into Pasternak's preferred residence, which—both before World War II and after—he was loathe to leave for visits to any of Moscow's attractions.[103] The importance of reasonably stable

---

*After Pasternak's parents and sisters left for Germany in 1921, the two brothers, Boris and Aleksandr, shared the apartment for a number of years. Around 1930, Aleksandr and his wife moved elsewhere. Sometime in the late 1920s or early 1930s, while Pasternak and his family continued to use a certain portion of the apartment, it became a communal apartment. Pasternak was still living there when he received the phone call from the Kremlin (see below). The background din (about which Pasternak complained in one of the accounts we have of this conversation) was a result of the communal arrangements and accounts for the confusion in Pasternak's mind at the time of the first call (cf. Ivo Fleischmann, "La visite chez le poète: Analyse d'un voyage" [about Fleischmann's visit to Pasternak in October, 1956], *Vagabondages* 5 [1978]: 42–43).

living conditions—including the availability of his own desk and study—became paramount to Pasternak (from that perspective Pasternak could exclaim, when visiting Mandelstam in 1933, that, having acquired his new apartment on Nashchokinskii Lane, his fellow poet "could now write poetry," a remark that incensed Mandelstam).[104] Pasternak's dacha eventually was designated No. 3, Pavlenko Street—the irony of his living on a street named for a tendentious party-line mediocrity did not escape many members of the Soviet literary community. The dacha came to be the main family abode, where Pasternak's second son, Leonid,* born in 1938 ("the first child of the year"), was to grow up.[105]

In the latter part of the 1930s nearly all creative tasks of Soviet writers were disrupted by a tragic course of events that crushed any optimism nurtured at recent forums and congresses. Most Soviet writers, including Pasternak, were traumatized by the episode in Soviet history known as the "Great Purge" or the "Great Terror"—a wave of state repression and killings that was triggered by the assassination of Sergei Kirov, a member of the Politburo, in December, 1934. The nightmare reached its peak in the years 1936 to 1938. Most members of the Central Committee of the party, several members of the Politburo, and many leading intellectuals were arrested and accused of sabotage, treason, preparation of terroristic acts, or espionage. Most of them were condemned to death or to long or indefinite imprisonment. As Stalin's dictatorial rule prevailed, there emerged an atmosphere of heightened insincerity and fictitiousness that in the Epilogue of *Doctor Zhivago* Pasternak denounced as "the reign of the lie."[106]

Pasternak was exposed to the Great Terror in its most virulent form when several of his friends or friendly fellow writers fell victim to it, including a number of prominent figures. Osip Mandelstam died in 1938 in a Siberian camp. Boris Pilniak disappeared in 1937. Isaak Babel was executed in 1941 as a Japanese spy. Nikolai Zabolotskii was arrested and exiled. The poet Nikolai Kliuev was arrested in 1934, exiled to Siberia, and died there in 1937. Iurii Olesha disappeared completely from the literary scene from 1938 to 1946. Vsevolod Meierkhold died in prison in 1940. In 1937 Titian Tabidze was arrested, tortured, and executed. Paolo Iashvili committed suicide in 1937. Pasternak's friend Aleksandr Afinogenov was "silenced" for a while. Mikhail Koltsov was arrested in 1938 and died four years later.

Pasternak's dauntless courage and independence of mind in defending some of those under fire and in refusing to conform made his existence precarious—as he promptly fell into disgrace—and turned his own survival into a paradox. Among the most signal of his courageous actions within this context are the following gestures: the promptness with which he flew to the defense of Mandelstam and stood by his side at various points between 1934 and 1938; his unequivocal refusal

---

*In the Clara Zetkin maternity home in Moscow, Zinaida Nikolaevna gave birth to Leonid precisely at midnight on December 31, 1937 (recorded as 00.00 hours on January 1, 1938). The rarity of this event made it newsworthy, whence the proclaiming of Leonid as "the first child of the year" by the press (*Vecherniaia Moskva*, January 2, 1938). Leonid Borisovich was to pursue a career in physics at the University of Moscow. He died in 1976 of an apparent heart attack while driving his car—a Moscow traffic death strangely reminiscent of Iurii Zhivago's.

Lavrushinskii Lane, where Pasternak had an apartment for twenty-five years in the apartment building of the Union of Writers. *Archives Georges Nivat.*

to sign certain documents that most of the leading Soviet writers endorsed, such as a letter approving the arrest and condemnation of Marshal Tukhachevskii and another condemning André Gide's book on the Soviet Union; his unflinching support of Tabidze and Iashvili and their families; and his willingness to intercede for various friends and acquaintances, such as Akhmatova's husband, Nikolai Punin (on whose behalf he successfully pleaded directly with Stalin).[107]

In May, 1934, Mandelstam, after reading to a small group of acquaintances his epigram referring to Stalin as "the mustachioed . . . Kremlin mountaineer" was subjected to a house search and then imprisoned and interrogated. The news of this arrest shook Pasternak.[108] Since the 1920s there had existed between the two poets a friendly dialogue, which, though reinforced by many letters and encounters in Moscow and Leningrad, was not marked by the natural, spontaneous communion that prevailed between, say, Mandelstam and Akhmatova.[109] After Mandelstam's arrest, as his widow later observed, "there was very good reason to keep right out of the whole business" in accordance with the widespread Soviet practice of avoiding "those stricken by the plague."[110] Nonetheless, with characteris-

Pond in Peredelkino, not far from Pasternak's dacha. *Photograph by Inga Morath. Cornell Capa/Magnum.*

tic generosity and self-forgetfulness, Boris Leonidovich took up a suggestion made by Nadezhda Mandelstam and rushed to the editorial offices of *Izvestiia*. There he begged Bukharin to intervene. Bukharin, even then reaching the end of his own rope, promptly wrote Stalin a letter in which he pleaded for lenient treatment of Mandelstam, on the grounds that he was an exceptionally talented poet. To back up his request with some concrete evidence (a method known to be Stalin's preference), Bukharin added in a concise postscript that Pasternak "shared his opinion" of Mandelstam's talent. In his quest for adequate protection for Mandelstam, Pasternak also approached Demian Bednyi, also at the suggestion of Mandelstam's wife. Bednyi had the rare advantage of being in favor with the regime for his intensely civic poetry while at the same time enjoying Pasternak's undivided esteem. Pasternak and Bednyi spent several hours driving around Moscow in Bednyi's car and discussing both Mandelstam's case and the plight of Soviet poetry; Bednyi opted to stay out of the case.[111]

The postscript in Bukharin's letter to Stalin had an unexpected consequence. One evening in late July, 1934, Pasternak received a telephone call from Stalin.[112] First of all, Stalin wanted to know why Pasternak was going out of his way to defend Mandelstam. To this the poet responded that he felt concern for the fate of a fellow poet, who was a good poet. Then the dictator came to the heart of the matter: Did Pasternak indeed believe that Mandelstam was a "genius"? Pasternak gave somewhat evasive answers, explaining that poetry was a matter as qualitative and elusive as a woman's beauty. Only at Stalin's insistence did Pasternak finally concede that he felt that Mandelstam was an exceptionally talented poet. Some critics have held that the poet's evasive response was detrimental to Mandelstam and obsequious to Stalin.[113] But both Mandelstam and his wife believed that Pasternak's approach in effect was the most appropriate to the occasion and saved his fellow poet.[114] Indeed, those familiar with Stalin's psychology could appreciate why this was so. While probably hoping that Mandelstam, if he was a truly great poet, could one day be induced to sing his praise, Stalin at the same time nurtured a pathological distrust of true greatness in every sphere. After Pasternak backed his fellow poet's talent, Stalin remarked, "Mandelstam will be all right."[115] Later in a letter Mandelstam's wife remarked about that conversation: "[Pasternak] conversed with his interlocutor as he conversed with everyone—with me, with Anna Andreevna [Akhmatova], with anyone. And precisely for that reason something was said in a most effective way [*zdorovo*]—unexpectedly, and most accurately. And all three of us [Akhmatova, Mandelstam, and she] valued this very much."[116]

Taking advantage of this unique opportunity, Pasternak tried to prolong the conversation, expressing to Stalin his wish to have a long talk with him—"about love, about life, about death." Thereupon Stalin is reported to have hung up abruptly,[117] robbing the poet of the inspiration he expected from an encounter with the great leader.* Frustrated, Pasternak felt unable to return to aesthetic

---

*Olga Ivinskaia is the only authority who claims that Pasternak repeatedly asserted that he had met Stalin once before, when, in the company of Maiakovskii and Esenin, he was invited to meet the leader in 1924 or 1925 (Olga Ivinskaya, *CAPT*, p. 58).

work for a prolonged period.[118] A curious consequence of the telephone conversation is that, as news of it spread around literary Moscow, the literati bestowed a halo on Pasternak that was to remain until he fell in disgrace in 1937.
Zinaida Nikolaevna reported that there was suddenly a sharp change in attitude
toward Pasternak at the Writers' Union: all its "orthodox" functionaries began
greeting him with smiles, shaking his hand, and asking about his health, and the
restaurant of the Writers' Club opened an account for him.[119]

Until Mandelstam's final exile Pasternak continued to show great courage in
his support of his confrère. Whereas most members of the Moscow intelligentsia—including Zinaida Nikolaevna—tended to avoid "plague" victims,
Pasternak went on seeing the Mandelstams.* He also endeavored to help them
financially whenever he could: in the summer of 1936 he gave five hundred rubles, which, together with a similar amount from Akhmatova, made it possible
for them to have a few weeks' rest in Zadonsk. His willingness to tender sympathy and help endured; Mandelstam's widow has reported that Pasternak was *the
only person* to come to see her on hearing of Mandelstam's death.[120]

At a time when things were going badly for Mandelstam—and none too easily
for himself—Pasternak had another opportunity to show his independence. The
French "fellow traveler" André Gide had been fêted in the Soviet Union from June
to August, 1936, but he noted flaws that marred his love story with Communism
in his volume *Return from the USSR* (*Retour de l'U.R.S.S.*), published in Paris in
November, 1937. As usual in such cases in the Stalinist era, Soviet writers were
called on to protest the book. Pasternak's name, however, was absent from the list
of the Moscow writers who in their session of April, 1937, denounced Gide's
"foul, slanderous book."[121] Pasternak simply refused to sign any document in-
criminating Gide's volume, claiming that he "had not read the book"[122] (in typical Soviet fashion the book was officially denounced, without being published and
without an opportunity for writers to read a translation). That was one of the
events that triggered the beginning of Pasternak's four-year disgrace.

Following on the heels of this incident, another episode created much upheaval
in the lives of the Pasternaks. In June, 1937, an official of the Writers' Union
came to their dacha in Peredelkino to have Pasternak sign a joint letter from Soviet writers endorsing the death sentence that had been meted out to Marshal
Tukhachevskii and seven other prominent military figures on charges of pro-
Fascist espionage. Tukhachevskii had been demoted and arrested in May, and on
June 12 he was executed with the others. Pasternak refused to sign the letter. He
is reported to have become incensed and to have told the functionary from the
Writers' Union:

The lives of people are disposed of by the government, not by private individuals. I know
nothing about them [the accused]. How can I wish their death? I did not give them life; I

---

*When the Mandelstams visited Pasternak in Peredelkino in the summer of 1937, his wife
"clearly wanted nothing to do with them." Many years later, when Nadezhda Mandelstam returned
from her Tashkent exile, Zinaida Nikolaevna said to her on the telephone, "Please don't come out
here to Peredelkino" (Nadezhda Mandelstam, *Hope*, pp. 298–99).

can't be their judge. I prefer to perish together with the crowd, with the people. After all, this is not like signing complimentary tickets for the theater.[123]

Pasternak later explained the circumstances of his decision and the ensuing developments:

My wife was pregnant. She cried and begged me to sign, but I couldn't. That day I examined the pros and cons of my own survival. I was convinced that I would be arrested—my turn had come. I was prepared for it. I abhorred all this blood and I couldn't stand it any longer. But nothing happened. I was told later that my colleagues had saved me—at least indirectly. Quite simply, no one dared to report to the hierarchy that I hadn't signed.[124]

On June 15—the day after his refusal to sign—Pasternak saw on the front page of *Literaturnaia gazeta* his signature, together with those of the forty-three other writers, at the bottom of the Soviet Writers' statement asking that Article 133 of Stalin's Constitution be applied to the eight "Fascist spies" and they be shot for plotting the downfall of the Soviet Union.[125] Again Pasternak persisted in his staunchness and rushed to town, protesting in the secretariat of the Union of Writers the unauthorized inclusion of his signature on the document[126]—very probably the merciful gesture of a fellow writer (presumably Aleksandr Fadeev).

Worse was still to come. In the summer of 1937 the news of Iashvili's suicide and of Tabidze's arrest hit Pasternak like a thunderbolt (only much later would he learn that Tabidze was cruelly tortured and then liquidated after two months in prison). The letters he forthwith addressed to the widows of the Georgian poets do not reflect the least indication of fear. Then began the regular financial support that he gave to Tabidze's widow, Nina, while also providing the two families with constant moral support (all of which was known to the authorities).[127]

Through these attitudes and gestures Pasternak was, of course, exposing himself more and more to the risk of arrest and punishment. He was fully aware of it. A memoirist well acquainted with the literary scene pointed out that, during the second half of 1939, Pasternak ran a real danger of being arrested and liquidated along with Babel and Vsevolod Meierkhold and that, together with the latter, the names of Pasternak and Olesha were being mentioned among those of members of an "organization" of intellectuals who were allegedly plotting a political diversion.[128] It is certain that during the 1930s Pasternak was on friendly terms with Meierkhold, whom he visited on many occasions.[129] He even pursued this dialogue in the late 1930s, undeterred by the serious "political" problems into which Meierkhold was running; thus he made a point of calling on Meierkhold on January 11, 1938, to commiserate about the closing down of the latter's theater, three days after it occurred.[130]

There is much evidence that Pasternak's position was becoming extremely delicate. At a plenary session of the board of the Union of Writers in early 1937, he was verbally attacked and covered with abuse—often a sign that some decisive political action was about to be taken against the writer.[131] The tragic fate of his erstwhile protector Bukharin—who was one of the key figures of the famous "show trials"* and was executed on March 14, 1938—certainly made matters worse for him, so much so, indeed, that one may wonder, How did it come about that Pasternak did survive the purges? Reviewing in his *Memoirs* similar seemingly unexplainable occurrences, Ilia Ehrenburg asks, "Why . . . did Stalin spare Pasternak who took his own independent line, but destroy [Mikhail] Koltsov who honourably carried out every task entrusted to him?"[132]

One possible explanation is that he was spared thanks to the intervention of Fadeev, whom Stalin liked and trusted. In 1939, Stalin had Fadeev appointed as secretary of the Writers' Union, a post which the novelist occupied for nearly two decades, functioning as a pillar of literary Stalinism. For all his staunchness in ideological matters, Fadeev had a special sympathy for Pasternak, whose verses he much admired, sometimes reciting them to a few chosen friends with or without the accompaniment of cognac.[133] That sympathy did not prevent Fadeev from occasionally attacking Pasternak at official meetings; he probably felt that on ideological grounds a few such attacks were expected of him in his official capacity. But in the daily run of life in Peredelkino, Fadeev evinced his sympathy by frequently visiting the Pasternaks, who would entertain him with great cordiality and in whose company he felt very happy. Zinaida Nikolaevna relates that Fadeev loved baked potatoes and she would prepare that dish for him. Fadeev (whose alcoholism was intensifying) would bring vodka to go with the baked potatoes, get drunk, and in that state speak his mind freely. The next day Pasternak would send some such message as, "Sasha, you were not at my house, and you said nothing. Boria."[134] Occasionally Fadeev went out of his way to do the Pasternaks special favors. Thus once during the war when Pasternak was away from Peredelkino, Fadeev had sixteen apple trees planted in Pasternak's garden so that the village council would not confiscate the land under a new ordinance regarding unused land.[135] In a number of ways it is clear that Fadeev functioned as Pasternak's protector or patron—much in the way Evgraf functioned for Zhivago in the novel, that very kind of relationship being characteristic of the era. Indeed, certain of Fadeev's distinguishing qualities—exceptionally handsome appearance, Siberian origin, and concern with Siberian themes—are echoed in Zhivago's benefactor.

The question also arises, Did Stalin himself function as the superprotector who from on high radiated the measure of leniency necessary for the wayward poet to survive? It is clear that Pasternak's message to the leader at the time of Stalin's wife's death must have made a lasting impression on the dictator. Also, as the poet himself indicated later, Bukharin's assessment of Pasternak in 1934 as the greatest living Russian poet probably impressed Stalin.[136] It is certain that Paster-

---

*Highlighting the Great Purge were the spectacularly orchestrated show trials of Grigorii Zinoviev, Grigorii Piatakov, and Nikolai Bukharin, which were attended by the foreign press and conveyed to the outside world the false notion that the forms of legality were being preserved in the prosecution of these three individuals (even that semblance of legality was missing from the trials of millions of others from whom confessions were forcefully extracted before they were summarily condemned).

nak's exceptionally active role in promoting Georgian poetry must have earned him a very special place in Stalin's books. Moreover, many points no doubt went to his credit when, in the January 1, 1936, issue of *Izvestiia*, the poet published a first-of-the-year dithyramb with an appropriately eulogistic mention of Lenin and Stalin. The poem was published side by side with another one by Bednyi, the "good-natured," cheerful civic poet, celebrating Stalin's notorious pronouncement, "Life has become better, comrades, life has become merrier."[137] This publication was the closest Pasternak came to the role of official bard and raises the disturbing question of the extent to which the poet participated in the adulation of Stalin that was all-pervasive in these years. Nina Tabidze felt that from approximately 1935 until 1937 Pasternak drew much closer to socialism and Stalin.[138] That closeness is reflected in the praise of Stalin's superhuman achievements in the *Izvestiia* poem.* Considering all these factors, it is fairly reasonable to infer that unusual and special tolerance was shown Pasternak during the Great Purge.

In the years 1935 to 1937 many of the most perceptive intellectuals either shared the euphoria about the regime or were made to bow to it. Zinaida Nikolaevna went through some of the outer motions of this attitude of adulation; she was reported to have declared, "My children love Stalin most of all, and me only second."[139] Even Mandelstam, at the nadir of his despair, composed an "Ode to Stalin."[140] Pasternak's good friend Afinogenov hailed the proclamation of Stalin's Constitution in November, 1936, with the words, "Now everything will go differently."[141] Up to about 1935, Pasternak himself had felt that the "years of cruelty" were coming to an end. But after the tragic fates of Tabidze and Iashvili, his eyes were opened. In conversations with friends he denounced the despotism of "this new Skalozub"† and pointed out that, if Stalin did not know of the crimes being perpetrated in his state, this was "also a crime, perhaps the greatest crime for a statesman." A similar degree of fearlessness was necessary for Pasternak to acknowledge the even greater degree of that virtue that he granted Mandelstam on one occasion in 1932, after his fellow poet had recited poems that constituted true political "exorcisms." Approaching Mandelstam, Pasternak told him: "I envy your freedom. . . . I need nonfreedom" (though the next few years were to prove clearly that Pasternak did not espouse any facile solution based on the choice of nonfreedom).[142]

It has been suggested that in the context of these years "a carefully cultivated irrational attitude . . . saved Pasternak's art and perhaps his life." Not too removed from that perception was the characterization of Pasternak as a "dacha-dweller of genius" ("*genialnyi dachnik*") by the Soviet critic Kornelii Zelinskii. These feelings have been echoed with a note of *poshlost* and coarseness by the recently arrived Soviet émigré Lev Navrozov, who has claimed that Pasternak survived by playing the role of the innocent or "village idiot" in a more or less con-

---

*The most embarrassing passages of this poem were omitted by the editors of the 1965 Soviet edition of Pasternak's *Collected Poetry* (*Stikhotvoreniia i poemy*).

†A martinet, a famous character in Aleksandr Griboedov's play *Woe from Wit* (1822–24).

scious way. That the silence practiced by Pasternak during those years was in effect a form of bravery is driven home by the comparison that Ivinskaia draws between the attitudes of two writers to the catastrophe of the Great Terror:

One [Aleksei Tolstoy] displayed the greatest lack of conscience, and cynicism, acclaiming the executioners in order to keep his estate, motorcars, and social status. The other [Pasternak] maintained a stubborn silence: all the forces of brutish coercion would not induce him to lie in support of injustice. But when he found it impossible to go on being silent, he bravely spoke the truth, knowing full well the risk not only to himself, but also to the life and freedom of his family.[143]

Pasternak had long been fully aware of the anguishing dilemma, which he was to solve with dignity and courage; that is made clear in a letter addressed in 1929 to a Russian émigré writer in which he remarked: "Should one suffer without falling prey to any illusions, or thrive while deceiving oneself and deceiving others?"[144]

As Pasternak insisted on following the voice of his conscience in such instances as the Tukhachevskii and Gide "affairs," whatever extent of goodwill that had been shown him was severely eroded.* As a punitive measure the establishment stopped printing his works. Thus at the close of the decade a time of material difficulties set in for the family of the writer in disgrace. When things became intolerable, Pasternak would take on some translation assignment.[145] Zinaida Nikolaevna went back to an old-time occupation, copying musical scores, which brought only a meager income. This situation continued for several years, until Pasternak's translation of *Hamlet*, published by the State Literature Publishing House (Goslitizdat) in 1941, somewhat improved the family's fortunes.[146]

In spite of all, the writer had not sold his soul. Its temporary mortgage to the Stalinian euphoria of the mid-1930s was a thing of the past. There began a silent confrontation between Stalin and the poet, who to many Soviet intellectuals became a symbol of heroic, passive resistance to the era's evil.

---

*Another act of great courage on Pasternak's part was his refusal (probably sometime between 1936 and 1938) to translate some youthful poems by Stalin for a Russian-language anthology being prepared by one of the state publishing houses—in spite of Stalin's alleged wish that Pasternak be the translator (Ivo Fleischmann, "La visite chez le poète: Analyse d'un voyage [about Fleischmann's visit to Pasternak in October, 1956], *Vagabondages* 5 [December, 1978]:45).

9

The War

A Liberation

1939–1945

The tragic and harrowing wartime period was a *living* one, and in this sense a free and blissful restoration of a feeling of community with everyone else.

Pasternak, quoted in *A Captive of Time*[1]

. . . when the war broke out, its real horrors, its real dangers, its menace of real death were a blessing compared with the inhuman reign of the lie, and they brought relief because they broke the spell of the dead letter.

Pasternak, *Doctor Zhivago*[2]

When war was declared between Germany and England in 1939, correspondence between Pasternak and his émigré relatives became rare and problematic. His two sisters had left Germany in the thirties to settle in England and had been joined there by their parents in 1938. Pasternak's mother, Rosa Isidorovna, died in 1939, and his father, Leonid Osipovich, continued working as a painter and illustrator, dispirited because the war made it impossible for him to return to Russia. Communications between Moscow and England were far from good, causing the poet considerable anxiety. Once in 1940 he said that he had received no reply from his father and sisters to a telegram he had sent them a month earlier. By the time the reply arrived, Pasternak had come to believe that they were dead.[3]

That Pasternak's closest relatives were émigrés gradually fostered the suspicion in the paranoid atmosphere of Stalin's regime that Pasternak was a foreign spy, a suspicion of which he was not aware at the time. Only after the war was Pasternak exposed to the consequences, when he was made to suffer the arrest of his friend Olga Ivinskaia, accused of being the accomplice of the "spy."

Germany's invasion of the Soviet Union, June 22, 1941, marked the end of Pasternak's period of disgrace. The declaration of war provided a welcome relaxation of the tense atmosphere for Russia's literati, and the consequent softening of formal restraints allowed them a greater freedom to write. That relaxation was also accompanied by heightened expectations: for a period of several years Pasternak hoped that the war would bring the resolution of the repression, which deeply upset him and which in a letter of September, 1941, he described as the "increasing, hopeless, intolerable spiritual unfreedom" of the era.[4]

Despite his deeply ingrained sympathy for German culture, Pasternak could not help but be revolted by the atrocities committed by the Nazi army. In the poem "A Terrible Tale," written in the winter of 1941, the poet refuses any pardon to those guilty of abominable crimes: "The cries of maimed children will be heard across the centuries."[5] Yet along with great suffering, the war paradoxically brought hope to the Russians. In the poem "1941" Iuliia Neiman offered a dramatic statement of the feeling of most Russians at the time:

> And causes were laid bare, effects revealed;
>
> . . . .
> The dubious yardsticks that we were measured by—
> Forms, questionnaires, long service, rank and age—
> Were cast aside and now we measured true:
> Our yardsticks in that year were valor, faith.[6]

This feeling of hope is also emphasized by a character in *Doctor Zhivago*: "When the war broke out, its real horrors, its real dangers, its menace of real death were a blessing compared with the inhuman reign of the lie, and they brought relief because they broke the spell of the dead letter."[7]

In the summer of 1941, as the advance of the German armies became an immediate threat to Moscow, the evacuation of the city began. In July, Pasternak helped his family move to the small Tatar town Chistopol, in the Urals, 650 kilo-

Photograph taken probably
in Chistopol, the small
town in the Urals to which
the Pasternaks were
evacuated in the early
1940s. *Ardis.*

meters from Moscow, with the other families of the Writers' Union. Zinaida
Nikolaevna was caught in an anguishing situation in leaving Moscow. She was
concerned for her oldest son, Andrian (Adik) Neigauz, terminally ill with tuberculosis of the spine. Boris Leonidovich eventually persuaded her to leave, taking
the care of Adik upon himself. He often visited the invalid at the hospital and
before joining his family in Chistopol delivered him to a clinic in Nizhnii Ufalei,
Cheliabinsk Region. That was the period when Pasternak became acutely aware
that Zinaida Nikolaevna was very authoritarian by nature and little attuned to his
endeavors and literary contacts. His home situation was viewed by friends as a
misfortune that at times elicited "immense pity" from them.[8]

Pasternak arrived in Chistopol in the late fall of 1941, joining the other writers,
and soon followed by his friend and confidant Aleksandr Gladkov. With the arrival of these evacuated Muscovites and Leningraders, the small provincial town
took on a peculiar appearance. In their elegant coats and plush hats the writers—
of whom there were several dozen, including Aseev, Fadeev, Leonov, Fedin, and
Shklovskii—wandered about the streets that the bountiful Russian rains had
turned into slush and met in gatherings: "As in the halls of the building of
Vorovskii Street [the Writers' Club in Moscow], not to meet with others two or
three times a day was almost impossible. All ate in the minuscule cafeteria, op-

posite the regional party office; all went to read the central newspapers; . . . all took books from the library of the Teacher's Center."[9]

Pasternak lived with his wife, his son Leonid, and his wife's son Stanislav (Stasik) Neigauz in a small, uncomfortable room in the house of a local family, the Vavilovs. The house was No. 75, at the end of Volodarskii Street, across from the town park.[10] His everyday life was more difficult than that of most of the other writers, for his writing was not yet acceptable to the party-controlled publishing houses. Consequently, his life-style contrasted sharply with the quasi-baronial status of Fedin, Leonov, and Aseev, who could afford many commodities that were beyond the means of less favored writers. Zinaida Nikolaevna was able to secure a position caring for children during the day, which entitled her to a mid-day meal, some of which she saved for her own children. Boris Leonidovich made the most of every possible moment to progress with his translation work. Even while waiting to eat at the Writers' Union cafeteria, he would consult his English dictionary and draft pages of his translation of *Antony and Cleopatra*. The poet often complained that his fingers would start freezing while he was writing in his poorly heated room. The only way to raise the temperature was to open the door to the communal kitchen, releasing the combined melodies of Primus stoves and a gramophone playing tangos. Yet on only one occasion was the poet known to complain of the noise and inconvenience, begging that the gramophone be silenced. The temperature was often $-30°C$. when he accompanied Gladkov to fetch wood, a chore most of the writers had to perform.[11]

While in Chistopol, Pasternak was assiduously reading a copy of Victor Hugo's *On Shakespeare* in the original. He remarked to Gladkov that "Hugo's book about Shakespeare is a treasure-house of thoughts, not only about Shakespeare, but about art in general." In particular, he was struck by Hugo's view that the genius is closest to the ordinary man, a tenet Pasternak embraced thereafter.[12] It is reasonable to surmise that Pasternak must have been especially influenced by Hugo's view of Shakespeare as the boundless elemental force that knows no reserve and his notion that "the simplicity of poetry is similar to an oak with many boughs."[13]

Pasternak spent two winters in Chistopol under such conditions. The town was near the Kama River, which had been the site of the Pugachëv rebellion in the eighteenth century, as he already knew from his stay in 1915.[14] Most writers later remembered their stay in Chistopol with hostility or boredom. Pasternak, however, shared the gratitude expressed in Aseev's poem "The Small Town on the Kama" for the shelter it afforded during the war (while he must have suffered from its stark continental climate, also noted in Aseev's poem: "Chistopol / Up to your neck in mud / Up to your belt in dust").[15] The materially and spiritually insecure new existence Pasternak viewed as a privileged chance for writers to acquire "inner independence," remarking in addition, "I'll always be grateful to Chistopol if only for that."[16] In later times he even mentioned Chistopol in the same breath as Pushkin's estate Mikhailovskoe—perhaps Russia's most famous prototype of the privileged creative haven, and a most apt analogue. It is clear that both Chistopol—whose run-of-the-mill life he believed provided "the best atmosphere for work"—and his rural retreat in Peredelkino blended in Pasternak's mind, being elaborated in his novel as Zhivago's artistic refuge, Varykino.[17] Pasternak did not remain year-round in the Urals, however. During the warmer months of the war years he divided his time between Moscow and his peaceful dacha in Peredelkino. That allowed him to maintain contacts with the war effort and the literary world, while permitting him occasional solitude to proceed with his writings.

Throughout World War II, Pasternak continued to stand aside in a courageous retirement, though any refusal to conform, even a passive one, was still potentially dangerous. In Peredelkino he devoted himself to translation work—a pursuit that both the Mandelstams and Akhmatova thought leads to the destruction of the creative force in the translator and, to that extent, "destroys literature" (especially in the repressive Soviet context). Although his translations often did not return substantial or even adequate income, they did provide some relief from financial hardship.

His *Selected Translations* were published in 1940,* but it was not until 1941 that his original work was accepted for publication. Pasternak was able to enhance his own situation with the produce of a vegetable garden beside his dacha (of course, gardening work, such as gathering and canning ripe cucumbers, meant that he sometimes had to postpone writing poetry as he would have wished to do). On his frequent trips to Moscow he received substantial rations from the Writers' Union; these he thoughtfully packed and sent to his family in Chistopol.[18]

War in Russia meant an end to the "inhuman reign of the lie" (to use the phrase from *Doctor Zhivago*) and thus a significant relaxation of the constraints under which writers were operating. The relaxation was notably marked by the appearance of *From Six Volumes*, by Anna Akhmatova. Since the appearance of her volume *A.D. 1921*, nothing by her, except for some significant studies of Pushkin, had been published during the Soviet period. The new volume contained a tribute to Pasternak, who, from the publication of her love lyrics in 1912–15, had viewed her as a master of Acmeism and admired the remarkably "simple means" she used in her craft.[19] They had developed friendly—if only intermittently revalidated—relations. Only with the appearance of *From Six Volumes*, however, did Pasternak become as fully attentive a reader of her verse as she thought he should be. He joined Fadeev in proposing this volume for a Stalin Prize.[20]

After spending some time in the hospital for treatment of an infection of the spinal nerve, Pasternak wrote Akhmatova in Leningrad, telling her that her book was a sensation in Moscow and had sold out. He proceeded to a critical discussion of her work and her influence on his own poetry volume *Above the Barriers* (1917). Pasternak saw in Akhmatova "a new artist," insofar as, he claimed, absolute realism now dominated her poetry over the earlier "impressionistic element." He assured her, "Apart from Blok no one has achieved *such* a mastery of the rhetoric of details and you are the only name there is, as far as having Pushkinian foundations is concerned."[21] During the war several letters were exchanged between the two

---

*The volume included translations of Heinrich von Kleist's play *The Prince of Homburg*, some of Shakespeare's sonnets, Keats's "Ode to Autumn," and poems by Paul Verlaine and Hans Sachs.

poets, reflecting a sincere and intense dialogue of two creative minds. Pasternak once wrote to the despondent Akhmatova, who was worried about the fate of her son serving in the armed forces, that her continuing duty toward the living was "to live and to want to live." Pasternak often cheered her up and helped her financially when she was ill. While acknowledging such help, Akhmatova was aware that Pasternak was a "charmer," whose sometimes exaggerated words of praise should not be taken at face value.[22]

While he was in Peredelkino, Pasternak's major achievement was his poetic interpretation of *Hamlet* for the Moscow Art Theater. Pasternak said of it: "*Hamlet* is my best achievement, I know this . . . . Up to now *Hamlet* has not been translated in this manner. It is the most subjective of Shakespeare's tragedies."[23] The popularity of Pasternak's creation was evidenced by its reception in the spring of 1940, when the poet gave two readings—the first at Moscow State University (MGU), on Hertzen Street, and the second at the Writer's Club, on Vorovskii Street. For an opportunity to hear his rendition of *Hamlet*, an enthusiastic audience of intellectuals and students "forced their way into the hall, crushed ushers aside."[24] After his reading at the university Pasternak was surrounded by his many women admirers, and he allowed himself to be carried away into discussions of Goethe, Johann Gottfried von Herder, and Shakespeare. He later said that on two or three such occasions during the war he found the experience of contact with such enthusiastic audiences overwhelming.[25] Much to Pasternak's chagrin his *Hamlet* was not produced because Stalin, approached by the actor Boris Livanov at a government reception, indicated that he was not overly pleased with certain themes, such as the abuse of princely power (the reason he also felt a distaste for *Macbeth* and the second part of Eisenstein's *Ivan the Terrible*); Stalin stressed that the play was "a pessimistic and reactionary one."[26] Nonetheless, copies of the book reached a wide audience—while the translator went on inveighing against the Moscow Art Theater for not giving his masterpiece a chance.[27] In a letter of May, 1942, Pasternak wrote: "Whether or not they give me a prize for it, whether or not they want to know about it, *Hamlet* spent an unheard-of, overwhelming winter at the front and in field hospitals, on the beds of the dying and in the context of forced evacuations."[28]

The appearance of Pasternak's *Hamlet* was greeted by many with enthusiasm. The well-known critic Nikolai Viliam-Vilmont* described it as "an outstanding phenomenon of Soviet culture" and added: "It is a remarkably mature and daring penetration into Shakespeare's poetic world.[29] . . . No Russian translator has been able to convey the tragic language of *Hamlet* with as much force and with such accurate coincidence with the original as Boris Pasternak. . . . One should point out that Boris Pasternak once more proved that he is the master, not the servant, of his poetic gift."[30] For all his praise, Viliam-Vilmont raised a query about the extent to which "a true fusion of two authorial personalities" had been achieved in Pasternak's creation, commenting: "Instead, what there is is one au-

*Nikolai Viliam-Vilmont was a friend of Pasternak's during their student days, and a friendly dialogue had been maintained between them since that time. Viliam-Vilmont's sister had married Pasternak's brother, Aleksandr.

thorial personality [Shakespeare], being submitted to another [Pasternak]."[31] In so doing Pasternak was utilizing the favorite method of the early-nineteenth-century poet-translator Vasilii Zhukovskii, an approach discarded by most translators after Zhukovskii.

The striking originality of Pasternak's *Hamlet* was singled out by M. Morozov, the eminent Shakespearean scholar.[32] Morozov made the careful distinction between the disillusion one felt because of specific flaws in the translation and the elation experienced because Pasternak, renouncing a literal rendering of the text, had penetrated the living essence of the play. The Danish prince had often appeared in translations as a manikin who spoke "poetic" but lifeless words. Pasternak's Hamlet, however, was a living image: "We feel him; he moves and breathes; his feelings, outbursts, and agitations are all alive."[33]

While recognizing that Pasternak's intent to make his *Hamlet* a genuine Russian dramatic work led to certain distortions of the essential flavor of Shakespeare's language, Morozov emphatically maintained that "only by overcoming pretended accuracy does one find the way to an adequacy of artistic impression." Mikhail Lozinskii, in his translation of *Hamlet*, created the feel of an epic; his language was pictorial. Pasternak, on the other hand, stressed the psychological; his language created emotion. Morozov concluded by saying that through Pasternak's translation the reader clearly "believes that not merely a great play has ended but a strong, enchanting, promising, and energetic human being has perished in that cruel dark world in which it was determined that Hamlet should live."[34]

Thus Pasternak's version of a Hamlet who attempts to maintain integrity in an atmosphere of corruption and decay may be likened to the poet's own uncompromising stance. Rather like Hamlet, who peremptorily stated: "You cannot play upon me," he refused to allow his skill to be "played upon" as an "instrument of the state in Stalinist Russia."[35] Pasternak's close involvement with *Hamlet* had an important side effect: it provided the poet with a vision of the Danish prince as the man born to set the times right, deriving inspiration from a great cause, and ready to stand apart from society in order to serve the people from which he had removed himself. This vision would soon be evolved in *Doctor Zhivago*, where in the poem "Hamlet" the poet gave a unique blending of Hamlet and Christ in the protagonist.

But such aesthetic pursuits as literary translation were soon disrupted by cataclysmic events even more formidable than those that shook the princedom of Helsingfors. Although Pasternak was spared direct exposure to much of the war's violence and confusion, his good fortune during that period could not withstand the great sorrows suffered by all when death becomes a part of everyday existence. Indeed, the death of Marina Tsvetaeva was not only his greatest loss of the war years but one to be felt throughout his life.

Tsvetaeva had returned to Moscow from Paris in 1939. The era had worked its havoc, and she found herself alone to carry a burden of loss and sorrow. Her husband, a former White Army officer, was arrested and shot, and her daughter disappeared, into a camp. In late summer, 1941, Tsvetaeva became another victim, taking her own life in flight from hopeless despair and poverty.[36]

Pasternak had made some attempts to alleviate her situation. Earlier in 1941, he had taken her to the State Literature Publishing House and introduced her to several of the editors. Two of them recall that she was asked to translate both Georgian and Yiddish writers. Unfortunately, Tsvetaeva was a perfectionist, translating extremely slowly and consequently earning less than the average professional. Pasternak also went to Aleksandr Fadeev, then secretary-general of the Union of Writers, in hopes of improving her living conditions in Moscow.[37] That effort too was unsuccessful.

Tsvetaeva left Moscow for a small provincial town, Elabuga-on-the-Kama, not far from Chistopol. She is reported to have wandered around Chistopol during her last days, begging for help.[38] Fellow writers, fearful of becoming involved with an émigré, leery of the bureaucracy, and tending to underestimate her plight, gave her no consolation. Marina Tsvetaeva, leaving only a callous son and her poetry, hanged herself on the last day of August, 1941.

Although Pasternak was in Moscow when Tsvetaeva died, he felt guilty that he had not somehow been able to help her. They had parted under rather disappointing conditions. Before she left Moscow, Tsvetaeva approached him for advice. He tried to dissuade her from going to the Tartar region but did not propose an alternative. It is evident from Tsvetaeva's later statements that she had anticipated an invitation to stay in Peredelkino. Possibly influenced by his wife's unaccepting attitude toward many of his intellectual friends, Pasternak remained silent. He saw Tsvetaeva and her son off at the Khimki River port in Moscow. It was their final meeting.[39]

On September 10, 1941, upon hearing of Tsvetaeva's suicide, Pasternak immediately wrote to Zinaida Nikolaevna. The letter was filled with guilt, self-accusation, and amazement. He was appalled by the inaction of writers in Chistopol, especially Aseev. He felt that they could have provided her with a loan, which he would have gladly reimbursed.[40] The poet held himself—as well as such fellow writers as Aseev, Fedin, and Fadeev—culpable for not trying to help her individually, in the face of an indifferent establishment. With typically excessive guilt, Pasternak probed his behavior, analyzing what he might have done, and exclaiming, "I loved her very much, and now I'm sorry that I did not look for occasions to tell her so, as often as it was necessary for her [to hear]."[41]

Pasternak wrote to his confidante Nina Tabidze that if Tsvetaeva—who was trying hard to escape from "godforsaken Elabuga" and had been refused a permit to settle in Chistopol—had held out for another month Fedin and he would have succeeded in arranging work and subsistence for her in Chistopol. He added: "It will always remain an unsolved mystery to me how her situation could have remained so desperate and without relief next to, and with the knowledge of, Trenev and Aseev, who are both laureates with literary prizes and have public influence and who both had a high opinion of her." He went on to say that his love for her and her work were so great that, even though he had been thousands of miles away from the scene of the tragedy, he felt he was "the only one to blame for this bitter sin of omission."[42]

During the years of their relationship Pasternak became aware that Tsvetaeva hid from the everyday world behind a creativity he later christened genius. She was one of the "Three Shadows" to whom he devoted a substantial section of *Sketch for an Autobiography*.[43] His great love, Ivinskaia, has said that he loved Tsvetaeva more than any other contemporary poet and thought her talent so immense that there was enough from which to carve genuine talent for ten men.[44] Ivinskaia has even speculated on the reasons why the love between Tsvetaeva and Pasternak was not consummated in a union and on the causes of the temporary break between them in the 1930s. She came to the conclusion that Tsvetaeva was "bold, decisive, and peremptory in a masculine way" while Pasternak was (in Tsvetaeva's words) "tortuously meek" in his approach to family life. As we may surmise, underlying the discussion of their divergent conceptions of "ordinary domestic life" was most likely Tsvetaeva's wish to convince Pasternak that he should put himself at a greater distance from his wife (perhaps even leave her) for the sake of a passionate dialogue (not necessarily a physical relationship) with Tsvetaeva—a step Pasternak would not take.[45]

Until the end of his days Pasternak never ceased to mourn Tsvetaeva's death. By finding and helping her daughter, Ariadna Efron, he attempted to ease the guilt he felt. He was able to establish contact with Ariadna, first while she was in camp and then in her place of exile far from Moscow, providing moral and material support to her during those most difficult years. After her release and return to Moscow, they became very close.[46] To Ariadna and others Pasternak proved his reverence for Tsvetaeva's memory when, in his *Sketch for an Autobiography*, he made poetry lovers both in the Soviet Union and abroad aware of her through his discussion of her art.[47]

Pasternak spent part of the winter of 1941–42 in Moscow, withstanding a climate that made Chistopol look inviting. The tradition goes that he greeted the New Year sleeping under the staircase in an unheated apartment building. He suffered hunger during this period, and friends dropped in occasionally with provisions.[48] In an enthusiastic attempt to contribute to Russia's war effort he enlisted in the Civil Defense Unit (Vsevobuch). In September, 1941, he wrote: "I am doing the same things as everybody else: fire-watching, drill, and shooting practice."[49] When the German air raids on Moscow began in July, he served as a fire watcher on the roof of the twelve-story writers' building on Lavrushinskii Lane. He considered the duty an act of service to his fellow men and performed it conscientiously. In late 1941 the building was hit by two incendiary bombs, and he was knocked unconscious.[50] The incident, described in a poem of 1943, he looked upon as a spiritual experience, later converting it to the spiritual values presented in the poem "Dawn," in *Doctor Zhivago*.*

From 1942, conditions improved for Pasternak. He began drawing a larger income, as a result of his greater output of translations and original work; thus the new edition of his translation of Kleist's *The Broken Jug* brought at least a subsistence income.

After Pasternak returned to Chistopol that winter, all the members of the writers' colony attended his reading in February, 1942, of excerpts from his transla-

*See Chapter 17.

tion of *Romeo and Juliet*, completed in the spring of 1941 but not appearing in
book form until 1943.[51] Pasternak achieved significant simplicity in his work because he adhered to a word-for-word translation, rather than elaborating on the
form as he had with *Hamlet*. The poet's comments on this play are relevant to the
way he handled his task. He tells us that in *Romeo and Juliet* "the form never asserts
itself at the expense of the infinitely discreet content. This is poetry at its best,
and like all such poetry it has the freshness and simplicity of prose. . . . It has the
very sound of high emotion and mortal danger overheard at night." Pasternak did
not, however, value this achievement as highly as his rendition of *Hamlet*.[52]

After this stay in Chistopol, Pasternak returned to Moscow to obtain more
commissions for translation and deliver the manuscript of *Early Trains* (*Na rannikh poezdakh*). The publication of *Early Trains* in the midsummer of 1943 ended
Pasternak's nine-year "creative silence." Reflecting on his anguish at becoming
the prisoner of a profession that left too little scope for his creative talent, he
remarked: "For six years I've been translating. I must at last write something."[53]
The appearance of *Early Trains* marks Pasternak's return to original work, the
beginning of efforts that would reach an apex in the completion of *Doctor Zhivago*.

Pasternak's war poetry did much to renovate his image as a poet close to the
everyday concerns of the Soviet people and therefore make his work more ideologically acceptable. Even his severest critic from the 1930s, Surkov, conceded that
there was a significant broadening of themes in Pasternak's poetry and that he was
becoming more closely associated with the concerns of the nation.[54] Later (in the
1960s), A. Abramov, in his *Lyric and Epic Poetry of the Great Patriotic War*, discussing Pasternak's wartime poem "Truth," stressed that the poet's craft underwent
an ideological "rearmament" in terms of both thematics and vocabulary.[55]

In December, 1942, Pasternak presented his latest version of *Early Trains* for a
poetry "evening" at the Writers' Club, attended by all of literary Moscow.[56] *Early
Trains* is a collection of poetry in four cycles, two written in 1936 ("The Artist"
and "Summer Notes"), two in 1941–42 ("Peredelkino" and "The War Months").
The poems, varied in content, are unified not so much by a common theme as by
an ineluctable unity of spirit, by the same deep reverence for nature, for friendship, for the people, for the dignity of the artist. The poem "On Early Trains" is
included in the cycle "Peredelkino," and shares many features with the other
poems. In sheer simplicity (it tells a story in almost conversational quatrains) it is
perhaps unexcelled in Pasternak's poetry and as such is representative of the poetic manner he tried to attain after 1940. It speaks of nature at the time of
awakening, early morning, bearing the idea of nature as eternally fresh and new,
of nature as wonder and marvel. The narrator as a totally passive recipient of impressions is another notable feature. Finally, the poem is pervaded by deep hu-
manitarian respect and admiration for the simple people of Russia.

The poem "The Old Park" in the "Peredelkino" cycle reflects Pasternak's interest in the effects of war on the intelligentsia. This poem describes the ancestral
Samarin estate both as Pasternak had seen it before the war and in its present
decimated condition, as a member of the Samarin family returns, injured, from
battle (Pasternak was clearly struck by this incident and by the death of another

member of the Samarin family, Iurii, who died of typhus after his return to Moscow in the late 1920s; the sad end of either or both of the Samarins appears to have suggested to him Zhivago's later life).

The cycle "The War Months" is also of interest in that it clarifies Pasternak's feelings about the war. It is a series of five poems, filled with unmasked hatred for the invader, deep sympathy for the victims of war, and praise for the heroic efforts of the Russian people. The poem "To the Memory of Marina Tsvetaeva" is attached to the end of this cycle. In it Pasternak conducts an internal monologue, trying to come to terms with the death of his old friend.

Pasternak's achievement in *Early Trains* was in his own perception a landmark in his progression toward new aesthetic values. Throughout the 1940s and 1950s he expressed personal dissatisfaction with the earlier innovative works that had won him fame. In the 1940s he told Gladkov: "For decades, I've lived on my credit, and so far have achieved nothing. . . . My future collected works have not yet been written."[57] From the 1930s Pasternak experienced a feeling of inadequacy, a lack of validity in his existence as a literary man. In the late 1950s he expressed the fear that foreign publishers would want to translate his early works, of years when he "knew neither how to write, nor to think, nor to speak."[58] Reflecting a desire to move away from the excesses of youthful modernism, Pasternak's feelings about his poetry of the years until 1932 parallelled those expressed by Jorge Luis Borges in this way: "I think that in my books of [the 1920s and 1930s] I committed almost all the literary sins: the love of form, of local color, the search for effect, and baroque style."[59] Such self-examination was followed in Pasternak's career by works stressing simplicity—*Second Birth* and his war poetry of the 1940s.

Writing in *Znamia* in 1943 about the "perfection of form" and the "purity of lines" of *Early Trains*, Pasternak's friend and fellow poet Pavel Antokolskii also had a word to say about the relationship of the poet's earlier achievement to that of his recent and future tasks. Antokolskii came to the conclusion that, impressive as it was, Pasternak's earlier work was the pledge of writing to be done "in a new notebook," in which the writer would convey an essential message about his time.[60]

Lyric poetry was not the only medium that Pasternak was exploring in order to convey that message. In 1942, after he developed misgivings about his role as the mere translator of Shakespeare's plays, he became very excited when he received an advance payment from the Novosibirsk Theater for an original play that was, he said, in progress and that he had begun mentioning as early as 1941.[61] He told various correspondents that he was completely engrossed with work on that play.[62] There is no evidence that the play ever materialized. It is clear, however, that during the war Pasternak was earnestly essaying diverse media—short lyrics, his long poem "Nightglow," a play, his novel—in his endeavor to find the form best suited to a description of the historical reality of the period.

Along with his desire to do original work, Pasternak had another *idée fixe*: to participate as an intellectual in the war effort. He wrote his wife, who was in Chistopol, of his hopes to get permission through Fadeev to go to the front. Before arriving in Chistopol for the winter, on December 20, 1942, he had applied

Pasternak with the critic
Semën Tregub, at the front
near Orel, September,
1943. Both were members
of a "brigade" of Soviet
writers on special mission.

Pasternak with his son
Leonid in Peredelkino,
1946. *Einaudi*.

for such permission, which materialized nine and a half months later.[63] He left on
August 28, 1943, to visit the divisions that had liberated Orel, accompanied by
other writers, including Vsevolod Ivanov, Konstantin Fedin, Konstantin Simonov, Raisa Azarch, Raisa Ostrovskaia, and Aleksandr Serafimovich.[64]

Semen Tregub, a writer on the staff of the army newspaper *Boevoe znamia* ("Battle Standard"), suggested that the writers collaborate on a book dealing with the
liberation of Orel. The command approved, and, beneath whizzing airplanes and
exploding projectiles, the plans for the book were earnestly discussed. The title
was unanimously decided: *V boiakh za Orel* (*In the Fighting for Orel*). The first part

Pasternak in his garden in
Peredelkino, late 1940s. *Einaudi.*

would describe in popular terms the tactical aspects of the battle, and the second
part would acquaint the reader with the people who had achieved the victory.
Before writing the book, the writers walked many kilometers over the terrain
around Orel. They discussed their future essays and verses with the heroes, eating
kasha from a communal pot and sleeping in the fields.[65]

Near the town of Zhizdra the enemy established a network of trenches and
blocked the city with infantry and antitank mines. When the Germans had been
beaten back, Pasternak met with the head of the Department of Propaganda,
Lieutenant Colonel Poedavshev. After they became acquainted, the poet asked to
be shown the Zhizdra fortifications. He wandered around the entrenchments; the
poem "Death of a Sapper" was born. Ivanov and Fedin went up in a rickety air-
plane to take a look at the battlegrounds. Fedin wrote eloquent documents inspired by his observation of several obliterated settlements. As for Serafimovich,
it seemed unwise for a man of his age to ride in such airplanes; he went instead to
visit the soldiers on the front. He, Ostrovskaia, Tregub, and Pasternak met with
soldiers, who recounted their part in the fighting and the inspiration provided by
the heroes of their favorite books. Before leaving the area, Pasternak wrote, in the
name of all writers in the group, the address containing their farewell message to
the troops.[66]

The book came out the following year as the Soviet army closed in on the German border. Written in the midst of action, *In the Fighting for Orel* has become a
bibliographical rarity. Decades after the freeing of Orel and the healing of many
wartime wounds, Soviet citizens could ponder the harrowing experience recorded
in this outstanding document.[67]

That memorable mission provided Pasternak with inspiration for later original work. He told about his journey in a report entitled "Visit to the Army," where he gave a description of the town of Chern.[68] He would also put the experience to use in the epilogue to *Doctor Zhivago*, in the description of Orel and Chern.[69]

At long last, Pasternak was reunited with his family, who had resettled in Moscow in the summer after the German offensive was broken. Extensive damage had been done both to the apartment on Lavrushinskii Lane and to the dacha in Peredelkino, and Zinaida Nikolaevna worked wonders, gradually restoring the two residences. In the meantime, they stayed in the Moscow apartment of their

Pasternak with his son Leonid and Nina Tabidze in front of the Pasternaks' dacha in Peredelkino, 1946. *Einaudi.*

Pasternak at his desk in his dacha, 1947. On the wall are paintings by his father.

friends the Asmuses, and the poet worked in his brother's room in a run-down building near Gogolevskii Boulevard.[70]

While staying in Moscow in 1944, Pasternak completed his translation of *Antony and Cleopatra*. He later commented that this work, together with *Julius Caesar*, comprised "the fruit of [Shakespeare's] study of plain everyday life. This study is pursued with passion by every representational artist. It is this pursuit which led to the naturalistic novel of the nineteenth century and which accounts for the even more convincing charm of Flaubert, Chekhov, and Leo Tolstoy."[71] The concern for the daily round that he read in Shakespeare was germane to his current approach to literary work.

In the first two issues of *Znamia* in 1944, both Pasternak's "A Translator's Notes" (on the art of translation) and the continuation of Simonov's popular *Days and Nights* (*Dni i nochi*) appeared. Also printed that year were various poems by Pasternak in such periodicals as *Literatura i iskusstvo* and *Literaturnaia gazeta*. In the previous year twenty-five pages of Pasternak's poetry—excerpts from *The Year 1905* and *Lieutenant Schmidt* and more recent poems—had been included in a collection of Soviet poetry published in Moscow.[72] It is clear that seeing his works published gave the poet hope that political conditions were changing for the better in Russia and induced in him a mood of great expectations about the postwar period—and probably some degree of leniency toward the shortcomings of the Soviet regime. Having lived through the worst of the war, Pasternak wrote to Nina Tabidze in 1944, "I . . . am myself by the nature of my profession under the influence of the mollifying power that teaches all-forgiveness."[73] However, the effect of the grim atmosphere in the latter part of the 1940s was to instill in him the courage to denounce the spiritual and human shortcomings of Stalinism.

Pasternak's most important original work emerging from the war years was *The Breadth of the Earth* (*Zemnoi prostor*).* It is a short collection of poems written in 1943–44 and presented in published form in 1945. Besides new poems, it contained others from the collection *Early Trains*. All the new poems in this collection directly or indirectly deal with war and form something of a victory march leading from the darkest days of the war to the sense of imminent triumph. Most of the poems, in quatrains of rhymed iambic tetrameters, recount wartime events, usually in terms of individual fates. The poems in the collection that do not deal directly with war are like hymns of praise and glory—one to past military heroes, one to southern Russia, one to victorious Leningrad, one to spring.

The Breadth of the Earth continued Pasternak's effort to attain an "unheard-of simplicity" (*neslykhannaia prostota*) in poetic manner. Here the forms are conservative, the images concrete, the meter regular, the thoughts direct and unadorned. Yet the poems are surcharged with genuine feeling, gained through the natural treatment of common but intense experiences of war. When the collection finally appeared in book form, it was printed on poor-quality paper, and the poet said that he experienced "physical revulsion" toward it.[74]

By the late summer of 1943, literary pursuits were overshadowed by the visibly

---

*The title of this volume has also variously been rendered as *Earth's Expanse*, *Terrestrial Expanse*, *Spacious Earth*, *The Vast Outdoors*, and *The Vastness of Earth*.

approaching conclusion to the German occupation in Russia and, ultimately, the end of the war. Intensified anticipation filled the time with bright hopes and feverish expectations. The general mood of joy and confidence also suffused Pasternak, whose enthusiasm for his long poem "Zarevo" ("Nightglow")* endured for a while after the publication of an excerpt in *Pravda* in October, 1943. "Nightglow" was intended to be a novel in verse recounting the realities of war and evaluating the postwar possibilities he expected; central to the poem's intent was an open polemic against the false art of the Stalinist period. Pasternak, however, was dissuaded by Fadeev from finishing the poem and by early 1944 had stopped work on it.[75] Later he was to give another reason—which does not necessarily conflict with the fact of Fadeev's intervention—for his loss of interest in the poem: "It was its very appearance in *Pravda*, for which it was being written, that put me off the idea of carrying on with it."[76]

Russia's losses during the war were great. Of her 200 million people, it was estimated that more than 20 million died. Besides the loss of human lives, the war destroyed approximately one-quarter of all property, 2,000 towns, 70,000 villages, 32,000 factories, and 84,000 schools. Damage to agriculture was equally severe. Stalin was determined that no time would be lost rebuilding the economy. The people, exhausted from years of overwork and privation, were now confronted with the massive job of reconstruction.

In this confusion the Pasternak family had to face a new tragedy, the death of Adik (Adrian), Zinaida Nikolaevna's son. Boris Leonidovich was at his side when he died. Adik's express wish was to have his remains cremated, a practice strictly against Soviet law. Once again Fadeev, fulfilling a function that foreshadowed that of the powerful and mysterious Evgraf in *Doctor Zhivago*, served as a thoughtful, silent benefactor and obtained official permission for Adik's wish to be carried out.[77]

It was at this time that Pasternak began to show an interest in the mechanisms whereby literary reputations are created. He paid special heed to the phenomen of the popularity of such writers as Simonov and Tvardovskii, professing immense admiration for the success of the latter's long poem *Vasilii Tërkin* in recapturing the modes and peculiarities of Russian folk idiom.[78] Tvardovskii's poem, based on his experience as a war correspondent and giving a colorful picture of the common Russian soldier, obviously provided Pasternak with an exemplar that, while being sincere and aesthetically remarkable, achieved both the "unheard-of simplicity" that Pasternak had been aiming at for several years and at the same time a broader appeal. He himself would soon receive more than his share of response from readers, both in his homeland and in time throughout Europe and the world. Work on *Doctor Zhivago* had begun.

---

*The title refers to the spectacular gun salutes marking the victories of the Red Army in the fall of 1943; the night sky over Moscow was almost continually lit up by them.

10

Toward *Doctor Zhivago*

1945–1957

I believe that since the war Russia has entered a period of integration. Something new comes forth, a new view of life, a sense among humanity of its own value.

Boris Pasternak[1]

To do his Hamlet deed, Pasternak had to write a big novel. By that deed he created a new myth of the writer, and we may conjecture that it will endure in Russian literature like other already mythical events: Pushkin's duel, Gogol's struggles with the devil, Tolstoy's escape from Iasnaia Poliana.

Czesław Miłosz[2]

Reason found it hard to accept that such an arbitrary method of rule could settle down as a system. As in previous years, every manifestation of it was still seen as a misunderstanding or as a ghastly accident of some kind. In other words, we looked for logic in unreason and tried to find justification for the unjustifiable.

Aleksandr Gladkov[3]

Pasternak called 1945 and 1946 his "years of deep spiritual crisis and change." He was "bothered by a sharp and tormenting awareness of a creative impasse"; he was dissatisfied with himself for failing to write his previously planned long poem "Nightglow" and original dramatic pieces for the theater. "My life," he wrote to his old friend Kruchenykh, "is painful and difficult, and not a trace is left of my former peacefulness and composure."[4] The notion of writing a full-scale prose work reflecting the experience of his generation had been a long-standing one. Now, with wartime impressions fresh in his mind and postwar Russia struggling around him, his ideas and perceptions were crystallizing into philosophical and literary material. He began composing sections of *Doctor Zhivago*, and, although he was tormented with doubts and uncertainties, he later said:

I wrote it with great ease. The circumstances were so definite, so fabulously terrible. All that I had to do was listen to their prompting with my whole soul and follow obediently their suggestions. The epoch contributed the main element to the novel—that element which constitutes the greatest difficulty given a freedom of choice: the delimitation of its content.[5]

Pasternak's sentiments concerning the war and its aftermath were mixed. At first his expectations were high, and he awaited new developments hopefully, as did many other Soviet intellectuals and foreign observers. Within a few years, however, he had become somber and pessimistic. The fears and anxieties rooted in prewar Stalinist conditions were very real and did not simply disappear. At one point during these years following the war Pasternak said to Gladkov: "Although the war and its tribulations had shattered the domination of all the contrived elements that were organically unsuited to the nature of man and society—elements that had gained such sway in our country—all the same, the inertia from the past prevailed."[6]

That such inertia would prevail was a possibility that Pasternak had kept in mind when during the war he had pessimistically told Gladkov: "If after the war, everything stays the same, I may find myself somewhere up north [that is, in a camp] among many of my old friends, for I won't be able to continue to be someone else."[7] In postwar Russia the high hopes of many of its citizens were not borne out by events; pressures to conform—to be "someone else"—continued to weigh heavily on artists and others, and some of Pasternak's worst fears materialized.

Yet there was a peculiar, endearing characteristic in Russia's condition in the postwar era that the poet found compelling. Pasternak at this point visualized Russia in terms not only of its suffering but also of its eventual and destined resurrection. He conceived of it not as a large stretch of populated land but personified, as a woman, much in the same way that Blok had before him. Resolving his faith in Russia's future proved to be a profound philosophical and aesthetic issue for him. His essentially optimistic conclusion about the outcome of the war he revealed in a statement to a visitor in June, 1958:

A war . . . is no game of chess; it doesn't merely end in the victory of white over black. Other things must come out of it. So many sacrifices cannot result in nothing.

I believe that since the war Russia has entered a period of integration. Something new comes forth, a new view of life, a sense among humanity of its own value.[8]

With the benefit of hindsight, very few observers would now recall evidence of significant "integration" taking place in the Soviet Union during that period. It was characteristic of Pasternak to need such a belief to function in the society in which he lived.

As Pasternak conceived the main framework of *Doctor Zhivago* in 1945–46 (when most of the "Poems of Iurii Zhivago" were written), it was to be a resolution of the crisis in Russia and of the effect of that crisis on the writer himself. The poem "Hamlet," written in 1946, reveals the profundity of that crisis, with its stark presentation of the spiritual anguish of a dramatis persona whose hopes for the establishment of justice in the state are dashed, with no chance for him to undertake any action that would further his ideals. The optimism that colored his proposed resolution is apparent in the epilogue to *Doctor Zhivago*, in a conversation between Gordon and Dudorov. Gordon reflects that the war came "as a breath of fresh air, a purifying storm, a breath of deliverance" and adds:

"The war has its special character as a link in the chain of revolutionary decades. The forces directly unleashed by the revolution no longer operated. The indirect effects of the revolution, the fruit of its fruit, the consequences of the consequences, began to manifest themselves. Misfortune and ordeals had tempered characters, prepared them for great, desperate, heroic exploits. These fabulous, astounding qualities characterize the moral elite of this generation."[9]

The striking optimism in such passages as this, the expectations for and belief in the future, were the spirit of Pasternak's life and work. He wrote to Nina Tabidze of the vitality of his hope and exultations:

One must write wonderful things, make discoveries, and see to it that wonderful things happen to you. That is life. The rest is rubbish. My oldest passion is art. . . . I and the circumstances of my life are ruled by it as unambiguously and firmly and with as much clarity as people were once upon a time ruled by religious convictions. The clarity of direction and aim makes everything easy for me. I am always ready for anything and I shall say thank you for everything to fate and heaven.[10]

In the fall of 1945, Pasternak was also working on several translations, notably Shakespeare's *Henry IV*, two poems by the Ukrainian poet Taras Shevchenko, and the Georgian Simon Chikovani's poem "Doubt." By the end of the year he had also translated almost all of the poetry of the Georgian Nikoloz Baratashvili. It was the centenary of Baratashvili's death, and Pasternak was expected to be an official delegate to the commemorative festivities in Tbilisi, Georgia. He had prepared for the journey since August, writing Chikovani of his eager anticipation of that visit because it would both provide him with a release from his labors and constitute "a journey within himself to himself."[11] Leaving his projects at his desk for two weeks in October, Pasternak renewed ties with Georgia. While he willingly participated in the celebrations, he disliked being himself the object of official honors and decorations; it is reported that he reacted with the utmost in-

Pasternak with Anna Akhmatova, ca. 1946–47. *Arthème Fayard.*

difference to a decoration the Hungarian government granted him just after the war.

Evidence of Pasternak's growing reputation abroad came soon after the war ended. His poetic achievement drew glowing praise from the Oxford scholar Cecil Maurice Bowra (praise that would be cited caustically in a negative article in *Znamia* in 1949), and editions of his prose and poetry came out in England and France, respectively.[12]

The poet's ties with the older literary generation were further loosened in 1945 with the death of Demian Bednyi. A Soviet poet-propagandist, Bednyi had been known for his strict adherence to the policy of the regime in power, despite the extreme right-wing views he had expressed in his prerevolutionary poetry. In Pasternak's view Bednyi was an earnest, sincere man regardless of his tendency to avoid troublesome situations.*

*See Chapter 8.

Bednyi, Maiakovskii, Esenin, and Tsvetaeva were gone, but Pasternak was focusing his efforts on a work that would bring back to life the whole earlier generation. Early in 1946 he wrote to Nadezhda Mandelstam that for three months, to the exclusion of any other project, he would concentrate on "something completely his own"—a prose work "about our life starting from Blok and finishing up with the present war, possibly in ten or twelve chapters." That panoramic description of the generation's endeavors, hopes, and trials was of course *Doctor Zhivago*, and he was making progress on it, in spite of many interruptions, about which he complained to his correspondent.[13]

Pasternak had to endure not only interruptions of his work but soon also attacks upon it, for in 1946 the infamous Zhdanov era (*zhdanovshchina*) began. Andrei Zhdanov, secretary of the Central Committee, was in charge of ideological affairs—in effect, a commissar of culture. He sought to rid Russian arts and letters of so-called Formalist [mostly modernist or overly theoretical], objectivist, and Western influences. In his efforts to restore strict party control over literature, Zhdanov chose as his principal targets Pasternak, Akhmatova, and Mikhail Zoshchenko. Fadeev, the secretary of the Writers' Union, publicly attacked the three writers; however, Pasternak received more lenient treatment than the others—very likely thanks to Fadeev's intercession. The Central Committee's resolution of August 14, 1946, entitled "On the Journals *Zvezda* and *Leningrad*," characterized Zoshchenko's writings as "vulgar and slanderous attacks" and those of Akhmatova as "devoid of principles and ideas." Zhdanov himself declared, "Our art is not a museum of historical weapons, but an arsenal meant for war."[14] Shortly afterward Akhmatova was expelled from the Writers' Union, and a meeting of the board, of which Pasternak was a member, was called in order to denounce her and Zoshchenko. Pasternak informed the board that he was suffering from radiculitis (spinal nerve inflammation), and was too ill to attend. For that intrepid act he was expelled from the board in August, 1946. Around that time Pasternak went to see Akhmatova and presented her with a thousand rubles to help her through a trying period. Even then he had fears that she might be forced into an early death.[15]

Despite the official disapproval hanging over him, Pasternak made a very successful appearance at a literary gathering late in August in Moscow's Hall of Columns. He continued his work on the translations from Georgian poets and later in the year wrote the first draft of "Notes on Translations from Shakespeare." That year he also composed an essay on modern Georgian poetry, whose appearance in print was quietly vetoed at the time.*

In the autumn of 1946, Pasternak's life took a dramatic turn. His encounter with Olga Vsevolodovna Ivinskaia opened a new chapter in both his emotional and his spiritual development; Ivinskaia was to become the poet's closest friend, adviser, assistant, lover, and muse. They met in October, 1946, in the editorial offices of *Novyi mir*, where the thirty-four-year-old Ivinskaia was in charge of the

---

*The essay was to be the introduction to *Georgian Poets*, an anthology of Pasternak's translations from the Georgian, slated for publication and Tbilisi. The essay appeared posthumously in 1966 (*Voprosy literatury* 1 [1966]).

new-authors section. Her duties consisted in evaluating incoming manuscripts and reporting on them to the newly appointed editor, Konstantin Simonov.[16]

The daughter of a provincial high-school teacher from Tambov who had moved to Moscow in 1915, Olga was partly of German and Polish descent (she used her mother's name). A fervent admirer of Pasternak's poetry since her adolescent days, when she began seeing him at literary gatherings, she had continued to view him as "a god" after friends helped her discover further merits in his art. That very month she had attended an evening in the Library of the Historical Museum at which Pasternak read from his translations and, upon returning home, had remarked to her mother, "I've just been talking to God!" She was therefore deeply moved when "God" walked into the editorial offices of the journal, stood there on the dark-red carpet, and smiled at her. Their conversation revealed to Pasternak that the young woman had a strong interest in his poetry, though she owned only one of his volumes. The very next day he remedied that by presenting her with copies of several more, and he soon started calling on her frequently at the journal.[17]

They met almost daily throughout the autumn—first beneath a statue of Pushkin, then outside her apartment—and went on long walks around Moscow. Early in 1947, Boris Leonidovich confessed to Olga his deep love for her. Before she could respond, Olga felt that she must tell him her unusual and complicated

Olga Ivinskaia, from a medallion made a number of years before Pasternak met her. *Arthème Fayard.*

life story; this she did in a written confession that "filled a whole school exercise book." She had been married twice; both her husbands had been members of the Communist party. Her first husband, Ivan Vasilevich Emelianov, had committed suicide by hanging in 1939. She later married Aleksandr Petrovich Vinogradov, though she knew that he had been Emelianov's rival and enemy, and she was not unaware of some of his shortcomings: behind an appearance of sincerity and generosity, Vinogradov could be treacherous (Olga believed that he had denounced her mother to the authorities for "slandering the Leader"). He acted as a faithful father, however, to Ivinskaia's daughter by her first marriage, Irina. In 1943 Vinogradov was killed at the front. Ivinskaia also mentioned love affairs of shorter duration. She explained the circumstances of her present life: she now lived in a top-floor apartment of a six-story apartment building on Potapov Street in central Moscow,* which she shared with Irina, age eight; her son by Vinogradov, age five; her mother, Mariia Nikolaevna, and her stepfather, Dmitrii Ivanovich Kostko.[18]

Rather than being deterred by Olga's "confession," Boris Leonidovich felt an intensified compassion and affection for the golden-haired young woman who had undergone such ordeals. The two met more and more often for long strolls, had "endless discussions" in which they tried to reach a decision about the future, and parted several times intending to meet again. For a long time during the first few months of 1947, Pasternak was torn between allegiance to his family and his new love. Long before Ivinskaia came into his life, his disaffection for Zinaida Nikolaevna had crystallized. He confessed to Ivinskaia that he had realized his mistake during the first year he lived with his second wife. Pasternak's friend of many decades Anna Akhmatova observed in 1940 that at the beginning, being blindly in love with Zinaida Nikolaevna, he failed to see what others around him had perceived—that she was "coarse and vulgar." Akhmatova also remarked that, although Pasternak now "said terrible things about her," he could not make up his mind to leave her for the sake of their child, Leonid, and because he "belonged to the race of conscientious men who cannot divorce twice." This interpretation suggests not so much a desire by Pasternak to preserve a façade of conventional morality as a reluctance to cause further disruptions in the family's life and the children's education.[19]

It is clear that Zinaida Nikolaevna was little attuned to Pasternak's spiritual and aesthetic pursuits at the time when he was conceiving and writing *Doctor Zhivago*. She was addicted to chain smoking and cardplaying; with such companions as Nina Tabidze; Leonidze's wife, Peputsa; the Selvinskiis; the Pogodins; the widow of the writer Trenev; and Iurii Krotkov,† she would sit up playing and

---

*Apartment 18, 9/11 Potapov Street.

†Owing to his friendly ties to the Tabidze family from his childhood, Krotkov had been readily admitted to the Pasternak household. It is clear that he had a number of conversations with Boris Leonidovich himself and carried on a friendly dialogue with Zinaida Nikolaevna both before and after Pasternak's death.

Krotkov was born in 1917 in Tbilisi, into a family that developed many close ties with government officials and party higher-ups—including Lavrenty Beria, who made young Krotkov his protégé. After literature studies in Moscow, he frequented the upper echelons of Soviet society and

smoking until dawn. Such idle occupations drew little sympathy from Pasternak. Her life-style led her to neglect her young son, Leonid, in the 1940s, according to comments by the poet's friends. Her rather brusque and authoritarian manner—which Pasternak related to the temperament of her father the gendarme colonel—was ill-oriented to his sensibilities. From now on, Pasternak would seek from Ivinskaia the spiritual and emotional solace that his wife had not given him in a long time.[20]

Pasternak could no longer resist what he felt to be a strong, sincere, authentic attachment. On April 4, 1947, he and Ivinskaia decided to accept fully their love for each other. On that day he inscribed the words "My life, my angel, I love you dearly" in a small red-bound volume of his verse that he presented to her. From then on he visited her more and more often in the apartment and stayed there when her children were away on excursions or vacations. Irina's initial deference toward the "living classic" who had entered her life soon turned into a more personal feeling; she gave the poet the nickname "Classoosha," an affectionate diminutive of "classic."[21]

With most of his friends Pasternak made no secret that Ivinskaia had become his great love and inspiration; her warmth and understanding filled the last thirteen years of his life. Early in 1948, at Pasternak's instigation, she left *Novyi mir*, where her closeness to him was making her situation increasingly difficult. He helped launch her career as literary translator, and, as a consequence of his efforts and her own diligence, by the 1950s she was well established in the profession. Their bliss was occasionally clouded by arguments, which often centered on Olga's feeling (reinforced by her mother's pleas) that Pasternak should make a clean break with Zinaida Nikolaevna and live with her.[22]

Making such a break, however, was just what the typically indecisive Pasternak found himself unable to do, despite an increasingly uncomfortable home life. When in the winter of 1948 Zinaida Nikolaevna found a letter from Olga on Pasternak's desk, relations between her and her husband changed, and there could never be a return to an atmosphere of trust between them. By and large Zinaida Nikolaevna seemed sufficiently content with her all-night poker and bridge games to go through the motions of domestic life and overlook her husband's relationship with Ivinskaia. At times, however, she became impatient with the situation and tried to force Pasternak to give up this new bond; once, during a serious illness of her son, Leonid, she extorted from him a promise to break with Ivinskaia. That promise Pasternak could not bring himself to keep.

---

cultural life and soon extended his circle of acquaintances to include foreign diplomats and dignitaries. His foreign ties were well exploited by the Soviet KGB, for whom he was an agent. Along with the usual spying and intrigue, his most spectacular caper was the blackmailing of French Ambassador Maurice Dejean. In similar operations he introduced foreign dignitaries to beautiful Soviet women (called "swallows" in Soviet secret-police jargon), who, under the watchful eyes of KGB cameras, seduced and compromised the unfortunate diplomats. In the 1950s, Krotkov wrote several anti-American plays, such as *John, a Soldier of Peace* (based on episodes from Paul Robeson's life).

For a discussion of Krotkov's activities as KGB agent see "KGB: The Swallows' Nest—Condensed from *KGB* by John Barron," *Reader's Digest*, August, 1970, pp. 201–29. See also Patricia Blake, "False Friend" [a review of Krotkov's *The Nobel Prize*, a fictionalized account of the last few years of Pasternak's life], *Time*, August 18, 1980, p. 148.

Inscription from Pasternak
to Olga Ivinskaia: "My life,
my angel, I love you truly.
4 April 1947," with a
postscript written in 1953:
"This inscription is eternal
and valid forever. And can
only grow stronger."
Arthème Fayard.

He went on dividing his time between two households and their distinctive atmospheres—and pets, the dacha in Peredelkino enlivened by the pranks of his favorite dog, Tobik, and Ivinskaia's apartment by the playfulness of her innumerable cats (whom he archly named for people he disliked).[23]

Even as his private life was undergoing turmoil, Pasternak's career as a Soviet poet continued to appear precarious. He spent the winter of 1946–47 preparing an edition of his collected poetry for the series "Selected Works by Soviet Writers." Early in 1947 the volume, entitled *Selected Verse* (*Izbrannye stikhotvoreniia*), was ready and copies had been printed when the authorities suddenly decided, in the wake of a speech by Zhdanov, to cancel publication. The edition was destroyed before it went on sale; only a few copies miraculously survived. The deci-

Ivinskaia fondling one of
the innumerable stray cats
she liked to bring into her
home. *Arthème Fayard.*

sion was obviously impelled not only by the Zhdanov speech but also by rumors circulating in Moscow that Pasternak had been put forward as candidate for the Nobel Prize for his poetry, a factor that could only have reflected negatively on the poet in the paranoiac and repressive atmosphere of the time.[24]

Such a setback did not stop Pasternak from working toward new goals. Regarding the new poems (part of the novel) that he was composing, he informed a correspondent: "I have again written a number of poems, and one of them ["Star of the Nativity"] is quite good."[25]

The uplift provided both by the public's acclaim and by his own confidence in his work in progress could not mask the signs of the literary and political storm that was gathering over him. From the beginning of March, 1947, he was abusively mentioned at various literary gatherings. The attacks were part of the general witch-hunt instigated by Zhdanov, now head of the Kominform, against any and all persons designated by him as "anti-Soviet." Pasternak was singled out for criticism on several occasions.[26]

Fadeev launched a virulent attack on Pasternak. "In his creative work," declared Fadeev, "he represents the spirit of individuality which is so profoundly alien to our society." At another point he even bluntly called Pasternak "the poet who refused to participate in the cruel war in which millions of our people shed their blood," adding the unfair comment, "When the war came to an end, Pasternak's contribution was seen to be only a handful of poems, none of them comparable with his best."[27]

It is ironic that Fadeev apparently did not believe what he officially proclaimed. How much he actually loved and admired Pasternak's poetry was brought to light in the confidences of a fellow writer:

> I remember a talk we had after Fadeev had been inveighing against the "aloofness from life" of certain writers, among whom he had named Pasternak. . . . Fadeev insisted on taking me to a corner café where, after ordering brandy, he said without preamble: "Would you like to hear some real poetry?" And he began to recite from memory verses by Pasternak, going on and on, only interrupting himself from time to time to say: "Wonderful stuff, isn't it?"[28]

Within the framework of Zhdanov's campaign there were, on and off during the period 1947 to 1949, many abuses of Pasternak in the Soviet press. The March, 1949, issue of *Zvezda* printed the minutes of a discussion "On Soviet Poetry," which in part condemned Pasternak for his interest in "denatured foreign trash" and urged him to learn to improve his "poetic version of the world . . . in the homeland [*u nas*]." Toward the end of 1948, Levin, the director of the Soviet Writer (Sovetskii pisatel), a publishing house, was denounced for "impudence" in attempting to republish works by Pasternak.[29]

One of the harshest direct attacks came in March, 1947, when the periodical *Culture and Life* (*Kultura i zhizn*) published a violent denunciation signed by Aleksei Surkov. The publication in a newspaper of an article devoted in whole to Pasternak was in itself a rare event for those years. As one of the ideologically staunchest members of the Union of Writers and defender of maximal fidelity to the party's objectives, over the decades Surkov often verbally jousted—sometimes in a virulent key—with Pasternak. In addition to their ideological differences, the events of the late 1940s and, especially, 1950s revealed in Surkov a strain of personal jealousy and hatred of the poet. Embittered by Surkov's behavior, Ivinskaia was to exclaim: "Surkov will be remembered only as the enemy of Pasternak, just as Bulgarin* is remembered only as the man who envied and vilified Pushkin." In his scathing attempt to intimidate the poet in *Culture and Life*, Surkov denied both that Pasternak wrote great poetry and that his voice was that

---

*Faddei Bulgarin (Tadeusz Bułharyn, 1789–1859): journalist and informer to the tsarist police, fought Pushkin and what he stood for.

Ivinskaia beside the pond in
Peredelkino. *Heinz Schewe.*

Pasternak with Ivinskaia
(*left*) and her daughter,
Irina. *Heinz Schewe.*

Pasternak with Ivinskaia in
Peredelkino. *Arthème
Fayard.*

"of the epoch"; he concluded by vehemently asserting that Soviet literature could
not reconcile itself with Pasternak's poetry.[30]

In the midst of this outcry the critic and literary scholar Anatolii Tarasenkov—
a fervent admirer of Pasternak's poetry and collector of his latest poems as well as
of clippings about him—was persuaded to howl with the wolves and joined the
outcry with derogatory articles on the poet. Such a phenomenon was by no means
untypical of the Stalin era and is part of the situation that in *Doctor Zhivago* was
described and presented as an illustration of the ancient adage about man being a
wolf to man.[31]

Pasternak was harassed economically as well as critically. He said of his finan-
ces, "Things got very bad for me." A contract negotiated in 1945 had failed to
materialize, and, as mentioned earlier, the edition of his *Selected Verse* had been
destroyed. In fact, from that time until 1954 none of Pasternak's original writings
was published in the Soviet Union; only his translations were printed. Gladkov
referred to the period as Pasternak's second period of disgrace.* The poet's need

*His first period of disgrace being the years 1936–40 (Aleksandr Gladkov, *Vstrechi*, p. 16).

for money worsened until, miraculously, he received a contract on April 20, 1947, for the translation of *Faust*. He greeted the contract with the comment, "They've decided not to make me starve." Something new and unfamiliar appeared in Pasternak's character as a result of these many pressures: he became somewhat irascible and even responded to acquaintances in sharp, angry tones.[32]

Translating *Faust* proved to be more than an economic respite; it helped free him socially and politically. In fact, during the political and economic tribulations of the Zhdanov campaign Pasternak became more inspired, more vital than ever. When Shostakovich was under attack the poet found the spirit to write him a letter "to cheer him up." Pasternak lucidly and boldly appraised Zhdanov's campaign thus: "We're living through a cultural reaction, not a cultural revolution."[33]

The poet continued to enjoy popular support. On January 30, 1948, he read

Pasternak in 1948. *Archives Hélène Zamoyska.*

his translation of *Antony and Cleopatra* to a crowd of actors of a Moscow theater. After reading the play, he was asked to read his own verse. He first read "Winter Night," "March," and "Holy Week" and then "Star of the Nativity," commenting that the last was influenced by Blok. "Miracle" and "Hamlet" he recited without looking at the text, and his reading of "Hamlet" was so unforgettable that it was clear that the poem was "a confession." He was obviously moved by the audience's warm reception, and his emotions bespoke how isolated such instances of public recognition were.[34]

When such opportunities arose, however, enthusiastic and often large audiences welcomed readings of Pasternak's poetry. Such an occasion came a few weeks after his visit to the actors. On February 23, 1948, he participated with about twenty other poets in a literary soirée that had been organized in the Polytechnic Museum, which had what was then the largest auditorium in Moscow, with the expectation that participants would speak up in favor of "peace and democracy" and denounce NATO. Although it was inattentive to officially recognized poets, the crowd, which had been drawn by his name on posters, rose and applauded when Pasternak came out onto the stage. When he was called to the rostrum, the audience "again went wild, clapping and shouting." As he read his verse, the hypnotized spectators called him out tirelessly for encores and shouted requests for particular poems, including notably Pasternak's version of Shakespeare's Sonnet 66, which afforded to many a politically relevant interpretation, heightened by the translator, of such phrases as "art made tongue-tied by authority." When he had trouble recalling a line, he was immediately prompted in unison by admirers from various parts of the hall; such sympathy and admiration brought tears to the poet's eyes as he stopped the recitation to exclaim, "Thank you, dear ones!" ("Spasibo, dorogie!"). In spite of the frantic efforts of the chairman to bring the proceedings to order, the meeting developed into a boisterous ovation for Pasternak. According to at least one eyewitness, part of the audience en masse accompanied the poet on his walk home.[35]

By May, 1948, Pasternak had made great progress on the manuscript of *Doctor Zhivago*, having completed the first section of the novel. He approached the process of revision with great strictness, and at the end of that process he had discarded approximately one-third of what he had written (including a long digression on the symbolic value of flowers in human passages). He met with Anna Akhmatova, who had recently arrived from Leningrad, and in his enthusiasm read her parts of *Doctor Zhivago* for hours at a stretch. On at least one occasion he read a chapter to a small group of listeners in the apartment of friends—a circumstance that was soon to be turned against Olga and him. It appears that reading aloud certain sections to friends helped Pasternak achieve greater critical perspective. In addition, he systematically sought the advice of certain trusted consultants, such as his long-term friend from Leningrad Sergei Spasskii, as well as Nina Skorbina, who passed on to him detailed comments. He seems to have "generously" given away to friends copies of the manuscript. And Ivinskaia has commented on the extent to which, over many years, he went on "endlessly" revising it.[36]

In spite of the controversies which surrounded him, the poet continued to be inspired and rejuvenated. Gladkov described him as "youthful-looking and handsome in his white panama and light suit" at an outing in May, 1948. His appearance was also surely a result of his love for Ivinskaia. They spent the summer together. She accompanied him to literary gatherings and poetry readings; they devoted many hours to walking and conversing. The "Poems of Iurii Zhivago," many of which had been written in 1946, Pasternak rewrote and revised during this time, continually inspired by her presence.[37]

A few months later, on August 31, Andrei Zhdanov died, and the way was clear for a purge of his followers in the political arena. Fadeev, who had been closely allied with Zhdanov, now softened his tone and recanted some of his criticisms of Pasternak.[38] Nevertheless, severe pressure on intellectuals, particularly Jewish ones, continued until Stalin's death.

In September a manuscript of the completed first part of *Doctor Zhivago* was circulating Moscow. Being with Ivinskaia and working with her on the manuscript had provided the support Pasternak needed to complete it. Ivinskaia, in fact, played a decisive part in shaping *Doctor Zhivago*: it has been correctly asserted that, belonging as she did to a generation younger than Pasternak's (and to that extent more sensitive to purely Soviet phenomena), she helped give the novel a more contemporary (and to that extent, more "Soviet") flavor. With intense devotion she also functioned as the secretary who twice retyped the manuscript of the book, as the literary agent who conducted essential and most delicate negotiations on his behalf with both Soviet and foreign publishers, and as the literary consultant and fellow translator whose knowledgeable advice he sought on many matters.[39] From the tremendous amount of effort Ivinskaia offered to the construction of *Doctor Zhivago*, she derived as much satisfaction as if the novel were her own. Her attitude toward the book has been described as "a settlement of accounts with everything she lived through, a devastating blow delivered to a hateful foe . . . the apotheosis of her life, her favorite child, delivered in pain and tears."[40]

For Pasternak also, *Doctor Zhivago* was a "settlement" of sorts—and even an attempt to make amends for the "wrongs" suffered by some of those closest to him. In a letter of November, 1948, he specifically mentioned the ludicrously inadequate rewards and cruel trials that an "outrageously dark and unjust life" meted out to such great artists as his father, Tsvetaeva, Iashvili, and Tabidze and commented that in writing the novel he felt like an "avenger" of the wrongs they had suffered, attempting to "get even for *them*." Thus both Ivinskaia and Pasternak had deeply personal reasons for creating in the novel a powerful artistic representation of the trials of their age.[41]

The significance of Ivinskaia as an inspiration for Pasternak is reflected in *Doctor Zhivago*. When speaking to certain visitors, the novelist simply equated Lara with Ivinskaia (thus, to one guest he said, "Lara exists. I want you to meet her. Here is her phone number . . ."). There are several direct parallels which reinforce this identification, such as their blonde hair and Ivinskaia's daughter, Irina, under the guise of Lara's daughter, Katenka. That Lara was none other than Ivinskaia was accepted within Pasternak's own family.[42] The truth, however, is more complex: Lara is in fact a composite portrait, combining elements of both Zinaida Nikolaevna and Olga Ivinskaia. Pasternak remarked to Nina Tabidze, whose radiant warmth and femininity he deeply admired, "In Lara there are many women. She is a composite . . . . Zina [Zinaida Nikolaevna] as well is in her, and you are too, Nina." Though Ivinskaia herself acknowledged this, she believed that she was the main inspiration for Lara, pointing out that her own childhood in Kursk resolved the clue in the statement, "You had come from Kursk," in one of the "Poems of Iurii Zhivago."[43] Indeed, such poems as "Separation" and "Bacchanalia" refer specifically to Ivinskaia. Pasternak's poem "August" concerns her alone, as homage to her courage and testimony of the poet's feelings for her,[44] expressed in the passage:

> Let us part now, you who threw
> Your woman's gauntlet to an abyss of degradations:
> I am the arena of your ordeal.
>
> Farewell, broad sweep of outspread wings
> Farewell to willfulness of soaring.[45]

While it is true that Ivinskaia's foreign background (half Polish, one-fourth German) is reflected in Lara's foreign ancestry, Zinaida Nikolaevna was also partly of foreign origin, and her youthful tribulations—as well as Olga Vsevolodovna's—are clearly reflected in Lara's life story. (As a matter of fact, Lara is portrayed as a contemporary of Pasternak's and Zinaida Nikolaevna's generation.) Pasternak remarked that his wife aided the development of Lara in that she was an "eternal, authentically Russian [*rossiiskoe*], enduring element."[46] At the same time, certain traits of Zinaida Nikolaevna—such as her passionate love of domestic work and her nest-building instinct—were embodied in the character of Tonia, Zhivago's wife.

In writing *Doctor Zhivago*, Pasternak was always concerned with "color and poetry." He believed that "thought draped itself in color and transformed itself in a vision of reality [a poetic image]." Therefore, he conceived of the novel as "a long narrative poem (*poema*), submitting to poetic intuition, which—in his opinion—is capable, more deeply than anything else, of expressing the atmosphere of life"[47]—a notion strongly reminiscent of Blok's conception in *Retribution*. The over-all poetic intuition as embodied in the "total conception" of the novel he later stated was far more important to him than any specific significance or symbolism of particular details.[48]

Doctor Zhivago may be most concisely characterized as Pasternak's spiritual history of the Russian revolution, presented in the form of the life story of a representative fictional hero, Iurii Zhivago. The author claimed that Zhivago was conceived as someone intermediate between himself and Blok, Esenin, and Maiakovskii.[49] This scion of the Russian intelligentsia is, successively, a doctor, a poet, a citizen in sympathy with the outbreak of revolution, a family man struggling to survive the material hardships of the early Soviet years, an involuntary member of the Red partisan army during the long civil war, a disgraced member of the former bourgeoisie, an internal refugee obliged by political dangers to part from the

The Russian Orthodox church in Peredelkino, where Pasternak frequently attended services during the last few years he was writing *Doctor Zhivago*. *Archives Jacqueline de Proyart.*

woman he loves, the extralegal husband of the daughter of a former family servant and—through all this—a man whose external life goes to seed while in his writings he keeps alive a full measure of spiritual and creative integrity.

Emotionally the novel's drama turns on Zhivago's fated, ideal love for Lara Guichard, a woman of a social class a step beneath his, whom Pasternak presents as variously emblematic of female wholeness, of Russia's suffering humanity in need of social justice, and of Iurii's passion for visionary integrity. The differing social origin of Zhivago's three "wives"; his displacements from Moscow to the Urals, back to Moscow, away to Siberia, and finally back to Moscow again; his experiences as citizen, doctor, and family man; the increasing hardships he sees and endures; and the varieties of people whose fates converge with his—all these embrace the experience of Russians-at-large during a half century of tumultuous change.

Through Zhivago's experiences and reflections Pasternak develops an evaluation of the revolution and its spiritual consequences which, without denying the historical inevitability of the upheaval, defends the enduring values of individual integrity, humanity, art, and responsiveness to the wholeness of the natural world. Dwelling on the consequences of political change, Pasternak questions the ultimate validity and efficacy of such approaches to the complexities of existence. Thus, while the novel is clearly a depiction of a particular social moment, its style and values make it a work that is at least as lyrical and spiritual as it is historical and political.

During the years he was composing *Doctor Zhivago*, Pasternak continued to work on translations of poems by Goethe (which were printed in *Novyi mir* in 1949) and further lyrics by Georgian poets that in 1949 were scheduled to be published by Sovetskii pisatel under the title *Three Georgian Poets*. The writing of his novel was closely and continuously intertwined with his work on the translation of *Faust*. By March, 1949, he had completed his translation of Act 1 of Goethe's masterpiece, which he had begun late in 1947 or early in 1948.[50]

Generally Pasternak's approach to *Faust* was to take in the gist of a passage and reproduce several lines closely and in vigorous and lively style; having thus constrained his options of rhyme and syntax, he transmuted the general content and the quality of the rest of the passage into a rather distant paraphrase redistributed over approximately the same footage, or metric length. Although this process results in certain textual and philosophical inaccuracies, the verbal felicity, sense of movement, and poetic integrity are admirably preserved. Pasternak's *Faust* was the only complete translation in Soviet times and to this date is generally recognized as the finest Russian translation.

Pasternak later claimed that translating *Faust* helped him creatively in the writing of *Doctor Zhivago*: "[*Faust*] helped me become bolder, freer, break up new paths not only in the sense of political or moral prejudices but also from the viewpoint of form. I freed myself from the impulse to be an original writer." The originality of *Zhivago* consists precisely in refusing to be original.[51] Translating *Faust* had a definite impact on his search for a straightforward, "nonoriginal" style, which he brought to a successful completion in the final draft of *Doctor Zhivago*.* However, even the labor on *Faust*, a work with which he empathized to a large degree, took its toll on Pasternak. Shortly after completing it, he wrote a friend that certain typical components of the translator's work had "devoured his personal means of expression" and that he had translated "too much."[52]

Some of these concerns were weighing on Pasternak's mind when on March 2, 1949, his friend and literary consultant Nina Skorbina visited him in his Moscow apartment and found that he seemed changed since the previous winter:

He seemed to me now other than during our last meetings. Not a magician, but an ordinary *homme de lettres*. Probably even he suffered from attacks of distrust in himself. Because he said right away as if answering an unvoiced reproach: "Perhaps I am a most ordinary writer. Perhaps I am simply a run-of-the-mill writer." . . . As always, he needed to be reassured.[53]

Pasternak told her that Anna Akhmatova and Olga Berggolts had called to tell him of the rumor circulating Leningrad that he had been arrested. Pasternak's friends were obviously concerned—Liliia Brik and Genrikh Neigauz had

---

*Concerning the simplicity typical of Pasternak's mature manner, see Chapter 18.

dropped by—and Pasternak himself was clearly worried. According to Skorbina, he felt that the talent and genius with which he was endowed could only make his fate worse; he could not even be sure that "they" would not treat him as they had treated many others. When Skorbina left, Pasternak gave her manuscripts of the first part of his novel and Act 1 of *Faust* with his corrections.[54]

Revision of his manuscripts could not take Pasternak's mind off serious worries. At the end of the month he told Skorbina: "At the publishers' the situation is mysterious. . . . all my editorial friends are putting on some sort of secretive airs." He hinted that Skorbina should buy his books while they were still available. Although he had finally taken at least a portion of Part One of *Faust* to the publishers, he said that it was "unknown whether they would publish it, and especially, whether they would pay."[55]

The assaults that Pasternak had anticipated were not long in coming. The blissful relationship between Pasternak and Ivinskaia was interrupted by an untoward event, through which the state manifested its apprehension of Pasternak's ideological independence. At eight on the evening of October 6, 1949, a group of security police burst into Ivinskaia's apartment on Potapov Street. Their six-hour search of the apartment focused on "everything connected with Pasternak." They arrested Ivinskaia, hoping to wrest from her some piece of information that would incriminate Pasternak as a spy or an enemy of the state. She was placed in solitary confinement in the Lubianka, the headquarters of the KGB.[56]

Ivinskaia's first interrogation was conducted by Minister of State Security Viktor Abakumov, who had obviously spent some time building a case against Pasternak. He was interested in "this novel Pasternak is passing around to people at the moment" and pressed her to make statements about what he referred to as the "anti-Soviet" nature of the novel. Ivinskaia remained silent. Because she was pregnant, she was given better rations and somewhat more humane treatment than that accorded other prisoners. Ivinskaia was soon handed over to her "regular" interrogator, A. S. Semionov. Hours of questioning and accusing went on night after night. Her stay in the Lubianka, however, was not altogether without benefit: while she was there, she met Trotsky's granddaughter Sasha Moglin and a group of doctors accused of plotting against Stalin, and she had ample opportunity to converse with them.[57]

Semionov tried to make the prisoner confess that Pasternak was a British spy—an absurd fabrication with no more basis than his relatives' prolonged residence in England. Semionov also tried to make her say that Pasternak's novel was "uncontemporary" because of the religious thematics of the poem "Mary Magdalene." After Semionov insisted that the poem was "un-Soviet," Ivinskaia explained to him the meaning of some of the poem's more recondite terms that had brought him to such a view. Semionov sometimes adopted a brutal tone, such as when he made coarse anti-Semitic remarks, saying, "I can't believe that a Russian woman like you could ever really be in love with this old Jew—there must be some ulterior motive here!"[58]

Her interrogator was not above subjecting Ivinskaia to sleep deprivation (a refined method of torture described earlier in the decade by Arthur Koestler in

Darkness at Noon). He once played a macabre joke on her. She was promised "a meeting with Pasternak" and sent to a dark room in another building where Pasternak was supposed to meet her, only to realize that she had been placed in a morgue. She was left there for a fairly long time, worrying that one of the corpses might be Pasternak's. There was also a confrontation between Ivinskaia and another prisoner, Sergei Nikolaevich Nikiforov (the assumed name of the former merchant Epishkin). Ivinskaia had known Nikiforov as a mild-mannered old man who came to her apartment to give English lessons to her daughter, Irina, but in prison he turned out to be an informer who testified to imaginary "anti-Soviet conversations" that he alleged had taken place between her and Pasternak. The impact on Ivinskaia of these shocking confrontations brought on a miscarriage, which occurred shortly after the confrontation with Epishkin. Pasternak did not learn of the miscarriage for some time.[59]

It has been reported that, when Pasternak heard of Ivinskaia's arrest, he wept and said: "Everything is finished now. They've taken her away from me, and I'll never see her again. It's like death—even worse." Thereafter, in conversations including those with "people he scarcely knew," he is reported to have referred to Stalin invariably as a "murderer." To a number of people in Moscow—friends and "even slight acquaintances"—Pasternak said that Ivinskaia would soon have her baby in jail. When in 1950 the poet was summoned to the Lubianka, he expected that he would be handed Ivinskaia's child and even informed Zinaida Nikolaevna—who greeted the information rather tempestuously—that they would have to look after the child. As it turned out, however, he was handed instead his letters to Ivinskaia, as well as books that he had inscribed to her (other of Pasternak's poems and notes were scrutinized during the interrogations and destroyed).* While he was at the Lubianka, Pasternak asked for paper and a pencil and wrote a note to the minister of state security, stating that if Ivinskaia was guilty of anything he was guilty too and requested to be put in prison in her stead. Nothing befell Pasternak, however, whereas Ivinskaia, having staunchly refused to incriminate him, was finally sentenced to five years in a hard-labor camp "for close contact with persons suspected of espionage"—a sentence passed under Article 58 of the Soviet Criminal Code, which dealt with political crimes.[60]

The arrest and subsequent condemnation of Ivinskaia was clearly a blow leveled at Pasternak. His own person remained inviolate, either because of a general recognition that arresting a writer of his stature would have unfavorable repercussions at home and abroad or because of the instructions allegedly issued by Stalin about him: "Do not touch this cloud-dweller."[61] The security forces knew where he would be most vulnerable, however, and took reprisals against the person closest to him. The deeper concern of the authorities was whether Pasternak's novel

---

*It was part of the standard legal procedure (seldom observed during the Stalin era) for the judiciary to return to a citizen those of his papers or documents that the interrogating or prosecuting agency no longer needed. This somewhat dramatic gesture of returning these documents to Pasternak reinforced the message being conveyed to him: he was implicated in the case against Ivinskaia, and, vulnerable as he was because of his feelings for her, he had better toe the line if he did not wish to see further reprisals taken against her—or even place himself in danger of being arrested as well.

would be the expression of the literary opposition. So paranoiac were the authorities that Pasternak's activity in "passing around" the novel contributed to creating and maintaining the suspicion against him. Ivinskaia's arrest was a punitive measure. As mentioned earlier, Pasternak never made any secret of his novel, even long before it was finished, and was always eager to tell his friends about its contents and to show them chapters.

Discussing the concern of the secret police about Pasternak, Ivinskaia later observed that "during the whole of his active life there was a file at the Lubianka on Pasternak in which not only everything he wrote was entered, but also every word ever uttered by him in the presence of innumerable informers." The minister of state security was zealously constructing a fully documented dossier on the poet for use when needed. Commenting on that state of affairs, Ivinskaia aptly observed that, just as in the case of Aleksandr Radishchev and Pushkin in the old days, "so now with Pasternak policemen were . . . trying to set themselves up as the best judges of the work of the writers, all the time keeping secret dossiers on them, and sometimes throwing them in jail."[62]

After Ivinskaia's arrest, Pasternak took it upon himself to care for her family out of his limited resources. Throughout her three-and-a-half-year absence he kept the family alive.[63] At the same time, perceiving that neither his worrying nor his endeavors (such as his letter to the minister of state security) were of any avail, Pasternak decided to invest all of his energies in the writing of the latter part of the novel, which he then conceived of as a monument to Ivinskaia.[64] The shock and anguish her arrest caused him provided the emotional thrust behind several episodes of *Doctor Zhivago*, especially in the scenes of Lara's departure and in the separation toward the end of the book. It was after her arrest that Pasternak wrote the poem "Parting," the following stanza of which reveals his immeasurable sorrow:

> And now, this flight of hers. Perhaps
> It had been forced upon her.
> This parting will consume them both
> And grief gnaw clean their bones.[65]

The anguish took its toll shortly. In 1950, Pasternak had a heart attack caused by thrombosis, followed by another in the fall of 1952.[66]

While Pasternak was helping her family survive, Ivinskaia had to submit to the fate the authorities had meted out for her. After a stay in a transit prison, Butyrki, she was sent to the hard-labor camp at Potma, in the Mordovian Republic,* completing her journey in a forced march across country. At Potma she was confined with various prisoners, chiefly "political," those who had also been sentenced under Article 58 of the Criminal Code. There began for her a grueling period; from seven in the morning until eight in the evening she had to work in the fields, on a gray and cracked earth and under a parching sun, driven by the abuse of her overseers. She had to keep up with the heavy quota imposed by an intense and somewhat sadistic female brigade leader—turning over and hoeing a

---

*About 500 kilometers southeast of Moscow.

certain number of cubic meters of soil baked hard by the sun. Among her companions were nuns, who suffered severe consequences for refusing to work and who "were kept alive by their faith" (according to Ivinskaia's account), and hefty western Ukrainian peasant women, who despised the "pampered ladies from Moscow." Ivinskaia managed to keep up her spirits by composing poetry laden with feeling. She preserved them in her memory, for she could not write them down. Because he was no "close relative," Pasternak's letters were forbidden, but between 1951 and 1953 five messages written by him and signed with her mother's name managed to reach her. In one such letter he conveyed his feelings in the third person:

I will never understand [Pasternak] and am against your friendship with him. . . . He lives in a fantastic world which he says consists entirely of you—yet he imagines this need not mean any upheaval in his family life, or in anything else. Then what does he think it means? I hug you, my purest dear. . . . [Signed] Your mama.

Such affectionate and often humorous notes went a long way toward supplying the prisoner with the courage necessary to survive.[67]

Ivinskaia was not the only camp inmate with whom Pasternak maintained a correspondence, though she was the one for whom he cared most dearly. As mentioned earlier, for years he kept up an epistolary dialogue with Ariadna Efron, Tsvetaeva's daughter, regularly sending her money and parcels. When she was released, she became a close friend of both Pasternak and Ivinskaia. In 1951, after the arrest of Nikolai Petrovich Bogatyrev, the son of the famous folklorist and an old friend, Pasternak immediately offered help and over the years wrote the prisoner and sent him copies of his translations of Shakespeare's plays and of *Faust*. Pasternak had still other ties with prisoners. In the late 1940s and early 1950s he was inundated with letters from the camps, and he replied, also sending food packages, books, and poetry. Receiving such letters, replying to the writers and sending them his poetry, knowing that contact with his art made life somewhat easier for them—all of this was of significance to Pasternak and provided, as he said, some relief for the "guilt" he felt at "not being together with them."[68] As Ivinskaia has clearly pointed out, such feelings about the tribulations of Pasternak's contemporaries were reflected in the poem beginning "My Soul, you are in mourning . . . ."*

Throughout this dark period in Soviet Russian history Pasternak was subjected to frequent critical attacks. The October, 1949, issue of *Znamia* printed an article by Anatolii Tarasenkov that declared: "Pasternak's artistic work is the most blatant example of rotten decadence. He himself, apparently sensing his alienation from the people, has ceased publishing new poems."[69]

After the publication of Pasternak's translation of *Faust*, there was an attack in the August, 1950 issue of *Novyi mir*, from the pen of critic Tamara Motyleva, who accused him of distorting Goethe's "social and philosophical meaning" in order to "defend the reactionary theory of 'pure art,'" of introducing "an aesthetic and

---

*Olga Ivinskaya, *CAPT*, pp. 124–31. For a discussion of this poem, see Chapter Fifteen.

individualist flavor into the text," and of attributing to Goethe "reactionary ideas." In a letter to a friend Pasternak wondered where Goethe's "progressive ideas" were. He then proceeded to fulfill a contract for a translation of the second part of *Faust*.[70]

In 1949 and 1950 especially, Pasternak sought to convey to his friends his philosophy of literature and human activity, perhaps to explain to them his chosen mode of existence—passing most of his time in Peredelkino, working on translations and on *Doctor Zhivago*, and continuing his innumerable friendships-by-mail. He was unwilling to write works of the kind that would find favor with the regime—not out of a desire to be an iconoclast but because his personality as a writer did not lend itself to expressions of patriotic fervor. For nothing in the world would he have traveled in the paths of such writers as Fedin and Aleksei Tolstoi—for whose aesthetic standards and willingness to conform he had little regard. He was equally reluctant to go after mere virtuosity; as he pointed out to a correspondent, "A good mastery of the pen, language, and a feeling for style," viewed as an aim in themselves, could easily supplant what he felt were the mainsprings of creativity: ". . . the long-discovered spiritual values which probably lie at the foundation of taste: love of people and gratitude to the past for its brilliance, next to a concern for repaying it with the same kind of beauty and warmth."[71]

Such thoughts echo formulations to be found in the pages of *Doctor Zhivago* and indicate that Pasternak liked to share and possibly formulate them with the most trusted of his correspondents at the same time he presented them in his manuscript. In a similar vein he wrote another correspondent in November, 1950:

If there is suffering anywhere, why should not my art suffer and myself with it? . . . I am speaking of the most artistic in the artist, of the sacrifice without which art becomes unnecessary and without which works of art are covered outside with a sprinkling of superficial talent, but inside stick to the ideas which mankind has known well and even outgrown since it emerged from savagery.[72]

Such a credo about art as a sacrifice was essential to the artist whose struggle to complete his work without compromise during those difficult years was in itself an act of heroism, of suffering for art's sake.

In 1949 the postwar purges began dying down. The following year Akhmatova was allowed to print a group of poems from the "Hail Peace" (or "Hail the World") cycle. The somewhat forced way in which these poems—inferior to her earlier achievement—were suffused with patriotic feelings made it clear that they were a command performance. Pasternak wrote to a friend that, while he rejoiced in this significant publication in the career of his previously silenced fellow poet, he could not but have misgivings about the kind of gesture that writing such a book represented; he hinted that the gesture was "repetitive" in relation to his own endeavors of twenty years before—an obvious allusion to his political stance in writing *Second Birth* (1932).[73]

But the lifting of the ban on the writers who had been attacked by Zhdanov was a slow process. None of Pasternak's original writings was published in 1950; he continued to work on translations. Part One of *Faust* was published in May, 1950, and Pasternak moved on to Part Two in December, qualifying the second part as "ridiculous stuff"—a reference to the thematic peculiarities of that part. He finished translating Part Two in 1951. It was estimated in Moscow that he earned 6,000 to 10,000 rubles a month ($1,500 to $2,500 in the Soviet exchange rate of the time).[74]

Despite his revived income, his friends apparently worried that he was being slighted in public recognition. There was even the imputation that he was a martyr to the cause of literary freedom. To such ideas the poet replied:

I have never considered myself in any way offended or passed over. If anyone thinks that to a detached observer I may appear to be a "martyr," then let me say that, first, I am not responsible for anyone's crazy ideas or ridiculous fancies and, secondly, it is sufficient that they who may be interested in such a theory should lift the ban on my books and let me mount the rostrum and this "semblance of martyrdom," which does *not exist* as far as I am concerned, will disappear by itself.[75]

Pasternak's forbearance and restraint cannot have been all "diplomatic," nor was he voicing such views out of sympathy or loyalty to the regime. One must conclude that such a statement was motivated by a spiritual acceptance of stark external circumstances—an acceptance that he felt strengthened his devotion to the task of completing *Doctor Zhivago.*

In 1951–52 there was no sign of relaxation of political tensions, and as Pasternak progressed on the novel, he was not encouraged by comments from writers or friends. In 1952 he wrote to his well-wisher Chikovani, whose verse he had admired since the 1930s and who had received the Stalin Prize in 1947: "Of those who have read my novel the majority are dissatisfied. They say it is a failure and that they expected more from me, that it is colourless, that it is not worthy of me, but I, acknowledging all this, just grin as though this abuse and condemnation were praise."[76] Cultural and aesthetic standards had not changed enough in the last years of Stalinism to allow for a spontaneous recognition of the merits of *Doctor Zhivago.* That same year, however, one bit of good news may have cheered him: the publication in New York of the collection *Muffled Voices,* which contained thirty-five poems by him.[77]

An enormously significant event in Soviet Russian history was the death in 1953 of Stalin at the age of seventy-four. Among the many changes that followed, restrictions on literature were eased, and more controversial and innovative literature and art began to appear. When Pasternak heard that Stalin was dead, he commented to Zinaida Nikolaevna that "a terrible man died, a man who drenched Russia in blood." Pasternak had long felt a horror of Stalin. Often in casual conversation he had concurred with Ivinskaia in her denunciations of Stalin and on one occasion had equated Stalinism with Shigaliovism."* The leniency with which Stalin is purported to have treated Pasternak did not diminish the

---

*The doctrine of Shigaliov, an unsavory character in Dostoevsky's *The Possessed*—a cold-blooded ideologist whose plans for the future happiness of mankind included the systematic sacrifice of millions of people. Pasternak asserted that even his Georgian poet friend Iashvili had been "bewitched" by the "Shigaliovism" that was so "prevalent" in 1937 (*Sketch for an Autobiography,* p. 90).

poet's sharp feelings about the tyrant. The hostility reached the point where Ivinskaia could speak of the "remarkable, silent duel" between Stalin and Pasternak.[78]

For Pasternak, Stalin's death had several significant consequences. First, in the amnesty that was granted to a great many prisoners, Ivinskaia was released and returned to Moscow within a matter of months. Second, after the death of the tyrant Fadeev gradually became aware of the untenable position in which he had put himself, having behaved over the past three decades as a docile instrument of Stalinism, with tragic consequences for many of the fellow writers above whom he had been placed. Fadeev—whose positive sides Pasternak knew and appreciated—later came to believe that, if he wanted to be honest and acknowledge the extent of his guilt, the only course of action left to him was suicide. Third, a process of liberalization was initiated after Stalin's death, which was soon termed the "Thaw" of the Soviet literary scene. Some highlights of the Thaw were the successful revival by the Moscow Satire Theater of Maiakovskii's *The Bathhouse*, an antiutopian play that challenged the foundations of Soviet life; the serialization of Ehrenburg's novelette *The Thaw*, an allegory of the post-Stalinian mood; and the publication by *Novyi mir* in December, 1953, of V. Pomerantsev's controversial essay "On Sincerity in Literature," and of Panfërov's *Mother Volga*, a depiction of the life of provincial party officials that proved so displeasing to authorities that its author was dismissed from the editorial board of the journal *Oktiabr* in 1954. These and similar events created a climate within which Pasternak felt that his novel might reasonably be expected to fit.[79]

At first, the phenomenon of the Thaw was welcome to him as to most other sincere Soviet intellectuals. They could only grieve for those who had disappeared under Stalin, details of whose fates were gradually revealed. Only in 1955, for example, did the Pasternaks find out with certainty that Titian Tabidze had died nineteen years before, and in October of that year Pasternak wrote Nina Aleksandrovna a heartfelt letter when he heard the report. Pasternak always was to give credit to Khrushchev for denouncing Stalin and for rehabilitating the Georgian's innocent victims. After the initial period of euphoria and high expectations wore off, however, the poet lost faith in any "thaw." As far as Khrushchev's personality was concerned, Pasternak was "staggered by [the leader's] verbosity and blustering boorishness." To Zinaida Nikolaevna, who was trying to make a case for Khrushchev's merits, the writer once observed, "After Stalin's death nothing has changed."[80]

Early in 1953, Pasternak spent several months in the Bolshevo Rest Home, near Moscow, recovering from the severe heart attack he had suffered in 1952. His first edition of the *Faust* translation and also the translations of several Shakespeare tragedies had just been published in Leningrad (a second edition of *Faust* would appear in 1955). He worked steadily on the novel, as well as on translations. The novel had priority over poetry; he even owned that he considered it his "sole business" and did not allow himself "to be distracted from it and to be squandered by poetry." Whatever lines of poetry entered his head he either discarded or remembered only in rudimentary form, without writing them down.

The short poems that he did compose that year he considered "second rate" in that they were "tender and musical, whereas poetry ought, in addition to music, to contain painting and meaning." It seems that more and more Pasternak was viewing his poetry as a training ground for his prose. According to Ivinskaia, he often said, "All my life I have wanted to write prose . . . writing verse is easier!" Having recovered from his heart attack, in 1953–54 he was giving all of his free time to the novel.[81]

After eight years of enforced creative silence, ten poems from *Doctor Zhivago* were published in the April, 1954, issue of *Znamia*. The poems were prefaced by the following note from the poet:

The novel will probably be completed in the course of the summer. It covers the period from 1903 to 1929, with an epilogue relating to World War II. The hero, Iu. A. Zhivago, a physician, a thinking man in search [of truth], with a creative and artistic bent, dies in 1929. Among his papers written in younger days, a number of poems are found, which will be attached to the book as a final chapter. Some of them are reproduced here.[82]

Official reaction to the poems was at best lukewarm. The same year, however, a collection including more favorably received poems—those dealing with war or revolution—was also printed by the Publishing House of Artistic Literature in Moscow. Discord was the keynote of the literary scene in 1954. The fluctuation of literary and political tides is indicated by two seemingly contradictory events that took place that year: the Stalinist Fadeev was replaced as secretary of the Writers' Union, while Aleksandr Tvardovskii, a leader in the fight for artistic freedom, was replaced by the more conservative Simonov as editor of *Novyi mir*. Nowhere were these contradictions better reflected than at the Second All-Union Congress of Soviet Writers that convened in December of that year and appeared in perspective as "an uneasy compromise between orthodoxy and liberalism." At the congress liberals made a strong case for increased concern with problems of form and technique, individual style and temperaments, human emotions and sincerity—at the same time rigid ideologists like Aleksei Surkov continued advocating the tightening of party control over literature.[83] In this ambiguous atmosphere Pasternak went on nurturing hopes for the publication of *Doctor Zhivago*.

At the same time his private life was undergoing new developments. Zinaida Nikolaevna had nursed her husband with the greatest devotion at the time of his heart attack in 1952, and she was hoping that his liaison with Ivinskaia—then still in the labor camp—was over. It is clear that in early 1953 he felt that out of gratitude to his wife, who "had saved his life," he should not continue his relation with Ivinskaia and broached the subject at the time to Ivinskaia's daughter, Irina. That did not prevent him from making endeavors to bring about Ivinskaia's release, however. In spite of Pasternak's "decision," as soon as Ivinskaia and he were reunited after her return to Moscow, they agreed they would live together "come what might, in any manner possible." The revived happiness of their association kept growing.[84]

The summer of 1954 was a time of particular joy and expectation for Pasternak

Pasternak near the dacha in
Peredelkino, 1954.
Einaudi.

and Ivinskaia. Ivinskaia's children were staying with her aunt in Sukhinichi, a circumstance that allowed the lovers to spend the summer together in Moscow. Once again Ivinskaia had become pregnant. Copies of the near-complete manuscript of the novel were circulating among various acquaintances, and many in Moscow were awaiting its publication in book form and in serial. The name of an editor was also frequently mentioned, for a large volume of Pasternak's poetry was being simultaneously prepared for publication. An unfortunate accident disrupted this hopeful atmosphere when, in the autumn of 1954, Ivinskaia gave birth to a stillborn child. Pasternak—who probably felt that the expected birth might have brought about a clearer solution to the problem of their future life together—was particularly distressed.

Overcoming her own depression, Ivinskaia started looking for an arrangement that would enable her and Pasternak to spend time together under the same roof. In the summer of 1955 she rented part of a dacha on the shore of the Lake of Izmalkovo, adjacent to Peredelkino. In the autumn they moved to a nearby dacha, surrounded by huge poplars, which became a regular abode for Ivinskaia's family—in addition to the apartment on Potapov Street. There Ivinskaia experienced "the happiness of daily communion" with Pasternak, under the benign eyes of their landlord, Sergei Kuzmich, and his family. In 1959, Ivinskaia moved to a larger house with its own garden plot on a hill in Peredelkino. In these successive abodes Pasternak and Ivinskaia kept open house on Sundays.[85]

Pasternak was still frowned upon by the Soviet literary hierarchy, as was testified to by the violent attacks made against him by the Soviet journalist Viktor Poltoratskii during an official tour in the United States in 1955. Nonetheless, his standing was still so high with those truly knowledgeable in things literary, even within the Eastern Bloc, that the German poet Bertolt Brecht, recipient of the Stalin Prize for 1955, insisted that Pasternak translate his acceptance speech into Russian. Pasternak agreed to do so only reluctantly—excerpts from Brecht's work published in an East German poetry anthology had conveyed to him the image of an over politicized poet with whom he felt little sympathy. Pasternak was to feel differently about Brecht and see in him more than a staunch ideologist after attending a successful 1956 performance of *The Caucasian Chalk Circle*, directed by Helene Weigel, Brecht's widow, and after reading more of the German poet's work.[86]

Occasional visits to Moscow theaters were a rare luxury for Pasternak. He spent the whole of 1955 working assiduously on *Doctor Zhivago*, having freed himself from the necessity of doing other work. He realized, however, that it was impossible to stretch such an "unpaid leave" over a period of many years, and he was eager to bring the task to completion. He told a correspondent that he considered it "his inner duty" to write the book, though for some time now he had been feeling that it was "absolutely inappropriate for publication," a reference both to the size of the manuscript, which was "very considerable in volume," and also, no doubt, to the misgivings he had about its acceptability in the context of Soviet publishing.[87]

At last, during the winter of 1955–56, Pasternak completed the manuscript of *Doctor Zhivago*. He proceeded to send copies to several Moscow publishers. By 1956 three copies of the novel were with individual publishers: one copy was in the possession of Simonov at *Novyi mir*; one of two handsomely bound brown volumes was at the journal *Znamia* (whose editor, Vadim Kozhevnikov, had begun reading it), and the other was with the State Publishing House for Literature (Goslitizdat). It was in the influential *Novyi mir* that Pasternak placed his chief hopes; he had negotiated a contract there at an earlier stage of his work on the novel.[88]

Shortly after completing *Doctor Zhivago*, Pasternak went for a walk in the woods near Peredelkino with his friend and neighbor Fedin and read to him the text, chapter after chapter. According to a letter Pasternak wrote to a French friend, Fedin wept at certain passages.[89] Later, however, when the editorial board of *Novyi mir* voted against publication of *Zhivago*, Fedin was in accord with the other board members.

By 1956 the party's attempts to control and censure literature had relaxed to such an extent and the defenders of literary freedom had become so outspoken that Pasternak had good reason to believe his novel would be published. Some of the works published that year created a stir in literary circles: *Znamia* finished the serialization of Ehrenburg's *The Thaw*; Semen Kirsanov's poem "Seven Days of the Week," a scathing condemnation of the inhumanity of Soviet bureaucracy, appeared; *Literaturnaia gazeta* printed an article on the Russian émigré Nobel Prize winner Ivan Bunin; and Valdimir Dudintsev's novel *Not by Bread Alone*, published in *Novyi mir*, sympathetically portrayed a talented man struggling with bureaucratic red tape. The two-volume almanac *Literary Moscow*, also appearing in 1956, was an almost defiant demonstration of the writers' belief in artistic liberty; its contents ranged from texts by long-silenced members of the prewar generation, such as Akhmatova, Pasternak, Nikolai Zabolotskii, Tsvetaeva, and Olesha, to pieces by some of the most daring new writers of the younger generation, such as the poets Evgenii Evtushenko and Robert Rozhdestvenskii and the prose writers Vladimir Tendriakov, Aleksandr Iashin, and Iurii Nagibin.[90]

An almost logical consequence of the Thaw was Fadeev's suicide in May, 1956. Fadeev was perhaps one of the most tragic victims of the Stalin years. Initially talented and sincere, he had become a moral and emotional cripple long before he physically perished. In 1955–56 he was acidly attacked for his many nefarious actions during the Stalin regime. The attack expressed the liberated spirit of the time; at the party congress that year the prominent novelist Mikhail Sholokhov asserted that Fadeev had allowed himself to be corrupted by his "love of power." It was also rumored that Fadeev had been asked to issue a third version of *The Young Guard*, to do away with the Stalinist-inspired revisions of the second edition. Since Khrushchev was also denouncing Stalinism, Fadeev may well have felt that there was no longer a place for prominent Stalinists in Russia. His alcoholism and the personal attacks upon him reinforced his sense of helplessness and led the former secretary of the Writers' Union to his tragic end.[91]

Pasternak's reaction to Fadeev's suicide revealed both his condemnation of his colleague's former actions and his deep sympathy for the way Fadeev had tried to "set things right" by his final dramatic gesture. All of this Pasternak expressed with courage and characteristic independence of mind. Upon first hearing of the event he remarked, "It absolves many of the wrongs he did, willingly or unwillingly." Later, while Fadeev's body lay in state in an open coffin in the Hall of Columns in Moscow, Pasternak, after looking closely at the dead man, said in a loud, clear voice for everybody around to hear: "Aleksandr Aleksandrovich has rehabilitated himself," upon which he bowed low before leaving. Under the immediate impact of Fadeev's suicide, Pasternak composed a whole new section for a chapter of *Doctor Zhivago* and inserted it into his draft.[92]

At the time of Fadeev's death Pasternak again had serious doubts about the possibility of his novel appearing in the Soviet Union, but he had not yet thought of having it appear abroad. Sergio d'Angelo had arrived in Moscow in March, 1956, as an emissary of the Italian Communist party, and entanglements began. He was keeping an eye out for manuscripts that might interest the well-known Milan publisher Giangiacomo Feltrinelli,* while working in the Italian section of Radio Moscow.[93]

In May, in an Italian-language broadcast, Radio Moscow announced the forth-

---

*Feltrinelli was born into one of Milan's wealthiest families, and as a young man avowed Socialism and then Communism. Paradoxically, however, it was as a capitalist publisher that this Marxist millionaire scored his greatest success, with such titles as *Doctor Zhivago* and Giuseppe di Lampedusa's *The Leopard*.

Pasternak, spring, 1956. *Archives*
Jacqueline de Proyart.

coming publication of *Doctor Zhivago*, "a novel written in diary form and span-
ning three-fourths of a century." The announcement struck d'Angelo as important, and he immediately went to Peredelkino, arriving on a beautiful May day.[94]

D'Angelo's concern took Pasternak completely by surprise—he had never
thought that the novel would be of interest to a foreign publisher, and he had
never considered approaching one. D'Angelo learned from Pasternak that there
had been no negative reaction to the novel from the tentative Soviet publisher and
then pointed out that the publication had been officially announced and there was
no reason not to have it published abroad. Pasternak agreed to this reasoning—
during the conversation he had made up his mind that the manuscript must be
published in the West if it could not be published in the Soviet Union. He entrusted a copy of the manuscript to d'Angelo, remarking to him, however, in jest:
"You are as of now invited to my execution." To Zinaida Nikolaevna, who
strongly opposed the action, Pasternak said, "I am a writer. I write in order to be
printed."[95]

A few days later, on a trip to Berlin, d'Angelo handed the manuscript to Feltrinelli, who set about having it translated. A formal contract between Pasternak
and Feltrinelli was negotiated by d'Angelo and signed by the writer on June 13,

1956. The contract gave Feltrinelli the rights to the Italian-language publication of *Doctor Zhivago* and all other "foreign" editions, but not the audiovisual and cinematographic rights, nor rights for any other work by Pasternak. Such rights were obtained only later by Feltrinelli.[96]

As soon as they found out about Pasternak's move, Ivinskaia and Nikolai Bannikov, Pasternak's friend and the editor of his poetry anthology at Goslitizdat, expressed anger that the writer had offered the novel to d'Angelo. In a note to Ivinskaia, Bannikov labeled Pasternak's action "treachery." From the viewpoint of the inner circle of his closest friends, however, his action was treachery only to the extent that it could well foil their efforts at having his works published in the Soviet Union. Upon discovering that the novel had been sent abroad, the hierarchy of the Writers' Union was dismayed, insofar as plans for a Soviet edition had not yet crystallized. Soviet officials, such as Dmitrii Polikarpov, head of the Cultural Section of the Central Committee of the Party, were concerned that, should an expurgated version of *Doctor Zhivago* be agreed to by a Soviet journal while the Italians published the full text, a politically embarrassing situation might ensue. In two conversations Polikarpov asked Ivinskaia to try her best to get the manuscript back from d'Angelo or to delay publication abroad. Ivinskaia, who wanted to try to assure maximum chances for a Soviet publication of the novel—even though in curtailed form, if worse should come to worse—agreed to make a compromise and ask Feltrinelli to delay the novel's appearance in Italy.[97]

Polikarpov instructed Anatolii Kotov, director of Goslitizdat, to take another look at the novel and make a contract with Pasternak. Kotov appointed as editor of the novel Anatolii Starostin, "a passionate admirer of Pasternak's work," who announced, "I shall make this into something that will reflect glory on the Russian people." As opposed to the leadership of the Writers' Union, which was hostile to the publication of the novel, Goslitizdat was eager to bring it out. Presumably on the basis of a sanction received from Polikarpov, the Foreign Section of the Union of Writers granted authorization for *Doctor Zhivago* to be published abroad. Thus Pasternak's action in handing over the manuscript to Feltrinelli in effect reactivated plans for its publication in the Soviet Union. It may be surmised, however, that, from the Writers' Union viewpoint, the promise to publish the novel was only a maneuver to gain time in the hope of recovering the manuscript from Feltrinelli and frustrating publication abroad. About that time the Soviet officials asked the Italian Communist party to delay the Italian publication; the party head, Palmiro Togliatti, met personally with Feltrinelli for that purpose. The Milan publisher promised to deal in a friendly and reasonable way with the Soviet officials.[98]

Pasternak's poetry continued to appear in Russian journals despite the problems involved in publishing *Doctor Zhivago*. In September a collection of his poems entitled "New Verses" appeared in *Znamia*. Goslitizdat agreed to publish a large volume of Pasternak's poetry (including all the Zhivago poems except "Hamlet"), to be edited by Bannikov. That collection never went beyond the stage of galley proofs. Two collections of Pasternak's poetry that had been announced in official Soviet bibliographic catalogues also never materialized.[99] Pasternak continued to work on *Sketch for an Autobiography*, which he intended as a preface to an edition of collected works, including *Doctor Zhivago* and recent poetry.

In September, Pasternak may have received a letter from the editorial board of *Novyi mir* explaining why they found the novel unsuitable for publication. Whether or not the letter was sent to Pasternak at that early date remains a question, but on October 25, 1958, after Pasternak had been awarded the Nobel Prize, a lengthy letter of rejection from the editorial board of *Novyi mir*, addressed to Pasternak and dated September, *1956*, was published in *Literaturnaia gazeta*. There is reason to believe that the letter was merely a fabrication to be used in the context of the 1958 campaign against Pasternak. D'Angelo held this suspicion because he saw Pasternak frequently from May, 1956, until the end of 1957, and the poet never mentioned such a document. Ivinskaia asserts that d'Angelo's suspicions may be well founded.[100]

Whether or not Pasternak received such a letter, it is clear that by the autumn of 1956 he had been told about the decision, and his hopes for the novel's publication were low (on behalf of *Novyi mir's* editorial board, Krivitskii was still, it is true, holding out to Ivinskaia the hope that excerpts might be printed). As early as the autumn of 1955, Pasternak had lamented: "I don't believe they will ever publish . . . [the novel]. I have come to the conclusion that I should pass it round to be read by all and sundry—it should be given to anyone who asks for it, because I do not believe it will ever appear in print." Yet up to January, 1957, Pasternak had some hope that there would be a Soviet edition of the novel. By February that hope had gone.[101]

Being aware that *Doctor Zhivago* might appear abroad, the authorities kept close vigilance over Pasternak's correspondence and then took more drastic measures: from November, 1956, until February, 1957, almost all of his incoming and outgoing mail was intercepted. During the winter of 1956–57, however, no obstacle was put in the way of his receiving visits from a number of foreigners. A Slavic scholar from France, Hélène Peltier, visited the Pasternaks and became a close friend of the poet. During her stay she met other artists at the dacha: Fedin, Ivanov, Akhmatova, the pianist Sviatoslav Richter, and the conductor Neigauz. Among others who visited Pasternak were Jean ("Dyma") Neuvecelle, son of the poet Viacheslav Ivanov, and the Slavic scholars Roman Jakobson and Michel Aucouturier.[102]

Also at that time he frequently saw another young Slavic scholar doing research in Moscow, Countess Jacqueline de Proyart, the curator of the Tolstoy Museum in Paris. She first came with friends to spend the evening of January 1, 1957, at the poet's dacha. Within the next few weeks she was to have many long conversations with Pasternak, who soon developed such a degree of friendship for and confidence in her that in early February he entrusted her with copies of both *Doctor Zhivago* and *Sketch for an Autobiography*. She took them with her when she returned to France and passed them on to the publisher Gaston Gallimard with the suggestion that they should be published in French. Pasternak signed a contract that spring with Gallimard either because, as Ivinskaia suggests, he felt closer to the French than to the Italian language or because he was disturbed by hearing of the many misprints going into the Italian edition.

Gallimard's copy of the manuscript had previously been in Simonov's possession (at some point it had been bound in blue); it was the most authoritative text of the novel, according to Pasternak. Proyart had offered to look after Pasternak's literary interests and author's rights in the West, and for that purpose the poet had signed a power of attorney and given it to her on February 7, 1957. Proyart most scrupulously and eagerly endeavored to fulfill this responsibility, in spite of many complications and difficulties that arose in dealing with Pasternak's Italian publisher. Only when those difficulties became insuperable did she ask Pasternak to sign a document releasing her from any legal responsibility for actions she had undertaken on his behalf, and this he did on April 12, 1960.[103]

During the winter of 1956–57, Goslitizdat—which had had a copy of *Doctor Zhivago* since 1955—entertained the notion of publishing a suitably edited version. Kornelii Zelinskii, a writer, publishing-house official, and old friend of Pasternak's, negotiated a contract for a version to be judiciously abridged by the editor A. I. Puzikov. Pasternak was very reluctant to accept such an abridgment and would doubtless have continued to fight vigorously for a version acceptable to him had he not become seriously ill in mid-February, 1957, suffering from what he thought was "neuritis" in the leg he had fractured in childhood. It is most likely that, had it not been for the illness, a solution would have been reached, and the novel would have been sent to the printer.[104]

Pasternak's condition was first diagnosed as acute arthritis, and he was hospitalized. In 1956, perhaps inspired by premonition, he had composed a deeply moving poem entitled "In Hospital," an intense religious evocation of an illness and stay in a hospital emergency ward.* Now the situation described in the poem became reality. Pasternak entered a branch of the Kremlin hospital at Uzkoe (formerly an estate of the princes Trubetskoi), reserved for particularly eminent Soviet figures. His condition became alarming; the physical pain was unbearable, and he thought he was dying. He stayed in the hospital for almost four months. To a correspondent the poet described the "mysterious ailment" in his right knee as combined meniscitis and sciatica, adding that the pain was so acute that he sometimes lost consciousness. The pain (which he believed to be neuralgia) was to continue after his release from the clinic. The alternate and far more plausible diagnosis is that Pasternak suffered from osteosarcoma close to the knee, which later would spread to the chest through metastasis, as we may now infer with hindsight.

On his hospital bed he listened to visitors' accounts of an event he would have given much to attend—the staging by the Moscow Art Theatre of Schiller's *Maria Stuart* in his translation, with the famous actress Alla Tarasova in the title

---

*For a discussion of this poem, see Chapter 17.

role. Pasternak continued writing, whenever the pain allowed, working on the one-volume edition of his poetry edited by Ivinskaia and Bannikov and writing several letters to Ivinskaia.[105]

The secretariat of the Writers' Union had him write to Feltrinelli and ask him to delay publication for six months. Radio Moscow and *Znamia* had spoken of the impending publication of the novel, but Pasternak's letter to Feltrinelli put an end to such announcements.[106]

Early in 1957, when the policies of the Soviet Union grew stricter as a result of the Hungarian uprising, Goslitizdat also requested a postponement of the Italian publication of *Doctor Zhivago* until September of that year—the projected time for the appearance of a Soviet edition. Feltrinelli was unaware that the Soviet publication was itself questionable and that the request was a ruse to gain time. Feltrinelli's theoretical and romantic approach to Marxism evidently made it hard for him to perceive some of the realities of Soviet literary politics.* He replied in a conciliatory tone that he would comply. In March, Pasternak again wrote the Italian publisher repeating the request for a delay, partly because of the dilatoriness of Soviet editors and partly because of his illness. Feltrinelli again agreed but set the beginning of September as the latest publication date.[107]

While he was recovering from his illness, Pasternak went over the text of *Sketch for an Autobiography*, which had been written in May and June, 1956. Toward the summer, on the advice of his doctors, he spent some time at the Uzkoe Resthouse near Moscow. When he returned from Uzkoe, he wrote poetry. One of the new poems was "Bacchanalia," in which he "paid his tribute" to an idea of "a mixture of frivolity and mystery" he had had in the late winter before his illness. He felt that this poem enabled him "to escape from this cluster of winter impressions" and continue with the other themes he wanted to treat in his forthcoming collection *When Skies Clear* (*Kogda razguliaetsia*).[108]

During the summer, while Zelinskii continued revising *Doctor Zhivago*, Aleksei Surkov, secretary of the Writers' Union, tried to prevent the publication of the novel in Italy. He presented Pasternak with an ultimatum: either sign a telegram to Feltrinelli asking him not to publish the novel because "its publication in its present form was not possible" or face the prospect of being arrested. He was given one or two days to make up his mind.

Pasternak found this decision agonizing. Because of his "proud" temperament he felt that sending the telegram would make him look a fool—asking Feltrinelli to stop publication of a work that he only recently had told the publisher was the main goal of his life.[109]

Ivinskaia and others made Pasternak see that he must sign the telegram, convincing him that Feltrinelli would not take it at face value. For one thing, the telegram was in Russian, and Feltrinelli and Pasternak had a prior understanding that the publisher was to accept as genuine only telegrams in French. Furthermore, contracts had been signed with publishers in other European countries,

---

*Thus, while the anti-Pasternak campaign was in full swing in the fall of 1958, Feltrinelli would observe that "the whole of the Pasternak affair" in the Soviet Union was merely a "struggle between factions" (Feltrinelli, letter of November 17, 1958, to Jacqueline de Proyart).

and publication could not be stopped at this stage anyway.* Pasternak signed the official telegram in Russian, and as soon as he had a chance he sent through Proyart a private message to Feltrinelli explaining the reasons for the telegram.[110] Those reasons were clarified in a letter he wrote to Proyart in November:

How happy I am that neither Gallimard nor Collins are allowing themselves to be taken in by the fraudulent telegrams which they [the Soviet authorities] forced me to sign under threat of being arrested, outlawed, and deprived of means of existence, and which I signed only because I have the assurance (which did not deceive me) that no one in the world would believe in these false texts, which were not composed by me but by agents of the state and forced upon me. In these telegrams forced upon me, I was told to request that publishers return to me the manuscripts of the novel so I could polish its style—only that, and for no other purpose. Have you ever seen a more touching concern for the beauty of [literary] works and authors' rights? And with what idiotic cowardice is all that being conducted. Under odious pressure I have been compelled to protest the violence [*sic*] and illegal nature of the fact that I am esteemed, recognized, translated, and published in the West. How impatiently am I awaiting the appearance of the novel!

Pasternak went on to say that it was useless to think that anything by him would be published in the Soviet Union because of deteriorating relationships between him and those in charge ("on se brouille avec moi de plus en plus").[111] Ivinskaia recalls that the tactics of official coercion and Pasternak's own yielding to pressures in signing the telegram left him with "scars that never healed."[112]

Another traumatic moment for Pasternak came on August 16, 1957, when a special, "enlarged" meeting of the Secretariat of the Union of Writers was convened to discuss his "behavior" in sending his manuscript abroad. Fearing that if Pasternak answered the summons to attend he would wax indignant and suffer a heart attack, Ivinskaia attended the meeting as his representative. Prodded and supported by venomous remarks from such writers as Vasilii Azhaiev, Sobolev, and Kataev, the chairman of the meeting, Surkov, vehemently denounced Pasternak's "treachery." Only isolated participants like Tvardovskii were prepared to give Ivinskaia a chance to speak. She and Anatolii Starostin did their best to present Pasternak's viewpoint, but in the end a very harsh motion of censure was passed against him. In its wake Pasternak remarked to his friend Gladkov, "They want to make a new Zoshchenko out of me."[113]

As the September publication date for the Italian edition neared, two high-ranking representatives of the Italian Communist party, Mario Alicata and Giovanni Sanna, went to Feltrinelli to insist that he abandon the project. Surkov, taking the opportunity of a meeting of Soviet and Italian poets and writers in Italy,† also saw Feltrinelli and renewed pressure on him to stop publication, warning of possible danger to Pasternak. To that Feltrinelli replied, "I have too

---

*Various European publishers, including Gallimard in France, Kuno Fischer in Germany, and Collins in England, were indeed proceeding with editions of the novel.

†Surkov himself had barred Pasternak from attending this meeting, though the Italian authorities had invited him. Moreover, crossing Akhmatova's name off the list of participants invited by the Italians, Surkov had summarily substituted his own name (this action triggered jokes in the Soviet literary community about the incongruous substitute the Italians would have for a lady of Akhmatova's charm).

high an opinion of the freedom writers enjoy in the Soviet Union to believe this."
By that time Feltrinelli was determined not to give in. He held back publication
for only a few weeks. An Italian writer passing through Moscow brought him a
note from Pasternak telling him to use his own judgment in the matter.[114]

When Surkov realized that he could not stop publication, he called a press
conference in Milan on October 19 and angrily claimed that the novel was being
published against the author's will; the action, he said, was a result of the cold
war. The press conference was reported in the Italian Communist organ *Unità*
three days later.[115]

In its summer, 1957, issue, the Polish literary journal *Opinie* published excerpts from *Doctor Zhivago*. In an accompanying note the editors explained that
they were giving a preview of a novel soon to appear in the Soviet Union—"a
broad, intricate story about the fate of the Russian intelligentsia and their ideological transformation, which was frequently accompanied by tragic conflicts." It
appears that plans were afoot in Poland for the publication of the entire novel but
that they were suspended for fear of endangering the poet. Pasternak did not ap-
prove of such timorous consideration; a visitor reported that he indicated in September of that year that "his Polish friends were doing him a disservice when—
fearing to hurt him—they abstained from releasing the novel."[116] For all the danger he would run, Pasternak would have preferred that his novel appear in Poland, as well as in western Europe.

In 1957, with Nikita Khrushchev firmly in power, the outward liberalism in
art and literature that had prevailed for two to three years disappeared. Khrushchev sharply criticized the novelist Vladimir Dudintsev, and Simonov, Dudintsev's publisher, lost his position as editor-in-chief of *Novyi mir*. In the August, 1957, issue of *Kommunist* the secretary-general of the party lashed out at
literary revisionists; Evgenii Evtushenko, Zinovii Rozhdestvenskii, and Ilia
Ehrenburg were among those individually censured. At a routine meeting in
Moscow of the Creative Intelligentsia in November of that year, Surkov deplored
the "exaggerated" praise that had been recently lavished on modernists silenced
under Stalin, including Tsvetaeva, Pasternak, Meierkhold, Pilniak, Bulgakov,
and Babel. Such an atmosphere was to alter the behavior of the literary hierarchy
toward Pasternak.[117]

Typical of the attitude of many rank-and-file Soviet *littérateurs* toward Pasternak was the caustic treatment the poet received in a book entitled *Satirical Verses*
that Sergei Vasilev published in September, 1957. Vasilev mockingly attributed
to Pasternak the following statement:

> What's this thing, called "here and now"?
> Dream-dust frail and momentary.
> From dacha-high I spit on thee
> And all that is contemporary.
> I spit on thee and soon I see
> Along the selfsame track
> My spittle dainty as can be
> Come bouncing up right back.[118]

The lampoon perpetuated a view that many in official Soviet literary circles had been voicing on and off since the 1930s—that Pasternak chose to remove himself from contemporary reality. In that autumn of 1957, Pasternak knew how to read such signs of the times as harbingers of the coming ostracism.

The coolness of the official attitude toward him did not mean that Pasternak was not receiving marks of interest and attention. On September 15, Evtushenko, accompanying a Slavic scholar from Italy, Angelo Maria Ripellino, paid a visit to the poet in Peredelkino. Ripellino reported that Pasternak told him how strongly he felt about the towering significance of his novel in comparison to his earlier work, exclaiming:

It hurts me to hear you speaking of my poetry and earlier merits (as if they could endure) with excessive kindliness, and in the same tone drop an allusion to my novel—whereas the novel and my past are two things which cannot be compared; and not only is this novel one hundred times more remarkable than everything I have done up to now: it is, as a matter of fact, the only work that bears any discussion, because its pages break up the continuity of development in the same way as did the changeover from steam to atomic energy; and whereas all my poetry—and with it all contemporary poetry—has dwindled, staying back on the river bank we have left behind, the novel, no matter how poor or weak, is the only light gleaming on that bank toward which we are sailing.[119]

Evtushenko has left a more subjective and impressionistic account of the visit and the atmosphere in which it took place. Pasternak's figure appeared to him as breathing a sparkling freshness, like freshly cut lilac. He was very effusive, and his mobile face was lit up with an amazingly childlike smile. "In effect," commented Evtushenko, "how much spiritual daring should one have in oneself to retain the ability to smile thus in such an unsmiling age!" Evtushenko—for whom this was the first of four encounters with Pasternak—later claimed that Pasternak acted on people who associated with him "not as a man but a fragrance, as a light, as a rustle." Interpreting in a *sui generis* manner Pasternak's imagery of the two river banks, the young poet claimed that because of the many years Pasternak had spent in isolation in his dacha (which gave him the precious ability to commune with himself and nature) he was to a good extent out of touch with many facets of contemporary existence. That existence appeared to him as "on the other bank of the river of time," distinguishable through thick haze, mostly thanks to his unusual spiritual insight (rather than actual acquaintance with that existence). Evtushenko did not mention that during the conversation Pasternak urged him not to dilute his own talent by capitulating and writing the verse the establishment wanted him to write.[120]

On November 10, 1957, *L'Espresso* published the first installment of a series of extracts from the novel, unfortunately choosing almost exclusively the anti-Soviet passages. On November 22, the first edition of the novel appeared in Italian under the title *Il Dottor Živago*. At a reception given that day at the Hotel Continental in Milan, which was attended by *le tout Milan*, Feltrinelli presented the book. The first printing of six thousand immediately sold out. It was followed by two other printings before the end of the month.[121]

Toward the end of 1957, Gerd Ruge, correspondent in Moscow for the West German radio network, set out to interview Pasternak in Peredelkino. The journalist "had not expected to find him at the front door, waving and smiling." Ruge reported: "I found one of the freest human beings I have ever known, using the word not to denote external freedom but as the attribute of someone sovereign, confident, open and true. . . . One does not get the impression of prolonged isolation." It is more than plausible to infer that Pasternak derived much of that freedom and confidence from his continuing "dialogue" with some of the greatest minds of all times. In his conversation with Ruge he discussed at length some of these major writers. While disapproving of the "Rilke cult" in the West, he was angered by the unjust and even nasty criticism of the Austrian poet coming from East Germany; although he admired much in the achievements of Proust, Mann, and Joyce, he found "something missing" in the works of all three of them—and the common missing element could be a "divine spark" linking literary creation with the transcendent. "He spoke of Goethe and Shakespeare as though they were his contemporaries and spoke about them in their own languages." When asked about the 1917 Revolution, Pasternak commented:

The proclamation, the tumult, the excitement are over. Now something else is growing, something new. It is growing imperceptibly and quietly, as the grass grows. It is growing as fruit does, and it is growing in the young. The essential thing in this epoch is that a new freedom is being born.

According to Ruge, Pasternak said that he was "grateful to his age and to his country, for his work and his strength had been shaped by them." Turning to *Doctor Zhivago*, Pasternak told his visitor that he did not deny one word of it but objected to people seeing it as an indictment of Soviet reality. "I deplore the fuss now being made about my book. Everybody's writing about it, but who in fact has read it? What do they quote from it? Always the same passages—three pages perhaps [the passages rich in ideological formulas], out of a book of 700 pages."[122]

While no word was being uttered in Moscow about a Soviet edition of *Doctor Zhivago*, Pasternak's name could still be seen there on title pages. In 1957, 25,000 copies of the third edition of his translation of *Faust* were published in Moscow. The State Publishing House of Artistic Literature published an *Anthology of Soviet Russian Poetry in Two Volumes* that included twelve poems by Pasternak (as well as four by Tsvetaeva).[123]

Early in 1958, following a recurrence of the ailment in his leg, Pasternak once again had to be hospitalized, this time until May. To a correspondent he complained that he had been robbed by illness of over three months of his life in time spent in the clinic.[124]

The decade of the 1950s had already brought Pasternak's greatest joys—his relationship with Ivinskaia and the printing of *Doctor Zhivago*—and such sorrows as Ivinskaia's arrest, the sharp decline in his health, and the continuing official attacks on his work. Ironically, in spite of official criticism that Pasternak did not write poetry that was accessible to the Russian masses, he had encountered cheering approval at every poetry reading (the sort of event that in Russia typically is attended by mass audiences). What Pasternak referred to as "the novel around the novel"—including the heartwarming developments and the intrigues surrounding the publication of *Doctor Zhivago*—was just beginning.[125]

11

The Pasternak Affair

1958–59

Nulle puissance humaine ne peut forcer le retranchement de la liberté du coeur.

[The liberty of the heart is a bulwark that no human force can storm.]

Bernard de Fontenelle[1]

The writer in no way considers his works as a *means*. They are *their own ends*, they are so far from being a means for himself and for others that, when necessary, he sacrifices *his* existence to *their* existence.

Karl Marx[2]

What you write about Stockholm [the possibility that Pasternak will be awarded the Nobel Prize] will never happen, because my government will never give its agreement to any distinction for me.

This and much else is grievous and sad. But you will never guess how insignificant is the place that these characteristics of the era occupy in my existence. And on the other hand, it's precisely these insurmountable fatalities that give life momentum, depth, and earnestness, and make it quite extraordinary—sovereignly joyful, magic, and real.

Pasternak (May, 1958)[3]

. . . in his declining days—when the authorities, to the accompaniment of much phony indignation, were planning to expel him from Russia—[Pasternak] carried a phial of poison in his pocket in order, if need be, to complete the long list of Soviet poets who committed suicide.

Abram Tertz (Andrei Siniavskii)[4]

In 1958 the Royal Swedish Academy voted to award Boris Pasternak the Nobel Prize for Literature in recognition of "his notable achievement in both contemporary lyrical poetry and the field of the great Russian [epic] narrative tradition."[5] The award brought a time of great tribulation for Pasternak as he became the center of a *cause célèbre*, the "Pasternak Affair." The episode was a conspicuous landmark between the publication of Zamiatin's *We* in 1924 and the appearance of Aleksandr Solzhenitsyn's *The Gulag Archipelago* in 1973 and was one engagement in the battle waged by Soviet writers to broaden the range of material that could be published in the Soviet Union.

Though there was no official comment in the months following the publication of *Doctor Zhivago* in Italy in November, 1957, party authorities—including Khrushchev—were attentive to both the foreign response to the novel and the preparation of various translations. Given this official silence and the hesitant attitude toward him, it is not surprising that in the months preceding the award Pasternak's literary activity (and thus his livelihood) remained dependent on translations. In 1958 several of his translations were published: Schiller's *Maria Stuart*, which came to be the standard translation for Soviet productions of the play; a new—and the last—edition of *Poems About Georgia and Georgian Poets*; and three long poems in an edition of *Selected Works* of the great Hungarian romantic poet Sándor Petofi. Because of the bleak outlook for publication of his novel in the Soviet Union, and out of concern for future income, in the spring Pasternak suggested to Goslitizdat that they reissue his Shakespeare translations.[6]

Though the brief post-Stalinism literary thaw had been followed by a much harsher ideological climate, there seems to have been an ambivalence in the demands for party-line socialist realism in 1958. Works by writers who had been subjected to criticism or censure, such as Vera Panova, Fedor Panfërov, and Anna Akhmatova, were published during the year. Such relaxation of attitudes was limited, however: Mikhail Zoshchenko died in that year, artistically broken and denied official forgiveness or honor, and the poet Nikolai Zabolotskii, who had been limited to publishing translations, also died during the year. Zabolotskii had never been officially expelled from the Writers' Union; nonetheless, his intensely personal and apolitical idealism had resulted in an enforced stay in Siberia from 1938 to 1946. Such treatment, along with his death from heart disease, suggests an uncomfortable resemblance to Pasternak's own circumstances. One can only conclude that in 1958, although the Soviet literary winter was not a painfully bitter one, it was cold and threatening. Perhaps the immense popularity of Vsevolod Kochetov's socialist-realist anti-Thaw novel *The Brothers Ershov*, is the best indication of the direction the wind blew from: in less than a month that scathing attack on what Kochetov portrayed as the arrogance of intellectuals sold a half million copies. The tightening of the screws on the literary scene was the result of the authorities' deep-seated uneasiness and their sense of their vulnerability in the aftermath of the 1956 revolts and of conflict among the elite of the Soviet hierarchy.[7]

Naturally in such a climate Pasternak's position could only be delicate. While no direct pressure was put upon him until the summer, he could not help but be

Pasternak at his desk, fall,
1958.

aware of unspoken pressures. Moreover, his health was poor. After his three-month stay in the hospital in early 1958 he continued to complain to correspondents of "terrible" bouts of neuritis in his leg. In May he even considered surgical removal of a meniscus from his knee, though by then his leg was much improved. His stay in the hospital had disheartened him, interfered with his writing, and discouraged long-range plans. He ascribed his depression to the danger that his physical condition would deteriorate and to strong fears of outside interference that would hamper his productivity.[8]

Interest in Pasternak's work abroad, enhanced by the publication of *Doctor Zhivago*, led to the publication (in March in the English periodical *Encounter* and shortly thereafter in *Die Zeit*) of Gerd Ruge's article about his interview with Pasternak the preceding winter. The article prompted the German poet Renate Schweitzer to write Pasternak. By April a correspondence had blossomed between the two poets. Pasternak took an interest in the religious symbolism pervading Schweitzer's verse.[9]

In their earliest correspondence he told Schweitzer that the basis of her admiration for his work was inadequate, inasmuch as she had not yet read *Doctor Zhivago*, which he believed was his crowning achievement. He felt that the novel was both deeper and "more modest" than his earlier work, and also was more successfully circumscribed in scope. He defined some of the aesthetic ideals that had inspired him, such as concern with clarity of expression and the poetic quality of historical existence and an involvement with important issues. In a letter to her a month later he predicted that his book would probably be attacked for its simple, naïve, transparent language and commonplace elements, while Communist critics would pounce on it for political reasons.[10]

Meanwhile Pasternak had received letters from admirers in France and Germany. In one of his replies he indicated that he felt a lessening of official pressure on him. The respite was to be only temporary, however, for in June, 1958, the French edition of *Doctor Zhivago*, published by Gallimard, renewed Western publicity, and therefore Soviet concern, about the book. Several French authors, including Albert Camus, sent him letters that in the warmth of their response to the book surprised and moved him.[11] By the middle of July, Pasternak was expressing concern about the repercussions that the French publication of *Doctor Zhivago* and of his *Sketch for an Autobiography* (which had also appeared in June) would have on him. It is not known whether Pasternak was aware of the interview broadcast on June 24 by Radio Warsaw in which Kornelii Zelinskii played down the significance of *Doctor Zhivago* and qualified his admiration of the lyric quality of Pasternak's poetry, criticizing it as too "remote . . . from contemporary themes." While Zelinskii's new attack on Pasternak was a relatively mild one, it indicated, well before the announcement of the Nobel Prize, the limits of the tolerance of Soviet officialdom. Thus Pasternak's anxiety seems to have been well founded. He was also apprehensive about the criticism of his work in the West— unavailable to him because of Soviet censorship. Although he felt that reading critical commentary on his own work provided a sort of "mirror effect" that was "unnatural," he was afraid that critics might be scolding him excessively.[12]

Despite Pasternak's fears, his stature was recognized almost everywhere. In August the publication of his 1932 poem "Waves" in the major Polish literary review *Twórczość* received favorable response. That summer the Soviet authorities, no doubt aware of Pasternak's increasing literary influence outside Russia, requested—with what he described as "earnest, threatening insistence"— that he visit some construction site, perhaps one on the Volga or Baku, so that he could write "something new" about such a locale. Panferov, who later claimed that he genuinely believed he was doing Pasternak a good turn, seems to have acted as the medium through which the request was conveyed to the poet. A strongly reluctant Pasternak begged off, pleading the continuing discomfort and weakness of his leg.[13]

In August, Pasternak asked Renate Schweitzer to keep him informed of the public's response to *Doctor Zhivago* after it appeared in West Germany. His concern about the reception of his novel intensified as the year progressed. In a letter to Eugene Kayden, an American translator of his poetry, he stressed how necessary it was for critics and readers to acknowledge the crucial place he felt the novel occupied in his literary achievement:

You say I am "first and last a poet, a lyric poet." Is it really so? And should I feel proud of being just that? . . . It hurts me to feel that I have not had the ability to express in greater fullness the whole of poetry and life in their complete unity. . . . What am I without the novel, and what have you to write about me without drawing upon that work, its terms and revelations?

He told another correspondent that he was concerned that the German translation of the novel, projected for publication by Fischer Verlag on August 17, would capture *Doctor Zhivago*'s most important elements: its content, its grasp of reality, and its originality of scope, representation, and tragic awareness.[14]

In England and the United States, meanwhile, the English translation of the novel was in preparation for publication in late September. Preceding that event both the London *Times* and *Saturday Review* gave the book favorable reviews. The *Times* even posed the following complimentary question: "A new version of *War and Peace?*" When the book did appear, in the translation by Max Hayward and Manya Harari, the *London Daily Express* gave it a great deal of publicity, commenting that "no novel this century has drawn such world-wide acclaim immediately on publication." Soon the most authoritative American critic of the era, Edmund Wilson, was to claim that "*Doctor Zhivago* will, I believe, come to stand as one of the great events in man's literary and moral history."[15]

Meanwhile, Pasternak's position at home seemed to be deteriorating. In August, 1958, according to Ivinskaia, a special meeting of the Secretariat of the Union of Writers was convened to discuss Pasternak's action in sending his manuscript abroad.[16] Also Pasternak's refusal to accommodate the official request for scenic writing appears to have brought economic reprisal. In a letter to the director of the publishing house that had issued *Poems About Georgia and Georgian Poets*, he said that he was "sorry that . . . his book had made such a terrible loss" and added:

Though I am forgotten to the point of complete obscurity, I did not think I had been forgotten so completely that my book would not go through at least ten editions, which would have covered your expenses [royalties owed to Pasternak] and the costs of publication. I realize, of course, that all this does not depend on you, for people in high office keep interfering with the future of literature; however, the rest are only too willing to follow them.[17]

Despite such efforts of Soviet literary commissars to restrict the circulation of Pasternak's works, interest in him among connoisseurs of Russian literature was growing. Many of the scholars participating in the International Congress of Slavists, convened in Moscow in August, 1958, were very eager to meet him. When some of them, including Arne Gallis, the Norwegian translator of *Doctor Zhivago*, requested through official channels a visit with Pasternak, they were summarily refused with the explanation that he was unwell. Not all the Slavists, however, were so easily put off; several, including Roman Jakobson, Henrik Birnbaum, and Nils Åke Nilsson (head of the Institute of Slavic Studies, in Stockholm), succeeded in meeting him in Peredelkino. To these visitors from Sweden, Pasternak conveyed some of his feelings about the possibility that the

Nobel Prize would be awarded to him. His visitors made those feelings known to appropriate officials in Stockholm. To one of the visitors Pasternak indicated that he would have no hesitation about receiving the prize; however, it struck the visitor that at that point Pasternak perhaps did not take such a possibility seriously.[18]

During the summer of 1958, Pasternak's candidacy for the Nobel Prize was debated frequently and seriously in various quarters. Five times since 1947 he had been nominated for the outstanding contribution to letters of his postrevolutionary poetry (in 1953 his candidacy, put forward by C. M. Bowra, had been turned down on the strange-enough grounds that he "was a Russian living in Russia");[19] now the impact of the publication of *Doctor Zhivago* coalesced a general movement toward Pasternak as the choice.* The many letters of admiration Pasternak was receiving from Germany, France, England, Italy, the United States, and Scandinavia attested to the impression the novel had made on men of letters. In September, 1958, Renate Schweitzer inquired through her journalistic contacts about a possible nomination of Pasternak for the Nobel Prize and learned that he was already being considered.[20]

During the period when the Swedish Academy was considering Pasternak's candidacy, its members sounded out various diplomatic officials about the putative reactions to such an award, inquiring also whether such a choice would be acceptable to them. Authoritative sources in Stockholm have confirmed that, in his dual capacity as member of the academy and secretary-general of the United Nations, Dag Hammarskjöld approached both the American and Soviet "camps" to learn their reactions to Pasternak's candidacy. John Foster Dulles is said to have been approached and to have responded positively. Soviet Foreign Minister Andrei Gromyko was asked whether his country would consider acceptable jointly granting the prize to Mikhail Sholokhov and to Pasternak. Gromyko made inquiries and then responded positively to Hammarskjöld (he is reported to have said, "Yes, Pasternak is well known as a good poet and translator, but Sholokhov is to us personally a greater writer"). By December the academy had decided to give the prize to Pasternak alone, postponing granting the prize to Sholokhov. This decision unleashed Soviet displeasure. The award of the prize to Pasternak alone, Surkov admitted in a conversation in 1959, had been considered by his country in terms of the politically oriented consultations that had taken place in 1958. Surkov added that, after the award was announced, his country just "had to do something"—take appropriate measures in response to what was viewed by its government as a political affront. Apparently Communist party ideologues believed that the West was going to use *Doctor Zhivago* as a weapon in an ideological battle and decided to take steps to counter that strategy. The mutual misunderstanding was typical of the cold war era; neither side was able to comprehend and deal with the other's viewpoint. Ironically, as the situation developed, the anti-Pasternak campaign that was to be unleashed in the Soviet Union would give the "anti-Soviets" among Western ideologues powerful ammunition.[21]

*The reason given by the academy in 1953 in turning down Pasternak's candidacy appears to stem from an overcautious desire to preserve Sweden's neutrality by not awarding the prize to a Soviet writer.

Among the many letters that Pasternak received at the beginning of October, 1958, was one from Alberto Moravia supporting his candidacy for the Nobel Prize. Pasternak wrote Renate Schweitzer to say that he hoped that Moravia would be the recipient, because if the award was given to him, it would cause discomfort not so much to himself as to others. Immediately upon receiving his letter, Schweitzer wrote to the Swedish Academy asking for a delay in his nomination. The academy did not receive her letter soon enough. [22]

Despite Pasternak's apprehension, recognition of his merits was gaining momentum. In October, Radio Warsaw broadcast a special program presenting a selection of his poems. It was one of the first signs of Polish cultural and ideological independence in the face of Moscow's official attitude toward Pasternak. In the more liberal atmosphere that arose in Poland after Władysław Gomułka's rise to power, Polish writers were concerned to strengthen their gains. The Poles' moral and material support to Pasternak had a significant impact on his fate. [23]

Even before parts of *Doctor Zhivago* were broadcast in Polish, the full text of the novel had become available throughout western Europe in the first of several editions in Russian. This edition, produced by Mouton, a scholarly publisher based in Holland, met the need for an edition in the original language—a technical prerequisite for consideration for the Nobel Prize. It also made available copies in Russian at the World's Fair held in Brussels in the fall of 1958—where hundreds of Soviet tourists bought them. When he heard that the edition had been produced without his permission, Feltrinelli was incensed, for technically it deprived him of the all-important copyright to the Russian-language edition. He apparently felt somewhat insecure about his claims to the latter, but he was prepared to fight for them (the matter was soon settled by an agreement between the two publishers). [24]

Shortly afterward, just before the appearance of the German translation, Friedrich Sieberg reviewed *Doctor Zhivago* in the *Frankfurter Allgemeine Zeitung*. He praised Pasternak's perspective on the events of the Revolution and pointed out that no critic or polemist had yet accomplished this feat. Not long afterward a West German radio broadcast provided detailed analyses of the novel. A few days before the announcement of the award Nils Åke Nilsson visited Pasternak. On Thursday, October 23, however, before Nilsson's written account of their conversation reached the press, Anders Österling, the permanent secretary of the Swedish Academy, dispatched a cable to the writer, and less than an hour later, at 3:20 P.M., he entered the sitting room of the Nobel Library and announced to the press simply, "It's Pasternak." Österling cited Pasternak's poetry, his translations of Shakespeare, and especially *Doctor Zhivago* as the basis upon which the academy had reached its decision. He likened the novel to the works of Tolstoy and added that it was "a great achievement to have been able to complete in difficult circumstances a work of such dignity, high above all party frontiers."

The initial reaction of the Western press was great pleasure, both because of the choice and because the academy had not been overcautious of Swedish neutrality in awarding the prize to a Soviet writer—the first such award in the academy's

Pasternak soon after the
announcement of the Nobel Prize
award. *Archives Jacqueline de
Proyart.*

history. Albert Camus, who had received the award in 1957, commented: "It is
the best choice that could have been made. I hoped for it and rejoice with all my
heart." François Mauriac, also a past recipient of the prize, said, "*Doctor Zhivago* is
perhaps the most important novel of our age."[25] When the press attaché at the
Soviet Embassy in Stockholm was informed, however, he evasively voiced what
had become the hackneyed official Soviet view: "As far as I know, Pasternak is
better known as a translator than as an author." More to the point, Artur Lundkvist, the Swedish left-wing writer and recipient of the 1958 Lenin Prize, gave an
indication of what the hard party-line response would be when he said that the
award was "an insult to the Russian nation." Moscow, however, remained silent;
no mention of the award was made in the media.[26]

On the following morning Pasternak, surrounded by friends and well-wishers

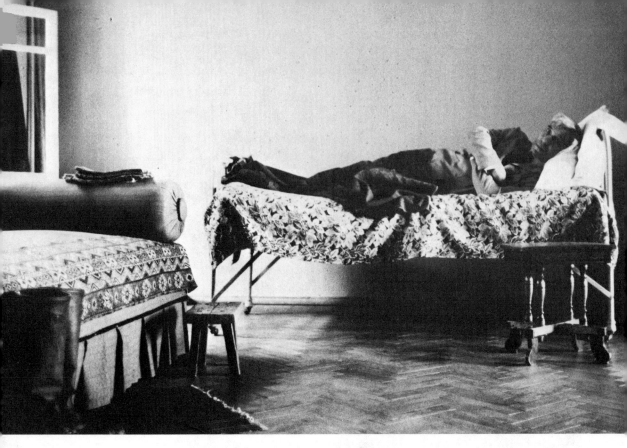

The poet in Peredelkino. *Cornell Capa/Magnum.*

at Peredelkino, received Østerling's cable. He told an English journalist: "This is a great joy for me. I don't feel any tremendous emotion. I'm just very glad." To a French correspondent he added, "For me this is more than just a joy; it is a moral support; say as well that my joy is solitary." Among the numerous cables he received from all over the world was one from the Polish Writers' Union. Unlike Radio Moscow, Radio Warsaw not only announced the award but also read an excerpt from Pasternak's poem "Chopin."[27]

As of October 24 it appeared that the Soviet government was preparing to accept the award to Pasternak, though perhaps only sedately and without enthusiasm. On that day Soviet Minister of Culture Nikolai Mikhailov, during an interview with a Communist correspondent, seemed to acknowledge its acceptance, while indicating that the award would be discussed at a meeting of the Soviet Writers' Union. Also on that day representatives of the Ministry of Culture appeared at Pasternak's home in Peredelkino, took pictures, and assisted foreign journalists, seeing to it that their telegrams passed censorship with minimum delay. With hindsight, it is reasonable to infer (and this interpretation is corroborated by statements made later by Secretary of the Writers' Union Surkov in a private conversation) that the development that irked the Soviet authorities was

Pasternak, 1958.

the appearance in the world press over the next few days of a number of statements by prominent Western political figures, interpreting the award in a political rather than a literary light. The impression these statements made in Moscow was that the novel was being exploited for political purposes and that a large-scale anti-Soviet campaign was under way.[28]

Kurt Wolff, a senior partner in Pantheon Books (the American publisher of *Doctor Zhivago*) and an internationally known publisher, wrote Pasternak about the appropriateness of the award: "In this case [genius] is being recognized as such. Your book is being read and loved for its remarkable lyric-epic-ethical qualities. (In six weeks, 70,000 copies—that is fantastic—and by the end of the year that will be 100,000 or more.)" Wolff added that he was reserving rooms for the two of them in Stockholm for the Nobel ceremonies starting on December 9.[29]

On October 25, the same day Wolff wrote to him, Pasternak sent Østerling the following cable of acknowledgment, written in English: "Immensely grateful,

Pasternak soon after receiving the announcement of the Nobel Prize award, October 23, 1958. *Henry Shapiro.*

Pasternak and his wife, Zinaida, celebrate the Nobel Prize award with the writer Kornei
Chukovskii, October 23, 1958. *Ludmilla T. Shapiro.*

touched, proud, astonished, abashed." Pasternak also made it clear to reporters
that it was too early to say whether or not he would attend the ceremonies in
Stockholm; he was probably waiting for some more specific reaction from the
Writers' Union before making definite plans. He did not have very long to wait,
for on the same day the Soviet response to the award began taking political and
censorious shape, and the media ended their silence. The leading literary journal,
Literaturnaia gazeta, published an article, under the headline "A Provocative Sally
of International Reaction," describing the award as "an inimical political act"
augmenting the cold war against the Soviet Union. It described the novel as
"counterrevolutionary," "slanderous," and inartistic.[30] The *Gazeta* also published
the letter of rejection for *Doctor Zhivago* purportedly sent to Pasternak by five
Novyi mir editors in September, 1956. (As was pointed out by a thoughtful annal-
ist of those years, it is doubtful whether the letter was actually the one composed
and sent in 1956.)[31] With the text of the letter was printed a cover letter sent to
the *Gazeta* by *Novyi mir*'s editorial board, continuing the attack:

It is quite obvious that this award has nothing at all in common with an impartial assessment of the literary merits of Pasternak's work itself, but is connected with the anti-

Soviet clamor which has been raised around *Doctor Zhivago*, and is purely a political act hostile to our country and aimed at intensifying the cold war. . . . It [the letter of rejection] explains convincingly enough why Pasternak's novel could have no place in a Soviet magazine, although naturally it does not express to the full the disgust and contempt which we, like all Soviet writers, feel over Pasternak's present shameful and unpatriotic attitude.[32]

Some of the shortcomings of the letter of rejection have been observed:

The editors' letter is on the whole a fair and truthful summary of the book. Zhivago is indeed the spokesman for Pasternak's viewpoint, and he is anti-Soviet and anti-Marxist. . . . The letter is not entirely accurate, however. In several details Pasternak might well claim to have been misrepresented, as when the editors incorrectly stress the material worries and the desire for comfort of some of the characters or dwell on Zhivago's vanity and ignore proofs of his altruism. [The letter] disagrees with Western opinion in one most important regard . . .: it takes for granted that, if the book expresses anti-Soviet sentiments, then without further argument it cannot be published.[33]

Radio Moscow also broke its silence to denounce "the award of the Nobel Prize for a mere mediocre work such as *Doctor Zhivago*" as "a hostile political act directed against the Soviet State."[34] Clearly at that time—the last phase of the cold war preceding the move toward rapprochement in the 1960s—the Soviet government was still reacting in an overly defensive way (to Western eyes, in a somewhat paranoid way) to moves that it viewed as threatening.

The impact of the award on public opinion in Moscow—especially among intellectuals—was considerable. The award was "the only topic" of every conversation in the capital—not the election of Cardinal Angelo Roncalli to the papacy, not the death in Leningrad of the eminent physiologist, Academician Leon Orbeli, nor even the award of the Nobel Prize for Physics to three Soviet scientists, Academician Igor Tamm, Pavel Cherenkov, and Ilia Frank (it is interesting to note that the Soviet government did not make the shadow of an objection to the awarding of the Nobel Prize to the three physicists).[35]

Thus within two days of receiving the most distinguished of literary prizes, Pasternak found himself in a situation that might best be described as the eye of a hurricane. While the winds of political rhetoric were raging about him, he was seemingly safe. But the barometric pressure had not yet reached bottom. In the following days the storm grew worse and sorely buffeted him. First, the verbal onslaught intensified. On October 26, *Pravda* printed an article signed by David Zaslavskii. The following excerpts are typical of both its tone and its intent:

[*Doctor Zhivago*] is a malicious lampoon on the Socialist Revolution, on the Soviet people, on the Soviet intelligentsia. The embittered philistine has given vent to his revengeful gall. . . . Pasternak's novel is low-grade reactionary hackwork molded into the form of a literary composition. . . . If even a spark of Soviet dignity had been left in Pasternak, if he had any writer's conscience and sense of duty to the people, he would have rejected this award so humiliating to him as a writer. But the inflated self-esteem of an offended and blatant philistine has left no trace of Soviet dignity and patriotism in Pasternak's soul. By all his activity, Pasternak confirms that, in our Socialist country, . . . he is a weed.[36]

Next, punitive measures were taken. On October 27 the Writers' Union, "bearing in mind Pasternak's political and moral downfall, his betrayal of the Soviet Union, Socialism, peace and progress," decided to "deprive Boris Pasternak of the title of Soviet writer and expel him from membership." Among those who voted for his expulsion—and who were therefore opposed to publishing Soviet editions of his poetry, fiction, or translations—were Valentin Kataev, Vera Panova, Leonid Sobolev, Vladimir Ermilov, Boris Polevoi, Sergei Smirnov, Aleksandr Iashin, and Nikolai Chukovskii (the son of Pasternak's sympathetic neighbor Kornei Chukovskii).* Such votes were invariably reported as "unanimous," without a trace of dissension. Many of those joining in the vote may have viewed it as a pro forma gesture unavoidable in the circumstances and not unduly harmful to Pasternak. On the other hand, it seems obvious that certain hard-core Communists among the writers were genuinely incensed, stressing that Soviet society had not given Pasternak "the right to make judgments about the Soviet way of life."

Rather than appearing in person, Pasternak sent the writers a letter expressing his indignation and reminding them of his continued willingness to compromise (to cut the "unacceptable" parts of his novel or donate the Nobel Prize money to an international peace fund). Although there is no extant copy of the letter, several who read it reported that it ended as follows: "I do not expect justice from you. You may have me shot, or expelled from the country, or do anything you like. All I ask of you is: do not be in too much of a hurry over it. It will bring you no increase either of happiness or of glory."[37]

The often base public assaults to which he and his novel were subjected hurt Pasternak deeply and aged him rapidly. He felt sincerely—as he had written to the head of the Cultural Department of the Central Committee, Dmitrii Polikarpov—that the novel was his supreme achievement and that because of it he considered that he did not have to repent of his life. Yet he was most slanderously abused in all sectors, and now he reacted according to his hypersensitive nature. He began carrying with him a fatal dose of Nembutal, and on October 28 he suggested to Ivinskaia that they die together as "a slap in the face" of their persecutors. Ivinskaia persuaded him to put aside that idea; in the meantime she sought advice—if only for tactical reasons—from Fedin and Polikarpov. When she told him about Pasternak's suggestion, Polikarpov urged her never to leave Pasternak's side; it is clear that Polikarpov was appalled by the possibility of a suicide, which he obviously feared would do great damage to the Soviet authorities.[38]

Under the pressure of the attacks leveled against him, Pasternak next decided to pursue a course that he believed would foil the authorities. On October 29, acting on his own and without consulting Ivinskaia or anyone else, he cabled Østerling a renunciation of the prize: "In view of the interpretation which this distinction has undergone in the community to which I belong, I must renounce

*The action meant depriving Pasternak of his livelihood.

Рисунок Бориса ЛЕО.

„ДЕЙЛИ ВРАЛЬ"

Б. ПАСТЕРНАК
ДОКТОР ЖИВАГО

РЕДАКТОР: — Вот как надо работать!

In the issue of November 10, 1958, the Soviet satirical journal *Krokodil* printed a cartoon depicting the editorial office of a scandal sheet dubbed *Deili vral* (*Daily Blat*, or *Rag*). The editor is holding a copy of Doctor Zhivago and commenting: "Good work!" or "That's the way to do it!"—meaning that the author of the novel did a good piece of slander, in the best traditions of the tabloid.

the undeserved prize which has been awarded me. Do not be offended by my voluntary refusal."[39] To an English correspondent he insisted that he had made his decision "quite alone" and without telling anyone, even close friends. Ivinskaia has commented that impulsive, solitary decisions about important matters were typical of Pasternak. We can now construe that his action came as a blow to the Soviet authorities. They had merely sought to humiliate him into recanting views espoused in the novel. One of the consequences for the Soviet Union was the loss of the considerable foreign currency the award represented.[40]

When Pasternak's refusal of the prize was made public, Nils Ståhle, director of the Nobel Foundation, announced that Pasternak's name would remain on the list of prizewinners with the notation that he had refused the award. He added, however, that Pasternak could not receive the prize money unless he attended the ceremonies in Stockholm on December 10.[41]

Pasternak's move was a great surprise to the Soviet hierarchy. At that time Khrushchev had made up his mind both to allow Pasternak to go abroad to accept the prize and to permit the novel to be published—or so he claimed in his memoirs. Khrushchev said that he had had the opportunity to allow publication of the novel but had "failed to act." He expressed regrets about that failure, adding, with his own brand of sincerity, "When dealing with creative minds, administrative measures are always most destructive and nonprogressive." While reminiscing, Khrushchev also expressed an awareness of the unfortunate consequences for the Soviet Union of the banning of *Doctor Zhivago*, acknowledging that "the decision to use police methods put a whole different coloration on the affair and left a bad aftertaste for a long time to come. People raised a storm of protest against the Soviet Union for not allowing Pasternak to go abroad to receive the prize."[42]

But such feelings that Khrushchev may have had about the "Pasternak Affair" had no impact on the campaign against the writer, which went on gathering momentum. On October 29—the same day on which Pasternak cabled his refusal to Østerling—the text of the Writers' Union statement of expulsion was printed in *Izvestiia*, and at an official meeting of Komsomol first secretary, Vladimir Semichastnyi, delivered the following vulgar diatribe, which was punctuated by loud applause:

As everybody who has anything to do with this animal knows, one of the peculiarities of the pig is that it never makes a mess where it eats or sleeps. Therefore if we compare Pasternak with a pig, then we must say that a pig will never do what he has done. . . . Pasternak, this man who considers himself among the best representatives of society, has fouled the spot where he ate and cast filth on those by whose labor he lives and breathes.

In conclusion Semichastnyi said that he was certain that the Soviet government would have no objection if Pasternak left for the "capitalist paradise."[43]

The Western press was, of course, scandalized by these tactics, and various groups of writers rallied together to protest the treatment Pasternak was receiving. On October 30 both the International PEN Club and a group of British writers sent telegrams to the Soviet Writers' Union. The PEN Club wired:

International PEN, very distressed by rumors concerning Pasternak, asks you to protect the poet, maintaining the right of creative freedom. Writers throughout the world are thinking of him fraternally.

The message from the British writers was as follows:

We are profoundly anxious about the state of one of the world's great poets and writers, Boris Pasternak. We consider his novel, *Doctor Zhivago*, a moving personal testimony and not a political document. We appeal to you in the name of the great Russian literary tradition for which you stand not to dishonor it by victimizing a writer revered throughout the entire civilized world.

Just a few among those signing the above cable were T. S. Eliot, Sir Maurice Bowra, Stephen Spender, Bertrand Russell, Aldous Huxley, Somerset Maugham, and C. P. Snow. The British Society of Authors also sent a cable of protest to the Soviet Writers' Union:

THE SOCIETY OF AUTHORS DEEPLY DEPLORE EXPULSION OF BORIS PASTERNAK BY THE SOVIET WRITERS' UNION AND STRONGLY URGE HIS REINSTATEMENT.[44]

Meaanwhile, however, the harassment was becoming even more severe. On October 30 Radio Moscow devoted all of its daily "literary" broadcast time to condemning Pasternak and the award, and on the following day a general meeting of Moscow writers was convened to pass judgment on him. The meeting lasted five hours, and had an estimated attendance of eight hundred (many members of the organization were absent—they may have chosen to boycott that meeting). The session was presided over by Sergei Sergeevich Smirnov, who with apparent gleefulness proceeded to indict Pasternak. Many came to the podium to deliver diatribes against the novelist, among them Lev Oshanin, Kornelii Zelinskii, Viktor Pertsov, Boris Slutskii, Anatolii Sofronov, Vladimir Soloukhin, Leonid Martynov, and Boris Polevoi. In the end the members passed a resolution asking the government to revoke Pasternak's Soviet citizenship because his conduct as a "man of letters was incompatible with the title of Soviet writer and citizen."[45]

While the campaign was continuing on its own momentum, new developments occurred. By now the Central Committee had decided that Pasternak's refusal of the prize was not quite adequate. As Ivinskaia put it, what the authorities really wanted was "to humble the poet, to force him to grovel in public." Though Polikarpov told Ivinskaia that Pasternak "must now say something," he chose not to put any direct pressure on the writer but rather used a subterfuge. At the prodding of an *agent provocateur*, a young lawyer and self-proclaimed admirer of Pasternak's poetry, Ivinskaia became convinced that only a letter to Khrushchev from the poet would save him from expulsion from the country. She found the whole situation "terrifying . . . threatening letters, a student demonstration against Pasternak, rumors that the house in Peredelkino would be sacked, the foul abuse by Semichastnyi {head of Komsomol Vladimir} and threat of expulsion," as well as her fears that Pasternak would commit suicide. Against the advice of her daughter and one or two friends, she drafted a letter to Khrushchev, and after many revisions Pasternak signed it. In the letter, delivered on October 31, Pasternak asserted that he could still work for the benefit of Soviet literature, and pleaded: "I am linked with Russia by my birth, life and work. I cannot imagine my fate separated from and outside Russia. . . . A departure beyond the borders of my country would be for me equivalent to death and I therefore request you not to take this extreme measure against me."

Although in her memoirs Ivinskaia called the letter a mistake and took the blame for it, it is clear that the trauma of leaving the country would have been too much for Pasternak and that there were few other choices open to the writer who had cried out that he "could not stand up any more to the hounding."[46] At the time neither Pasternak nor Ivinskaia viewed the letter as either a capitulation or a recantation of the message of *Doctor Zhivago*.

On the same day the letter was delivered, an official caravan was sent to fetch Pasternak from Peredelkino. The writer was in good spirits. He expected to confront Khrushchev and resolve his predicament—but he took his heart medication along should the meeting prove upsetting. Instead of Khrushchev, it was Polikarpov who received him—in the company of a mysterious person whom for a time at least Ivinskaia thought to be Mikhail Suslov, a member of the Politburo. Polikarpov's handling of the meeting—notably his comment to Pasternak that the writer had "stuck a knife in Russia's back" proved too exasperating to the writer, who stormed out of the room. The point of the meeting was to convey to Pasternak a reply to his letter: he was to be allowed to remain in the Soviet Union. Ivinskaia was told that a condition was appended to that decision: in the near future Pasternak would have to sign another public statement.[47]

At the end of his conversation with Ivinskaia, Polikarpov indicated that he considered the issue closed but that it was too late for him to stop publication in the next day's *Literaturnaia gazeta* of materials critical of Pasternak, reflecting what he termed "the wrath of the people." The newspaper's issue of November 1 did indeed contain a full-page feature of testimonies and rage and indignation directed against the writer by a number of readers, including an excavator operator, a *kolkhoz* chairman, old-age pensioners, and a salesgirl from a bookshop, none of whom could say that they had read the novel. All the published opinions were negative—the paper refrained from printing any of the numerous positive letters it had received, though copies of many of them reached Pasternak. The writer was sometimes moved to tears by statements he found in his mail, such as: "You must not feel lonely. You have probably never before in your life had so much sympathy from people unknown to you as at the moment," and, "Millions of Russian people are happy at the appearance in our literature of a truly great work. History will not treat you harshly. [Signed] The Russian People."[48]

The outside world formed only a schematized picture of Pasternak's trials. When it published Pasternak's letter to Khrushchev on November 2, Tass added in a note that the poet had neither applied for nor been denied a visa for foreign travel and made the callous comment: "In the event of Pasternak's expressing a wish to leave the Soviet Union forever, the State . . . will not raise any obstacles." Such a heavy-handed statement was probably thought necessary to set at rest any conjectures abroad that the writer was not free to leave the country.[49]

The Western literary world was dismayed by the events surrounding Pasternak and could understand them only as persecution. The Association of Swedish Authors, a group of Norwegian writers, and the Icelandic Socialist writer Halldór Laxness sent indignant telegrams of protest. Perhaps to counter these gestures,

Mikhail Sholokhov, the Soviet Union's preferred candidate for Nobel honors, granted a telephone interview to the Swedish Socialist paper *Aftonbladet*, in which he insisted that Pasternak got the prize not because of *Doctor Zhivago*'s artistic value but because of its "anti-Soviet tendency" and that the Writers' Union's decision to expel him was "absolutely just." He also insisted that Pasternak's expulsion would not expose him "to any material pressure"; it would simply "bring a moral pressure to bear on his conscience, on his patriotic mind."[50]

Nonetheless, if the Polish Writers' Union had not commissioned translations from Pasternak, his livelihood would have been painfully curtailed. Just before the announcement of the award, with concerned foresight his Polish friends had requested him to translate Juliusz Słowacki's *Maria Stuart*. Pasternak was fully aware of the support that this request represented and later told a reporter that, during the difficult times of 1957–58, "only the Polish poets remembered me. They asked our writers to ask me to translate Juliusz Słowacki's *Maria Stuart* because they wanted me to have work."[51]

On November 4, Polikarpov asked Ivinskaia to have Pasternak compose the additional statement he had mentioned. Polikarpov and Ivinskaia held a session during which Pasternak's draft went through many modifications. From the session a document emerged that the writer signed on November 5, to be published in *Pravda* the next day. The statement was said to have been made of the author's own free will, without any outside pressure. In it Pasternak claimed that he had "never had the intention of harming . . . [his] State or his people" and that he had been misled in assessing as "a literary distinction" a prize that turned out to be a political gesture with dire consequences. He said once more that he had turned down the prize "on . . . [his] own initiative and without any compulsion." Referring to the warning in the *Novyi mir* rejection letter about possible misinterpretation of the novel, Pasternak said:

. . . if one bears in mind the conclusions arising from the critical analysis of the novel, it follows that I supposedly adhered in the novel to the following erroneous theses. It seems that I assert that any revolution is a historically illegitimate phenomenon, that the October Revolution was one of such illegitimate events, that it brought Russia misfortunes and led the Russian traditional intelligentsia to its destruction.

It is clear to me that I cannot accept such assertions carried to absurdity. Yet my work . . . gave rise to such grievous interpretation, and . . . I rejected the prize.

If the publication of the book had been suspended, as I asked my publisher in Italy to do . . . , I would probably have succeeded at least partially in correcting this.

At the end of the statement was a protestation, demeaning in its incongruity and reminiscent of a schoolboy's contrition after a stupid prank: "I believe I shall find the strength to restore my good name and the confidence of my comrades."[52]

The unwitting Western reader may misinterpret the conciliatory and self-justificatory tone of Pasternak's document, contrasting it with the bold defiance that has characterized Solzhenitsyn's attitude. A clearer view is that the two writers waged the same battle with equal courage, the one "relaying" the other at the necessary moment. Going through the motion of expressing public remorse was the only feasible step for Pasternak at that particular point in the battle. It would be wrong for the Western reader to conclude that Pasternak, in renouncing the Nobel Prize, was behaving like any other Soviet writer in recanting his "sins," even though with a little less groveling. Within their own cultural context, Soviet readers are experts at deciphering such public pronouncements and seldom take the ritual gestures at face value, whereas the Western reader in his naïveté may all too easily misinterpret the semiotics of this particular "genre" by assuming an abject degree of submissiveness in Pasternak. Pasternak wrote this letter of submission both because he found it difficult to endure further harassment and because he felt it his duty to consider all those dependent on him.[53] It must have occurred to him that Ivinskaia would be defenseless if he was expelled from the country. He was, in fact, being blackmailed into compliance by an implied threat to someone dear to him. The treatment that was meted out to Ivinskaia within weeks of Pasternak's death is ample proof that his fear was valid.

Viewed from another angle, the letter sums up the ambiguity of the distinction bestowed upon Pasternak by the Nobel Prize: honor and distress commingled. It has been felt by some that, in proclaiming recognition of Pasternak's deserts, non-Soviet literati—and specifically the jury of the Swedish Academy—chose to disregard Russian sensitivity about internal conditions and unwittingly unleashed a storm of irreparable damage whose human cost was incalculable. Such an interpretation overlooks an essential aspect of the realities involved—that the international fame and recognition bestowed on Pasternak by the prize automatically endowed him with an immunity that no other Soviet writer then enjoyed and that only one other colleague, Solzhenitsyn, was to acquire in his turn in later years. Besides—and this is the argument that would have been closest to Pasternak's own heart—it is neither right nor feasible to escape one's fate, "the order of the acts" referred to in Pasternak's "Hamlet." His contemporary and sympathizer Nadezhda Mandelstam phrased it slightly differently: she felt that it was almost inevitable for a poet to arouse enmity at some point or other, and pointed out that this finally happened "even to Pasternak, who, for so long and with such skill—the same skill with which he charmed all who met him—had avoided provoking the blind fury of the philistines."[54] It would seem unfair to lay undue blame at the door of the Swedish Academy, which spent much thought and time in consultations East and West before making the award and was utterly dismayed by the recrudescence of Stalinism during the *Zhivago* affair, which most observers would not have thought possible.

A number of vexations punctuated the anti-Pasternak campaign of those days. In the fall of 1958 his name was omitted from posters announcing the plays being performed in his translations at the Moscow Art Theater and the Malyi Theater. Also, one evening that fall, some drunken hooligans came by and hurled stones into the windows of Pasternak's dacha, yelling anti-Semitic slogans. A microphone was planted in Ivinskaia's dacha—which Pasternak would humorously greet each day—and both he and Ivinskaia were clumsily followed by KGB agents on their outings. In a comment on that campaign, and in particular on the

Soviet writers' frenzied denunciations, a witness remarked: "That was the last recurrence of that great fear which was left to us as a legacy of the years of Stalin's cult. . . . People were purely and simply seized by the well-known, obnoxious, sticky fear."

During the trying days of late 1958 and early 1959, only a handful of acquaintances and friends dared visit Pasternak (Fedin and many other writers stopped greeting him). Among the staunchest of those intimates were Nikolai Bogatyrev (who was to die in mysterious circumstances in 1976), Ariadna Efron, and Viacheslav (to his friends, "Koma") Ivanov, the son of the novelist Vsevolod Ivanov. Ivanov had moved into Aleksandr Afinogenov's dacha after the latter's death in the early 1940s, becoming Pasternak's next-door neighbor and, in time, close friend. Among those who came to visit the poet during those months "when no one dared to cross the Pasternaks' threshold" were the sculptor Zoia Maslenikov and her husband, an architect. They appeared at the dacha, introduced themselves, and expressed their warm sympathy for the writer, with whom they soon developed friendly relations. In 1958, Pasternak sat for Zoia Maslenikov, who did a bronze bust of him, now in the study of the dacha in Peredelkino.[55]

After the publication of Pasternak's letter to *Pravda*, the direct attacks on him seemed to come to an end. He could hardly be considered a free agent, however, as he made clear in a later statement to a reporter:

My house was a real hospital at that time. They gave me a woman doctor as nurse. I told her she could go home as she did not need to worry about me. But she did not go. Apparently she was not allowed to because she was under orders. Maybe they feared I would commit suicide. I was always surrounded by doctors. They even slept under my roof.[56]

Throughout November, Pasternak kept silent; the Western dailies and periodicals kept their reportage to noncontroversial subjects such as book sales; Soviet comments dwindled to an occasional satiric thrust.* Although Kochetov went on to label Pasternak "a renegade" in the press, and the regime's devoted poet-feuilletonist Sergei Mikhalkov continued to publish lampoons about him, in the course of November the campaign slowly died down.[57]

In December, Pasternak complained that interest in *Doctor Zhivago* had brought feverish translation of his earlier works—works that he felt demonstrated an expressionistic disintegration of form† and weakness of content. He also complained about the prosy translations of the poetry at the end of some

---

*The November 10 issue of the Soviet satirical journal *Krokodil* printed a caricature depicting the editorial office of a scandal sheet dubbed *Deili vral* (*Daily Blat*, or *Rag*): the editor holds in his hands a copy of *Doctor Zhivago* and comments: "Good work!"

†In the sense in which Erich Kahler has perceived a gradually intensifying disintegration of form in twentieth-century art, as the aesthetics of modernism kept dictating a bolder and bolder departure from the earlier belief in the need for the unity—and significance—of form (see Erich Kahler, *The Disintegration of Form in the Arts*, New York: George Braziller, 1968). This disintegration of form Pasternak viewed (as he wrote in the same letter to Renate Schweitzer) as related to the current reduced emphasis on content (*Inhalt*), and increased "emptiness" (*Leere*)—or lack of "significance"—of the work. Concerning the aesthetic issue of Pasternak's strong feeling about the primacy of content in the work of art, see Chapter 18.

foreign editions of *Doctor Zhivago*. In Moscow, meanwhile, a congress of Soviet writers met and applauded both the increase in party control over literature and a denunciation of Pasternak. Earlier the same day *Pravda*, no doubt with the upcoming Nobel ceremonies in mind, published an article calling Pasternak a "traitor" and a "symbol of decadence." [58]

In the early days of December, Pasternak again received evidence from Poland of warm recognition and support. At a UNESCO conference in Warsaw on December 6 the three hundred participants applauded enthusiastically when Antoni Slonimski dedicated one of his poems to Pasternak. Slonimski, chairman of the Polish Writers' Union, compared Pasternak to Diogenes—one who had criticized the defects of his times and had been subjected to humiliation and sarcasm. The comparison met with warm approval. [59]

At the Nobel ceremonies on December 10, Østerling noted Pasternak's absence: "The laureate has, as is known, announced that he does not wish to accept the prize. This renunciation in no way changes the validity of the distinction. It remains only for the Swedish Academy to state with regret that it was not possible for the acceptance to take place." [60]

Later, near the end of the month, Pasternak told a German correspondent that he had finished his translation of Słowacki's *Maria Stuart*. He also expressed his gratitude for the "courageous and honorable attitude" of the Polish friends who stood at his side and supported him "in difficult circumstances." Pasternak added that he considered *Doctor Zhivago* "the work of his life," but he characteristically noted that publishers need not "reach into the moth-proof box" of his earlier achievements for a follow-up to it, and remarked, "I am not dead yet. I am still working." Becoming specific about a work he had recently completed, Pasternak indicated that, if his friendly foreign publishers really wanted to publish another of his works, he was recommending "a small collection of apolitical and very personal poems" that he had passed on to Jacqueline de Proyart. That collection, which he still referred to as *In the Interlude* (*V pereryve*) was in fact published in 1960 under the alternate title *When Skies Clear* (*Kogda razguliaetsia*). [61]

Thus at the end of the year Pasternak was set on moving on. First, however, he received some year-end tributes to *Doctor Zhivago* from England, Poland, Italy, and the United States. On December 21 and 28 the London *Sunday Times* reviewed the "books of the year" and said unhesitatingly that "*Doctor Zhivago* is the novel of the year." The Polish weekly *Polityka* published the results of a questionnaire circulated among its readers. From the survey it was apparent that Polish writers considered *Doctor Zhivago* one of the most significant books of 1958, even though they could read the full text only in foreign-language editions. In Italy the novel won the 1958 Bancarella Prize—a best-seller award and one of Italy's two most significant literary prizes. In the United States, Kurt Wolff paid this tribute to the novel: "In my opinion it is the most significant novel that I have had the happiness and honour to publish during a long period of activity as a publisher." Finally, for John Strachey, the novel was the culminating expression of what he called the literature of the strangled cry—the other instances of this literature, discussed with *Doctor Zhivago* in Strachey's *The Strangled Cry*, being Arthur

Koestler's *Darkness at Noon*, George Orwell's *1984*, and Whittaker Chambers's *Witness*.[62]

Continued press coverage of *Doctor Zhivago* marked the beginning of 1959. Within two years of the original Italian publication the novel was to appear in twenty-five languages—including the major European languages, as well as Hebrew, Arabic, Turkish, Persian, Japanese, Chinese, Vietnamese, Indonesian, Hindi, and Gujarati. One Russian edition had been published by Feltrinelli in 1957, and the University of Michigan Press edition materialized in 1958. By January, 1959, 300,000 copies of the French translation had been sold, and by April, 260,000 copies had been sold in England. While it was hailed by many militants of the cold war as a political statement, hundreds of writers praised the novel on grounds ranging from moral and aesthetic to sentimental. In contrast, a sharp reaction emanated from Israel: Prime Minister David Ben-Gurion denounced it as "one of the most despicable books about Jews ever written by a man of Jewish origin"—an opinion based on a narrow reading of certain passages in the book.* The British publisher Collins estimated that by May more than £250,000 in royalties had accumulated in the West for the author. Copies were selling on the black market on Kuznetskii Bridge in Moscow for 1,500 old rubles ($150 at the official rate).[63]

Though Pasternak was still under surveillance, he continued to write. On February 2 the *London Daily Telegraph* quoted Pasternak as saying that, although writing a sequel to *Doctor Zhivago* was one of his long-term projects, he was now writing poetry. "To write prose, in which you follow out your thoughts to the end, demands an atmosphere of security. That is what I do not have at the moment. It is easier for me in my present circumstances to write poetry," he said.[64]

Early in 1959, Pasternak wrote (in English) to a foreign correspondent about the anxiety and the emotional strain under which he lived:

You will never imagine the ignominious treatment to which . . . I am subjected [with only brief respites]. You cannot imagine to what extent my [ability to correspond is] difficult [*sic*] and limited. And I have to remain silent about it. . . . I will never travel as long as the circumstances are as tense as they are and as long as one is not able to read reports which are openly sincere and inspired by real ideas. . . . How grateful I am to you . . . for having admitted that there are maybe grey and somber days in my life, full of unknown mysteries, so different from what people think about my life and of what has been written. Days of a heavy sadness without cause, of an undefinable reticence, self-respect insulted, of a shapeless inexistence.

Later in the year, the poet also owned that during three months of 1959—from February through April—all his mail "mysteriously and completely disappeared."[65] Such enforced isolation from the West could only reinforce his despondency.

Pasternak's acute depression and even anguish brought on by the harassment to which he had been subjected were embodied in the first version of his poem "The Nobel Prize," which was completed by early February. On the spur of the mo-

---

*For a discussion of Judaic values and "the Jewish question" in *Doctor Zhivago*, see Chapter 17.

Pasternak with Irina,
Ivinskaia's daughter.
Arthème Fayard.

ment he gave a copy of the poem to journalist Anthony Brown of the *London Daily Mail*, asking him to take it to Jacqueline de Proyart. Little did the poet foresee that, instead, Brown would commit a grievous indiscretion and publish it in the *Daily Mail* on February 11.[66] Millions of readers could learn of Pasternak's agony and anguish for the future:

> I am lost like a beast in an enclosure,
>   Somewhere are people, freedom and light.
> Behind me is the noise of pursuit,
>   And there is no way out.
>
> Dark forest by the shore of the lake,
>   Stump of fallen fir tree,
> Here I am cut off from everything,
>   Whatever shall be is the same to me.

> But what wicked thing have I done,
>   I, the "murderer" and "villain"?
> I, who force the whole world to cry
>   Over the beauty of my land.
>
> But, in any case, I am near my grave,
>   And I believe the time will come,
> When the spirit of good will conquer
>   Wickedness and infamy.[67]

The day after its appearance the poem was read and discussed in the British House of Lords. Its publication created a strong current of pity for Pasternak among readers of the world press. In presenting it to his readers, Brown commented that "sections of the Government and the Soviet Writers' Union press for [Pasternak's] ejection from his home, forfeiture of all royalties on his poems and translations in the Soviet Union—which would make him penniless—and possible imprisonment for 'literary deviation.'" The newspaper also reported that "Pasternak has become an outcast. His fellow-writers leave him alone severely."[68]

In addition to his despondency, Pasternak also experienced very intense emotional strain produced by a serious quarrel with Ivinskaia. The writer, more and more disgruntled by what he viewed as his wife's antagonism, had finally made plans to leave the "big dacha" in Peredelkino, and go with Ivinskaia to Tarusa to spend the winter with Konstantin Paustovskii. Ivinskaia welcomed the plan. Then on the morning of January 20, the day fixed for their departure, Pasternak said that he did not have the nerve to leave his family. Ivinskaia, who had been looking forward to being married to Pasternak at long last, was incensed. After a tempestuous argument she said that she was leaving Pasternak and departed for Moscow.* Pasternak's despair was reflected in two stanzas added to a revised version of "The Nobel Prize," completed by March, in which he lamented the circumstance that made the hour even darker: "My right hand is no longer with me— / My dear friend is with me no more." There was another serious quarrel with Ivinskaia in February and March, 1959, but Ivinskaia soon forgave Pasternak, and their association continued.[69]

Intertwined with this crisis in his private life were the serious difficulties which the writer then had to face as a result of two indiscretions he had committed: the release of "The Nobel Prize" and an interview with a British journalist from the *London News Chronicle*, in which he outlined his conception of the writer as "the Faust of modern society" and vowed that the Union of Writers would never succeed in making him go down on his knees before them. Polikarpov was outraged by these indiscretions, which amounted to a complete denial of the version of recent events that he had tried to convey to the world press. Pasternak was summoned to a Soviet criminal court, subjected to a formal interrogation, and ac-

---

*As Ivinskaia points out, marriage to Pasternak would have meant for her the protection to be derived from bearing his name. Such protection in fact remained lacking—and later, after Pasternak's death, this circumstance facilitated the authorities' plan to arrest her. For more details about this episode, see Chapter 12.

Pasternak with Georges Nivat, a young Slavic scholar, who during his stay in Moscow became engaged to Irina. *Archives Georges Nivat.*

Pasternak with Ivinskaia. *Archives Georges Nivat.*

cused of high treason for slandering the Soviet regime. Pasternak refused to sign a statement promising not to meet foreigners but did give Prosecutor General Roman Rudenko his verbal assurance to that effect. Back at his dacha, Pasternak put up on his front door a notice in English, French, and German: "Pasternak does not receive. He is forbidden to receive foreigners." Within about ten days Ivinskaia was also summoned to court and told not to see foreigners.[70]

In his isolation Pasternak nevertheless continued to write. The London *Times* published an item from Moscow, dated February 13, in which Pasternak said that he was working on a new book "about human conditions at the present time, . . . which I accept, extol, and must write about." Furthermore, in spite of the renewed political pressure, Pasternak hoped to be reinstated in the Writers' Union. It turned out that a price was exacted for reinstatement: the poet should write an "appropriate" work—an ode to the Soviet sputniks or possibly an open "peace letter" to India's Prime Minister Jawaharlal Nehru. After some hesitation Pasternak concluded that such a step was beneath his dignity as a writer, and he was never reinstated in the Union of Writers.[71]

If government officials offered a glimmer of hope for Pasternak's eventual reentry to the Writers' Union, they nonetheless completely smothered any hope of further foreign contact. In mid-February, the *Manchester Guardian* in several articles reported an effort by Priscilla de Villalonga (the wife of the exiled Spanish writer José-Luis de Villalonga), who was visiting Moscow, to arrange some lecture tours for Pasternak in the United States and Great Britain. The picture becomes unclear at this point. According to one source, Pasternak was unwilling to leave Russia without the assurance that he would be allowed to return. Although some said that there was no basis for the rumor that such lecture tours were being seriously considered, the Soviet Embassy in East Berlin is alleged to have annulled a visa previously issued by the Soviet Embassy in Paris to José-Luis de Villalonga, who wanted to make contact with the Soviet minister of culture to organize a tour for Pasternak in the West. It was also reported that Villalonga predicted that such a tour could raise a million dollars for a "Pasternak Foundation" to aid deserving writers.[72]

In February, Polikarpov asked Pasternak to absent himself from the capital from February 21 to March 3, during the visit to Moscow of British Prime Minister Harold Macmillan, so that he would not be descended upon by journalists accompanying Macmillan or asked to meet some member of the official party. It was hinted that he might give an interview that he would later regret. He complied with this "request" (later making it clear to a friend that he was not given much choice) and decided to go with Zinaida Nikolaevna to visit Nina Tabidze in Georgia. On February 14, the Pasternaks arrived in Georgia, having taken advantage of a recently inaugurated air service between Moscow and Tbilisi. For the first time in his life Pasternak made a plane trip, on board a Tupolev-104. He became ill before the end of the two-hour flight, a reaction that his Georgian friends later interpreted as a symptom of more serious illness, soon to progress rapidly.

The Pasternaks spent three weeks with the Tabidzes on Gogebashvili Street in

Pasternak in front of the dacha in Peredelkino. *Cornell Capa/Magnum.*

Tbilisi. The poet took walks with Nina Tabidze or with her daughter, Nitochka. It was reported that he was "unusually happy" during this stay. "His lips smiled, his eyes smiled, his voice smiled." Pasternak was met warmly by Georgian intellectuals; both his *Poems About Georgia* and *Georgian Poets* (in his Russian translations) had appeared in 1958, and these publications deepened the sympathy and respect Tbilisi intellectuals felt for him. Although the Union of Georgian Writers had been instructed not to organize any meetings in his honor, many came to see him—including the poet Leonidze, at whose house the Pasternaks had stayed in 1931 and whose guest Zinaida Nikolaevna would be again after her husband's death. Nina Tabidze tried her best to divert him from his anxiety. Half in joke she referred to him as "the third Russian poet in disgrace that Georgia received" (the others had been Pushkin and Lermontov).[73]

In spite of these friendly efforts, the pressure was obviously heavy. A visitor, the journalist Patricia Blake, reported that on Easter Pasternak greeted her from the top step of the porch (not having invited her in) and read a letter she had for him. She said that, "although he was deeply sun-tanned and looked astonishingly young for a man of sixty-nine, she was shocked by the immense weariness in his face, in his whole bearing." He spoke to her of how cautious he had to be: "I am in serious trouble. . . . I am not permitted to see foreigners. . . . Please forgive me for my terrible rudeness." Blake reported that, when she left Pasternak, plain-clothes policemen followed her as far as the railway-station platform. Because of the continued surveillance and pressure from authorities, as well as the importunity of certain visitors, until later in 1959 the poet was reluctant to see any strangers. It was reported that in September a hand-lettered sign in Russian hung on his door reading: "Journalists and others, please go away. I am busy." In spite of the sign, however, Pasternak at times relented and had visitors for long conversations.[74]

To the dismay of most Western readers of *Doctor Zhivago*, the novelist Mikhail Sholokhov, a mouthpiece for the Soviet establishment, denounced Pasternak at a press conference held in London in April. At the meeting Sholokhov referred to the author of *Doctor Zhivago* as a "poet of old maids" and called the work a "shapeless" novel that slandered Russian intellectuals. He added that if it were published in Russia his readers would beat him.[75]

By the time the Third Writers' Congress convened in Moscow in May, 1959, a vigorous campaign against sundry literary "revisionists"—such as Ehrenburg, Simonov, and Evtushenko—had reached its climax. Soon, however, Khrushchev's desire to present an appearance of adopting milder policies toward the intelligentsia (after the post-Hungary hardening of the line) led to a effort at reconciliation between party authorities and writers. As a consequence of that new situation—and also very probably as a result of Khrushchev's displeasure at Surkov's mishandling of the "Pasternak Affair"—Surkov was replaced by Fedin as secretary of the Writers' Union.*

---

*During a five-hour interview in Moscow with British Member of Parliament R. H. S. Crossman in August, 1958, Surkov readily admitted that he was "chiefly responsible" for the ban on Pasternak's novel (R. H. S. Crossman, "London Diary," *New Statesman*, November 29, 1958, p. 751).

There is good reason to believe that during the second half of the year government surveillance of Pasternak lessened, at least to the extent that he could resume his correspondence. Nonetheless, in a letter to a foreign woman friend he referred to his "semiprison" condition and suggested that she postpone a planned trip to see him because he might have to refuse her entry into his house. Although he told some correspondents that he was joyous about the success of his novel overseas, he told Renate Schweitzer that he felt he should suppress those feelings to make room for energies that could lead to new literary productions.[76]

Early in the summer of 1959 he revealed that, because he was unable to receive his royalties from the West, he had to spend most of his time on translations to provide for his family. He denied the rumor that he was working on a translation of Rabindranath Tagore. According to a well-informed Western source, in August he was again receiving royalties for plays performed in his translations. One play in particular was singled out: Schiller's *Maria Stuart*. On one occasion funds from abroad—royalties from the sales of *Doctor Zhivago*, "a fairly substantial sum"—were deposited for Pasternak in the State Bank (Gosbank). The poet, under pressure from the authorities, had to renounce them.[77]

Meanwhile, Pasternak's influence continued to grow. Two young Soviet poets, Ivan Kharabarov and Iurii Pankratov,* got into trouble for spreading a "Pasternak cult." They often visited Pasternak in Peredelkino, adorned their apartments with his pictures, and obtained a copy of his novel from which they read excerpts to students enrolled at the Gorky Literary Institute in Moscow. When they refused to go to the virgin lands of central Asia to expiate their crimes, both were excluded from the Komsomol and from the Union of Writers. Another fact seemed to indicate that Soviet authorities were still cautious in dealing with Pasternak: in September his nephew Nicolas Slater (the son of Lydia Pasternak-Slater), who had received a scholarship from the British Ministry of Education, was refused a visa to the Soviet Union. Pasternak, however, felt relaxed enough to make his first public appearance since the awarding of the Nobel Prize. On September 11 he attended the Moscow performance of the New York Philharmonic Orchestra, conducted by Leonard Bernstein. After the concert Pasternak went up to Bernstein and embraced him.[78]

In September, 1959, Khrushchev appears to have asked his son-in-law Aleksei Adzhubei (the editor of *Izvestiia*) for an opinion on *Doctor Zhivago*. Adzhubei reported that there was nothing fundamentally wrong with the novel, that he thought it could very well have been published with the omission of three to four hundred words. At the thought that so much unnecessary turmoil had been caused by overzealous dogmatists, Khrushchev exploded and ordered the dismissal of Semichastnyi, head of the Komsomol. At that point Khrushchev appears to have given the green light for the writer's readmission to the Writers' Union,† thus putting an end to the harshest reprisals against him.[79]

Disregarding these oscillations in the official attitude toward him, Pasternak pursued his literary contacts with the West. As these contacts grew, he received

---

*Both were classmates of Ivinskaia's daughter, Irina, at the Gorky Institute of World Literature in Moscow.

†Pasternak's reinstatement never took place, for reasons explained earlier.

from his correspondents a number of books to which the average Soviet intellectual did not have access. Thus (as I verified during a visit to the Pasternak family in Peredelkino in 1962) the poet had on his shelves several volumes by Pierre Teilhard de Chardin, including *Le phénomène humain*; several of Virginia Woolf's novels; D. H. Lawrence's *The Plumed Serpent*; two different editions of Paul Claudel's complete works; an edition of Friedrich Nietzsche's letters; Lawrence Durrell's *Justine* and *Balthazar*; individual works by such authors as Pär Lagerkvist and the French theologian Jean Daniélou; and a number of modern American novels in the Gallimard editions (many of these books had been sent to him by Jacqueline de Proyart). Concerning the works of certain contemporary French and Scandinavian writers, he wrote to one correspondent that, despite the novelty and stylistic majesty he found in many of them, none were really exciting or relevant to the new paths he was exploring.[80]

A major achievement of Pasternak's in the 1950s was the poetry grouped under the title *When Skies Clear* (*Kogda razguliaetsia*). In its fullest edition this collection comprises forty-four poems related by a fuguelike composition. Jacqueline de Proyart has analyzed the work in a perceptive structural and thematic study. Here the main interlocutors in the poet's dialogue are woman, nature, death, and God. The feminine element is present in many guises—the women in the poet's childhood, his apprenticeship in passion, woman's Evelike role in his life—but passion is portrayed here in a far more subdued vein than in *My Sister, Life*. Nature, even more pervasive, occupies about half the space in the collection—the usual proportion in Pasternak. All the seasons are represented in an order reflecting careful structural concern rather than the calendar. The landscapes depicted are mostly Pasternak's natural paradise of Peredelkino—Lake Izmalkovo, the River Setun, the mushrooms in the nearby forest, haystacks in the field. In a striking cultural insight wheat fields are seen as a page of man's writing. The natural experience is far from being merely picturesque and pleasurable, however; foul weather, disease, and death are part of it, and Proyart's careful reconstruction of the cycle's composition has shown how these elements reflect Pasternak's experience of the years 1956 through 1959.[81]

At a deeper level, nature is viewed as a long religious service that the poet-worshiper has attended. The abundant and heartwarming response of thousands of his readers reveals to Pasternak another aspect of "God's world." "In Hospital" provides a full acknowledgment of divine providence. Cosmic gratitude for natural and supernatural experiences pervades the collection in a devotional note that often borders on ecstasy; thus a meditation on Poland and Georgia evokes a vision of ultimate harmony between man and the elements.

It has been pointed out that the "child's freshness, the wonder, the strong joy of acclamation of a world just created" so characteristic of Pasternak's earlier poetry are absent from *When Skies Clear*. It is true that here we see far less buoyancy than before and less of an active desire to "transform the given world into something new and intense and extraordinary."[82] Yet the poet still seeks, in a more mature and refined way, to identify and understand the constant flow of changes affecting the world and to radiate this understanding. While the narrator reveals an aware-

Pasternak being presented
with a Russian-language
edition of *Doctor Zhivago*,
the first he had seen, 1959.
Ralph E. Matlaw.

ness of the aging process, in *When Skies Clear* he is not resigning from his former mission, only seeking to accomplish it from a different vantage point. He endeavors to communicate to his readers his mature vision of the values that inform an infinite universe. In essence, the deeper message of the collection is similar to that of *Doctor Zhivago*: from death arises a new life of greater awareness. The poet feels a responsibility to enhance others' awareness of this rebirth. In this connection, the artist's vocation is shown as having its moral imperative: fame "is not a pretty sight," while the artist's only fulfillment lies in eschewing appearance for the sake of true being, which is achieved by the most rigorous and honest work. Authenticity is attained only if the artist pursues the aim of creation, which is "gift of self." The ultimate transfiguration of nature and self through art conceived as a superior, demanding mission fraught with renunciation is the culmination of the book's message.[83]

Another of Pasternak's major achievements of the decade was *Sketch for an Autobiography*. Composed at the instigation of his editor Bannikov and completed in May–June, 1956, under the title "In Lieu of a Foreword" it was originally intended to serve as a preface to the collection of earlier and more recent poems that Pasternak hoped to publish simultaneously with *Doctor Zhivago*. Pasternak corrected the proofs in November, 1957. The following year—the publication of the volume in the Soviet Union having become impossible because of the appearance abroad of the novel—Pasternak changed his plans and authorized publication of the more recent poetry as a separate volume (which appeared as *When Skies Clear*), while the introduction also appeared separately as *Essai d'autobiographie*, published by Gallimard in the summer of 1958. Toward the end of the year Feltrinelli published the two texts together in Italy as *Autobiografia e nuovi versi*. The publisher hoped thereby to secure international rights for both works. Unlike *Doctor Zhivago*, *Sketch for an Autobiography* was to be published in the Soviet Union several years after the author's death (an attempt to print it in the third volume of the almanac *Literaturnaia Moskva* in 1957 failed, but it was published with a few abridgments in *Novyi mir* in January, 1967).[84]

Although thirty years separate *Sketch for an Autobiography* from *A Safe-Conduct*, the second autobiography covers the same period of the author's life, updated only with one section on Paolo Iashvili and Titian Tabidze. *Sketch for an Autobiography* neither repeats nor continues *A Safe-Conduct*; as Aleksandr Gladkov put it, "It represents as it were a musical variation on it." Whereas the earlier volume mingles a description of the origins of Pasternak's poetry with broader aesthetic and cultural considerations, the later text is almost exclusively a discussion and reevaluation of those artists who influenced Pasternak. The *Sketch* reads like an intimate, intent (albeit impressionistic) conversation about people and places. Pasternak omitted much of what could not but shape him as an artist—his experiences in Moscow and Chistopol during World War II and his translations of Shakespeare—as if (it has been suggested) "selecting and retaining only that which, in his life, led him to compose *Doctor Zhivago*."[85]

Beginning with a criticism of what he called the "unnecessary mannerisms" marring the earlier volume, Pasternak penned his second autobiography in clear, lucid prose ("I was born in Moscow on January 29, 1890 . . ."). *Sketch for an Autobiography* is divided into five sections. The first, "Infancy," is filled with Pasternak's early impressions, ranging from nannies and domestic scenes to his father's artistic activities. Here the author mentions Tolstoy twice, as a portent of his eventual devotion to literature and as a very real indication of the inspiration, moral as well as aesthetic, that Tolstoy provided. In "Scriabin," Pasternak lovingly describes the famous composer's music and personality (both were fresh and original), as well as Scriabin's hold on his imagination. But—perhaps more important—he says that Scriabin proved to him that, with the means that were at the disposal of his predecessors, a great artist can renew an art form "from its very foundations."[86]

"The Nineteen Hundreds" opens with a description of events of the 1905 Revolution, the political turmoil of the period being an appropriate introduction to the literary turmoil that began then. There is a tension in this section, produced by the repeated alternation of the old and the new. Characteristic of the older generations are Tolstoy—whose death, a symbol of the passing of a generation, is described—as well as Belyi, to whom Pasternak ascribes "all the marks of genius," and Blok, whom he views as exemplary and endowed with the earmarks of a great poet. Within the context of his discoveries as a young poet, Pasternak also analyzes Rilke's poetry, which struck and amazed him in the same way that his first encounter with Blok's poems did—through "the urgency of what they had to say, the absoluteness, the gravity, the direct purposefulness of their language." The significance for Pasternak of Rilke's poetic diction was such that, to prove his point, he translated two examples of the latter's poems, quoting them in this text. In contrast to the uniqueness of these talents, Pasternak underscores the helplessness and inarticulateness—at that particular time—of the "new" Russian poets, a censure from which he absolves the early production of both Tsvetaeva and, surprisingly, the mediocre Aseev.[87]

Pasternak then gives a single-page account of his summer at the University of

Pasternak in his garden, 1959.
Ardis.

With Heinz Schewe, after a performance in Moscow of *Faust* by the Hamburg Theater
Company. *Heinz Schewe.*

After the performance of *Faust*, Pasternak congratulates the actors. *Heinz Schewe.*

Pasternak in Peredelkino. *Archives
Hélène Zamoyska.*

Marburg (compared with forty-odd pages in *A Safe-Conduct*). The major emphasis
in this section, "Before the First World War," is on Maiakovskii, whose *early*
lyrical poetry the author viewed as "beautifully modelled, majestic, demonic,
and, at the same time, infinitely doomed, perishing, almost calling for help."
Pasternak was alienated by Maiakovskii's later poetry, however, and states over
and over that his connections with him have been exaggerated. His new attitude
toward his fellow poet is marked by an intentional dryness of tone and a definite
toughness. Perhaps the most important part of this section is a short disquisition
on suicide, which reveals Pasternak's belief in the vital importance of the continuity of inner existence; for him memories create this continuity, which is so
necessary for survival—those who abandon their past, their memories, abandon
their reason for existence. This is a deeply personal passage; Pasternak is contrasting his ability to survive with the suicides of his fellow poets Maiakovskii and
Esenin.[88]

The "Three Shadows" discussed in the conclusion are Tsvetaeva, Iashvili, and
Tabidze. Pasternak writes: "The fate of these two men, and that of Marina
Tsvetaeva, was to become my greatest sorrow." As has been noted, however, Pasternak "does not dwell on their deaths . . . but on the richness of life they gave
him." Pasternak discusses the poetry of all three (Tsvetaeva's in the most depth)
and relates memories of his friendship with each. Strengthened by his memories

of these friends and others from his past, Pasternak seems in calm possession of himself and ready for what fate has in store for him. *Sketch for an Autobiography* "memorializes the dead," but more important, by calling off the names of the dead, Pasternak both illustrates (as he had in *A Safe-Conduct*) his belief in the continuity of art in history and traces his own artistic genealogy.[89]

Doctor Zhivago, *When Skies Clear*, and *Sketch for an Autobiography* had now been published. By the autumn of 1959 the main episodes of the "Pasternak Affair" were over—but not without irreversible consequences to Pasternak's health. Thus, in November, 1959, he mentioned to a Belgian correspondent that he was neglecting "the signals" his heart was giving him. Around the same time, in a letter to another Western correspondent, he alluded to his impending death. He elaborated at some length the background of this premonition:

A short time ago I began to notice now and then a disturbance at the left side of my breast. This is allied to the heart—I am telling no one about it as, if I do mention it, I shall have to give up my habitual daily routine. My wife, relatives, friends will stand over me. Doctors, sanatoriums, hospitals crush out life before one is yet dead. The slavery of compassion begins.

Rumors concerning the writer's failing health began circulating; the word cancer was mentioned.[90]

In the latter part of 1959, Pasternak was again occasionally seen in town at cultural events. A particularly significant and moving occasion for him was the visit he paid in December to a performance of *Faust* by a Hamburg company, directed by Gustaf Gründgens at Moscow's Central Children Theater on Sverdlov Square. The warm, spirited conversation that he continued with director and actors until the middle of the night prompted him to invite some of them to visit him in Peredelkino within a few days (but that plan had to be given up, for he feared Zinaida Nikolaevna's opposition to the visit).[91]

Pasternak's life continued outwardly unchanged: he saw visitors and attended to his voluminous correspondence (it has been estimated that from October, 1958, until his death he received between twenty and thirty thousand letters). When in January, 1960, Renate Schweitzer wrote him that she planned a visit to Moscow in the near future, he responded enthusiastically, looking forward to acquainting her with Zinaida Nikolaevna, Ivinskaia, his home, and his daily life. The letter concluded with a paragraph expressing dismay that he was unable to get on with his work, feeling that he was duty-bound to continue writing because of the praise bestowed on *Doctor Zhivago*. The next month—less than three months before his death—he voiced similar feelings when (in a letter written in English) he expressed hopes of retrieving his true self from "this long and continuing period of letter writing, boring trouble, endless thrusting rhyme translations, time robbing and useless, and of the perpetual selfreproof because of the impossibility to advance the longed for, half begun, many times interrupted, almost inaccessible new manuscript [a historical drama of Russia in the 1860s]." It is clear that, because of such obligations and the financial duress which made it necessary for him to earn a living by translation work, until his death Pasternak was tormented by his inability to further his creative work.[92]

By the end of the decade worldwide recognition and fulfilment had come to Pasternak. He had won the Nobel Prize, about which, according to a fellow poet's testimony, he "had dreamed."[93] There were to be tragic sequels to the "Pasternak Affair": the writer's death and the subsequent fate of Ivinskaia and her daughter.

12

The End and Its Aftermath

1960–

His stature as a great and exquisite poet is one point which needs no abiding of judgement. Russia, once so generously rewarded by God with poets (to quote Gogol), can (but does not) boast of the two (just two) surviving today.* Pasternak is Russia's only living male poet of stature and authenticity, and the very last of Russia's intellectuals.

Bernard Gilbert Guerney[1]

[The poem "August"] is only a dream, and now I've put it down on paper it won't come true. But even so—how good it would be to die at this God-given time of year, when the earth pays people back a hundredfold, makes good its debts in full and rewards us with unbelievable generosity. The sky is as blue as it can ever be, the water so eagerly reflects the fantastically coloured rowan trees, turning them upside down. The earth has given its all and is ready for a breathing space.

Boris Pasternak[2]

For half a century now I have often found myself suddenly muttering some poem of Pasternak's. You cannot banish those poems from the world: they are alive.

Ilia Ehrenburg[3]

*The other Russian poet "of stature and authenticity" whom Guerney had in mind was Anna Akhmatova.

On his seventieth birthday, February 10, 1960, Pasternak was showered with testimonies of affection and admiration from all over Russia and the world. He was
still receiving an average of thirty letters a day, and on this special occasion special
tokens of recognition reached him, including a silver candlelighter, a valuable old
engraving from Jena, and many records and books. While comforted by these
gestures of thoughtfulness, he was not so keen on receiving congratulations, for
the very reason that, just as he was reluctant to accept the process of aging in
general, so he was unwilling to "take kindly the counsel of the years."[4]

Until almost the very end, Pasternak managed to maintain an extraordinarily
youthful appearance. Until well after sixty, he had a good figure, looked healthy
and slender, was swift and agile—until the late 1950s he would "run" rather than
walk around Peredelkino, a habit that reflected his peculiar kind of restlessness.
The few streaks of gray that had barely touched his hair in the early 1940s had
become a white mane, yet without altering the youthful appearance of his face.
He maintained his good health through his simplicity, modest life-style, and
brisk regimen. Before his leg began giving him trouble, he would get up early, do
gymnastics, have a hearty breakfast, and then sit down to work. Before the mid-
day meal, even in freezing winter weather, he washed at the outdoor pump in his
yard in Peredelkino; in the spring, as soon as the snow began to recede, he would
go to the Setun to immerse his head in its icy waters. After his meal he would take
a brief siesta before going back to his desk, where he worked until nine or ten in
the evening.[5] Only very seldom did he watch television—the set in their living
room served mainly for the entertainment of Zinaida Nikolaevna.

An important break in the daily routine was the long, sometimes more than
two-hour walk he took in Peredelkino or the surrounding countryside. Tidily
attired in the familiar old jacket and trousers, he walked around Lake Izmalkovo
or to the neighboring village, Choboty, or even farther, deep into the forest. During these walks he stopped to talk to those he met, gazing at them with his large,
radiant dark-hazel eyes with an air of trustfulness. To the children who sometimes followed him he gave candy from the supply stuffed in his pockets. In his
peculiar baritone drone, with a deep nasal timbre and resonant, long-drawn-out
vowels, Pasternak addressed those he met. The poet spoke to them all, the lowly
and the poor, listened with a child's simplicity, gave advice, and helped them
when he could—evidently trying to meet the standards he held up in such a
poem as "The Change" (1958). Whereas when speaking to fellow artists Pasternak was so carried away with breathless excitement and enthusiasm that he conducted monologues (seeming to require charmed listeners rather than partners in
a dialogue), with the simpler neighbors it appears that he evolved another mode
of communication.

During his walks the poet would indulge in his favorite sensory experiences:
the smell of freshly laundered linen drying in the breeze, the sight and smell of
autumn bonfires of leaves in the gardens, and the many sensations provided by all
the seasons, as conveyed in *When Skies Clear.*[6]

One key element of Pasternak's mental and physical health was the aptitude for
work (which has been described as "boundless"), patience, and endurance embod-

AMERICAN ACADEMY OF ARTS AND LETTERS
NATIONAL INSTITUTE OF ARTS AND LETTERS

IN RECOGNITION OF
CREATIVE ACHIEVEMENT IN THE ARTS

BORIS PASTERNAK

WAS ELECTED TO HONORARY MEMBERSHIP
NEW YORK   FEBRUARY   MCMLX

PRESIDENT OF THE ACADEMY   PRESIDENT OF THE INSTITUTE

SECRETARY   SECRETARY

The publication of *Doctor Zhivago* brought various awards. Pasternak was extremely proud of this certificate, which reached him just three months before his death. *Arthème Fayard.*

ied in him. Everyday work at his desk he viewed as a vital duty, to which he sacrificed pastimes he felt unnecessary. In the 1930s he had stopped reading newspapers, and toward the end of his life he no longer listened to the radio (he once remarked that life became "transparent" if instead of working one just looked for news, living off the echo of something taking place elsewhere). Beside intellectual endeavor work in his garden was an essential activity. He sometimes helped Zinaida Nikolaevna gather brushwood, but most often and regularly from the first days at Peredelkino he would till the field, growing cucumbers, vegetable marrows, and potatoes. At times it seemed to him that this work was something visible and real, as opposed to "all the rest," which looked like "something insubstantial, vague, and confused." During the many difficult days he endured, labor in the garden helped take his mind off his concerns. Rummaging in the soil with his hands and perceiving nature as something palpable and akin to him gave him a feeling of plenitude. On hot July days his friend Chukovskii would often see him working on the potatoes he had planted himself, while the sun burned his bare back.[7]

While for a long time such a way of life provided the necessary external sta-

Pasternak working in the vegetable garden in front of his dacha, 1958. *Cornell Capa/Magnum.*

bility, grappling with his latest self-assigned creative task proved an ordeal. The last few months of Pasternak's life were a time of agonizing mental strain, compounded by an eagerness to complete his work in progress, the dramatic trilogy *The Blind Beauty* (*Slepaia krasavitsa*). He felt duty-bound to write this work, to repay the recognition and affection that had come to him from over the world with the appearance of *Doctor Zhivago*. Despite failing health, during the last year of his life he often sat at his desk until two or three in the morning to further this task.[8]

Nadezhda Mandelstam was both inaccurate and unfair when she wrote that Pasternak "in his old age . . . took it into his head to write a melodrama of a traditional kind." The idea of writing a play had first occurred to the writer at the beginning of World War II, when he had devoted much time and energy to composing a play about the war. After the publication of *Zhivago* he had taken up the endeavor again, in a new conception. *The Blind Beauty* was unfinished at his death in 1960. There were only fragments of the first play in a projected trilogy—a two-scene prologue, an incomplete first act, and notes on how the rest of the drama was to be developed. On the aesthetic plane the fragments we have are certainly not on a par with Pasternak's best work, though it is difficult to say what the tone and structure of the completed trilogy would have been.[9]

The Blind Beauty is a historical drama concerned with serfdom and the serf theater laid in nineteenth-century Russia but suggesting a parallel with the contemporary scene. In its completed form it was to be Pasternak's statement on freedom and Russia's cultural tradition. Pasternak was fascinated by the institution of slavery in Russia as it approached emancipation and the effect the time of transition must have had upon the artist. The play's characters talk much about freedom—especially social freedom—but after the emancipation soon realize that real freedom can be found only in art. An impassioned love story was to have been included in the drama, along with the reenactment of actual historical events of the period.[10]

In the trilogy Pasternak is also suggesting a parallel between two radically different spheres of existence: art and history. In the play we see history in flux as Russia moves toward emancipation—a sort of social redemption. Its parallel in the twentieth century is the movement of art toward freedom from repression and censorship. Yet, for the poet, art is not on a parallel plane with history, but on a higher one. We see this through the allegorical figure Lusha, a young, pregnant serf who is blinded when an *objet d'art* shatters. The other "blind beauty" is Russia, which, as Pasternak said to a visitor, has been "oblivious for so long of its own beauty, of its own destinies." In the play Agafonov, an actor, is responsible for curing Lusha of her blindness, as art will cure Russia of her blindness. From the fragments of the trilogy that we have, it is clear that Pasternak saw art as the one thing of permanence and value in a constantly changing society.[11]

Pasternak in his study in Peredelkino. *Cornell Capa/Magnum.*

In addition to *The Blind Beauty*, Pasternak also planned further prose works, in which he wanted to show "what can be achieved through extreme stylistic restraint (*sderzhannostiu sloga*)." The poet's other plans included the elaboration of his notes on his translations of Shakespeare and Goethe into a longer article.[12]

The poet's commitment to these projects is all the more remarkable when one considers that, besides dealing with almost constant pressure from the regime, he was aware that his own health was failing and thus doubly concerned about the future of his family and friends. He wrote in August, 1959: "The vise has not been loosened. My situation is worse, more intolerable and dangerous than I am able to tell you or than you could imagine." He was also concerned about the possible fate of his works. He decided to put the manuscript of *The Blind Beauty* in a safe place. In April, 1960, he entrusted it to Ivinskaia.[13]

In spite of his many concerns, Pasternak continued working and kept up contacts and correspondence with friends, artists, and writers both in the Soviet Union and in the West. One of these friends, Renate Schweitzer, was able to visit Pasternak in April, 1960, and her account of that visit provides great insight into his life during the last months. An interesting sidelight to this literary friendship is that apparently Pasternak experienced some unease upon meeting her in person. He broached the matter in a letter to her, though concluding that her visit would cause no disharmony or tension that could threaten the members of his household. In a later letter, however, which arrived after Schweitzer had left Berlin, Pasternak asked her to forgo the visit. Their correspondence had begun when he was in physical pain and mental desperation. Schweitzer's unrestrained admiration for his work and her compassion for his oppressed life had provided him with occasional relief from depression. Their correspondence also reveals Pasternak's artistic agonies and his attempts to dispel his fears of artistic inadequacy and to confirm, within himself, his greatness. It should also be pointed out that the Pasternak-Schweitzer correspondence—like Pasternak's with certain other women friends—was marked by a somewhat exalted tone and occasionally veered into the sentimental (Pasternak must have had misgivings about that dimension, for he felt guilty in regard to Ivinskaia about this exalted platonic friendship; some of his letters to Schweitzer pronounce an end to such an involvement).[14]

Renate Schweitzer spent Easter Sunday (April 17, 1960) with the Pasternaks in Peredelkino. She was surprised by his declining health, noticing, for example, his pallor. Talking with Zinaida Nikolaevna, she expressed some anxiety about Pasternak's meager diet. The poet's wife affirmed that he never ate much, often just soup. Pasternak admitted to her that his health was not good, describing to her the hardships of his stay in the Moscow clinic in 1958 and adding, "It was a terrible situation, I wouldn't want to relive it."[15]

The visit was equally revealing about Pasternak's work. Schweitzer expressed her surprise at the diversity of titles in Pasternak's library, which, in addition to copies of *Zhivago* in various translations, contained almost exclusively English, German, and French authors. Pasternak explained, "Owning these books constitutes one of my crimes!"[16]

Renate had brought several books to her friend. Pasternak was most interested in *Civilization and Ethics*, by Albert Schweitzer (Renate's putative remote "cousin," with whom she corresponded). Pasternak said that he felt a kinship with Schweitzer's philosophy, especially with his "reverence for life" and his concern for the suffering of others (emphasizing the suffering of women and children).[17]

Pasternak then asked her to distribute five thousand dollars (from the royalties accrued to him in the West) to people he considered needy. Renate interpreted this gesture as a manifestation of Tolstoy's influence on Pasternak, for Tolstoy too had renounced possessions in his later years. Pasternak told her, "Money is only of value insofar as it provides freedom and peace for work, work which is an obligation of man." Such a gesture was very much in keeping with the generosity and concern for others that Pasternak had shown for many years; for decades he had given liberally to those in need, including the Mandelstams, Akhmatova, and Belyi's widow, and had arranged for such benefits as a pension direly needed by an aged writer.[18]

After that memorable Easter Sunday (spent partly at Ivinskaia's dacha and partly at the "big dacha" with the Pasternak family), Renate Schweitzer left for Moscow. It is clear that the visit was an emotional strain for Pasternak. The two of them made plans for her next visit, to be in the summer of the same year. Schweitzer did not suspect that she would not see Pasternak again. As a farewell gift Pasternak presented her with a copy of *When Skies Clear*, with an inscription reiterating an image used in the poem "Winterlight": spots left on the wall by dead moths who had lost nocturnal battles with the poet for the kingdom of lamplight.[19]

For Pasternak himself, darkness was slowly conquering the kingdom of the lamplight. Pressures, worry, and illness had so debilitated him that he had great difficulty working. Nonetheless, in April he managed some final letters to Schweitzer, expressing optimism about the future: ". . . there is so much to come, so much that will happen." The optimism proved ill-founded. On April 25, Pasternak wrote her that he had been bedridden for five days with extreme pain in the chest, back, and left shoulder. He mentioned their "charity project" but said that it would be some time before he could arrange to have the money sent to her. He added that the memory of their recent meeting was a consolation to him in his suffering and emotionally thanked her for their friendship.[20]

Pasternak's final illness was signaled by a series of blackouts early in May. On May 6 he sent Schweitzer a telegram, telling her that he had been bedridden again for three weeks, this time with increasing pain. Even in these last days Pasternak endeavored to continue some of his correspondence, showing his sensitivity and concern for the needs of his friends.[21]

Pasternak apparently disliked the attention of doctors. Several sources note that he tried to hide the gravity of his condition from those around him and also from the officials, probably out of an attempt to protect his family. He expressed fears about his family's fate in the event of his death. As his condition grew worse, however, Pasternak at last acknowledged that he needed medical attention. He allowed himself to be taken to a hospital, but—it is reported—was refused admittance to the Kremlin Clinic (it is unclear whether or not for political reasons). On May 17 he had another severe attack, and this time nurses were sent to his bedside. His problem was diagnosed as a heart condition. On May 27, the famous heart specialist Nikolai Petrov (who charged five hundred rubles—over five hundred dollars—a visit) discovered that Pasternak also had cancer of the lungs, a condition of at least two years' duration. The diagnosis came too late, for the malignancy had spread to his heart,[22] with widespread infection. Priscilla Johnson, a correspondent for *Harper's Magazine*, was sought out in Moscow and asked whether she could obtain some ampuls of aureomycin or penicillin for him. The antibiotics were eventually obtained from a Western embassy.

As the poet's condition worsened, Ivinskaia asked that the news be communicated to the outside world. Through the good offices of the West German journalist Heinz Schewe—in whom Pasternak and Ivinskaia had the fullest trust—many of the writer's friends, including Renate Schweitzer, were kept informed of the progress of his final illness.[23]

At home, family and friends gathered about the dying poet, who lay in an oxygen tent in the music room, on the ground floor of the dacha (to which he had been moved earlier to be spared climbing the stairs). A doctor and nurses were in residence. Constant visitors included Pasternak's brother, Aleksandr, and his family; Pasternak's first wife, Evgeniia Vladimirovna; his son Evgenii, his stepson Stanislav Neigauz, and their families; and old friends Genrikh Neigauz, Nina Tabidze, Valentin Asmus, and Nikolai Viliam-Vilmont. Many of them stayed in the Pasternak dacha. Ivinskaia's daugher, Irina, was also at the dacha much of the time. During Pasternak's extremity his wife reportedly offered to call Ivinskaia to his bedside, but he refused. Later one of Pasternak's nurses relayed to Ivinskaia that the poet was afraid his debilitated condition would cause Ivinskaia to love him less or leave her with bad memories. Pasternak sent her reassuring notes, however, when he was permitted a pencil.[24]

Although thus surrounded by thoughtful presence during his final days, in the end Pasternak slipped quietly away when the family was out of the room for a few moments. Only a nurse was present when he drew the last breath, at 11:20 P.M. on May 30, 1960.[25]

Thus Pasternak's tormented last days ended quietly. Priscilla Johnson described the spring morning in Peredelkino that followed, full of the beauty the poet had loved: "It was a hot day, almost like mid-summer. The apple trees outside the Pasternak dacha were a mass of pink and white blossoms. Underfoot the grass was thick with clover and dandelions, buttercups and forget-me-nots."[26]

Ripples of the news began spreading from Peredelkino to friends and fellow artists. Some of his friends, including Konstantin Paustovskii, came by the poet's home that very morning. Ordinary people heard the news in their own way. On May 31 a handwritten scrap of paper was anonymously posted next to the ticket window at the Kiev Railroad Station, where suburban passengers bought their tickets for Peredelkino. The sign read:

At four o'clock on the afternoon of Thursday, June 2, the last leavetaking of Boris Leonidovich Pasternak, the greatest poet of present-day Russia, will take place.

The announcement also noted that one could reach Peredelkino from the Belorussian Station (though this alternative route meant a longer walk, the information would be useful should the authorities try to change the train schedules to discourage people from attending the funeral). Several times over a three-day period the sign was removed by some watchful official, always to be promptly replaced by a similar one posted by an unknown hand.[27]

News of Pasternak's death spread among the people through such anonymous messages and word of mouth. The literary community learned of it through a formal notice that appeared in the journal *Literature and Life* on June 1. The same announcement was reprinted at the bottom of the back page of *Literaturnaia gazeta* on June 2. It read:

The Board of the Literary Fund of the USSR announces the death of Boris Leonidovich Pasternak, writer and member of the Literary Fund, who passed away on May 30 in the seventy-first year of his life after a prolonged and serious illness. The board expresses its sympathy to the family of the deceased.

The phrase "member of the Literary Fund" is interesting. The Literary Fund was (and is) simply an organization which provides mutual aid or social services to writers. Mediocre writers unworthy of full membership in the Writers' Union were provided Literary Fund services. Since Pasternak had been expelled from the Writers' Union with great fanfare in 1958, the phrase had humiliating overtones. Some have suggested, on the other hand, that it was more fitting for the announcement of the poet's death to be issued by the Literary Fund (which was endowed with great respect because of its prerevolutionary antecedents and relative independence) than for the announcement to have come from the Writers' Union, to which Pasternak had never been close in spirit.[28]

Despite such efforts to downplay Pasternak's death, his funeral ceremony was fraught with meaning for both the many Russians and the foreigners who attended. Musicians were among the first to pay tribute to Pasternak. Four leading pianists—Stanislav Neigauz, Andrei Volkonskii, Mariia Iudina, and Sviatoslav Richter—performed at the dacha before the burial, paying tribute to Pasternak and in memory of his love of music. Richter played Chopin, about whom the poet had written an essay. The tribute of these artists lasted several hours. At the conclusion of Chopin's "Marche Funèbre," the coffin was borne out by several men, including Pasternak's sons. The other pallbearers included the writer Lev Kopelev (soon to become a dissident) and Andrei Siniavskii and Iulii Daniel, Pasternak's disciples and friends (who were later prosecuted for their intellectual independence, in a trial that received international attention).[29]

Among the mourners that day were many other artists and writers: Chukovskii (who carried one of the funeral wreaths that preceded the coffin), Veniamin Kaverin, Liubov Ehrenburg (whose husband was in Stockholm), Neigauz, and

Pasternak's funeral, June 2, 1960. At 4:00 P.M. the coffin is carried out of the dacha. The pallbearers in front are the poet's sons, Leonid (*left*) and Evgenii. *Heinz Schewe.*

At the gravesite. Among the mourners (*left to right*): Ivinskaia, Heinz Schewe, Irina (*behind her mother's shoulder*), Pasternak's stepson Stanislav Neigauz, Zinaida Pasternak, and the poet's younger son, Leonid. *Heinz Schewe Collection.*

At the gravesite. Zinaida Pasternak is second from the right. *Heinz Schewe Collection.*

Asmus. Also present were certain future "dissident" writers, such as Arkadii Belinkov.[30]

The funeral itself was a study in contrasts. In perspective it appears to have been the first significant political demonstration of the new—post-Thaw—Soviet intelligentsia, bolder and more conscious of the values it stands for. It was also the occasion for a spontaneous outpouring of thousands of ordinary Russians—including workers and peasants, as well as students. Thus the shadow of the police state, whose political pressure many see as the catalyst that brought on the poet's illness and death, fell across his funeral as well.

As Pasternak's coffin was being carried out of the house, accompanied by throngs of grieving students and friends, a large black limousine suddenly appeared. A well-known official of the Writers' Union stepped out and suggested that the heavy coffin might better be placed on top of the car for the rest of the journey. The students shouted him down, and the procession continued on its way to the Peredelkino cemetery, on the hillside facing the house. The procession walked at a brisk pace—so rapidly that to many it carried an impression of unseemly haste. Most of the large crowd followed the coffin on the road, while many others took a shortcut across a field.[31]

The ceremony itself was simple but extremely moving. There was no *panikhida* or Orthodox funeral service (the rites of the Orthodox church [*moleben*] had been performed quietly the evening before at the dacha; they had ended with the words, "May the memory of Boris Leonidovich, who is worthy of praise, remain with us forever"). At the graveside Pasternak was not accorded the ceremonies

Pasternak's grave and monument, at the foot of the three pines which the poet loved and which he could see from his window. The bas-relief is by sculptor Sara Lebedev. *Inge Morath. Cornell Capa/Magnum.*

270

normally accompanying the funeral of a member of the Writers' Union.[32] Asmus delivered the eulogy (reported by a journalist as follows:

We have come to bid farewell to one of the greatest of Russian writers and poets, a man endowed with all the talents, including even music. One might accept or reject his opinions, but as long as Russian poetry plays a role on this earth, Boris Leonidovich Pasternak will stand among the greatest.

His disagreement with our present day was not with a regime or a state. He wanted a society of a higher order. He never believed in resisting evil with force, and that was his mistake.

I never talked with a man who demanded so much, so unsparingly, of himself. There were but few who could equal him in the honesty of his convictions. He was a democrat in the true sense of the word, one who knew how to criticize his friends of the pen. He will forever remain as an example, as one who defended his convictions before his contemporaries, being firmly convinced that he was right. He had the ability to express humanity in the highest terms.

He lived a long life. But it passed so quickly, he was still so young and he had so much left to write. His name will go down forever as one of the very finest.

To some who were there, the eulogy sounded formal and restrained—such restraint being perhaps due in part to the presence of many foreign journalists and photographers, and especially of a small team of KGB informers, clicking away unabashedly with their cameras. In spite of the surveillance, the funeral was deeply emotional and meaningful. An actor from the Moscow Art Theater gave a recitation of Pasternak's poem "Hamlet," and the lips of many of the mourners moved in silent unison with the words.[33]

Many have said that Pasternak's funeral "evoked in a startling, almost awe-inspiring fashion, the funeral of Zhivago himself." At the funeral copies of the prophetic poem "August" were distributed as the poem, along with others, was recited.[34] As one person would finish reciting a poem, another would begin. At one point a young man in working clothes stood up and shouted: "Thank you in the name of the working man! We waited for your book. Unfortunately, for reasons that are well known, it did not appear. But you exalted the name of 'writer' higher than anyone." Toward the end of the funeral a seminarian came forth, wept, and spoke some incoherent words. A highly dramatic moment then occurred as a voice in the crowd cried, "Poet byl ubit!" ("The poet was killed!"). The crowd responded: "*Pozor! Pozor! Pozor!*" ("Shame [on them]!").[35]

Almost everyone brought flowers, and when the coffin was finally lowered into the grave, everyone began passing flowers on to each other, over the heads of the crowd. For a few moments distant onlookers had the impression of a sea of flowers floating above the assembled crowd. Then the grave was transformed into a huge mound of flowers.[36]

Afterward, the people refused to leave, staying at the grave until the evening, reading poetry, mainly Pasternak's verse. Most of those who stayed were students, young men and women. Thus did the Russian people say farewell to Pasternak.

Moved by these and other testimonies of affection, the Pasternak family members in Peredelkino, Moscow, and Oxford, England, expressed their gratitude in the *Times* (London) for the sympathy of people the world over. [37]

In contrast to those who, by attending the funeral, proved they were standing by their aesthetic and political opinions, other prominent literary figures chose to ignore Pasternak's funeral, thereby making another kind of statement—one supporting the official attitude toward Pasternak and his work. Among the latter was Konstantin Fedin, who had been one of the negotiators in the endeavors to suspend publication of *Zhivago*. Fedin had lived next door to Pasternak in Peredelkino for twenty-three years, but in 1957 he had stopped speaking to the poet, and on the day of the funeral he did not simply stay away but hid. Many writers noticed that the windows of his dacha were hung with blankets, as if to shut out all sight and sound and knowledge of what was happening outside. He said that he "had the flu" and had known nothing of the arrangements for the funeral. [38] Aseev's conspicuous absence was possibly a manifestation of what one observer called his "Salieri complex." *

Many writers, however, not only took an active part in the funeral but also went to visit the family afterward. To visit and show support for the family was, in effect, to make still another statement, for the months that followed the funeral were to bring hardship to those closest to the poet, just as he had long feared.

Immediately after the funeral the secret police began hunting for any remaining scraps of Pasternak's writings. The manuscript of *The Blind Beauty*, which the poet had left with Ivinskaia, was seized by the police two days after his death. Some time thereafter, Ivinskaia gave Heinz Schewe a typewritten copy of the play for safekeeping, not publication; she ultimately secured a written promise from Feltrinelli not to publish it without her permission. Schewe promptly took the manuscript to West Germany, where he deposited it in a safe, postponing any idea of publication so as not to endanger Ivinskaia. [39]

Ironically, while the authorities were making a systematic effort to seize and discredit Pasternak's work, the Writers' Union made a token gesture of honoring the poet, giving his widow a thousand rubles for a monument for the grave. She used the money to commission the sculptor Sara Lebedev to create a simple white tombstone, showing the head of the poet in bas-relief and bearing the inscription "Boris Pasternak 1890–1960." [40]

With this gesture made, the regime's next move was to try to discredit Pasternak by vilifying Ivinskaia. Pasternak had often observed that only his relationship with her had saved her from harassment. Pasternak had made her his literary executor and heir and had entrusted her with financial matters having to do with publication of his books abroad. She was thus an easy target for the authorities. Following Pasternak's instructions, she had become involved in transactions that had a necessarily clandestine nature because of the peculiarities of the Soviet regime: "smuggling" his manuscripts out of the country and secretly ac-

---

*Gladkov, *Vstrechi*. The allusion is to Pushkin's interpretation of Antonio Salieri's legendary jealousy of Mozart.

cepting royalties. These activities the KGB would use and embellish to try to discredit her.[41]

Vast sums of royalty money had been accumulating for Pasternak in the West. Soon after publishing *Doctor Zhivago*, Feltrinelli apparently suggested depositing some of the royalties in the Moscow State Bank.* Polikarpov, of the Central Committee, counseled Pasternak not to do so, but to arrange for his foreign transactions to be made in a less conspicuous manner, lest an awkward scandal arise. Thus before Pasternak's death some friends of d'Angelo, a couple named Benedetti, were delivering Soviet currency directly to an emissary appointed by Pasternak. The money was used to support both Pasternak households. In addition, Ivinskaia has said, Pasternak gave away over $100,000 of his foreign royalties, chiefly to strangers who showed an interest in his work or wrote him letters of encouragement. Ivinskaia had taken on much of Pasternak's financial and publishing negotiations because she was familiar with the operations of the publishing world and was concerned for Pasternak's health.[42]

Her arrest, two months after the poet's death, was a typical KGB entrapment. The Benedettis asked Ivinskaia and her daughter to pick up a suitcase of unspecified contents. Even before the women had opened the suitcase, police appeared. The suitcase proved to be stuffed with rubles thoughtlessly dispatched by Feltrinelli. Again Ivinskaia's house was searched. A package of Pasternak's papers and letters escaped confiscation in the house of a neighbor, a dressmaker, who assumed that the package contained fabric.[43]

Ivinskaia was charged not only with committing currency offenses in connection with the royalties of *Doctor Zhivago* but also with deceiving Pasternak for reasons of personal profit. It is incredible that the government would expect the world to believe that she had deceived the poet, when earlier from 1948 to 1953, she had been punished in his stead while refusing to incriminate him. Though after her arrest she admitted to receiving money from foreign sources, she made the admission under very difficult circumstances, knowing that her daughter had also been arrested and that other members of her family faced persecution. Irina's welfare was the only consideration that kept Ivinskaia from admitting almost anything that her interrogators suggested—she was even accused of writing *Doctor Zhivago* herself. It was no longer necessary to condemn Pasternak. Surkov retracted his statements against Pasternak and maintained that Ivinskaia was the "adventuress who got him to write *Doctor Zhivago* and then to send it abroad so she could enrich herself." She no longer seemed to care about her own fate, feeling that since Pasternak's death she "had lost her place in life." She surrendered to a "dazed sense of despair" and apathy.[44]

A passage from *Zhivago*, composed at the time of Ivinskaia's first imprisonment, was again timely: "One day Larisa Feodorovna went out and did not come back. She must have been arrested in the street at that time. She vanished without

---

*Years later Pasternak's remaining royalties became the subject of a lawsuit between Feltrinelli and his former associate d'Angelo. Feltrinelli also blamed d'Angelo's indiscretion for Ivinskaia's second prison term (cf. *Sunday Times* [London] *Weekly Review*, May 31, 1970).

a trace and probably died somewhere, forgotten as a nameless number on a list that afterwards got mislaid, in one of the innumerable mixed or women's concentration camps in the north."[45]

One person who might have helped Ivinskaia and her daughter was Georges Nivat, Irina's fiancé, a graduate student of Russian literature working in Moscow. As a Frenchman, he was a natural liaison with the foreign press. He knew the details of the situation well and could have defended the women against the charges. His visa was not renewed, however, and after unpleasant complications he was forced to return to France.[46]

Although official sources held forth with self-righteous indignation about the charges against Ivinskaia, they did not reveal the date of the trial, the conviction, or the resulting sentence until six weeks after the two women were sent to Siberia. Ivinskaia was sentenced to eight years' imprisonment, and her daughter to three. The punishment severely damaged Irina's career as a student of Asian languages and traumatized the lives of both.[47]

On January 21, 1961, Radio Moscow made a series of broadcasts in Italian, German, and English denouncing Ivinskaia and accusing her of swindling Pasternak's rightful heirs, and of accepting shipments of rubles and Western commodities smuggled past customs. The broadcast in Italian commented, "The dream of fantastic riches impelled her to crime." The broadcast in English said that "Olga Ivinskaia, although she was a professional literary translator, was attracted by an entirely different phase—finance."[48]

Newspapers throughout the Western world expressed doubt about the charges and dismay at the imprisonment. The *Times* (London) declared, "The radio statement is much too vindictive in its wording and too melodramatic to be swallowed whole in the West," and wondered why the trial had not been open to the public. It pointed out that Pasternak had not received any of the blame or recrimination. The *Manchester Guardian* headlined one article on the subject "Almost Certainly a Frame-Up," and commented: "At most she may have received modest gifts from the West at a time when Pasternak was in great difficulties because Soviet royalties on his translations had been cut off."[49]

The *New Statesman* had another theory. It observed that, since Pasternak had entrusted Ivinskaia with his financial affairs, he might have appointed her executrix of his will to make it possible for her and her daughter to receive royalties from his books. Otherwise the two women could not legally inherit anything. Neither of them could claim to be a relative; Pasternak had never adopted Irina, though he had often expressed the intention of doing so. The article underlined that the confession and admission of guilt the authorities had extracted from Ivinskaia contained a hint of duress.[50]

Within a few months, however, Western newspapers ceased expressing concern over Ivinskaia's fate. As it turned out, Ivinskaia and her daughter were quietly released before the ends of their terms—Irina in 1962, and her mother in 1964. In due time Ivinskaia, resettled in Moscow, resumed her career as literary translator. Among other things, Pasternak's restoration to acceptability if not favor helped bring about their release.

A rare photograph. *Left to right*: Pasternak's first wife, Evgeniia Vladimirovna; Boris's son Evgenii Pasternak; Evgenii's son Boris (Boris); Evgenii's wife, Elena, holding their younger son, Petia (Petr). Photograph taken ca. 1964. *Private collection.*

While Pasternak's relatives did not suffer arrest, duress, or imprisonment, they nevertheless came under pressure. Although his books were being sold all over the world, the family's financial situation was critical. The Literary Fund charged sixty rubles a month rent on the dacha and additional rent for another wing of the house.* The poet's widow simply did not have the money. Pasternak's son Leonid, a junior scientific associate at the Crystallography Institute of the Academy of Sciences, drew a stipend of only eighty-four rubles a month. Stanislav Neigauz, Zinaida Nikolaevna's son by her first marriage, and Pasternak's older son, Evgenii, tried to help, but they were supporting families of their own.

Some of her relatives advised Zinaida Nikolaevna to give up the dacha, but she refused to consider it. There she could preserve at least something of the past and the sense of Pasternak's presence. She was also afraid that if they left for a time the dacha might be burglarized or the authorities might take the dacha away from them—another step toward destroying the poet's legacy.[51]

During the second half of 1961 several writers, including Ehrenburg, Chukovskii, Aleksandr Tvardovskii, and Konstantin Paustovskii, wrote to Khrushchev asking for financial help for Pasternak's family. In response to these appeals one of

---

*This was apparently in accordance with accepted practice—the dacha was rent-free only as long as Pasternak was alive.

Khrushchev's assistants called the Literary Fund, which lent the family three thousand (new) rubles. The widow had no way to repay the loan, however. Several times she petitioned for a pension, but in vain. A pension could be granted only by the Writers' Union, with Polikarpov's approval. That made the situation doubly difficult; Polikarpov had a long-standing dislike for Zinaida Nikolaevna, whom he viewed as overly blunt and lacking in cultural refinement.[52]

During Zinaida Nikolaevna's period of desperate straits in 1962–63, she asked Aseev for a loan. His wife replied by sending the widow only two hundred rubles accompanied by an offensive note. Life soon became so precarious for the household that Zinaida Nikolaevna considered selling a collection of about seventy-five of Pasternak's letters of particular literary significance. After several difficult years of widowhood, Zinaida Nikolaevna died on June 27, 1966, from kidney disease. She was buried next to the poet in the Peredelkino cemetery.[53]

The treatment of Pasternak's family was a concomitant of the official policy of downgrading the poet and his works. That policy was kept alive in the 1960s through the vigilance of Pasternak's old and influential enemy Surkov, who, for example, included Pasternak with Tsvetaeva, Mandelstam, and Khlebnikov among poets who were "facing the past" and were therefore not good examples for Communist poets, who must "face the future." Praise from critics inside the Soviet Union was excised, as in the case of the fourth edition of *Faust*, published just two months before Pasternak's death. The introduction, by Viliam-Vilmont, was included, but the last two pages were cut, including this significant passage: "Boris Pasternak made *Faust* into a live manifestation of Russian poetry. . . . the essential has been achieved—the poetical metamorphosis, the new Russian recreation [*perevyrazhenie*] of *Faust*, remarkable by the force of its verse and style."[54]

Outside the Soviet Union, however, sales of Pasternak's works continued to rise. In 1960, the *New York Herald Tribune* noted that 330,000 copies of *Doctor Zhivago* had been sold in Great Britain, with accrued royalties of £23,000 (as reported in the *Daily Telegraph*), and that over a million copies had been sold in the United States.[55]

At some time during this period the official attitude toward Pasternak and his works began to change slightly. The loud denunciations before and after his expulsion from the Writers' Union in 1958 ceased. His partial "rehabilitation" was quiet, however, and only a few writers dared praise his work. More evidence of the softening toward Pasternak was forthcoming in January, 1962, when a German-language broadcast by Radio Moscow gave a summation of the official view in response to a question from a German listener. *The Year 1905* and *Lieutenant Schmidt* were declared to be the acme of the poet's work: "These two poems, which flowed from the pen of a master craftsman of the poet's craft and which sing of the Russian people's revolutionary heroism, have become part of the treasure of Soviet poetry forever." The broadcast went on to say that later in his life Pasternak displayed a weakness of vision and understanding about the revolutionary destiny of the Russian people and to criticize *Doctor Zhivago* as "artistically clumsy and philosophically weak." The announcers protested as totally false the claim of the "reactionary Western press" that Pasternak's work was banned. On the contrary, his translations were still being published, *Faust* had come out in a fourth edition, and shortly after his death a volume of his selected works had been issued in a large printing. The tenor of the broadcast was that Pasternak was a gifted poet but limited in his capacity to think in political terms.[56]

In August, 1962, another broadcast by Radio Moscow, this time to English listeners, also devoted some time to Pasternak. The announcer, praising a new Russian edition of Shelley's poems, said, "I want to single out the brilliant translations of Boris Pasternak, especially that of the 'Ode to the West Wind' which is perhaps the most difficult from the translator's point of view."[57] In September a one-volume edition of Kleist's plays was published in Moscow, including three plays in Pasternak's translations, *The Broken Jug*, *Robert Guiscard*, and *The Prince of Homburg*, yet another indication that the rehabilitation of the writer was under way.[58]

The change toward Pasternak was accompanied by a shift in attitude toward other writers as well. This period saw the first Soviet publication of the works of Ivan Bunin, the only other Russian Nobel Prize–winning author (1933). The publication of Aleksandr Solzhenitsyn's *One Day in the Life of Ivan Denisovich* (1963) constituted the first important landmark since *Doctor Zhivago* in the struggle of Russian writers for freedom of expression.[59] These developments were occurring in a less monolithic artistic atmosphere; in 1962 debates over the program of the party's Twenty-second Congress had revealed the first open split in Soviet literature since the abolition of literary factions in 1932.

In January, 1962, Ilia Ehrenburg, whose novel *The Thaw* had symbolized an era, addressed an audience of students and other young people in the main hall of the Polytechnical Museum in Moscow. He had recalled that in 1960 there was only a brief four-line announcement of Pasternak's death and that some prominent writers of the day had refrained from attending the funeral. "A great Russian poet has died!" Ehrenburg exclaimed, and his statement brought prolonged applause. He added: "Why applaud now? . . . You should choose the moment when it is decent to applaud. . . . The way in which Pasternak's death was announced was unworthy of him."[60]

In 1963, Ehrenburg's memoirs, whose publication had been delayed for ideological reasons, finally appeared. In them Ehrenburg gave new viewpoints on several writers, including Pasternak. In the following passage Ehrenburg at least praised *Doctor Zhivago* for its lyric qualities:

It was its artistic untruth which struck me about the novel. I am convinced that Pasternak wrote it sincerely; it contains some marvellous pages on nature and love; but too many pages are devoted to things the author did not see or hear. Some wonderful poems are included; they underline, as it were, the spiritual inaccuracy of the prose.[61]

This ambiguous statement is typical of Ehrenburg's behavior in delicate situations; while trying to bestow some praise on Pasternak, he expressed some reservations that were attuned to the official Soviet position. Nonetheless, Ehrenburg accomplished infinitely more toward the rehabilitation of Pasternak than had the overcautious Aseev, who for many years had been a close associate of the poet.*

Gradually the atmosphere was being cleared of paranoid feelings about Pasternak. In an article in *Literaturnaia gazeta*, Lev Ozerov called for the publication of works by Pasternak and other poets—such as Belyi and Mandelstam—"known only by name, and by critical admonishments." Ozerov went on to say:

If we do not publish and explain these poets, those who speculate on the slowness of publishing houses . . . will give them popularity in their own fashion. . . . Thus are sometimes false idols created within certain segments of our literary youth. . . . We should explain cultural phenomena, not evade them, still less suppress them.[62]

It is reasonable to infer that such stimuli gradually paved the way for the publication of Pasternak's poetry, *Poems and Long Poems* (*Stikhotvoreniia i poemy*), released in an edition of forty thousand by the publishing house Soviet Writer in the well-known series the Poet's Library (Biblioteka poeta) in 1965, with a perceptive and substantive introduction—a high-water mark of critical insight—by Andrei Siniavskii.†

Yet while more liberal minds were "rehabilitating" Pasternak, certain typically conservative minds conditioned by the regime downplayed the importance of the new editions of Pasternak's work. From 1960 on, rumors sporadically circulated Moscow that *Doctor Zhivago* would be published in the Soviet Union, though a critic writing in *Znamia* in 1962 had commented that "*Doctor Zhivago* has been forgotten."[63] The publication has never materialized. The novel was published in Yugoslavia in 1962, in Serbo-Croatian, an event clearly indicative of the degree of intellectual liveliness and ideological independence achieved by the Yugoslavs (rights for the edition had been purchased from Feltrinelli in 1958, but the Yugoslav authorities held up publication for four years).[64]

In spite of the official ban, *Doctor Zhivago* was and is read in the Soviet Union, both foreign editions and typewritten copies put out by the *samizdat*, the underground network of do-it-yourself publishing. Readers often sit up at night to read or copy the manuscripts. Young Soviet readers, whose opinions were surveyed by a Western source in 1965, expressed warm reactions to the novel, contradicting the official view that young readers could not understand it. One student commented that *Doctor Zhivago* must have been considered "dangerous" because it treats of "spiritual elements and psychological situations" that *Homo sovieticus* is not supposed to know of or experience. Another reader confessed to having sat up three nights reading the novel and having been fascinated to discover that there exist "real Russian people," not just the "puppets" generally found in Soviet novels.[65]

That writers in the Soviet Union still recognize Pasternak's contribution and

---

*Aseev died in 1963, and others of Pasternak's contemporaries followed him in death in the 1960s: Akhmatova in 1966, Ehrenburg in 1967, and Sergei Bobrov in 1971.

†Not long after the introduction appeared in print, Siniavskii was sent to a prison camp for his "criminal" publication of literary texts abroad.

their debt to it is also apparent in both poetry and criticism. Pasternak has greatly influenced younger writers, though in his lifetime he strongly rejected any position as a "leader." Like Pushkin and Chekhov (and unlike Tolstoy), Pasternak did not conceive of himself as a "master" with "precepts." He once said in a conversation with his friend Gladkov, "There is something false in the pose of the writer claiming to be a master of life (*uchitel zhizni*)." He told Evtushenko, "I have not intended to lead anyone anywhere, for the poet is simply a tree, which rustles on and on, but does not propose to lead anyone anywhere."[66]

On the other hand, as early as the 1940s, Pasternak himself had postulated the existence of followers when he remarked: "I am writing *Doctor Zhivago* about people who could be representatives of my school—if I had such a school."[67] Despite his later disclaimers, Pasternak does indeed have such heirs and disciples; foremost among them are Andrei Voznesenskii, Bella Akhmadulina, Evgenii Evtushenko, and Iosif Brodskii.

Pasternak evidently had a real liking for Voznesenskii, who "from his schooldays" had shown his verse to the older poet and who until the autumn of 1958 had been a frequent visitor at the dacha in Peredelkino. Five months after Pasternak's death Voznesenskii managed to publish an homage under the guise of a tribute to Tolstoy on the occasion of the fiftieth anniversary of his death. Voznesenskii's poem, nominally dedicated to Tolstoy, said in part:

> They bore him to no entombment
> They bore him to enthronement.
>
> . . . .
> The lilac at his doorstep burned . . .
> A fountain of falling stars soaked in sweat,
> His back steamed
> Like a loaf in the oven.
>
> . . . .
> In his flight is his victory;
> In his retreat, an ascent
> To pastures and planets
> Far from lying ornament.*

In a press conference in Paris in 1962, Voznesenskii announced that Pasternak's "gigantic" stature loomed very large on the poetic horizon for him and his contemporaries. Reviewing Pasternak's posthumous collection of translations *Starry Skies* (*Zvëzdnoe nebo*) in 1968, Voznesenskii quoted Pasternak's poem "Hamlet"— still not allowed in print in the Soviet Union—in such a way that it might appear to be a quotation from Pasternak's translation of the play. The rest of his article was pervaded by a very warm regard both for Pasternak's achievement as a re-creator of foreign poets' works and for the writer's own works, including *A Safe-Conduct*.[68]

As early as 1958, Bella Akhmadulina, in her poem "Winter Day," had described an old man "still youthful-looking"—evidently Pasternak. Her poem

---

*That is, the false art of other, less authentic or demanding artists.

"Peredelkino," published in 1962, clearly concerned an encounter with Pasternak in Peredelkino, while her piece "Chapters from a Poem" (subtitled "About Pasternak") was a prose and verse account of her encounter with the poet. In her poem "Bad Spring" (1967) she praised the "neat outline and simplicity of [Pasternak's] greatness" and devoted to him the poem "Snowstorm" (1968).[69]

Resorting to a subterfuge similar to the one used by Voznesenskii, Evtushenko published his own tribute to Pasternak in the form of a poem, "The Fence," disguised under a "false" dedication to the poet Vladimir Lugovskoi. Evtushenko devoted to Pasternak (whose inspiration he had previously acknowledged) several pages of his *Precocious Autobiography*, which he published in the West without the consent of Soviet authorities.[70]

The poem "We Buried the Old Man . . . ," published in *Novyi mir* in 1964 by still another young poet, Vladimir Kornilov, has unmistakable allusions to Pasternak's funeral, though Pasternak is unnamed. The poem stresses the "high simplicity" of that funeral, "without any flag, without any bronze," and describes the swaying coffin as a boat carrying its passenger from death to immortality. It pictures the dead man buried in flowers up to his chest—indeed, lifted on that sea of flowers noted by other observers at Pasternak's funeral.[71]

Besides influencing younger poets, Pasternak's legacy has also been reflected in literary criticism. Certain of the Georgian critic Georgii Margvelashvili's phrases could almost have been written by Pasternak: "Man is not only and not merely the son of Nature; he is the son of History as well." In *Doctor Zhivago* Pasternak had written, "Man lives not only in nature, but in history." Margvelashvili, commenting on Leonidze's poetry, repeats a leitmotiv from *Doctor Zhivago*: "Death is called life." Margvelashvili also sees certain dimensions of Leonidze's work, such as his conception of history strongly colored by everyday life, as clearly reminiscent of Zhivago's—and Pasternak's—own.[72]

Even conservative critics have gradually begun, however timidly, to acknowledge Pasternak's significance. Thus, in an article published in the late 1960s, the scholar Mikhail Khrapchenko acknowledged as "indubitable" the "profound spiritual and aesthetic influence of the best works" of Esenin, Akhmatova, and Pasternak. Khrapchenko also referred to the criticism of A. I. Metchenko, who, in such a conservative journal as *Oktiabr*, endeavored to "annex" Pasternak to the tradition of "socialist literature" and thereby rehabilitate him. In 1969, Nikolai Rylenkov devoted a few sensitive and enlightened pages to Pasternak in an essay "The Poet's Second Life," which dealt with the literary afterlife of such poets as Afanasii Fet, Bunin, Akhmatova, and Pasternak.[73]

Most strikingly, Pasternak's achievement has been a beacon for Solzhenitsyn in his continuing struggle against the ideological and aesthetic sclerosis produced by Stalinism and its aftermath. Although Solzhenitsyn claims that he would never have written the letter to Khrushchev that Pasternak penned at the height of the anti-*Zhivago* campaign, he has acknowledged clearly that Pasternak "opened the way for literature and blocked the path of its enemies" and "looked on present reality from the point of view of eternity."[74]

Bust of Pasternak by Los
Angeles sculptor Carole
Shultz. *Photography © Steve
Lawrence.*

In the 1970s two remarkable documents on Pasternak from the Soviet Union
have come to us, thoughtfully edited by Max Hayward. The first of these was the
memoir *Meetings with Pasternak*, composed by Pasternak's friend the dramatist
Aleksandr Gladkov. The manuscript found its way to the West, where it was
published in Russian in 1973 and in English in 1977. Based on the many conversations between Gladkov and the poet over nearly a quarter of a century, it
provides enlightening insights into Pasternak's thoughts and concerns, as well as
circumstances of his personal and professional life.[75]

We owe the second volume of testimony to the unflagging concern and energy
of Ivinskaia throughout the difficult years that followed her release from the

prison camp in 1964. During those years her consuming concern was the writing of her memoirs, which were aimed at giving the full and truthful picture of her association with Pasternak, and of the many trials the poet and she had to face. Her manuscript was completed in 1972, but because of its frankness and explicitness its appearance in the Soviet Union was unthinkable. It was published abroad in 1978, in Russian and in Western European languages, under the title *A Captive of Time* (*V plenu vremeni: gody s Borisom Pasternakom*).

The book is a mine of information on Pasternak. For all its vibrancy, however, it seethes with subjective emotionalism and is marked by contradictions. With some aptness it has been described by Christopher Ricks as "swirling, repetitive, artless, indignant, alive." Often Ivinskaia's florid style comes dangerously close to *poshlost*. While she idealizes her relationship with Pasternak (brushing aside his misgivings and feelings of guilt, which she indirectly admits), her justificatory claims are now and then interspersed with regrets that her memories of the last few years of his life were marred by serious quarrels. Ivinskaia's worshipful portrayal of Pasternak as an unworldly figure who had the courage of his convictions is counterbalanced by the revelation of flaws and weaknesses, such as his childish petulance and very worldly vanity. The author's vision of her rival Zinaida Nikolaevna as moved "only by the slyest attention to self-interest" has been described as smacking of "provincial vulgarity." In her craving for recognition, Ivinskaia perhaps overlooked that her own apotheosis, already "beautifully accomplished in Pasternak's poems to her and in the novel," might best have been left to stand alone.[76]

Although the timing of future recognition of Pasternak's work by the conservative critics of his own country and the form it will take remain a matter of conjecture, poetry lovers both within and outside the Soviet Union recognize his greatness. As early as 1954 the eminent Polish writer Czesław Miłosz predicted that Pasternak's genius would eventually be fully recognized and claimed that a statue of Pasternak would stand one day in Moscow.[77]

As of now, continuing popular recognition is apparent in private and public readings of Pasternak's poetry, such as those that take place at his grave from time to time. In 1971 a special occasion marked the eleventh anniversary of Pasternak's death: one night in the late fall of that year over a thousand young people gathered in the woods near Sofrino, a village outside Moscow, and under an autumn rain listened intently to a recital of the "Poems of Iurii Zhivago" "interspersed with passages from some of the abusive attacks—including Semichastnyi's speech—made against Boris Leonidovich at the height of the campaign against him." Two girls sang "Winter Night," accompanying themselves on the guitar.[78]

It is young admirers such as these who began the now traditional yearly pilgrimage to Pasternak's grave. In his article "Pasternak's Children," published in the *Observer* in 1963, John Strachey described the beginning of that tradition. To Strachey the tradition proved that, "after forty years of Stalinist education, a sensitive, a gifted, a Pasternakian intelligentsia has suddenly appeared in Russia." In his book *The Russians*, Hedrick Smith described the pilgrimage as it is held today:

I remember well one cool spring day, May 30, the anniversary of Pasternak's death, . . . going to . . . Peredelkino, where scores of Muscovites, young and old, were making their annual pilgrimage to the grave of Boris Pasternak. . . . On the white tombstone . . . people quietly laid their unpretentious bouquets. . . . Those who came ranged from elderly women in baggy coats to . . . modish young women . . . or young men carrying attaché cases. . . . In a society where the state ritually causes millions to mark so many anniversaries and holidays for its own political ends and reputation, this seemed all the more meaningful an occasion because it had been forgotten by the state and remembered by private individuals.

Such a pilgrimage is some indication of resoluteness and willingness to take risks, especially when one considers that, well known to the Moscow intelligentsia, shortly after Pasternak's funeral the KGB installed a hidden microphone near his tomb.

Flanked by three tall pines, the stark white tombstone with its relief of the poet's craggy head stands out sharply. Since the funeral the grave has been kept meticulously clean by one of Pasternak's devoted admirers—an ordinary workman in baggy trousers and muddy shoes. The thousands of visitors who come to the grave on May 30 shower the tombstone with tulips and other showy blossoms, but also with hand-picked buttercups, lilies of the valley, and dandelions.[79]

Part Two

Pasternak's Historical Universe

An Interpretation

Pasternak on the bench in his garden in
Peredelkino, October, 1958. Cornell Capa: "I
visited Boris Pasternak on the day of his invitation
to go to Stockholm to accept the Nobel
Prize. . . . It was a cold 'moody day,' and when
we completed a walk in a garden, he rested on the
bench." *Cornell Capa/Magnum.*

Introduction

Ever since Kant, fundamental dichotomies similar to the Kantian opposition of nature and freedom have attracted thinkers. Nature and history appeared to Pasternak as the two obvious and convenient poles for the definition and evaluation of reality—two poles to which, in *Doctor Zhivago*, he refers implicitly and explicitly in communicating to us his vision of man. "Man does not live in nature, but in history." Such is one of Pasternak's fundamental affirmations, the import of which may well be ambiguous. The aim of the chapters that follow will be to try to elucidate, with reference to the history of ideas and to aesthetics, what these two polarized notions of nature and history mean to Pasternak.

Like Pasternak's poetry, *Doctor Zhivago* is essentially a hymn to life, a song to celebrate "my sister, Life." It is a rapt meditation, but it is also a desperate claim in favor of that mysterious original force by one who is alarmed by the menace directed against life and its manifestations. Pasternak's attitude toward the entity he calls "life" makes it necessary to pose certain questions regarding what has been called by some his vitalism, by some his pantheism, and by some his naturalism—and these questions are raised in the chapter that follows.

The world of nature is not, however, the last word for Pasternak, for whom history is "a second universe," a world of values in which man is called upon to live. The discussion of this pole of history and its values is initiated in Chapter 14.

Pasternak himself enumerates those values that constitute the diverse dimensions of the world of history, and each of them is examined in turn as it appears in his works: the idea of the free personality, love of one's neighbor, the idea of life as sacrifice (Chapters 15, 16, and 17).

In Chapter 18, which deals with Pasternak's aesthetics, I endeavor to show that for Pasternak art is the higher sphere where the values of the "universe of history" find their fulfillment. While being the culmination of the universe of history, art (thanks to the realistic method as it is understood by Pasternak) also holds the potential of maximum faithfulness to natural reality, to the pole of nature. Thus is a reconciliation of the two worlds achieved.

13

Zhivago Versus Prometheus

The Poetics of Nature

". . . life is never a material, a substance to be molded. If you want to know, life is the principle of self-renewal, it is constantly renewing and remaking and changing and transfiguring itself, it is infinitely beyond your or my obtuse theories about it."

Pasternak, *Doctor Zhivago*[1]

Various commentators, from Marina Tsvetaeva to Andrei Siniavskii, have pointed out that in Pasternak's poems the lyrical voice is that of Nature herself, rather than that of the poet. Nature herself—landscape—is the chief lyrical character in Pasternak. Other poets wrote about nature, but, in Tsvetaeva's original formulation, no one but Pasternak wrote nature (or "painted nature": *pisal prirodu*). According to such logic, Pasternak's poetry is nature transcribed.[2]

I would like to discuss here Pasternak's philosophy of natural authenticity, as propounded at a climax in his poetic career, that is, in *Doctor Zhivago*, and to show how this desire for fulfillment through natural values clashes in the novel with the Promethean dream of the Soviet era, since this conflict can be seen as a basic tension in Pasternak's book.

In his poetry nature remains a live, unpredictable force, which opens up perspectives to us by revealing itself in ever-fresh outbursts. These eruptions often take the form of squalls, whirlwinds, "luminous downpours" (to borrow a phrase from Tsvetaeva) that thrust themselves unexpectedly on the poet's perception and create an animistic universe.[3] The reader is spellbound by this cascade of elemental forces and may feel that wonder is the only possible reaction. Sooner or later, however, he may be tempted to look for some orientation within this elemental surge. At times the universe he is shown has a definitely pantheistic coloration. This pantheism is consciously felt by Iurii Zhivago, who sums up Pasternak's view of nature when he says, "'. . . all the time, life, one, immense, identical throughout its innumerable combinations and transformations, fills the universe and is continually reborn.'"[4]

More often, though, when pondering Pasternak's view of nature, one is reminded of eighteenth-century vitalism, an immediate precursor of Kantianism—a philosophy with which Pasternak was thoroughly familiar. In its broad sense "vitalism" may best serve to designate the "live" attitude, the lifelike and life-responsive sensibility characteristic of Pasternak.* This is a vitalism which, sometimes in a defensive and sometimes in an offensive key, militates against the current mechanistic view of the natural and social worlds, just as Bergsonism appeared as a reaction against such schematized dogmas of the nineteenth century as positivism, determinism, and Théodule Ribot's associationism in psychology.

Such a reaction to prevalent mechanistic preconceptions is not new; it has occurred time and again over the centuries. The Renaissance provides the example of an enthusiasm for "Mother Nature," whose concrete and "truthful" image both Christians and Aristotelians tried to re-create to counter scholastic abstractions. Various conceptions succeed one another as one notion of nature is shattered and another takes its place. Eighteenth-century naturalism itself surely represents a protest of conscience and imagination against the mechanized and suitably deanimated nature of the physicists. Whereas Descartes, Galileo, and Kepler conceived of the world of nature as a construct of mathematics and mechanics in

---

*Within the framework of a strictly philosophical discussion, it would be necessary to speak of—rather than Pasternak's vitalism—his "hylozoism," similar to the doctrine of the Ionians of ancient Greece, that is, the doctrine that all matter is animated or endowed with life.

which the principles inherent in man-made machines were seen to operate on a universal scale, Leibniz and Newton reverted to *finality* in nature. Pre-Romantics from Rousseau to Diderot launched a conscious reaction against an overly schematized and mechanized view of nature summed up in neat formulas.[5]

In Russia in the mid-nineteenth century, the essential spokesman of the anti-mechanization attitude is, of course, Dostoevsky's "underground man," who indicted the mechanistic philosophy of Vissarion Belinskii's followers and the intellectualist materialism of Nikolai Chernyshevskii. Resolutely denouncing the limitations of "the laws of nature," the underground man believed that freedom is preferable to the most efficient "scientific" organization of man's existence.

Now, much in the same way as Bergson's *élan vital* arose to challenge the "established" world of Auguste Comte and Ribot, the passionate and explicit dissent in *Doctor Zhivago*—which is the condensation of an element implicit in his earlier poetry—is one of the strongest voices raised in our century against the excesses of a technological society. The ancient struggle between the two attitudes is sharply rejoined when Pasternak denounces the so-called transformation of nature by technology.

The charter of Pasternak's views is to be found in a dialogue between Iurii Zhivago and Liberius Averkevich, the head of the "forest brotherhood." Exasperated by the latter's blinkered and blundering enthusiasm, Zhivago cannot restrain his feelings any longer:

"Reshaping life! People who can say that have never understood a thing about life—they have never felt its breath, its heartbeat—however much they have seen or done. They look on it as a lump of raw material that needs to be processed by them, to be ennobled by their touch. But life is never a material, a substance to be molded. If you want to know, life is the principle of self-renewal, it is constantly renewing and remaking and changing and transfiguring itself, it is infinitely beyond your or my obtuse theories about it."[6]

The programmatic nature of this statement is so striking and forceful that it was quoted a few years ago as an epigraph to an article on "the new genetics" in *Time* magazine.[7]

Thus what Pasternak calls life is an autonomous and original force, irreducible to categories, be they political, industrial, or economic. This phenomenon of life is both solemn and intoxicating; it is, in Zhivago's eyes, a gift.[8] It is a force that cannot long be countered, a flow impossible to contain, an upsurge that sooner or later breaks and swallows up the petty barriers erected against it.

In many ways this elemental life-force is reminiscent of Bergson's *élan vital*. When talking of life, Bergson uses images that are very close to those of Pasternak: life appears to him as "an immense wave moving forward," as "a force" at work, "trying to free itself from its bonds and also to go beyond," as "an immense current," as an "inner thrust." What characterizes this force in Bergson's eyes is its irreducibility to physicochemical causes or phenomena; he insists on its absolute originality and unpredictability.[9] It is interesting to note this similarity and bear in mind that, as Pasternak himself tells us, "a large group were carried away by Bergson" at the University of Moscow when he was studying there.[10]

A few years before that, Pasternak as a schoolboy had been "intoxicated" with Knut Hamsun, one of the representatives of "the newest literature."[11] This was the time when, in the wake of the 1905 Revolution, the more idealistic elements of the intelligentsia developed a veritable cult around Hamsun, whom they christened "the bard of love and nature."[12] In the works of the Norwegian novelist a sentimental conception of nature leads to a somewhat artless glorification of natural life and the peasant. Characteristically, Hamsun was worshiped in the early decades of the century by the same readers who adored the youthful Hermann Hesse, Władysław Reymont's *Peasants*, and Pearl Buck's *The Good Earth* (the half-digested leavings of writers like these were later picked up and vulgarized by Nazi ideologues as grist for their blood-and-soil mill). Hamsun's idolatry of nature is, however, a genuine reaction against various aspects of life in society, of organized urban culture—industry, the natural sciences, positivism—in a word the organization of life "in the Swiss fashion," according to Hamsun's own words. This romanticizing primitivism is connected with his conception of life as a huge force, so vast that it "can afford to waste" (*Vagabonds*), a view to which Pasternak's concept is strikingly similar. The works of Hamsun about which Pasternak the adolescent "raved" included *Mysteries* (1892), whose lyrical hero probes the mystical connection between man and nature; *Pan* (1894), which—together with its hero, Lieutenant Glahn, a gentle, sensitive lover of nature—won great acclaim in Russia; and *Victoria* (1898), a depiction of a lyrical and asocial dreamer, Johannes. The Hamsunian hero is an aesthete who willingly gives himself over to the intoxication derived from nature—a characteristic also present in Iurii Zhivago.

The cyclical rebirth of vitalism expresses the perennial distrust that those sensitive to the authenticity of life feel when confronting mechanization. It reflects rebellious life itself putting mechanics in its place. Interestingly, however, a vitalistic protest like Pasternak's does not preclude any feeling for the poetry of industrialized urban life: "nature" for Pasternak specifically includes urban landscapes. Although he never adopted the principle propounded by Maiakovskii in 1914 that "the town must take the place of nature," Pasternak clearly loved the topography of Moscow and on occasion celebrated the charms specific to the metropolis.[13] He understood, and did not seem to regret, that urban settings and modes of living have come to be an essential component of the twentieth-century experience. That is shown by his ardently sensitive and evocative descriptions of Moscow in *Doctor Zhivago*, exemplified by the following passage from Zhivago's Varykino diary, which starts with a brief critical-aesthetic statement:

"Pastoral simplicity doesn't exist in those conditions [modern urban life]. When it is attempted, its pseudo-artlessness is a literary fraud, not inspired by the countryside but taken from the shelves of academic archives. The living language of our times, born spontaneously and naturally in accord with its spirit, is the language of urbanism.

"I live at a busy intersection. Moscow, blinded by the sun and the white heat of the asphalt-paved yards, scattering reflections of the sun from its upper windows, breathing in the flowering of clouds and streets, is whirling around me, turning my head and telling me to turn the heads of others by writing poems in its praise. For this purpose, Moscow has brought me up and made me an artist.

"The incessant rumbling by day and night in the street outside our walls is as inseparable from the modern soul as the opening bars of an overture are inseparable from the curtain, as yet secret and dark, but already beginning to crimson in the glow of the footlights." [14]

Some may wonder whether such a fascination with Moscow is not at variance with the cult of the natural life. Such doubt loses force when one notices how little attention is paid in the above passage to everyday aspects of mechanized urban life and how exclusively it focuses on certain overwhelming sensory perceptions—the intersection of planes of light and sound. This is indeed the reaction of a "poet of nature" to the sharp, sensuous jolts he experiences in an urban environment. Zhivago's apprehension of these phenomena of light and sound reduces the city to a particularly crude and violent form of nature, like a network of bare canyons roaring with waterfalls.

Yet at other moments Pasternak observes that the technological civilization of the twentieth century, condensed nodelike in the urban industrial centers, disrupts man's "natural" mode of life and perverts its values. He protests the modern trend toward abstract specialization and divorce from the organic human community:

In those days [the early 1920s] everything became a speciality, including versification and the art of translation; theoretical studies were written on all possible subjects, and institutes were founded right and left. There arose all sorts of Palaces of Thought, Academies of Artistic Ideas. [15]

Pasternak sounds most Bergsonian when he proclaims that automation in all its forms—including "belonging to a type," being justified only by one's specialty—entails a refusal to progress spiritually and is the very antithesis of the spirit of continuous creation. The mechanization that comes from extreme specialization takes man further and further away from fulfillment in a "natural" context. Marx placed relationships of economic production in the foreground, seeing in them the fundamentals of human reality; Pasternak feels that labor relationships are neither the single nor the fundamental link between man and reality. We are reminded that besides work—whose humane value is asserted in Pasternak's novel if only by the constant endeavors of Zhivago—there exist other values, values of love, contemplation, and aesthetic creation, which constitute vital planes of communication with nature. The aesthetic joys of creation, as well as such values as sacrifice and abnegation—all of which are central in *Doctor Zhivago*—cannot possibly be reduced to work relationships. An important factor in the novel tempering what spontaneous enthusiasm men might feel for their "tooled-up" and engine-propelled civilization is the gradual economic and technological disintegration in Russia. The depiction of this débâcle culminates in Pasternak's pronouncements on collectivization: "the collective squandering of thousands" and the "failure" of collectivization. [16]

Work and exertion become highly desirable for Pasternak when they are no longer means of achieving power but are the instruments of reconciliation with nature. That is attested to most strikingly by the lyric soliloquy that Pasternak puts in the mouth of Zhivago upon his resettlement in the Urals:

"What happiness, to work from dawn to dusk for your family and yourself, to build a roof over their heads, to till the soil to feed them, to create your own world, like Robinson Crusoe, in imitation of the Creator of the universe, and, as your own mother did, to give birth to yourself, time and again.

"So many new thoughts come into your head . . . when your mind has set you a task that can be achieved by physical effort . . ., when for six hours on end you dig or hammer, scorched by the life-giving breath of the sky. . . . The town recluse whipping up his nerves and his imagination with strong black coffee and tobacco doesn't know the strongest drug of all—good health and real necessity." [17]

Elsewhere Pasternak hinted that "the vast, thousand-mile expanse of arable Russia, the Russia of peasant villages which feed the small area of urban Russia and work for it," was the country's true life stream. [18]

Alarmed by the decay of people's ability to recognize the rhythm of Nature and live in harmony with her, Pasternak advocates a return to Nature—Cicero's "non desiderabis artifices si sequeris naturam." Zhivago sounds very much like Isak of Sellanraa, the hero of Hamsun's epic hymn *Growth of the Soil*, when he sings the blessings that human labor can confer on the soil when it collaborates closely with nature. One could apply to Zhivago the statement that Hamsun makes about Isak: "A tiller of the ground, body and soul; a worker on the land without respite. A ghost risen out of the past to point the future, a man from the earliest days of cultivation, a settler in the wilds, nine hundred years old, and, withal, a man of the day." [19] In Pasternak's eyes agricultural life was indeed a privileged form of partnership—"uncontrollable, unpredictable, and often cruel"—between man and nature. [20] This was no abstract credo to him; Pasternak himself toiled extensively in the fields of Peredelkino for several days at a time and during a good part of the year. [21]

Doctor Zhivago is a commentary on the experience of today's Prometheus. The Soviet era is characterized by its faith in the operational virtues of a science and technology oriented toward *possessing* the world through the mediation of labor. The Soviet Prometheus is represented by the collective engineering designing and designed to reshape life, and he idealizes the toil of mind and hand that goes with this reshaping. Prometheus is an upstart whose audacity must always arouse a serious fear: Will man know how to use the power he has stolen from the gods? Pasternak certainly never shared the enthusiasm of either the seventeenth century or the Soviet twentieth century for man's vocation as "maître et possesseur de la nature," as Descartes put it. Prometheus, therefore, is the real villain in *Doctor Zhivago*; the novel describes the disintegration of what are to its author fundamental natural values. It rejects the claim that the Soviet era is achieving a revaluation of man through technology, through the new power that man has acquired.

Thus Pasternak's novel is a warning against the social utopias that the Promethean myth can inspire. This myth, man's dream of the conquest of nature, lends
itself to a collective dream compensation by suggesting a magic or automatic promotion of man and thereby inflaming popular imagination and playing into the
hands of the mechanizers, deceiving or themselves deceived. Far from being a
purely modern fancy, this "promotion" is found in the genesis of fairy tales as
explained by Roman Jakobson. Jakobson refers to Boris Sokolov's definition of the
fairy tale, "a type of dream-compensation," and himself calls the fairy tale "a
dream about the conquest of nature, . . . a dream about the triumph of the
wretched, about the metamorphosis of a hind into a tsar." It is worthy of note
that, immediately after giving this definition, he goes on to comment: "The actual {that is, current} technical and social reconstruction, therefore, easily gives
new attributes to the tale. In the newest tale records we find an aeroplane with
levers (to direct it to right and to left,) instead of the wooden eagle on which the
hero traveled before." [22] The very terms used by Jakobson in this passage—and
elsewhere in the same essay—cast light on *Doctor Zhivago*. In point of fact, the
novel does describe, from Zhivago's vantage point, the current "technical and
social reconstruction" attempted by Communism in Russia. Zhivago does see the
whole era, not without initial enthusiasm or bemusement, as "the epoch of the
effacement of borders between utopia and reality," as Jakobson puts it; he experi-

ences, together with the Russian people, the frustration of many of its "hopes and longings." The venture of technical reconstruction, the venture of promoting the new dream in Russia, threatens and finally shatters Zhivago's hopes of fulfillment and authenticity through his natural philosophy. Such contemporaries of Pasternak as Leonid Leonov reacted against the pervasive "technological mentality" of the Stalin era,[23] but, going beyond Leonov's conservationist attitude, Pasternak in his novel provides the philosophical foundations for a paratechnological approach toward life in society. The warning he issues on this subject is among the rare ones made during his era.

Opposing current technological utopias, Pasternak reasserts the organic conception of nature—an entity accessible through the medium of human labor, but also through that of contemplation, communion, and aesthetic creation, innocent of any dream of conquest. This conception, as it emerges from Zhivago's diary, is based on a harmonious balance between an implicit theory of leisure (essentially consonant with Josef Pieper's enlightened philosophy of leisure) and a vision of the authenticity of work. Toward the end of his life Pasternak was to discover that this philosophy of natural authenticity was closely attuned to that of Albert Schweitzer, in whose doctrine of "affirmation of life," of "reverence for life," he discerned a striking corroboration of his own vision.[24]

14

The Voice of the Street

The Poetics of History

[History] . . . is the centuries of systematic explorations of the riddle of death, with a view to overcoming death.

Doctor Zhivago[1]

[History is] another universe, made by man with the help of time and memory in answer to the challenge of death.

Doctor Zhivago[2]

Doctor Zhivago is a political novel in the same sense that *A Tale of Two Cities*, *Le Rouge et le Noir*, or, for that matter, *War and Peace* are political novels. It diagnoses the effect political situations have on men and women. But, contrary to Dickens, Stendhal, and Tolstoy who handle the intrusion of politics as an extraneous assault, as a physical penetration which, however ruthless, cannot change the texture of human lives, Pasternak sees this intervention as a chemical, nay, a nuclear process affecting and destroying the living tissue of reality.

Victor Frank[3]

In Pasternak's work the street can sometimes be a variation on a *topos* of the urban landscape, as in the fresh and original statement, "I come from the street, where the poplar is amazed,"[4] where the street's feelings are conveyed through the poplar's amazement. The street, metonymically speaking, can also stand for the many simple people active in it; in this sense, the voice of the street makes itself heard through their viewpoint.

In *Doctor Zhivago* we have a broad, complex spectrum of ideological and political views, with interesting shifts in the views of individual characters (such as Antipov-Strelnikov, Kologrivov, Komarovskii, and Tiverzin). Most of the characters show deep concern for what happens in Russia, and the behavior of the more "popular" characters provides clear evidence of the concern of the street for events in the street. The voice of elemental, rural Russia, which was heard so strongly in Pilniak's *The Naked Year* (1921), is similarly present in Pasternak's novel.

Over the decades the poet's famous exclamation in *My Sister, Life*, "What millennium is it . . . out there [*na dvore*]?"[5] has often been inaccurately interpreted as reflecting the persona's remoteness from or standoffishness about current events. Characters in *Doctor Zhivago* manifest considerable involvement in the events *na dvore*, "out there" in the street. In particular, some of the voices from the street deserve to be heard carefully—those that set forth Pasternak's conception of history.

His views are presented in a few key passages by various spokesmen; Nikolai Nikolaevich Vedeniapin, Zhivago's uncle, a priest returned to lay status who has become an apostle of a Tolstoyan type of socialism; Zhivago himself; Lara; and the remarkably well-read girl of Iuriatin, Sima Tuntseva. These characters express opinions that variously reflect the fundamental attitude of the author; to that extent *Doctor Zhivago* is even an overly "monologal" novel, in the terminology of the Soviet scholar Mikhail Bakhtin.*

Zhivago's conception of man's spiritual destiny is closely linked to the gradual disruption of the pact he originally concluded with socialism. As disillusion followed disillusion, he opened his eyes to the trickery underlying Bolshevik dogmatism and evolved his own more authentic vision of man. As we consider the stages of the hero's fascination for the social ideas of his time, it is therefore important to trace the chain of upheavals that Pasternak and his generation experienced, to see how his views gradually evolved, later to be reflected in the novel.

The world in which Pasternak grew up and which left its imprint on him was that of the Russian intelligentsia before 1914. Because both his parents were distinguished artists, Pasternak grew up in an extremely cultivated and cosmopolitan milieu of artists and intellectuals. The dazzling inspiration of Scriabin vied with the philosophical conversation of Tolstoy and the magic of Vrubel's coloring, to leave indelible marks in the mind and heart of the poet. Some of his subsequent reactions and views are clearly indicative of his early life in that milieu.

---

*Bakhtin coined the terms *monologal* and *dialogal* in his fundamental work *Problems of Dostoevsky's Poetics* (*Problemy poetiki Dostoevskogo*, Leningrad, 1929).

It would be wrong, however, to see Pasternak as simply an anachronistic survivor of a past epoch and its bourgeois culture, a judgment that has become a commonplace of Soviet Pasternak criticism and is also the basis of Issaac Deutscher's critique of *Doctor Zhivago* as a work archaic in both idea and style.[6] The vigor with which the writer denounces the defects of the old regime, especially its social privileges and the omnipotence of money, is sufficient proof to the contrary. One could not seriously contend that Pasternak has given an idealized image of tsarist Russia, much less that *Doctor Zhivago* is, as Deutscher argues, conditioned by a nostalgic desire for return to a bourgeois accommodation to that past.[7] Some would much rather accuse him of making concessions to socialist realism when in the first part of *Doctor Zhivago* he depicts a world in which men of doubtful reliability lead prodigal millionaires to their ruin or wealthy bachelors play the evil geniuses of young orphans. Also in *Doctor Zhivago* the novelist gives the floor to the businessman Samdeviatov, who in discussing the old regime finally explodes: "Gluttons and parasites sat on the backs of the starving workers and drove them to death, and you imagine things could stay like that? Not to mention all the other forms of outrage and tyranny. Don't you understand the rightness of the people's anger, of their desire for justice, for truth?"[8] These words from a man prospering under the new conditions created by Bolshevism echo the judgment of Zhivago, the young doctor returning from the German front in 1917: ". . . there really was something unhealthy in the way rich people used to live. Masses of superfluous things. Too much furniture, too much room, too much emotional refinement, too many circumlocutions. I'm very glad we're using fewer rooms. We should give up still more."[9] Here the voice of the street denounces the bankruptcy of values of the old regime.

Although he does not follow the official Marxist point of view about the timeliness of the Revolution in all its aspects, Pasternak does nonetheless agree that it was a pressing social necessity. The heroes of *Doctor Zhivago*, like an important segment of Russian student youth at the beginning of the century, turn to socialism in their search both for an absolute and for a method of curing the country's political ills. Socialism is for them "'the sea of life, the sea of spontaneity, . . . life as you see it in a great picture, transformed by genius, creatively enriched. Only now [since the revolution] people have decided to experience it not in books and pictures but in themselves, not as an abstraction but in practice.'"[10] In the beginning this enthusiasm is manifested in a wild admiration for the Revolution, which has suddenly "exploded right into the very thick of daily life." Zhivago, for his part, manifests an attachment to the Revolution in the first months following the establishment of the new regime by sustaining a humble fidelity to his work at the hospital, while the "fashionable" doctors drop "those people" (they ask Zhivago, "So you're working for *them?*").[11] As Raymond Aron has pointed out, the political and artistic avant-gardes have often been able to play a common game, since they dream of an adventure carried out in common with an eye to the same liberation: "The artist denounces the Philistine, the Marxist, the bourgeoisie. They can think of themselves solidary in the same combat against the same enemy."[12] That this alliance is based on a misapprehension we shall have occasion to see in Pasternak and the Russian intelligentsia.

The search for an absolute—that is what socialism was for many of Pasternak's generation. In an article on Pasternak entitled "Le Don Quichotte de notre temps," the French critic Jean Duvignaud writes that "this distance between Zhivago and the world, this distance between Pasternak and Soviet society, is the very distance which separates Cervantes and his dreams." Duvignaud continues:

Like all writers attracted to socialism and revolution, . . . Pasternak dreamed of a complete, absolute communication between men, . . . a world was going to appear in which each consciousness, transparent to other consciousnesses, would be fully recognized for what it is. A world was going to be born in which man, communicating freely with man delivered from his "alienation," would find the spontaneity and innocence characteristic of a humanistic society.[13]

Alas, this lovely dream was soon to collide with a materialization quite different from what was expected. In Zhivago's opinion (and in this respect he is symbolic of Pasternak), socialism, the "sea of life," would but generate a fermenting of elementary forces *directed toward a greater flowering of life*. Reality proved Zhivago wrong.

The exalting episode of the abortive Revolution of 1905 could sustain such hopes. To that event Pasternak dedicated "The Year 1905." In the poem the poet perceives as "through a dream" the past and present of the eternal Russian Revolution. The vision is not focused around the revolutionary intelligentsia. Besides Sofiia Perovskaia and the heroic students, the muzhiks, the factory workers, and the sailors of the *Potemkin* stand in the foreground. As Benjamin Goriély rightly noted, the events of 1905, contemporary with Pasternak's youth, are described in the exalted tone of youth, well suited to the psychology of the Russia of the time. As he commented, they were "youth of the bourgeoisie, youth of the intellectuals, youth of the working class, youth of the political parties, youth of ideas. What an intoxicated snowfall!"[14] The poet sees in the riot the unleashing and explosion of a profound, uncontrollable force, symbolized by fire, "the inferno . . . flooding and swelling" in the last pages of the poem. The work constitutes both a rupture with his previous poetry and an attempt at conciliation with the regime.

The next important episode was the War of 1914, a cataclysm to which Pasternak apparently traced all the evils that befell his generation. One of the indirect sequels of the war was the launching of the Revolution of 1917.

While Pasternak (as he has been reproached) fails to treat in sufficient detail some of the most exciting and controversial issues that agitated Moscow in 1917,[15] he excels in conveying the atmosphere in Moscow during the years immediately following the Revolution and the long series of mishaps of the "forest brotherhood" in Siberia. For many topical and anecdotic details of Chapter 7 of the novel ("Train to the Urals"), Pasternak very skillfully utilizes historical sources, such as an account entitled "A Journey from Petersburg to Siberia in January 1920," published at the time in an émigré publication of documents.[16] These are particularly successful instances of transmutation of experience into art, of documentary into fiction.

It was unfair to reproach Pasternak, as did the editorial board of *Novyi mir*, for giving a completely distorted image of the events of 1917. In the open letter they addressed to Pasternak in November, 1958, they termed a grievous fault the manner in which he mixed up the revolutions of February and October, 1917, lumping them together instead of depicting them separately and showing all the differences in social significance that created an enormous distance between the one, a bourgeois revolution, and the other, a proletarian revolution. It is interesting to note that a Communist free from allegiance to Moscow Bolshevism such as Isaac Deutscher also reproaches Pasternak for confusing the two revolutions. The truth is that Pasternak "strode through history," as Yves Berger put it.[17] His aim was to write a *sui generis* epic, not a pedestrian chronicle. Was it therefore necessary for him to define the heroes' attitude toward "the overthrow of autocracy, the coming to power of Kerensky, the July events, Kornilov's revolt, the October uprising, the seizure of power by the Soviets, and the disbanding of the Constituent Assembly," as the *Novyi mir* editors would have him do?

One should point out in this connection that Pasternak does have specific merits as a chronicler. Those merits were singled out by a competent observer, who praised the poet's description of "Russian geo-strategy." Few students of literature might think to look up the January, 1960, issue of the *Revue de défense nationale* for the article of a French strategy expert, Colonel Jacques Dinfreville, entitled "The Partisan War in *Doctor Zhivago*."[18] Dinfreville congratulates the novelist on the detailed report he has provided of the combat methods of the partisan army. The military leaders seem intensely alive, he emphasizes, having no appearance of "made-up characters"; surrounded by their military specialists (*spets*), "bodyguards, spies, agents provocateurs," they conduct their campaign vigorously. At a disadvantage because of their unhomogeneous army, to which the central powers grant but few resources, they use "a scientific technique of coercion" on their men and absolutely classical guerrilla tactics on the enemy. The author of the novel rightfully emphasizes the determining factor of morale, and he does not forget to recall the topographic peculiarities of the taiga, the unusual setting. This perceptive analysis rightfully "rehabilitates" Pasternak as a chronicler.

It is not, however, at the level of chronicle writing that Pasternak most intensely revives the events of 1917 but in poetry of a paradoxically intimate and delicate turn whose musing seeks out the profound afflatus at work in the overthrow of every order, including the political. Sir Maurice Bowra reminds us that for Pasternak, as well as for other Futurists (Maiakovskii and Khlebnikov in particular), "the Revolution was a prodigious manifestation of natural forces which had hitherto lain dormant in Russia," a manifestation completely in accord with Pasternak's dynamic conception of life. Pasternak's poetry contains some of the characteristics of the revolutionary period that inspired it, but they are reworked after his own fashion, which is quite different from Maiakovskii's.

Pasternak lived his political experience so intensely that he expressed external events as he felt them, eager to gather their meaning through the framework of his own dialectic, whence the transposition of these events onto the palette—so limited at first glance—of his lyric emotion. From this perspective the importance of historic events seems to be reduced to that of natural events. As one commentator observed: "This is precisely the importance that [Pasternak] finds in them. They are indeed natural events and therefore full of majesty and mystery. They are a special manifestation of the strange powers that can be observed in physical nature."[19] Commenting on the poem "Summer" (composed in 1917), Bowra emphasizes that the political events, forming part of the harmonious rustic scene, "are also its climax and its culmination." What must be augured from the dawn and the rising breeze, symbols of a new order, in the poem "May It Be" of 1919? Pasternak is convinced, as Bowra says, "that such an eruption of natural forces must in the end be right and prevail, he finds in them a source of vitality and energy. What matters for him is this release of nature's powers which bring man closer to itself."[20]

To the very extent that he considers political events *from afar,* as though they were a faraway realm, Pasternak can say that in *My Sister, Life* (the collection containing "Summer" and "May It Be") he has succeeded in creating "expressions not in the least contemporary as regards poetry." Such poetry exemplifies the ideal he opposes to that of Maiakovskii. It is not at all surprising, then, that the poet who had sung only a certain exotic quality of the Revolution, the philosopher who meditated only on its logical presuppositions and historical preparation, should be brought brutally back to earth when confronting his dreams with the realization of that revolution and its sordid, shabby aspects. Nadezhda Mandelstam has discussed the uncanny idealistic fascination exerted on Mandelstam, Pasternak, and others—"the most worthy" of their generation—by the very notion of revolution. According to her, they "feared the Revolution might pass [them] by if, in [their] short-sightedness, [they] failed to notice all the great things happening before our eyes."[21]

Disillusionments kept accumulating for the intelligentsia overtaken by the events of the Revolution—that intelligentsia of which Pasternak was an integral part and of which Iurii Zhivago is the symbol. Of the whole process of establishing Marxism in Russia, the part that weighs heaviest on Zhivago is the dragging out of the transition period, with its sequel of disorders and confusion—a situation that exemplifies what the political scientist G. Ferrero labeled "destructive revolution."* For decades the Soviet rulers loudly proclaimed the need for transforming the country, preparing the way for Marxism, and building the city of the future, and during all those years the Russians were obliged to live a life of sacrifice in what were often inhuman conditions, hoping that their grandchildren would see paradise realized on earth. In the name of this people too long deluded,

*According to Ferrero, "destructive revolution" (as opposed to "constructive revolution") is caused by "the collapse of one principle of legitimacy and the absence of a legitimacy of replacement." It is to the destructive revolution that he attributes "the responsibility for terror, wars, and tyranny" (Raymond Aron, *L'opium des intellectuels* [Paris: Calmann-Lévy, 1955], p. 19).

Zhivago explodes: "Man is born to live, not to prepare for life." For the Communists, "transitional periods, worlds in the making, are an end in themselves." These passages awaken an echo of Camus's voice accusing the revolutionaries of sacrificing living men to an allegedly absolute good, to a historical end.

The transitional period is indefinitely prolonged because "those who inspired the revolution aren't at home in anything except change and turmoil." It is an epoch when true values go unutilized, when only "the resourceful" succeed. Russia is governed "by civilians [and] lawyers." The cruel struggle between Reds and Whites, an ethic of reprisals, the reigning terror, and famine soon drive out all civilization. "That period confirmed the ancient proverb, 'Man is a wolf to man.' . . . The laws of human civilization were suspended. The jungle law was in force."[22]

Once a regime has been set up under these conditions—or, rather, in spite of them—what are its far-reaching repercussions on human life? Two fundamental criticisms emerge from Pasternak's work: the Soviets force the hand of life, of reality and they choke off all flowering of the personality, the normal condition of life in society. By their intransigence the Soviets overturn the universally accepted norms of life and the most natural features of interpersonal relations: "It isn't natural, it's like the ancient Roman virtue. . . . They are made of stone, these people, they aren't human, with all their discipline and principles."[23]

Having left a starving Moscow, Zhivago, on his way to the Urals with his family, no longer recognizes the habitual face of things or the accustomed behavior of men: "Where is reality in Russia today? . . . Reality has been so terrorized that it is hiding. . . . what's going on isn't life—it's madness, an absurd nightmare." Nothing now functions according to human laws. The Soviet ideologists portrayed in *Doctor Zhivago* (nonparty men though they are) behave like fanatics, concentrating wholly on their program, thinking only of realizing their theories. Carried away by their fixed ideas and their will to alter everything to accord with those ideas, they are blind to the real facts: "What kind of people are they, to go on raving with this never-cooling, feverish ardor, year in, year out, on nonexistent, long-vanished subjects, and to know nothing, to see nothing around them?"[24]

On closer examination, however, was not the disillusionment of the intelligentsia inevitable? The editors of the French magazine *Arguments*, having emphasized that "Pasternak belongs . . . among those who, at a certain moment in their lives, thought that Communism represented a 'chance' for humanity," are satisfied with adding, "We would be inclined to say that in order to understand Pasternak and his novel, one must have gone through the Communist experience, or have come quite close to it."[25] It seems to me that whether we are Marxists, non-Marxists, or ex-Marxists, the essential question is, Why does Zhivago abandon socialism? Why is he *necessarily* disappointed by its practical application?

Renato Poggioli has correctly pointed out that "Ivan Karamazov accepted God while rejecting the world He had created: Doctor Zhivago similarly accepts the postulate of the revolution while rejecting many of its corollaries."[26] Stalinism is certainly a corollary that Zhivago finds most offensive. If another commentator could say that *Doctor Zhivago* is not so much an *anti-* as a *pre-*Soviet novel, it is because its heroes, in their political views, certainly go as far as the whole pre-revolutionary Russian intelligentsia did, but never much further. The socialism that Pasternak portrays in his poem "Waves" is clearly presented as a remote and, ultimately, unrealizable ideal, which the poet is inclined to contrast with all the pettiness around him. It is an ideal that essentially belongs to the "faraway realm of socialism" but that, paradoxically and unexpectedly, turns out to be close at hand. Its nature is essentially hazy because it is seen through a smoky screen of theoretical discussions.

In brief, the intelligentsia's disappointment with the liberation process was the inevitable consequence of its dream of a far-too-ideal liberation. The kind of revolution they had in mind never materialized because its very conception was mythical. Though it was a congenital necessity, the revolution that actually occurred, unforeseeable by the idealistic intelligentsia, was to give birth to tyrannical power. As Raymond Aron has pointed out: "Revolutionary power is by definition tyrannical power. . . . The tyrannical phase lasts for a shorter or longer time depending on the circumstance, but it can never be dispensed with."[27]

In a fictional context Pasternak denounces the basic misapprehension of the believers in the abortive Revolution of 1905:

By virtue of a self-deception permissible in our day too, they [these intellectuals] imagined that the Revolution would be staged again, like a once temporarily suspended and later revived drama with fixed roles, that is, with all of them playing their old parts. This illusion was all the more natural that, believing deeply in the universally popular nature of their ideals, they all held the opinion that it was necessary to test their own conviction on living people. Becoming convinced of the complete and, to a certain extent, environmental oddity of the Revolution from the standpoint of the average Russian outlook, they could justly be puzzled as to where fresh amateurs and devotees for such a specialized and subtle undertaking could emerge.[28]

Confident that socialism would resemble something like a play given by a handful of conscientious amateur actors reciting the "lines"—the formulas—memorized in prewar salons and cafés, the intelligentsia was bound to find the interlude following the October Revolution extravagant or grotesque. The intelligentsia represented by Zhivago adhered to a liberalism that, though generous, was in the last resort inadequate in the face of the eruption of disturbing social and political phenomena in the wake of 1917.

In the plot of *Doctor Zhivago*, Pasternak gives an interesting insight into the social psychology of the generation depicted in the novel. The social movement is from the aristocratic mansions of the Zhivago and Gromeko families to the outdoor life of Zhivago's daughter, the laundry girl Tania, a waif roaming the streets; from the "upstairs" level of the Gromeko townhouse to the "downstairs" level of the lodge of the porter Markel. In the first part of the book Markel is already the mediator between the Gromeko and Zhivago families and the events in the street. In the latter part of the novel it is Markel's daughter, Marina—no longer the aristocratic Tonia or the *déclassée* Lara—who is the feminine presence in Zhivago's life, mediating between him and everyday realities. The pervasive presence of the new social reality, as represented by Tania and Marina, is shown as necessary, though a piece of the disruptive pattern of events.

Although the Revolution is presented as much-needed "surgery," the protagonists see the ensuing upheavals as a vast, fundamental uprooting, necessarily wasting vital substance and constituting a rupture in a sort of original pact between man and the world. Pasternak's catastrophic outlook in *Doctor Zhivago* is closely linked to his conception of fate. The theme of fate is not explicitly developed in the novel; it is more an "atmosphere" in which events unfold, a structuring principle of the plot. In this connection one critic distinguishes two possible conceptions of fate: the first (the Greek *anagkē*), as a blind, capricious force; the second, as a reasonable law of being, an objective order of life. The latter conception, based on a mysterious bond between necessity and liberty, between the objective order of the world and man's creative will, is undoubtedly the one prevailing in *Doctor Zhivago*. It seems to me, however, that the two conceptions are in fact closely linked in the novel; the protagonists see events as having "the strangeness of the transcendental, as if they were snatches torn from lives on other planets that had somehow drifted to earth." [29] The cataclysms of World War I and of the Revolution are seen as an apocalypse; here fate is made implacable (although rational in a certain sense), and the frightened creatures can only go to ground in some corner spared from divine wrath. From the portrayal of these cataclysmic events it thus becomes clear that Pasternak relates very strongly to them as a participant (whereas Tolstoy, as Victor Frank noted, merely conveys God's eye view of history). [30] This refutes the main thesis of Deutscher's argument about the characters' nonparticipation in revolutionary events. True, the participants are everyday people, not extraordinary actors like Kutuzov, Napoleon, and Alexander, and they do not participate in the action of major battle scenes. Unlike the protagonists in *War and Peace*, Pasternak's approach—the description of the Revolution from the viewpoint of the common man, a rather insignificant historical figure—is nonetheless a valid approach to epic depiction. To be sure, such an approach has cheated the aesthetic preferences of a reader like Akhmatova, who was unhappy that Pasternak's protagonist was such an ordinary, run-of-the-mill, unstriking person; she could not agree with Pasternak's concept of Zhivago as an "average" man, feeling that literature should raise its heroes above the crowd. [31] In Pasternak's view Zhivago was truly the man in the street.

In the foregoing discussion of Pasternak's attitude vis à vis historical developments in his country, a few of the observations about his vision could have been formulated from a Marxist or near-Marxist viewpoint; they have, in fact, been put forward (in a more damaging form) by hostile critics in *Pravda* and *Literaturnaia gazeta*. Do Marxists, however, offer anything in the way of a more coherent, reasonable attitude toward history? It is fitting that we examine this matter here, since it is in its confrontation with Marxism that Pasternak's humanism takes on all its meaning and implications—not because it exists and is valid only as a counter truth or antidote, but because any form of humanism wishing to assert itself as such in the twentieth century must do so in terms of Marxism in one way or another and define its position in relation to that dogma. Raymond Aron asserts: "Every action in the middle of the twentieth century implies and involves taking a position with regard to the Soviet venture. To elude this taking of a position is to elude the tyranny of historical existence." [32] What is true of action is at least as true of intellectual reflection. Thus Sartre, in his *Critique de la raison dialectique*, points out how imperative it is to take into account "the reality of Marxism." [33]

In *Doctor Zhivago*, Pasternak depicts all the stages of enthusiasm for Marxist doctrine experienced by his heroes (as Deutscher pointed out, Pasternak portrays no Communist party member in good standing [34]—Strelnikov is the strongest ideological antithesis to Zhivago). Iurii Zhivago has no difficulty subscribing to Strelnikov's assessment of Marxism made shortly before he kills himself. Against the debauchery, depravity, and social injustice in the disreputable and poor districts of every capital, displayed flagrantly, barricades and socialist publicists were in the last resort powerless. "Marxism arose, it uncovered the root of the evil and it offered the remedy, it became the great force of the century." [35]

Zhivago's experiences from 1917 on do not permit him to go further, however, than those concessions to Marxism. As he witnesses the practical application of Marxism, his opposition increases. It is a radical opposition, because beyond the Soviets' concrete realizations, it is directed against the philosophy underlying them. For Zhivago, "Marxism is too uncertain of its ground to be a science. Sciences are more balanced, more objective. I don't know a movement more self-centered and further removed from the facts than Marxism." [36] The problem Pasternak raises in this passage is that of "scientific socialism," the claims of Marxism to be a scientifically proved system, and we know how fundamental is that claim for the champions of Marxism-Leninism. [37]

It is not appropriate here to attempt another "final" evaluation (after so many others) of the claim put forward for Marxism. I will restrict myself to underlining certain limitations of the Marxist conception of history, insofar as the latter is brought up for discussion in Pasternak's novel. It is worthwhile attempting to clarify the seemingly paradoxical reproach that Pasternak, through his characters, addresses to the Bolsheviks: he accuses them of disregarding history by remaining at the level of nature—such, in effect, is the meaning of the reminder that "man does not live in nature but in history." [38]

This reproach seems astonishing at first sight if one considers the cardinal importance of history for the forefathers of Bolshevism. For Marx, reason must emerge from history. Because he situates the historical process objectively, outside the mind, Marx makes the mind subject to various phenomena of history. Because of the, for Marx, completely materialistic character of the content of history, production relations and social reality strictly determine human consciousness and consequently every event of history. And when, in *Economic-Philosophic Manuscripts of the Year 1844*, Marx makes it clear that Communism will be the end of the conflict between man and nature, does he not thereby grant that at the end of the historical process man will be in nature? [39] History therefore has a physical teleology, just as its content is made up of the sum of physical determinisms. The historical outcome of the dialectic will be an adequation of consciousness to its content, and vice versa, and therefore a return to the undifferentiated condition of animal life.

When, on the other hand, Pasternak says that man is in history, he does not mean a historicity that excludes transcendence, in the Marxist manner. For the Marxists, indeed, man is so essentially historical that social practice is identified with human reality, and all transcendence is rigorously excluded.

In the last analysis, the schematic and verbalistic aspects of the Hegelian-Marxist conception of history made it scientifically inexact. As Sartre points out in the *Critique of Dialectical Reason*, history as it is actually lived offers resistance to a priori schemata.[40] It is indeed possible to discard such schemata and perceive history in the broader perspective of human evolution. That is Pasternak's position, considering history as a kind of organic phenomenon. Pasternak does not envisage history according to any preestablished schema; he grasps it in its total ordination. As a growing organism, humanity advances—with much bumping and groping, it is true. Pasternak does not consider history as the materiality of the various empirical facts composing it; history manifests itself in its orientation, according to its spiritualized, transfigured sense. There is no doubt that he thus comes close to Berdiaev, with whose works, however, he was not well acquainted.*

Is it not this attitude that he has in mind when he talks about the historical method of the Marburg school, which consists in considering the logical significance of this or that period of history? History is of interest to the historian only to the extent that it can be "laid bare to [his] logical commentary,"[41] and not through its specificity or historicity in itself. Besides, man's historicity has too often been reduced to the simple consciousness of historicity. In seeking the meaning of history in history alone, a certain kind of humanism failed grossly. Thus the spectacle of history induces the Marxist to adopt a relativizing conception of man: he is only the product of the material content of the world, which is historically manifested according to the dialectical process. This minimizing conception runs the risk of giving rise to skepticism about man within man himself. Pasternak has, on the contrary, an absolutizing conception of history, in the sense that for him history, the meeting place of the temporal and the eternal, is what reveals man in his true dimensions. For him, man's historical dimension is not so radical and obvious that it is rigorously proved by action unfolding itself. If it were, it would be condemned to total "exteriority." Indeed, such a radical historicism would be characterized by temporal dispersion and would lead in the end to the suppression of history.

In *Doctor Zhivago*, Pasternak formulated his conception of history. When collated, "Father" Vedeniapin's reflections and Iurii Zhivago's tirades, as well as Sima Tuntseva's digressions, form a surprisingly coherent vision of history. There

---

*From his study *The Meaning of History* (1923), it is clear that for Berdiaev history is the highest spiritual reality, and as such is not given empirically in the form of simple material facts, because it does not exist in that way. Historical memory, in spiritualizing and transfiguring it, reveals what constitutes its inner nature and shows itself truly endowed with a soul.

are thus grounds, here again, to consider these three characters as spokesmen of the view of the author. We do not find in Pasternak as well-developed or systematic a statement as the one Tolstoy gives in the epilogue of *War and Peace*, a veritable treatise on the meaning of history. Pasternak proceeds in the manner of an impressionist painter: many strokes create the total impression if one just stands back far enough. The many lyrical and symbolic allusions represent an aesthetic system effective enough to make us overlook the absence of a systematic statement in the fashion of Tolstoy's epilogue.

Pasternak talks about a primitive state in which nature asserted itself in its absolute virulence: "Nature hit you in the eye so plainly and grabbed you so fiercely and so tangibly by the scruff of the neck that perhaps it really was still full of gods. Those were the first pages of the chronicle of mankind, it was only just beginning."[42] It is truly the epoch of the alienation of man, who felt so out of place on a hostile earth, of the alienation in the cosmogonies then flourishing, by which man related himself, as well as the earth, to the "spirits of fire and water."

The first great civilizations led to a religious syncretism; the plurality of gods in Rome abolished the reign of fear: "This ancient world [the world of cosmogonies] ended with Rome, because of overpopulation. Rome was a flea market of borrowed gods and conquered people."

The ransom for that liberation was severely felt, however, because it occurred only as a result of the human promiscuity of a decayed civilization, the vestige of a "high-class culture" in the process of disappearing—to use Oswald Spengler's terminology. Rome was

a bargain basement on two floors, earth and heaven, a mass of filth convoluted in a triple knot as in an intestinal obstruction. Dacians, Herulians, Scythians, Sarmatians, Hyperboreans, heavy wheels without spokes, eyes sunk in fat, sodomy, double chins, illiterate emperors, fish fed on the flesh of learned slaves. There were more people in the world than there have been ever since, all crammed into the passages of the Coliseum, and all wretched.[43]

All that the ancients knew was

blood and beastliness and cruelty and pockmarked Caligulas who do not suspect how untalented every enslaver is. They had the boastful dead eternity of bronze monuments and marble columns.[44]

Such contrasts may seem exaggerated; however, they must be put into context. The two passages above are inserted into an argument whose essential aim is to describe a more humane conception of history and civilization that took shape after the Roman era. What Pasternak is stigmatizing, in relegating them to the past from which they arose, are the tribal alienation, "the reign of numbers," the "patriarchal alienation" of a degrading submission to rulers and tyrants, and the pompous inanity of a national glory that enslaves what is noblest in man. Declamations about leaders and peoples belong "to the Biblical times of shepherd tribes and patriarchs."[45] The "Caligulas" referred to in *Doctor Zhivago*—the rulers and tyrants who demand such degrading submission—stand for one particular infamous leader toward whom Pasternak personally felt "horror": Stalin. That is clear from statements Pasternak made to Gladkov during World War II.[46]

That *Doctor Zhivago* is in a very specific sense a condemnation of the Stalinist era of Communism has not escaped an observer as sensitive to ideology as Deutscher, who reproached Pasternak with projecting the "horrors of the Stalin era" on to the early era of Bolshevik rule.[47] Incidentally, Deutscher's acknowledgment that in his portrayal of postrevolutionary events Pasternak in effect described the Stalinist era and dwelled on it is a contradiction of his own statement that Pasternak's mind "had stopped" in the early 1920s and that the writer had thus misinterpreted "the calendar of the revolution."[48] Deutscher completely missed the plain fact that one of Pasternak's conscious aims in writing *Doctor Zhivago* was to denounce the horrors of Stalinism. It is really Deutscher who betrays ignorance of the *Soviet* calendar: in the early 1950s (and even at the time of the Thaw) it was still inconceivable to provide an explicit description of the Stalin era in a literary work. Thus Pasternak's subterfuge, ostensibly giving a description of the 1920s but in effect portraying Stalinism. This approach also reflects a feeling that Pasternak must have had: that the horrors of Stalin's days had their roots in the first few years of Bolshevik rule.

Doctor Zhivago is the orchestration of a deep-seated ideological conflict that affected the whole of Russia. To the extent that it reflects that conflict, the novel is the voice of Russia—while it is also the culmination of what has been termed the "remarkable, silent duel" that opposed Pasternak and Stalin.[49] From the memoirs of both Aleksandr Gladkov and Olga Ivinskaia it is clear that Pasternak saw the writing of *Doctor Zhivago* as an act of political courage. In the novel Pasternak denounced the philistinism (*meshchanstvo*) of Soviet literature and culture under Stalin. In the mid-1950s he was strongly critical not only of the excesses of the cult of personality (*lichnost*) but also of the continued facelessness (*bezlichie*) and uniformity of the crass and shallow obscurantism that, through sheer inertia, continued under Khrushchev. His view is clear in a poem he penned in 1956:

> The cult of personality's been unthroned
> But the cult of hollow words holds sway
> And the cult of faceless philistines, perhaps,
> Has magnified a hundredfold . . . .[50]

According to Zhivago, Stalinism was culturally bankrupt because it made an organized effort to revive an era rendered obsolete by the spiritual progress of mankind: ". . . Rome was at an end. The reign of numbers was at an end. The duty, imposed by armed force, to live unanimously as a people, as a whole nation, was abolished. Leaders and nations were relegated to the past."[51] The divergence between Stalin's and Zhivago's philosophies has to do with the respective significance they grant to the rights of *homo publicus* as opposed to *homo privatus*. Such a conflict is similar to the one set forth by Arthur Koestler in *Darkness at Noon* (1941), for decades the only full-length treatment—and then in fictional form— of the plight of Pasternak's protector Bukharin.

In Pasternak's view the key factor in the history of mankind that generated a new attitude was Christianity—the successor of such decisive spiritual moments as Egypt, Greece, and the theology of the Old Testament.[52] Against the background of this still new though ancient and hallowed ideology, Stalinism appears regressive. Christianity is presented in *Doctor Zhivago* as a spiritual "high deed" or prowess* "still being accomplished by all who are inspired" and "not yet superseded by anything else." It is depicted as a practice and an endeavor indissolubly linked to a new humanism, to the promotion of "individual human life." It is Christ who established history as it is understood today: "Christ's gospel is its foundation . . . . There was no history in this sense among the ancients." In striking phrases Pasternak defines what history is for him: "History . . . is the centuries of systematic explorations of the riddle of death, with a view to overcoming death." History is "another universe, made by man with the help of time and memory in answer to the challenge of death."[53] This is the goal that polarizes higher human activities, the ultimate triumph of life, in its most immediate as well as its more advanced forms.

The "impetus" moving in this direction requires a "spiritual equipment": it is again to the Gospel that Pasternak traces its fundamental ideas. These ideas are:

> . . . To begin with, love of one's neighbor, which is the supreme form of vital energy. Once it fills the heart of man it has to overflow and spend itself. And then the two basic ideals of modern man—without them he is unthinkable—the idea of free personality and the idea of life as sacrifice.[54]

These three values—love of one's neighbor, the free individual, and life as sacrifice—are the pivotal points in Pasternak's convictions.

---

* The Russian original has the word *rabota*, but it is used in a way suggestive of *podvig*—the term traditionally used in the context of Russian Orthodox spirituality to denote a spiritual "high deed" or prowess (sometimes almost superhuman in scope).

15

Individual Human Life

A Personalist Philosophy

What an enormously significant change! How did it come about that an individual human event, insignificant by ancient standards, was regarded as equal in significance to the migration of a whole people? Why should it have this value in the eyes of heaven? . . . Something in the world had changed. Rome was at an end. The reign of numbers was at an end. . . . Leaders and nations were relegated to the past. They were replaced by the doctrine of individuality and freedom. Individual human life became the life story of God.

Doctor Zhivago[1]

In modern times the adherents of Marxism have extolled praxis—action in the world with the aim of transforming it—but they disregard the fact that if man has acquired a historical role he can fulfill it only as a person. The etymology of the word *person* tells us that it refers to someone who has a role to play. Having a role implies a dignity superior to that of an instrument or a means; it implies demands that will break biological egoism by transcending the narrow limits of individuality. A historical role in this sense obviously can be assigned only to a person, not to the masses. For man to become conscious of his historic role, of his basic historicity, he must tear himself away from the state in which he stagnates—undifferentiated from the beings around him—to discover a unity of events, to see in the present, beyond its ambiguity, a possibility of transcending the past and an orientation toward the future.

Moreover, the prerequisite for the creativity and human inventiveness to which the advance of science bears witness (and which lie at the foundation of Soviet technological rationalism) is scope for the originality of the human mind. During Pasternak's lifetime Soviet Marxists obstinately refused to recognize this originality reposing in *persons* and hence oppose any promotion of human individuality and "interiorism" (in the sense of Teilhard de Chardin's *intériorité*). Originality and internalization are in fact complementary qualities that combine to make the "I" an absolute irreducible to the determinants of any objectivizing science.

Pasternak calls for the "I" to be given the same rank of *absolute source* in the political domain as it enjoys in metaphysics. He shows himself to be more Hegelian than Marxist in the sense that for him the union of the rational and the real (a problem that every philosophy since Hegel must address) is not accomplished by a critique of institutions with a view to their practical transformation but results from the spontaneity of the mind considering its liberty in the world. For Pasternak, however, this union is accomplished not through any sort of dialectic development but by an intuitive insight characteristic of his spiritual monism. This intuition brings about its own integration into the world and its own objectivization.

Pasternak's subjectivism is best revealed in his poetry. He is, of course, eager to capture natural reality, but it is his appreciation of things that gives them value and reality; they derive their unifying principle from man's consciousness. In the final analysis, the medium is the soul of the poet, who transforms nature according to his own peculiar vision.

Pasternak has therefore often been reproached for confining nature and life within the limits of an intimate and comfortable niche. The poet is as fascinated as a Mallarmé by all that the gray tranquillity of a garden can conceal. His professed aim is to crowd onto the narrow canvas of his poem a line of bushes along the river, leaves sculptured in snow, an entire city, even the whole world:

> I squeeze a world in stanzas:
> Snow town and frozen sea
> of roofs; riverside sculpture
> of bush and fallen tree.[2]

That the symphonic world at large is thus sometimes transposed into a willfully symbolic and intimate melodic line is one of the triumphs and paradoxes of Pasternak's poetry.

It has been said that the meaning of *Doctor Zhivago* can be reduced to an analysis of the precipitation of historical events in terms of individual destinies. This interpretation applies even more persuasively to Pasternak's poetry, especially to his later poetry, where images become more "internalized," as is apparent in his cycle *When Skies Clear*. For Pasternak, natural or historical events clearly are symbolic of individual destiny. Thus in the poem "Round the Turning" the poet's whole future lies waiting for him hidden in the depths of the forest, as certain as a pledge, ineluctable, unquestionably unfolding before his eyes. The same theme occurs in "Fulfillment," where the poet reads his future in the pattern of a jay's flight, and the echo sent back by the forest becomes a valid confirmation supplied by the world.[3]

Often a process of intense internalization takes place in the course of a poem, at the end of which the poet reveals a profound truth, an anguish that has gripped his life. He leads up to it gradually, starting with the description of a landscape. Thus in a poem of 1932 the process, beginning with an evocation of mountain scenery, is marked by the increasingly compelling tone of the remarks the poet exchanges with his companion. These remarks lead to the tragic confession: "I am thrown into life, which in the flood of days rolls the flood of species, and it is harder for me to hew out mine [my life] than with scissors to cut the waves."[4]

The subjective mood sometimes has a Baudelairean tinge, as in the poem "Soul" of the mid-1950s, in which the poet's soul is in mourning "for agonized lives"—those of his friends who fell victim to a "skinflint time." Bent down under the weight of these friends' agony, all the persona's soul can do is function as "a harp of bitterness" in singing the praises of those dead, "Embalming their bodies / In dedicated verse," and (in a striking image) grinding the whole age "to a heap of compost." The starkness of the poem is enhanced by the metaphors presenting the soul as a "funeral urn" and a "morgue."[5] The poem has very specific concrete, historical connotations. The unnamed departed who are mourned here are Tsvetaeva, Tabidze, Iashvili, Maiakovskii, and the poet's many other friends and acquaintances who met with tragic fates under Stalin.*

This grievous or even mortuary note, however, is exceptional in Pasternak. More often he sings the artist's vocation, a poetic *topos* also permeated by a concern with the artist's creative individuality. In the poem "Night" the whole firmament and the creatures beneath it, the pilot's night flight, moving trains, Paris nightclubs, locomotive drivers throwing coal into the furnace, all the lights and fires aglow on all continents are present in the artist's awareness as he meditates in his garret. This accounts for the cosmic intensity of the task pursued by the worker struggling against sleep; and it explains the intensity of the exhortation addressed to him by the poet:

*See Chapter 10.

Work; watch;
Don't waver, work.
Wrestle with sleep
Like planet and pilot
There's no surrender
To sleep, artist,
Eternity's hostage,
Captive to time.[6]

The artist (the symbol of man in his essence, who is creative man) appears as the prophet, the seer such as the Romantics—Pushkin, Victor Hugo—saw him. At the same time, however, he is a microcosm, the summary of all human experience, the product of the entire universe.

The all-encompassing subjectivism to be found in Pasternak's work is bound to raise certain reservations. While it extols a contemplation that fosters the deepening of the self's experience and the transfiguration of daily existence, it also leads to an extremity of individualism, a self-withdrawal of the *individual* called to the broadening role of the *person*, the citizen, the biblical "neighbor." Ultimately, the happiness sought by the protagonists of *Doctor Zhivago* may well be the kind that leads to disappointment—insofar as that happiness hinges upon personal fulfillment, to the detriment of action in common cause.

It should be said, in reply to this objection, that *Doctor Zhivago* is a protest and a reaction—at times embittered—against the abuses of systematic social engineering. It appeared, we must not forget, after forty years of a Communist regime that through continuous propaganda strove to turn the goal of reshaping the world into the focal point of the average citizen's existence and in the process libeled and thwarted his profoundest and most deeply rooted natural aspirations. One should also emphasize again how chimerical were the enforced collective dreams to which Pasternak's generation fell prey—dreams against which the heroes of *Doctor Zhivago* often protest in profound *cris du coeur* tinged with sharp irony:

The riddle of life, the riddle of death, the enchantment of genius, the enchantment of unadorned beauty—yes, yes, these things were ours. But the small worries of practical life—things like the reshaping of the planet—these things, no thank you, they are not for us.[7]

Still, professions of faith of this kind are hardly proof against the charge of naïve escapism, of clinging passionately to profound values like the contemplation of the riddle of life and death, genius, and the admiration of beauty, with scarcely any reference to the political, economic, and social realities on which these values are founded. Is not Pasternak's attitude, then, one of extreme introversion and just as reprehensible as the one he denounces? If the Soviets are alienated from realities of the psyche in their economic and social planning ("the reshaping of the planet"),[8] is not Pasternak a victim of the opposite "idealistic alienation?"

To deal with this objection, let us try to determine the exact nature of the "detachment" or "solitude" that Pasternak makes a fundamental characteristic of his heroes.

If for Marx the only things that count are relationships arising from production, that is, subject-object relationships (the object—material goods—having priority over the conscious subject), for Pasternak all that counts, as we have seen, is the relationship that arises from love. Now this relationship is essentially that of subject-subject, and its very depth and intensity demands—besides "attachment"—a certain degree of "interiority" (David Riesman's "inner-directedness"),[9] a certain extent of "detachment" in the very interest of those loved. This concept is clarified when one considers Gabriel Marcel's distinction between two kinds of detachment, the spectator's and the saint's: "The saint's detachment occurs . . . within reality itself . . . . This detachment is a participation, the highest there is. The spectator's detachment is the exact opposite, it is a desertion that is not only ideal [that is, on the plane of the mind, of ideas] but real."[10] It is obvious that the detachment of Iurii Zhivago, who withdraws to think and create and whose work will later be precious and instructive to the public, can be equated to that of the saint in that it yields the highest social utility. It is criticism that liberates by creative example.

In this same order of ideas Sartre indicates in what sense there exists a solitude that is *project* (or *pro-ject* [*pro-jet*]—according to the full semantic value of the term, which corresponds to the Heideggerian *Ent-wurf*). In Sartre's vocabulary solitude is isolation felt within a "serial group" (*groupement sériel*) or a society that is passively accepted (*collectif inerte*). Each member of this *collectif inerte* is basically isolated despite the physical presence of the other members; he remains unbound to them. On the other hand, the individual who is part of a group in the real sense of the word (that is, a society in which each of its members spiritually participates instead of merely acquiescing) projects "his own action in the *praxis* of the group." This individual fulfills his role spontaneously and will not feel isolated even if he is physically separated from the other members of the community. There exists, therefore, an "isolation" that is a presence and a bond. Even in certain cases where the individual looks detached or isolated, the subjective aspect of this attitude is a necessary element of the "objective" process (from objectivization to objectivization). History takes place wherever individual freedoms clash with each other and then become "common" within groups.[11]

Thus Pasternak speaks of a personal liberty concentrated in solitude. The community of men is organically viable and dynamic only because each individual is independent and has the latitude to satisfy his needs and pursue his interests. Pasternak's *individualism* is closely connected to his vitalism, as discussed earlier. Pasternak shared the creed (propagated by Zhivago in his pamphlets), fostering individuality as "the biological basis of the organism."[12] In this regard, it is useful to recall that, even on the basis of considerations concerning a possible level of infracellular individuality, a biologist like Georges Canguilhem has come to the conclusion that individuality is not a limit or a boundary. This amounts to a claim that in biology we can believe in the existence of infracellular individualities because "the individual necessarily supposes in himself his relationship to a larger being, he calls for, he *demands* . . . a continuous background against which his discontinuity will stand out."[13] Individuality understood in this way must be called, on a human level, *personality*. It should be stressed that Pasternak's individualism is based on the recognition of the individual as *person* (with rights and duties), not on an exaltation of the individual as representative of the biological ego and the egoism of the body.

Moreover, on occasion Pasternak exhibits a note of clearly impersonal pantheism that is far from exalting the singularity or uniqueness of the individual. In this connection it is interesting to consider the lecture on "Symbolism and Immortality" that Pasternak gave in Moscow in 1913. In his *Sketch for an Autobiography* he gives the following account of it:

I argued that [the fundamental subjectivity of our perceptions] was not the attribute of every individual human being, but was a generic and supra-personal quality, that it was the subjectivity of the world of man and of humanity at large. I suggested . . . that after his death every person leaves behind him a part of that undying, generic subjectivity which he possessed during his lifetime. The main object of my paper was to advance the theory that perhaps this preeminently subjective and universally human corner or separate part of the soul has since time immemorial been the sphere of action and the main subject of art. That, besides, though the artist was of course mortal like the rest of mankind, the joy of living experienced by him was immortal, and that other people a century later might through his works be able to experience something approaching the personal and vital form of his original sensations.[14]

The same doctrine is found in *Doctor Zhivago*, as, for example, when young Iurii Zhivago admonishes Anna Ivanovna Gromeko at her bedside:

. . . all the time, life, one, immense, identical throughout its innumerable combinations and transformations, fills the universe and is continually reborn. You are anxious about whether you will rise from the dead or not, but you rose from the dead when you were born and you didn't notice it.[15]

These lines and those that follow are characteristic of Pasternak's views. He admits of no afterlife for the individual conscience; he expressed himself clearly on this point on many occasions, such as, in his speech at a meeting of Soviet writers in 1936, in his allusion to "the false [religious] superstructure of the immortality of the soul."[16]

This conviction, however, is less important to Pasternak than the conception of the person that he adopted from Christianity. In his mind, the utmost development of personality coincides with the utmost response of the individual to "tradition" (*traditsiia*) in the sense almost of "revelation"—and the imperative of love for others. This he makes clear in an eloquent passage in *A Safe-Conduct*:

To all of us tradition has appeared; to all it has promised a face; to all, each in a different way, it has kept its promise. We have all become people only to the measure in which we have loved people and had the opportunity to love.

Unfortunately, human beings have too often refused this "tradition":

315

Instead of a face [most] preferred facelessness, afraid of the sacrifices that tradition demands from childhood. To love selflessly and unreservedly, with a strength equal to the square of the distance, this is the task of our hearts while we are children.[17]

If personality is a direct function and manifestation of love, it now seems clear why Pasternak protested so much against the loss of personality exacted and brought about by a totalitarian regime. The statement in *Doctor Zhivago* about gregariousness being "always the refuge of mediocrities" has sometimes been quoted. It corresponds to a firmly established notion of Pasternak's, for we find it expressed in only slightly different words in a short prose text published by him before the war, "The Haughty Pauper": "Belonging to a type is equivalent to lacking naturalness, and the only people who live according to types are those who deliberately go against nature to put on such a pose." Zhivago will say: "Belonging to type is the death of man, his condemnation."[18]

Pasternak's personalism can be seen as organized around a poetics of the homecoming, as has been suggested by one critic, who pointed out that the historical theme in *Doctor Zhivago*

opposes the frantic home-destroying motion of the Revolution to the values embodied in the home symbol: serenity, order, and loyalty to the past. On the religious level, the home symbol expresses the Christian view of man "at home in history" and at home even in death in a cosmic process paternally ordered by God. Finally [for Zhivago] art is a homecoming in that it is a return to the primordial archetypes, restoring one's contact with the intimations of the sacred experienced in childhood."[19]

It should be worthwhile to pursue the consideration (scarcely attempted yet) of this poetics of "homecoming" in *Doctor Zhivago* in terms of Gaston Bachelard's category of *intimité* or *intériorité*, as set forth through a number of concepts or archetypes (the native home, the "Jonas complex," the grotto, the labyrinth)—in a word, in terms of the Bachelardian dialectics of involution.[20]

At the beginning of this chapter I indicated in what sense Pasternak is nearer to Hegel than to Marx in his conception of the spirit. It was a mere suggestion, not a strict philosophical comparison with Hegel, since there is scant reason to relate Pasternak, who has so little of the dogmatic turn of mind, with Hegel. Here it should be emphasized once more that Pasternak is not a systematic philosopher and that comparisons with formal philosophers suggest themselves only because of the philosophic orientation of his pronouncements. With this reservation one may say that his views of freedom and history are often similar to those of his near-contemporary Benedetto Croce. For Croce, freedom plays an essential role in history insofar as it is the moral ideal of humanity and an eternal creative principle. Croce, like Hegel, sees reality as the mind unfolding through conflicts, but he stresses the mind's unity and originality, since to him it reaches far beyond narrow Hegelian rationality and encompasses the unconscious, nature, art, and intuition. This view is very close to Pasternak's conception of freedom. As Alexander Gerschenkron has pointed out, the freedom that is so essential to him is most clearly manifest in "Garden of Gethsemane," one of the "Poems of Ivrii Zhivago":

When the hour on the Mount of Olives had drawn to its close; when all the doubts have
been resolved, the fears suppressed, and the last hopes extinguished; when what has been
written is about to be fulfilled, it is still "in voluntary pain" to glorify "the terrible majesty" of what has been preordained as the "march of centuries" that Jesus is ready for his
cross. And this is the last word and the summary of the parable which is this novel.[21]

Gerschenkron's view is that Pasternak intended the novel to be a parable signify-
ing the death of the Russian intelligentsia and its entombment in the sepulcher,
with a promise of ultimate resurrection. According to this arresting interpretation, the apotheosis of a will freely choosing its own end should not surprise us,
coming as it does from one of the disciples of the Marburg philosopher Hermann
Cohen. Gerschenkron quotes Kant and Cohen to illustrate how this influence is
linked with Cohen's interpretation of the *Critique of Pure Reason*:

Cohen taught him well "was der Alte meinte" in propounding the Third Antinomy in
the *Critique of Pure Reason*. The causal determination of the phenomena and the normative freedom of the noumena receive their active resolution in the methodological dichotomy of *Sein und Sollen*. Man is a norm-making creature. He may know a great deal about
the causal world; he may be deeply impressed with the grandeur of the creation and with
what he believes to be the world's predetermined course, and he may mold his norms
accordingly. Yet the attempt to obliterate the duality of causality and imputation by substantive *Gleichschaltung* must fail. Norm-making in its deepest essence is and remains a
free activity. Whatever the strength of the causal world and its power over the individual,
it cannot destroy the normative world of individual freedom.[22]

Although these affinities should not be used to make Pasternak into a formal
philosopher or the heir of a philosophical school in the strict sense of the term,
such an interpretation casts light on a vital aspect of his creative mind. Zhivago,
the hero of "voluntary acceptance," is the apotheosis of Pasternak's personalism.

16

Dissolving in All Others

Community and
Suprapersonal Values

Zhizn ved tozhe tolko mig
Tolko rastvorenie
Nas samikh vo vsekh drugikh
Kak by im v darene.

[For life, too, is only an instant,
Only the dissolving of ourselves
In the selves of all others
As if bestowing a gift.]

> Pasternak, "Wedding"[1]

Skvoz proshlogo peripetii
I gody voin i nishchety
Ia molcha uznaval Rossii
Nepovtorimye cherty.

[Through all the past tribulation,
The years of war and privation,
All through, hushed, I recognized
Russia's unique features.]

> Pasternak, "On Early Trains"[2]

Zhivago's immersion in the past, in the visions of his childhood, and in his memories of Old Russia is an act of re-creative memory, a return to the source of creativity, true originality, true existence.

> René E. Fortin[3]

We have seen that Pasternak treats personality as an absolute. It should be made explicit, however, that this absolute derives its value from the recognition that it guarantees and conditions social values. Pasternak's personalism is far from the extreme of asocial individualism, because, even while extolling the individual values menaced by Sovietism, Pasternak is convinced of the privileged role of the cultural community as a whole and thus defends what Max Scheler called the "*Volk*-oriented way of thinking" (*Volksgesinnung*). He jealously asserts the rights of that community by arguing that in certain deviations of individualism, such as the personality cult, the object of the cult exceeds the role normally devolving upon personality and encroaches on the rights of the community and of each individual within it.

Pasternak even goes so far as to label "shabby improvisations" the activities of the heads of state, who are almost deified by the Soviets and are generally conceded certain skills as organizers in the West. Here Pasternak in effect espouses Max Scheler's distinction between mere *Führer* and authentic *Vorbilder* (exemplary models). We will return later to the privileged role that, according to Pasternak, belongs to genius (the equivalent of Scheler's *Vorbild*). All Führers are anathemas to him. The politician is great only as an incarnation of the virtues of the people, since the people alone really "make" history.[4]

The reason for this is that, in Pasternak's eyes, life is something great and beautiful that evolves spontaneously, and as a rule rather slowly. Trying to rush this evolution by means of great upheavals is a ridiculous quest. Society grows and changes eternally of its own accord. Here Pasternak remains in the Tolstoyan tradition of denying warriors and statesmen the roles of initiators and innovators:

No single man makes history. History cannot be seen, just as one cannot see grass growing. Wars and revolutions, kings and Robespierres, are history's organic agents, its yeast. But revolutions are made by fanatical men of action with one-track minds, geniuses in their ability to confine themselves to a limited field. They overturn the old order in a few hours or days, the whole upheaval takes a few weeks or at most years, but the fanatical spirit that inspired the upheavals is worshipped for decades thereafter, for centuries.[5]

In the novel, Strelnikov, in his great tirade on the Revolution, casts Lenin, the idol of the revolutionaries, in a secondary role. Lenin was only the individual "who fell upon the old world as the personified retribution for its misdeeds"— Lenin, who personified the whole of nineteenth-century revolutionary aspirations and endeavors, "the whole of the workers' movement of the world, the whole of Marxism in the parliaments and universities of Europe, the whole of this new system of ideas with its newness, the swiftness of its conclusion, its irony, and its pitiless remedies elaborated in the name of pity."[6]

If we take this view to be Pasternak's, we cannot help comparing it with that of a prominent Western historian of Soviet Russia, E. H. Carr. According to Carr, the individuals who launch decisive events in history are conditioned by the circumstances and the milieu to which they belong and do not in any way "transcend" that milieu. All things considered, such individuals succeed in modifying the course of history only because they reflect and personify the aspirations of their generation. In Carr's view Stalin's most decisive quality was that he was the least Europeanized and the least intellectual of all the Russian politicians of his generation, and thus the most similar to the great mass of Russians, of whom he seemed the perfect reflection.[7]

If Stalin is for Carr the epitome of "positive" qualities (insofar as he is the exemplar of "Russianness"), Lenin is for Strelnikov the incarnation of something essentially negative. The same can be said of the image of Stalin that can be distilled from the novel. In the two passages from *Doctor Zhivago* quoted above and in various other passages throughout the novel (for instance, the one concerning the cruel "Caligulas who had no idea how inferior the system of slavery is"), Pasternak stigmatizes Stalin, though without naming him.[8]

In setting forth his theory of history ("No single man makes history. History cannot be seen, just as one cannot see grass growing"), Pasternak makes the following statement: "Tolstoy thought of it in just this way, but he did not spell it out so clearly. He denied that history was set in motion by Napoleon or any other ruler or general, *but he did not develop his idea to its logical conclusion.*"[9] The last assertion seems somewhat surprising. Pasternak seems to have left out of account the whole epilogue of *War and Peace*, which is a body of argument notably more elaborate than the reflections that Pasternak offers (in basic agreement with Tolstoy) at various points throughout his novel. It is worth trying to present the points Tolstoy made before taking up Pasternak's remark about him.

Tolstoy begins the epilogue of *War and Peace* with a consideration of "the mysterious forces that move humanity." He goes on to claim that the theory of an "ordination" of history, so dear to historians, necessarily involves the concepts of chance and genius. Since the final aim of history is in fact inscrutable to us, there is no reason to seek at all costs an element of genius in Alexander or Napoleon. No, the real meaning of history lies elsewhere: "The fundamental and essential significance of the European events of the beginning of the nineteenth century lies in the movement of the mass of the European peoples from west to east and afterwards from east to west." Only an inexplicable series of chances permits Napoleon's growing success, and thereby the chance factor is adduced by Tolstoy to eliminate the genius factor.

Just as Pasternak will later use the image of the forest to prove that final ends and general aims are inscrutable to man, Tolstoy uses a comparison borrowed from apiculture: "All that is accessible to man is the relation of the life of the bee to other manifestations of life. And so it is with the purpose of historic characters and nations." Modern history, Tolstoy emphasizes, has rejected the traditional theory of the mainspring of history (persons endowed with divine power and moved directly by the will of the divinity), as well as the explanatory principle of the ancient *fatum*. It leads to the same results, however, since it claims that men are led by single individuals, and asserts the existence of a determined end toward which nations and humanity proceed. When Tolstoy notes the "strangeness and absurdity" of the answers offered by historians, he strikes a vein that will be resumed later by Valéry.[10]

The question that should be asked, Tolstoy claims, is this: "What is the power that moves peoples"—the force that "has appeared . . . instead of a divine power?" Would this force be "a power inherent in heroes and rulers?" But what is power, exactly? Jurists answer that power is the sum of the wills of the masses transferred to their delegates. Thus we approach the extremely delicate and complex problem of the relationship between rulers and the masses. Precisely to what extent do the former represent, and *continue in the course of time to represent*, the will of the masses? Historians invent abstractions (liberty, equality, evolution, progress, civilization) and identify these abstractions with the goal toward which history moves. Once this framework is established, historians tell us of the lives and activities of monarchs, writers, and reformers. But this kind of history remains a history of monarchs, and so on; it is not the history of the life of the people. The life of the people is not contained in the life of a few men, for the connection between those men and the people has not been found.[11]

Thus we still face the problem of power. Tolstoy concludes that power is the fixed relationship between an order given (by a ruler) and the event that follows: "This relation of the men who command to those they command is what constitutes the essence of the conception called power." He adds:

The movement of nations is caused not by power, nor by intellectual activity, nor even by a combination of the two as historians have supposed, but by the activity of *all* the people who participate in the events, and who always combine in such a way that those taking the largest direct share in the event take on themselves the least responsibility and vice versa.

The mainspring of history must be the free will of each of those participating in it: "A man is only conscious of himself as a living being by the fact that he wills. . . . But his will—which forms the essence of his life—man recognizes (and can but recognize) as free. . . . A man having no freedom cannot be conceived of except as deprived of life." In a statement that reveals how much the Russian intelligentsia was permeated by German philosophy, Tolstoy declares:

History examines the manifestations of man's free will in connection with the external world in time and in dependence on cause, that is, it defines this freedom by the laws of reason, and so history is a science only in so far as this free will is defined by those laws.

All things considered, the law of inevitability in history does not destroy but strengthens the foundation on which the institutions of church and state are erected.[12]

Such are Tolstoy's positions, forming the conclusion of the epic that served to illustrate them. *War and Peace* must have been familiar to Pasternak from his childhood. Moreover, Tolstoy's influence is unquestionably evident in the various passages from Pasternak quoted in this chapter. But it is piquant to record Pasternak's reproach to Tolstoy that "he did not carry his reasoning to its conclusion." Most aspects of Pasternak's reasoning are to be found in Tolstoy's. Both use metaphors of organic nature to explain the movement of history (the bees in Tolstoy, grass in Pasternak); Zhivago's "Robespierres" and Strelnikov's Lenin correspond to Tolstoy's Napoleon; and Tolstoy would indeed have joined Pasternak in calling revolutionaries "geniuses of self-limitation" (*genii samoogranicheniia*) and would gladly have applied the term to Napoleon. The new feature in Pasternak is his explanation of how the periods between revolutions are sacrificed to the "spirit of single-mindedness" (*dukh ogranichennosti*) that inspired the upheavals.[13]

For Pasternak, as for Tolstoy, the progress of history is the progress of a people or a community as a whole, deriving essence from the free collaboration of each individual in that community. It is interesting to compare Pasternak's conception of the role of the individual to other conceptions of the same period. It might be said, for example, that Pasternak, although rejecting Marxism as well as any dialectical interpretation of history, is in a sense situated midway between the two possible interpretations of Marxist dialectic as analyzed by Michel Collinet in *Du Bolchévisme*. On one side we have Kautsky and the Mensheviks, who consider man as essentially an object of history, led by its dialectic. On the other side we have Lenin and Trotsky (continuing a basic attitude implicit in Napoleon and Cromwell, as Collinet points out) envisaging man as being above all a *subject* of history, an *acting* subject, representing as he does the incarnation of the universal dialectic.[14]

We have said that Pasternak does not envisage history as a dialectic—as is obvious in his argument based on the image of the forest. In this sense he is nearer to the Aristotelian conception of evolution through quantitative variations than to the Heraclitean view that pervades Hegel's dialectics. From that viewpoint he in effect adopts a metaphysic of laissez faire, upon which socialism à la Rosa Luxemburg or à la Kautsky is also based. Although believing deeply in human liberty as the foundation for man's status as subject, he stops short of Lenin's "interventionist" audacity. Even if history does move in the direction of bettering the lot of the masses, he feels that it is completely useless and beside the point to give history a hand through organization. Pasternak's "liberal conservatism" requires that established authority be limited to a laissez-faire policy in the style of François Quesnay. Every conservatism, such as Quesnay's, is based (more or less unconsciously) on the concept of a "natural and essential order in human societies," an order that flowers in the harmony of spontaneous relationships created among men living in society. This harmony is identical to the natural order of things and far superior to any system artificially conceived and imposed. Thus Zhivago exclaims: "So why substitute this childish harlequinade of immature fantasies"— for life itself, for the breathtaking phenomenon of life? The Soviets, Zhivago states elsewhere, "are made of stone. . . . they aren't human, with all their discipline and principles." From this point of view, direct or indirect intervention by the state, in whatever form, must be limited to the indispensable minimum. That is why Pasternak's heroes remain unreconciled to the tyranny exercised by the Soviet state.[15]

It would be simplistic to deduce from Pasternak's "individualism" (which, as we have seen, is actually a rich, authentic personalism) the absence of any communal dimension. Rather, he has a tendency to overvalue the cultural riches belonging to the nation in its own right, while appearing very reserved toward that objectivized—and often imperfect—embodiment of the nation which is the state.

Because of his very real conservatism on the one hand and his reflexes of a dissident intellectual on the other, Pasternak has a strong propensity to distinguish sharply between the ideological state—the symbol of organization and regimentation in all its forms—and the nation—the reservoir of original, organic forms. It is a distinction that would be much more difficult to establish in a country like Great Britain, where, some claim, a fusion has taken place between the spirit of the state and that of the nation. It is, however, the sort of distinction that is imperative in a country in political transition, and still more so in a country with a coercive regime.

It is not surprising that the deep love for the Russian nation that pervades Pasternak's novel is colored on occasion by nostalgia for a past in which Russia, the country and the people, formed a harmonious whole. Pasternak himself apparently shares the feelings of Galuzina, the grocer's wife, who evokes a happier time for which certain rural communities are still yearning: "And everything in those days had been fine and rich and seemly . . . everything had rejoiced her heart." The people, middle class or peasant, gave an impression of "wealth"; they had an enterprising spirit and an aptitude for healthy, constructive work. "Now everything had lost its glamour, nothing but civilians left, lawyers and Yids clacking their tongues day and night" (this is not anti-Semitism or disapproval of the other categories of people mentioned; it is an expression of dissatisfaction with a situation controlled by intellectuals, who are always "clacking their tongues"). To Galuzina this behavior is in sharp contrast to old times, when, it seemed to her, there was less verbosity and more effective activity.[16]

Besides alienation from the state, there is alienation from society. Pasternak's heroes strongly reject the main tenets of Soviet society: the "social system based on such a false premise, as well as its political application, [that is,] the elevation of man above the rest of nature, the modern coddling and worshipping of man, never appealed to them." It should be stressed that this idea of the predictable alienation of "collective"—and collectivized—man, once he is established as the sole depository of values, goes back to Marx. Such a notion constitutes a gratuitous anticipation of the future, from the vantage point of overly rational reason.[17]

Freeing himself of any allegiance to the tyrannical state and rejecting the false worship of collective man, Zhivago (symbol in this regard of Pasternak) maintains and cherishes a deep attachment for what might be called "natural groupings" or basic groups: family, profession, and city. The disruptions of Zhivago's family life occur under the pressure of exceptional circumstances, and his successive efforts to build a new hearth can be seen as the workings of an instinctive desire to try to find meaning and anchorage in a "natural unit." His professional activity as a doctor he continues with unremitting devotion at every stage of his life (except during the final Moscow episode). The significance that Zhivago himself attaches to this attitude becomes clear when he insists that he wishes to be

active as "a farmer or a doctor" (*selskim trudom ili vrachebnoi praktikoi*), while planning some vital intellectual project. His unusual acuity (he is a "marvellous diag-
nostician") and effectiveness in fulfilling this social role is stressed more than once
in the novel.[18]

Pasternak's whole novel moves in the direction of a rediscovery of certain "natural" values once extolled by Pushkin but forgotten in Russia in the accelerated
rhythm and agitation of modern life. Thus Zhivago notes in his diary: "Only the
familiar transformed by genius is truly great. The best object lesson in this is
Pushkin. His works are one great hymn to honest labor, duty, everyday life!" All
of this is very well expressed in the stanzas in which Pushkin tells of Eugene
Onegin's ambitions:

> Now my ideal is the housewife,
> My greatest wish, a quiet life
> And a big bowl of cabbage soup.

Pasternak is concerned with reestablishing the essential components of human
life, the family and work, what Pierre-Frédéric Le Play called in the last century
the "permanent needs inseparable from human nature."[19]

This authentic social life, completely organic and spontaneous, flourishes in the bosom of the community, where daily activities and the ideal inspiring them become fused. When all is said and done, the main character of Pasternak's novel is Russia—a character whose psychology is studied with love and subtlety. The ideal community, the Russian nation as seen by the heroes of the novel, possesses a characteristic *Volksgeist*. The Russian people—in the sense of the German word *Volk* as used by Herder and later by Fichte—is the essential source of positive— and, as it were, organic—values, of all that Gustave Thibon in his social essays designates by the terms "depth" or "density" (*épaisseur*).[20]

The love Iurii Zhivago feels for Russia is a profound, authentic feeling. It is also (to use a Western term) a *committed* love, as we shall soon see. Pasternak could easily have put in Zhivago's mouth this stanza from one of his poems of 1941:

> Through all the past tribulation,
> The years of war and privation,
> All through, hushed, I recognized
> Russia's unique features.[21]

17

The Fire of Thy Hands

The Religious Dimension

Konchaias v bolnichnoi posteli,
Ia chuvstvuiu ruk Tvoikh zhar.
Ty derzhish menia, kak izdele,
I priachesh, kak persten v futliar.

[I feel your warm hands hold me
Here in the ward, replace
Their handiwork, your ring
Inside death's jewel case.]

Pasternak, "In Hospital"[1]

I was born a Jew. My family was interested in music and art and paid little attention to religious practice. Because I felt an urgent need to find a channel of communication to the Creator, I was converted to Russian Orthodox Christianity. But try as I might, I could not achieve a complete spiritual experience. Thus I am still a seeker.

Pasternak (1959)[2]

I believe that Pasternak's religious feelings were akin to those of Leo Tolstoy or Albert Einstein.

Olga Ivinskaia[3]

A discussion of the significance of religion for Pasternak requires an evaluation of the part it played in *Doctor Zhivago*, which in most respects represents a summation of his *oeuvre*. Max Hayward has said that, unlike Dostoevsky's Prince Myshkin, "Zhivago is not a Jesus-like figure. He is more like an apostle, one of those disciples who could not keep awake during the vigil of Gethsemane, referred to in the last poem at the end of the novel". This statement brings up extremely thorny problems: whether Zhivago is a Christlike figure and whether the novel's "message" is essentially a religious one. Many Western critics have disagreed with Hayward in this regard and adopted a religious interpretation. Thomas Merton, for example, not only found in *Doctor Zhivago* "a deep and uncompromising spirituality" but also believed that the book was "deeply religious and even definitely Christian." In a sensitive commentary Pasternak's sister Josephine terms such sometimes indiscreet insistence by many Christianity-oriented critics an "avid grabbing of Christologists" after the novel. There has even been a somewhat uncritical book-length essay interpreting *Doctor Zhivago* in a Christological perspective.[4]

If Zhivago were a symbol of Christ, however, and Pasternak's novel were in fact centered around a religious message, how could we explain why many theologians have strong reservations about elements they find untenable from a strictly dogmatic point of view? Could it be that Pasternak is preaching a highly personal and paradogmatic religion?

In 1957, a few months after Feltrinelli published *Il dottor Živago*, an Italian Jesuit, U. A. Floridi, wrote in *Civiltà Cattolica*: "The abundance of religious elements in this latest work of Pasternak's does not in itself justify our proclaiming his faith in God and the supernatural." Though at times we might be inclined to do so, "at other moments we . . . would resolutely deny his faith." Floridi's main criticism is that Pasternak is painting a Christ who is "emphatically human," as well as offering "a Christianity interpreted in a new key." Floridi finds some extenuating circumstances to explain the author's lack of dogmatic solidity: ". . . it must be said that Pasternak is a poet, a thinker, a Russian, and what is more, that he is obligated to live under an atheistic Communist regime." The whole of this appraisal, by a specialist in dogma, fails to show adequate sensitivity to what appears to other Christian theologians as an essentially Christian attitude.[5]

A Russian Orthodox priest, however, D. V. Konstantinov, has expressed similar reservations vis-à-vis Pasternak's religious attitude: the philosophical-religious ideas with which Pasternak's novel is saturated, he declares, "bear little resemblance to the teachings of the Orthodox Church." He wonders whether, instead of belief based on dogma, it is not merely simple religiosity that we find in Pasternak. Commenting on certain passages in the novel (particularly Sima Tuntseva's "exegeses"), Father Konstantinov notes, "It is not altogether a matter of religion here, but only of a conception of religion, a personal philosophic interpretation of certain Christian dogmas and gospel stories." He also asks, Does not a rationalism à la Renan emerge from those pages of *Doctor Zhivago* that make of Christ a historic personage of the first rank but nothing more? Does not the novel's Nikolai Nikolaevich Vedeniapin express the rationalist view in his homilies about immortality?

In connection with the question of immortality, Konstantinov, although otherwise noting the importance of the theme of resurrection in Pasternak, regrets the rejection of any *personal* immortality in the book. He quotes, however, significant extracts from a work by the theologian V. Slavinskii, who stresses that "the most profound definitions of the Church mention not the immortal soul, but the resurrection of the dead and life eternal in Christ or God. Simple immortality of the soul," Slavinskii continues, "representing a prolongation of individual life, so to speak, is not declared as dogma, although it is a sort of popular belief." From such a perspective Pasternak would appear not to have taken such great liberties with dogma after all.

The chief aim of Konstantinov's article is to connect the philosophical-religious themes of *Doctor Zhivago* with the development of a certain religious feeling among Soviet intellectuals. Even the title of the article is suggestive in this respect: "*Doctor Zhivago* and the Search for God in the USSR." The novel can be considered, it says, the very history of the search for God by the Russian intelligentsia of the last generation. Konstantinov notably alludes to the theory of the quasi-organic growth and development of the human mind popular in the circles of the Leningrad intelligentsia in the 1930s.[6]

Some other points in Pasternak's would-be Christian attitude might well attract the attention of a scrupulous theologian. Thus, in parts of the novel, Pasternak's concept of the supernatural seems to boil down to a heightened consciousness of the apocalyptic upheavals experienced by a given generation. That attitude sometimes leads to a "catastrophic" point of view. As L. A. Zander points out, there is a distinction, of course, between the blind, capricious force of the Greek *moira* and the Hegelian-Christian conception of fate; Zander believes that the latter prevails in Pasternak—fate as a reasonable law of being, an objective order of life.[7] It is perfectly true that Pasternak stresses the mysterious link between the objective order of the world and the undertaking of the individual. Do we not, however, find in his novel the concept of a fate that is both *rational* and implacable, and does not the characters' highly developed awareness of this fate inspire in them a sort of apocalyptic terror? Meanwhile, there is an unassailable internal logic in the novel: it would be idle to keep recalling the existence of a constructive Christian economy to those living under the sign of the Beast, following with anguish the struggle of the Angel and the Dragon.

Another potentially controversial point is Pasternak's overt identification of the essence of the "progress" represented by Christianity with "the doctrine of individuality and freedom . . . individual human life."[8] Here again, as with the problem of the historic person of Christ, the novelist's position is perfectly tenable from a humanistic viewpoint. The question is whether it is theologically tenable. Is it tenable for a believer in the Christian revelation—in which the revealed truth concerns essentially the specific nature of the religious element, rather than its equation with some humanistic belief?

It is certain that historically the elevation of the position of the individual has been indissolubly linked with Christian civilization; the individual became privileged through Christianity because of his immediate and necessary relationship with God. Not everyone would agree, however, that the personal dimension starts with the New Testament. For Vladimir Solovёv, for example, the main constituents of the religion of the Old Testament are the personal relationships between God and his people—patriarchs, prophets, and rulers who "believe in a personal God and live personally in that faith." Another theologian, Romano Guardini, insists that it is false "to limit the essence of Christianity to the individual's place at the center of religious consciousness" or to any other single aspect of the religion. Rather than reduce Christianity to an exaltation of the individual, one could, objectively speaking, assert the contrary of such a position and define the core of Christianity as the discovery of the religious community and of community rather than personal values. Besides, Christian "personal religion" is concerned with theological individuality, whose correlate is unity in Christ. Far from biological, material individuality, whose correlate is terrestrial society (*Gesellschaft*), theological individuality cannot be reduced to personal, spiritual individuality, whose correlate is spiritual society (*Gemeinschaft*).[9]

The unorthodox nature of Pasternak's orthodoxy can be seen as related to his Jewish origins. Because of his Jewish cultural background, Christianity necessarily remained for him "the object of a rare and exceptional inspiration," as he himself put it.* Boris Leonidovich's parents were liberal Jews who did not participate very actively in the rites of the synagogue. On the other hand, Ida Vysotskaia recalled that, unlike her own family—atheistic for three generations—the Pasternak household had remained far more traditional in its Judaism. Leonid Osipovich's home was imbued with the spirit of Tolstoy and his sincere, upright religion. During the first few decades of his career, Leonid Pasternak's awareness of Judaic life had been dormant, and his main concern had been assimilation into the mainstream of Russian life (however, he claimed that during that period well-to-do Russian Jewry was completely indifferent to the work of Russian-Jewish artists, did nothing to foster it, and thus did not even provide an opportunity for them to pay special attention to Jewish themes or perspectives). Beginning around 1910, he nonetheless experienced an awakening of interest in Judaic values that impelled him to write a commentary on the Judaic atmosphere in Rembrandt, especially conceived as a semipopularized text to be translated into Hebrew for the sake of "the Jewish masses."[10]

Because of the milieu in which he grew up, it could well be that, much like Mandelstam,† Pasternak felt slightly ill at ease or misplaced as a Jew—that uneasiness perhaps being reflected in young Misha Gordon's misgivings in *Doctor Zhivago*: "What did it mean to be a Jew? What was the purpose of it? What was the reward or the justification of this defenseless challenge, which brought nothing but grief?" Mandelstam, however, never felt the need to draw closer to Christianity, remarking about his fellow poet: "Why did he, Pasternak, have to change his religion? What does he need intermediaries for, when he has his art?"

---

*See Chapter 1.

†Mandelstram's biographer has remarked: "Mandelstram felt vaguely misplaced as a Jew, the victim of a slightly comic but also unpleasant and even shameful miscalculation by Fare" (Clarence Brown, *Mandelstram* [Cambridge: Cambridge University Press, 1973], p. 20).

It is clear that, at least toward the end of his life, Pasternak sometimes endeavored to "repress" or disclaim his Jewish origin.[11]

Within the framework of Pasternak's exposure to Judaic influences, it is appropriate to say something more of the impression made on him by his revered mentor Hermann Cohen, the leader of Neo-Kantianism in Marburg and a towering figure in German philosophy for several decades.* Cohen dealt with religion in such writings as *Die Religion der Vernunft aus den Quellen des Judentums* (1922) and *Deutschtum und Judentum* (1915), the principles of which had certainly matured by the time he exerted the influence on him that Pasternak claimed he did (1912). *Deutschtum und Judentum* attempts a reconciliation between *Deutschtum* (developed by Cohen as an ideology that now appears to us typical of the Bismarck era) and *Judentum*, whose originality and specificity are asserted, although with a high-mindedness that admits of a conciliatory, irenic attitude toward Christianity—viewed as the historical intermediary (*Vermittler*) between Judaism and Germandom. The universalism derived from Judaism becomes the basis for the typically Kantian notion of religion "within the bounds of reason" propounded by Cohen.[12] What Pasternak may have learned from Cohen is the philosopher's uncompromising belief in supreme values that can be traced to Judaism—notably faith in the pure spirituality of God.

Like Christian believers, some Jewish believers have "avidly grabbed" after Pasternak. They too endeavored to show that his inspiration was religious—and, in their interpretation, specifically Judaic. Thus M. Z. Ben-Ishaj has dwelled on the importance of the Jewish background and Judaic affinities in the lives of the Pasternaks. He gave details about Leonid's and Boris's contacts with the Jewish writer David Frischman late in 1910 and claims that at that time Leonid Osipovich drew much closer to Jewish circles. He also attempts to make much of Cohen's visit to Moscow in May, 1914, claiming that Cohen "won over" many Russian Jews who were on the verge of apostasy. The thesis that Pasternak's spiritual inspiration was primarily Judaic is sharply belied by the negative reaction of characters in *Doctor Zhivago* (obviously speaking for the author) to Jewish culture, which they considered a separate and separatist tradition. Indeed, the reaction was depicted as so negative that the book was violently attacked in Israel, especially by David Ben-Gurion, who in 1959 called it as "one of the most despicable books about Jews ever to be written by anyone of Jewish origin." It is clear that Ben-Gurion's ire was triggered by the "anti-Zionism" pervading many pages of *Doctor Zhivago*, such as the passage where Misha Gordon cries out to all Jews: "Come to your senses, stop. Don't hold on to your identity. Don't stick together, disperse. Be with all the rest. You are the first and best Christians in the world. You are the very thing against which you have been turned by the worst and weakest among you." Misha Gordon's message is part of Pasternak's over-all message—that Judaism has been outdated in Christianity and should therefore be viewed as anachronistic. In private conversation Pasternak claimed that nothing was more alien to him than Jewish nationalism, asserting: "I am in favor of full assimilation of the Jews, and to me personally Russian culture is the only one that

*See Chapter 4.

appears as the native one." Besides, someone so oriented toward spiritual values as Pasternak could have had little sympathy for the traditionally secular dimension of Zionism.[13]

While Pasternak's rejection of Judaism in favor of Christianity is undeniable, it would be wrong to conclude that there are no traces of the Judaic legacy in Pasternak's work. In an interesting study Judith Stora suggested that this legacy, specifically the substratum of Judaic values in *Doctor Zhivago*, is seen in the prophetic idea of universal happiness; the primacy of earthly life as contrasted to an afterlife; rejection of the Platonic dualism of body and soul (for example, Sima Tuntseva's diatribe against the repression of the flesh); the stressing of the everyday details that give life its richness and fecundity; and the insistence on the primacy of action (as in Zhivago's speech to the bedridden Anna Ivanovna Gromeko)—all typically Judaic attitudes.[14]

The first person to bring young Pasternak to Christianity was his nursemaid Akulina Gavrilovna. Pasternak clearly claimed that she baptized him and reared him as a Christian, and that around 1910 to 1912—the decisive period in the shaping of his world view—he was nurtured mostly on a Christian inspiration. For a long time, however, circumstances did not permit him to become associated with the Russian Orthodox church or liturgy. His first marriage, with Evgeniia Lourié, who was Jewish, gave him no opportunity to draw nearer to the Christian creed. Thus around 1929 he could confide to a friend of the family: "I grew up and was educated in [the context of] Christian culture and attitudes. I very nearly became a [Russian] Orthodox; perhaps, in order to take the final step, I would only need one thing—to marry an Orthodox."[15] One can surmise that Pasternak's marriage in the early 1930s to Zinaida Nikolaevna, a Russian Orthodox, helped him take the final step he claimed that he had not yet taken by 1929.

One may also reasonably infer that it was in the 1930s that Pasternak took that final step. While in his pre-Zhivago poetry there are only rare references to New Testament values—such as an occasional reference to the values of the Sermon on the Mount—it is only with *Doctor Zhivago* that Christ appears as a major presence. It is clear that by the 1950s the onion-shaped blue cupolas of the Russian Orthodox Patriarchal Church of the Transfiguration, which the writer could see from the windows of his dacha, had become a meaningful symbol for him. Especially during the period when he was composing *Doctor Zhivago*, he became thoroughly familiar with Orthodox ceremonies and customs, which he lovingly attended in the village church (peasant women in Peredelkino believed that he had been christened). In a private conversation Ehrenburg tried to explain that Pasternak drew closer to Christianity because he wanted to identify himself more fully with the Russian people. On a rather flat and analytical level one could detect in Pasternak some evidence of the wish to be "as fully Russian as any Russian"—to "overcompensate" for an initial religious lack by fully espousing Orthodoxy, which he saw both as a spiritual force and as a component of the Russian ethos. It is more enlightening, however, to dwell on Pasternak's discovery of Orthodox spiritual values.[16]

Rather than being connected with individual aspects of church dogma, Pasternak's religious preoccupation differed little from that which engrosses the medi-

cal student Iurii Zhivago to the point of disturbing him deeply during his dissection session: the mystery of life and death. Iurii finally solves the problem by
resolutely deciding that death is nonexistent: "There will be no death, says St.
John. His reasoning is quite simple. There will be no death because the past is
over; that's almost like saying there will be no death because it is already done
with, it's old and we are bored with it. What we need is something new, and that
new thing is life eternal." Such progress in relation to death—or rather, the victory over death—was one of the favorite themes of Nikolai Fëdorov, the brilliant,
obscure librarian of the Rumiantsev Museum, who exerted great influence on the
Dostoevsky of *The Brothers Karamazov*, as well as on Shestov, Berdiaev, and Maiakovskii.* For Fëdorov, the first duty of the "new man" is to overcome the forces of
nature, and his main task is to bring about the resurrection of the dead. "Liberty
without absolute power over the natural world is the same as liberating serfs
without giving them land." To achieve this absolute power, man must stamp out
the various natural phenomena and calamities that chain him to death. Man must
try to destroy "the power that death has over life." Fëdorov preached a "philosophy of the common cause," a collective struggle to annihilate death (the latter
being the result of nonfraternal relations among men).[17]

Such is essentially the message of Pasternak's novel. Life must pass through
suffering, since only through suffering can it surmount death, and surmounting
death is its principal task. The theme of the duel between life and death—of the
ultimate victory over death, thanks to Zhivago's "spiritual feat" (*podvig*)—is central to *Doctor Zhivago* (of course, the theme of victory over death is a fundamentally Christian one, receiving special and forceful orchestration in Fëdorov). It is
announced in the first lines of the novel, where life is threatened by death. Death
is actually shown burying life: "'Kogo khoroniat?' . . . 'Zhivago'" ("'Whom are
they burying?'" . . . "'Zhivago'" ["'the Living One'"]).* The book opens with
the scene of the burial of Mariia Zhivago (whose death is soon to be followed by
the death of Zhivago's father) and concludes with that of Iurii Zhivago, as if to
emphasize that the essential part of human reality is condensed into a brief combat with death. Edmund Wilson drew attention to the frequency of scenes of
death or burial in the book, and indeed one could draw up a long list of such
passages: death scenes, war scenes, massacres, executions, atrocities committed
by Reds and Whites.[18]

Of all the authors whom he read in his discovery of the supernatural and of the
spiritual value of individual destiny, Pasternak was most influenced by Rilke.

---

*Leonid Pasternak drew what is believed to be the only extant portrait of Fëdorov (Leonid Pas-
ternak, *ZAP*, pp. 142–44).

*To many Russian readers the name Zhivago is strongly reminiscent of such Old Church
Slavonic phrases as "Syn Boga zhivago," as they occur in the Russian Orthodox service (cf. Luke
24:5 and Rev. 7:12). The surname Zhivago, while not common, was borne by a few members of
the Moscow *haute bourgeoisie* before the Revolution. In a private letter Pasternak sharply denied that
any religious symbolism was attached to his hero's name, which he referred to as "a name like any
other name." He viewed as appropriate this name that could well have belonged to "someone quite
unknown" from "either . . . the merchant class or . . . the semi-intelligentsia" (Olga Ivinskaia,
CAPT, p. 183). Pasternak's pronouncement clashes with Edmund Wilson's interpretation (cf. Edmund Wilson, "Doctor Life and His Guardian Angel," *New Yorker*, November 15, 1958).

Pasternak seems to have experienced a great spiritual affinity with Rilke's thorough abandon—as expressed in "Der Lesende"—to overwhelming cosmic or spiritual forces that it would be both wrong and useless for man to try to oppose. But the decisive force that moved Pasternak in this direction was the deep emotion with which he became aware of the miraculous orientation of his own life. The introduction to *Spektorskii* (1931), recalling a providential convergence of events that led to the composition of that poem, and the poet's experiences during the period from 1939 to 1942 marked the crystallization of that discovery, as witnessed in "Dawn" ("*Rassvet*"), one of "The Poems of Iurii Zhivago":

> You were the be-all in my destiny.
> Then came the war, the devastation,
> And for a long, long time there was
> No word from you, not even a sign.
>
> And after many, many years
> I find again your voice disturbs me.
> All night I read your testament—
> And found my consciousness returning.[19]

The Augustinian—or Pascalian—atmosphere in this poem indicates that Pasternak was undergoing some *nuit de feu*. It is very clear that the poem was conceived from a traumatic yet uplifting experience that Pasternak underwent in December, 1941, during a night of heavy bombardment while he was on duty on the roof of a building in Moscow.*

Although, as we have seen, Pasternak's religious views coincided in many essentials with those of Fëdorov, he did not profess a "tragic" philosophy as Fëdorov did. His inner life was always marked by a striving toward free and new truths. That instead of the socialist revolution he propounded an authentic social revolution must originate from within. Pasternak aspired to achieve some *podvig*, or spiritual prowess, according to the Russian ascetic tradition. This urge is crystallized in key attitudes of certain of his fictional characters. Thus in *A Tale* we have the *podvig* ascribed to that mysterious character Igrek Tretii ("Y3"). A fictitious creation of the protagonist Serëzha, Y3 is distinguished by an art that is "born of the richest, bottomlessly sincere, terrestrial poverty." Animated by the highest spiritual motives, he puts himself up for auction to achieve authenticity. He chooses exterior, physical servitude because he has discovered within himself that he has "no current value in that large issue in which man has been printed. That he must make himself a commodity of exchange, and they must help him in this."[20]

This radically spiritual attitude is all the more vital to Pasternak since the "spirituality" or "morality" thus achieved is an essential requirement for another form of fulfillment or authenticity—genius. That is made clear in a passage of *A*

---

*See Chapter 9. I share with George Katkov (a connoisseur of Pasternak's work, who in 1956 had a long conversation with the poet in Peredelkino) this impression about the genesis of this poem (George Katkov, letter of spring, 1961, to the author).

Safe Conduct where, talking of his youthful infatuation with historical symbolism, he observes: "I did not know [at that time] that the essence [of genius] lies in the experience of real biography and not in symbolism refracted in a figurative way. I did not know that, as distinct from the primitives, its roots lie in the rough directness of the moral instinct." [21]

Such an attitude, prevalent in Pasternak's fiction of the 1920s, becomes even more central to the design of *Doctor Zhivago*. The whole of Zhivago's behavior appears to be a *podvig*. Without going so far as to choose abjection like the holy eccentrics of whom Russia has produced many examples (the "fools in Christ" who took Saint Paul's words about the folly of the cross at face value), Zhivago nonetheless performs a certain *podvig*. His own particular holy deed consists in remaining faithful throughout his life to what he believes in, even though it turns him into a personal and social failure from the viewpoint of "the wisdom of this world." Thereby the tragedy of his life takes on a deep philosophical meaning, a meaning beyond its dramatic overtones and the "factual" elements of a personal and social downfall.

The desire to reenact the *podvig* of the Lord himself—Christ the personal God—is crystallized in Iurii Zhivago. Zhivago has been likened to Don Quixote, to Onegin, to Oblomov. How much deeper and truer, though, is the clue that Pasternak himself gives us about the meaning of Zhivago's life in "Hamlet" (which opens the cycle of poems at the end of the book), a poem that also reveals the deepest strivings of Pasternak himself:

> . . . .
> If thou be willing, Abba, Father,
> Remove this cup from me.
>
> I cherish this, Thy rigorous conception,
> And I consent to play this part therein;
> But another play is running at this moment,
> So, for the present, release me from the cast.
>
> And yet, the order of the acts has been schemed and plotted,
> And nothing can avert the final curtain's fall.
> I stand alone. All else is swamped by Pharisaism.
> To live life to the end is not a childish task. [22]

Such an experience does not stop at the threshold of a burning revelation. It recaptures the essence of the Christian attitude: loving compliance, in spite of the flesh's disgust, with what the Father's supreme will has ordained. Continuously revealing new dimensions, the beautiful lines of "Magdalene" provide both a vibrant illustration of intense personal emotion and a compendium of Christology:

> . . . .
> When I, before the eyes of all, have grown into one
> With Thee, even as scion and tree,
> Because my yearning is beyond all measure.

> When, Jesus, I embrace Thy feet
> As I support them on my knees
> It may be that I am learning to embrace
> The squared beam of the Cross.[23]

This seems to be the fundamental note of Pasternak's spirituality.

The poet sometimes states with astonishment and almost with fear (though never foundering in metaphysical anguish) that death hides everywhere in nature (as may be seen in several of "The Poems of Iurii Zhivago"), but his spirituality is by no means based on a Tolstoyan preoccupation with death. Thomas Merton has aptly remarked that

the problematical quality of Pasternak's "Christianity" lies in the fact that it is reduced to the barest and most elementary essentials: intense awareness of all cosmic and human reality as "life in Christ," and the consequent plunge into love as the only dynamic and creative force which really honors this "Life" by creating itself anew in Life's—Christ's—image.[24]

Thanks to this "plunge into love," Pasternak participates in intense creativity as envisioned by Christianity, whose authentic meaning he has discovered. It is important to note that by his own admission he had been attracted toward "mysticism and superstition" from early childhood. Later he went much beyond the facility of sentimental or superstitious religiosity. Pasternak had great admiration for the sincerity of Blok's and Esenin's religious and liturgical inspiration, which to them was on the level of a linguistic reality rather than of personal spiritual experience; however, he certainly goes more deeply than Blok into the poignant truthfulness of a Christian vision closely linked with actual personal experience. As Merton remarked:

Like Dostoevsky, Pasternak sees life as a mystic, but without the hieratic kenoticism of the *Brothers Karamazov*. The mysticism of Pasternak is more latent, more cosmic, more pagan, if you like. It is more primitive, less sophisticated, free and untouched by any hieratic forms. There is therefore a "newness" and freshness in his spirituality that contrasts strikingly with the worn and mature sanctity of Staretz Zossima purified of self-consciousness by the weariness of much suffering.[25]

Merton would agree that at times it may not be easy to discern in Pasternak the specificity of Christian theology or even of the supernatural. That however, comes as no surprise to the reader who has been accustomed to finding in almost every Russian "ideology," whatever its origin or orientation, a warm (and often quasi-spiritual) glow of charity. We find it in the cosmic pity evidenced by Dostoevsky and even in the fundamental element of brotherly concern for mankind present in Kropotkin and the Russian anarchists. This warm feeling of love is certainly essential in Pasternak.

Merton described another interesting aspect of Pasternak's spirituality:

. . . though Pasternak is deeply and purely Christian, his simplicity, untainted by ritualistic routine, unstrained by formal or hieratic rigidities of any sort, has a kind of *pre-Christian* character. In him we find the ingenuous Christianity of an *anima naturaliter*

Christiana that is not perfectly at home with dogmatic formulas, but gropes after revealed truth in its own clumsy way. And so in his Christianity and in all his spirituality Pasternak is exceedingly primitive. [26]

In the sense that Pasternak was an *anima naturaliter Christiana* (as opposed to an *anima dogmatice Christiana*), it is very likely that Cohen's nonsectarian attitude may have instigated Pasternak's effort to develop a nondogmatic, nondenominational, eclectic approach to religious values during his later years—his most intensely religious period. At that time he expressed great interest in Albert Schweitzer's spiritual world, after reading the Western thinker's *Civilization and Ethics*, sent to him from Germany. In keeping with Pasternak's "undogmatic" approach to Christianity was the interest (which he expressed during the same period) in the writings of the French Jesuit anthropologist and philosopher Pierre Teilhard de Chardin. He felt great affinity for Teilhard's untraditional presentation, based upon both theological and other philosophical considerations, of a "dynamic generosity" at work in the cosmos. Czesław Miłosz was therefore perfectly justified in referring to the "latent 'Teilhardism' of *Doctor Zhivago*." [27]

Indeed, the undogmatic ecumenicity of Pasternak's views is so patent that the Indian essayist N. K. Gupta could, from an "Indian viewpoint," see in him a kindred soul. Gupta was particularly attracted by certain notions underlying *Doctor Zhivago*, for example, the notion of the unity of the world, and the conception of life as a rhythmic whole—besides detecting in specific poems by Iurii Zhivago "the eternal note of sadness" that Matthew Arnold had heard and felt in the lines of Sophocles. [28]

In a striking illustration of Péguy's claim that "the revolution should be a moral one or should not be at all," Pasternak, never the rebel but always intensely the revolutionary, proposed moral revolution to an era that believed only in the economic one. Our age easily condemns the "moral revolutionary," reproaching him unjustly for being socially useless: the mob howls and demands efficacy, economic justice, and the liberation of Barabbas. Pasternak, overflowing with love, radiates perhaps the only revolutionary force capable of changing the world. This religion of love transfigures his idea of personality, enriching it with warmth and generosity. If it is correct to assume that liberty is the source of the intelligibility of history and must be based on generosity, then Pasternak knew how to convince us that the inner revolution has its origins in love.

According to Pasternak, the future—and in particular the more or less immediate future of the human species—will see the triumph of love. "After the era of the locomotive will come the era of love." It is from this perspective that Pasternak could propose to a French musician an ideal of greatness and a program of life and action based on that ideal:

Greatness, greatness, above all else. Art is its language, its expression. Sublimity manifested off-handedly, with nonchalance—that is beauty.
One must be great. One must be born great or learn to achieve greatness. One learns by a lifetime of pity for women and children, by a life of goodness bestowed on others and experienced by them.

One must be great. Which greatness do I mean? . . . The greatness opposed to pettiness, to mediocrity, to sterility, to the verbose hysteria of every second-rate art.

One must be free, sovereignly, like a king. Not from the influences of one's age, the
prevailing customs—but from one's own acquired perfections, free from oneself.

One must have moved mountains—actually moved them, and not merely claimed to
have done so; and having moved them, one must go on to new goals.[29]

If the revolution preached by Pasternak is to be a moral, not an economic, one,
the freedom toward which he was striving is likewise moral, rather than political
or social (as this statement shows clearly). The freedom he wishes to achieve is a
freedom of the heart; it is synonymous with an active love based on an ideal of
"greatness and devotion."

Such freedom and love hinge upon personal contact with God. If sometimes it
surprises us to read Pasternak's vigorous attacks on personal survival in all its
forms, and if it surprises us to hear him style himself "almost an atheist," let us
remember the mystical vision of this quasi-atheist who saw the centuries "like the
rungs of the divine ladder" and who sought traces of the presence of the Creator
everywhere.[30]

If at times the Pasternakian Christ seems simply a conceptual moment, that
impression does not endure when one is confronted with the tense invocation the
poet wrote in 1956—an invocation directed to an unquestionably personal, life-
giving Creator in the climax of the poem "In Hospital." In the poem are commingled recognition of the perfection of the Lord's ways,* gratitude for God's
"rich gifts" to the poet, and acceptance that He can take back his gift—the poet's
life:

> I feel your warm hands hold me
> Here in the ward, replace
> Their handiwork, your ring,
> Inside death's jewel case.[31]

Such a heightened sense of the spiritual significance of life so pervaded Pasternak's
vision of the world that he considered even the aesthetic endeavor as a reenactment of Christ's deed, as he clearly expressed in a letter he wrote late in his life:

The chief spirit of my experiences or tendencies (philosophy I have none) is the understanding of art, of creative embodiment and inspiration as an offer of concentrated abnegation in a *far and humble likeness* with the Lord's Supper and the Eucharist, that the
pictorial side of our culture, the figures and images of the European history have a certain
relation or are in a certain sense a kind of Imitation de Jésus-Christ, that the Gospels are
the foundation of what is called in the realm of writings, realism."[32]

---

*In Pasternak's poem the formulation "How perfect are Your ways, / O Lord . . ." strikes one as
very similar to the opening lines of the Psalm recited in the traditional Synagogue Service: "How
lovely are Your ways, O Lord, / Your tents, O Israel. . . ." For more information on the circumstances of the composition of the poem, see p. 217.

18

The Poet as Critic

Views on Art and Literature

. . . art has two constant, two unending concerns: it always meditates on death and thus always creates life.

Doctor Zhivago[1]

For Pasternak history is "the centuries of systematic explorations of the riddle of death, with a view to overcoming death."[2] Art, as it creates life, is the most effective instrument in this quest, leading most directly to victory over death.

In this chapter I will discuss Pasternak's critical-aesthetic views as they are inspired by the intuition of a dynamic generosity operating and manifest in life-creating artistic activity. Several moments or aspects of this intuition will be examined in turn: the notion of dynamism that Pasternak shared with some of the Futurists early in the century; Pasternak's interpretation of what he labels "realism" in Verlaine, Chopin, and Pushkin; his insistence on a "realistic" aesthetics as the surest method of conveying the force underlying reality; his original characterization of the aesthetic function as a para-cognitive process; his conception of autonomous forces at work in language. The intuition of a dynamic generosity operating in artistic creation underlies all these aspects and is the cornerstone of Pasternak's originality—whether the poet's inspiration of the moment is Futurist, Bergsonian, or Christian. Also addressed is the question of the artist's paradoxical evolution from a young Futurist poet-theoretician insisting upon the primacy of an often wildly experimental form over content, to a mature Pasternak proclaiming the primacy of experience, of content over form.

In the ensuing presentation of some of Pasternak's critical-aesthetic statements, no claim will be made that they add up to a rationally developed critical edifice; indeed, his poetic idiom and symbol-laden formulations are often a handicap to rational understanding of his aesthetic insights. He may also resort to the question-begging use of such terms as "reality," "truth," "life," "nature," without clearly defining them; however, if we accept these terms as summations endowed with persuasive poetic logic, they are enlightening metaphors.

Pasternak's first concern with the theory of art was through "dynamism," an aesthetic dimension he encountered while he was in the ranks of the Russian Futurist movement early in the century. Even if he did not accept all the tenets of the Italian Futurists, at least the following cardinal point of Marinetti's "Manifeste futuriste" of 1909 certainly proved congenial to the young Russian Futurist: "The poet," Marinetti wrote, "must give himself with frenzy, with splendor, and with lavishness, in order to increase the enthusiastic fervor of the primordial elements." The manifesto written by Pasternak and published in 1916 under the title "The Black Goblet" in a Moscow literary almanac presents Pasternak's own views and indicts two revered schools of aesthetics still holding sway at the time: Impressionism in painting and the Symbolist movement in poetry.[3]

Pasternak here formulates a sharp, sometimes caustic critique of certain metaphoric criteria of "mobility" and dynamism which were applied to art at the time. In addition to the Russian Symbolists, Pasternak attacks the Peredvizhniki (Itinerants), painters belonging to the Society of Itinerant Exhibitions, innovators in Russian art during the third quarter of the nineteenth century.* The Futurist criticism contained in the manifesto is directed against painters of the generation of Vasilii Surikov and Ilia Repin. What Pasternak criticized above all was a cer-

---

*See Chapter 1.

tain attitude common to the old guard of the Itinerants, based essentially on the materialist aesthetics bequeathed by the nineteenth-century critics Vissarion Belinskii, Nikolai Dobroliubov, and Nikolai Chernyshevskii: the misuse in art of certain social and historic postulates and criteria that had become moral concerns of a popular, democratic humanism. The whole of the manifesto consists of a single metaphor developed at length, through which Pasternak criticizes the extreme "mobility" (*podvizhnost*) of these Peredvizhniki. Pasternak explains how such a systematic mobility runs the risk of immobility (*nepodvizhnost*)—that is, artistic ultraconservatism or staleness. He reproaches the Impressionists and Symbolists for their much-too-ample palette, for the extreme thematic saturation customary in their works. This generation of "packers," he asserts, is good only at hastily packaging the riches of the world, trying to amass the whole of its wealth in their works.

The criticisms and warnings put forward in this document are also aimed at "the current theory of a popular form of Futurism," according to which "the rhythm of life must be stolen from the automobile engine," that is, from contemporary technical constructs. Here Pasternak is obviously serving as spokesman for the faction of Futurism led by Khlebnikov (Cubofuturism) and endorsing their contempt for certain slogans of Marinetti and the other Italian Futurists, in particular "the aesthetics of the machine." He emphasizes how utterly useless and senseless it is for a lyric poet to ape the dynamics appropriate to technical fields or to history. The reaction of the Russian Futurists to Marinetti's "aesthetics of speed" is strikingly similar to feelings voiced at the same time in England in the Vorticist manifesto: "*Automobilism* Marinettiism bores us. We don't want to go about making a hullabaloo about motor cars, anymore than about knives and forks, elephants or gaspipes." Considering Pasternak's rejection of the aesthetics of speed in this text, it is paradoxical that Ehrenburg, a fellow writer sympathetic to his achievement, characterized Pasternak's rhythm as "the rhythm of our day, violent and wild in its speed."[4]

Furthermore, Pasternak suggests, dynamism is neither an original discovery nor an exclusive privilege of the Futurists. Is not their dynamism an imitation or, at the very least, a reflection of that true characteristic of (Russian) Symbolism, anticipation, a tension of expectancy relating the present to the future? Futurism, after all, is the close kindred and heir of Symbolism and Impressionism: it has retained the symbolist device of "packaging," as well as the dynamic anticipation of the future.[5]

After pointing out the hereditary links between Impressionism and Futurism, however, Pasternak singles out the originality of Futurism. It orients itself unambiguously "towards the rediscovered pole" of authentic "Lyricism," which was magnetic to the members of Centrifuge, a Futurist group. According to them, "Lyricism" was "something that made genuine poetry possible."[6]

Pasternak evolved his personal notion of dynamism within the framework of a more elaborate aesthetics, which gradually took shape in the early and mid-1920s, and was set forth notably in *A Safe-Conduct*. Here we encounter the fundamental insistence, characteristic of his post-Futurist period, on actual experience as the origin of all art. To him art must grasp reality; its purpose lies in launching "the content of experience onto the track and into the chase after life." It is every-day reality that must be grasped—innate reality, human reality. Art is "set by the clock of the living race which strikes with the generations." Poetry is born from experience, from the infinitely complex dimension that exists at the heart of that experience; it is born "from the conflicting currents of these trends, from the difference in their flux, from the falling behind of the more tardy and from their accumulation behind, on the deep horizon of remembrance."[7] For Pasternak art must be an authentic transposition of that same dynamic process, reality.

To "embrace and enhance life," * Pasternak has evolved a method whose foundations are expounded in *A Safe-Conduct*. He claims that if there is representation in art it is subject to transposition; it should aim not at representing the cold axles of reality but at changing them to hot ones. Art "is concerned not with man but with the image of man. The image of man, as becomes apparent, is greater than man."[8] Therefore, the goal of art is to convey that "disproportionate" image.

Now this image of man can come into being only in the act of transition:

Focused upon a reality that has been displaced by feeling, art is a record of this displacement. It copies it from nature. How then does nature become displaced? Details gain in sharpness, each losing its independent meaning. Each one of them could be replaced by another. Any one of them is precious. Any one, chosen at random, will serve as evidence of the state which envelops the whole of transposed reality. When the signs of this condition are transferred onto paper, the characteristics of life become the characteristics of creation. The latter stand out more sharply than the former.[9]

For Pasternak, life is a never-ending outburst whose motion never ceased to fascinate him: "I loved movement in its most diverse manifestations—manifestations of power, reality. I loved to seize this whirling world as it was rushing head-long, and reproduce it" (such was the statement he made toward the end of his life). Thus the Pasternakian process of creation, described in the passage from *A Safe-Conduct* above, essentially takes its origin from a displacement, from movement. This description of the process of creation is necessarily reminiscent of Bergson's view that "beauty belongs to form, and every form owes its origin to the movement whereby this form is outlined: form is nothing but recorded movement." Also, after an interval of several decades Paul Klee was to give, in his *Théorie de l'art moderne* (1965), an interesting corroboration of Pasternak's statement when he observed that "a work of art is born in movement, it itself is a fixed movement, and it is interpreted with the movement of the eye."[10]

"Art is interested in life at the moment when the ray of power *is passing through it*," Pasternak writes, and he elaborates on the meaning he gives to this notion of power as follows:

I would take the concept of power in that widest sense in which theoretical physics takes it, only with the difference that it would be a question of its voice, its presence . . . in the context of self-awareness power is called feeling.[11]

* Compare the formulation by Antony Burgess, discussed below.

This power which for Pasternak is the source of art is renamed "feeling" and is equivalent to what he calls the joy of existence, as we shall see. This notion of power or force as the source of art is reminiscent of the romantic concept of power of some nineteenth-century writers, such as Turgenev.*

Yet another fundamental aspect of the aesthetic function as viewed by Pasternak should be mentioned, in which the dynamic significance that art has for him can clearly be seen. For Pasternak there exists a profound correspondence between the aesthetic process—the creation and contemplation of the work of art—and the religious attitude. In other words, the creation of art is characterized by the same dynamic nature that can be discerned in such other fundamental "historical" functions of the Pasternakian universe as religion. In the religious sphere this dynamism takes the form of an essentially *generous* attitude, a gift of self—whether it be man giving himself up to others, as in the poem "Wedding"; or God giving life to man, as illustrated in the stanzas of "In Hospital"; or "Magdalene" (one of "The Poems of Iurii Zhivago"). Thus Pasternak's religion is essentially active rather than contemplative, and is defined by a movement *ad extra*, by a generous tension of each person toward other persons. (That such a fundamental analogy—as is outlined here—between the aesthetic function and the religious experience is based on a "principle of generosity" common to both has also been suggested by Bergson.)[12]

With time Pasternak placed less of an exclusive focus on art's dynamic qualities. In a deeply sympathetic and sensitive article written in 1944, Pasternak praises Verlaine's *realism* for having succeeded in that difficult task of refracting life, while safeguarding its most characteristic elements in their authenticity. In Pasternak's view, Verlaine knew how to convey in poetry the ringing of bells, the fragrance of France, the song of the birds; he knew how to re-create the silence of the stars and of torrid midday and how to bring alive the tenacious torment of suffering, the cruel experience of the loss of God, the infidelity of a woman, the hostility of a town; the poet's unexpected simplicity aimed essentially at granting full voice and hearing to the life abounding in him. Thus the turbulence prevailing in Verlaine's soul was reflected in his poetry with compelling force. Here Pasternak focuses on the same aspects that the contemporary French critic Antoine Adam has singled out as representing the core of Verlaine's achievement.[13]

According to Pasternak, Verlaine's realism is manifested in his style: instead of writing in words, he writes in whole sentences, harmonious French sentences full of precision and zest, and the many different qualities of the language of the Paris he knew so well come straight from the streets of the city to lodge in his poetry. That is perhaps the most questionable statement that Pasternak makes in the article; whether we consider Verlaine's impressionistic poems or his other poetry, the poet's obvious and deliberate lexical and technical experimentation appears hardly to be compatible with an intent to convey the "language of the streets" with any sort of "realistic truthfulness" (as Pasternak would have him do). Pasternak's description of Verlaine as fundamentally a realist comes as a surprise.

---

*For a discussion of Pasternak's notion of an original life-force indicating the similarity of some of his formulations with some of Bergson's, see Chapter 13.

Among recent critics Octave Nadal labels Verlaine's technique as "musical impressionism" and sees in him an artist for whom modulation is more important than representation and a seer for whom the dream world (*le songe, la rêverie imaginante*) was the only truth. Antoine Adam claims that Verlaine went beyond Impressionism, reverting to the strains of "*le grand lyrisme romantique.*" [14] Nowhere but in Pasternak do we find anything like "realism" adduced as a critical category appropriate to the evaluation of Verlaine's achievement. We are bound to conclude that Pasternak does not make use of any of the objective notions that critics apply to Verlaine's art and that few critics ever defined realism as Pasternak does: as the capture by means of privileged images of the dynamics of life, without any special claims to strict objectivity.

From the 1920s on, Pasternak's concern for a content as rich and profound as possible in a work of art is manifested many times over in declarations of what he terms *realism*. In his view this realism is applicable to all forms of art, even to those in which its presence or role is not readily distinguishable. Thus, even though "nowhere are conventionality and ambiguity so much condoned" as in the world of music, the music of Bach and Chopin "abounds in details and produces the impression of a chronicle of their lives. With them more than anyone else, reality emerges through sound." [15]

In Pasternak's article on Chopin we find the following interesting definition of realism: "In any art whatsoever, realism is not a separate development, but consists of a special degree of art, of an unusual vein of precision in the artist." In contrast to the "romantic" artist, who stops at the threshold of this the supreme requirement of realism, the realistic artist is constrained by its severity. For the artist scrupulously faithful to realism, "his method is his cross":

Artistic realism . . . is a depth of biographical impression acting as the main impulse in the artist's life, pushing him into innovation and originality.

Chopin's work, for example, is:

thoroughly original not because it is dissimilar from that of his rivals, but because it is similar to nature, the model after which he wrote. It is always biographical, not because of egocentricity, but because like other great realists Chopin looked on his life as a means of knowing every kind of life on earth. [16]

In this vein Pasternak indicates how Chopin tried all his life to avoid "departing from the truth," to accomplish his task with rigorous fidelity, transmitting to the world the tidings, the message of historic importance his melody brings to us, a message that is the melody itself. The very kind of music criticism that Pasternak indulges in here shows clearly that he is among those who believe that music is a language of feeling. Unless we agree that music is the *exposition* of feelings, or at least believe in some concept of musical semantic, we are bound to feel uneasy about the notion that there is a "message" in music and the consequent (and perhaps somewhat willful) labeling of Chopin as a "realist." That for Pasternak music is a language based on specific "inner correspondences . . . with the surrounding external world" also appears very clearly in his commentaries on Scriabin's music (Pasternak is not alone in interpreting music along these lines: Susanne Langer has stressed that Schopenhauer treated music "as a real semantic" and shows that for Wagner music "is not self-expression, but *formulation and representation* of emotions, moods, mental tensions and resolutions").[17]

Other aspects of the claims made in the Chopin article may make the critical reader uncomfortable—above all, Pasternak's distinction between "realistic" and "romantic" art, the latter term being used almost as a synonym for second-rate, facile art, insofar as it indulges in flight into the unreal or fantastic. Arbitrary as it may seem, however, this distinction is essential to Pasternak's critical-intuitive approach, and it can be clarified best through examining more of his own statements on the relationship between reality and art and on his feelings about the romantic or "fantastic."

In the crisp stanzas of the poem "Posle viugi" ("After the Storm," 1958) Pasternak compares the hand of the artist to a powerful solvent, an agent even more efficacious than the storm at giving to all a new and authentic coloring, at washing and transforming everything. From the artist's chemical process "life, reality, and actual experience" emerge radiant, cleansed of the dust and mud that usually (such as before the storm) mask their dazzling clarity from us. Inspired by his "realistic" aesthetics, in *Doctor Zhivago*, Pasternak set himself the task both to describe the Russian reality of the past fifty years and to characterize and emphasize "reality as such, reality itself, reality as a philosophic phenomenon or category—reality in itself."[18] This underlying task is to Pasternak of the essence of every great realistic work of art. By the "cardinal" element Pasternak means "the characterization of reality as such; almost as . . . a philosophic category."[19] The inclusion of "reality as such" or "reality in itself" in the basic aesthetic categories strikes the modern critic as outdated. Russia often finds ways of being anachronistic, however, sometimes quaint and remarkable ways; here Pasternak continues a certain nineteenth-century tradition—that of, say, Turgenev's hypostatized use of the concept of reality.*

It is this love of reality in its authentic form that produces in Pasternak a marked repugnance for the fantastic, as exemplified by the following passage from a letter:

> I have never liked nor even understood the fantastic or romantic elements in themselves (nor have I believed in their existence) as an independent domain. I have never liked nor understood the strangeness of E. T. A. Hoffman or Carlo Gozzi, for example. For me art is a possession, and the artist is a man attached, stricken, possessed by reality, by an everyday existence which appears even more fairy-like to a lively and expanded sensitivity precisely because of the unretouched, prosaic element.[20]

The term "romantic elements," used here as synonymous to "the fantastic," applies best to the "strangeness" of E. T. A. Hoffman and Carlo Gozzi, and, in Russian literature, to, say, the romanticism of Prince V. F. Odoevskii. Pasternak

---

*Victor Terras has pointed out that for Turgenev "reality" (*deistvitelnost*) is a "hypostatized and revered concept" and that Henry James had a similar conception of reality (Victor Terras, "Turgenev's Esthetic and Western Realism," *Comparative Literature* 22 [Winter, 1970]: 29).

views Nikolai Gogol as a realist; he praises Gogol highly for his supremely honest method and for his strikingly truthful and effective aesthetic. Pasternak extols Gogol's and Dostoevsky's striking and effective depictions of St. Petersburg, for example, as the highest ideal of artistic truthfulness. Pasternak defines this ideal through a "negative" counter definition when he says that it would be both base (*nizko*) and dishonest (*bessovestno*) to give any depiction of the contemporary world that was less colorful and overwhelming than these two Russian masters' portrayal of the city. Pasternak's view of Gogol coincided with that of the nineteenth-century Russian critics who saw him as a realist; as they did, he ignored the Surrealist in Gogol.[21]

Elsewhere—notably in the article on Chopin, as we have seen—Pasternak equates "romantic" with "cheap, facile" art. This attitude coincides perfectly with the prevailing one in the eighteenth and nineteenth centuries.* Furthermore, Pasternak rejected what he labeled the "romantic attitude," somewhat narrowly defining it as one founded on the "notion of biography as spectacle," on the cult of the artist's ego, and on the concept of the artist as a "visual-biographical emblem." This attitude Pasternak denounced in *A Safe-Conduct*, claiming that, instead, the poet should be a "living personality," involved in the pursuit of cognition of a special kind.[22] Once we are agreed about the inadequacy—and occasional arbitrariness—of many current textbook definitions of such critical terms, we shall feel no need to reject as invidious Pasternak's own contradistinction between what he terms "romantic" and "realistic." We should bear in mind that for Turgenev as well "romanticism" was a negative concept; he defined it as essentially "individualism and subjectivism (and, by implication, daydreaming, idle speculation, self-love, egocentrism, inaction, and other vices)." (From the viewpoint of Pasternak's definitions, it is paradoxical that the exceptional and the bizarre are to be found in the poetics of writers whom we normally associate with "realism"—writers such as Maupassant and the Goncourt brothers. For these writers, seeking out the unusual and bizarre was part of their pursuit of truthfulness to reality.)[23]

During a conversation in 1958, Pasternak emphasized to what extent the forms we are presently seeking in art fail to do justice to the accumulation of experience and thought—the *content*—that recent years have bequeathed us. It is not "rightist or leftist tendencies," he added, or the struggle between those tendencies that constitute art; it is the biographic and mental *content* (experience and thought), fully elaborated and deepened.[24] (His phraseology—when he tells us to forget about "tendencies" and concentrate on "content"—is strikingly reminiscent of a statement by Henry James: "There are no tendencies worth anything but to see the actual or the imaginative . . . and to paint it.")[25]

Pasternak's assertion that contemporary art forms cannot encompass the accu-

---

*In a study of Friedrich Schlegel, Hans Eicher outlined the historical development of the term *"romantic"* [*romantisch*], showing how it came to mean "fantastic," "marvelous," "miraculous," "fanciful," "improbable," "exotic," and so forth, and pointing out that in these senses the word was used by eighteenth-century Rationalists pejoratively and that it retained these connotations into a much later period (Hans Eicher, *Friedrich Schlegel* [New York, 1970], p. 51; see also Blok's article "O romantizme," *Sobranie sochinenii*, VI [Moscow-Leningrad, 1962], p. 359).

mulated experience of recent years will certainly not go unchallenged. The Western reader may feel impelled to cite the achievement of James Joyce, which precisely *does* seem to consist in the invention of a form adequate to the "new accumulated content" of the modern era. It is a sad paradox of the literary scene in Russia that even a sophisticated reader like Pasternak was probably not familiar enough with this achievement to hold it up as an outstanding solution to the problem he was considering. As we shall see, however, he did provide a solution of his own to the current impotence of form—at least as it most affected his own writing.

From the 1930s, Pasternak stressed the importance of content in the above sense as the essential substance of a work of art. In *Doctor Zhivago* it is content that, like a philosopher's stone, animates and transforms the work of art; it is on content that art, "acting as a restricted and 'concentrated' virus,"* works the alchemy from which the work of art is born. It is essentially in relation to content that Pasternak extols "a principle that is present in every work of art, a force applied to it and a truth worked out in it." And it is content in its richness and its wholeness that the artist must grasp within his art. The doctrine of the cardinal importance of content in art is diametrically opposed to views the artist held as a young man. Here we see an interesting paradox in the evolution of Pasternak from Futurist poet-theoretician—insisting on the importance of the "work as such," of form as such, of sheer sound—to believer in the primacy of experience-content (*Erfahrungsinhalt*)—an aesthetic preference in the mature Pasternak that reconciles him with the great Russian tradition (recall, for example, Turgenev's exclamation: "Tolstoy's greatest virtue is . . . that his stuff smells of life").[26]

"All great art tries to convey an integral vision of the world," writes Pasternak, but it always does so "in relation to the philosophy of its time and, for that reason, with different means." Thus the nineteenth century, represented by Tolstoy and Dostoevsky, Henry James and Dickens, Flaubert and Maupassant, tried to render the background of reality and the substratum of existence through a doctrine of causality based on "the belief that objectivity was determined and ruled by an iron chain of causes and effects." In a letter to Stephen Spender (written in English), Pasternak said that, in the eyes of these writers,

all appearances of the moral and material world were subordinate to the law of sequels and retributions. And the severer and more inflexible was an author in showing such consequences (of characters and conducts) the greater a realist he was esteemed. The tragic bewitching spell of Flaubert's style or Maupassant's manner roots [sic] in the fact that their narratives are irrevocable like verdicts or sentences, beyond recall.

For Pasternak the substratum of reality is far indeed from being governed by the immovable limits of some fixed determinism. At the summation of a lifelong study of reality, having considered the best means of rendering its lines of force, he asserts (in his idiosyncratic English) that he has come "to results if not di-

---

* With this phrase I try to render the idea underlying Pasternak's original: ". . . *nechto uzkoe i sosredotochennoe*" (*Doktor Zh* [Milan: Feltrinelli, 1957], p. 291).

ametrically opposite to the tendencies of the named masterpieces [of the nine-teenth century], at least to quite different observations than those of our predecessors and teachers." [27]

Indeed, the striking thing about Pasternak is the spontaneous spark of that movement he calls life, a spark whose unexpectedness and strangeness, as he wrote Spender, have always seemed characteristic to him, whether in his own experience or that of his contemporaries and intimates:

. . . from my earliest years [I have] been struck by the observation that existence was more original, extraordinary, and inexplicable than any of its separate astonishing incidents and facts. I was attracted by the unusualness of the usual." [28]

To another interlocutor, Ralph Matlaw, Pasternak also said that for him realism and the pursuit of "reality" lay not in the enhancing of the inexorable causality depicted by Balzac, Stendhal, Tolstoy, and Flaubert but

in the multiplicity of the universe, in the large number of possibilities, in a kind of spirit of freedom, a coincidence of impulses and inspirations (not *religious* inspiration, just inspiration—*vdokhnovenie*). Even modern science and mathematics . . . (about which Pasternak claimed he knew next to nothing) is moving in that direction, away from simple causality. Whatever happens, for example loss or destruction in nature or life, it is just one of the many things that happen. . . . Nature is much richer in coincidences than is our imagination. If all these possibilities exist, reality must be the result of choice, of a choice deliberately made. [29] [The comments are Matlaw's.]

Awareness of the unpredictability and unusualness of life led Pasternak to eschew nineteenth-century aesthetics based on "accentuating the fixed statics of *anagkē*, of natural laws, of settled moral regularity" (in his own words) and to follow, as he wrote to Spender, a completely different, more selective aesthetic method:

To attain a true resemblance between the imitative efforts of art and the truly tasted and experienced order of life it would me not suffice [*sic*] to put my representation in a vivid instantaneous motion. I would pretend [he means "claim"] (metaphorically) to have seen nature and universe themselves not as a picture made or fastened on an immovable wall, but as a sort of painted canvas roof or curtain in the air, incessantly pulled and blown and flapped by a something of an immaterial unknown and unknowable wind.

Pasternak's desire to render the peculiarly "original, extraordinary, and inexplicable" character of life with its constant turbulence accounts for the use of a striking device in *Doctor Zhivago*. To this desire he attributed

the not sufficient tracing of characters I was reproached with (more than to delineate them I tried to efface them) . . . the frank arbitrariness of the "coincidences" (through this means I wanted to show the liberty of being, its verisimilitude touching, adjoining improbability).

These are the coincidences that Gleb Struve, in his lucid "The Hippodrome of Life," demonstates to be, indeed, part of the basic fabric of the novel and one of the important devices Pasternak uses to convey the force of predestination as the human corollary to the "theory of relativity" that governs the physical universe as a whole though without determining its every particular movement.[30]

More than once in Pasternak's career the pressure of a broader portion of reality, complex and moving and newly perceived, brought an explosion of poetic form. The new spheres of reality revealed to him in the 1940s (an important aspect of which is mentioned in "Dawn", one of "The Poems of Iurii Zhivago") forced him to achieve the "unheard-of simplicity" that he had been dreaming of since 1932. In the mid-1940s, with the discovery of more complex areas of life, he decided that he must discard lyric poetry in favor of prose, the better to communicate his new experiences. The decision is reminiscent of the choice Pushkin made in the late 1820s. It is worthwhile studying the few recorded instances when a great poet abandoned verse for a more directly referential and propositional (and less metaphoric and less essentially rhythmic) discourse like prose. In 1935, Roman Jakobson had indicated that the prose of Briusov, Belyi, Khlebnikov, Maiakovskii, and Pasternak—"that remarkable colony of modern poets"—was already opening up "hidden paths to a revival of Russian prose" and declared that "Pasternak's prose is the characteristic prose of a poet in a great age of poetry." Jakobson pointed out that in a general way "there is an undeniably closer relationship on the one hand between verse and metaphor, on the other, between prose and metonymy." Jakobson characterized Pasternak's art as essentially metonymic (as opposed, say, to Maiakovskii's metaphorical style).[31] One may therefore say that according to the logic implicit in Jakobson's article (although he did not himself make the deduction) it was inevitable that Pasternak's fundamental reliance on metonymy should prompt him to make a decisive choice for the kind of writing that most naturally hinges upon metonymy.

We are fortunate to have the following transcription of Pasternak's comments on the most important revolution in his own aesthetic:

I believe that it is no longer possible for lyric poetry to express the immensity of our experience. Life has grown too cumbersome, too complicated. We have acquired values which are best expressed in prose. I have tried to express them through my novel. . . . I feel [*Doctor Zhivago*] has more value than those early poems. It is richer, more humane than the works of my youth. I believe that prose is today's medium, elaborate, rich prose like Faulkner's. Today's work must re-create whole segments of life.[32]

Pasternak's new arrangement of creative priorities was confirmed in a statement he made in 1953 indicating that he was "immersed" in his prose novel, which he viewed as his "sole business" to the extent that he did not allow himself "to be distracted from it and to be squandered on poetry."

The paradox of Pasternak's realism, then, is that it is a genuine, deep (very defensible) realism and yet is the opposite of that realism of writers such as Flaubert who insist on a strict causality, and who bend to an idolatry of form in striving for an objective, *impersonal* art. Pasternak's realism is the realism of an intuitionist—a *post-Modernist* realism. This realism of Pasternak's insists on the decisive role of experience-content, on *personal*, biographical content; it increasingly tries to encompass the great complexities of experience; it chafes, then, under the strictures of form. For him, in other words, experience-content must rule; form must be subordinated to the primary demands of experience. It was this sense of realism that led Pasternak from poetry to prose.

Henry James called prose "the most independent, most elastic, most pro- digious" of literary forms. It is true that today the "super-genre" of the novel, this broadest, most polyvalent, most protean form, is truly a cosmopolis that welcomes and encompasses a multitude of specific forms, intentions, styles, and tones. Remarkably enough, Pasternak achieved an aesthetically satisfying form, adequate to the new accumulative content that loomed so large in his awareness. Of course, *Doctor Zhivago*, being the recapitulation of a vision, is certainly an "expansive" novel whose aesthetic is removed from, say, James's endeavor to create a refined and stringent form—but then Pasternak's "expansive" form, un- like James's, was part of Pasternak's dual sense of art. For him art, in conveying the multifaceted movements of experience-content, would both embrace and en- hance life; for him art was both the communication of his intuitive realism and the celebration of life as inherently creative and good. Unfortunately, however, there was no guarantee that his experience-content would necessarily lead to such a celebration. Indeed, of all the comments that have been made about Pasternak's novel, the following by Anthony Burgess perhaps best sums up the achievement it represents within its genre, while at the same time placing it in its literary and historical context:

The two "big" European novels which have, in a sort of delayed action, appeared since the war—Thomas Mann's *Doctor Faustus* and Boris Pasternak's *Doctor Zhivago*—both record failure on the part of Germany and Russia respectively to counter the self-destructive urge which appeared at a moment of historical crisis: they are both massive works, and they approach traditional greatness, but they are as much cries of despair as exuberant shouts of acceptance. Perhaps the times are no longer propitious to the production of masterpieces which both embrace and enhance life.[33]

Pasternak's endeavor to "embrace and enhance life" can be traced back to this decisive critical-aesthetic statement he made in *A Safe-Conduct*:

We cease to recognize reality. It presents itself in some new category. This category seems to us to be its, not our, condition. Except for this condition everything in the world has been named. It alone is unnamed and new. We try to name it. The result is art.

The statement contains important implications with regard to Pasternak's paracognitive notion of art. Discussing the first two sentences of this passage, Fedor Stepun pointed out the typically Kantian character of the concept of cate- gory that Pasternak uses here to define art. Stepun compared this formula to a definition of Heinrich Rickert's: "To know the world is to make it unknowable." This comparison is most interesting, because for the neo-Kantian Rickert human knowledge can only be a simplification, a transformation of reality.

The parallel between Pasternak and Kant is of even greater interest. Let us go back to the passage from *A Safe-Conduct*: "This category [in which the world that he has ceased to know presents itself to the artist] seems to us to be its, not our, condition." Stepun comments:

This thought is obviously linked to Kant's distinction, according to which the world, which appears to the naïve observer as a kind of reality independent of man, in fact constitutes one of his creations, an informing (*oformlenie*) of the world by the forms of time and space, causality and eternity, inherent in the consciousness.

This is admirably said. Though without naming them, Stepun then proceeds methodically from the "Transcendental Esthetic" to the "Transcendental Analytic" of the *Critique of Pure Reason*:

[This consciousness which informs the world] is not the consciousness of empiric man alone, but of man with a capital M, so to speak, who in Kant bears the name "transcendental subject," in Fichte "absolute ego," in Hegel "absolute spirit," and in Pasternak "the image of man which is greater than man." It is this image which creates the world of art.[34]

If we wish to define Pasternak's position in the light of comparison with Kant, we must first face the problem of determining the nature of the subject that "enjoys" (rather than knows) and creates the work of art. For Pasternak it is not an empirical subject (a solution rejected by Stepun), not a purely logical, transcendent subject (a solution adopted by the Neo-Kantian Marburg school and forming the perspective taken by Stepun). Ignoring such scholastic distinctions, Pasternak conceives of a subject possessing a spontaneous intuition—a subject that, beyond theoretical knowledge and practical action, possesses an aesthetic (artistic) intuition that is autonomous and distinct from the faculties of knowledge and action:

There is no doubt about it: reality is broken up. And in breaking up, it gathers around two opposite poles: Lyricism and History. Both are equally a priori and absolute.[35]

According to this division of Pasternak's (which at first sight does not coincide with the structure of Kant's system), lyricism and history could not be more clearly opposite and distinct from each other. Pasternak finds the essential postulate "of the category of originality" inherent in lyricism. Authentic lyricism is "the truly a priori condition of the possibility of the subjective. . . . The subjective originality of Futurism," he specifies, "is by no means the subjectivity of the individual. This subjectivity must be understood as a category of lyricism itself—of the Original in its ideal sense" (in this text *Original* has a meaning similar to that of Plato's and Schopenhauer's "archetypes" and "the ideal").

The a priori and the absolute of lyricism, therefore, constitute a world apart that has nothing to do with the world of history. That is why the true Futurist, perched in the citadel of lyricism, never lets himself be lured into "preparing history in view of tomorrow" (which would be tantamount to accepting the etymology of his name in a simplistic sense). History is something completely different. "The a priori of history is terrible, and history has its heroes." But keep it separate from lyricism. The (Russian) Symbolists, victims of a sad confusion, are the ones who have reintroduced the phantom of history into lyricism; it is they who "have given way to the misleading suggestions" of the former by illegitimately enlarging the proper domain of the latter.

Yes, the two universes are distinct, and Pasternak, assimilating reality with history, affirms in his youthfully grandiloquent ardor that the Futurist "diagrams" have nothing to do with the structure of reality: lyricism is qualitatively different from the objective world; it "makes an attempt against reality." In short, Pasternak writes, "in art we see an improvisation of an absolutely unique kind, the execution of which requires only brilliance of execution." It is worth noting that fifteen years or so after he made these pronouncements Pasternak had apparently abandoned such rigorous, polarized contradistinctions and held that art and reality do intersect; thus in *A Safe-Conduct* he wrote: ". . . a part of [Khlebnikov's] merit remains inaccessible to me even now, for the poetry that I understand proceeds after all in history and in collaboration with real life."[36] This change is in keeping with the general trend of the evolution of his aesthetic from a cult of the word and form to an insistence upon experience and content.

Considering the dichotomy forcefully proclaimed by Pasternak at a time when, fresh from Marburg, he readily dichotomized, it is worth trying to link these divisions to Kantianism, which had so clearly influenced him earlier. For Kant, history is a circumscribed domain that deals only with phenomenal manifestations of the liberty of the will, without being able to tell us anything about its profound causes (even though, paradoxically, he sees in liberty the element that constitutes history, and recognizes no history outside the manifestations of human liberty). For him human liberty, at least on the personal level, is often exercised irrationally, even savagely, anarchically. Is not Pasternak's absolute pole of lyricism a replica or analogy of the spontaneous "lawless" liberty of Kant's acting subject? That would be the domain of the "aesthetic subject" (that is, possessing artistic intuition) as Pasternak sees it. It is a subject that, for good reason, cannot be assimilated to Kant's acting subject. Kant has devoted a separate work to the "aesthetic" subject, his *Critique of Judgment*.

We may gain further understanding of Pasternak's theory of art if we examine it in the light of the *Critique of Judgment*. In this work Kant is primarily concerned with elaborating the logical status that may be accorded to judgments predicating the concepts of the beautiful and the sublime. In the perspective of what Kant calls "aesthetic finality," aesthetic judgments, although they are not cognitive and do not ascribe an objective quality to their object, lay claim to a universal validity. The problem that interests Kant from the point of view of judgment and that he resolves in a certain sense through the principle of reflective judgment also interests Pasternak, primarily from the point of view of the creative process and artistic expression.

Pasternak has emphasized the essential spontaneity of the authentic work of art, which is infinitely beyond poor human techniques. "In art," he writes, "man is silent and the image speaks."[37] The sources of art correspond to a latent truth inherent in the world which will inform the expression of the artist much more than that expression will confer a structure upon some vague inspiration.

It is to this perspective that we must link Pasternak's concept of the primacy and autonomy of language, considered as a cardinal aspect of creation and a decisive factor in the whole process of inspiration. This process is described in *Doctor Zhivago* as a moment when

the relation of the forces that determine artistic creation is, as it were, reversed. The dominant thing is no longer the state of mind the artist seeks to express but the language in which he wants to express it. Language, the home and receptacle of beauty and meaning, itself begins to think and speak for man and turns wholly into music, not in terms of sonority but in terms of the impetuousness and power of its inward flow.[38]

Dale Plank's study *Pasternak's Lyric* contains an original interpretation of this comment on autonomous forces at work in language, which the author applies to Pasternak's poetics. Plank takes up Roman Jakobson's subtle hint that "the *agens* is excluded from Pasternak's thematics," and in the chapter entitled "The Voice of the Image" concludes that "the voice becomes not that of the poet, but that of the subject of the poem." While I cannot fully agree with his effort to work out a theory of "phonetic significance" (using as a point of departure the Russian Formalist Osip Brik's article "Sound Repetitions"), it seems to me that Plank is perfectly right when he sees the poet's will and intention as actually "replaced" by a "purposive energy of sounds, words, and images." That is in keeping with Victor Erlich's statement that in Pasternak's poetics "the last word belongs to poetry rather than the poet." The "impetuousness and power" of language are for Pasternak closely related to those qualities in the realities described. That is made clear by a passage from the same context in *Doctor Zhivago* indicating the real motivation behind Iurii Zhivago's aesthetic strivings:

He had striven constantly for an unconspicuous style. . . . Last night he had tried to convey, by words so simple as to be almost like childish babble and suggest the directness of a lullaby, his feelings of mingled love and fear and anguish and courage, in such a way that it should speak for itself, almost apart from the words.[39]

This statement is unambiguous: the reality to be conveyed clearly determines the form. Indeed, the power of the emotion almost does away with language by making it "unconspicuous," by speaking almost "independently of the words." In this perspective Pasternak envisages an original and eternal being of language that seeks, like a *bonum diffusivum sui*, to be realized by man. When he thus dwells on the autonomous forces at work in language, Pasternak—with no critical or scholarly pretensions—proves to be heir to a tradition going back to Plato, who in *Ion* depicts the poet as one possessed by divine inspiration. This tradition includes such diverse figures as Herder, for whom language springs of necessity from man's innermost nature, this process being a conspicuous illustration of the Herderian notion of *das Naturwüchsige;* Friedrich Schlegel, who terms language "the collective memory of the human race"; Wilhelm von Humboldt, who views language not as a *Werk* (*ergon*), but as a dynamic activity (*Tätigkeit, energeia*); the pan-logician Hegel, for whom language is the vehicle by which to reach the highest and deepest realities; Karl Vossler, who speaks of "the autonomy of . . . [the] intuitive, classical, creative will" of language.[40]

Of course, for the Russian Futurists, poetic speech was an end in itself. However, rather than being an echo of Khlebnikov's somewhat arrogantly and flamboyantly proclaimed slogan of the "self-oriented" or "self-sufficient" word (*samovitoe slovo*), Pasternak's statement about the autonomous forces at work in language appear in both tone and content, to be more akin to, say, the formulations contained in Novalis's "Monolog," a summation of the poet's views on the spontaneous creativity at work in language—(*die*) *Eingebung der Sprache* and (*die*) *Wirksamkeit der Sprache* being key concepts used there.[41] In contrast to poet-theoreticians like Maiakovskii and Valéry, who—diverse as they were in many respects—agree in insisting that poetry is primarily a matter of technical skill, Pasternak stresses the primacy of inspiration, resuming in this respect a romantic attitude (kept alive by Russian Symbolists dwelling on the role of "poetry as magic").[42]

Pasternak, in his idea of perception, maintains that intuition must grasp the whole margin of reality that eludes cognition (*poznanie*). His conception, never developed into an explicit theory, would have us believe that the mind (Kant's *Gemüt*) possesses, beyond spatiality and temporality, a sort of third form with a corresponding system of categories appropriate to it, the whole of which permits aesthetic apprehension. For Pasternak, such aesthetic apprehension appears to be endowed with its own form and categories and constitutes an autonomous, para-cognitive process. According to Pasternak, this autonomous aesthetic faculty plays an essential, irreplaceable role, because for him consciousness, which proceeds by means of simple representations, shows itself inadequate to grasp life and nature. These are beyond truth, beyond the true word resulting from the act of knowing:

What is it the honest man does when he speaks *only* the truth? While he is telling the truth time goes by; in that time life moves ahead. His truth lags behind, it deceives. Is this the way man must speak, everywhere and always?[43]

Art is therefore situated beyond truth, because art aims not only at giving a simple image to represent man (which could be accomplished by means of the understanding) but also at giving a larger representation of man, an image of man that is greater than man. This enlarged image emerges only in the act of transition, and art is the only faculty capable of grasping and rendering that transition. Thus in Pasternak a cinematic or dynamist perspective, in profound analogy with the Bergsonian attitude, colors a manifestly Neo-Kantian view of the problem. If an intuitionist is defined as someone for whom art is the most important cognitive activity of man, then it does not appear that Pasternak should be so labeled, insofar as he does not claim that the aesthetic function should altogether supplant the rational process but indicates that it should supplement it. Indeed, we have every reason to believe that Pasternak developed his own views on the special role of the aesthetic function, without being in any way indebted to the monistic theories of Schelling, according to which the act of the imagination is not just an act of cognition in the strictest sense of the word but also the most vital act of cognition the human mind can perform. Nor do we have evidence that Pasternak was acquainted with the critical writings of Coleridge, and thus the coincidences in their statements are even more striking. For Coleridge, who identified the "philosophic imagination" with the "highest intuitive knowledge," poetry is a sublime way of knowledge, far superior to the understanding and its concern for expressing truth; however, for him imagination does perform the feat of conveying truth in an even more compelling way than understanding.[44]

As we have seen, art for Pasternak consists in recapturing the movement of emotion, the movement of life. The lines of force of that movement constitute the form of art, a form that resides neither in the delineation of contours nor even in the disposition of parts but is an organic principle of cohesion of content and an internal law of its unfolding. The organic nature of the work of art was emphasized by Pasternak as early as 1921 in "Some Tenets." There he insisted that the various components of the work as a whole should be a matter of indifference to the artist, provided that the whole is authentic. Such a statement sounds like an echo of the indifference to form peculiar to Wordsworth and other Romantics. For Pasternak it is essential that poor imitations or anything unusual or false (such as bad taste, which is taste for the mediocre or the average) not be interposed between the artist and what he is expressing. Thus authentic art "expresses the joy of existence," which is the most profound principle animating living beings. Art, in its search for beauty, always finds it in this joy of existence, since "beauty is delight in form," and that form in turn is "the key of organic life, since no living thing can exist without it." The similarity of the work of art to an organism was probably first suggested by Aristotle in his *Poetics* and was later taken up by Kant, though somewhat hesitatingly—he did not go all the way to equate art with organism. Pasternak's wholehearted advocacy of such an equation is most strongly reminiscent of Coleridge's unambiguous declaration: "The organic form is innate; it shapes as it develops itself from within, and the fullness of its development is one and the same with the perfection of its outward form."[45]

These deliberations have a direct bearing on Pasternak's conception of the critique of art. For him it is the critic's duty to stress that the artist cannot work to order and that his essential virtues should be great freedom and audacity in the exercise of imagination. Furthermore, the nature of the primary inspiration of art (animated reality) and its goal (beauty, symbol of the infinite in art), as well as the organic character of the work itself, do not permit the work to be dissected or categorized. As a poet-critic, Pasternak protested the jargon that tends to creep into literary criticism and criticism in general (thereby echoing some of Tolstoy's pronouncements in *What Is Art?* in a less virulent key). For him criticism, in its ignorance of man, "weaves a tissue of inventions and calumnies with regard to specializations"—and Pasternak discusses some of the effects of this pernicious jargon.[46]

Because the initial content and foundation of art is the "joy of existence," the work of art has no other object than creating the ever-renewed surge and drive of existence reaching after beauty. On the strength of this premise Pasternak could say that art is infinite (*beskonechno*). As long as art exists, it will endeavor to seize and render the lines of force that animate life, to recapture beauty. Such statements by Pasternak are spontaneous elaborations of the same intuition that Keats had conveyed in a slightly different formulation: "What the Imagination seizes as Beauty must be Truth."[47]

Pasternak saw the evolution of his own aesthetic as a gradual departure from the formal, technical experimentation characterizing his poetry of the second decade of the century and a progression toward a more "realistic" art, capable of conveying forcefully the experience of his generation. He commented on this evolution when, as a mature artist, he branded (perhaps with excessive severity) the overly ornamental and *recherché* aspects of his early verse and strictured the "desire for effects" of his early art, the "deplorable and annoying" features of most of his earlier work, the "unnecessary mannerism" that he felt "marred" *A Safe-Conduct* (1931). He believed that he had gradually drawn closer and closer to the "unheard-of simplicity" mentioned in a poem of 1932, to a drastic economy of means that permitted the historic reality experienced by his generation ("a world of hitherto unknown aims and aspirations, problems and exploits") to be refracted in his later art, specifically in *Doctor Zhivago*. Characteristically, he praised most highly those poets (Pushkin, Verlaine, Rilke, Blok), those prose writers (Gogol, Tolstoy, Dostoevsky, Chekhov), and those musicians (Bach, Chopin, Scriabin) who in his view had been most successful in fostering the irruption of reality into the texture of their art, without being primarily concerned with technical innovation. As a mature artist Pasternak believed that excessive preoccupation with technical experiments is characteristic of a sickly or dying art while great art is that which is so possessed by the overwhelming force of experience and feeling that it forgets the technical aspects of expression. Paradoxically, while denouncing what he labeled "romantic" art, Pasternak continued a typically Romantic attitude by valuing content over form. Pasternak's own aesthetic evolution (from excessive ornamentation and affectation to "unheard-of simplicity") appeared to him a "privileged" pattern, which he tended to project into his portrayal of masters he admired. Thus in his Varykino diary Zhivago (who appears clearly to speak for Pasternak) views the evolution of Pushkin's aesthetic as a gradual departure from the voices of his Arzamas period (imitative approach to art, excessive use of mythology, bombast, faked epicureanism and sophistication, affectation of wisdom), until the poet knew how to allow "air, light, the noise of life, reality" to "burst into his poetry from a street as through an open window." Even though it may be to a point marred by "affective fallacy," such criticism is very enlightening.[48]

The points adduced here can only reinforce Victor Terras's view that "Pasternak's aesthetic is certainly closer to the romantic than the Kantian aesthetics." In view of the mature Pasternak's (somewhat invidious) denunciation of "romanticism" as second-rate art, it is all the more paradoxical that at the time of *My Sister, Life* he should have taken as terms of reference such inveterate Romantics as Heine, whose talent has egotistic and at times destructive components, and Nikolaus Lenau, the poet of egoistic, introspective, and passive *Weltschmerz*. It is also striking that even during World War II, when he was translating Sándor Petöfi's verse, Pasternak owned that he took delight in the Hungarian's "gypsy, exuberant spirit." One writer suggested that Pasternak was a *neo*-Romantic (insofar as his thematics are more oriented toward the familiar than the exotic). We must perforce conclude that Pasternak was a Romantic *malgré lui.*[49]

While denouncing the "romantic" attitude and extolling fidelity to "reality," Pasternak's critical statements often appear to have a romantic or Platonizing coloration, such as his proclamations of belief in transcendent values (beauty) or ideals ("the image of man" that is "greater than man"). Too, his reliance upon a "prelinguistic" inspiration directly determined by reality is at variance with his statements on the specifically poetic or mythmaking functions of language. These various approaches of his cannot be fully reconciled, and such contradictions in his statements remain unresolved.

Going beyond such paradoxes, however, for Pasternak the aesthetic function, like the religious attitude, is characterized by a creative tension *ad extra*—that of the artist's subjectivity, stronghold of the world of "history," toward the fundamental "otherness" of natural reality. Forgetting or outgrowing his youthful, belligerent distinction between lyricism and history, Pasternak stresses the dichotomy of nature and history, best formulated in the statement by a character from *Doctor Zhivago*: "Man does not live in nature but in history." By then the term "history," having shed its Kantian connotations, had a purely positive meaning for Pasternak, since it denotes the sphere of highest human achievements. The polarity between nature and history is at the heart of Pasternak's work from the 1940s. Nature for Pasternak maintains the dynamism that was an integral part of the earlier "lyricism," but now, instead of irreconcilable polarity, there is synthesis, and at this point of synthesis of nature and history, life becomes art. To illustrate this synthesis Pasternak wrote *Doctor Zhivago*. Pasternak's poetics of nature has been discussed earlier;* his poetics of history finds its culmination in the aesthetic realm. The artist's subjectivity—the epitome of the world of *history*—strives for the otherness of *natural* reality. This is in agreement with Pasternak's statement that art finds metaphor in nature and reproduces it faithfully; metaphor is not invented by art, nor is it the product of subjectivity (characteristic of the world of history): it is the encounter of subjectivity with what is different from it, with the otherness it finds in nature. Metaphor—also described by Pasternak as "the shorthand of a great personality and of its spirit"—is achieved by art through the fusion of subjectivity and this otherness. Iurii Zhivago believed that "art has two constant, unending concerns: it always meditates on death and thus always creates life."[50] By meditating on death—a necessity and a law of the world of nature—art generates new life, transcending the physicochemical aspects of nature. Thus only within the aesthetic function can a reconciliation of the two worlds of nature and history be achieved. The mature Pasternak, while achieving this reconciliation, continues to stress as the main axis of his aesthetics that the primary function of art is to communicate authentic emotion and experience. Thereby is the reconciliation between nature and history achieved.

*See Chapter 13.

Appendices

Appendix 1

Chronology of
Pasternak's Life

I said that an intelligent person could always look up dates and things in a good encyclopedia or in any manual of Russian literature. He [my publisher] said that a student would not be necessarily an intelligent person and anyway would resent the trouble of having to look up things.

Vladimir Nabokov *

The Chronology of Nabokov's *Nikolai Gogol* was introduced at the express wish of the publisher, and in spite of the author's initial reluctance. Not so in this volume: the labor of compiling this Chronology cannot be blamed upon, or traced back to, a sadistic suggestion of the publisher's—it was brought upon my head by my own doing. The compilation was begun in 1960–61; in 1962 an excerpted version was composed with the collaboration of Michael Henry Heim and privately published in Germany.

Naturally, this chronology suffers from an almost unavoidable defect of the genre—near-telegraphic style. "Hero experiences unrequited love"—such might be a horribly inadequate entry the reader would find under the spring of 1912. He will discover a rather more complex presentation of that episode in Chapter 4.

---

* Vladimir Nabokov, *Nikolai Gogol* (New York: New Directions, 1959), p. 152.

1889   February 14: Marriage of painter Leonid Osipovich Pasternak and pianist Rosa Isidorovna Kaufman.

1890   February 10 (January 29 O.S.): Birth of Boris, the Pasternaks' first child, in Moscow in Lyzhin House, a building facing the seminary on Oruzheinyi Lane.

1892   Boris's father is invited with other artists to illustrate a deluxe edition of Leo Tolstoy's *War and Peace*.

1893   Birth of Boris's brother, Aleksandr.

Akulina Gavrilovna joins Pasternak household as Boris's nurse.

Pasternak family moves to Meshchanskaia Street.

November: Death of Peter Ilych Tchaikovsky (erroneously given as 1894 in *Sketch for an Autobiography*).

1894   Leonid Pasternak accepts chair at Moscow School of Painting, Sculpture, and Architecture. Family moves to lodgings provided by the school at 21 Miasnitskaia Street.

From the balcony of the School of Painting family watches Alexander III's funeral procession.

November 23: Tolstoy and two of his daughters attend concert at the Pasternaks' at which Rosa Isidorovna performs.

November: Death of Anton Rubinstein, who had fostered Rosa Pasternak's career as a pianist.

1896   From the apartment balcony the Pasternaks view the coronation ceremonies of Nicholas II.

1898   July: Leonid Pasternak executes an often-reproduced drawing of his son Boris busily sketching.

Fall: Leonid Pasternak goes to Iasnaia Poliana to collaborate with Tolstoy on *Resurrection*, for which he does a series of remarkable illustrations.

1899   Rainer Maria Rilke's first trip to Russia, during which he visits the Pasternaks.

1900   Birth of Boris's sister Josephine.

Rilke's second trip to Russia.

Summer: Leonid Pasternak takes the family to Odessa for the summer. On the train the family meets Rilke and Lou Andreas-Salomé, who are on their way to call on Tolstoy at Iasnaia Poliana.

1901   Boris admitted to second-year German Classical Grammar School (Moscow Fifth Gymnasium).

Spring: Visits the Moscow circus, where a "tropical drum parade" starring "Amazons from Dahomey" makes a vivid impression on him.

Winter: The Pasternaks move to a new apartment specially fitted for them in the main building of the School of Painting.

1902   Birth of Lydia, the Pasternaks' fourth child.

Rilke sends inscribed copy of *Das Buch der Bilder* to Leonid Pasternak.

1903   Late spring: At the dacha rented by his father on the Obolenskoe estate near Maloiaroslavets, Boris has his first encounter with composer Aleksandr Scriabin, who becomes a friend of the family and Pasternak's "god." Boris hears long discussions between his father and Scriabin.

Autumn: Falls from a horse and fractures a leg. In Moscow begins serious study of musical composition under Iurii Engel and Reinhold Glière.

December: Scriabin takes leave of the Pasternak family before his departure for Switzerland. Boris comes across an inscribed copy of Rilke's *Mir zur Feier* in his father's library.

1904   February 19: Scriabin leaves for Switzerland.

1905   January–October: Events of the 1905 Revolution make a vivid impression on Boris (later to be described in *The Year 1905*). Pasternak is among the student demonstrators and is whiplashed by a mounted Cossack. Vladimir Maiakovskii, still a gymnasium student, also takes part in the demonstrations.

October: Boris visits his uncle Aleksandr and aunt Klavdiia in Petersburg, attends Vera Komissarzhevskaia's theater, reads novels by Knut Hamsun and Przybyszewski, and strolls around the city.

Develops a passionate interest in Aleksandr Blok's poetry.

December: In Moscow, Maxim Gorky meets several times with Leonid Pasternak and asks him to contribute to journals of political satire. The family leaves for an extended sojourn in Berlin.

Rilke's *Das Stunden-Buch* appears.

1906   The Pasternaks stay first at the Hotel Am Knie in Berlin-Charlottenburg and thereafter at 112 Kurfürstenstrasse.

January: Gorky leaves Russia, arrives in Berlin, where Leonid Pasternak sketches his portrait. Boris has his first encounter with Gorky.

March 6: Execution of rebel Lieutenant Pëtr Petrovich Schmidt and other mutinous sailors on Berezan Island, an event later described in Pasternak's *Lieutenant Schmidt*.

Summer: The family stays in Goehren, a small resort town on Rügen Island, where Pasternak continues music lessons with the composer Engel.

1907   Winter: The Pasternaks return to Moscow, where Rilke's poetry enters Pasternak's life.

Boris joins Serdarda, a society devoted to literary experimentation.

Tutors Ida Davidovna Vysotskaia.

1907–
1908   Discovers poetry of Innokenti Annenskii and similarities between his own and Annenskii's styles.

Frequently sees members or friends of Serdarda: Arkadii Gurev; Sergei Makovskii, future editor of journal *Apollon*; Sergei Bobrov, an ardent believer in Pasternak's poetry, who tends to isolate Pasternak from the older literary generation; S. N. Durylin; and A. I. Kozhebatkin.

1908   May: Graduates from gymnasium with gold medal. In contrast to his dutiful completion of academic work, Maiakovskii engages in illegal activities and does not graduate from gymnasium.

Becomes acquainted with many persons in the literary world. Continues for a time to work as a private tutor.

1908–
1909   Inner drama drives Pasternak to abandon a musical career. Durylin detects quality in his first literary essays; his influence is decisive in inducing Pasternak to give up music in favor of poetry.

Enters University of Moscow School of Law.

1909   January: Scriabin returns from abroad. Rehearsals of Scriabin's *Poem of Ecstasy* begin, attended by Boris. On Scriabin's advice transfers from School of Law, where he has been studying for a semester, to historical-philological faculty to study philosophy.

February 2: "Futurist Manifesto," by Filippo Marinetti, published in *Le Figaro* in Paris.

Develops more serious interest in literature, reads Rilke's *Mir zur Feier* to Serdarda circle, delves more deeply into Blok and Andrei Belyi, admiring their "profundity and wonder."

1910   November 2: Accompanies his father, summoned to make a drawing of

Tolstoy on his deathbed in Astapovo, and witnesses funeral procession.

Hails Belyi's novel *The Silver Dove* as a landmark. Maiakovskii leaves the gymnasium and studies painting, first at the Stroganov Institute of Applied Arts, then at the Moscow School of Painting. Velimir Khlebnikov initiates the Futurist movement. Posthumous publication of Annenskii's *The Cypress Chest*. Publication of Rilke's *Die Aufzeichnungen des Malte Laurids Brigge*, which is to influence Pasternak, and Mikhail Kuzmin's "Concerning Beautiful Clarity." First nonfigurative canvasses of Mikhail Larionov and Nataliia Goncharova mentioned by Pasternak among landmarks of artistic life. Death of actress Komissarzhevskaia and of painter Mikhail Vrubel.

1911 Summer: The Pasternaks move to new quarters opposite the Church of Christ the Savior—No. 14 Volkhonka Street, Apartment 9.

Autumn: Rosa Isidorovna suffers her first heart attack and takes the cure at Bad Kissingen, Germany.

1912 Early May: Leaves for Marburg, Germany, to study philosophy under Hermann Cohen.

May 9: Registers at University of Marburg for the summer semester. Takes up residence in guesthouse at No. 15, Gisselbergerstrasse.

July: Visited by Ida Vysotskaia, who refuses his marriage proposal. Decides to abandon philosophy. Begins intense devotion to poetry.

August 3: Withdraws from University of Marburg.

Early August: Journeys through Basel to Milan, then on to Venice, Florence, and Pisa, where he meets his parents. Returns to Moscow, where he prepares for his philosophy examinations.

1913 Discusses Rilke's poetry with the poet Emile Verhaeren, who is sitting for his father.

February: In the studio of the sculptor Konstantin Krakht, he reads to Symbolist circle his paper "Symbolism and Immortality," in which he speaks of a generic immortality in man.

Late spring: Takes state examinations in philosophy. Graduates from the university.

Summer: Reads Fëdor Tiutchev and writes poetry at his parents' dacha in Molodi. Tutors in home of Moritz Philipp.

Five poems printed in first issue of Moscow almanac *Lirika*, promoted by a group of young writers of the same name whose leaders are Bobrov and Nikolai Aseev (the Lirika group later merges with Centrifuge).

1914 Spring: Takes part in activities of Centrifuge, a group of literary innovators.

May: First acquaintance with Maiakovskii's poetry, to which he is attracted.

At a café in the Arbat has first encounter with Maiakovskii, whom he knew by sight at the gymnasium.

Summer: Stays on the estate of Lithuanian poet Jurgis Baltrušaitis, working as a private tutor. Translates Heinrich von Kleist's *Der zerbrochene Krug* for Moscow Chamber Theater.

July: Outbreak of World War I. Boris is called up and goes to Moscow but is exempted from military service because of childhood leg accident. Maiakovskii is also exempted.

August: Anti-German demonstrators burn and loot the home of Moritz Philipp, destroying Pasternak's books and manuscripts.

Autumn: Continues working as tutor to Walter Philipp in the Philipp family's new apartment.

First collection of verse *Twin in the Clouds* published by Lirika with friendly preface by Nikolai Aseev. Three poems published in collection *Rukonog* by Centrifuge (Moscow).

1915   April 14: Death of Scriabin.

May: Pasternak's translation of Kleist's *The Broken Jug*, edited by Gorky, appears in Gorky's *Sovremennik*. On May 8, not knowing who edited his translation, Pasternak writes to Gorky to complain that his text has been tampered with.

Autumn: Travels to Urals. Maiakovskii writes *War and the Universe*.

December: Appearance of almanac *Vzial*, edited by Osip Brik, containing programmatic statement by Maiakovskii and poetry by Pasternak.

Three poems published in *Vesennee Kontragenstvo muz*.

Winter: Spends first winter in the Urals. Begins *Over the Barriers*.

1916   Continues work on *Over the Barriers*.

January: Maiakovskii sends Pasternak a copy of *Simple as Mooing*, containing, in Pasternak's view, Maiakovskii's "first and brightest experiments."

Spring–summer: In Moscow, works as tutor for Philipp family.

Publication: Verse published in the second collection of Centrifuge.

Winter, 1916–17: Works at the Ushkov chemical plant on the Kama River in the Urals. For a while manages the local draft board. Composes poetry, the notebook of which is later lost.

1917   March: News of the revolution in Petrograd reaches Ushkov factories in the Urals. Pasternak undertakes the return trip to Moscow in a covered cart with runners, stopping at the Izhevsk ordnance works. In Moscow, stays with his parents on Volkhonka Street.

Summer: In a dacha in Molodi rented by his parents, composes *My Sister, Life*.

July: On the advice of Valerii Briusov, Ilia Ehrenburg establishes contact with Pasternak.

Fall–winter: Stays for a while on Lebiazhii Lane, then on Gagarin Lane, and finally in a room on Sivtsev Vrazhek overlooking the Arbat.

October 16–19: First conference of the new Proletkult (Proletarian Cultural and Educational Organization).

Appearance of his second collection of verse, *Over the Barriers*, published by Centrifuge.

1918   Late January: At the apartment of M. Tsetlin attends a "meeting of two generations of poets," at which Konstantin Balmont and Maiakovskii read their poetry to Vsevolod Ivanov, Andrei Belyi, Jurgis Baltrušaitis, Vasilii Kamenskii, Ilia Ehrenburg, Marina Tsvetaeva, and Aleksei Tolstoy.

Mid-March: With Gorky's assistance obtains work as a foreign-press screener in the Library of Commissariat for Education.

March: Publication of Blok's *The Twelve*.

May 17: Publication of Boris's "Dialogue" and dramatic fragments in *Znamia truda*.

Summer: Spends a few days at dacha rented by his parents near Ochakovo station.

Visits Gorky to discuss publication of a novel by Boris Pilniak in the almanac *Dom iskusstv*. Learns that Gorky edited his translation of *The Broken Jug*.

November: Ends employment with Commissariat for Education.

December 26–28: "Without Love" published in short-lived Social Revolutionary newspaper *Volia truda*.

Works on *My Sister, Life*, "Letters from Tula," and "The Childhood of Liuvers."

Returns to live in parents' apartment on Volkhonka Street.

Other publications: "Apelles' Mark" (first story in prose), in *Znamia truda*;

poetry in *Vesennii salon poetov* and *Proletarii*.

1919   January 30: Publication of Imaginist manifesto "Deklaratsiia."

1920   Reads to Maiakovskii verse from *My Sister, Life*. Maiakovskii's reaction is "ten times what [I] had ever hoped to hear from anyone" (Pasternak's remark).

1921   Pasternak's mother suffers serious heart attack. Family leaves for Germany, where they remain. Pasternak and brother, Aleksandr, remain in Moscow, in apartment on Volkhonka Street.

February 5: Apologizes to Gorky for his letter of May, 1915, complaining about editorial changes in his translation of *The Broken Jug*.

February 11 and 13: In his speech "On the Calling of the Poet," read at Pushkin House, Blok says, "Peace and freedom are taken away!"

March 2: Regular literary Wednesday of the House of the Press devoted to Pasternak. Actress V. Alekseeva-Meshieva reads from his unpublished poems; Maiakovskii participates in discussion.

April 1: Maiakovskii anonymously publishes his longer poem *150,000,000* and reads it to Pasternak, who finds it "uncreative." The beginning of Pasternak's estrangement from Maiakovskii's poetry.

May 7: With Maiakovskii attends poetry readings by Blok at the Polytechnic Museum and Dante Alighieri Society. Converses with Blok, who says that he has heard "many good things" about Pasternak.

August: Nikolai Gumilev shot without trial for "counterrevolutionary" activities. His former wife, Anna Akhmatova, suffers deep depression.

August 7: Blok dies in Petrograd.

October 16: At Lenin's entreaty Gorky leaves Soviet Union.

November: Pasternak listed as one of the contributors to the Moscow Association of Futurists' (MAF) Publishing House and is announced as planning a volume to be entitled *Lirika* (*Lyric Poetry*).

1922   Spring: Buys Tsvetaeva's *Versts* and is "instantly won over by its great lyrical power." Begins correspondence with her.

Marries painter Evgeniia Vladimirovna Lourié.

July 23: Death of Futurist poet Khlebnikov.

August 15: Pasternak and his wife go to Germany for ten-month stay, mainly in Berlin. He sees several other Russian writers, temporary or permanent émigrés: Tsvetaeva, Belyi, Ehrenburg, Vladislav Khodasevich, Aleksei Tolstoy, Igor-Severianin, and Gorky.

Fall: Makes contacts with Russian publishers in Berlin. His third collection of verse, *My Sister, Life: Summer, 1917* published by Grzhebin (Berlin, Petrograd, and Moscow), establishing him as a poet.

September 25: At Grzhebin's meets with Khodasevich (who had emigrated in June) and Belyi to discuss a celebration in honor of Gorky to take place on October 1.

October: Maiakovskii leaves Russia on his first trip abroad for a ten-week stay in Berlin—where Pasternak and he are in contact—and Paris.

Other publications: "Letters from Tula," published in vol. 1 of almanac *Shipovnik* (Moscow). Article "Some Tenets" published in vol. 1 of the collection *Sovremennik* (Moscow). "The Childhood of Liuvers" published in vol. 1 of the almanac *Nashi dni* (Moscow).

Publishes his translation of Goethe, *The Mysteries* (which he later referred to as "awful"). Poetry published in *Poetry of Revolutionary Moscow*, edited by Ehrenburg.

1923   January: Publication of fourth collection of verse, *Themes and Variations*, by Gelikon (Berlin).

February: Pilgrimage to Marburg.

March: Publication of first issue of journal *Lef*, founded by Maiakovskii.

March 12: Pasternak's father paints his portrait.

Mid- or late March: Pasternak leaves Berlin for Moscow.

April–May: Second issue of journal *Lef* contains his poem "May Day," written at the specific request of Maiakovskii—probably his first practice of *littérature engagée*.

September 23: Birth of Evgenii, his first son.

Publication of second edition of *My Sister, Life*. Begins work on longer poem "High Malady."

1924   January 21: Death of Lenin.

Publication of fragments of *High Malady* in first volume of *Krug*. Continues work on the poem, which contains a section devoted to Lenin's speech at the Ninth Congress of Soviets. Begins work on *Spektorskii*.

Story "Aerial Ways" appears in *Russkii sovremennik*.

1925   Central Committee of the Communist party issues liberal resolution "Manifesto on Literature."

Pasternak begins work on longer poems *The Year 1905* and *Lieutenant Schmidt*.

December: Sergei Esenin, a poet highly esteemed by Pasternak, commits suicide.

Publications: Pasternak's poems "A Stifling Night" and "Sailing Away" appear in sixth issue of journal *Commerce* (Paris), make an impression on Rilke. Illustrated edition of *Carrousel: Verse for Children* appears (Leningrad). Chapters 1–3 of *Spektorskii* appear in vol. 2 of almanac *Kovsh* (Leningrad); Chapter 4, in vol. 4. Volume of prose *Aerial Ways* (containing "Il Tratto di Apelle," "Letters from Tula," "The Childhood of Liuvers," and "Aerial Ways") published by Krug (Moscow and Leningrad).

1926   Pasternak's wife and son visit abroad.

February: Writes letter to Rilke.

March 14: Rilke writes Leonid Pasternak that Boris's "youthful fame" has reached him—that he has become acquainted with Boris's verse in two Western European publications.

September 20: At "evening" in Polytechnical Museum, Maiakovskii delivers a report "How to Write Poetry," devoted in part to a discussion of Pasternak's poetry.

December 29: Death of Rilke in sanatorium in Valmont.

Publications: Longer poem *Lieutenant Schmidt* serialized in *Novyi mir*. Selected Verse published by Uzel (Moscow).

1927   Works on *The Year 1905*.

The last friendly references to Pasternak in Maiakovskii's speeches. The break between them becomes final.

February: Reads Tsvetaeva's "Poem of the End" and on the same day receives news of Rilke's death (Pasternak's "Posthumous Letter to Rilke," written between 1931 and 1937, will describe the impact of Rilke's death).

Fall: Publication of *The Year 1905*.

September 20: Sends copy of *The Year 1905* to Gorky with inscription "To Aleksei Maksimovich Gorky, [who is] the greatest expression and justification of the epoch, with respectful and deep expression."

Begins work on *A Safe-Conduct*.

Publication of *My Sister, Life*, and *Themes and Variations* (Moscow and Leningrad).

1928   Complete version of *High Malady* appears in *Novyi mir*.

1929   Conflict between "proletarian writers" and "fellow travelers."

Publications: *A Tale* in *Krasnaia niva*, *Literaturnaia gazeta* (with an excerpt from "Nochnoi nabrosok"), and *Novyi mir*; *The Zoo* (verse for children); *Selected Verse*, from *Over the Barriers*, *My Sister, Life*, and *Themes and Variations* (Moscow); *A Safe-Conduct*, part 1 (*Zvezda*); volume of selected poetry, *Over the Barriers*.

1930   April 14: Maiakovskii commits suicide.

Summer: The Pasternaks visit friends in Irpen: V. F. Asmus and his wife and G. G. Neigauz and his wife, Zinaida Nikolaevna. Pasternak draws closer to Zinaida.

September 29: The Pasternaks return to Moscow.

Publications: *Two Volumes: Verse*, second edition; *The Year 1905*, second edition.

1931   Parts from wife, Evgeniia Vladimirovna, who keeps their son, Evgenii.

Makes first trip to the Caucasus for a six-month stay, accompanied by Zinaida Nikolaevna Neigauz (now separated from Neigauz) and her two sons. Stays at house of poet Paolo Iashvili and his wife. Develops friendship with Iashvilis, the Tabidzes, Simon Chikovani, and the Leonidzes. Begins translating Georgian poets.

Publications: *A Safe-Conduct* and novel in verse, *Spektorskii* in book form; *A Safe-Conduct*, parts 2 and 3, in *Red Virgin Soil*; excerpt from part 3 of *A Safe-Conduct* and "First Meetings with Maiakovskii" in *Literaturnaia gazeta*; second edition of *Over the Barriers*.

1932   April 23: Creation of Union of Writers by the Central Committee, which simultaneously dissolves all existing literary associations.

Summer: Pasternak goes on "mission" under auspices of Union of Writers. Visits a region near Sverdlovsk on the banks of Lake Shartash.

October 21: Resumes work after four-day stay in Leningrad.

November 10: Attends evening of Osip Mandelstam's poetry at offices of *Literaturnaia gazeta*; tells Mandelstam: "I envy you your freedom. For me you are a new Khlebnikov. And just as alien to me as he is. I need nonfreedom."

Publications: *Second Birth*; third edition of *The Year 1905*.

1933   October: Lives in apartment on Volkhonka Street.

November: Goes on mission to Georgia with delegation of Soviet writers. Delegation is briefly received by Stalin.

Publications: Single-volume edition of *Verse* (*Stikhotvoreniia*), Leningrad; *Longer Poems* (*Poemy*), published by Sovetskaia literatura (Moscow); *Aerial Ways* (containing "Childhood of Liuvers," "Apelles' Mark," "Aerial Ways") published by Gosudarstvennoe izdatelstvo khudozhestvennoi literatury (Moscow); *Selected Verse* (*Izbrannye stikhi*), Sovetskaia literatura (Moscow); *Little Book for Children* (*Knizhka dlia detei*), Sovetskaia literatura (Moscow).

1934   January: Moves into apt. provided by Union of Writers on Tverskoi Boulevard.

Marries Zinaida Nikolaevna in a civil marriage.

Continues translating Georgian poetry and working on his own prose.

Late March: Suffers from heart ailment, is instructed to give up tea, smoking, and (temporarily) work.

May 13: Mandelstam arrested after reading an anti-Stalin epigram to several fellow writers. Pasternak goes to Nikolai Bukharin at *Izvestiia* to ask him to intercede for Mandelstam.

May: Bukharin writes to Stalin on behalf of Mandelstam, praising his merits and adding postscript: "And Pasternak shares this opinion." Stalin telephones Pasternak to ask for his opinion of Mandelstam's poetry.

August 17–September 1: First All-Union Congress of the Union of Soviet Writers. In his speech to the congress, Bukharin singles out Pasternak as "one of the most remarkable craftsmen of verse of our day."

August 18: In his opening address to the congress, Gorky formulates the doctrine of "socialist realism," which is adopted as binding for all members of the union.

August 29: Pasternak delivers a speech at the congress.

August 31: In an article in *Pravda*, Gorky suggests that a group of writers, including Pasternak, go to Georgia to arrange for the translation of Georgian poetry into Russian.

September: On their way back to Moscow from the congress, Pasternak and his wife spend almost a month at the Odoevo rest home.

Early fall: Makes trip to Georgia.

Publications: *A Tale* (Leningrad); single-volume edition of *Selected Verse* (Moscow); second edition of *Second Birth*.

1935   March: Titian Tabidze and Paolo Iashvili visit Moscow.

Late spring: Pasternak stays in sanatorium near Moscow, under treatment for nervous condition caused by acute and prolonged insomnia. He is ordered to leave for Paris to take part in the International Congress of Writers for the Defense of Culture (June 21–25) as a representative of the Soviet Writers' Union.

June: Leaves by train with Isaac Babel. Has one-day stopover in Berlin, where he sees his sister Josephine and brother-in-law. Arrives in Paris.

June 24: Delivers much-applauded speech at congress.

Goes to Meudon to visit Tsvetaeva. Ac-

companies her on excursion to Saint-Gilles-sur-Vie. Sees Russian artist Iurii Annenkov.

June–July: Returns by boat via England. His condition worsens. In Leningrad is too ill to join other writers on the train to Moscow. Zinaida Nikolaevna stays with him in Leningrad until he is better.

Summer: Stays in various rest homes.

October 6: Writes to a friend: "I am still far from well, but I have made up my mind to pay no attention to my heart, my liver, my sleep, or my nerves."

Publications: *Poets of Georgia*, translated by Pasternak and Nikolai Tikhonov; Czech-language editions of *A Safe-Conduct*, with a preface by Roman Jakobson, and of a collection of verse, *Lyrika*, translated by Joseph Hora (Prague). Second enlarged edition of *Verse* (Moscow).

1936   Moves into No. 72 in the apartment house of the Union of Writers, 17 Lavrushinskii Lane, Moscow, which he will keep until his death.

February: Participates in the Plenary Session of Board of Union of Writers in Minsk. In speech "On Modesty and Boldness," replies to Aleksandr Bezymenskii, who has criticized him for not traveling and reading his poetry.

March 5: At the home of Vsevolod Meierkhold talks with André Malraux, who then leaves to see Gorky in the Crimea.

June 18: Death of Gorky.

Summer: Pasternak, Akhmatova, and others send money to the Mandelstams. Pasternak visits Georgia, works on the poetic cycle "Travel Notes." Stays in the dacha he has been assigned in the Writers' Village in Peredelkino, where he will spend the summers until 1941 and live most of the year thereafter.

Height of the "Great Purge," which counts among its victims Mikhail Koltsov, Babel, and Pilniak.

Publications: Third, enlarged edition of 1933 one-volume *Verse*.

1937   Nikolai Zabolotskii is sent to a concentration camp.

Early May: Marshal Mikhail Tukhachevskii is arrested.

May: Date of the last surviving poem by Mandelstam, whose exile sentence ends on May 16.

June 12: Execution of Marshal Tukhachevskii.

June: Pasternak refuses to sign with other writers a letter to *Pravda* condemning actions of Marshal Tukhachevskii and other generals accused of participating in a military conspiracy. Without his knowledge, his colleagues add his name to list of signatories.

July 21: Titian Tabidze is arrested. He dies in a few weeks as a result of torture.

July 22: Upon learning of Tabidze's arrest, Iashvili commits suicide.

August 28: Pasternak writes long letter of condolence to Iashvili's widow. From then on, gives the Tabidze and Iashvili families all the material and moral support he can.

August: Nikolai Kliuev dies in Siberia.

October: A new edition of *Georgian Lyric Poets* is released for publication (Moscow), much shorter than the 1935 edition—all the poems by Tabidze and Iashvili have been omitted.

December 31: Birth of Leonid, Pasternak's second son.

Publications: *1905, Lieutenant Schmidt* (Moscow). Short prose "Iz novogo romana o 1905 g." in *Literaturnaia gazeta*.

1938   Continuation of the Great Purge, with the arrests of many writers.

March 14: Execution of Bukharin, Pasternak's erstwhile protector.

May 2: Mandelstam's second and last arrest, deportation to Siberia.

December: Publication in *Literaturnaia gazeta* of two novelistic fragments: "A District Behind the Front" and "A December Day 1905."

1939   June 12: Tsvetaeva returns to the Soviet Union after seventeen years as an émigrée.

August 23: Pasternak's mother dies in Streatham Hill, London.

September: Declaration of war makes it impossible for Leonid Pasternak to return to the Soviet Union.

1940   Spring: Pasternak reads his translation of *Hamlet* to enthusiastic audiences in overcrowded halls at Moscow State University on Herzen Street and at Writers' Club on Vorovskii Street.

Publications: Translations (works of Kleist, Shakespeare, Raleigh, Byron, Keats, Sándor Petöfi, Becher, Hans Sachs).

1941   Spring: Translation of *Hamlet* completed. Excerpt from *Romeo and Juliet* published (issued in book form in 1943). Continues work on his long prose text (to become *Doctor Zhivago*).

June 22: Germany invades the Soviet Union.

Early summer: Evacuation of Pasternak family and families of other writers to Chistopol, in the Urals. Pasternak returns to Moscow.

August 31: Marina Tsvetaeva commits suicide in Elabuga, a small town near Chistopol.

Late September: Pasternak takes Andrian (Adik) Neigauz (son of Zinaida Nikolaevna by her first marriage), terminally ill with tuberculosis of the spine, to clinic in Nizhnii Ufalei, Cheliabinsk Region.

October: Moscow is threatened by German armies. Pasternak undergoes training for civil-defense service.

Fall: Continues to work on his translation of Shakespeare whenever possible in Moscow and Chistopol.

November 4: His friend and next-door neighbor in Peredelkino, Aleksandr

Afinogenov, is killed by a bomb in Moscow.

December: Completes translation of *Romeo and Juliet*. Has financial difficulties.

Winter, 1941–42: Stays with his family in Chistopol.

Publications: Both the full edition of his translation of Shakespeare's *Hamlet* and shorter edition, *Scenes from the Tragedy "Hamlet"*; new edition of his translation of Kleist's *The Broken Jug* (Moscow and Leningrad); English translation of *The Childhood of Liuvers* appears under the title *Childhood* in Singapore.

1942   Winter: Receives advance from Novosibirsk Theater for play he is writing. Writes two poems to the memory of Tsvetaeva.

February 26: All members of the writers' colony in Chistopol attend Pasternak's reading of excerpts from his translation of *Romeo and Juliet*.

Spring: Returns to Peredelkino.

Late October: After stay in Chistopol, returns to Moscow for a few weeks. Is commissioned to do more translations. Manuscript of *Early Trains* is delivered to publishing house.

October 23: Reads his translation of *Romeo and Juliet* at the All-Union Theatrical Society in Moscow.

December 15: At a poetry evening in Writers' Club in Moscow attended by all of literary Moscow Pasternak reads from his latest verse, soon to appear in book form as *Early Trains*.

Ca. December 20: Leaves Moscow for Chistopol.

Winter, 1942–43: Stays with family in Chistopol.

1943   February: Soviet victory in Stalingrad.

Summer: The Pasternaks resettle in Moscow.

Zinaida Nikolaevna restores their property in Peredelkino and the apartment on Lavrushinskii Lane.

August–September: With other writers visits the front near Orel, an experience soon described in his documentary story "A Trip to the Front."

Publications: Collection of poetry *Early Trains* (nine years after the appearance of his last book).

1944   Soviet territory freed from Germans.

Publications: Cycle of poems "Spring 1944"; second translation of *Romeo and Juliet*; translation of Shakespeare's *Antony and Cleopatra*.

1945   Death of Zinaida Nikolaevna's son Andrian Neigauz.

Early February: Publication of his collection of poetry *The Breadth of the Earth*, which is adversely received by official critics but promptly sells out.

May 8: Victory of the Allies over Germany.

May 31: Death of Boris's father, in Oxford.

October 21: In response to official invitation, stays two weeks in Tbilisi, Georgia, to participate in celebrations in honor of the one hundredth anniversary of the death of the poet Baratashvili.

Publications: Translation of Shakespeare's *Othello* (two different editions, Moscow); *The Collected Prose Works* (*A Safe-Conduct*, "Apelles' Mark," "Aerial Ways," "Letters from Tula," "The Childhood of Liuvers"), translated into English by L. Drummond (London); *Selected Verse and Poems* (from *Over the Barriers*; *My Sister, Life*; *Second Birth*; *Early Trains*; *The Breadth of the Earth*; *The Year 1905*; *Lieutenant Schmidt*, Moscow).

1946   Makes a public appearance with other writers at a literary evening in the Hall of Columns in Moscow, reads his poetry, and receives an ovation.

June: Writes introduction to his translations from Shakespeare.

August 1: Beginning of "Zhdanov era" (*zhdanovshchina*): Secretary of Central Committee Andrei Zhdanov launches campaign against "cosmopolitanism" in Soviet arts and letters.

Pasternak claims he has radiculitis, unable to attend meeting of Board of Union of Writers at which Anna Akhmatova and Mikhail Zoshchenko are condemned.

First Secretary of Union of Writers Aleksandr Fadeev makes speech criticizing Pasternak's work.

October: Pasternak has first encounter with thirty-four-year-old Olga Vsevolodovna Ivinskaia in the editorial offices of *Novyi mir*, where she works.

Fall: Calls daily on Ivinskaia, first at *Novyi mir*, then at her apartment.

Winter, 1946–47: Regime adopts a hard-line attitude: a campaign is conducted against "decadent" and "cosmopolitan" writers.

1947   Spring: Tells Ivinskaia of his love for her. Torn between feelings for his family and love for her.

Has financial difficulties. Reopens negotiations with Detgiz Publishing House concerning a translation of *King Lear* (fall, 1945 contract had remained inactive because of Pasternak's involvement in other matters).

April: Pasternak and Ivinskaia accept their love for each other.

Obtains contract for translation of Goethe's *Faust*, easing financial difficulties.

Publications: *Georgian Poets*.

1948   Works on *Doctor Zhivago*.

January 30: Reads to actors in a Moscow theater his translation of *Antony and Cleopatra* and selections from "The Poems of Iurii Zhivago."

February 23: During literary evening, "For Peace, for Democracy," at Polytechnical Museum, audience stands and applauds him as he comes to rostrum. After he reads his poetry, repeated shouts for encore.

Summer: Spends summer in town with Ivinskaia.

August 31: Death of Zhdanov, who had launched attacks against Pasternak and Akhmatova.

Recantation and self-criticism by Fadeev and others who had earlier attacked Pasternak.

Publications: Translation of Shakespeare's *King Henry the Fourth*, parts 1 and 2 (Moscow); Translation of Petöfi's *Selected Works*.

1949   October 6: At 8:00 P.M., Ivinskaia is arrested in her apartment on Potapov Street and is taken to Lubianka Prison, where she is held for several months for interrogation.

Publications: Translation of *King Lear* published both by GIKhL (Moscow) and by Detgiz (Moscow and Leningrad). Two-volume *William Shakespeare in Boris Pasternak's Translation* (Moscow).

1950   Soon after Ivinskaia's arrest, Pasternak suffers heart attack.

Supports Ivinskaia's family during her absence.

Work on *Doctor Zhivago*, at which he had been busy since 1945, is interrupted.

Mid-autumn: Suffers another heart attack.

1951   After spending a year in Lubianka Prison—during which she refuses to incriminate Pasternak—Ivinskaia is transferred to a concentration camp.

Publications: Translation of Shakespeare's tragedies (Moscow and Leningrad).

1952   Summer: Writes poetry.

September: Suffers from insomnia. Suffers serious heart infarct.

November–December: Recovers in hospital.

1953   January: Suffers serious heart infarction.

March: Spends some time in Bolshevo Rest Home, near Moscow.

March 5: Death of Stalin. With ensuing relaxations, Pasternak resumes work on *Doctor Zhivago*.

Ivinskaia is amnestied. Pasternak declares that they will live together.

Spring: Back at work at his desk in Peredelkino.

September: Adheres to a "carefully regulated rigid regime of work." Is "immersed" in his novel, which he considers his "sole business," at the expense of poetry.

November: Publication of his translation of Goethe's *Faust*.

1954   April: Journal *Znamia* publishes ten poems from *Doctor Zhivago* with a foreword by the author that the writing of the novel is expected to be completed in the summer. The poems receive adverse reaction from the press.

Summer: Spends summer with Ivinskaia in Moscow—her children stay with an aunt in Sukhinichi.

Fall: Ivinskaia gives birth to stillborn child. Goes to work for Goslitizdat as translator-consultant.

Winter: Publication of Ehrenburg's novel *The Thaw*.

1955   While on tour in the United States, Soviet journalist V. Poltoratskii vehemently attacks Pasternak.

Begins poems that will be part of the collection *When Skies Clear*.

Fall: After renting several other dachas, Ivinskaia moves to one belonging to Sergei Kuzmich. There she holds open house on Sundays with Pasternak.

Manuscript of *Doctor Zhivago* completed.

Publications: *A Safe-Conduct*, in *Opalnye povesti* (Sbornik), edited by V. A. Aleksandrova (New York).

1956   Begins work on *Sketch for an Autobiography* intended as a preface to a col-

lected edition of his works, including *Doctor Zhivago* and recent poetry.

February 25: Nikita Khrushchev denounces Stalin at a secret session of the Twentieth Party Congress.

April: *Znamia* publishes part 2 of Ehrenburg's *The Thaw*; the thaw he predicts seems to be materializing.

Pasternak sends manuscript of *Doctor Zhivago* to the editorial board of the journal *Novyi mir*.

The Italian Communist Sergio d'Angelo, who is to leave the party at the time of the Hungarian Revolution, hears in Moscow of the impending publication of Pasternak's book in the Soviet Union. He makes contact with the author and—in his capacity as representative of Italian publisher Feltrinelli—reaches an agreement on the publication of the book in the West.

May: Pasternak doubts the possibility of publication of the novel in Soviet Union.

Suicide of novelist and former Secretary of Union of Writers Aleksandr Fadeev.

June: D'Angelo delivers a typescript of *Doctor Zhivago* to Feltrinelli in Berlin.

September: Purported date of letter addressed by the editorial board of *Novyi mir* to Pasternak explaining its refusal to publish *Doctor Zhivago* and calling the novel "an unqualified apology" for an egocentric member of the old intelligentsia.

Hélène Peltier meets writers Konstantin Fedin, Vsevolod Ivanov, and Anna Ahkmatova and pianists Sviatoslav Richter, and Genrikh Neigauz at the Pasternaks.

A collection of "New Verses" appears in *Znamia*.

Fall: A contract is signed with the State Publishing House for an abridged version of *Doctor Zhivago*.

November: For several months Pasternak's incoming and outgoing mail is intercepted.

December: Pasternak falls ill; plans for publication of *Doctor Zhivago* are postponed. Spends winter in Kremlin clinic and asks Feltrinelli to delay publication for six months.

1957 January–March: Revises his translation of Schiller's *Maria Stuart* for the stage. Falls ill; has extensive stay in clinic. Writes poem "In Hospital."

March: Again is forced to write Feltrinelli to ask for delay of publication of *Doctor Zhivago*. Feltrinelli sets the beginning of September as the latest date for the Italian edition. He has concluded or is about to conclude the contracts transferring translation rights for the novel to various foreign publishers (Gallimard in France, Kuno Fischer in Germany, and Collins in England).

Spring: Recovering from his illness, Pasternak continues writing *Sketch for an Autobiography*.

Attends a performance of Bertolt Brecht's *The Caucasian Chalk Circle*, in which Brecht's widow Helene Weigel performs.

June: Khrushchev succeeds in eliminating his rivals. The outward liberalism, that had reigned for two or three years in literature and the arts disappears.

The secretary-general of the party sharply criticizes Dudintsev.

Summer: On the advice of his doctors, rests in the sanatorium of the Academy of Sciences in Uzkoe, near Moscow.

Party officials decide not to publish *Doctor Zhivago* in the Soviet Union.

Kornelii Zelinskii continues revision of *Doctor Zhivago* with a view to submitting an abridged version for publication in the Soviet Union. Meanwhile, Aleksei Surkov, secretary of the Writers' Union, tries to prevent publication of the novel in Italy.

Pasternak is persuaded by Zelinskii and other writers to send telegram to Feltrinelli asking him to stop publication and return the manuscript.

Feltrinelli refuses to suspend Italian publication.

Two leading members of the Italian Communist party and Aleksei Surkov, who hints that something may happen to Pasternak if publication proceeds, continue to press Feltrinelli to abandon the project. By this time, Feltrinelli is determined to continue and decides to hold back publication for only a few weeks.

Pasternak sends note to Feltrinelli by an Italian writer, telling him to use his own judgment in the matter.

August 30: Writes to Nina Tabidze, rejoicing over publication in Leningrad and Tbilisi of her poetry in "The Poet's Library" series.

Fall: In spite of treatment in Uzkoe, his condition remains very serious (his main ailment is nerve inflammation in his leg).

November 10: *L'Espresso* publishes the first installment of a series of extracts from the novel, choosing almost exclusively the anti-Soviet passages.

November 22: The first edition of the novel appears in Italian under the title *Il Dottor Živago*. The printing of 6,000 is immediately sold out and is followed by two more printings before the end of the month.

November 27: At a Moscow meeting of Creative Intelligentsia, First Secretary of Writers' Union Surkov protests attempts "to canonize the work of Pasternak" and others, such as Tsvetaeva.

Publications: Translation of Goethe's *Faust* (parts 1 and 2, Moscow); Twelve poems in *Anthology of Soviet Russian Poetry in Two Volumes* (Moscow).

1958 *Doctor Zhivago* appears in England, the United States, Germany, France, Spain, Portugal, Brazil, Sweden, Denmark, Norway, Finland, Israel, Turkey, and Iran.

Winter: Pasternak stays in hospital until May.

April: Carries on correspondence with Renate Schweitzer.

May–June: After leaving hospital, writes several poems.

August: Is asked by government to visit various construction sites so that he can write about them later. Declines because of leg trouble.

October 14: Death of poet Nikolai Zabolotskii.

October 23: Pasternak awarded the Nobel Prize for Literature for *Doctor Zhivago*.

October 25: Union of Writers, Radio Moscow, and *Literaturnaia gazeta* announce and condemn the award. The secretary of the Swedish Academy receives Pasternak's message of acceptance.

October 26: David Zaslavskii's letter vehemently attacking Pasternak appears in *Pravda*.

October 27: Pasternak is deprived of the title of Soviet writer and is expelled from the Union of Writers.

October 29: Pasternak renounces the Nobel Prize; *Izvestiia* publishes the announcement by the Union of Writers on the expulsion of Pasternak.

October 30: The International PEN Club and a group of British writers plead with the Union of Soviet Writers to protect Pasternak.

October 31: Eight hundred writers of the Moscow branch of the Writers' Union appeal to the government to deprive Pasternak of his Soviet citizenship; Khrushchev receives a letter from Pasternak with plea not to expel him from Russia.

November 1: *Literaturnaia gazeta* devotes a full page to anti-Pasternak letters.

November 2: Tass announces that if Pasternak wishes to receive the prize in person the government will not prevent him from leaving the country.

November 6: Pasternak's letter of No-

vember 5, in which he acknowledges his "mistakes," is published in *Pravda*. Direct attacks seem to end, but Pasternak is kept under close surveillance, and doctor is sent to stay with him.

Begins work on dramatic trilogy *A Blind Beauty*.

Other Publications: *Poems About Georgia: Georgian Poets* (Tbilisi; only three thousand copies are sold); Translation of Schiller's *Maria Stuart*; *Sketch for an Autobiography* in foreign languages.

1959   February 11: *Daily Mail* publishes Pasternak's poem "The Nobel Prize." Shortly thereafter Pasternak is summoned to court and questioned on a treason charge; is released after a day's interrogation.

Renewed political pressure on Pasternak; he stops seeing foreign visitors.

February–March: During British Prime Minister Harold Macmillan's visit to Moscow, the Pasternaks comply with a request by the authorities that they stay away from the capital. They fly to Tbilisi, where they visit Nina Tabidze. For three months all of Pasternak's mail disappears.

April: Mikhail Sholokhov denounces Pasternak in a press conference in London.

May: Government surveillance of Pasternak lessens somewhat.

Summer: Unable to receive royalties from the West, Pasternak does translations to support his family.

August: Pasternak again receives royalties for foreign plays being performed in his translations.

September 11: Pasternak's first public appearance since the awarding of the Nobel Prize: he attends a concert in Moscow by the New York Philharmonic under the direction of Leonard Bernstein. He has a long conversation with Bernstein, which leads to a friendly correspondence.

Fall: His health declines. He gives the rights for the first performance of *The*

Blind Beauty to Stockholm's Drama-tikse Theater.

Works on *The Blind Beauty* and a translation of Juliusz Słowacki's *Maria Stuart*.

Publications: Last collection of poems, *When Skies Clear*; *Doctor Zhivago* (in the Netherlands, France—in Polish; in India—in Hindustani and Gujarati; in Egypt, and in Japan); abridged editions (in Vietnam and Taiwan); Russian-language edition by Société d'Édition et d' impression mondiale (Paris); *An Autobiographical Sketch* (*Sketch for an Autobiography*) in Germany and England; last edition of *Poems About Georgia and Georgian Poets*.

1960   Early Spring: Pasternak looks forward to coming visit of German friend Renate Schweitzer.

Complains to Schweitzer in a letter that he is unable to progress with his work.

Easter dinner at Peredelkino, attended by Renate Schweitzer, Nina Tabidze, and Genrikh Neigauz and his wife.

April–May: Bedridden for three weeks in extreme pain.

May: Early in month Pasternak suffers from series of blackouts.

May 17: Pasternak has severe attack, diagnosed as heart attack.

May 27: Pasternak's illness diagnosed as lung cancer; tumor has already spread to heart.

May 30: Pasternak dies at 11:40 P.M.

June 1: *Literatura i zhizn* carries a four-line announcement of the poet's death by the Board of the Literary Fund.

June 2: *Literaturnaia gazeta* carries the same announcement. Pasternak's funeral held at 4:00 P.M. in Peredelkino.

Mid-August: Ivinskaia arrested.

Early September: Ivinskaia's daughter arrested.

December 7: Trial of Ivinskaia and daughter.

December 12: Ivinskaia and daughter deported to Siberia.

Publications: Essay (in German) on Chopin. Fourth edition of translation of *Faust*. English edition of *When Skies Clear*, with parallel texts (London).

Appendix 2

Chronology of Pasternak's Works

1914	*Bliznets v tuchakh* (*Twin in the Clouds*)	1931	*Okhrannaia gramota* (*A Safe-Conduct*) *Spektorskii* (*Spektorskii*)
1915	*Temy i variatsii* (*Themes and Variations*)	1932	*Vtoroe rozhdenie* (*Second Birth*)
1916	"Istoriia odnoi kontraoktavy" ("History of a Counter-Octave"; published in 1974)	1934	*Povest* (*A Tale*; published as *The Last Summer*)
1917	*Poverkh barerov* (*Over the Barriers*)	1937	"Iz novogo romana o 1905 gode" ("From a New Novel About the Year 1905")

1914   *Bliznets v tuchakh* (*Twin in the Clouds*)

1915   *Temy i variatsii* (*Themes and Variations*)

1916   "Istoriia odnoi kontraoktavy" ("History of a Counter-Octave"; published in 1974)

1917   *Poverkh barerov* (*Over the Barriers*)

1918   "Bezliube" ("Without Love")

"Pisma iz Tuly" ("Letters from Tula"; published in 1922)

"Detstvo Liuvers" ("The Childhood of Liuvers"; published in 1923)

1922   *Sestra moia—zhizn: leto 1917 goda* (*My Sister, Life: Summer, 1917*)

"Neskolko polozhenii" ("Some Tenets")

1923   "Apellesova cherta" ("Apelles' Mark"; published in 1918)

1924   "Vozdushnye puti" ("Aerial Ways")

Vysokaia bolezn (*High Malady*)

1925   *Rasskazy* (*Short Stories*)

1927   *Deviatsot piatyi god* (*The Year 1905*; contains "The Year 1905" and "Lieutenant Schmidt")

1931   *Okhrannaia gramota* (*A Safe-Conduct*)

Spektorskii (*Spektorskii*)

1932   *Vtoroe rozhdenie* (*Second Birth*)

1934   *Povest* (*A Tale*; published as *The Last Summer*)

1937   "Iz novogo romana o 1905 gode" ("From a New Novel About the Year 1905")

1938   "Uezd v tylu" ("A District Behind the Lines")

1939   "Nadmennyi nishchii" ("The Arrogant Pauper")

"Tetia Olia" ("Aunt Olga")

1943   *Na rannikh poezdakh* (*Early Trains*)

1945   *Zemnoi prostor* (*The Breadth of the Earth*)

1957   *Doktor Zhivago* (*Doctor Zhivago*)

1958   *Avtobiograficheskii ocherk* (*Sketch for an Autobiography*; published in England as *An Essay in Autobiography* and in the United States as *I Remember: Sketch for an Autobiography*)

1959–60   *Kogda razguliaetsia* (*When Skies Clear*)

Slepaia krasavitsa (*The Blind Beauty;* published in 1969)

Abbreviations Used in Notes

See Bibliography for full citations of works.

WORKS BY PASTERNAK

Doctor Zhivago	*DZh*
Doktor Zhivago (Russian-language edition)	*Doktor Zh*
I Remember: Sketch for an Autobiography (in the text referred to as *Sketch for an Autobiography*)	*IR*
Letters to Georgian Friends	*LGF*
A Safe-Conduct	*SC*
Sochineniia (*Works*; three-volume edition, Ann Arbor, 1961)	*Works*
Stikhotvoreniia i poemy (*Longer Poetry and Poems*; Moscow, 1965)	*STIKHP*

WORKS BY OTHERS

Aleksandr Gladkov, *Vstrechi s Pasternakom* (*Meetings with Pasternak*)	*Vstrechi*
Olga Ivinskaya, *A Captive of Time*	*CAPT*
Part 1 (*Grani* 60 [1960])	*KROT 1*
Part 2 (*Grani* 63 [1967])	*KROT 2*

Iurii Krotkov, "Pasternaki"	
Part 1 (*Grani* 60 [1960])	*KROT 1*
Part 2 (*Grani* 63 [1967])	*KROT 2*
L[eonid] O[sipovich] Pasternak, *Zapisi raznykh* let (*Notes of Various Years*)	*ZAP*

RUSSIAN PERIODICALS FREQUENTLY CITED

For the convenience of the reader, in the text some of the titles are cited in English.

Izvestiia (*News*)
Krasnaia nov (*Red Virgin Soil*)
Literatura i iskusstvo (*Literature and Art*)
Literaturnaia gazeta (*Literary Gazette*)
Molodaia gvardiia (*Young Guard*)
Na postu (*On Guard*)
Na literaturnom postu (*On Literary Guard*)
Novyi mir (*New World*)
Novyi Lef (*New Lef*)
Pechat i revoliutsiia (*Press and Revolution*)
Pravda (*Truth*)
Voprosy literatury (*Questions of Literature*)
Znamia (*Banner*)
Zvezda (*Star*)

Notes

Note: Translations of titles of works appear in the Bibliography

PREFACE

1. Boris Pasternak, "Gamlet," *Doktor Zh*, p. 532; "Hamlet," *DZh*, p. 523.
2. Boris Pasternak, "Byt znamenitym nekrasivo," *STIKHP*, p. 447.
3. L. Fleishman, "K kharakteristike rannego Pasternaka," *Russkaia literatura* 12 (1975): 80.
4. Pasternak, "Byt znamenitym nekrasivo," p. 448; Boris Pasternak to J. de Proyart, August 20, 1959, in Jacqueline de Proyart, *Pasternak*, pp. 37–38; (hereafter BP/J. de Proyart, etc.); BP/ Hermann Bauer, April 17, 1959 (unpublished).
5. BP/Titian and Nina Tabidze, November 6, 1933, in Boris Pasternak, *LGF*, p. 51.
6. The December, 1962, issue of the journal *Novyi mir* in which this short novel was printed actually appeared early in 1963.
7. John Strachey, "Pasternak's Children," *Observer*, May 5, 1963.

CHAPTER I

1. Boris Pasternak, *IR*, pp. 40–41.
2. Boris Pasternak, *STIKHP*, p. 426 (my translation).
3. Nadezhda Mandelstam, *Hope Against Hope*, p. 154 (hereafter cited as *Hope*).
4. Pasternak, *IR*, p. 20.
6. Leonid Osipovich Pasternak, "Vier Fragmente aus meiner Selbstbiographie," in Max Osborn, *Leonid Pasternak*, p. 58; "Mastityi L. Pasternak," *Rubezh* 28 (Kharbin, June 1, 1933) (my translation).
7. Lydia Pasternak Slater, "Letter to the Editor," *New York Times Book Review*, October 29, 1961, p. 50.
8. L. Pasternak, *ZAP*, p. 59.

9. B. Pasternak, *IR*, pp. 21, 23, 26–27, 31.
10. Ibid., pp. 32, 26 (translation modified).
11. Ibid., p. 20.
12. Ibid., p. 31; BP/J. de Proyart, May 2, 1959, in Boris Pasternak, *Works*, 1:xi.
13. B. Pasternak, *IR*, pp. 24–25, 40–41.
14. Ibid., p. 22 (translation modified).
15. Boris Pasternak, *SC*, p. 22.
16. *SC*, p. 22.
17. B. Pasternak, *IR*, pp. 20–21.
18. Guy de Mallac, "A Russian Impressionist: Leonid Osipovich Pasternak, 1862–1945," *California Slavic Studies* 10 (1977): 99–100; L. Pasternak, "Vier Fragmente," pp. 86–90; L. O. Pasternak, "My Meetings with Tolstoy," *Russian Review* 19 (April, 1960): 122–31; L. Pasternak, *ZAP*, pp. 184–86.
19. B. Pasternak, *IR*, p. 17 (translation modified).
20. Ibid., pp. 27–28; L. Pasternak, *ZAP*, pp. 192–98.
21. B. Pasternak, *SC*, p. 21; L. Pasternak, "Vier Fragmente," pp. 94–106; Rilke/Sophie Schill, May 20, 1900, quoted in Christopher J. Barnes, "Boris Pasternak and Rainer Maria Rilke: Some Missing Links," *Forum for Modern Language Studies* 8 (January, 1972): 61–78.
22. A. von Gronicka, "Rilke and the Pasternaks: A Biographical Note," *Germanic Review*, December, 1952, p. 268.
23. Ingeborg Schnack, *Rainer Maria Rilke: Chronik seines Lebens und seines Werkes*, 1:256.
24. B. Pasternak, *SC*, p. 29.
25. BP/parents, 1936, quoted by Lydia Pasternak Slater, trans., in Introduction, Boris Pasternak, *Fifty Poems*, p. 16.
26. B. Pasternak, *IR*, pp. 33–34; Nadezhda Mandelstam, *Hope Abandoned*, trans. Max Hayward, p. 79.
27. G. Kurlov, "O Pasternake," *Russkaia mysl*, no. 1288 (November 18, 1958) (my translation).
28. Boris Pasternak, *DZh*, p. 120.

CHAPTER 2

1. Tsvetaeva/L. O. Pasternak, October 11, 1927, quoted in "Pisma Mariny Tsvetaevoi," *Novyi mir*, April, 1969, p. 202; Marina Tsvetaeva, *Neizdannye pisma*, p. 252.

2. Boris Pasternak, *IR*, p. 76; BP/parents, 1936, quoted by Lydia Pasternak Slater, trans., in Introduction, Boris Pasternak, *Fifty Poems*, p. 16.

3. Tsvetaeva/L. O. Pasternak, October 11, 1927, quoted in "Pisma Mariny Tsvetaevoi," *Novyi mir*, April, 1969, p. 202; Marina Tsvetaeva, *Neizdannye pisma*, p. 252.

4. Leonid Osipovich Pasternak, "Vier Fragmente aus meiner Selbstbiographie," in Max Osborn, *Leonid Pasternak*, p. 44.

5. Ibid.; BP/Hermann Bauer, April 17, 1959, unpublished (in Bauer's possession).

6. L. Pasternak, *ZAP*, p. 11.

7. Ibid., p. 13.

8. Ibid., p. 16.

9. Ibid., pp. 30–31.

10. Ibid., pp. 38–41, 45–51.

11. Guy de Mallac, "A Russian Impressionist: Leonid Osipovich Pasternak, 1862–1945," *California Slavic Studies* 10 (1977): 102.

12. Ibid.

13. L. Pasternak, *ZAP*, p. 33.

14. O. Bachmann, *Rosa Koffmann: Eine biographische Skizze, nebst Auszug einiger Rezensionen*, pp. 18–25.

15. Ibid., pp. 18–25.

16. *Illustriertes Extra Blatt* (Vienna), April 20, 1883, quoted in Serge Levitsky, "Rose Koffman-Pasternak: la mère du poète," *Slavic and East-European Studies* (Montreal) 8 (1963): 73–80.

17. L. Pasternak, *ZAP*, pp. 104, 151–52.

18. Josephine Pasternak, "Last Years," in *Leonid Pasternak, 1862–1945*, catalogue of exhibition of March–May, 1969.

19. B. Pasternak, *IR*, p. 25.

20. Boris Pasternak, *SC*, p. 36.

21. Cf. *Russkie Vedomosti*, March, 1895; October 14, 1895; January 17, 1904; October, 1908; and *Russkoe Slovo*, February, 1910.

22. Levitsky, "Rose Koffman-Pasternak," pp. 73–80.

23. J. Pasternak, "Last Years."

24. Leonid Pasternak, *ZAP*, p. 58.

25. C. M. Bowra, "Leonid Pasternak," in *Memorial Exhibition of Paintings and Drawings by Leonid Pasternak, 1862–1945*, catalogue of exhibition of April, 1958, in the Ashmolean Museum, Oxford University.

26. L. Pasternak, *ZAP*, pp. 225–26.

27. A. Sidorov, *Russkaia grafika nachala XX veka: Ocherki, istorii, i teorii*, p. 50.

28. Ibid., p. 105.

29. N. M. Moleva and E. M. Beliutin, *Russkaia khudozhestvennaia shkola vtoroi poloviny XIX–nachala XX veka*, p. 256.

30. "Boris Pasternak's Father," *Time*, August 24, 1962, p. 48; Igor Grabar, "Pamiati Leonida Pasternaka," *Sovetskoe Iskusstvo*, no. 28 (July 13, 1945), p. 4; L. Pasternak, *ZAP*, pp. 238–40.

31. M. F. Shemiakin, "Vospominaniia," in I. S. Zilbershtein and V. A. Samkov, eds., *Valentin Serov v vospominaniiakh, dnevnikakh, i perepiske sovremennikov*, 2:231.

32. V. A. Serov, *Perepiska, 1884–1911*, pp. 180–81; Moleva and Beliutin, *Russkaia . . . shkola*, p. 366; Zilbershtein and Samkov, *Valentin Serov*, 1:375.

33. S. A. Shcherbatov, *Khudozhnik v ushedshei Rossii*, p. 30; Moleva and Beliutin, *Russkaia . . . shkola*, p. 256.

34. Bowra, "Leonid Pasternak."

35. Ivan Lazarevskii, "L. O. Pasternak," *Novyi zhurnal dlia vsekh*, no. 9 (1909), p. 82.

36. BP/L. O. Pasternak, 1936, in B. Pasternak, *Fifty Poems*, Introduction, p. 16.

37. L. Pasternak, *ZAP*, p. 80.

38. Camilla Gray, *The Great Experiment: Russian Art, 1863–1922*, pp. 38, 45.

39. Ibid., p. 70.

40. Ibid., pp. 92, 128.

41. Val. Bulgakov, "L. O. Pasternak," *Iskusstvo*, July, 1961, p. 67.

42. L. Pasternak, *ZAP*, pp. 215–42.

43. De Mallac, "A Russian Impressionist," pp. 107–108; L. Pasternak, *ZAP*, pp. 95–96.

44. L. Pasternak, *ZAP*, p. 148; de Mallac, "A Russian Impressionist," p. 100.

45. L. S. Fleishman, "Marginalii k istorii russkogo avangarda," introductory article in N. M. Oleinikov, *Stikhotvoreniia*, p. 14; *Leonid Pasternak, 1862–1945*, catalogue of exhibition of works held at Crawford Centre, University of Saint Andrews (Scotland), January 28–February 25, 1978, pp. 11–13; BP/parents, 1936, in B. Pasternak, *Fifty Poems*, Introduction, p. 16.

46. Josephine Pasternak, "Three Suns," in Paul J. Mark, ed., *Die Familie Pasternak: Erinnerungen, Berichte*, p. 8; Anatolii Lunacharskii, "Ocherk rus-

skoi literatury revoliutsionnogo vremeni" [1963], *Literaturnoe Nasledstvo* 82 (1970):229; Anthony Brown, "Pasternak: On My Life Now," *London Daily Mail*, February 12, 1959; Jacqueline de Proyart, *Pasternak*, p. 19; BP/Leonid Pasternak, 1934, quoted in Mark, *Die Familie Pasternak*, p. 107; BP/O. Freidenberg, November 30, 1948, quoted in Elliott Mossmann, ed., "The Unpublished Letters of Boris Pasternak," *New York Times Magazine*, January 1, 1978, p. 29.

47. BP/Livanov, September 14, 1959, quoted in Olga Ivinskaya, *CAPT*, p. 303.

CHAPTER 3

1. Boris Pasternak, *SC*, p. 25.
2. Ibid., p. 74.
3. Iurii Annenkov, "Boris Pasternak," in *Dnevnik moikh vstrech: Tsikl tragedii*, 2:158.
4. Aleksandr Pasternak, "Leto 1903 goda: Iz zapisei o dalekom proshlom," *Novyi mir* 1 (January, 1972):203–11.
5. Pasternak, *SC*, p. 22.
6. Boris Pasternak, *IR*, pp. 36–37 (translation modified).
7. Ibid., pp. 37–38.
8. Faubion Bowers, *Scriabin: A Biography of the Russian Composer, 1870–1915*, 1:342, 2:9.
9. Pasternak, *SC*, p. 23.
10. Ibid., pp. 23–24.
11. Cf. Bowers, *Scriabin*, 2:11–13.
12. Ibid., pp. 13, 47–49, 53, 92, 95, 98–99, 118, 215.
13. Boris Pasternak, *DZh*, pp. 6–11, 40–43.
14. Bowers, *Scriabin*, 2:60.
15. Ibid., pp. 128–29.
16. Jacqueline de Proyart, "Une amitié d'enfance," *Boris Pasternak, 1890–1960: Colloque de Cerisy-la-Salle (11–14 septembre 1975)*, ed. Michel Aucouturier, p. 518.
17. Pasternak, *IR*, p. 54.
18. Cf. Boris Pasternak, *The Year 1905*, in *STIKHP*, pp. 245–70.
19. N. M. Moleva and E. M. Beliutin, *Russkaia khudozhestvennaia shkola vtoroi poloviny XIX–nachala XX veka*, p. 281; Leonid Pasternak, *ZAP*, p. 60.
20. Moleva and Beliutin, *Russkaia . . . shkola*, p. 281.
21. B. Pasternak, *IR*, p. 47.
22. Cf. L. Pasternak, *ZAP*, pp. 69–70; Moleva and Beliutin, *Russkaia . . . shkola*, p. 281.

23. Aleksandr Leonidovich Pasternak, letter of January 10, 1963, to author; Robert C. Williams, *Culture in Exile: Russian Émigrés in Germany, 1881–1941*, p. 14.
24. B. Pasternak, *IR*, p. 55.
25. All details concerning the stay in Berlin were supplied by Pasternak's brother (Aleksandr Leonidovich Pasternak, letter of January 10, 1963, to author); cf. B. Pasternak, *IR*, pp. 38–39; and Leonid Pasternak, *ZAP*, pp. 69–70.
26. B. Pasternak, *IR*, p. 39.
27. G. Kurlov, "O Pasternake," *Russkaia mysl*, no. 1288 (November 18, 1958).
28. B. Pasternak, *SC*, p. 28; B. Pasternak, *IR*, pp. 57–58.
29. B. Pasternak, *IR*, p. 59.
30. Ibid., pp. 58–61; B. Pasternak, *SC*, p. 29.
31. B. Pasternak, *IR*, pp. 56, 61; B. Pasternak, *SC*, p. 29; Christopher J. Barnes, "Boris Pasternak and Rainer Maria Rilke: Some Missing Links," *Forum for Modern Studies* 8 (January, 1972): 62.
32. Bowers, *Scriabin*, 2:174, 183, 190.
33. A. Pasternak, "Leto 1903 goda," pp. 206–207.
34. Bowers, *Scriabin*, 2:183, 194; James Lyons, "Alexander Skryabin," *American Record Guide*, January, 1972, p. 748.
35. B. Pasternak, *IR*, pp. 39–40.
36. Ibid., pp. 39, 41.
37. B. Pasternak, *SC*, pp. 27–28; B. Pasternak, *IR*, p. 41.
38. B. Pasternak, *IR*, pp. 41–42.
39. Kornei Chukovskii, "Boris Pasternak (1890–1960)," in Boris Pasternak, *Stikhi*, p. 18.
40. Kurlov, "O Pasternake."
41. Josephine Pasternak, "Three Suns," in Paul J. Mark, ed., *Die Familie Pasternak*, p. 8; Lydia Pasternak Slater, "La Poésie de Boris Pasternak," in ibid., p. 138; Lydia Pasternak Slater, "Prix Nobel de littérature 1958 (Notes fragmentaires)," in ibid., p. 162.
42. Christopher J. Barnes, "Letter to the Editor: Skryabin and Pasternak," *Musical Times* (London), January, 1972, p. 268.
43. Ibid.; Annenkov, "Boris Pasternak," pp. 157–58; Aleksandr Gladkov, *Vstrechi*, pp. 10, 31, 99; *Le Figaro littéraire*, October 3, 1959.
44. Barnes, "Skryabin and Pasternak," p. 268.
45. BP/S. N. Durylin, March 27, 1950, *Voprosy literatury* 9 (1970):168; Bowers, *Scriabin*, 1:320.

46. B. Pasternak, *SC*, p. 31.

47. BP/K. G. Loks, January 21, 1917, *Voprosy literatury* 9 (1972): 155.

48. Josephine Pasternak, "Neunzehnhundert-Zwolf," *Alma Mater Philippina* [Marburg], Winter, 1971–72, p. 40; Kurlov, "O Pasternake."

CHAPTER 4

1. Nikolai Aseev, "Melody or Intonation?" in Donald Davie and Angela Livingstone, eds., *Pasternak: Modern Judgements*, p. 79.

2. D. S. Mirsky, *A History of Russian Literature*, p. 503; Boris Pasternak, *IR*, pp. 62, 86; Boris Pasternak, *SC*, p. 31.

3. Pasternak, *IR*, pp. 48–49.

4. BP/unidentified fellow poet, fragment, n.d., *Paris Review* 24 (1960): 71.

5. Pasternak, *IR*, p. 49.

6. Ibid., p. 50.

7. Boris Pasternak, *DZh*, pp. 79–80, 160–61, 518.

8. Pasternak, *IR*, p. 52.

9. Hélène Peltier, as reported in Ig. Opishnia, "Ben Gurion osuzhdaet B. Pasternaka: Pasternak i molodezh," *Vozrozhdenie* 87 (1959): 144.

10. Henry Gifford, "Pasternak and the 'Realism' of Blok," *Oxford Slavonic Papers* 13 (1967): 96.

11. Pasternak, *IR*, p. 51.

12. Aleksandr Blok, *Sochineniia v dvukh tomakh*, (Moscow, 1955) 1:378.

13. Pasternak, *IR*, p. 68.

14. BP/S. N. Durylin, March 27, 1950, *Voprosy literatury* 9 (1972): 168.

15. D. Burliuk, A. Kruchenykh, V. Maiakovskii, and V. Khlebnikov, "Poshchechina obshchestvennomu vkusu" (December, 1912), in Vladimir Markov, ed., *Manifesty i programmy russkikh futuristov*, pp. 50–51.

16. Pasternak, *IR*, p. 58.

17. Rita Wright-Kovaleva, "Mayakovsky and Pasternak: Fragments of Reminiscence," *Oxford Slavonic Papers* 13 (1967): 123.

18. Boris Pasternak, "U sebia doma," *STIKHP*, pp. 144–45.

19. G. Kurlov, "O Pasternake," *Russkaia mysl*, no. 1288 (November 18, 1958).

20. Pasternak, *IR*, p. 57.

21. P. A. Zhurov, "Dve vstrechi s molodym Klychkovym," *Russkaia literatura* 2 (1971): 149.

22. Boris Pasternak, "Pervye opyty Borisa Pasternaka," ed. E. V. Pasternak, *Trudy po znakovym sistemam*, part 4, *Uchenye zapiski Tartuskogo gosudar-stvennogo universiteta*, no. 236 (1969), p. 264.

23. Boris Pasternak, *SC*, pp. 35, 38–39.

24. Ibid., p. 36.

25. Ibid., pp. 36–37.

26. Cf. Andrei Belyi, *Mezhdu dvukh revoliutsii*; Alfred Rammelmeyer, "Die Philipps-Universität zu Marburg in der russischen Geistesgeschichte und schönen Literatur," *Mitteilungen Universitätsbund Marburg* 2–3 (1957): 70–77.

27. See Ingeborg Schnack, *Marburg: Bild einer alten Stadt, Impressionen und Profile.*

28. B. Pasternak, *SC*, pp. 40–43.

29. BP/Hermann Bauer, April 17, 1959, unpublished (in Bauer's possession).

30. B. Pasternak, *SC*, p. 41.

31. Erika F. Sheikholeslami, "Pasternak's Unpublished Essay 'About the Object and Method of Psychology' and Its Relation to Pasternak's Aesthetics," paper delivered at the New England Slavic Conference, Amherst, Mass., April 15, 1978.

32. BP/Hermann Bauer, April 17, 1959, unpublished.

33. Sheikholeslami, "Pasternak's Unpublished Essay."

34. Julius Ebbinghaus, "Hermann Cohen als Philosoph und Publizist," *Archiv für Philosophie* 6 (1956): 109–22; Henri Dussort, *L'École de Marbourg*, ed. J. Vuillemin.

35. José Ortega y Gasset, "Meditación del Escorial" (1950), *Obras completas*, 2: 558.

36. José Ortega y Gasset, "Prólogo para alemanes," *Obras completas*, 8: 27.

37. B. Pasternak, *SČ*, p. 44.

38. Andrei Belyi, "Premudrost," *Urna* (Moscow, 1910), pp. 63–64 (my translation).

39. Nina Berberova, *The Italics Are Mine*, p. 201.

40. Jacqueline de Proyart/author, November 10, 1975; information received from I. D. Vysotskaia-Feldzer in 1964, 1975.

41. B. Pasternak, *SC*, p. 45.

42. Jacqueline de Proyart, "Une amitié d'enfance," *Boris Pasternak, 1890–1960: Colloque de Cerisy-la-Salle (11–14 septembre 1975)*, ed. Michel Aucouturier, p. 518.

43. Ibid., p. 519.

44. B. Pasternak, *SC*, p. 45.

45. B. Pasternak, *DZh*, p. 40.

46. Olga Ivinskaya, *CAPT*, pp. 12–13; B. Pasternak, *SC*, p. 48.

47. B. Pasternak, *SC*, p. 49.

48. Proyart, "Une amitié d'enfance," p. 518.

49. B. Pasternak, *SC*, pp. 52, 59.

50. Ibid., p. 59; cf. Fr. Grundlach, comp., *Catalogus Professorum Academiae Marburgensis, 1527–1910*, p. 299.

51. B. Pasternak, *SC*, p. 50; cf. V. Erlich, "Strasti razriady (Zametki o Marburge)," *Boris Pasternak, 1890–1960: Colloque de Cerisy-la-Salle (11–14 septembre 1975)*, pp. 281, 287. Pasternak made it clear that he began writing the poem under the immediate impact (*pod naporom*) of the refusal (conversation of January, 1957, with Proyart, conveyed to author).

52. Stanzas 1 and 4 were not included in the 1928 version of the poem; cf. Viktor Erlich, "Strasti razriady," and Olga Hughes, "Stikhotvorenie Marburg i tema 'vtorogo rozhdeniia' v tvorchestve Pasternaka," *Boris Pasternak, 1890–1960: Colloque de Cerisy-la-Salle (11–14 septembre 1975)*, pp. 281–302.

53. Boris Pasternak, "Marburg," *STIKHP*, pp. 107–109.

54. Vladimir Maiakovskii, "Kak delat stikhi?" ("How Verses Are Made"), *Polnoe sobranie sochinenii*, 12:93.

55. B. Pasternak, "Marburg," *STIKHP*, pp. 107–109.

56. Proyart, "Une amitié d'enfance," p. 519.

57. Ibid., p. 519.

58. Hughes, "Stikhotvorenie Marburg."

59. Andrei Siniavskii, remark made at *Boris Pasternak, 1890–1960: Colloque de Cerisy-la-Salle (11–14 septembre 1975)*.

60. B. Pasternak, *SC*, p. 55.

61. BP/K. G. Loks, July 15, 1912, unpublished (Pasternak family archive, Moscow).

62. Ibid., p. 62.

63. Hermann Bauer/BP, April 5, 1959, unpublished; cf. B. Pasternak, *SC*, p. 62.

64. BP/Hermann Bauer, April 17, 1959, unpublished (in Hermann Bauer's possession).

65. Georgii Adamovich, "Temy," in *Vozdushnye puti: Almanakh*, ed. R. N. Grynberg (New York: Chekhov Publishing House, 1960), 1:43.

66. René Le Senne, *Traité de caractérologie*.

67. Carl G. Jung, *Psychological Types*, trans. G. Godwin Baynes, pp. 181–82, 508–509, 567–69.

68. Boris Pasternak, *LGF*, p. 137.

69. Tsvetaeva/L. O. Pasternak, February 5, 1928, in Marina Tsvetaeva, *Neizdannye pisma*, p. 256.

70. Simon Karlinsky, *Marina Cvetaeva: Her Life and Art*, p. 25.

71. B. Pasternak, *IR*, p. 73; Josephine Pasternak, "Neunzehnhundert-Zwölf," *Alma Mater Philippina* [Marburg], Winter, 1971–72, p. 42.

72. Lucy Vogel, "Lightning Flashes of Art: Blok's Essays on Italy," *Italian Quarterly* 20 (Summer–Fall, 1976): 19–30.

73. B. Pasternak, *SC*, p. 71.

74. B. Pasternak, *IR*, p. 76.

CHAPTER 5

1. Iurii Annenkov, "Boris Pasternak," *Dnevnik moikh vstrech: Tsikl tragedii*, 2:152.

2. Boris Pasternak, *IR*, p. 76.

3. Ibid., pp. 76–77.

4. Jacqueline de Proyart, "Une amitié d'enfance," *Boris Pasternak, 1890–1960: Colloque de Cerisy-la-Salle (11–14 septembre 1975)*, ed. Michel Aucouturier, p. 518.

5. Lydia Pasternak, "Prix Nobel de littérature 1958," *Die Familie Pasternak*, p. 159; cf. Boris Pasternak, *SC*, pp. 30–31.

6. Boris Pasternak, review of Maiakovskii's *Prostoe kak mychanie*, "Kriticheskie etiudy," *Literaturnaia Rossiia*, March 19, 1965, pp. 18–19.

7. Pasternak, *IR*, p. 82; cf. "Uezd v tylu," *Works*, 3:330.

8. "Uezd v tylu," *Works*, 3:333; Elliot Mossmann, ed., "The Unpublished Letters of Boris Pasternak," *New York Times Magazine*, January 1, 1978, p. 24.

9. Pasternak, *IR*, p. 76.

10. Ibid., p. 56.

11. Boris Pasternak, "Pervye opyty Borisa Pasternaka," ed. E. V. Pasternak, *Trudy po znakovym sistemam, IV*.

12. Christopher J. Barnes, "Boris Pasternak and Rainer Maria Rilke: Some Missing Links," *Forum for Modern Studies* 8 (January, 1972):65.

13. Michel Aucouturier, *Pasternak par lui-même*, p. 32.

14. Angela Livingstone, "Pasternak i Rilke," *Boris Pasternak, 1890–1960: Colloque de Cerisy-la-Salle (11–14 septembre 1975)*, pp. 431–39.

15. Barnes, "Boris Pasternak and Rainer Maria Rilke," p. 66.

16. Rainer Maria Rilke, *Briefe aus Muzot 1921 bis 1926*, p. 364.

17. BP/Rilke, April 12, 1926, Rilke Archives in Fischerhude; see Barnes, "Boris Pasternak and Rainer Maria Rilke," pp. 67–71, 77–78; Boris Pasternak, Untitled article, *Chitatel i pisatel*, nos. 4–5 (February 11, 1928); Boris Pasternak, "Boris

Pasternak About Himself and His Readers," trans. and ed. Gleb Struve, *Slavic Review* 23 (March, 1964): 125–28.

18. Barnes, "Boris Pasternak and Rainer Maria Rilke," p. 76.

19. Pasternak, unpublished letter of December 10, 1955, quoted in ibid., p. 61.

20. Aucouturier, *Pasternak par lui-même*, p. 32.

21. Pasternak, *IR*, pp. 61–62.

22. Fedor Stepun, *Das Antlitz Russlands und das Gesicht der Revolution: Aus meinem Leben, 1884–1922*, p. 190.

23. Pasternak, *IR*, p. 62.

24. Central State Archive of Literature and Art (TSGALI), Archive Group 1085 (R. M. Glier), storage unit 1143, folio 8.

25. Boris Pasternak, *DZh*, pp. 67–68.

26. Pasternak, *IR*, p. 64.

27. L. Fleishman, "K kharakteristike rannego Pasternaka," *Russkaia literatura* 12 (1975): 82; Pasternak, *SC*, p. 35.

28. Vladimir Markov, *Russian Futurism: A History*, pp. 230–35; Pasternak, *IR*, pp. 78–79.

29. Pasternak, *IR*, p. 86.

30. Ibid., pp. 86–87; *Literaturnoe nasledstvo* 70 (1963): 296.

31. Boris Pasternak, *STIKHP*, p. 702.

32. Pasternak, *SC*, p. 81.

33. Nikolai Aseev, *Sobranie sochinenii v piati tomakh*, 1:8.

34. Ibid.; E. Mustangova, *Literaturnyi kritik* 12 (1935).

35. Nikolai Aseev, "Melody or Intonation," in Donald Davie and Angela Livingstone, eds., *Pasternak: Modern Judgements*, pp. 77–78; Christopher J. Barnes, "Boris Pasternak: A Review of Nikolai Aseev's Oksana (1916)," *Slavica Hierosolomytica* 1 (1977): 297–99.

36. Pasternak, *IR*, pp. 53, 106; Pasternak, *SC*, p. 81; Pasternak, "Drugu, zamechatelnomu tovarishchu," *Works*, 3:161–62; Barnes, "Boris Pasternak: A Review," pp. 299–301.

37. BP/Vladimir Pozner, 1929, *Le Monde*, November 15, 1969; Barnes, "Boris Pasternak: A Review," p. 298; Aleksandr Gladkov, *Vstrechi*, p. 34.

38. V. Katanian, *Maiakovskii: Literaturnaia khronika*, 4th ed., p. 43; Markov, *Russian Futurism*, pp. 241, 245.

39. Gladkov, *Vstrechi*, pp. 117, 128.

40. Viktor Shklovskii, *Gamburgskii shchet*, p. 19; Ilia Ehrenburg, "Otstaivat chelovecheskie tsennosti," *Sobranie sochinenii v deviati tomakh*, 6:604.

41. Pasternak, *SC*, p. 83; Vladimir Markov, *The Longer Poems of Velimir Khlebnikov*, pp. 16, 20, 205–206; Boris Iakovlev, "Poet dlia estetov (Zametki o Velimire Khlebnikove i formalizme v poezii)," *Novyi mir*, no. 5 (May, 1948), p. 211.

42. Iakovlev, "Poet dlia estetov," pp. 22–26; Osip Mandelstam, *O Poezii*, p. 47; L. Fleishman, "Marginaliia k istorii russkogo avangarda: Vstupitelnaia statia," in N. M. Oleinikov, *Stikhotvoreniia*, pp. 3–4; Christopher J. Barnes, "The Poetry of Boris Pasternak, with Special Reference to the Period 1913–1917," (diss., Cambridge University), pp. 245–68.

43. Pasternak, *IR*, pp. 91–93; Pasternak, *SC*, p. 79; Edward J. Brown, *Mayakovsky: A Poet in the Revolution*, pp. 131–32, 181; V. Koxhinov, "Dostoevskii ili geroi Dostoevskogo," *Voprosy literatury* 9 (1966): 108–109; Pasternak, *DZh*, p. 177.

44. Pasternak, *SC*, p. 83.

45. Barnes, *The Poetry of Boris Pasternak*, pp. 274–356.

46. Pasternak, *IR*, p. 96; Pasternak, *SC*, p. 87.

47. Pasternak, *IR*, pp. 79–80.

48. Ibid., p. 81.

49. Annenkov, "Boris Pasternak," 2:157.

50. Pasternak, *SC*, pp. 57–58.

51. L. Livshits, *Polutoraglazyi strelets*, p. 98.

52. Pasternak, *SC*, p. 85.

53. Konstantin Paustovsky, *The Story of a Life*, trans. Joseph Barnes, p. 276.

54. BP/parents, December 9, 1916, Mossmann, "The Unpublished Letters of Boris Pasternak," pp. 11–12.

55. Lydia Pasternak Slater, "Prix Nobel de littérature 1958 (Notes fragmentaires)," in Paul J. Mark, ed., *Die Familie Pasternak: Erinnerungen, Berichte*, p. 161; L. O. Pasternak, 1919 sketch, "Boris Pasternak Writing with a Cigarette in His Right Hand," no. 72, in *Leonid Pasternak, 1862–1945*, catalogue of exhibition at University of Saint Andrews (Scotland), January 28–February 25, 1978, p. 22.

CHAPTER 6

1. Marina Tsvetaeva, "Svetovoi liven: Poeziia vechnoi muzhestvennosti," *Epopeia* 1 (Berlin, February, 1922): 162.

2. Boris Pasternak, *STIKHP*, p. 631.

3. Nadezhda Mandelstam, *Hope*, p. 190.

4. BP/S. Chikovani, October 6, 1957, Boris Pasternak, *LGF*, pp. 166–67.

5. Cf. Roman Jakobson, "The Prose of the Poet Pasternak," in Donald Davie and Angela Livingstone, eds., *Pasternak: Modern Judgements*, p. 147.

6. A. D. Siniavskii, "Poeziia Pasternaka," Pasternak, *STIKHP*, p. 14.

7. Nadezhda Mandelstam, *Hope Abandoned*, pp. 331, 459; Tsvetaeva, "Svetovoi liven: Poeziia vechnoi muzhestvennosti," *Epopeia* 2 (1922): 10–33; Tsvetaeva/BP, November 19, 1922, in Marina Tsvetaeva, *Neizdannye pisma*, pp. 273–74; Osip Mandelstam, "Notes on Poetry," *Russian Literature Triquarterly* 6:418; D. S. Mirsky, *A History of Russian Literature*, p. 501.

8. Boris Pasternak, *SC*, p. 88.

9. Vera Aleksandrova, "Po literaturnym adresam poeta," *Vozdushnye puti: Almanakh*, ed. R. N. Grynberg (New York: Chekhov Publishing House, 1960), 1:120–21.

10. Simon Karlinsky, *Marina Cvetaeva: Her Life and Art*, pp. 44–45.

11. Aleksandr Pasternak/author, January 10, 1963. In the aesthetic elaboration of this episode in *Spektorskii*, Pasternak dates it otherwise; cf. Pasternak, *STIKHP*, p. 304.

12. Cf. Guy de Mallac, "A Russian Impressionist: Leonid Osipovich Pasternak, 1862–1945," *California Slavic Studies* 10 (1977): 106; Pasternak, *STIKHP*, p. 304; BP/Mandelstam, September 19, 1924, August 16, 1925, "Pisma B. L. Pasternaka O. E. i N. Ia. Mandelstam," *Vestnik russkogo studencheskogo khristianskogo dvizheniia* 104–105 (1972): 233, 237–40; Aleksandr Pasternak/author, January 10, 1963.

13. Boris Pasternak, response of March 12, 1919, to Poetry Section, Moscow Professional Union of Writers, Gorky Institute of World Literature [IMLI], Moscow, Archive Group 120, Storage Unit 18, in Milan Djurčinov, "Dva priloga za B. A. Pasternak," *Godishen zbornik na filozofskiot fakultet na univerzitetot vo Skopje* 26 (1974): 363.

14. BP/Tsvetaeva, June 6, 1922, Tsvetaeva, *Neizdannye pisma*, p. 266.

15. "Bezliube," *Volia truda* 60 (November 26, 1918) and 62 (November 28, 1918); Boris Pasternak, *Works*, 1:321–27.

16. Max Hayward, Introduction, Boris Pasternak, "Without Love," *Partisan Review* 3–4 (1961): 363; George Katkov, " 'Bezliube'—rannii nabrosok *Doktora Zhivago*," *Boris Pasternak, 1890–1960: Colloque de Cerisy-la-Salle (11–14 septembre 1975)*, ed. Michel Aucouturier, pp. 329–35. (George Katkov had originally edited and published "Bezliube" ["Without Love"], with an introduction, in *Novyi zhurnal* 62 [1960]: 10–11.)

17. Pasternak, *Works*, 2:53–82, 137–50.

18. A. Lezhnev, "Boris Pasternak," in Davie and Livingstone, *Pasternak: Modern Judgements*, p. 93.

19. Mikhail Kuzmin, "Govoriashchie," *Uslovnosti*, pp. 158–61; Gorkii/BP, October 4, 1927, *Literaturnoe nasledstvo* 70 (1963): 296; Kn. D. Sviatopolk-Mirskii, "Boris Pasternak: Raskazy," *Sovremennye Zapiski* 25 (1925): 544.

20. Cf. William Edgerton, "The Serapion Brothers: An Early Soviet Controversy," *American Slavic and East European Review* 8 (1948): 1.

21. Boris Pasternak, *IR*, p. 105.

22. Kornelii Zelinskii, *Na rubezhe dvukh epokh: Literaturnye vstrechi 1917–1920 godov*, pp. 208–209; Ilia Ehrenburg, *People and Life, 1891–1921*, trans. Anna Bostock and Yvonne Kapp, pp. 244–49; V. Katanian, *Maiakovskii: Literaturnaia khronika*, 4th ed., p. 94.

23. *ROSTA Art Bulletin*, March 3, 1921; Katanian, *Maiakovskii*, p. 143.

24. Pasternak, statement of March 12, 1919, in Djurčinov, "Dva Priloga," p. 363.

25. Vasilii Barsov, "O Pasternake: Moskovskie vpechatleniia," *Grani* 40 (1958): 102.

26. Ibid., pp. 107–109.

27. V. Katanian, "Ne tolko vospominaniia," *Russian Literature Triquarterly* 13 (Fall, 1975): 477.

28. Tsvetaeva/BP, July 7, 1922, Tsvetaeva, *Neizdannye pisma*, p. 273.

29. Pasternak, *IR*, p. 107.

30. Karlinsky, *Marina Cvetaeva*, p. 56; Pasternak, *IR*, pp. 107–108.

31. Pasternak, *IR*, p. 108; Karlinsky, *Marina Cvetaeva*, p. 230; Aleksandr Gladkov, *Vstrechi*, p. 53.

32. Karlinsky, *Marina Cvetaeva*, p. 56; Pasternak, *STIKHP*, p. 661.

33. *Literaturnoe nasledstvo* 70:300, 307–308; Karlinsky, *Marina Cvetaeva*, pp. 64–65.

34. Cf. "Spektorskii," Pasternak, *STIKHP*, pp. 326–32; Olga Raevsky Hughes, "Pasternak and Cvetaeva: History of a Friendship," *Books Abroad* [later *World Literature Today*] 44 (Spring, 1970): 219–20.

35. Tsvetaeva, *Neizdannye pisma*, pp. 265–84; Hughes, "Pasternak and Cvetaeva," pp. 218–19.

36. Tsvetaeva/BP, March 10, 1923, and May 29, 1926, Tsvetaeva, *Neizdannye pisma*, pp. 289, 301; Tsvetaeva/R. Gul, 1923, Karlinsky, *Marina Cvetaeva*, p. 56.

37. Tsvetaeva/Aleksandr Bakhrakh, October 4, 1923, A. Bakhrakh, "Pisma Mariny Tsvetaevoi," *Mosty* 6 (1961):338; Tsvetaeva/BP, March 9, 1923, Tsvetaeva, *Neizdannye pisma*, p. 285.

38. Karlinsky, *Marina Cvetaeva*, p. 61.

39. BP/Literature Department of People's Commissariat of Education, June, 1920, *New York Times Magazine*, January 1, 1978, p. 13.

40. Elliot Mossmann, ed., "The Unpublished Letters of Boris Pasternak," *New York Times Magazine*, January 1, 1978, p. 24; Pasternak, *Works*, 2:343–44; Rita Wright-Kovaleva, "Pasternak and Mayakovsky: Fragments of Reminiscence," *Oxford Slavonic Papers* 13 (1967):114–17. According to Evgenii Pasternak, Pasternak's marriage took place as early as January or February, 1922.

41. Iurii Krotkov, *KROT 1*, p. 67; Charles Vildrac, *Pages de journal, 1922–1966*, p. 51.

42. Nina Berberova, *The Italics Are Mine*, p. 155.

43. Pasternak, *STIKHP*, p. 207.

44. Tsvetaeva/BP, June 28, 1922, Tsvetaeva, *Neizdannye pisma*, p. 270.

45. Leonid Pasternak, *ZAP*, pp. 101, 240.

46. Krotkov, *KROT 1*, p. 50.

47. Robert C. Williams, *Culture in Exile: Russian Émigrés in Germany, 1881–1941*, pp. 111–16; Katanian, *Maiakovskii*, p. 174.

48. Cf. Williams, *Culture in Exile*, pp. 131–36.

49. Viktor Shklovskii, *Zoo, or Letters Not About Love*, trans. and ed. R. Sheldon, pp. 27–30.

50. Katanian, *Maiakovskii*, p. 172.

51. Ehrenburg, *Memoirs, 1921–1941*, p. 20.

52. Williams, *Culture in Exile*, pp. 245–52, 261.

53. Berberova, *The Italics Are Mine*, p. 156; Katanian, *Maiakovskii*, pp. 171–72.

54. Berberova, *The Italics Are Mine*, pp. 170–71, 199–200; Jacqueline de Proyart, "Une amitié d'enfance," *Boris Pasternak, 1890–1960: Colloque de Cerisy-la-Salle (11–14 septembre 1975)*, p. 589.

55. Shklovskii, *Zoo*, pp. 62–63.

56. Ibid.

57. B. Pasternak, *SC*, p. 62; Renate Schweitzer, *Freundschaft mit Pasternak: Ein Briefwechsel*, p. 134.

58. Tsvetaeva/BP, March 3, 1923, March 9, 1923, Tsvetaeva, *Neizdannye pisma*, pp. 283–84.

59. Tsvetaeva/R. Gul, Tsvetaeva, *Letters to R. Gul*, no. 178, quoted in Karlinsky, *Marina Cvetaeva*, p. 56.

60. Berberova, *The Italics Are Mine*, p. 165; Boris Zaitsev, "Pasternak i revoliutsii," *Dalekoe*, pp. 115–16.

61. Schweitzer, *Freundschaft mit Pasternak*, p. 134.

62. L. Pasternak, *ZAP*, p. 158.

63. Tsvetaeva/BP, March 9, 1923, Tsvetaeva, *Neizdannye pisma*, pp. 285, 288.

64. Nikolai Aseev, "Melody or Intonation," in Donald Davie and Angela Livingstone, eds., *Pasternak: Modern Judgements*, p. 81.

65. D. S. Mirsky, *A History of Russian Literature*, ed. Francis J. Whitfield, p. 501; Tsvetaeva/BP, March 9, 1923, Tsvetaeva, *Neizdannye pisma*, p. 288.

66. Krotkov, *KROT 1*, pp. 56–57; Hedrick Smith, *The Russians*, p. 102.

67. B. Pasternak, *STIKHP*, p. 239.

68. Semen Chikovani, *Mysli, vpechatleniia, vospominaniia*, pp. 60–61; B. Pasternak, *STIKHP*, pp. 243–44; Anatolii Lunacharskii, "Tezisy o politike RKP v oblasti literatury," typescript, 1925, and "Na fronte iskusstva," typescript, 1926, *Literaturnoe nasledstvo* 74 (1965):31, 41.

69. Lydiia Chukovskaia, *Zapiski ob Anne Akhmatovoi: I, 1938–41*, p. 53; Gleb Struve, *Russian Literature Under Lenin and Stalin, 1917–1953*, pp. 77–79, 89–91; Edward J. Brown, *The Proletarian Episode in Russian Literature, 1928–1932*, pp. 39–43; *Izvestiia*, July 1, 1925.

70. B. Pasternak, *STIKHP*, pp. 655–56.

71. BP/Gorkii, October 10, 1927, *Literaturnoe nasledstvo* 70:297–98.

72. Tsvetaeva/BP, December 11, 1927, Tsvetaeva, *Neizdannye pisma*, p. 301.

73. Katanian, *Maiakovskii*, p. 291; A. Lezhnev, "Boris Pasternak (K vykhodu 'Dvukh knig' i '1905 goda')," *Krasnaia nov* 8 (1926):215–19; A. Lezhnev, "Boris Pasternak: 1, Dve knigi, Stikhi, 2 1905 god," *Pravda*, December 28, 1927; Tsvetaeva/BP, December 28, 1927, Tsvetaeva, *Neizdannye pisma*, p. 288; N. Otsup, "O Borise Pasternake," *Zveno* 5 (1928):260–66.

74. BP/Gorkii, November 16, 1927, *Literaturnoe nasledstvo* 70:303.

75. Tsvetaeva/L. O. Pasternak, January 10, 1928, Tsvetaeva, *Neizdannye pisma*, p. 310.

76. BP/Gorkii, October 13, 1927, *Literaturnoe nasledstvo* 70:298.

77. *Lef* 2 (May 1, 1923).

78. Brown, *Mayakovsky*, p. 213.

79. A. Lezhnev, *Sovremenniki: Literaturno-kriticheskie ocherki*, p. 73.

80. *Lef* 1 (1923).

81. Vladimir Maiakovskii, "Vystuplenie na dispute 'Lef ili blef?'" *Literaturnoe nasledstvo* 65:62–63.

82. K. G. Loks, "Epopeia Selvinskogo (B. Pasternak)," *Krasnaia nov* 3 (1927):236.

83. BP/V. P. Polonskii, June 1, 1927, *Novyi mir*, October, 1964, pp. 195–96.

84. Shklovskii, *Zoo*, p. 193.

CHAPTER 7

1. George Reavey, ed., "Exegi Monumentum," in *The Poetry of Boris Pasternak, 1914–1960*, p. 54.

2. BP/S. D. Spasskii, January 3, 1928, *Voprosy literatury* 9 (1969):166.

3. Kn. D. Sviatopolk-Mirskii, "'1905 god' Borisa Pasternaka," *Versty* 3 (1928):150–54; Ilia Ehrenburg, *People and Life, 1891–1921*, trans. A. Bostock and Y. Kapp, p. 283.

4. Zh. Elsberg, "Mirovospriiatie B. Pasternaka," *Na literaturnom postu* 7 (April, 1930):42–50, translated in Edward J. Brown, *The Proletarian Episode in Russian Literature, 1928–1932*, pp. 148–49.

5. V. Shklovskii, *Gamburgskii shchet* (Leningrad: Izdatelstvo pisatelei v Leningrade, 1928), p. 119.

6. K. Zelinskii, *Kriticheskie pisma: Kniga vtoraia*, p. 256.

7. Gleb Struve, *Russian Literature Under Lenin and Stalin 1917–1953*, p. 188; BP/S. D. Spasskii, January 3, 1928, *Voprosy literatury* 9 (1969):166.

8. Maksim Gorkii, "Predislovie k povesti Pasternaka 'Detstvo Liuvers,'" *Literaturnoe nasledstvo* 70 (1963):309.

9. Czesław Miłosz, "On Pasternak Soberly," *Books Abroad*, 44 (Spring, 1970):201.

10. V. Pertsov, *Literaturnye zapiski, God dvadtsatyi, Almanakh odinnadtsatyi*, pp. 357–58.

11. BP/Spasskii, January 3, 1928, and March 30, 1929, *Voprosy literatury* 9 (1969):166–69.

12. Iurii Krotkov, *KROT 2*, pp. 58–59.

13. BP/Spasskii, September 29, 1930, *Voprosy literatury* 9 (1969):170–72.

14. Krotkov, *KROT 1*, p. 66.

15. BP/Spasskii, September 29, 1930, *Voprosy literatury* 9 (1969):170–72.

16. Pasternak, statement under the rubric "Pisateli o sebe," *Na literaturnom postu*, 1929, nos. 4–5; cf. Boris Pasternak, *STIKHP*, p. 671.

17. Pasternak, untitled statement, *Chitatel i pisatel*, nos. 4–5 (February 11, 1928), Gleb Struve, trans. and ed., "Boris Pasternak About Himself and His Readers," *Slavic Review* 23 (March, 1964):127–28.

18. "Interes k Pasternaku," *Novoe russkoe slovo*, December 31, 1958; Aleksandr Gladkov, *Vstrechi*, p. 12.

19. Pasternak, *Spektorskii*, in *STIKHP*, p. 318.

20. A. Selivanovskii, "Poeziia opasna?" *Literaturnaia gazeta*, August 15, 1931; Lidiia Chukovskaia, *Zapiski ob Anne Akhmatovii: I, 1938–41*, pp. 129–30.

21. Michel Aucouturier, "The Metonymous Hero, or the Beginnings of Pasternak the Novelist," *Books Abroad* [later *World Literature Today*] 44 (Spring, 1970):222–27.

22. *Krasnaia gazeta*, January 31 and February 2, 1930; *Leningradskaia pravda*, February 3, 1930; *Rabochii i teatr*, February 5, 1930.

23. V. Katanian, *Maiakovskii: Literaturnaia khronika*, p. 418.

24. Vladimir Maiakovskii, *The Bedbug and Selected Poetry*, ed. Patricia Blake, p. 313; Viktor Frank, "Realizm chetyrekh izmerenii (Perechityvaia Pasternaka)," *Izbrannye stati*, ed. Leonard Schapiro, pp. 71–76.

25. Boris Pasternak, *SC*, p. 94.

26. Rita Wright-Kovaleva, "Mayakovsky and Pasternak, Fragments of Reminiscence," *Oxford Slavonic Papers* 13 (1967):131–32; Boris Pasternak, *IR*, p. 99.

27. Pasternak, *SC*, p. 77.

28. Ibid., pp. 77–97; Pasternak, *IR*, pp. 88–100; Wright-Kovaleva, "Mayakovsky and Pasternak," p. 132.

29. Ilia Ehrenburg, *People and Life, 1891–1921*, trans. A. Bostock and Y. Kapp, p. 283.

30. Wright-Kovaleva, "Mayakovsky and Pasternak," p. 132.

31. Pasternak, *SC*, p. 84.

32. Ibid., p. 86.

33. Pasternak, *IR*, pp. 94–96.

34. Liliia Iurevna Brik, "Chuzhie stikhi, Glava iz vospominanii," *V. Maiakovskii v vospominaniiakh sovremennikov*, pp. 341–44.

35. V. Pertsov, *Maiakovskii: Zhizn i tvorchestvo, 1925–1930*, pp. 121, 125–27.

36. Gladkov, *Vstrechi*, p. 14.

37. Pasternak, *SC*, p. 86.

38. Ehrenburg, *People and Life*, p. 284.

39. Pasternak, *IR*, p. 100.

40. V. A. Katanian, "O Maiakovskom i Pasternake," *Russian Literature Triquarterly* 13 (Fall, 1975): 503.

41. Pasternak, *IR*, p. 98.

42. Edward J. Brown, *Mayakovsky: A Poet in the Revolution*, pp. 350–51.

43. Pasternak, *IR*, p. 98.

44. Sergei Kosman, *Maiakovskii: Mif i deistvitelnost*, p. 67; V. Pertsov, *Maiakovskii: Zhizn i tvorchestvo v poslednie gody 1925–1930*, p. 363.

45. Nina Skorbina, "Boris Pasternak: Vstrechi i pisma," *Novoe russkoe slovo*, February 18, 1973.

46. Pasternak, *SC*, p. 96.

47. Valentin Kataev, *The Grass of Oblivion*, p. 199.

48. Pasternak, *SC*, p. 97.

49. Ibid., p. 80.

50. Gladkov, *Vstrechi*, p. 14; A. Lezhnev, *Sovremenniki: literaturno-kriticheskie ocherki*, p. 74.

51. Maiakovskii, "Lef ili blef?" *Literaturnoe nasledstvo 65 (Novoe o Maiakovskom)*, p. 56.

52. Boris Pasternak, *DZh*, p. 296.

53. Pasternak, statement to Z. I. Konchalovskaia; Pasternak/P. N. Medvedev, 1929, in G. G. Superfin, "B. L. Pasternak, Critic of the 'Formalist Method,'" *Trudy po znakovym sistemam* 5 (1971); Nancy Beveridge, trans., *Russian Literature Triquarterly* 6 (1973): 607–609; Nadezhda Mandelstam, *Hope Abandoned*, p. 295.

54. Iurii Krotkov, conversation of 1975 with author; Ivinskaya, *CAPT*, p. 26; Mandelstam, *Hope Abandoned*, p. 215.

55. Krotkov, *KROT 1*, pp. 67–68.

56. Ibid.

57. Pasternak, *IR*, pp. 111–12.

58. Krotkov, *KROT 1*, p. 68; Pasternak, *IR*, pp. 111–12.

59. Svetlana Allilueva, *Twenty Letters to a Friend* (New York: Discus/Avon, 1968), p. 78.

60. Pasternak, "Liubit inykh tiazhelyi krest . . . ," *STIKHP*, p. 359.

61. Krotkov, *KROT 1*, p. 68.

62. Information conveyed by Evgenii Borisovich Pasternak to author.

63. Krotkov, *KROT 1*, p. 71.

64. Tsvetaeva/Anna Tesková, March 20, 1931, Marina Tsvetaeva, *Pisma k Anne Teskovoi*, pp. 90–91.

65. Ida Davidovna Feldzer, recollections as communicated to author in 1975 through Jacqueline de Proyart.

66. Krotkov, *KROT 1*, p. 64.

67. Ibid.

68. Pasternak, "Posleslovie," *Okhrannaia gramota*, *Works*, 2 : 344.

69. Krotkov, *KROT 1*, p. 66.

70. BP/Z. N. Pasternak, 1930–31, ibid., p. 69.

71. BP/Z. N. Pasternak, June 9, 1931, Pasternak, "Iz pisem k zhene," *Vestnik russkogo studencheskogo khristianskogo dvizheniia* 106 (1972): 204.

72. Krotkov, *KROT 1*, p. 69; Georges Nivat, "Pasternak dans l'Oural en 1932," in *Boris Pasternak, 1890–1960: Colloque de Cerisy-la-Salle (11–14 septembre 1975)*, ed. Michel Aucouturier, p. 521.

73. Ibid.; BP/Paolo Iashvili, July 30, 1932, Pasternak, *LGF*, pp. 39–40.

74. Boris Pasternak, *DZh*, p. 9; Krotkov, *KROT 1*, p. 69.

75. Krotkov, *KROT 1*, pp. 69–70; Lotte Schwarz, "Rencontres," *Esprit*, September, 1976, pp. 236–37; Nivat, "Pasternak dans l'Oural en 1932," p. 521.

76. Krotkov, *KROT 1*, p. 70; Nivat, "Pasternak dans l'Oural en 1932," p. 522.

77. Boris Pasternak, postscript to Soviet Writers' letter to Stalin, *Literaturnaia gazeta*, November 17, 1932.

78. Krotkov, *KROT 2*, p. 63.

79. Zelinskii, *Kriticheskie pisma*, pp. 242, 244.

80. Pasternak, *SC*, p. 91.

81. Yuri Olesha, "Speech to the First Congress of Soviet Writers," *Envy and Other Works*, pp. 216–19.

82. Veniamin Kaverin, *Prolog: Putevye rasskazy*; Ronald F. Walter, "The Prose Fiction of Veniamin Kaverin: An Interpretive Study" (Ph.D. diss., Indiana University, 1974), pp. 89–103.

83. Zelinskii, *Kriticheskie pisma*, pp. 242–57; A. Bem, "Boris Pasternak: Vtoroe rozhdenie," *Sovremennye zapiski* 51 (1933): 454.

84. Bem, "Boris Pasternak," pp. 454–56; Zelinskii, *Kriticheskie pisma*, pp. 242, 245; Chukovskaia, *Zapiski*, pp. 124–25.

85. Zelinskii, *Kriticheskie pisma*, pp. 243–44.

86. Pasternak, *STIKHP*, p. 358; Chukovskaia, *Zapiski*, p. 134.

87. Pasternak, *STIKHP*, p. 371.

88. Ibid., p. 350.

89. Ibid., pp. 343–52.

90. Nina Berberova, *The Italics Are Mine*, p. 318.

91. Zelinskii, *Kriticheskie pisma*, pp. 249–57.

92. Czesław Miłosz, conversation with author.

93. Miłosz, "On Pasternak Soberly," p. 204.

94. Pasternak, *Works*, 2:354–58.

95. Aleksandr Gladkov, *Vstrechi*, p. 15; "Interes k Pasternaku," *Novoe russkoe slovo*, December 31, 1958; BP/G. Reavey, March 6, 1933, in Elena Levin, "Nine Letters of Boris Pasternak," *Harvard Library Bulletin* 15 (1967): 324.

96. BP/Spasskii, January 3, 1928, *Voprosy literatury*, 9 (1969): 166.

97. Pasternak, *IR*, p. 19.

98. Pasternak, *SC*, pp. 21–22.

99. Ibid., p. 30.

100. Ibid., p. 29.

101. Ibid., p. 40–41.

102. Ibid., pp. 76–97.

103. Cf. ibid., p. 31.

104. Gladkov, *Vstrechi*, p. 15.

CHAPTER 8

1. Boris Pasternak, "Hamlet," *DZh*, p. 523.

2. Nina Skorbina, "Boris Pasternak: Vstrechi i pisma," *Novoe russkoe slovo*, February 18, 1973.

3. Clarence Brown, *Mandelstam*, p. 90.

4. An estimate taking into account unpublished materials.

5. Aleksandr Blok, vol. 6 in *Sobranie sochinenii v vosmi tomakh*, ed. V. N. Orlov et al., pp. 468–69; Cf. Boris Pasternak, *IR*, pp. 53–54.

6. Kornei Chukovskii, *Vysokoe iskusstvo*, vol. 3 in *Sobranie sochinenii*, p. 341; E. Etkind, "Poeticheskii perevod v istorii russkoi literatury," *Mastera russkogo stikhotvornogo perevoda*, pp. 68–71.

7. Iu. Levin, "Russkie perevody Shekspira," *Masterstvo perevoda: Sbornik shestoi*, p. 24.

8. Henry Gifford, *Pasternak: A Critical Study*, p. 161; Brown, *Mandelstam*, p. 90.

9. P. Karp, "Zhizn, a ne slovesnost," *Zvezda* 2 (1968): 220.

10. Iurii Krotkov, *KROT 1*, p. 42.

11. *Literaturnaia Gruziia*, no. 8 (1968).

12. A. N. Afinogenov, diary entry for September 21, 1937, *Stati, Dnevniki, Pisma, Vospominaniia*, p. 152.

13. Aleksandr Gladkov, *Vstrechi*, p. 51.

14. Ibid., pp. 32, 51, 54–55.

15. BP/A. O. Naumova, May 23, 1942, *Masterstvo perevoda: Sbornik sedmoi*, p. 342.

16. Etkind, "Poeticheskii perevod," p. 70.

17. Boris Pasternak, *Works*, 3:191.

18. Pasternak, conversation of August 13, 1959, with Z. A. (private information).

19. Cf. Etkind, "Poeticheskii perevod," p. 67.

20. Levin, "Russkie perevody Shekspira," p. 24.

21. Cf. Etkind, "Poeticheskii perevod," p. 70–71.

22. Ibid., p. 69; A. Fedorov, "Neobychnaia antologiia," *Masterstvo perevoda: Sbornik sedmoi*, p. 278; Etkind, "Ob uslovno-poeticheskom i individualnom (Sonety Shekspira v russkikh perevodakh)," *Masterstvo perevoda: Sbornik shestoi*, p. 146.

23. A. Finkel, "66-i sonet v russkikh perevodakh," *Masterstvo perevoda: Sbornik shestoi*, p. 173.

24. Etkind, "Ob uslovno-poeticheskom i individualnom," p. 146.

25. Gifford, *Pasternak*, p. 151; V. Levik, "Nuzhny li novye perevody Shekspira?" *Masterstvo perevoda: Sbornik shestoi*, p. 95; Pasternak, "Translating Shakespeare," *IR*, pp. 141–46.

26. Boris Pasternak, "Neskolko slov o novoi gruzinskoi poezii (Zamechaniia perevodchika)," *Voprosy literatury*, January, 1966, pp. 170–72; Pasternak, *IR*, pp. 112–18; Pasternak, telegram to Union of Georgian Writers, *Na rubezhe Vostoka* 5 (1936).

27. Pasternak, "Neskolko slov o novoi gruzinskoi poezii," p. 170.

28. A. Tarasenkov, "O gruzinskikh perevodakh Pasternaka," *Znamia*, September, 1935, pp. 204–205.

29. Vl. Ognev, "U karty sovetskoi poezii," *Masterstvo perevoda: Sbornik shestoi*, pp. 288–89.

30. D. Mirskii, "Pasternak i gruzinskie poety," *Literaturnaia gazeta*, October 24, 1935.

31. Gladkov, *Vstrechi*, p. 90.

32. Pasternak, "Translating Shakespeare," *IR*, p. 142.

33. Gifford, *Pasternak*, p. 161.

34. Vladimir Markov, "An Unnoticed Aspect of Pasternak's Translations," *Slavic Review*, October, 1961, p. 508.

35. Pasternak, *Works*, 2:198, 295–339; Editorial "Predislovie," Boris Pasternak, *Fragmenty romana*, ed. Christopher J. Barnes and Nicholas J. Anning, pp. 3–4.

36. Boris Pasternak, "Pered razlukoi," *Fragmenty romana*, p. 9.

37. Nadezhda Mandelstam, *Hope*, p. 299.

38. Vítězslav Nezval, *Neviditelná Moskva*, p. 93.

39. Pasternak, unpublished letter of (December ?) 1937, in response to an inquiry from *Litera-*

turnaia gazeta, Archive of Gorky Institute of World Literature (IMLI), Moscow.

40. Josephine Pasternak, "Patior," *London Magazine* 4 (September, 1964):47.

41. BP/L. O. Pasternak, 1934, quoted in "Introduction," Boris Pasternak, *Fifty Poems*, trans. Lydia Pasternak Slater, p. 16.

42. BP/L. O. and R. I. Pasternak, 1937, ibid., p. 17.

43. BP/Titian and Nina Tabidze, April 8, 1936, Boris Pasternak, *LGF*, p. 66.

44. BP/J. Hora, November 15, 1935, *Plamen* 7 (1963), supplement; A. Selivanovskii, "Pasternak," *Literaturnaia entsiklopediia* (1934), 8:465–71; D. Mirskii, "Pasternak i gruzinskie poety."

45. Aleksei Surkov, "Chto zhe takoe formalizm?" *Golosa vremeni: Zametki na poliakh istorii literatury 1934–1965* (Moscow: Sovetskii pisatel, 1965), p. 137.

46. G. Adamovich, "Nesostoiavshaiasia progulka," *Sovremennye zapiski* 59 (1935):295.

47. BP/Titian and Nina Tabidze, November 6, 1933, Pasternak, *LGF*, p. 51.

48. Ilia Ehrenburg, *Memoirs: 1921–1941*, p. 270.

49. Nezval, *Neviditelná Moskva*, p. 93.

50. Robert Payne, *A Portrait of André Malraux*, pp. 188–91.

51. Gustav Regler, *The Owl of Minerva*, pp. 204–207.

52. Anatolii Iakobson, *Konets tragedii*, p. 179.

53. Aleksei Surkov, "Derzhat liricheskii porokh sukhim!" [speech at First Congress of Soviet Writers, 1934], *Golosa vremeni*, p. 74.

54. B. Pasternak, *Works*, 3:217–18.

55. N. Bukharin, "Poetry, Poetics, and the Problems of Poetry in the USSR," A. Zhdanov et al., eds., *Problems of Soviet Literature: Reports and Speeches at the First Soviet Writers' Congress*, pp. 233–40.

56. Edward J. Brown, *Mayakovsky: A Poet in the Revolution*, p. 370.

57. Pasternak, *IR*, pp. 100–101.

58. Ilia Ehrenburg, speech at First Congress of Soviet Writers, 1934, *Sobranie sochinenii v deviati tomakh*, 6:522–23.

59. Ehrenburg, *Memoirs*, p. 270.

60. Ibid., p. 272.

61. B. Pasternak, *IR*, p. 108.

62. Ehrenburg, *Memoirs*, p. 304; cf. Olga Ivinskaya, *CAPT*, pp. 70–71.

63. J. Pasternak, "Patior," pp. 45–46.

64. Iurii Krotkov, *KROT 1*, pp. 70–71.

65. J. Pasternak, "Patior," p. 46.

66. Tsvetaeva/A. Tesková, February 15, 1936, Marina Tsvetaeva, *Pisma k Anne Teskovoi*, p. 134.

67. J. Pasternak, "Patior," p. 45.

68. Ibid., pp. 45–48.

69. Regler, *The Owl of Minerva*, p. 231; Ehrenburg, *Memoirs*, p. 304; *Poslednie novosti* (Paris), June 22, 1935.

70. André Malraux, *Anti-Memoirs*, p. 398; Charles Vildrac, *Pages de journal, 1922–1936*, pp. 90–91.

71. Ehrenburg, *Memoirs*, p. 305; George Reavey, Introduction, *The Poetry of Boris Pasternak, 1914–1960*, p. 54.

72. Ehrenburg, *Memoirs*, p. 305; Ehrenburg, "Pisma s mezhdunarodnogo kongressa pisatelei," *Literaturnyi kritik* 8 (1935):17; Ehrenburg, "Pismo s kongressa: IV," *Izvestiia*, June 25, 1935.

73. I. Luppol, ed., *Mezhdunarodnyi kongress pisatelei v zashchitu kultury. Parizh, iiun 1935: Doklady i vystupleniia*, pp. 358, 185–87; Ilia Ehrenburg, "Pismo s kongressa: V. Poslednee zasedanie," *Izvestiia*, June 27, 1935.

74. Ehrenburg, *Memoirs*, pp. 304–305.

75. Boris Pasternak, "Slovo o poezii," in Gleb Struve, ed., *Sbornik statei, posviashchennykh tvorchestvu Borisa Leonidovicha Pasternaka*, p. 9; Reavey, Introduction, *The Poetry of Boris Pasternak*, p. 53.

76. Ehrenburg, "Pisma s mezhdunarodnogo kongressa," p. 20.

77. Malraux, *Anti-Memoirs*, p. 398.

78. Ehrenburg, *Memoirs*, p. 306.

79. Pasternak, *IR*, p. 108; Nina Berberova, *The Italics Are Mine*, p. 203.

80. Simon Karlinsky, *Marina Cvetaeva: Her Life and Art*, pp. 66, 69–70.

81. Pasternak, *IR*, pp. 108–109; Tsvetaeva/Tesková, July 16, 1937, Marina Tsvetaeva, *Pisma k Anne Teskovoi*, p. 154.

82. Tsvetaeva/BP, October, 1935, "Pisma Mariny Tsvetaevoi," *Novyi mir*, April, 1969, p. 198.

83. Tsvetaeva/A. Tesková, July 2, 1935, February 15, 1936, Tsvetaeva, *Pisma k Anne Teskovoi*, pp. 126, 134; Tsvetaeva/BP, October, 1935, "Pisma Mariny Tsvetaevoi," p. 198; J. Pasternak, "Patior," p. 48; Olga Ivinskaya, *CAPT*, p. 51.

84. Iurii Annenkov, "Boris Pasternak," *Dnevnik moikh vstrech: Tsikl tragedii*, 2:163.

85. Ehrenburg, *Memoirs*, p. 221; interview with Ida Davidovna Feldzer by Jacqueline de Proyart, fall, 1976 (information conveyed to author).

86. Annenkov, "Boris Pasternak," pp. 163–65.

87. BP/Z. N. Pasternak, July 10, 1935, Boris Pasternak, "Iz pisem k zhene," *Vestnik russkogo studencheskogo khristianskogo dvizheniia* 106 (1972): 213–16.

88. Ehrenburg, *Memoirs*, p. 308.

89. Krotkov, *KROT 1*, pp. 70–71; BP/T. Tabidze, October 6, 1935, Boris Pasternak, *LGF*, p. 62; Lydia Pasternak Slater, conversation with author, summer, 1979.

90. BP/Tabidze, October 6, 1935, Pasternak, *LGF*, pp. 61–62.

91. Krotkov, *KROT 1*, p. 71.

92. Surkov, "K narodnoi poezii sotsializma," *Golosa vremeni*, pp. 114–15.

93. B. Pasternak, "O skromnosti i smelosti," *Works*, 3:220–21.

94. Ibid., 219–24.

95. BP/J. Hora, November 15, 1935, supplement to *Plamen*, July, 1963.

96. Krotkov, *KROT 1*, p. 71.

97. B. Pasternak, *Works*, 3:218–19.

98. Ibid., p. 220.

99. Aleksandr Afinogenov, diary entry for September 21, 1937, *Stati, Dnevniki, Pisma, Vospominaniia*, p. 152.

100. Olga R. Hughes, *The Poetic World of Boris Pasternak*, p. 139.

101. Leonid Borisovich Pasternak/author, January 14, 1963.

102. Kornei Chukovskii, "Boris Pasternak (1890–1960)," in Boris Pasternak, *Stikhi*, pp. 5–11.

103. Afinogenov, *Stati, Dnevniki*, p. 152.

104. Nadezhda Mandelstam, *Hope*, p. 150; Brown, *Mandelstam*, p. 131.

105. *Vechernaia Moskva*, January 2, 1938.

106. Pasternak, *DZh*, p. 507.

107. Krotkov, *KROT 2*, p. 64; Ivinskaya, *CAPT*, p. 125.

108. Krotkov, *KROT 2*, pp. 61–62.

109. Nadezhda Mandelstam, *Hope Abandoned*, p. 230.

110. Mandelstam, *Hope*, pp. 25–27.

111. Ibid., p. 145.

112. Accounts of this episode are to be found in ibid., pp. 25–27, 145–49, 214; Krotkov, *KROT 2*, p. 62; Ivinskaya, *CAPT*, pp. 60–67; Ivo Fleischman, "La visite chez le poète: Analyse d'un voyage" [about Fleischman's visit to Pasternak in October, 1956], *Vagabondages*, 5 (1978): 43–45.

113. Gladkov, *Vstrechi*, p. 23; Krotkov, *KROT 2*, p. 63.

114. Mandelstam, *Hope*, p. 148.

115. Ibid., pp. 146, 148, 214.

116. Gladkov, *Vstrechi*, p. 23; Mandelstam, *Hope*, p. 146.

117. Krotkov, *KROT 2*, p. 62; Mandelstam, *Hope*, p. 146.

118. Mandelstam, *Hope*, pp. 148, 299.

119. Krotkov, *KROT 2*, p. 62.

120. Mandelstam, *Hope*, pp. 131, 144, 298–99; Brown, *Mandelstam*, p. 132.

121. *Literaturnaia gazeta*, April 6, 1937.

122. Gladkov, *Vstrechi*, p. 11.

123. Krotkov, *KROT 2*, pp. 63–64.

124. Nils Åke Nilsson, "Pasternak: 'We Are the Guests of Existence,'" *Reporter* 19 (November 27, 1958):34.

125. "Ne dadim zhitia vragam Sovetskogo Soiuza" (June 11, 1937), *Literaturnaia gazeta*, June 15, 1937.

126. Krotkov, *KROT 2*, pp. 63–64.

127. Ivinskaya, *CAPT*, pp. 125–26; Pasternak, *LGF*, pp. 70–76, 79–87, 89–97; Krotkov, *KROT 2*, p. 64.

128. Gladkov, *Vstrechi*, pp. 135–36.

129. Ibid., pp. 9–10.

130. L. Snezhnitskii, "Poslednii god," in M. A. Valentii et al., eds., *Vstrechi s Meierkholdom: Sbornik vospominanii*, p. 565.

131. Gladkov, *Vstrechi*, pp. 10–11.

132. Ilia Ehrenburg, *Post-War Years, 1945–1954*, trans. Tatyana Shebunina, p. 277.

133. Ibid., p. 165.

134. Krotkov, *KROT 2*, pp. 65–66.

135. Ibid.

136. Boris Pasternak, conversation of August 30, 1959, with Henrik Birnbaum (information conveyed to author by H. Birnbaum).

137. Boris Pasternak, "Ia ponial, vsë zhivo . . . ," *Izvestiia*, January 1, 1936; Boris Pasternak, *STIKHP*, pp. 554–55, 702–703; Demian Bednyi, *Izbrannoe*, p. 254.

138. Krotkov, *KROT 2*, p. 63.

139. Mandelstam, *Hope*, p. 45.

140. "Mandelstam's 'Ode to Stalin,'" *Slavic Review*, December, 1975, pp. 683–91.

141. Mikhail Koriakov, "Afinogenov i Pasternak," *Novyi zhurnal* 56 (1959): 170.

142. Gladkov, *Vstrechi*, pp. 32, 54; Krotkov, *KROT 2*, p. 63; Ivinskaya, *CAPT*, pp. 81, 86; Brown, *Mandelstam*, p. 129.

143. Czesław Miłosz, "On Pasternak Soberly," *Books Abroad* [now *World Literature Today*] 44 (Spring, 1970):204; Kornelii Zelinskii, *Kriticheskie pisma: Kniga vtoraia*, p. 256; Lev Navrozov,

The Education of Lev Navrozov, pp. 276–78; Ivinskaya, *CAPT*, p. 248.

144. BP/Vlad. Pozner, 1929, *Le Monde*, November 15, 1969, supplement.

145. Afinogenov, *Stati, Dnevniki*, p. 152; Krotkov, *KROT 2*, p. 65.

146. Krotkov, *KROT 2*, p. 65.

CHAPTER 9

1. Olga Ivinskaya, *CAPT*, p. 81.

2. Boris Pasternak, *DZh*, p. 507.

3. BP/Z. Akhmatova, November 1 [?], 1940, Boris Pasternak, "Unpublished letters to Akhmatova; Unpublished Reviews of Akhmatova," *Russian Literature Triquarterly* 9 (1974): 528.

4. BP/A. N. Pasternak, September 12, 1941, Boris Pasternak, "Iz pisem k zhene," *Vestnik russkogo studencheskogo khristianskogo dvizheniia* 106 (1972): 224.

5. Boris Pasternak, "Strashnaia skazka," *STIKHP*, pp. 408–409.

6. Iuliia Neiman, "1941," trans. W. N. Vickery, *Partisan Review* 3–4 (1961): 475.

7. Pasternak, *DZh*, p. 507.

8. Iurii Krotkov, *KROT 2*, p. 66; BP/N. Tabidze, March 20, 1942, Boris Pasternak, *LGF*, pp. 89–90; Lydiia Chukovskaia, *Zapiski ob Anne Akhmatovoi: I, 1938–41*, pp. 18, 89.

9. Aleksandr Gladkov, *Vstrechi*, p. 17.

10. R. Porman, "B. L. Pasternak v Chistopole," *Russkaia literatura* 3 (1966): 193.

11. Gladkov, *Vstrechi*, pp. 18–21, 25–26.

12. Ibid., pp. 30, 33, 39; Boris Pasternak, *Works*, 3: 171, 205; Semen Tregub, "Voenno-polevoi soiuz pisatelei," *Sputniki serdtsa*, p. 203.

13. Victor Hugo, *William Shakespeare: Oeuvres complètes*, 12: 240–41.

14. Boris Pasternak, *IR*, p. 82; BP/N. Tabidze, March 20, 1942, Pasternak, *LGF*, p. 90.

15. Nikolai Aseev, "Gorodok na Kame," *Stikhotvoreniia i poemy*, pp. 321–25.

16. Gladkov, *Vstrechi*, pp. 36, 62.

17. Ibid., p. 113.

18. Nadezhda Mandelstam, *Hope Abandoned*, pp. 262–63; Chukovskaia, *Zapiski*, pp. 89, 164; Krotkov, *KROT 2*, p. 66.

19. Pasternak, *IR*, p. 82; BP/Akhmatova, July 28, 1940, Pasternak, "Unpublished Letters to Akhmatova," pp. 525–26.

20. Mandelstam, *Hope Abandoned*, p. 230; Chukovskaia, *Zapiski*, pp. 146–47, 164.

21. BP/A. Akhmatova, July 28, 1940, Pasternak, "Unpublished Letters to Akhmatova," pp. 525–26; Chukovskaia, *Zapiski*, pp. 146–47.

22. Pasternak, "Unpublished Letters to Akhmatova," pp. 522–33; Chukovskaia, *Zapiski*, pp. 53, 77–78, 189–90.

23. Gladkov, *Vstrechi*, p. 51.

24. Ibid., p. 11; Krotkov, *KROT 2*, p. 61.

25. Gladkov, *Vstrechi*, p. 11; BP/N. Ia. Mandelstam, June 10, 1943, Boris Pasternak, "Pisma B. L. Pasternaka O. E. i N. Ia. Mandelstam," *Vestnik russkogo studencheskogo khristianskogo dvizheniia* 104–105 (1972): 243.

26. Gladkov, *Vstrechi*, pp. 31–33, 81; Ivinskaya, *CAPT*, p. 303; Krotkov, *KROT 2*, p. 65.

27. Gladkov, *Vstrechi*, p. 33.

28. BP/Z. O. Naumova, May 23, 1942, "K perevodam shekspirovskikkh dram (Iz perepiski Borisa Pasternaka)," *Masterstvo perevoda: Sbornik shestoi*, p. 342.

29. N. Viliam-Vilmont, "'Gamlet' v perevode Borisa Pasternaka," *Internatsionalnaia literatura*, nos. 7–8 (1940), p. 291.

30. Ibid., p. 290.

31. Ibid., p. 291.

32. M. Morozov, "'Gamlet' v perevode B. Pasternaka," *Teatr*, February, 1941, pp. 144–47.

33. Ibid., pp. 144–46.

34. Ibid., pp. 145–47.

35. William Shakespeare, *Hamlet*, act 3, sc. 2, lines 354–55. Cf. Anna Kay France, "Boris Pasternak's Interpretation of Hamlet," *Russian Literature Triquarterly* 7 (1974): 204.

36. Simon Karlinsky, *Marina Cvetaeva: Her Life and Art*, pp. 101–102, 195; Ivinskaya, *CAPT*, pp. 162–64.

37. Ivinskaya, *CAPT*, pp. 163–65.

38. Ibid., pp. 150, 175.

39. Ibid., p. 167.

40. BP/Z. N. Pasternak, September 10, 1941, Pasternak, "Iz pisem k zhene," pp. 222–23.

41. Gladkov, *Vstrechi*, pp. 52–53.

42. BP/N. Tabidze, March 20, 1942, Pasternak, *LGF*, pp. 90–91.

43. Pasternak, *IR*, pp. 105–11, 115.

44. Ivinskaya, *CAPT*, p. 158.

45. Ibid., p. 168.

46. Ibid., pp. 127, 129–30.

47. Pasternak, *IR*, pp. 105–11, 115; Karlinsky, *Marina Cvetaeva*, p. 112.

48. "The Passion of Yurii Zhivago," *Time*, December 15, 1958, p. 54; Gladkov, *Vstrechi*, pp. 31, 47.

49. Ivinskaya, *CAPT*, p. 73; Krotkov, *KROT 2*, p. 66.

50. Ivinskaya, *CAPT*, pp. 72–73; Pasternak, *STIKHP*, pp. 558–60.

51. Gladkov, *Vstrechi*, pp. 55–56.

52. Boris Pasternak, "Translating Shakespeare," *IR*, p. 133.

53. Gladkov, *Vstrechi*, pp. 63, 86, 90.

54. A. Surkov, "S narodom i dlia naroda," *Golosa vremeni*, p. 183.

55. A. Abramov, *Lirika i epos velikoi otechestvennoi voiny: Problematika, stil, poetika*, p. 187.

56. Gladkov, *Vstrechi*, p. 76.

57. Ibid., p. 51.

58. Ibid., pp. 97–98.

59. Aurelio di Sovico, "Poet of Perplexity: Reflections on the Pleasures of Writing" [on Jorge L. Borges], *Il Mondo*, January 22, 1976; reprinted in *Atlas World Press Review*, April, 1976, p. 48.

60. P. Antokolskii, "Boris Pasternak," *Znamia* 9–10 (1943):316.

61. BP/Z. N. Pasternak, July 20, 1941, Pasternak, "Iz pisem k zhene," p. 220; Gladkov, *Vstrechi*, p. 68.

62. BP/A. O. Naumova [June or July] 1942, unpublished; BP/M. M. Morozov, July 15, 1942, P. G. Antokolskii/BP, July 9, 1942, "K perevodam shekspirovskikh dram (Iz perepiski Borisa Pasternaka)," pp. 347, 350–51.

63. BP/Z. N. Pasternak, November, 1942, "Stikhi i proza," *Novyi mir*, January, 1965, p. 164.

64. Tregub, "Voenno-polevoi soiuz," pp. 197–98; Nikolai Mazurin, "Orel—god 1943-i," *Literaturnaia Rossiia* 31 (August 2, 1968):5; Ivinskaya, *CAPT*, p. 73.

65. Mazurin, "Orel"; Tregub, "Voenno-polevoi soiuz," pp. 200–203; Semen Tregub, "Tri stikhotvoreniia Borisa Pasternaka," *Literaturnaia Rossiia* 9 (February 23, 1968):22–23; Ivinskaya, *CAPT*, p. 74; Boris Pasternak, "Osvobozhdennyi gorod," *Novyi mir*, January, 1965, p. 164.

67. Tregub, "Voenno-polevoi soiuz," p. 204.

68. Boris Pasternak, "Poezdka v armiiu," *Works*, 3:162–66.

69. Pasternak, *DZh*, pp. 509–12.

70. Krotkov, *KROT 2*, pp. 69, 85–86, 99.

71. Pasternak, "Translating Shakespeare," *IR*, p. 138.

72. Boris Pasternak, "Ozhivshaia freska," *Literatura i iskusstvo*, April 15, 1944; Boris Pasternak, "Zimnie prazdniki," *Literaturnaia gazeta*, November 11, 1944; Gladkov, *Vstrechi*, p. 99; V. Kazin and V. Pertsov, eds., *Sbornik stikhov* (Moscow: Oriz, 1943).

73. BP/N. Tabidze, March 30, 1944, Pasternak, *LGF*, p. 96.

74. Gladkov, *Vstrechi*, p. 101.

75. Pasternak, *STIKHP*, p. 703; Gladkov, *Vstrechi*, pp. 91–93; Ivinskaya, *CAPT*, pp. 139–40.

76. Ivinskaya, *CAPT*, p. 140.

77. Krotkov, *KROT 1*, p. 56; *KROT 2*, p. 66; BP/N. Ia. Mandelstam, 1945, Pasternak, "Pisma B. L. Pasternaka O. E. i N. Ia. Mandelstam," p. 244.

78. Gladkov, *Vstrechi*, pp. 94–95; Nadezhda Mandelstam, *Hope*, p. 276.

CHAPTER 10

1. Nils Åke Nilsson, "Pasternak: 'We Are the Guests of Existence,'" *Reporter* 19 (November 27, 1958):34–35.

2. Czesław Miłosz, "On Pasternak Soberly," *Books Abroad* [now *World Literature Today*] 44 (Spring 1970):205.

3. Aleksandr Gladkov, *Vstrechi*, p. 102.

4. Ibid., pp. 103–104.

5. BP/F. A. Stepun, June 1958, F. A. Stepun, "B. L. Pasternak," *Novyi Zhurnal* 56 (1959).

6. Gladkov, *Vstrechi*, p. 114.

7. Ibid., p. 11.

8. Nilsson, "Pasternak: 'We Are the Guests of Existence,'" p. 34.

9. Boris Pasternak, *DZh*, p. 508; cf. Olga Ivinskaya, *CAPT*, p. 75.

10. BP/Nina Tabidze, first half of 1948, April 5, 1949, Boris Pasternak, *LGF*, pp. 118–19.

11. BP/S. I. Chikovani, August 3, 1945, Pasternak, *LGF*, p. 100.

12. Iurii Krotkov, *KROT 1*, p. 58.

13. BP/Nadezhda Mandelstam, January 26, 1948, Nadezhda Mandelstam, *Hope*, p. 299.

14. Resolution of Central Committee of CPSU, August 14, 1946, "On the Magazines *Zvezda* and *Leningrad*," quoted in Gleb Struve, *Russian Literature Under Lenin and Stalin 1917–1953*, pp. 350, 353–55; Vera Alexandrova, *A History of Soviet Literature, 1917–1964: From Gorky to Solzhenitsyn*, pp. 284–85.

15. Ivinskaya, *CAPT*, p. 122.

16. Ibid., pp. 3–4.

17. Ibid., pp. 6–12.

18. Ibid., pp. 12–17.

19. Ibid., pp. 17–18; Lidiia Chukovskaia, *Zapiski ob Anne Akhmatovoi: I, 1938–41*, p. 89.

20. Krotkov, *KROT 1*, pp. 42–65; Chukovskaia, *Zapiski*, p. 89; Ivinskaya, *CAPT*, p. 18.

21. Ivinskaya, *CAPT*, pp. 19–22.

22. Ibid., pp. 21–22; Gladkov, *Vstrechi*, p. 120.

23. Krotkov, *KROT 1*, p. 72; Ivinskaya, *CAPT*, pp. 22–23.

24. Gladkov, *Vstrechi*, pp. 110, 132.

25. BP/M. N. Chikovani, February 25, 1947, Pasternak, *LGF*, p. 116.

26. Ivinskaya, *CAPT*, pp. 76–77; Gladkov, *Vstrechi*, pp. 109–10, 132.

27. Struve, *Russian Literature*, p. 355; Gladkov, *Vstrechi*, pp. 109–10.

28. Ilya Ehrenburg, *Post-War Years, 1945–1954*, trans. Tatyana Shebunina, p. 165.

29. "O sovetskoi poezii," *Zvezda*, March, 1949; Max Hayward, "Notes and Comments," in Aleksandr Gladkov, *Meetings with Pasternak: A Memoir*, p. 198.

30. A. Surkov, "O poezii B. Pasternaka," *Kultura i zhizn* 8 (March 21, 1947): 2; Gladkov, *Vstrechi*, p. 16; Ivinskaya, *CAPT*, pp. 205, 209.

31. Gladkov, *Vstrechi*, pp. 107–108; Nadezhda Mandelstam, *Hope Abandoned*, p. 479.

32. Gladkov, *Vstrechi*, pp. 110–11.

33. Ibid., p. 111; Ivinskaya, *CAPT*, p. 122; L. Plotkin, "A. A. Zhdanov i voprosy literatury," *Zvezda* 10 (1947).

34. Gladkov, *Vstrechi*, pp. 116–20.

35. Mark Shcheglov, "Studencheskie tetradi," entry for February 23, 1948, *Novyi mir*, June, 1963, p. 138; Hayward, Introduction, in Gladkov, *Meetings with Pasternak*, pp. 20–23.

36. Ivinskaya, *CAPT*, pp. 97, 189–92; Gladkov, *Vstrechi*, pp. 120–21; Nina Skorbina, "Boris Pasternak: Vstrechi i pisma," *Novoe russkoe slovo*, February 18, 1973.

37. Gladkov, *Vstrechi*, p. 120; Ivinskaya, *CAPT*, p. 20.

38. Krotkov, *KROT 2*.

39. Gladkov, *Vstrechi*, pp. 120–22; BP/Z. A. Maslenikova, October 17, 1958; Krotkov, *KROT 1*, p. 63; Ivinskaya, *CAPT*, pp. 38–39, 194, 196–204, 215–20.

40. Krotkov, *KROT 1*, p. 73.

41. BP/Olga Freidenberg, November 30, 1948, in Elliot Mossman, ed., "The Unpublished Letters of Boris Pasternak," *New York Times Magazine*, January 1, 1978, p. 29.

42. BP/Georges Nivat, conversations of 1959–60; Nilsson, "Pasternak: 'We Are the Guests of Existence,'" p. 34; Hélène Peltier, "Ma rencontre avec l'auteur du 'Docteur Jivago,'" *Figaro littéraire*, November 1, 1958; Ivinskaya, *CAPT*, pp. 184–85.

43. Krotkov, *KROT 1*, p. 74; Pasternak, *DZh*, p. 526; Ivinskaya, *CAPT*, pp. 184–85.

44. BP/Georges Nivat, conversation of 1959; cf. Ivinskaya, *CAPT*, pp. 43–44.

45. Pasternak, *DZh*, p. 541.

46. Krotkov, *KROT 1*, p. 74.

47. Ibid., pp. 44–45.

48. Cf. Ralph Matlaw, "A Visit with Pasternak," *Nation*, September, 1959, p. 134–35.

49. BP/unknown student, 1948, Ivinskaya, *CAPT*, p. 183.

50. BP/S. I. Chikovani, April 24, 1949, Pasternak, *LGF*, p. 120; Skorbina, "Boris Pasternak."

51. Pasternak, conversation with Z. A. Maslenikova, October 17, 1958.

52. Skorbina, "Boris Pasternak."

53. Ibid.

54. Ibid.

55. Ibid.

56. Ivinskaya, *CAPT*, pp. 83–86.

57. Ibid., pp. 91–102.

58. Ibid., pp. 99–101.

59. Ibid., pp. 102–106.

60. Ibid., pp. 86–87, 107–109, 117.

61. Ibid., pp. 132–34.

62. Ibid., pp. 96–102.

63. Ibid., p. 119.

64. BP/Georges Nivat, conversations of 1959; BP/Renate Schweitzer, conversations of 1960.

65. Pasternak, *DZh*, p. 544.

66. Ivinskaya, *CAPT*, pp. 90, 119.

67. Ibid., pp. 109–19.

68. Ibid., pp. 127–28.

69. Anatolii Tarasenkov, "Zametki kritika (B. Pasternak)." *Znamia*, October, 1949, p. 163; Gladkov, *Vstrechi*, p. 16.

70. Ivinskaya, *CAPT*, p. 79.

71. BP/N. G. Vachnadze, December 31, 1949, Pasternak, *LGF*, p. 122.

72. BP/R. K. Mikadze, November 18, 1950, ibid., p. 130.

73. BP/Nina Tabidze, April 6, 1950, ibid., pp. 125–26.

74. *Figaro littéraire*, November 1, 1958.

75. BP/Nina Tabidze, April 6, 1950, Pasternak, *LGF*, p. 126.

76. BP/S. I. and M. N. Chikovani, June 14, 1952, ibid., pp. 142–43.

77. Vladimir Markov, ed., *Priglushennye golosa*.

78. Krotkov, *KROT 2*, p. 63; Ivinskaya, *CAPT*, pp. 125, 133, 135, 144.

79. George Gibian, "The Climax with *Doctor*

Zhivago," Interval of Freedom: Soviet Literature During the Thaw, 1954–1957, pp. vii–viii, 3, 9; Walter N. Vickery, *The Cult of Optimism: Political and Ideological Problems of Recent Soviet Literature*, p. 49.

80. BP/Nina Tabidze, 1955, Pasternak, *LGF*, pp. 160–61; Ivinskaya, *CAPT*, pp. 141–42; Krotkov, *KROT 2*, p. 59.

81. BP/Nina Tabidze, September 30, 1953, Pasternak, *LGF*, pp. 155–56.

82. Boris Pasternak, *Znamia*, April 1954, p. 192.

83. *Antologiia*; Vickery, *The Cult of Optimism*, pp. 53–73.

84. Ivinskaya, *CAPT*, pp. 24–26, 36.

85. Ibid., pp. 35–41; Gladkov, *Vstrechi*, p. 16.

86. Gerd Ruge, "A Visit to Pasternak," *Encounter* 54 (March, 1958).

87. BP/Zelma Fedorovna Ruoff, December 10, 1955.

88. Ivinskaya, *CAPT*, pp. 193–95, 202; BP/J. de Proyart, conversation of January, 1957.

89. Pasternak, conversations of 1959–60 with Georges Nivat.

90. Gibian, *Interval of Freedom*, pp. 10, 14–15; Vickery, *The Cult of Optimism*, pp. 82–83.

91. Edward J. Brown, *Russian Literature Since the Revolution*, rev. ed., pp. 178–79.

92. Ivinskaya, *CAPT*, p. 141.

93. Ibid., pp. 196–99; Sergio d'Angelo, "Der Fall Pasternak—Zehn Jahre danach," *Osteuropa*, July, 1968, p. 490.

94. Ivinskaya, *CAPT*, pp. 196–97; d'Angelo, "Der Fall Pasternak," p. 490.

95. Ivinskaya, *CAPT*, pp. 196–97; d'Angelo, "Der Fall Pasternak," p. 490; Krotkov, *KROT 1*, p. 73; *KROT 2*, p. 73.

96. Ivinskaya, *CAPT*, p. 201; d'Angelo, "Der Fall Pasternak," p. 490; private sources.

97. Ivinskaya, *CAPT*, pp. 199–203.

98. Ibid., pp. 202–205; d'Angelo, "Der Fall Pasternak," pp. 490–91; Hayward, "Notes and Comments," in Aleksandr Gladkov, *Meetings with Pasternak*, p. 201.

99. *Novye knigi* 31 (1957); *Sovetskie knigi* 87 (1957); d'Angelo, "Der Fall Pasternak," p. 493.

100. D'Angelo, "Der Fall Pasternak," p. 491; Ivinskaya, *CAPT*, p. 207.

101. Ivinskaya, *CAPT*, pp. 194–95; Pasternak, conversation of early February, 1957, with Jacqueline de Proyart.

102. BP/Maurice Nadeau, February 4, 1957, *Les Lettres nouvelles*, November, 1961, pp. 7–8 (the letter reached Nadeau in April, 1960); Hélène Peltier, "Ma rencontre avec l'auteur du 'Docteur Jivago.'"

103. Ivinskaya, *CAPT*, p. 350; J. de Proyart/G. de Mallac, September 19, 1977.

104. Ivinskaya, *CAPT*, pp. 193–94, 374–75; Robert Conquest, *The Pasternak Affair: Courage of Genius*, p. 64.

105. Ivinskaya, *CAPT*, pp. 206, 371–77; J. de Proyart/G. de Mallac, September 19, 1977.

106. Ivinskaya, *CAPT*, p. 196; Conquest, *The Pasternak Affair*, p. 64; d'Angelo, "Der Fall Pasternak," p. 491.

107. Ivinskaya, *CAPT*, p. 207; Conquest, *The Pasternak Affair*, p. 64.

108. Ivinskaya, *CAPT*, pp. 375–76; Leonid Borisovich Pasternak/G. de Mallac, January 14, 1963; BP/Nina Tabidze, August 21, 1957; Pasternak, *LGF*, pp. 162–63.

109. Ivinskaya, *CAPT*, pp. 205, 210; d'Angelo, "Der Fall Pasternak," pp. 491–92.

110. Ivinskaya, *CAPT*, p. 211; d'Angelo, "Der Fall Pasternak," p. 492.

111. BP/J. de Proyart, November 3, 1957 (unpublished, communicated to author by Jacqueline de Proyart).

112. Ivinskaya, *CAPT*, pp. 210–11.

113. Meeting of August 16, 1957, in Gladkov, *Vstrechi*, pp. 126–27; Ivinskaya, *CAPT*, pp. 211, 215–19.

114. Ivinskaya, *CAPT*, p. 211; d'Angelo, "Der Fall Pasternak," pp. 492–93.

115. *Unità*, October 22, 1957.

116. *Opinie*, July–September, 1957; Angelo Maria Ripellino, "Una Visita a Pasternak," *Corriere della Sera*, April 21, 1963.

117. For background information on that period, see Gibian, *Interval of Freedom*, pp. 18–24; Vickery, *The Cult of Optimism*, pp. 89–95.

118. Sergei Vasilev, "Minuta otkroveniia (Boris Pasternak)," *Satiricheskie stikhi*, pp. 11–12.

119. Ripellino, "Una Visita a Pasternak," *Corriere della Sera*, April 21, 1963.

120. Evgenii Evtushenko, *Avtobiografiia*, pp. 118–22.

121. *L'Espresso*, November 10, 1957; *Corriere della Sera*, November 23, 1957.

122. Ruge, "A Visit with Pasternak," p. 22.

123. *Antologiia russkoi sovetskoi poezii v dvukh tomakh*, ed. V. A. Lugovskoi et al.

124. BP/J. de Proyart, May 8, 1958.

125. BP/Kurt Wolff, October 3, 1958, unpublished.

CHAPTER II

1. Bernard Le Bovier de Fontenelle, "De la connaissance de l'esprit humain: Fragment," *Œuvres complètes*, ed. G. B. Depping, 2:412.

2. Karl Marx, "Verhandlungen des 6. rheinischen Landtags: Erster Artikel. Debatten über Pressfreiheit und Publikation der Landständischen Verhandlungen," *Rheinische Zeitung*, May 5, 1842.

3. BP/Kurt Wolff, May 12, 1958, Kurt Wolff, *Briefwechsel eines Verlegers: 1911–1963*, p. 479.

4. Abram Tertz [Andrei Siniavskii], "The Literary Process in Russia," *Kontinent I*, p. 88.

5. Anders Østerling, "Announcement," *Roger Martin du Gard, Gabriela Mistral, Boris Pasternak*, Nobel Prize Library, pp. 219, 221 (slightly different formulations of the award citation are to be found on these pages).

6. BP/A. I. Puzikov, Olga Ivinskaya, *CAPT*, p. 214.

7. Much of the background on the literary scene of that period is discussed in: George Gibian, *Interval of Freedom: Soviet Literature During the Thaw, 1954–1957*, pp. 18–22.

8. BP/Aleksandr Bisk, February 24, 1958, *Novoe russkoe slovo*, March 16, 1958; BP/Renate Schweitzer, April 3, 1958, Renate Schweitzer, *Freundschaft mit Pasternak*, p. 11; Ivinskaya, *CAPT*, pp. 214–15; BP/R. Schweitzer, May 29, 1958, June 20, 1958, Schweitzer, *Freundschaft*, pp. 18, 20–21.

9. Gerd Ruge, "A Visit to Pasternak," *Encounter*, March, 1959; Schweitzer, *Freundschaft*, p. 56.

10. BP/R. Schweitzer, April 3, May 7, 1958, Schweitzer, *Freundschaft*, pp. 11–12, 47.

11. BP/Kurt Wolff, July 10, 1958, unpublished.

12. BP/R. Schweitzer, July 12, 1958, Schweitzer, *Freundschaft*, p. 28.

13. Gerd Ruge, *Boris Pasternak: A Pictorial Biography*, pp. 107ff.; BP/Kurt Wolff, August 19, 1958, unpublished; Ivinskaya, *CAPT*, pp. 214–15; Fedor Panfërov, conversation with Max Hayward, 1960.

14. BP/R. Schweitzer, August 12, 1958, Schweitzer, *Freundschaft*, p. 31; BP/Eugene Kayden, August 22, 1958, Boris Pasternak, "Pasternak on Poetry," *Poems*, trans. E. M. Kayden, pp. vii–ix.

15. *Times* (London), September 4, 1958; *London Daily Express*, September 25, 1958; Edmund Wilson, "Doctor Life and His Guardian Angel," *New Yorker*, November 15, 1958, p. 238.

16. Ivinskaya, *CAPT*, pp. 215–19.

17. BP/M. I. Zlatkin, September 2, 1958, Boris Pasternak, *LGF*, pp. 171–72.

18. Pasternak, conversation of August 30, 1959, with Henrik Birnbaum; Nils Åke Nilsson/author, March 22, 1976.

19. Anders Østerling/J. de Proyart, April 16, 1963, unpublished; Ivinskaya, *CAPT*, p. 220; Sir Maurice Bowra/author, June 25, 1963, unpublished.

20. Anders Østerling, quoted by David Floyd, *Daily Telegraph* (London), October 24, 1958; Schweitzer, *Freundschaft*, p. 48.

21. Nils Åke Nilsson/author, March 22, 1976; cf. Nils Åke Nilsson, "Ovädret förbi, Pasternak inte tabu," *Stockholm Expressen*, May 25, 1959.

22. BP/R. Schweitzer, October 9, 1958, Schweitzer, *Freundschaft*, pp. 53, 54.

23. BP/R. Schweitzer, October 21, 22, 1958, Schweitzer, *Freundschaft*, p. 61; Ivinskaya, *CAPT*, p. 231; Conquest, *The Pasternak Affair*, pp. 58–59.

24. Ivinskaya, *CAPT*, pp. 350–51.

25. *Frankfurter Allgemeine Zeitung*, October 4, 1958; Nils Åke Nilsson, "Hos Boris Pasternak," *Bonniers litterära magasin* 27 (1958); same item, *Dagens Nyheter*, October 23, 1958; cf. *Die Welt* [Hamburg] October 24, 1958; *London Daily Mail* October 24, 1958; *Le Monde* [Paris], October 28, 1958; Conquest, *The Pasternak Affair*, p. 201.

26. Anders Østerling; *London Daily Telegraph*, October 24, 1958; *Le Monde*, October 25, 1958.

27. *Manchester Guardian*, October 25, 1958; *Le Monde*, October 26, 27, 1958; Conquest, *The Pasternak Affair*, pp. 59, 92; *New York Times*, October 27, 1958; *Sunday Times* (London), October 26, 1958.

28. Nilsson, "Ovädret förbi."

29. Kurt Wolff/BP, October 25, 1958, Kurt Wolff, *Briefwechsel*, p. 480.

30. *Le Monde*, October 25, 1958; D. Zaslavskii, *Literaturnaia gazeta*, October 25, 1958; cf. Conquest, *The Pasternak Affair*, pp. 131ff.

31. George Gibian, *Interval of Freedom: Soviet Literature During the Thaw, 1954–1957*, p. 155.

32. Conquest, *The Pasternak Affair*, pp. 139ff.

33. Gibian, *Interval of Freedom*, p. 156.

34. *Daily Telegraph* (London), October 25, 1958.

35. Aleksandr Gladkov, *Vstrechi*, p. 146.

36. D. Zaslavskii, "Shumikha reaktsionnoi propagandy vokrug literaturnogo sorniaka," *Pravda*, October 26, 1958, trans. in Conquest, *The Pasternak Affair*, pp. 167ff.

37. V. Zorza, "Pasternak Acceptance Angers 'Pravda,'" *Daily Telegraph* (London), October 27, 1958; *Literaturnaia gazeta*, October 29, 1958; Nadezhda Mandelstam, *Hope*, p. 83; Ivinskaya, *CAPT*, pp. 227–28, 251–59.

38. Conquest, *The Pasternak Affair*, pp. 175ff.; Ivinskaya, *CAPT*, pp. 233–35.

39. Pasternak, telegram to Østerling, *Times* (London), *Le Monde*, October 30, 1958.

40. *Manchester Guardian*, October 30, 1958; Ivinskaya, *CAPT*, p. 232; Conquest, *The Pasternak Affair*, p. 93.

41. *Times* (London), October 30, 1958.

42. Nikita S. Khrushchev, *Khrushchev Remembers*, pp. 76–77.

43. Conquest, *The Pasternak Affair*, pp. 175–76.

44. *Times* (London), *Le Monde*, October 30, 1958.

45. Ivinskaya, *CAPT*, pp. 234, 236–41.

46. Ibid., pp. 232–34, 238–41.

47. Ibid., pp. 261–68; Heinz Schewe, *Pasternak privat*, pp. 25–29.

48. Ivinskaya, *CAPT*, pp. 268–75.

49. Conquest, *The Pasternak Affair*, pp. 177–78.

50. *Times* (London), October 31, 1958; *Le Monde*, November 1, 1958; Conquest, *The Pasternak Affair*, pp. 74ff.

51. BP/R. Schweitzer, October 21–22, 1958, Schweitzer, *Freundschaft*, p. 61; Conquest, *The Pasternak Affair*, p. 58; Ivinskaya, *CAPT*, p. 231.

52. Ivinskaya, *CAPT*, pp. 277–80; Conquest, *The Pasternak Affair*, pp. 178ff.

53. Ivinskaya, *CAPT*, pp. 244–46.

54. Boris Pasternak, "Hamlet," in "Poems of Iurii Zhivago," *DZh*, p. 523; Mandelstam, *Hope*, p. 225.

55. Gladkov, *Vstrechi*, pp. 144–45, 147; Henrik Birnbaum, conversation with author; Iurii Krotkov, *KROT 2*, pp. 76–78.

56. *Manchester Guardian*, December 22, 1958; *Le Monde*, December 23, 1958 (both quoting from *Welt am Sonntag* [Hamburg]).

57. Gladkov, *Vstrechi*, p. 146.

58. BP/R. Schweitzer, December 5, 1958, Schweitzer, *Freundschaft*, p. 63; *Pravda*, December 8, 1958.

59. *Le Monde*, December 7, 1958; *Süddeutsche Zeitung* (Munich), December 8, 1958.

60. *Le Monde*, December 11, 1958.

61. *Manchester Guardian*, December 22, 1958, quoting *Welt am Sonntag* [Hamburg]; *Le Monde*, December 23, 1958, quoting *Welt am Sonntag*.

62. *Süddeutsche Zeitung*, January 12, 1959; John Strachey's article was later included in *The Strangled Cry*, pp. 44–77.

63. *Times* (London), January 22, 1959; *Le Monde*, March 18, 1959; *New York Herald Tribune*, May 2, 1959; Krotkov, *KROT 1*, p. 46; Ivinskaya, *CAPT*, pp. 212, 402. *Sunday Times* (London), April 19, 1959; *London Evening Standard*, February 6, 1959.

64. *London Daily Telegraph*, February 11, 1959.

65. Pasternak, letters of January 27, early February, and November 22, 1959, to a Belgian correspondent, Marnix Gijsen, "A Note on Pasternak," *Books Abroad* [now *World Literature Today*] 35 (1961): 132–33.

66. Jacqueline de Proyart, statement to author.

67. *London Daily Mail*, February 11, 1959.

68. *London Daily Mirror*, February 12, 1959; *London Daily Mail*, February 11, 12, 1959.

69. Ivinskaya, *CAPT*, pp. 297–99; Max Hayward, "Notes and Comments," Ivinskaya, *CAPT*, p. 404; Boris Pasternak, *Works*, 3 : 107–108.

70. Ivinskaya, *CAPT*, pp. 293–94; Hayward, "Notes and Comments," Ivinskaya, *CAPT*, pp. 404–405; Schweitzer, *Freundschaft*, pp. 68, 76, 125.

71. *Times* (London), February 14, 1959; *New York Herald Tribune*, February 17, 1959; Schewe, *Pasternak privat*, pp. 15–16.

72. *Manchester Guardian*, February 23, 1959; *Le Monde*, February 24, 1959; *Times* (London), February 23, 1959.

73. Ivinskaya, *CAPT*, p. 300 [it is difficult to accept Ivinskaia's chronology]; Krotkov, *KROT 1*, pp. 36–49; Leonid Borisovich Pasternak/author, March, 1963.

74. Patricia Blake, "We Don't Breathe Easily," *Harper's Magazine*, May, 1961, p. 121; Jhan Robbins, "Boris Pasternak's Last Message to the World," *New York Herald Tribune*, August 7, 1960, p. 5; Ivinskaya, *CAPT*, pp. 293–94; Ralph E. Matlaw, "Visit with Pasternak," *Nation*, September 12, 1959, p. 134.

75. *New York Herald Tribune*, April 29, 1959.

76. Schweitzer, *Freundschaft*, pp. 78–79.

77. Victor Zorza, "Royalties for Pasternak,"

Manchester Guardian, August 22, 1959; *New York Herald Tribune*, April 5, 1959; Krotkov, *KROT 1*, p. 60.

78. *Sunday Times* (London), August 16, 1959; *Frankfurter Allgemeine Zeitung*, August 25, 1959; *Le Monde*, September 8, 1959; *Le Figaro littéraire*, October 3, 1959; *Schweizer Allgemeine Zeitung*, 1959.

79. Moscow correspondence by Harrison E. Salisbury, published in the *New York Times* and quoted in *Le Figaro littéraire*, October 3, 1959.

80. BP/J. de Proyart, January 17, 1960, Jacqueline de Proyart, *Pasternak*, p. 240; BP/R. Schweitzer, October 9, 1958, Schweitzer, *Freundschaft*, p. 52.

81. Pasternak, *Works*, 3:59–110; Jacqueline de Proyart, "La nature et l'actualité dans l'œuvre de Boris Pasternak (Réflexions sur la structure du cycle *Kogda razguljaetsja*)," *Boris Pasternak, 1890–1960: Colloque de Cerisy-la-Salle (11–14 septembre 1975)*, ed. Michel Aucouturier, pp. 373–410.

82. Angela Livingstone, "Pasternak's Last Poetry," *Meanjin Quarterly* 22 (1963): 388, 395.

83. Pasternak, *Works*, 3:62; cf. Proyart, "La nature et l'actualité," p. 405.

84. Pasternak, *Works*, 2:350–53; Proyart, "La nature et l'actualité," p. 405; Ivinskaya, *CAPT*, pp. 209, 360–62, 412.

85. Gladkov, *Vstrechi*, p. 129.

86. Boris Pasternak, *IR*, pp. 19–44.

87. Ibid., pp. 49–50, 53, 56, 62, 121.

88. Ibid., p. 93; Gladkov, *Vstrechi*, p. 129.

89. Sherman Paul, "An Art of Life: Pasternak's Autobiographies," *Salmagundi* 14 (1970): 31; Pasternak, *IR*, p. 121.

90. *Literaturnaia Moskva: Almanakh*.

91. Schewe, *Pasternak privat*, pp. 34–42; Ivinskaya, *CAPT*, p. 174.

92. Ivinskaya, *CAPT*, p. 275; BP/Thomas Merton, February 7, 1960, Thomas Merton, "Postscript to the Pasternak Affair," *Disputed Questions*, pp. 218–19.

93. N. N-ko [*sic*], "Moi vstrechi s Annoi Akhmatovoi," *Novoe russkoe slovo*, March 13, 1966.

CHAPTER 12

1. Bernard Gilbert Guerney, ed., "Boris Leonidovich Pasternak," in *An Anthology of Russian Literature in the Soviet Period from Gorki to Pasternak*, p. 416.

2. Pasternak, statement to Ivinskaia, Olga Ivinskaya, *CAPT*, pp. 43–44.

3. Ilia Ehrenburg, *People and Life, 1891–1921*, trans. A. Bostock and Y. Kapp, p. 286.

4. Heinz Schewe, *Pasternak privat*, pp. 16–20; Ivinskaya, *CAPT*, p. 313.

5. Aleksandr Gladkov, *Vstrechi*, pp. 20, 126; Kornei Chukovskii, "Boris Pasternak (1890–1960)," in Boris Pasternak, *Stikhi*, pp. 5–6; Schewe, *Pasternak privat*, p. 12; Iurii Krotkov, *KROT 2*, p. 61.

6. Chukovskii, "Boris Pasternak," pp. 5–6; Krotkov, *KROT 1*, pp. 40, 42, 44, 65; Krotkov, *KROT 2*, pp. 60–61; Gladkov, *Vstrechi*, pp. 11–12, 61, 116, 126; Ehrenburg, *People and Life*, p. 281.

7. Gladkov, *Vstrechi*, pp. 44, 112; Krotkov, *KROT 1*, p. 57; Krotkov, *KROT 2*, pp. 60–61, 67; Chukovskii, "Boris Pasternak," p. 6; Aleksandr Afinogenov, *Stati, Dnevniki, Pisma, Vospominaniia*, p. 152; Jhan Robbins, "Boris Pasternak's Last Message to the World," p. 5.

8. BP/R. Schweitzer, June 15, 1959, in Renate Schweitzer, *Freundschaft mit Pasternak*, pp. 83–84; Krotkov, *KROT 2*, pp. 61, 78–79; Ivinskaya, *CAPT*, pp. 309–12.

9. Gladkov, *Vstrechi*, pp. 55, 68, 74, 79, 82, 89, 125, 146; Nadezhda Mandelstam, *Hope Abandoned*, p. 362; Ivinskaya, *CAPT*, p. 309.

10. Ivinskaya, *CAPT*, pp. 309–10; Olga Carlisle, "Three Visits with Boris Pasternak," *Paris Review* 24 (Summer–Fall, 1960): 45–69.

11. Carlisle, "Three Visits," pp. 61–66.

12. Gladkov's notes of his conversation of February, 1961, with Pasternak's neighbor Vsevolod Viacheslavovich Ivanov, in Gladkov, *Vstrechi*, pp. 147–48.

13. Pasternak, quoted in *Encounter*, August, 1960; Robert Conquest, "Le sort d'Olga Ivinskaia," *Preuves* 126 (December, 1961): 67; Ivinskaya, *CAPT*, p. 319; Georges Nivat/author, June 30, 1976.

14. BP/R. Schweitzer, January 25, April 14, 1960, in Schweitzer, *Freundschaft*, pp. 110–11, 138–39; Ivinskaya, *CAPT*, pp. 316–17.

15. Schweitzer, *Freundschaft*, pp. 120–24, 135; R. Schweitzer, conversation with author, September, 1975.

16. Schweitzer, *Freundschaft*, p. 122.

17. Ibid., p. 133; Albert Schweitzer/R. Schweitzer, September 14, 1960, unpublished.

18. Schweitzer, *Freundschaft*, pp. 133–34.

19. Ibid., pp. 135–38.

20. BP/Schweitzer, April 25, 1960, in Schweitzer, *Freundschaft*, pp. 140–41.

21. Pasternak, telegram to Schweitzer, May 6, 1960; Schweitzer, *Freundschaft*, p. 141.

22. Krotkov, *KROT 2*, pp. 81–83; Schweitzer, *Freundschaft*, p. 124.

23. Priscilla Johnson, "Letter from Moscow," *Harper's Magazine*, May, 1961, p. 141; Ivinskaya, *CAPT*, p. 386; Schweitzer, *Freundschaft*, pp. 140–41.

24. Krotkov, *KROT 1*, pp. 63–64; Ivinskaya, *CAPT*, p. 320.

25. Krotkov, *KROT 1*, pp. 63–64; Ivinskaya, *CAPT*, p. 323; Georges Nivat, conversation with author.

26. Johnson, "Letter from Moscow," p. 141.

27. Ibid.

28. *Literatura i zhizn*, June 1, 1960; *Literaturnaia gazeta*, June 2, 1960; Max Hayward, "Notes and Commentaries," in Ivinskaya, *CAPT*, pp. 406–407.

29. Nivat, conversation with author; Schewe, *Pasternak privat*, pp. 48–49.

30. Ivinskaya, *CAPT*, pp. 325–32; Conquest, *The Pasternak Affair*, p. 186; Gladkov, *Vstrechi*, p. 154; Krotkov, *KROT 2*, p. 87.

31. Johnson, "Letter from Moscow," p. 141; Ivinskaya, *CAPT*, pp. 329–30; eyewitnesses Arkadii Belinkov, Nataliia Belinkov, Georges Nivat, Vladimir Lefebvre, and Jeremiah Schneiderman.

32. Winthrop Knowlton, "A Pilgrim at the Grave of Boris Pasternak," *Los Angeles Times*, February 5, 1978; Thomas Merton, "Postscript to the Pasternak Affair," in Merton, *Disputed Questions*, p. 294.

33. Johnson, "Letter from Moscow," pp. 144–45; eyewitnesses Vladimir Lefebvre and Nataliia Belinkov.

34. Merton, "Postscript," p. 293; L. S. Fleishman, "Avtobiograficheskoe i 'Avgust' Pasternaka," *Slavica Hierosolymitana* 1 (1977): 194–98; Olga R. Hughes, *The Poetic World of Boris Pasternak*, p. 163; Ivinskaya, *CAPT*, p. 324.

35. Johnson, "Letter from Moscow," p. 145; eyewitness Vladimir Lefebvre.

36. Nataliia Belinkov; Schewe, *Pasternak privat*, pp. 48–49.

37. *Times* (London), June 29, 1960.

38. Pasternak, conversation of August 30, 1959, with Henrik Birnbaum; "Letter from Veniamin Kaverin to Konstantin Fedin of 25 January 1968," *Survey* 68 (July, 1968): 115; eyewitness Arkadii Belinkov.

39. Nivat/author, June 30, 1976; Ivinskaya,

CAPT, p. 336; Schewe, *Pasternak privat*, p. 30.

40. Krotkov, *KROT 1*, p. 57.

41. Ivinskaya, *CAPT*, pp. 333–49; Conquest, *The Pasternak Affair*, pp. 111–28; Schewe, *Pasternak privat*, p. 52.

42. Ivinskaya, *CAPT*, pp. 333–49; Schewe, *Pasternak privat*, pp. 69–71.

43. Ivinskaya, *CAPT*, pp. 338–42.

44. Conquest, *The Pasternak Affair*, pp. 181–89; Ivinskaya, *CAPT*, p. 345.

45. Boris Pasternak, *DZh*, p. 503.

46. Ivinskaya, *CAPT*, pp. 336, 427; Conquest, *The Pasternak Affair*, pp. 111, 188.

47. Conquest, *The Pasternak Affair*, p. 111; Schewe, *Pasternak privat*, pp. 70–71; Ivinskaya, *CAPT*, pp. 349–60, 409–10.

48. Radio Moscow, broadcasts in Italian, German, and English, January 21, 1961; Conquest, *The Pasternak Affair*, pp. 109–14.

49. *Times* (London), January 23, 1961; *Manchester Guardian*, January 23, 1961.

50. *New Statesman* (London), February 3, 1961.

51. Krotkov, *KROT 1*, pp. 50, 59; Zinaida Nikolaevna Pasternak, conversation with author, May, 1963.

52. Krotkov, *KROT 2*, pp. 57–58.

53. Ibid.

54. Aleksei Surkov, *Komsomolskaia pravda*, May 9, 1963; Aleksei Surkov, Foreword, *Golosa vremeni: Zametki na poliakh istorii literatury, 1934–1965*, p. 7; N. Viliam-Vilmont, Introduction, Johann Wolfgang von Goethe, *Faust*, trans. Boris Pasternak, 3d ed.

55. *New York Herald Tribune*, November 18, 1960.

56. Radio Moscow, German-language broadcast, January 11, 1962.

57. Radio Moscow, English-language broadcast for Great Britain and Ireland, August 7, 1962.

58. Geinrikh Kleist, *Pesy*, ed. A. Dymshits.

59. Ivan Bunin, *Sobranie sochinenii*; Aleksandr Solzhenitsyn, "*Odin den Ivana Denisovicha*," *Novyi mir*, January, 1963.

60. *New York Herald Tribune*, January 8, 1962; *Le Monde*, January 9, 1962.

61. Ilia Ehrenburg, "Liudi, gody, zhizn," *Novyi mir*, April, 1962, p. 50.

62. Lev Ozerov, *Literaturnaia gazeta*, June 12, 1962.

63. Mekhti Gussein, "Stranitsy dnevnika," *Znamia*, March, 1962, p. 110.

64. Krotkov, *KROT 2*, p. 80; Boris Pasternak, *Doktor Živago*, trans. Olga Vlatkovič. Belgrade: Prosveta, 1962.

65. K. Pomerantsev, "Vo chto verit sovetskaia molodezh?" *Novyi zhurnal* 78 (1965): 152–53.

66. Gladkov, *Vstrechi*, pp. 114–15; Evgenii Evtushenko, *Avtobiografiia*, p. 120.

67. Gladkov, *Vstrechi*, p. 104.

68. Ivinskaya, *CAPT*, pp. 147–48; Andrei Voznesenskii, "Molodye—o sebe," *Voprosy literatury*, September, 1962, p. 123; Krotkov, *KROT 2*, p. 78; Andrei Voznesenskii, "Listia i korni," *Literatura i zhizn*, November 20, 1960; Andreii Voznesenskii, "Leaves and Roots," trans. Stanley Kunitz, in Ivinskaya, *CAPT*, p. 406; Andrei Voznesenskii, press conference, Paris, December 20, 1962; Andrei Voznesenskii, "Nebo Borisa Pasternaka," *Inostrannaia literatura*, February, 1969, pp. 98–101.

69. Bella Akhmadulina, *Oznob*, pp. 177–80; Bella Akhmadulina, *Izbrannye stikhi*, pp. 154–58.

70. Evgenii Evtushenko, "Ograda," *Sobranie sochinenii v trekh tomakh*, pp. 111–13; Evtushenko, *Avtobiografiia*, pp. 118–22.

71. Vladimir Kornilov, "My khoronili starika," *Novyi mir*, December, 1964.

72. Georgii Margvelashvili, "V mire obrazov Georgiia Leonidze," *Literaturnaia Gruziia*, May, 1964, pp. 63–68.

73. M. B. Khrapchenko, *Tvorcheskaia individualnost pisatelia i razvitie literatury* (Moscow: Sovetskii pisatel, 1975), pp. 201–203; Nikolai Rylenkov, "Vtoraia zhizn poeta," *Dusha poezii: Portrety i razdumia*, pp. 252–57.

74. Aleksandr Solzhenitsyn, *Bodalsia telenok s dubom: Ocherki literaturnoi zhizni*, pp. 14, 130–31, 144–45.

75. Gladkov, *Vstrechi*; Alexander Gladkov, *Meetings with Pasternak*, trans. and ed. Max Hayward.

76. Christopher Ricks, "Pasternak: A Prince Among Survivors," *Sunday Times* (London), April 16, 1978; Olga Ivinskaia, *V plenu vremeni: Gody s Borisom Pasternakom*; Ivinskaya, *CAPT*.

77. Czesław Miłosz, "On Pasternak Soberly," *Books Abroad* [now *World Literature Today*] 44 (Spring, 1970): 201.

78. Ivinskaya, *CAPT*, pp. 366–67.

79. John Strachey, "Pasternak's Children," *Observer* (London), May 5, 1963; Klaus Mehnert, "Pasternaks Enkel," *Ost-Europa*, July, 1968, pp. 502–505; Hedrick Smith, *The Russians*, pp. 398–99; Knowlton, "A Pilgrim."

CHAPTER 13

1. Boris Pasternak, *DZh*, p. 338.

2. Andrei Siniavskii, "Poeziia Pasternaka," Boris Pasternak, *STIKHP*, pp. 9–62; Marina Tsvetaeva, "Svetovoi liven," *Epopeia* 2 (1922): 10–33.

3. Cf. C. M. Bowra, "Boris Pasternak, 1917–1923," *The Creative Experiment*, p. 147.

4. Pasternak, *DZh*, pp. 67–68.

5. Cf. Robert Lenoble, *Esquisse d'une histoire de l'idée de nature*, pp. 217–38, 279–364.

6. Pasternak, *DZh*, p. 338.

7. "Man into Superman: The Promise and Peril of the New Genetics," *Time*, April 19, 1971.

8. Pasternak, *DZh*, pp. 297, 338.

9. Henri Bergson, *L'évolution créatrice*, pp. 31, 266; Henri Bergson, *L'énergie spirituelle*, pp. 19, 21.

10. Boris Pasternak, *SC*, p. 22.

11. Boris Pasternak, *IR*, p. 54.

12. Kornelii Zelinskii, "Sumerki Gamsuna," *Na rubezhe dvukh epokh: Literaturnye vstrechi 1917–1920 godov*, pp. 96–103.

13. Vladimir Markov, *Russian Futurism: A History*, p. 242.

14. Pasternak, *DZh*, pp. 488–89.

15. Ibid., p. 474.

16. Ibid., pp. 242, 507.

17. Ibid., p. 277.

18. Pasternak, *IR*, p. 65.

19. Knut Hamsun, *Growth of the Soil*, p. 252.

20. Pasternak, statement to Jhan Robbins, fall, 1959, Jhan Robbins, "A Visit to Pasternak," p. 5.

21. Iurii Krotkov, *KROT 2*, pp. 60–61, 66–67; Aleksandr Gladkov, *Vstrechi*, p. 112.

22. Roman Jakobson, "On Russian Fairy Tales," in *Russian Fairy Tales* [selected from Afanasev collection], trans. Norbert Guterman, p. 650.

23. Kendall E. Bailes, "The Politics of Technology: Stalin and Technocratic Thinking Among Soviet Engineers," *American Historical Review* 79 (April, 1974): 445–69.

24. Josef Pieper, *Leisure: The Basis of Culture*, trans. Alexander Dru, intro. T. S. Eliot; Renate Schweitzer, *Freundschaft*; Albert Schweitzer, *Out of My Life and Thought: An Autobiography*, trans. C. T. Campion, pp. 116–28, 154–58.

CHAPTER 14

1. Boris Pasternak, *DZh*, p. 10.

2. Ibid., p. 66.

3. Victor Frank, "Boris Pasternak" (paper read at Pasternak Symposium, Saint Antony's College, Oxford University, December, 1962).

4. Boris Pasternak, *STIKHP*, p. 187.

5. Ibid., p. 111.

6. Isaac Deutscher, "Pasternak and the Calendar of the Revolution," *Partisan Review*, Spring, 1959; quoted in Donald Davie and Angela Livingstone, eds., Pasternak: *Modern Judgements*, pp. 240–58.

7. Ibid., pp. 243, 248.

8. Pasternak, *DZh*, p. 261.

9. Ibid., p. 170.

10. Ibid., p. 147.

11. Ibid., p. 197.

12. Raymond Aron, *L'Opium des intellectuels*, pp. 54–55.

13. Jean Duvignaud, "Le Don Quichotte de notre temps," *Arguments*, December, 1958, p. 7.

14. Benjamin Goriély, trans., untitled introductory study of *The Year 1905*, in Boris Pasternak, *L'An 1905*, p. 23.

15. Deutscher, "Pasternak and the Calendar," p. 246.

16. Andrei Levinson, "Poezdka iz Peterburga v Sibir v ianvare 1920 g.," *Arkhiv russkoi revoliutsii*, 3d ed., 3:190–209.

17. Yves Berger, *Boris Pasternak*, p. 75.

18. Jacques Dinfreville, "La Guerre des partisans dans le Docteur Jivago," *Revue de défense nationale*, January, 1960, pp. 4–50.

19. C. M. Bowra, "Boris Pasternak, 1917–23," *The Creative Experiment*, p. 150.

20. Ibid., p. 153.

21. Nadezhda Mandelstam, *Hope*, p. 126.

22. Pasternak, *DZh*, pp. 296–97, 310, 378.

23. Ibid., pp. 299, 301.

24. Ibid., pp. 224, 260, 381–82.

25. Editorial, *Arguments*, December, 1958, p. 2.

26. Renato Poggioli, "Boris Pasternak," *Partisan Review* 25 (Fall, 1958):549.

27. Aron, *L'Opium des intellectuels*, p. 50.

28. Boris Pasternak, *The Last Summer*, pp. 31–32.

29. L. A. Zander, "Filosofskie temy v romane B. L. Pasternaka 'Doktor Zhivago,'" *Vestnik russkogo studencheskogo khristianskogo dvizheniia* 1, no. 52 (1959):40.

30. Frank, "Boris Pasternak."

31. Olga Ivinskaya, *CAPT*, p. 190.

32. Aron, *L'Opium des intellectuels*, p. 66.

33. Jean-Paul Sartre, *Critique de la raison dialectique*, 1:15, 23, 107, 139.

34. Deutscher, "Pasternak and the Calendar," p. 253.

35. Pasternak, *DZh*, p. 460.

36. Ibid., p. 259.

37. V. I. Lenin, *Chto takoe "Druzia naroda" i kak oni voiuiut protiv sotsial-demokratov?* vol. 1 of *Polnoe sobranie sochinenii*, 5th ed., pp. 139–40.

38. Pasternak, *DZh*, p. 10.

39. Karl Marx, *Ökonomisch-philosophische Manuskripte aus dem Jahre* 1844, in Karl Marx and Friedrich Engels, *Historisch-kritische Gesamtausgabe*, ed. V. Adoratskii, 3:111–23, 150–72.

40. Sartre, *Critique de la raison dialectique*, p. 81.

41. Boris Pasternak, *SC*, p. 39.

42. Pasternak, *DZh*, p. 43.

43. Ibid.

44. Ibid., p. 10.

45. Ibid., pp. 10, 43, 412–13.

46. Aleksandr Gladkov, *Vstrechi*, p. 54.

47. Deutscher, "Pasternak and the Calendar," pp. 254–55.

48. Ibid., p. 240.

49. Ivinskaya, *CAPT*, p. 135.

50. Ibid., p. 142.

51. Pasternak, *DZh*, p. 413.

52. Ibid., p. 411.

53. Ibid., pp. 411, 43, 413, 10, 66.

54. Ibid., p. 10.

CHAPTER 15

1. Boris Pasternak, *DZh*, pp. 412–13.

2. Boris Pasternak, "Posle viugi," *STIKHP*, pp. 473–74.

3. Boris Pasternak, "Za povorotom," ibid., p. 481; Boris Pasternak, "Vse sbylos," ibid., p. 482.

4. Boris Pasternak, "Poka my po Kavkazu lazaem," ibid., p. 370.

5. Boris Pasternak, "Dusha," ("Soul"), in Boris Pasternak, *Kogda razguliaetsia: Poems, 1955–1959*, trans. Michael Harari, p. 17.

6. Boris Pasternak, "Noch" ("Night"), ibid., p. 61.

7. Pasternak, *DZh*, p. 502 (translation modified).

8. Ibid.

9. David Riesman, with Reuel Denney and Nathan Glazer, *The Lonely Crowd: A Study of the Changing American Character*, pp. 13–15, 113–18.

10. Gabriel Marcel, *Être et avoir*, pp. 25–26.

11. Jean-Paul Sartre, *Critique de la raison dialec-*

tique, vol. 1, *Théorie des ensembles pratiques*, pp. 61, 66, 310, 406–407.

12. Pasternak, *DZh*, p. 474.

13. Georges Canguilhem, *Connaissance de la vie*, p. 86.

14. Boris Pasternak, *IR*, pp. 63–64.

15. Pasternak, *DZh*, pp. 67–68.

16. Boris Pasternak, "O skromnosti i smelosti," *Works*, 3:223.

17. Boris Pasternak, *SC*, p. 22.

18. Pasternak, *DZh*, p. 9; Boris Pasternak, "Nadmennyi nishchii," *Works*, 2:300; Boris Pasternak, *Doktor Zh*, p. 306.

19. René E. Fortin, "Home and the Uses of Creative Nostalgia in *Doctor Zhivago*," *Modern Fiction Studies* 10 (1974):203–209.

20. Gaston Bachelard, *La Terre et les rêveries du repos*.

21. Alexander Gershenkron, "Notes on *Doctor Zhivago*," *Modern Philology* 58 (February, 1961).

22. Ibid., pp. 199–200.

CHAPTER 16

1. Boris Pasternak, *Doktor Zh*, p. 543; Boris Pasternak, *DZh*, p. 535.

2. Boris Pasternak, *STIKHP*, p. 405.

3. René E. Fortin, "Home and the Uses of Creative Nostalgia in *Doctor Zhivago*," *Modern Fiction Studies* 20 (1974):209.

4. Pasternak, *DZh*, pp. 465–66, 472–73; Max Scheler, *Le Saint, le génie, le héros* [*Vorbilder und Führer*].

5. Pasternak, *DZh*, p. 454.

6. Ibid., p. 461.

7. Edward Hallett Carr, *A History of Soviet Russia*, vol. 3, *Socialism in One Country, 1924–1926*, pp. 176–77.

8. Pasternak, *DZh*, p. 10; cf. Aleksandr Gladkov, *Vstrechi*, p. 54.

9. Pasternak, *DZh*, p. 454.

10. Leo Tolstoy, *War and Peace*, trans. Louise Maude and Aylmer Maude, pp. 1253, 1256–60, 1264, 1313–14; Pasternak, *DZh*, pp. 453–54; Paul Valéry, *Regards sur le monde actuel*, rev. ed.

11. Tolstoy, *War and Peace*, pp. 1316, 1317, 1323–28.

12. Ibid., pp. 1328, 1333, 1335, 1337, 1338, 1348–51.

13. Pasternak, *Doktor Zh*, p. 466.

14. Michel Collinet, *Du Bolchévisme: Evolutions et variations du Marxisme-Léninisme*.

15. Luigi Einaudi, ed., Preface, *François Ques-*

nay et la physiocratie, p. ix; Charles Gide, *Principes d'économie politique*, 22d ed., p. 10; Pasternak, *DZh*, pp. 297, 301.

16. Pasternak, *DZh*, p. 310.

17. Ibid., pp. 501–502.

18. Ibid., pp. 106–107, 284, 407.

19. Ibid., p. 285; A. S. Pushkin, "Otryvki iz puteshestviia Onegina," *Sobranie sochinenii v desiati tomakh*, 4:188; Pierre-Frédéric Le Play, *La Constitution essentielle de l'humanité*.

20. Gustave Thibon, *Diagnostics: Essai de physiologie sociale*.

21. Pasternak, *STIKHP*, p. 405.

CHAPTER 17

1. Boris Pasternak, "V bolnitse" ("In Hospital"), in Boris Pasternak, *Kogda razguliaetsia: Poems, 1955–1959*, trans. Michael Harari, p. 75.

2. Boris Pasternak, statement to Jhan Robbins, fall, 1959, Jhan Robbins, "Boris Pasternak's Last Message to the World," *New York Herald Tribune*, August 7, 1960, p. 5.

3. Olga Ivinskaya, *CAPT*, p. 137.

4. Max Hayward, "Pasternak's 'Dr. Zhivago,'" *Encounter* 56 (May, 1958):43; Thomas Merton, *Disputed Questions*, pp. 29–31; Josephine Pasternak, "Patior," *London Magazine* 4 (September, 1964); Giuseppe di Leonardo, *Il Cristianesimo del* Dottor Zivago.

5. U. A. Floridi, S.J., "Un messaggio di risurrezione della Russia sovietica," *Civiltà Cattolica*, January 18, 1958; Boris Pasternak, *DZh*, p. 43.

6. D. V. Konstantinov, "*Doktor Zhivago* i bogoiskatelstvo v SSSR," *Vestnik Miunkhenskogo Instituta po izucheniiu SSSR*, no. 2 (1959), pp. 76–84; Viktor Slavinskii, *Dialektika sovremennosti*, pp. 102–103.

7. L. A. Zander, "Filosofskie temy v romane B. L. Pasternaka *Doktor Zhivago*," *Vestnik russkogo studencheskogo khristianskogo dvizheniia* 1, no. 52 (1959):40.

8. Pasternak, *DZh*, p. 413.

9. Vladimir Soloviev, "O khristianstve," *Dukhovnye osnovy zhizni, 1882–1884*, part 2, chap. 2, sec. 4; Romano Guardini, *Das Wesen des Christentums*, pp. 7–8; Karl Rahner, *Gefahren im heutigen Katholizismus*.

10. Jacqueline de Proyart, "Une amitié d'enfance," *Boris Pasternak, 1890–1960: Colloque de Cerisy-la-Salle (11–14 septembre 1975)*, p. 518; Guy de Mallac, "A Russian Impressionist: Leonid

Osipovich Pasternak, 1862–1945," *California Slavic Studies* 10 (1977); L. Pasternak/Ch. N. Bialik, February, 1923, *Slavica Hierosolymitana* 1 (1977): 306–308.

11. Pasternak, *DZh*, p. 13; Nadezhda Mandelstam, *Hope*, p. 262; Olga Ivinskaya, *CAPT*, p. 138.

12. Alexander Altmann, "Judaism and World Philosophy," in Louis Finkelstein, ed., *The Jews: Their History, Culture, and Religion*, 3d ed., 2: 992–93; Jehuda Melber, *Hermann Cohen's Philosophy of Judaism*.

13. M. Z. Ben-Ishaj, "With Pasternak in Moscow," *Ha-doar*, December 12, 1958; *Evening Standard* (London), February 6, 1959; Pasternak, *DZh*, p. 123; Aleksandr Gladkov, *Vstrechi*, pp. 49, 112.

14. Judith Stora, "Pasternak et le judaïsme," *Cahiers du monde russe et soviétique* 9 (1968): 353–64; Iu. Margolin, "Perechityvaia 'Doktora Zhivago,'" *Novoe russkoe slovo*, December 17, 1961.

15. Statement by Pasternak to Mme Z. I. Kanchalovskii, 1929–30.

16. Boris Pasternak, "Balzac," *STIKHP*, pp. 204–205; Iurii Krotkov, *KROT 1*, pp. 53–54; Georges Nivat, conversation with author; Ilia Ehrenburg, conversation with Dr. George Katkov, 1950s, quoted in G. Katkov/author, spring, 1961.

17. Pasternak, *DZh*, p. 3; Edmund Wilson, "Legend and Symbol in Doctor Zhivago," *Encounter* 12 (June, 1959): 5.

19. Rainer Maria Rilke, *Gesammelte Werke*, 3: 135, 137–38; Boris Pasternak, "Avtobiograficheskii ocherk," *Works*, 2: 20–22; Boris Pasternak, Introduction, *Spektorskii*, *STIKHP*, p. 304; Pasternak, "Dawn," in "The Poems of Iurii Zhivago," *DZh*, pp. 549–50.

20. Boris Pasternak, *The Last Summer*, trans. George Reavy, p. 78 (translation modified).

21. Boris Pasternak, "Okhrannaia gramota," *Works*, 2: 263–64 (author's translation).

22. Pasternak, "Hamlet," in "The Poems of Iurii Zhivago," *DZh*, p. 523.

23. Pasternak, "Magdalene," in ibid., p. 525

24. E.g., "False Summer," "Autumn," "August," "Encounter," in ibid.

25. Boris Pasternak, *IR*, pp. 40, 94; Merton, *Disputed Questions*, p. 13.

26. Merton, *Disputed Questions*, p. 15.

27. BP/R. Schweitzer, in Renate Schweitzer, *Freundschaft mit Pasternak*, p. 133; BP/J. de Proyart, January 17, 1960, in Jacqueline de Proyart, *Pasternak*, p. 240; Czesław Miłosz, "On Pasternak Soberly," *Books Abroad* [now *World Literature Today*] 44 (Spring, 1970): 208.

28. Nolini Kanta Gupta, "Boris Pasternak: An Indian Viewpoint," *Russian Review* 19 (July, 1960): 248–53.

29. BP/J. de Proyart, 1959, Pasternak, *Works*, 1: xiv; Boris Pasternak, "Dédicace à un musicien français," *Pasternak Speaks* (London Discurio— William Lennard Concerts, Ltd.), record no. L7/001; for translation of French original, see Guy de Mallac, *Boris Pasternak*, pp. 100–101.

30. Gerd Ruge, "A Visit to Pasternak," *Encounter* 10 (March, 1958): 22–25.

31. Boris Pasternak, "V bolnitse" ("In Hospital"), *Poems, 1955–1959*, pp. 72–75.

32. BP/unidentified correspondent, early 1959, in James H. Billington, *The Icon and the Axe: An Interpretive History of Russian Culture*, p. 779.

CHAPTER 18

1. Boris Pasternak, *DZh*, p. 90.

2. Ibid., p. 10.

3. F.-T. Marinetti, "Manifeste futuriste," *Le Figaro*, February 20, 1909; see also Emilio Marinetti, *Le Futurisme*; Boris Pasternak, *Works*, 3: 147–51.

4. The First Vorticist Manifesto, *Blast*, no. 1 (1914); Ilia Ehrenburg, "Boris Pasternak," *Portrety russkikh poetov*.

5. Vladimir Markov has analyzed the complex and changing attitudes of the Futurists toward self-styled Russian "Impressionism." See Vladimir Markov, *Russian Futurism: A History*, pp. 1–28, 31, 146, 198, 382.

6. The background of Pasternak's statement is clarified in ibid., pp. 228–75.

7. Boris Pasternak, *SC*, pp. 30–32; translation modified.

8. Ibid., pp. 32, 59.

9. Ibid., p. 72.

10. Letter cited by Jacqueline de Proyart in Preface, Boris Pasternak, *Works*, 1: xiv; Henri Bergson, *La Pensée et le mouvant*, p. 279; Paul Klee, *Théorie de l'art moderne*.

11. Pasternak, *SC*, pp. 71–72.

12. "Toute chose manifeste, dans le mouvement que sa forme enregistre, la générosité infinie d'un principe qui se donne. Et ce n'est pas à tort qu'on appelle du même nom le charme qu'on voit au mouvement et l'acte de libéralité qui est carac-

téristique de la bonté divine" (Bergson, *La Pensée et le mouvant*, p. 279); see also Chapter 17.

13. Boris Pasternak, "Paul-Marie Verlaine," *Works*, 3:168–71; Antoine Adam, *Verlaine*, rev. ed., p. 172.

14. Octave Nadal, *Paul Verlaine*, pp. 119, 94, 21; Adam, *Verlaine*, p. 169.

15. Boris Pasternak, "Chopin," *Works*, 3:171. All quotations from this article are given here in Paul Schmidt's translation (with occasional slight modification) in "Chopin," *Partisan Review* 21 (1964):405–409.

16. Pasternak, "Chopin," trans. Schmidt, pp. 405–406.

17. Boris Pasternak, *IR*, p. 43; Suzanne K. Langer, *Philosophy in a New Key: A Study in the Symbolism of Reason, Rite, and Art*, 2d ed., pp. 186–89.

18. Pasternak, letter dated Spring, 1959, quoted by Jacqueline de Proyart in Preface, Pasternak, *Works*, 1:xviii.

19. BP/Stephen Spender, August 22, 1959, cited in *Encounter* 83 (August, 1960):4 (*Encounter* faithfully reproduced the original letter as Pasternak wrote it in English).

20. BP/J. de Proyart, late 1959, quoted in Preface, Pasternak, *Works*, 1:xx.

21. Pasternak, *Works*, 2:52; Pasternak, *IR*, p. 122.

22. Pasternak, *SC*, p. 129 ("biography as a spectacle" or "a scenic conception of biography": *zrelishchnoe ponimanie biografii*).

23. Victor Terras, "Turgenev's Esthetic and Western Realism," *Comparative Literature* 22 (Winter, 1970):24; Erich Auerbach, *Mimesis: The Representation of Reality in Western Literature*, p. 439.

24. Interview (in German) recorded by Erik Mesterton and edited as a record, with other recordings of Pasternak's voice, *Pasternak Speaks* (London: Discurio—William Lennard Concerts, Ltd.), record no. L7/001.

25. Henry James, "The Great Form: A Letter to the Deerfield Summer School," in *The Future of the Novel: Essays on the Art of Fiction*, ed. Leon Edel, p. 29.

26. Pasternak, *DZh*, p. 281; Roman Jakobson, *Noveishaia russkaia poeziia*, p. 7; Victor Erlich, *Russian Formalism: History—Doctrine*, 2d ed., p. 45; Donald Davie, Foreword, in Donald Davie and Angela Livingstone, eds., *Pasternak: Modern Judgements*, p. 13; statement quoted by Terras in "Turgenev's Esthetic and Western Realism," p. 29.

27. BP/Stephen Spender, August 22, 1959, *Encounter* 82 (August, 1960):4 (Pasternak's English).

28. Ibid., pp. 4–5.

29. Ralph Matlaw, "A Visit with Pasternak," *Nation*, September 12, 1959, p. 134.

30. BP/Stephen Spender, August 22, 1959, *Encounter* 82 (August, 1960); Gleb Struve, "The Hippodrome of Life: The Problem of Coincidences in *Doctor Zhivago*," *Books Abroad* [now *World Literature Today*] 44 (Spring, 1970):231–36.

31. Pasternak, "Volny," *Vtoroe rozhdenie*, *Works*, 1:327; Roman Jakobson, "Randbemerkungen zur Prosa des Dichters Pasternak, *Slavische Rundschau* 6 (1935); quoted in translation in Davie and Livingstone, eds., *Pasternak: Modern Judgements*, pp. 136, 144.

32. Olga Carlisle, "Three Visits with Boris Pasternak," *Paris Review* 24 (1960):58–59; Boris Pasternak, *LGF*, pp. 155–56.

33. Anthony Burgess, *The Novel Now*, p. 19.

34. Pasternak, *SC*, p. 70 (translation modified); Fedor Stepun, "B. L. Pasternak," *Novyi Zhurnal* 56 (New York, 1959).

35. Pasternak, "Chernyi bokal," *Works*, 3:150.

36. Ibid.; Pasternak, *SC*, p. 121.

37. Pasternak, *SC*, p. 92.

38. Boris Pasternak, *Doktor Zh*, p. 448; *DZh*, p. 437.

39. Dale L. Plank, *Pasternak's Lyric: A Study of Sound and Imagery*, pp. 5, 90; V. Erlich, "'Life by Verses': Boris Pasternak," in *The Double Image*, p. 153; Pasternak, *DZh*, pp. 440–41 (translation modified).

40. Karl Vossler, *The Spirit of Language in Civilization*, trans. Oscar Oeser, p. 234.

41. The notion of *samovitoe slovo* was brought up by Khlebnikov and other Futurists in "A Slap in the Face of Public Taste" ("Poshchechina obshchestvennomu vkusu") and other pronouncements, reprinted in Vladimir Markov, ed., *Manifesty i programmy russkikh futuristov*; Novalis, *Schriften*, ed. Paul Kluckhohn and Richard Samuel, vol. 2, *Das philosophische Werk*, pp. 672–73.

42. One of the most important "anti-inspirational" statements by Valéry is his well-known "Poésie et pensée abstraite," in which he stresses that a poem is essentially a construct ("une sorte de machine à produire l'état poétique au moyen des mots") and the product of technical activity (Valéry, "Poésie et pensée abstraite," *Œuvres* 1:1314–39). An important statement by Maiakovskii is to

be found in his *Sobranie sochinenii*, 5:426 (this passage is discussed in Erlich, *Russian Formalism*, pp. 48–49). Some remarks by Osip Brik, as when he insists on the need for "an understanding of the laws of creation to replace a 'mystical' penetration into the 'secrets' of creation," corroborate the opinions of both Valéry and Maiakovskii; cf. also Brik's statement: "Poets do not invent themes. . . . The poet's work begins with the working out of the theme, with the discovery of a corresponding literary form" (O. M. Brik, "The Formal Method," September, 1923).

43. Pasternak, *SC*, p. 60.

44. When Coleridge identifies the "philosophic imagination" with the "highest intuitive knowledge," he blends views borrowed from Schelling with his own Neoplatonism (on occasion, such as in *Biographia Literaria*, vol. 12, he refers to passages from Plotinus, e.g., *Enneads* 5.5.8); see also Samuel Taylor Coleridge, *Lectures upon Shakespeare and Other Dramatists*, in *Complete Works*, vol. 4 (New York: Harper and Brothers, 1854), p. 55.

45. Boris Pasternak, "Neskolko polozhenii," *Works*, 2:154; Address of August 29, 1934, to First Congress of Writers of the Soviet Union, ibid., pp. 223–24; Pasternak, *Doktor Zh*, p. 466; René Wellek, "Immanuel Kant's Esthetics and Criticism," in *Discriminations: Further Concepts of Criticism*, p. 132; Coleridge, *Lectures*, p. 32.

46. Pasternak, "Neskolko polozhenii," *Works*, 3:154.

47. Ibid.; John Keats, letter of November 22, 1817; cf. Turgenev's identification of art with the pursuit of "beauty" and "truth" as discussed in Victor Terras, "Turgenev's Esthetic and Western Realism," *Comparative Literature* 22 (Winter, 1970): 27.

48. For Boris Pasternak on "desire for effects" (*stremlenie k effektam*), see *Works*, 2:41; *IR*, p. 96; *Works*, 1:1; *IR*, pp. 19, 122; *Works*, 2:13; *IR*, pp. 42–43; *DZh*, pp. 283–84.

49. Victor Terras, "Boris Pasternak and Romantic Aesthetics," *Papers on Language and Literature* 2 (1967):42–56; Aleksandr Gladkov, *Vstrechi*, p. 32.

50. Pasternak, *DZh*, pp. 10, 90; Pasternak, *Works*, 3:194.

Bibliography

For the convenience of the reader, titles of works in Russian in most of the sections have been translated into English.

WORKS BY PASTERNAK

Pasternak's works have been quoted primarily from the following editions:

Sochineniia [*Works*]. Edited by Gleb Struve and Boris Filippov. 3 vols. (Ann Arbor: University of Michigan Press, 1961): vol. 1, *Stikhi i poemy, 1912–1932* [*Poetry, 1912–1932*]; vol. 2. *Proza 1915–1958: Povesti, rasskazy, avtobiograficheskie proizvedeniia* [*Prose, 1915–1958: Stories and Autobiographical Works*]; vol. 3: *Stikhi 1936–1959, Stikhi dlia detei, Stikhi 1912–1957, ne sobrannye v knigi avtora. Stati i vystupleniia* [*Poetry, 1936–1959; Poetry for Children; Uncollected Verse, 1912–1957; Articles and Addresses*].
Stikhotvoreniia i poemy [*Poems and Long Poems*]. Edited by L. A. Ozerov. Moscow-Leningrad: Sovetskii pisatel, Biblioteka poeta, bolshaia seriia, 1965.
Doktor Zhivago. Milan: Feltrinelli, 1959.

The following English translations have been used:

Doctor Zhivago. Translated by Max Hayward and Manya Harari. Includes "The Poems of Yurii Zhivago," translated by Bernard Gilbert Guerney. New York: Pantheon Books, 1958.
I Remember: Sketch for an Autobiography. Translated and edited by David Magarshack; includes "Translating Shakespeare," by Manya Harari. New York: Meridian Books, 1960.
The Last Summer [*Povest*]. Translated by George Reavey, introduction by Lydia Slater. Revised translation. London: Penguin Books, 1960.
A Safe-Conduct. Translated by Angela Livingstone. In Boris Pasternak. *The Collected Prose Works of Boris Pasternak*. Edited by Christopher J. Barnes. New York: Praeger, 1977.

Below is a selective list of works by Pasternak that are not included in either of the editions of his works listed above:

"Anketa sektsii poetov" ["Response to the Questionnaire of the Poetry Section"] (1919) and "Avtobiografiia" ["Autobiography"] (1923). Edited by Milan Djurčinov. "Dva priloga za B. L. Pasternak." *Godishen zbornik na filozofskiot fakultet na univerzitetot vo Skopje* 26 (1974): 359–65.
The Blind Beauty. Translated by Manya Harari and Max Hayward. New York: Harcourt, Brace and World, 1969. (*Slepaia krasavitsa*, the original text, was issued in a limited edition, edited by Christopher J. Barnes and Nicholas J. Anning, by Collins and Harvill, London, the same year.)
"Boris Pasternak About Himself and His Readers." Translated by Gleb Struve. *Slavic Review* 23 (March, 1964): 125–28.
"Dramatic Fragments." Translated and edited by Christopher Barnes. *Encounter*, July, 1970, pp. 15–21.
Fragmenty romana [*Fragments of a Novel*]. Edited by Christopher Barnes and Nicholas J. Anning. London: Collins and Harvill, 1973.
Die Geschichte einer Kontra-Oktave. Translated by Heddy Pross-Weerth, postscript by Evgenii Pasternak. Frankfort on the Main: Suhrkampf, 1975.
"Kriticheskie etiudy" [including "Vladimir Maiakovskii: *Prostoe, kak mychanie*," "Zametki perevodchika," and "Shopen"]. *Literaturnaia Rossiia*, March 19, 1965, pp. 18–19.
Letters to Georgian Friends. Translated and edited by David Magarschack. New York: Helen and Kurt Wolff/Harcourt, Brace and World, 1968.
"Novogodnee pozhelanie" ["Wishes for the New Year," December 20, 1957]. *Literaturnaia Rossiia*, January 1, 1965, p. 9.

"O predmete i metode psikhologii" ["About the Object and Method of Psychology"]. Edited, with a commentary, by S. G. Gellershtein. *Slavica Hierosolymitana* 4 (1979): 274–85.

La Reazione di Wassermann: Saggi e materiali sull'arte. Edited by Cesare G. De Michelis. Padova: Marsilio, 1970.

"Simvolizm i bessmertie: Tezisy" ["Symbolism and Immortality: Main Points in Outline"]. In L. Fleishman, *Stati o Pasternake*. Bremen: K-Presse, 1977.

"Slovo o poezii" ["Allocution About Poetry"]. Speech delivered in June, 1935. In *Sbornik statei, posviashchennykh tvorchestvu B. L. Pasternaka* [*A Collection of Articles Devoted to B. L. Pasternak's Work*]. Edited by Gleb Struve. Munich: Institut po izucheniiu SSSR, 1962.

"Stikhi i proza" ["Verse and Prose"]. *Novyi mir* [*New World*], January, 1965, pp. 163–84.

"Pervye opyty Borisa Pasternaka" ["Boris Pasternak's First Literary Endeavors"]. Edited by E. V. Pasternak. *Trudy po znakovym sistemam, IV.* Uchenye zapiski Tartuskogo gosudarstvennogo universiteta, 236. [*Studies on Semiotic Systems, Volume 4.* Scholarly Proceedings of Tartu State University, issue 236.] Tartu, 1969.

Below is a selected list of English-language editions of Pasternak's poetry.

Fifty Poems. Translated by Lydia Pasternak Slater. London: Unwin Books, 1963.

In the Interlude. Translated by Henry Kamen. Oxford: Oxford University Press, 1962.

Poems. Translated by Eugene M. Kayden. 2d ed. Yellow Springs, Ohio: Antioch Press, 1964.

Poems, 1955–1959. Translated by Michael Harari. London: Collins and Harvill, 1960.

The Poems of Dr. Zhivago. Translated, with commentary, by Donald Davie. New York: Barnes and Noble, 1965.

The Poetry of Boris Pasternak, 1914–1960. Translated by George Reavey. New York: Putnam's, Capricorn, 1959.

Sister My Life: Summer, 1917. Translated by P. C. Flayderman. New York: Washington Square Press, 1967. Bilingual edition.

BOOKS ABOUT PASTERNAK

Andreev, G., M. Slonim, B. Zaitsev, et al. *Delo Pasternaka* [*The Pasternak Affair*]. Munich: TsOPE, 1958.

Aucouturier, Michel. *Pasternak par lui-même*. Ecri-

vains de toujours, no. 66. Paris: Seuil, 1963.

———. *Boris Pasternak, 1890–1960: Colloque de Cerisy-la-Salle (11–14 septembre 1975)*. Edited by Michel Aucouturier. Paris: Institut d'études slaves, 1979.

Berger, Yves. *Boris Pasternak*. Poètes d'aujourd'hui. Paris: Seghers, 1958.

Birnbaum, Henrik. *Doktor Faustus und Doktor Schiwago*. Lisse: Peter de Ridder, 1976.

Bodin, Per Arne. *Nine Poems from Doktor Živago: A Study of Christian Motifs in Boris Pasternak's Poetry*. Stockholm Studies in Russian Literature, no. 6. Stockholm: Almqvist and Wiksell, 1976.

Borowsky, Kay. *Kunst und Leben: Die Ästhetik Boris Pasternaks*. Hildesheim: Georg Olms, 1976.

Conquest, Robert. *Courage of Genius: The Pasternak Affair*. London: Collins and Harvill, 1961.

Dal, Elena. *Nekotorye osobennosti zvukovykh povtorov Borisa Pasternaka* [*Certain Peculiarities of Sound Repetitions in the Work of Boris Pasternak*]. Göteborg: Institutum Slavicum Universitatis Gothoburgensis, 1978.

Davie, Donald. *The Poems of Doctor Zhivago*. New York: Manchester University Press, Barnes and Noble, 1965.

———, and Angela Livingstone, eds. *Pasternak: Modern Judgements*. Introduction by Donald Davie. London: Macmillan, 1969.

De Michelis, Cesare G. *Pasternak*. Florence: La Nuova Italia, 1968.

Döring, Johanna Renate. *Die Lyrik Pasternaks in den Jahren 1928–1934*. Slavistische Beiträge, no. 64. Munich: Otto Sagner, 1973.

Dyck, J. W. *Boris Pasternak*. World Authors Series, no. 225. Boston: Twayne, 1972.

Erlich, Victor, ed. *Pasternak: A Collection of Critical Essays*. Englewood Cliffs, N.J.: Prentice-Hall, 1978.

Fleishman, Lazar. *Boris Pasternak v dvadtsatye gody* [*Boris Pasternak in the 1920s*]. Munich: Wilhelm Fink, 1980.

———. *Stati o Pasternake* [*Articles About Pasternak*]. Bremen: K-Presse, 1977.

France, Anna Kay. *Boris Pasternak's Translations of Shakespeare*. Berkeley: University of California Press, 1978.

Gifford, Henry. *Boris Pasternak: A Critical Study*. New York: Cambridge University Press, 1977.

Gladkov, Alexander. *Meetings with Pasternak: A Memoir*. Translated and edited by Max Hayward. New York: Harcourt Brace Jovanovich, 1977.

———. *Vstrechi s Pasternakom* [*Meetings with Pasternak*]. Paris: YMCA Press, 1973.

Hughes, Olga R. *The Poetic World of Boris Pasternak*. Princeton, N.J.: Princeton University Press, 1974.

Ivinskaya, Olga. *A Captive of Time*. New York: Doubleday, 1978.

———. *V plenu vremeni: Gody s Borisom Pasternakom* [*A Captive of Time: My Years with Boris Pasternak*]. Paris: Arthème Fayard, 1978.

Krotkov, Yuri. *The Nobel Prize: A Novel*. Translated by Linda Aldwinckle. New York: Simon and Schuster, 1980.

Leonardo, Giuseppe di. *Il cristianesimo del Dottor Živago*. Rome: Ciranna, 1960.

Mallac, Guy de. *Boris Pasternak*. Classiques du XXe siècle, no. 57. Paris: Editions Universitaires, 1963.

Nilsson, Nils Åke, ed. *Boris Pasternak: Essays*. Stockholm: Almqvist and Wiksell, 1976.

Pasternak, Boris, and Thomas Merton. *Six Letters*. Lexington: King Library Press, University of Kentucky, 1973.

Payne, Robert. *The Three Worlds of Boris Pasternak*. New York: Coward-McCann, 1961; Bloomington: Indiana University Press, 1963.

Plank, Dale L. *Pasternak's Lyric: A Study of Sound and Imagery*. The Hague: Mouton, 1966.

Pomorska, Krystyna. *Themes and Variations in Pasternak's Poetics*. Lisse: Peter de Ridder, 1975.

Proyart, Jacqueline de. *Pasternak*. Paris: Gallimard, 1964.

Rowland, Mary F., and Paul Rowland. *Pasternak's Doctor Zhivago*. Preface by Harry T. Moore. Carbondale: Southern Illinois University Press, 1967.

Ruge, Gerd. *Pasternak: A Pictorial Biography*. London: Thames and Hudson, 1958.

Ruoff, Z. F. *"Doktor Zhivago" kak zavershenie poetiki Borisa Pasternaka* [*"Doctor Zhivago" as the Culmination of Boris Pasternak's Poetics*]. Moscow: Samizdat, 1961–62.

———. *Pasternak i Rilke*. Moscow: Samizdat, 1968–69.

Schewe, Heinz. *Pasternak privat*. Hamburg: Christians Verlag, 1974.

Schweitzer, Renate. *Freundschaft mit Pasternak*. Vienna: Kurst Desch, 1963.

Struve, G. P., ed. *Sbornik statei, posviashchennykh tvorchestvu Borisa Leonidovicha Pasternaka* [*Collection of Articles on Boris Pasternak's Work*]. Munich: Institut po izucheniiu SSSR, 1962.

Van Damme, Jos. *Boris Pasternak*. Brugge: Desclée de Brouwer, 1965.

Vukanovich, E. I. *Zvukovaia faktura stikhotvorenii sbornika "Sestra moia zhizn"—B. L. Pasternaka* [*The Sound Texture of the Poems in B. L. Pasternak's Collection "My Sister Life"*]. Lansing, Mich.: Russian Language Journal, 1971.

Zendejas, Francisco. *La Pasión de Pasternak*. Mexico City: Libro Mex, 1958.

OTHER BOOKS CITED

Abramov, A. *Lirika i epos velikoi otechestvennoi voiny: Problematika, stil, poetika* [*The Lyric and Epic Poetry of the Second World War: Problematics, Style, Poetics*]. Moscow: Sovetskii pisatel, 1972.

Adam, Antoine. *Verlaine*. Rev. ed. Paris, 1953.

Afinogenov, A. N. *Stati, dnevniki, pisma, vospominaniia* [*Articles, Diaries, Letters, Reminiscences*]. Moscow: Iskusstvo, 1957.

Akhmadulina, Bella. *Izbrannye stikhi* [*Selected Verse*]. Moscow: Gosudarstvennoe izdatelstvo khudozhestvennoi literatury, 1975.

———. *Oznob* [*Shiver*]. Frankfort on the Main: Posev, 1966.

Alexandrova, Vera. *A History of Soviet Literature 1917–1964: From Gorky to Solzhenitsyn*. Garden City, N.Y.: Doubleday, 1963.

Allilueva, Svetlana. *Twenty Letters to a Friend*. New York: Discus, Avon, 1968.

Annenkov, Iurii. *Dnevnik moikh vstrech: Tsikl tragedii* [*A Diary of My Encounters: Cycle of Tragedies*]. 2 vols. New York: Inter-Language Literary Associates, 1966.

Aron, Raymond. *L'Opium des intellectuels*. Paris: Calmann-Lévy, 1955.

Aseev, Nikolai. *Sobranie sochinenii v piati tomakh* [*Collected Works in Five Volumes*]. Moscow, 1963.

———. *Stikhotvoreniia i poemy* [*Poems and Longer Poems*]. Leningrad: Sovetskii pisatel, 1967.

Auerbach, Erich. *Mimesis: The Representation of Reality in Western Literature*. Garden City, N.Y.: Doubleday, 1957.

Bachelard, Gaston. *La Terre et les rêveries du repos*. Paris, 1948.

Bachmann, O. *Rosa Hoffman: Eine biographische Skizze, nebst Auszug einiger Rezensionen*. Odessa: L. Nitzsche, 1885.

Bednyi, Demian. *Izbrannoe* [*Selected Works*]. Moscow, 1950.

Belyi, Andrei. *Mezhdu dvukh revoliutsii* [*Between Two Revolutions*]. Moscow, 1934.

Berberova, Nina. *The Italics Are Mine*. New York: Harcourt, Brace and World, 1969.

Bergson, Henri. *L'Énergie spirituelle*. Paris: Alcan, 1919.

———. *L'Évolution créatrice*. Paris: Alcan, 1907.

———. *La Pensée et le mouvant*. Paris: Alcan, 1934.

Billington, James H. *The Icon and the Axe: An Interpretive History of Russian Culture*. New York: Knopf, 1966.

Blok, Aleksandr. *Sobranie sochinenii v vosmi tomakh* [*Collected Works in Eight Volumes*]. Edited by V. N. Orlov et al. Moscow: Gosudarstvennoe izdatelstvo khudozhestvennoi literatury, 1960–63.

Bowers, Faubion. *Scriabin: A Biography of the Russian Composer, 1870–1915*. 2 vols. Tokyo: Kodansha, 1969.

Bowra, C. M. *The Creative Experiment*. London: Macmillan, 1949.

Brown, Edward J. *Mayakovsky: A Poet in the Revolution*. Princeton, N.J.: Princeton University Press, 1973.

———. *The Proletarian Episode in Russian Literature, 1928–1932*. New York: Columbia University Press, 1953.

———. *Russian Literature Since the Revolution*. Rev. ed. New York: Collier, 1969.

Bunin, Ivan Alekseevich. *Sobranie sochinenii v deviati tomakh* [*Collected Works in Nine Volumes*]. Edited by A. S. Miasnikov et al. Moscow: Gosudarstvennoe izdatelstvo khudozhestvennoi literatury, 1965–67.

Burgess, Anthony. *The Novel Now*. London: Faber, 1967.

Canguilhem, Georges. *Connaissance de la vie*. Paris: Hachette, 1952.

Carlisle, Olga. *Poets on Street Corners*. New York: Random House, 1969.

Carr, Edward Hallett. *Socialism in One Country, 1924–1926*. Vols. 5–6 in *A History of Soviet Russia*. 7 vols. New York: Macmillan, 1951–60.

Chikovani, Semen. *Mysli, vpechatleniia, vospominaniia* [*Thoughts, Impressions, Recollections*]. Moscow: Sovetskii pisatel, 1968.

Chukovskaia, Lidiia. *Zapiski ob Anne Akhmatovoi: I, 1938–41* [*Notes About Anna Akhmatova: I, 1938–41*]. Paris: YMCA Press, 1976.

Chukovskii, Kornei. *Sobranie sochinenii* [*Collected Works*]. Vol. 3, *Vysokoe iskusstvo* [*A Lofty Art*]. Moscow, 1966.

Coleridge, Samuel Taylor. *Complete Works*. Vol. 12, *Biographia Literaria*. New York: Harper and Brothers, 1854.

———. Vol. 4, *Lectures*. New York: Harper and Brothers, 1854.

Collinet, Michel. *Du Bolchévisme: Évolution et variations du marxisme-léninisme*. Paris: Le Livre Contemporain, Amiot-Dumont, 1957.

Conquest, Robert. *The Pasternak Affair: Courage of Genius*. Philadelphia: Lippincott, 1962.

Dussort, Henri. *L'École de Marbourg*. Edited by J. Vuillemin. Paris: Presses Universitaires de France, 1963.

Ehrenburg, Ilia. *Memoirs, 1921–1941*. Cleveland: World, 1963.

———. *People and Life, 1891–1921*. Translated by Anna Bostock and Yvonne Kapp. New York: Knopf, 1962.

———. *Portrety russkikh poetov* [*Portraits of Russian Poets*]. Berlin, 1923.

———. *Post-War Years, 1945–1954*. Translated by Tatiana Shebunina. Cleveland: World, 1967.

———. *Sobranie sochinenii v deviati tomakh* [*Collected Works in Nine Volumes*]. Moscow: Khudozhestvennaia literatura, 1965.

Einaudi, Luigi, ed. *François Quesnay et la physiocratie*. Paris: Institut national d'études démographiques, 1958.

Erlich, Victor. *The Double Image*. Baltimore, Md.: Johns Hopkins Press, 1964.

———. *Russian Formalism: History—Doctrine*. 2d ed. The Hague, 1965.

Evtushenko, Evgenii. *Avtobiografiia* [*Autobiography*]. London: Flegon, 1964.

———. *Sobranie sochinenii v trekh tomakh* [*Collected Works in Three Volumes*]. Moscow: Khudozhestvennaia literatura, 1974.

Finkelstein, Louis, ed. *The Jews: Their History, Culture, and Religion*. Vol. 2. New York: Harper, 1960.

Fontenelle, Bernard Le Bovier de. *Œuvres complètes*. Edited by G. B. Depping. Vol. 2. Geneva: Slatkine, 1968.

Frank, Viktor. *Izbrannye stati* [*Selected Articles*]. Edited by Leonard Schapiro. London: Overseas Publications Interchange, 1974.

Frumkin, Jacob, G. Aronson, and A. Goldenweiser, eds. *Russian Jewry, 1860–1917*. Translated by Mirra Ginsburg, New York: Yoseloff, 1966.

Gibian, George. *Interval of Freedom: Soviet Literature During the Thaw, 1954–1957*. Minneapolis: University of Minnesota Press, 1960.

Gide, Charles. *Principes d'économie politique*. 22d ed. Paris: Larose et Forcel, 1920.

Gladkov, Aleksandr. *Meetings with Pasternak: A Memoir*. Translated and edited by Max Hayward. New York: Harcourt, Brace, 1977.

———. *Vstrechi s Pasternakom* [*Meetings with Pasternak*]. Paris: YMCA Press, 1973.

Goethe, Johann Wolfgang von. *Faust*. Translated

by Boris Pasternak. 3d ed. Moscow: GIKHL, 1957.

Grabar, I. E., V. N. Lazarev, A. A. Sidorov, and O. A. Shvidovskii, eds. *Istoriia russkogo iskusstva* [*History of Russian Art*]. Vol. 10, pts. 1 and 2. Moscow: Nauka, 1968–69.

Gray, Camilla. *The Great Experiment: Russian Art, 1863–1922*. New York: Abrams, 1962.

Grigorenko, V. V., N. K. Gudzii, et al., eds. *V. Maiakovskii v vospominaniiakh sovremennikov* [*V. Maiakovskii in the Reminiscences of Contemporaries*]. Moscow: Gosudarstvennoe izdatelstvo khudozhestvennoi literatury, 1963.

Grundlach, Fr., comp. *Catalogus Professorum Academiae Marburgensis, 1527–1910*. Marburg, 1927.

Guardini, Romano. *Das Wesen des Christentums*. 5th ed. Würzburg: Werkbund-Verlag, 1958.

Guerney, Bernard Gilbert, ed. *An Anthology of Russian Literature in the Soviet Period from Gorki to Pasternak*. New York: Random House, 1960.

Hamsun, Knut. *Growth of the Soil*. New York: Knopf, 1930.

Holthusen, Johannes. *Twentieth Century Russian Literature: A Critical Study*. New York: Ungar, 1972.

Hugo, Victor. *William Shakespeare: Oeuvres complètes*. Vol. 12. Paris: Club français du livre, 1969.

Iakobson, Anatolii. *Konets tragedii* [*The End of the Tragedy*]. New York: Chekhov, 1973.

Jakobson, Roman. *Noveishaia russkaia poeziia* [*The Russian Poetry of Most Recent Times*]. Prague, 1921.

James, Henry. *The Future of the Novel: Essays on the Art of Fiction*. Edited by Leon Edel. New York: Vintage, 1956.

Jung, Carl G. *Psychological Types*. Translated by G. Godwin Baynes. New York: Harcourt, Brace, 1926.

Karlinsky, Simon. *Marina Cvetaeva: Her Life and Art*. Berkeley: University of California Press, 1966.

Kataev, Valentin. *The Grass of Oblivion*. New York: McGraw-Hill, 1970.

Katanian, V. *Maiakovskii: Literaturnaia khronika* [*Maiakovskii: A Literary Chronicle*]. 4th ed. Moscow: Gosudarstvennoe izdatelstvo khudozhestvennoi literatury, 1961.

Kaverin, Veniamin. *Prolog: Putevye rasskazy* [*Prologue: Travel Stories*]. Moscow: Goslitizdat, 1931.

Khrapchenko, M. B. *Tvorcheskaia individualnost pisatelia i razvitie literatury* [*The Writer's Creative Individuality and the Development of Literature*]. Moscow: Sovetskii pisatel, 1975.

Khrushchev, Nikita S. *Khrushchev Remembers*. Boston: Little, Brown, 1974.

Klee, Paul. *Théorie de l'art moderne*. Paris, 1965.

Kleist, Geinrich. *Pesy* [*Plays*]. Edited by A. Dymshits. Moscow: Iskusstvo, 1962.

Kosman, Sergei. *Maiakovskii: Mif i deistvitelnost* [*Maiakovskii: Myth and Reality*]. Paris: Maison du livre étranger, 1968.

Kuzmin, Mikhail. *Uslovnosti* [*Conventions*]. Petrograd: Poliarnaia zvezda, 1923.

Langer, Suzanne K. *Philosophy in a New Key: A Study in the Symbolism of Reason, Rite, and Art*. 2d ed. New York, 1951.

Lenin, V. I. *Polnoe sobranie sochinenii* [*Complete Works*]. 5th ed. 55 vols. Moscow: Gosudarstvennoe izdatelstvo politicheskoi literatury, 1967.

Lenoble, Robert. *Esquisse d'une histoire de l'idée de nature*. Paris: Albin Michel, 1969.

Leonid Pasternak, 1862–1945. Catalogue of exhibition of works by Leonid Pasternak organized by Oxford University Press, in London, March 20–May 30, 1969. Introduction, "Last Years," by Josephine Pasternak. London: Oxford University Press, 1969.

Leonid Pasternak, 1862–1945. Catalogue of exhibition of works by Leonid Pasternak held at Crawford Centre for the Arts, University of Saint Andrews [Scotland], January 28–February 25, 1978. Preface by John Steer, Introduction by Larissa Salmina-Haskell, "The Life of Leonid Pasternak" by Jennifer Bradshaw. Saint Andrews: Crawford Centre for the Arts, 1978.

Le Play, Pierre-Frédéric. *La Constitution essentielle de l'humanité*. Tours: Mame, 1881.

Le Senne, René. *Traité de caractérologie*. Paris: Presses Universitaires de France, 1945.

Lezhnev, A. *Sovremenniki: Literaturno-kriticheskie ocherki* [*Our Contemporaries: Literary-Critical Essays*]. Moscow: Krug, 1927.

Lindstrom, Thaïs S. *A Concise History of Russian Literature*. Vol. 2, *From 1900 to the Present*. New York: New York University Press, 1978.

Livshits, Benedikt. *Polutoraglazyi strelets* [*The One-and-a-half-eyed Archer*]. Leningrad: Izdatelstvo pisatelei v Leningrade, 1933.

Literaturnoe nasledstvo 65 (Novoe o Maiakovskom) [*Literary Heritage, Vol. 65: New Materials on Mayakovskii*]. Moscow: Akademiia Nauk, 1958.

Lugovskoi, V. A., et al., eds. *Antologiia russkoi sovetstoi poezii v dvukh tomakh* [*Anthology of Soviet*

Russian Poetry in Two Volumes]. Moscow, 1957.

Luppol, I., ed. *Mezhdunarodnyi kongress pisatelei v zashchitu kultury, Parizh, iiun 1935: Doklady i vystupleniia* [*The International Congress of Writers for the Defense of Culture, Paris, June, 1935: Addresses and Speeches*]. Moscow: Gosudarstvennoe izdatelstvo khudozhestvennaia literatura, 1936.

Maiakovskii, V. V. *Polnoe sobranie sochinenii* [*Complete Works*]. Moscow: Gosudarstvennoe izdatelstvo khudozhestvennoi literatury, 1959. [See also under Mayakovsky, Vladimir.]

Malraux, André. *Anti-Memoirs*. New York: Holt, Rinehart, and Winston, 1968.

Mandelstam, Nadezhda. *Hope Abandoned*. Translated by Max Hayward. New York: Atheneum, 1974.

————. *Hope Against Hope: A Memoir*. Translated by Max Hayward. Introduction by Clarence Brown. New York: Atheneum, 1970.

Mandelstam, Osip. *O poezii* [*On Poetry*]. Leningrad: Akademiia, 1928.

Marcel, Gabriel. *Être et avoir*. Paris: Aubier-Montaigne. 1935.

Marinetti, Filippo Tommaso. *Le Futurisme*. Paris: Sansot, 1910.

Mark, Paul J., ed. *Die Familie Pasternak: Erinnerungen, Berichte*. Geneva: Poésie Vivante, 1975.

Markov, Vladimir. *Russian Futurism: A History*. Berkeley: University of California Press, 1968.

————, ed. *The Longer Poems of Velimir Khlebnikov*. Berkeley: University of California Press, 1968.

————, ed. *Manifesty i programmy russkikh futuristov* [*Manifestos and Programs of the Russian Futurists*]. Munich: Wilhelm Fink, 1967.

————, ed. *Priglushennye golosa* [*Muffled Voices*]. New York: Chekhov, 1952.

Marx, Karl, and Friedrich Engels. *Historisch-kritische Gesamtausgabe*. Edited by V. Adoratskii. Berlin: Marx-Engels-Verlag, 1932.

Mayakovsky, Vladimir. *The Bedbug and Selected Poetry*. Translated by Max Hayward and George Reavey, edited by Patricia Blake. New York: World, 1969. [See also under Maiakovskii, Vladimir.]

Melber, Jehuda. *Hermann Cohen's Philosophy of Judaism*. New York: Jonathan David, 1968.

Memorial Exhibition of Paintings and Drawings by Leonid Pasternak, 1862–1945. Catalogue of exhibition held in the Ashmolean Museum, Oxford, April, 1958. Essay, "Leonid Pasternak," by C. M. [Sir Maurice] Bowra. Oxford: Ashmolean Museum, 1958.

Merton, Thomas. *Disputed Questions*. New York: Farrar, Straus and Cudahy, 1960.

Mirsky, D. S. *A History of Russian Literature: From Its Beginnings to 1900*. Edited by Francis J. Whitfield. New York: Knopf, 1949.

————. *A History of Russian Literature* [including *A History of Russian Literature* and *Contemporary Russian Literature*]. Edited by Francis J. Whitfield. New York: Knopf, 1969.

Moleva, N. M., and E. M. Beliutin. *Russkaia khudozhestvennaia shkola vtoroi poloviny XIX—nachala XX veka* [*The Russian Artistic School from the Second Half of the Nineteenth Century to the Beginning of the Twentieth*]. Moscow: Iskusstvo, 1967.

Nadal, Octave. *Paul Verlaine*. Paris, 1961.

Navrozov, Lev. *The Education of Lev Navrozov*. New York: Harper and Row, 1975.

Nezval, Vítězslav. *Neviditelná Moskva* [*Invisible Moscow*]. Prague, 1935.

Novalis [pseud. Baron Friedrich von Hardenberg]. *Schriften*. Edited by Paul Kluckhohn and Richard Samuel. Stuttgart, 1965.

Oleinikov, N. M. *Stikhotvoreniia* [*Poems*]. Edited by Lazar Fleishman.

Olesha, Yuri. *Envy and Other Works*. Garden City, N.Y.: Doubleday, 1967.

Ortega y Gasset, José. *Obras completas*. 11 vols. Madrid: Revista de Occidente, 1946–49.

Osborn, Max. *Leonid Pasternak*. Warsaw: Stybel, 1932.

Pasternak, L[eonid] O[sipovich]. *Zapisi raznykh let* [*Notes of Various Years*]. Moscow: Sovetskii khudozhnik, 1975.

Paustovsky, Konstantin. *The Story of a Life*. Translated by Joseph Barnes. New York: Pantheon, 1964.

Payne, Robert. *A Portrait of André Malraux*. Englewood Cliffs, N.J.: Prentice Hall, 1970.

Pertsov, V. *Literaturnye zapiski, God dvadtsatyi, Almanakh odinnadtsatyi* [*Literary Notes: Almanac No. 11*]. Moscow: Gosudarstvennoe izdatelstvo khudozhestvennoi literatury, 1937.

————. *Maiakovskii: Zhizn i tvorchestvo, 1925–1930* [*Maiakovskii: His Life and Work, 1925–1930*]. Moscow, 1972.

————. *Maiakovskii: Zhizn i tvorchestvo v poslednie gody, 1925–1930* [*Maiakovskii: His Life and Art in the Last Years, 1925–1930*]. Moscow: Nauka, 1965.

Pieper, Josef. *Leisure: The Basis of Culture*. Translated by Alexander Dru, introduction by T. S. Eliot. New York: New American Library, 1963.

Poggioli, Renato. *The Poets of Russia, 1890–1930.* Cambridge, Mass.: Harvard University Press, 1960, pp. 321–42.

Pushkin, A. S. *Sobranie sochinenii v desiati tomakh* [*Collected Works in Ten Volumes*]. Moscow: Gosudarstvennoe izdatelstvo khudozhestvennoi literatury, 1960.

Rahner, Karl. *Gefahren im heutigen Katholizismus.* Einsiedeln: Johannes Verlag, 1950.

Reavey, George. *The Poetry of Boris Pasternak, 1914–1960.* New York: Putnam's, Capricorn, 1960.

Regler, Gustav. *The Owl of Minerva.* New York: Farrar, Straus and Cudahy, 1960.

Riesman, David, with Reuel Denney and Nathan Glazer. *The Lonely Crowd: A Study of the Changing American Character.* New Haven, Conn.: Yale University Press, 1950.

Rilke, Rainer Maria. *Briefe aus Muzot 1921 bis 1926.* Leipzig, 1935.

———. *Gesammelte Werke.* 6 vols. Leipzig: Insel-Verlag, 1927.

Roger Martin du Gard, Gabriela Mistral, Boris Pasternak. Nobel Prize Library [published under the sponsorship of the Nobel Foundation and the Swedish Academy]. New York: Alexis Gregory; Del Mar, Calif.: CRM, 1971.

Rylenkov, Nikolai. *Dusha poezii: Portrety i razdumia* [*The Soul of Poetry: Portraits and Meditations*]. Moscow: Sovetskii pisatel, 1969.

Sartre, Jean-Paul. *Critique de la raison dialectique.* Vol. 1, *Théorie des ensembles pratiques.* Paris: Gallimard, 1960.

Scheler, Max. *Le Saint, le génie, le héros* [*Vorbilder und Führer*]. Paris: Emmanuel Vitte, 1958.

Schewe, Heinz. *Pasternak privat.* Hamburg: Christians, 1974.

Schnack, Ingeborg. *Marburg: Bild einer alten Stadt. Impressionen und Profile.* Hanau: Peters, 1964.

———. *Rainer Maria Rilke: Chronik seines Lebens und seines Werkes.* 2 vols. Frankfort on the Main: Insel, 1975.

Schweitzer, Albert. *Out of My Life and Thought: An Autobiography.* Translated by C. T. Campion. New York: American Library, 1953.

Selz, Peter. *German Expressionist Painting.* Berkeley: University of California Press, 1974.

Serov, V. A. *Perepiska, 1884–1911* [*Correspondence, 1884–1911*]. Moscow: Iskusstvo, 1937.

Shcherbatov, Kn. Sergei. *Khudozhnik v ushedshei Rossii* [*The Artist in Bygone Russia*]. New York: Chekhov Publishing House, 1955.

Shklovskii, Viktor. *Gamburgskii shchet* [*The Hamburg Reckoning*]. Leningrad: Izdatelstvo pisatelei v Leningrade, 1928.

———. *Zoo, or Letters Not About Love.* Translated and edited by R. Sheldon. Ithaca, N.Y.: Cornell University Press, 1971.

Sidorov, A. *Russkaia grafika nachala XX veka: Ocherki, istorii, i teorii* [*Russian Graphic Arts of the Beginning of the Twentieth Century: Essays, History, and Theories*]. Moscow: Iskusstvo, 1969.

Slavica Hierosolymitana: Slavic Studies of the Hebrew University. Vol. 1, edited by L. Fleishman, O. Ronen, and D. Segal. Jerusalem: Magnes Press, Hebrew University, 1977.

Slavinskii, Viktor. *Dialektika sovremennosti* [*Dialectics of the Contemporary Era*]. Buenos Aires, 1955.

Slonim, Marc. *Soviet Russian Literature: Writers and Problems, 1917–1967.* London: Oxford University Press, 1973.

Smith, Hedrick. *The Russians.* New York: Quadrangle, New York Times, 1977.

Soloviev, Vladimir. *Dukhovnye osnovy zhizni* [*The Spiritual Foundations of Life*]. Moscow[?], 1882–84.

Solzhenitsyn, Aleksandr. *Bodalsia telenok s dubom: Ocherki literaturnoi zhizni* [*The Calf and the Oak: Essays About Literary Life*]. Paris: YMCA Press, 1975.

Stepun, Fedor. *Das Antlitz Russlands und das Gesicht der Revolution: Aus meinem Leben, 1884–1922.* Munich: Kösel, 1961.

Strachey, John. *The Strangled Cry.* New York: William Sloane, 1962.

Struve, Gleb. *Russian Literature Under Lenin and Stalin, 1917–1953.* Norman: University of Oklahoma Press, 1971.

Surkov, Aleksei. *Golosa vremeni: Zametki na poliakh istorii literatury, 1934–1965* [*Voices of the Age: Marginal Remarks About the History of Literature, 1934–1965*]. Moscow: Sovetskii pisatel, 1965.

Thibon, Gustave. *Diagnostics: Essai de physiologie sociale.* Paris: Librairie de Médicis, 1942.

Tolstoy, Leo. *War and Peace.* Translated Louise Maude and Aylmer Maude. New York: Simon and Schuster, 1942.

Tregub, Semen. *Sputniki serdtsa* [*Traveling Companions of the Heart*]. Moscow: Sovetskii pisatel, 1964.

Tsvetaeva, Marina. *Neizdannye pisma* [*Unpublished Letters*]. Paris: YMCA Press, 1974.

———. *Pisma k Anne Teskovoi* [*Letters to Anna Tesková*]. Prague: Academia Praha, 1969.

Valentei, M. A., et al., eds. *Vstrechi s Meierkholdom: Sbornik vospominanii* [*Meetings with Meier-*

khold: A Collection of Reminiscences]. Moscow: Vserossiiskoe teatralnoe obshchestvo, 1967.

Valéry, Paul. *Oeuvres.* Vol. 1. Paris: Gallimard, édition Pléïade, 1957.

—————. *Regards sur le monde actuel.* Rev. ed. Paris: Gallimard, 1945.

Vasilev, S. A. Satiricheskie. *Stikhi* [*Verses*]. Moscow: Khudozhestvennaia literatura, 1957.

Vickery, Walter N. *The Cult of Optimism: Political and Ideological Problems of Recent Soviet Literature.* Bloomington: Indiana University Press, 1963.

Vildrac, Charles. *Pages de journal, 1922–1966.* Paris: Gallimard, 1968.

V. Maiakovskii v vospominaniiakh sovremennikov [*V. Maiakovskii According to the Reminiscences of Contemporaries*]. Moscow: Gosudarstvennoe izdatelstvo khudozhestvennoi literatury, 1975.

Vossler, Karl. *The Spirit of Language in Civilization.* Translated by Oscar Oeser. London, 1932.

Wellek, René. *Discriminations: Further Concepts of Criticism.* New Haven, Conn.: Yale University Press, 1970.

Williams, Robert C. *Culture in Exile: Russian Emigrés in Germany, 1881–1941.* Ithaca, N.Y.: Cornell University Press, 1972.

Wolff, Kurt. *Briefwechsel eines Verlegers, 1911–1963.* Frankfort-on-the-Main: Heinrich Scheffler, 1966.

Zaitsev, Boris. *Dalekoe* [*Faraway Realm*]. Washington, D.C.: Inter-Language Literary Associates, 1965.

Zelinskii, Kornelii. *Kriticheskie pisma: Kniga vtoraia* [*Critical Letters: Second Book*]. Moscow: Sovetskaia literatura, 1934.

—————. *Na rubezhe dvukh epokh: Literaturnye vstrechi 1917–1920 godov* [*On the Boundary Between Two Epochs: Literary Encounters of the Years 1917–1920*]. Moscow: Sovetskii pisatel, 1959.

Zhdanov, A., et al., eds. *Problems of Soviet Literature: Reports and Speeches at the First Soviet Writers' Congress.* Moscow: Cooperative Publishing Society of Foreign Workers in the USSR, 1935.

Zilbershtein, I. S., and V. A. Samkov, eds. *Valentin Serov v vospominaniiakh, dnevnikakh, i perepiske sovremennikov* [*Valentin Serov Through the Reminiscences, Diaries, and Correspondence of Contemporaries*]. 2 vols. Leningrad: Khudozhnik RSFSR, 1971.

BOOKS CONSULTED

Akademiia nauk SSSR, Institut mirovoi literatury im. A. M. Gor'kogo. *Literaturno—esteticheskie kontseptsii v Rossii kontsa XIX–nachala XX v.* Moscow: Nauka, 1975.

Aleksandrov, V. *Liudi i knigi: Sbornik statei.* Moscow: Sovetskii pisatel, 1956.

—————. *The Tukhachevsky Affair.* Translated from the French by John Hewish. Englewood Cliffs, N.J.: Prentice-Hall, 1964.

Anikst, A. *Tvorchestvo Shekspira.* Moscow: Izdatelstvo khudozhestvennoi literatury, 1963.

Bakhtin, Mikhail. *Problemy poetiki Dostoevskogo* [*Problems of Dostoevsky's Poetics*]. Leningrad, 1929.

Benois [Benua], Alexandre. *Memoirs.* Translated by Moura Budberg. London: Chatto and Windus, 1960.

Berdiaev, Nikolai. *The Meaning of History.* Translated by George Reavey. Cleveland: Meridian Books, 1962.

Blake, Patricia, and Max Hayward, eds. *Dissonant Voices in Soviet Literature.* New York: Harper, 1964 [reprint ed].

Bowlt, John, trans. and ed. *Russian Art of the Avant-Garde: Theory and Criticism, 1902–1934.* New York: Viking, 1976.

Brown, Clarence. *Mandelstam.* Cambridge: Cambridge University Press, 1973.

Buckman, David. *Leonid Pasternak: A Russian Impressionist, 1862–1945.* London: Maltzahn Gallery, 1974.

Certkov, Leonid. *Rilke in Russland auf Grund neuer Materialien.* Austrian Academy of Sciences, Philosophical-Historical Section, Proceedings, vol. 301. Vienna: Verlag der Österreichischen Akademie der Wissenschaften, 1975.

Cohen, Hermann. *Deutschtum und Judentum.* Giessen, 1915.

—————. *Kant's Begründung der Ethik.* Berlin, 1877.

Conquest, Robert. *The Great Terror: Stalin's Purge of the Thirties.* Rev. ed. Harmondsworth: Penguin, 1971.

Crowley, Edward L., and Max Hayward, eds. *Soviet Literature in the 1960's.* New York: Praeger, 1964.

Dudintsev, Vladimir. *Not by Bread Alone.* New York: Dutton, 1957.

Fedorov, Nikolai Fedorovich. *Filosofiia obshchego dela.* Vol. 1, Vernyi, 1906; vol. 11, Moscow, 1913.

Gasparov, M. L. *Sovremennyi russkii stikh: Metrika i ritmika.* Moscow: Nauka, 1974.

Gifford, Henry. *The Novel in Russia: From Pushkin to Pasternak.* New York: Harper and Row, 1964.

Goncharov, B. P. *Zvukovaia organizatsiia stikha i problemy rifmy.* Moscow: Nauka, 1973.

Grabar, I. E. *Valentin Aleksandrovich Serov: Zhizn i tvorchestvo 1865–1911 [Valentin Aleksandrovich Serov: His Life and Art, 1865–1911].* Moscow: Iskusstvo, 1965.

Hayward, Max, and Leopold Labedz, eds. *Literature and Revolution in Soviet Russia, 1917–62.* London: Oxford University Press, 1963.

Kozmin, B. P. *Pisateli sovremennoi epokhi.* Moscow, 1928.

Lo Gatto, Ettore. *Storia della letteratura russa contemporanea.* Milano: Nuova Accademia, 1958.

McLean, Hugh, and W. N. Vickery, trans. and eds. *The Year of Protest: 1956.* New York: Random House, 1961.

Maguire, Robert A. *Red Virgin Soil: Soviet Literature in the 1920's.* Princeton, N.J.: Princeton University Press, 1968.

Mandelstam, Nadezhda. *Mozart and Salieri.* Translated by Robert A. McLean. Ann Arbor, Mich.: Ardis, 1973.

Mannheim, Karl. *Ideology and Utopia.* New York: Harcourt, Brace, 1936.

Margvelashvili, Georgii. *Svet poezii.* Tbilisi: Literatura da khelovneba, 1965.

Martin, Marianne W. *Futurist Art and Theory, 1909–1915.* Oxford: Clarendon Press, 1968.

Medvedev, Roy. *Let History Judge.* New York, 1971.

Menshutin, A., and A. Siniavskii. *Poeziia pervykh let revoliutsii, 1917–1920.* Moscow: Nauka, 1964.

Pasternak, L. O. *Rembrandt i evreistvo v ego tvorchestve [Rembrandt and the Jewish Ethos in His Work].* Berlin: S. D. Saltzmann, 1923.

Poggioli, Renato. *The Poets of Russia, 1890–1930.* Cambridge, Mass.: Harvard University Press, 1960.

Pozner, Vladimir. *Panorama de la littérature russe contemporaine.* Paris: Kra, 1929.

Reck, Vera T. *Boris Pilniak: A Soviet Writer in Conflict with the State.* Montreal: McGill–Queen's University Press, 1975.

Redko, A. E. *Literaturno-khudozhestvennye iskaniia v kontse XIX–nachale XX veka.* Leningrad: Seiatel, 1924. Reprint. Bradda Books, 1973.

Russkaia literatura kontsa XIX–nachala XX v. 1908–1917. Moscow: Nauka, 1972.

Schnack, Ingeborg. *Marburg: Bild einer alten Stadt: Impressionen und Profile.* 2d ed. Hanau: Peters, 1964.

Schuhl, P. M. *Machinisme et Philosophie.* 2d ed.

Paris: Presses Universitaires de France, 1947.

Serge, Victor. *The Case of Comrade Tulayev.* Translated by Willard R. Trask. New York: Doubleday, 1950.

Serov, V. A. *Vospominaniia [Reminiscences].* Moscow: Iskusstvo, 1947.

Shaikevich, B. A. *Ibsen i russkaia kultura. Ocherki.* Kiev: Izdatelstvo pri kievskom gosudarstvennom universitete, 1974.

Shcherbatov, Sergei. *Khudozhnik v ushedshei Rossii.* New York: Chekhov, 1955.

Shklovskii, Viktor. *Mayakovsky and His Circle.* Translated and edited by Lily Feiler. New York: Dodd, Mead, 1972.

Shoshin, V. A. *Poet i mir. O tvorcheskoi individualnosti v sovetskoi poezii.* Moscow: Nauka, 1972.

Slonim, Marc L. *Modern Russian Literature from Chekhov to the Present.* New York: Oxford University Press, 1953.

Solzhenitsyn, Aleksandr. *Bodalsia telenok s dubom: ocherki literaturnoi zhizni.* Paris: YMCA Press, 1975.

Součková, Milada. *A Literary Satellite: Czechoslovak-Russian Literary Relations.* Chicago: University of Chicago Press, 1970.

Spasskii, Sergei. *Maiakovskii i ego sputnikii: vospominaniia.* Leningrad: Sovetskii pisatel, 1940.

Sviatopolk-Mirskii, Kn. Dmitrii, comp. *Russkaia lirika: malenkaia antologiia ot Lomonosova do Pasternaka.* Paris: Franko-russkaia pechat, 1924.

Vildrac, Charles. *Russie neuve.* Paris: Émile-Paul, 1937.

Vinogradov, V. V. *Stilistika, Teoriia poeticheskoi rechi, Poetika.* Moscow: Izdatelstvo Akademii nauk SSSR, 1963.

Vogel, Lucy E. *Aleksandr Blok: The Journey to Italy.* Ithaca: Cornell University Press, 1973.

Vykhodtsev, P. S. *Russkaia sovetskaia poeziia i narodnoe tvorchestvo.* Moscow: Akademiia nauk SSSR, 1963.

Zavalishin, Vyacheslav. *Early Soviet Writers.* Studies of the Research Program on the U.S.S.R., no. 20. New York: Frederick A. Praeger, 1958.

CHAPTERS AND
ARTICLES IN ENGLISH

Alliluyeva, Svetlana. "To Boris Leonidovich Pasternak." *Atlantic,* June, 1967, pp. 133–40.

Altmann, Alexander. "Judaism and World Philosophy." In Louis Finkelstein, ed. *The Jews: Their History, Culture, and Religion.* 3d ed. Vol. 2. New York: Harper and Brothers, 1960.

Arndt, Walter. "Dr. Zhivago—Freedom and Unconcern." *South Atlantic Bulletin* 25 (May, 1959): 1–6.

Aseev, Nikolai. "Melody or Intonation?" In Donald Davie and Angela Livingstone, eds. *Pasternak: Modern Judgements*. London: Macmillan, 1969.

Aucouturier, Michel. "The Legend of the Poet and the Image of the Actor in the Short Stories of Pasternak." *Studies in Short Fiction* 3 (1966): 225–35.

———. "The Metonymous Hero, or the Beginnings of Pasternak the Novelist." *Books Abroad* [now *World Literature Today*] 44 (Spring, 1970): 222–27.

Bailes, Kendall E. "The Politics of Technology: Stalin and Technocratic Thinking among Soviet Engineers." *American Historical Review* 79 (April, 1974): 445–69.

Barnes, Christopher J. "Boris Pasternak: The Musician-Poet and Composer." *Slavica Hierosolymitana* 1 (1976): 317–35.

———. "Boris Pasternak: A Review of Nikolai Aseev's *Oksana* (1916)." *Slavica Hierosolomytica* 1 (1977): 293–305.

———. "Boris Pasternak and Rainer Maria Rilke: Some Missing Links." *Forum for Modern Language Studies* 8 (January, 1972): 61–78.

———. "Letter to the Editor: Skryabin and Pasternak." *Musical Times*, January, 1972, p. 268.

———. "The Original Text of 'O skromnosti i smelosti'" ["On Modesty and Boldness"]. *Slavica Hierosolymitana* 4 (1979): 294–303.

———. "Pasternak as Composer and Scriabin-Disciple." *Tempo: A Quarterly Review of Modern Music* 121 (June, 1977): 13–25.

Ben-Ishaj, M. Z. "With Pasternak in Moscow." *Ha-doar*, December 12, 1958.

Berger, Yves. "Boris Pasternak" [Introduction] in *Boris Pasternak*. Poètes d'aujourd'hui. Paris: Pierre Seghers, 1958.

Berlin, Isaiah. "The Energy of Pasternak." *Partisan Review* 17 (September–October, 1950): 748–51.

Blake, Patricia. "New Voices in Russian Writing." *Encounter*, April, 1963.

———. "We Don't Breathe Easily." *Harper's Magazine*, May, 1961.

"Boris Pasternak's Father." *Time*, August 24, 1962.

Bowra, C. M. "Boris Pasternak, 1917–1923." In *The Creative Experiment*. London: Macmillan, 1949.

———. "Leonid Pasternak." In *Memorial Exhibition of Paintings and Drawings by Leonid Pasternak, 1862–1945*. Catalogue of exhibition of April, 1958, in the Ashmolean Museum, Oxford University.

Brown, Alec. "On Translating Pasternak." In Boris Pasternak. *Safe Conduct: An Early Autobiography and Other Works*. Translated by Alec Brown. London: Elek Books, 1959.

Brown, Anthony. "Pasternak: On My Life Now." *London Daily Mail*, February 12, 1959.

Bukharin, N. "Poetry, Poetics, and the Problems of Poetry in the USSR." In A. Zhdanov et al., eds. *Problems of Soviet Literature: Reports and Speeches at the First Soviet Writers' Congress*. Moscow: Cooperative Publishing Society of Foreign Workers, 1935.

Carlisle, Olga. "Three Visits with Boris Pasternak." *Paris Review* 24 (Summer–Fall, 1960): 45–69.

Chukovskii, Kornei. "Boris Pasternak (1890–1960)." In Boris Pasternak, *Stikhi* [*Works*]. Moscow: Khudozhestvennaia literatura, 1966.

Cohen, J. M. Introduction. In Boris Pasternak, *Prose and Poems*. Edited by Stefan Schimanski. London: Ernest Benn, 1959.

Davie, Donald. Introduction. In *Pasternak: Modern Judgements*. Edited by Donald Davie and Angela Livingstone. London: Macmillan, 1969.

Deutscher, Isaac. "Pasternak and the Calendar of the Revolution." *Partisan Review* 26 (Spring, 1959): 248–65. Reprinted in Donald Davie and Angela Livingstone, eds. *Pasternak: Modern Judgements*. London: Macmillan, 1969.

Di Sovico, Aurelio. "Poet of Perplexity: Reflections on the Pleasures of Writing" [on Jorge L. Borges]. *Il Mundo*, January 22, 1976. Reprinted in *Atlas World Press Review*, April, 1976.

Dyck, J. W. "Boris Pasternak: The Caprice of Beauty." *Canadian Slavonic Review* 16 (1974): 612–26.

Edgerton, William. "The Serapion Brothers: An Early Soviet Controversy." *American Slavic and East European Review* 8 (1948).

Erlich, Victor. "The Concept of the Poet in Pasternak." *Slavonic and East European Review* 37 (June, 1959): 325–35.

———. "'Life by Verses': Boris Pasternak." In Victor Erlich. *The Double Image*. Baltimore: Johns Hopkins Press, 1964.

Fortin, René E. "Home and the Uses of Creative Nostalgia in *Doctor Zhivago*." *Modern Fiction Studies* 20 (1974): 203–209.

France, Anna Kay. "Boris Pasternak's Interpretation of *Hamlet*." *Russian Literature Triquarterly* 7 (1974).

Frank, Victor S. "Boris Pasternak." Paper read at Pasternak Symposium, Saint Anthony's College, Oxford University, December, 1962.

———. "The Meddlesome Poet: Boris Pasternak's Rise to Greatness." *Dublin Review* 232 (Spring, 1958): 49–58.

Gerschenkron, Alexander. "Notes on Doctor Zhivago." *Modern Philology* 58 (February, 1961): 194–200. Reprinted in Alexander Gerschenkron. *Economic Backwardness in Historical Perspective*. Cambridge, Mass.: Harvard University Press, 1962.

Gibian, George. "The Climax with *Doctor Zhivago*." In George Gibian. *Interval of Freedom: Soviet Literature During the Thaw, 1954–1957*. Minneapolis: University of Minnesota Press, 1960.

Gifford, Henry. "Doctor Zhivago: A Novel in Prose and Verse." In *The Novel in Russia: From Pushkin to Pasternak*. New York: Harper and Row, Colophon Books, 1965.

———. "Pasternak and the 'Realism' of Blok." *Oxford Slavonic Papers* 13 (1967): 96–106.

Gijsen, Marnix. "A Note on Pasternak." *Books Abroad* [now *World Literature Today*] 35:2 (1961).

Goriély, Benjamin. Introduction. In Boris Pasternak. *L'An 1905*. Translated and with a study by Benjamin Goriély. Paris: Editions Debresse, 1958.

Grigorieff, Dmitry Felix. "Pasternak and Dostoevskij." *Slavic and East European Journal* 17, n.s., 3 (1959): 335–42.

Gronicka, A. von. "Rilke and the Pasternaks: A Biographical Note." *Germanic Review* (December, 1952).

Guerney, Bernard Gilbert. "Boris Leonidovich Pasternak." In Bernard Gilbert Guerney, ed. *An Anthology of Russian Literature in the Soviet Period from Gorki to Pasternak*. New York: Random House, 1960.

Gupta, Nolini Kanta. "Boris Pasternak: An Indian Viewpoint." *Russian Review* 19 (July, 1960): 248–53.

Hampshire, Stuart. "*Doctor Zhivago*: As from a Lost Culture." *Encounter* 11 (November, 1958): 3–5.

Harari, Manya. "Pasternak." *Twentieth Century* 164 (December, 1968): 524–28.

Harris, Jane Gary. "Pasternak's Vision of Life: The History of a Feminine Image." *Russian Literature Triquarterly*, no. 9 (1974), pp. 389–421.

Hayward, Max. "Introduction to Boris Pasternak's 'Without Love.'" *Partisan Review* 3–4 (1961).

———. "Notes and Comments." In Aleksandr Gladkov. *Meetings with Pasternak: A Memoir*. New York: Harcourt, Brace, 1977.

———. "Notes and Comments." In Olga Ivinskaya. *A Captive of Time*. New York: Doubleday, 1978.

———. "Pasternak's *Dr. Zhivago*." *Encounter* 10 (May, 1958): 38–48.

Howe, Irving. "Freedom and the Ashcan of History." *Partisan Review* 26 (Spring, 1959): 249–75. Reprinted in Donald Davie and Angela Livingstone, eds. *Pasternak: Modern Judgements*. London: Macmillan, 1969.

Hughes, Olga Raevsky. "Pasternak and Cvetaeva: History of a Friendship." *Books Abroad* [now *World Literature Today*] 44 (Spring, 1970): 218–21.

Jackson, Robert L. "*Doktor Živago* and the Living Tradition." *Slavic and East European Journal* 4 (1960): 103–18.

Jakobson, Roman. "On Russian Fairy Tales." In *Russian Fairy Tales* [selected from Afanasev collection]. London: Routledge, n.d.

———. "The Prose of the Poet Pasternak." In Donald Davie and Angela Livingstone, eds. *Pasternak: Modern Judgements*. London: Macmillan, 1969.

James, Henry. "The Great Form: A Letter to the Deerfield Summer School." In Leon Edel, ed. *The Future of the Novel: Essays on the Art of Fiction*. New York: Vintage, 1956.

Johnson, Priscilla. "Letter from Moscow." *Harper's Magazine*, May, 1961.

Kalb, Marvin. "Pasternak's Russia." *Saturday Review*, March 11, 1967, pp. 70–87.

Kaverin, Veniamin. Letter of January 25, 1968, to Konstantin Fedin. *Survey*, no. 68, July, 1968.

Kermode, Frank. "Pasternak's Novel." *Spectator* (London), September 5, 1958, p. 315.

Knowlton, Winthrop. "A Pilgrim at the Grave of Boris Pasternak." *Los Angeles Times*, February 5, 1978.

Levin, Elena. "Nine Letters of Boris Pasternak." *Harvard Library Bulletin* 15 (1967).

Lezhnev, A. "The Poetry of Boris Pasternak." In Donald Davie and Angela Livingstone, eds. *Pasternak: Modern Judgements*. London: Macmillan, 1969.

Livingstone, Angela. "Allegory and Christianity in *Doctor Zhivago*." *Melbourne Slavonic Studies* 1 (1967): 24–33.

———. "Pasternak's Last Poetry." *Meanjin Quarterly* 22 (1963): 388–96.

Lora, Guillermo. "El Caso Pasternak." In *La Frus-*

tración del novelista Jaime Mendoza. La Paz: Editorial Masas, 1964.

Lyons, James. "Alexander Skryabin." *American Record Guide*, 1972.

Magidoff, Robert. "The Life, Times, and Art of Boris Pasternak." *Thought* 42 (Autumn, 1967): 327–57.

Mallac, Guy de. "A Russian Impressionist: Leonid Osipovich Pasternak, 1862–1945." *California Slavic Studies* 10 (1977): 87–120.

Mandelstam, Osip. "Notes on Poetry." *Russian Literature Triquarterly* 6.

"Mandelstam's 'Ode to Stalin.'" *Slavic Review*, December, 1975, pp. 683–91.

"Man into Superman: The Promise and Peril of the New Genetics." *Time*, April 19, 1971.

Markov, Vladimir. "Notes on Pasternak's *Dr. Zhivago*." *Russian Review* 18 (January, 1959): 14–22.

———. "An Unnoticed Aspect of Pasternak's Translations." *Slavic Review*, October, 1961.

Matlaw, Ralph. "A Visit with Pasternak." *Nation*, September 12, 1959, pp. 134–35.

Matthewson, Rufus W., Jr. "Pasternak: 'An Inward Music.'" In *The Positive Hero in Russian Literature*. 2d ed. Stanford: Stanford University Press, 1975.

Merton, Thomas. "Boris Pasternak and the People with Watch Chains." *Jubilee*, July 1959, pp. 19–31.

———. "The Pasternak Affair." In *Disputed Questions*. New York: Farrar, Straus and Cudahy, 1960.

———. "The Pasternak Affair in Perspective." *Thought* 34 (1959): 485–517.

———. "Postscript to 'The Pasternak Affair.'" *Disputed Questions*. New York: Farrar, Straus and Cudahy, 1960.

Miłosz, Czesław. "On Pasternak Soberly." *Books Abroad* [now *World Literature Today*] 44 (Spring, 1970): 200–209.

Mossman, Elliot, trans. and ed. "Unpublished Letters of Boris Pasternak." *New York Times Magazine*, January 1, 1978, pp. 9–13, 24–33.

Muchnic, Helen. "Boris Pasternak and the Poems of Yurii Zhivago." In *From Gorky to Pasternak: Six Writers in Soviet Russia*. New York: Random House, 1961.

———. "Pasternak in His Letters" [review of Boris Pasternak. *Letters to Georgian Friends*. Translated by David Magarshack. Harcourt, Brace and World] *New York Review of Books*, November 7, 1968, p. 10.

———. "Toward an Analysis of Boris Pasternak." *Slavic and East European Journal* 2 (1957): 101–105.

Neiman, Iuliia. "1941." Translated by W. N. Vickery. *Partisan Review* 3–4 (1961).

Nilsson, Nils Åke. "Life as Ecstasy and Sacrifice: Two Poems by Boris Pasternak." *Scando-Slavica* 5 (1959): 180–98.

———. "Pasternak: 'We Are the Guests of Existence.'" *Reporter* 19 (November 27, 1958): 34–35.

Obolensky, Dimitri. "The Poems of Doctor Zhivago." *Slavonic and East European Review* 40 (December, 1961): 123–25.

Olesha, Yuri. "Speech to the First Congress of Soviet Writers." *Envy and Other Works*. Garden City, N.Y.: Doubleday, 1967.

Østerling, Anders. "Announcement." *Roger Martin du Gard, Gabriela Mistral, Boris Pasternak*. Nobel Prize Library [published under the sponsorship of the Nobel Foundation and the Swedish Academy]. New York: Alexis Gregory, 1971; Del Mar, Calif.: CRM, 1971.

Palmer, Christopher. "A Note on Skryabin and Pasternak." *Musical Times*, January, 1972, pp. 28–30.

"The Passion of Yurii Zhivago." *Time*, December 15, 1958, pp. 50–56.

Pasternak, Josephine. "Last Years." In *Leonid Pasternak, 1862–1945*. Catalogue. London: Oxford University Press, March–May, 1969, pp. 2–4.

———. "Patior." *London Magazine* 4 (September, 1964): 41–57.

———. "Three Suns." In Paul J. Mark, ed. *Die Familie Pasternak: Erinnerungen, Berichte*. Geneva: Poésie Vivante, 1975.

Pasternak, Leonid Osipovich. "My Meetings with Tolstoy." *Russian Review* 19 (April, 1960).

Pasternak-Slater, Lydia. "Letter to the Editor." *New York Times Book Review*, October 29, 1961, p. 50.

Paul, Sherman. "An Art of Life: Pasternak's Autobiographies." *Salmagundi* 14 (1970).

Poggioli, Renato. "Boris Pasternak." *Partisan Review* 25:4 (Fall, 1958): 541–54.

Rannit, Aleksis. "The Rhythm of Pasternak: 1. His Early Poetry, 1912–1924." *Bulletin of the New York Public Library* 63 (November, 1959): 555–67.

———. "The Rhythm of Pasternak: 2. Poet in Search of His Place 1924–1936." *Bulletin of the New York Public Library* 64 (August, 1960): 437–51.

Reavey, George. "Exegi Monumentum." *The Poetry of Boris Pasternak, 1914–1960*. Edited by George Reavey. New York: Putnam's, Capricorn, 1960.

Reavey, George. Introduction. *The Poetry of Boris Pasternak, 1914–1960*. Edited by George Reavey. New York: Putnam's, Capricorn, 1960.

————. "A Note on Boris Pasternak." *Noonday* 1 (1958): 115–18.

Reeve, F. D. "*Doctor Zhivago*: From Prose to Verse." *Kenyon Review* 22 (Winter, 1960): 123–36.

Ricks, Christopher, "Pasternak: A Prince Among Survivors." *Sunday Times* (London), April 16, 1978.

Ripellino, A. M. Introduzione. In Boris Pasternak. *Poesie*. Nuova collana di poeta tradotti. 2d ed. Milan: Giulio Einaudi, 1957.

Robbins, Jhan. "Boris Pasternak's Last Message to the World." *New York Herald Tribune*, August 7, 1960, p. 5.

Ruge, Gerd. "A Visit to Pasternak." *Encounter* 10 (March, 1958): 22–25.

Sheikholeslami, Erika F. "Pasternak's Unpublished Essay 'About the Object and Method of Psychology' and Its Relation to Pasternak's Aesthetics." Paper delivered at the New England Slavic Conference, Amherst, Mass., April 15, 1978.

Šilbajoris, Rimvydas. "The Conception of Life in the Art of Pasternak." *Books Abroad* [now *World Literature Today*] 44 (Spring, 1970): 209–14.

————. "Pasternak and Tolstoj: Some Comparisons." *Slavic and East European Journal* 11 (1967): 23–34.

Strachey, John. "Pasternak's Children." *Observer* (London), May 5, 1963.

————. "The Strangled Cry." *Encounter* 15 (December, 1960): 23–37.

Struve, Gleb. "The Hippodrome of Life: The Problem of Coincidences in Doctor Zhivago." *Books Abroad* [now *World Literature Today*] 44 (Spring, 1970): 231–36.

————. "Sense and Nonsense About Doctor Zhivago." In *Studies in Russian and Polish Literature in Honor of Wacław Lednicki*, edited by Z. Foleiewski et al. The Hague: Mouton, 1962.

————, trans. and ed. "Boris Pasternak About Himself and His Readers." *Slavic Review* 23 (March, 1964): 125–28.

Terras, Victor. "Boris Pasternak and Romantic Aesthetics." *Papers on Language and Literature* 3 (1967): 42–56.

————. "Boris Pasternak and Time." *Canadian Slavic Studies* 2 (Summer, 1968): 264–70.

————. "Turgenev's Esthetic and Western Realism." *Comparative Literature* 22 (Winter, 1970).

Tertz, Abram. "The Literary Process in Russia." In *Kontinent I*. New York: Anchor Books, 1976.

Vogel, Lucy. "*Lightning Flashes of Art*: Blok's Essay on Italy." *Italian Quarterly* 20 (Summer–Fall, 1976): 19–30.

Wain, John. "The Meaning of *Dr. Zhivago*." *Critical Quarterly* 10 (1968): 113–37.

Weidlé, Wladimir. "A Contemporary's Judgment." *Books Abroad* [now *World Literature Today*] 44 (Spring, 1970): 215–17.

Wellek, René. "Immanuel Kant's Esthetics and Criticism." *Discriminations: Further Concepts of Criticism*. New Haven, Conn.: Yale University Press, 1970.

Wilson, Edmund. "Doctor Life and His Guardian Angel." *New Yorker*, November 15, 1958, pp. 213–38.

————. "Legend and Symbol in *Doctor Zhivago*." *Encounter* 12 (June, 1959): 5–16; *Nation*, April 25, 1959, pp. 363–73. Reprinted with postscript in Edmund Wilson. *The Bit Between My Teeth: A Literary Chronicle of 1950–1965*. New York: Farrar, Straus and Giroux, 1965.

Wrenn, C. C. "Boris Pasternak." *Oxford Slavonic Papers* 2 (1951): 82–97.

Wright-Kovaleva, Rita. "Mayakovsky and Pasternak: Fragments of Reminiscence." *Oxford Slavonic Papers* 13 (1967).

Zaslove, Jerald. "*Dr. Zhivago* and the Obliterated Man: The Novel and Literary Criticism." *Journal of Aesthetics and Art Criticism* 26 (1967): 65–80.

Zorza, Victor. "Pasternak Acceptance Angers 'Pravda.'" *London Daily Telegraph*, October 27, 1958.

————. "Royalties for Pasternak." *Manchester Guardian*, August 22, 1959.

SELECTED CHAPTERS
AND ARTICLES
IN RUSSIAN

For a listing of 442 bibliographical items in Russian about Pasternak, see N. A. Troitsky. *Boris Leonidovich Pasternak, 1890–1960: A Bibliography of the Works of B. Pasternak and Literature About Him Printed in Russian*. Ithaca, N.Y.: Committee on Soviet Studies, Cornell University, 1969, pp. 85–126.

Adamovich, Georgii. "Nesostoiavshaiasia progulka" ["A Canceled Stroll"]. *Sovremennye zapiski* [*Contemporary Notes*] 59 (1935): 288–96.

———. "Temy" ("Themes"). In R. N. Grynberg, ed. *Vozdushnye puti: Almanakh* [*Aerial Ways: An Almanac*]. New York: Chekhov Publishing House, 1960.

Aleksandrova, V. "Po literaturnym adresam poeta (B. Pasternak)" ["Investigating the Literary Addresses of the Poet (B. Pasternak)"]. *Vozdushnye puti* [*Aerial Ways*] 1 (1960): 118–34.

Annenkov, Iurii. "Boris Pasternak." *Dnevnik moikh vstrech: Tsikl tragedii* [*Diary of My Encounters: A Cycle of Tragedies*]. Vol. 2. New York: Inter-Language Literary Associates, 1966.

Antokolskii, P. "Boris Pasternak." *Znamia* [*Banner*], nos. 9–10 (1943), pp. 312–16.

Aseev, N. "Organizatsiia rechi (B. Pasternak)" ["The Organization of Speech (B. Pasternak)"]. *Pechat i revoliutsiia* [*Press and Revolution*] 6 (1923): 71–78. Reprinted as "Melodika ili intonatsiia?" ["Melody or Intonation?"] *Dnevnik pisatelia* [*Diary of a Writer*]. Leningrad, 1929.

Barnes, Christopher J. "Boris Pasternak i Revoliutsiia 1917 goda" ["Boris Pasternak and the 1917 Revolution"]. *Boris Pasternak, 1890–1960: Colloque de Cerisy-la-Salle (11–14 septembre 1975)*. Edited by Michel Aucouturier. Paris: Institut d'études slaves, 1979.

———, and Nicholas J. Anning. Editorial "Predislovie" [Editorial "Foreword"]. Boris Pasternak, *Fragmenty romana* [*Fragments of a Novel*]. Edited by Christopher J. Barnes and Nicholas J. Anning. London: Collins and Harvill, 1973.

Barsov, Vasilii. "O Pasternake: moskovskie vpechatleniia" ["On Pasternak: Moscow Impressions"]. *Grani* [*Facets/Boundaries*] 40 (1958): 102–16.

Bem, A. "Boris Pasternak: Vtoroe rozhdenie" ["Boris Pasternak: A Second Birth"]. *Sovremennye zapiski* [*Contemporary Notes*] 51 (1933): 454–56.

Brik, Liliia Iurevna. "Chuzhie stikhi: Glava iz vospominanii" ["Others' Poems: A Chapter from Reminiscences"]. *V. Maiakovskii v vospominaniiakh sovremennikov* [*V. Maiakovskii as Remembered by his Contemporaries*]. Moscow: Gosudarstvennoe izdatelstvo khudozhestvennoi literatury, 1963.

Briusov, V. "Vchera, segodnia i zavtra russkoi poezii (B. Pasternak)" ["Yesterday, Today, and Tomorrow of Russian Poetry (B. Pasternak)"]. *Sobranie sochinenii v 7-i tomakh* [*Collected Works in 7 Volumes*]. Vol. 6. Moscow, 1975. Originally appeared in *Pechat i revoliutsiia* [*Press and Revolution*] 7 (1922): 57–58.

Bulgakov, Val. "L. O. Pasternak." *Iskusstvo* [*Art*], July, 1961.

Burliuk, D., A. Kruchenykh, V. Maiakovskii, and V. Khlebnikov. "Poshchechina obshchestvennomu vkusu" ["A Slap in the Face of Public Taste"]. In Vladimir Markov, ed., *Manifesty i programmy russkikh futuristov* [*Manifestos and Programs of the Russian Futurists*]. Munich: Wilhelm Fink, 1967, pp. 50–51.

Chelionati. "Liriki" ["Lyric Poets"]. *Moskovskie mastera: zhurnal iskusstv* [*Moscow Craftsmen: A Journal of the Arts*]. Moscow: Vesna, 1916.

Chukovskii, Kornei. "Boris Pasternak (1890–1960)." In Boris Pasternak. *Stikhi* [*Verse*]. Moscow: Khudozhestvennaia literatura, 1966. Reprinted in Kornei Chukovskii. *Sobranie sochinenii v 6-1 tomakh* [*Collected Works in 6 Volumes*]. Vol. 5. Moscow: Izdatelstvo Khudozhestvennaia literatura, 1967.

Ehrenburg, Ilia. "Boris Leonidovich Pasternak." *Portrety russkikh poetov* [*Portraits of Russian Poets*]. Berlin: Argonavty, 1922.

———. "Pisma s mezhdunarodnogo kongressa pisatelei" ["Letters from the International Writers' Congress"]. *Literaturnyi kritik* [*Literary Critic*] 8 (1935): 3–21.

———. "Pismo s kongressa: IV" ["Letter from the Congress: IV"]. *Izvestiia* [*News*], June 25, 1935.

———. "Pismo s kongressa: V. Poslednee zasedanie" ["Letter from the Congress: V. Final Session"]. *Izvestiia* [*News*], June 27, 1935.

Elsberg, Zh. "Mirovospriiatie B. Pasternaka" ["B. Pasternak's Perception of the World"]. *Na literaturnom postu* [*On Literary Guard*] 7 (April, 1930): 42–50.

Erlich, V. "Strasti razriady (Zametki o *Marburge*)" ["Discharges of Passion (Notes on 'Marburg')"]. *Boris Pasternak, 1890–1960: Colloque de Cerisy-la-Salle (11–14 septembre 1975)*. Edited by Michel Aucouturier. Paris: Institut d'études slaves, 1979.

Etkind, Efim. "Ob uslovno-poeticheskom i individualnom (Sonety Shekspira v russkikh perevodakh)" ["On the Conditionally Poetic and the Individual (Shakespeare's Sonnets in Russian Translations)"]. *Masterstvo perevoda: Sbornik shestoi* [*The Craft of Translation: Sixth Collection*]. Pp. 142–47. Moscow, 1968.

———. "Pasternak, novator poeticheskoi rechi"

["Pasternak as Innovator in the Sphere of Poetic Speech"]. *Boris Pasternak, 1890–1960: Colloque de Cerisy-la-Salle (11–14 septembre 1975)*. Edited by Michel Aucouturier. Paris: Institut d'études slaves, 1979.

———. "Poeticheskii perevod v istorii russkoi literatury" ["The Poetic Translation in the History of Russian Literature"]. *Mastera russkogo stikhotvornogo perevoda [Masters of Russian Verse Translation]*. Leningrad: Sovetskii pisatel, 1968.

Fedorov, A. "Neobychinaia antologiia" ["An Unusual Anthology"]. In *Masterstvo perevoda: Sbornik sedmoi [The Craft of Translation: Seventh Collection]*. Moscow, 1970.

Finkel, A. "66-i sonet v russkikh perevodakh" ["The Sixty-sixth Sonnet in Russian Translations"]. *Masterstvo perevoda: Sbornik shestoi [The Craft of Translation: Sixth Collection]*. Moscow, 1968.

Fleishman, L. S. "Avtobiograficheskoe i 'Avgust' Pasternaka ["The Autobiographical Element in Pasternak's 'August'"]. *Slavica Hierosolymitana* 1 (1977): 194–98.

——— "Fragmenty 'futuristicheskoi' biografii Pasternaka" ["Fragments of Pasternak's 'Futuristic' Biography"]. *Slavica Hierosolymitana* 4 (1979): 79–113.

———. "K kharakteristike rannego Pasternaka" ["Toward a Characterization of the Early Pasternak"]. *Russian Literature* 12 (1975): 79–126.

———. "Marginaliia k istorii russkogo avangarda: Vstupitelnaia statia" ["Marginal Remarks on the History of the Russian Avant-Garde: Introduction"]. In N. M. Oleinikov, *Stikhotvoreniia [Poems]* (Studien und Texte, no. 5 [1975]). Bremen: Verlag K-Presse.

Frank, Victor. "Realizm chetyrekh izmerenii (Perechityvaia Pasternaka)" ["Realism in Four Dimensions (Rereading Pasternak)"]. *Izbrannye stati [Selected Articles]*. Edited by Leonard Shapiro. London: Overseas Publications Interchange, 1974.

———. "Vodianoi znak (Poeticheskoe mirovozzrenie Pasternaka)" ["The Watermark (The Poetic World View of Pasternak)"]. *Sbornik statei, posviashchennykh tvorchestvu B. L. Pasternaka [A Collection of Articles Devoted to the Work of B. L. Pasternak]*. Munich: Institut po izucheniiu SSSR, 1962.

Gavruk, Iu. "Nuzhen li novyi perevod 'Gamleta' na russkii iazyk?" ["Is a New Russian Translation of *Hamlet* Necessary?"]. *Masterstvo perevoda: Sbornik shestoi [The Craft of Translation: Sixth Col-*

lection of Articles]. Moscow: Sovetskii pisatel, 1968.

Gorkii, Maksim. "Predislovie k povesti Pasternaka 'Detstvo Liuvers'" ["Foreword to Pasternak's Short Story 'The Childhood of Liuvers'"]. *Literaturnoe Nasledstvo [Literary Heritage]* 70 (1963): 308–10.

Grabar, Igor. "Pamiati Leonida Pasternaka" ["Memories of Leonid Pasternak"]. *Sovetskoe Iskusstvo [Soviet Art]*, no. 28, (July 13, 1945).

Gussein, Mekhti. "Stranitsy dnevnika" ["Pages of a Diary"]. *Znamia [Banner]*, March, 1962, p. 110.

Hughes, O. R. "Stikhotvorenie Marburg i tema 'vtorogo rozhdeniia' v tvorchestve Pasternaka" ["The Poem 'Marburg' and the Theme of the 'Second Birth' in Pasternak's Works"]. *Boris Pasternak, 1890–1960: Colloque de Cerisy-la-Salle (11–14 septembre 1975)*. Edited by Michel Aucouturier. Paris: Institut d'études slaves, 1979.

Iakovlev, Boris. "Poet dlia estetov (Zametki o Velimire Khlebnikove i formalizme v poezii)" ["A Poet for Aesthetes (Notes about Velimir Khlebnikov and Formalism in Poetry)"]. *Novyi mir [New World]* 5 (May, 1948): 207–31.

"Interes k Pasternaku" ["Fascination with Pasternak"]. *Novoe russkoe slovo [New Russian Word]*, December 31, 1958.

Karp, P. "Zhizn, a ne slovesnost" ["Life, but Not Literature"]. *Zvezda [Star]* 2 (1968): 220–22.

Katanian, V. A. "Ne tolko vospominaniia" ["Not Only Remembrances"]. *Russian Literature Triquarterly* 13 (Fall, 1975): 477–95.

———. "O Maiakovskom i Pasternake" ["On Maiakovskii and Pasternak"]. *Russian Literature Triquarterly* 13 (Fall, 1975): 499–518.

Katkov, George. "'Bezliube'—rannii nabrosok *Doktora Zhivago*" ["Without Love—An Early Sketch Toward *Doctor Zhivago*"]. *Boris Pasternak, 1890–1960: Colloque de Cerisy-la-Salle (11–14 septembre 1975)*. Edited by Michel Aucouturier. Paris: Institut d'études slaves, 1979. "Bezliube" originally published in *Novyi zhurnal [New Review]* 62 (1960): 10–11.

Khalafov, K. "O muzyke stikhov Pasternaka" ["On the Music of Pasternak's Verse"]. *Mosty [Bridges]* 8 (1961): 120–29.

Konstantinov, D. V. "Doktor Zhivago i bogoiskatelstvo v SSSR" ["Doctor Zhivago and the Search for God in the USSR"]. *Vesnik Instituta po izucheniiu SSSR [Bulletin of the Institute for the Study of the USSR]* 2 (1959): 75–86.

Koriakov, M. "Afinogenov i Pasternak" ["Afinogenov and Pasternak"]. *Novyi zhurnal* [*New Review*] 56 (1959): 159–86.

———. "Stalin i Pasternak" ["Stalin and Pasternak"]. *Novoe russkoe slovo* [*New Russian Word*]. January 23 and 30, 1966.

———. "Termometr Rossii u Pasternaka" ["Russia's Thermometer as Reflected in Pasternak"]. *Novyi zhurnal* [*New Review*] 55 (December, 1958): 130–41.

Kornilov, Vladimir. "My khoronili starika" ["We Buried the Old Man"], in "Chetyre stikhotvorenii" ["Four Poems"]. *Novyi mir* [*New World*], December, 1964, pp. 83–84.

Kozhinov, V. "Dostoevskii ili geroi Dostoevskogo" ["Dostoevskii or Dostoevskii's Hero"]. *Voprosy literatury* [*Questions of Literature*], no. 9 (1966), pp. 208–09.

Krotkov, Iurii. "Pasternaki." Part 1, *Grani* [*Facets/Boundaries*] 60 (1966); Part 2, *Grani* 63 (1967).

Kurlov, G. "O Pasternake: Iz gimnazicheskikh vospominanii" ["About Pasternak: A Page from Reminiscences of my Schooldays"]. *Russkaia mysl* [*Russian Thought*] 1288 (November 8, 1958).

Kuzmin, M. "Krylati gost, gerbarii i ekzamen" ["The Winged Visitor, the Herbarium, and the Examination"]. *Zhizn iskusstva* [*Life of Art*], July 18, 1922.

Lazarevskii, Ivan. "L. O. Pasternak." *Novyi zhurnal dlia vsekh* [*New Journal for Everyone*] no. 9 (1909).

Levik, V. "Nuzhny li novye perevody Shekspira?" ["Are New Translations of Shakespeare Necessary?"]. In *Masterstvo perevoda: Sbornik shestoi* [*The Craft of Translation: Sixth Collection*]. Moscow, 1968.

Levin, Iu. "Russkie perevody Shekspira" ["Russian Translations of Shakespeare"]. In *Masterstvo perevoda: Sbornik shestoi* [*The Craft of Translation: Sixth Collection*]. Moscow, 1968.

Lezhnev, A. "Boris Pasternak." In *Sovremenniki: literaturno-kriticheskie ocherki* [*The Contemporaries: Critical-Literary Essays*]. Moscow: Krug, 1927, pp. 32–54.

———. "Boris Pasternak (K vykhodu 'Dvukh knig' i '1905 goda')" ["Boris Pasternak (On the Publication of 'Two Books' and '1905')"]. *Krasnaia nov* [*Red Virgin Soil*] 8 (1926): 205–19.

———. "Boris Pasternak: 1. Dve knigi. Stikhi. 2. 1905 god" ["Boris Pasternak: 1. Two Books.

Verse. 2. 1905"]. *Pravda* [*Truth*], December 28, 1927.

Loks. K. G. "Epopeia Selvinskogo (B. Pasternak)" ["Selvinskii's Epic (B. Pasternak)"]. *Krasnaia nov* [*Red Virgin Soil*] 3 (1927): 236.

Lunacharskii, Anatolii. "Na fronte iskusstva" ["On the Front of Art"; typescript, 1926]. *Literaturnoe nasledstvo* [*Literary Heritage*]. Moscow: Nauka, 1965, 74: 41.

———. "Ocherk russkoi literatury revoliusionnogo vremeni" ["A Sketch of Russian Literature of the Revolutionary Period"; 1922]. *Literaturnoe nasledstvo* [*A. V. Lunacharskii, neizdannye materialy*] [*Literary Heritage (A. V. Lunacharskii: Unpublished Materials)*]. Moscow: Nauka, 1970, 88: 229–30.

———. "Tezisy o politike RKP v oblasti literatury" ["Theses About the Politics of the R(ussian) C(ommunist) P(arty) in the Area of Literature"; typescript, 1925], *Literaturnoe nasledstvo* [*Literary Heritage*]. Moscow: Nauka, 1965, 74: 31.

Maiakovskii, Vladimir. "Vystuplenie na dispute 'Lef ili blef?'" ["Appearance at the Debate Lef (Left Flank) or a Bluff?"]. *Literaturnoe nasledstvo* [*Novoe o Maiakovskom*] [*Literary Heritage (New Materials About Maiakovskii)*]. Moscow: Akademiia nauk SSSR, 1958, 65: 56, 62–63.

Mandelshtam, Osip. "B. Pasternak." In *O poezii* [*On Poetry*]. Leningrad: Akademiia, 1928.

———. "Buria i natisk." *Russkoe iskusstvo* [*Russian Art*] 1 (1923): 75–82. Translated by Clarence Brown as "Storm and Stress" in *Russian Literature Triquarterly* 1 (Fall, 1971): 154–62.

Margolin, Iu. "Perechityvaia 'Doktora Zhivago'" ["Rereading *Doctor Zhivago*"]. *Novoe russkoe slovo* [*New Russian Word*], December 17, 1961.

Margvelashvili, Georgii. "V mire obrazov Georgiia Leonidze" ["In the World of Georgii Leonidze's Images"]. *Literaturnaia Gruziia* [*Literary Georgia*], May, 1964, pp. 63–68.

Markov, Vladimir. "Mysli o russkom futurizme" ["Thoughts on Russian Futurism"]. *Novyi zhurnal* [*New Review*] 38 (1954): 169–81.

———. "Sovetskii 'Gamlet' (B. Pasternak)" ["The Soviet *Hamlet* (B. Pasternak)"]. *Grani* 45 (1960): 119–124.

"Mastityi L. Pasternak" ["The Eminent L. Pasternak"]. *Rubezh* [*Boundary*] 28 (June 1, 1933).

Mazurin, Nikolai. "Orel—god 1943-i" ["Orel—1943"]. *Literaturnaia Rossiia* [*Literary Russia*] 31 (August 2, 1968): 5.

Mirskii, D. S. "Pasternak i gruzinskie poety"

["Pasternak and the Georgian Poets"]. *Literaturnaia gazeta* [*Literary Gazette*], October 24, 1935. See also Sviatopolk-Mirskii, kn.D.

Metchenko, A. "O sotsialisticheskom realizme i sotsialisticheskom iskusstve" ["On Socialist Realism and Socialist Art"]. *Oktiabr* [*October*], no. 6 (1967), pp. 185–200.

Morozov, M. "'Gamlet' v perevode Borisa Pasternaka" ["*Hamlet* in Boris Pasternak's Translation"]. *Teatr* [*Theater*], February, 1941, pp. 144–47.

"Ne dadim zhitia vragam Sovetskogo Soiuza" ["We Will Not Give Quarter to the Enemies of the Soviet Union"]. *Literaturnaia gazeta* [*Literary Gazette*], June 15, 1937.

N-ko, N. [*sic*]. "Moi vstrechi s Annoi Akhmatovoi" ["My Meetings with Anna Akhmatova"]. *Novoe russkoe slovo* [*New Russian Word*], March 13, 1966.

Ognev, Vl. "U karty sovetskoi poezii" ["By the Map of Soviet Poetry"]. In *Masterstvo perevoda: Sbornik shestoi* [*The Craft of Translation: Sixth Collection*]. Moscow, 1968.

Opishnia, Ig. "Ben Gurion osuzhdaet B. Pasternaka: Pasternak i molodezh" ["Ben Gurion Condemns B. Pasternak: Pasternak and Young People"]. *Vozrozhdenie* [*Rebirth*] 87 (1959): 143–45.

"O sovetskoi poezii" ["On Soviet Poetry"]. *Zvezda* [*Star*], March, 1949.

Otsup, N. "O Borise Pasternake" ["On Boris Pasternak"]. *Zveno* [*Link*] 5 (1928): 260–66.

Ozerov, L. "Neokonchennaia piesa B. Pasternaka" ["An Unfinished Play by Boris Pasternak"]. *Prostor* [*Wide-Open Spaces*], no. 10, (1969), pp. 45–47.

Pasternak, Aleksandr. "Leto 1903 goda: Iz zapisei o dalekom proshlom" ["The Summer of 1903: From Notes on a Distant Past"]. *Novyi mir* [*New World*] 1 (1972): 203–11.

"Poezdka iz Peterburga v Sibir v ianvare 1920 g." ["A Trip from Petersburg to Siberia in January, 1920"]. *Arkhiv russkoi revoliutsii* [*Archive of the Russian Revolution*] 3 (1922): 190–209.

Pomerantsev, K. "Vo chto verit sovetskaia molodezh?" ["In What Does Soviet Youth Believe?"]. *Novyi zhurnal* [*New Journal*] 78 (1965): 140–58.

Porman, R. "B. L. Pasternak v Chistopole" ["B. L. Pasternak in Chistopol"]. *Russkaia literatura* [*Russian Literature*] 3 (1966): 193–95.

Pravdukhin, V. "V borbe za novoe iskusstvo (B. Pasternak)" ["In the Struggle for a New Art (B. Pasternak)"]. *Sibirskie ogni* [*Siberian Lights*] 5 (1922): 174–78.

Selivanovskii, A. "Pasternak, Boris Leonidovich." *Literaturnaia entsiklopediia* [*Literary Encyclopedia*] 8 (1923): 465–71.

———. "Poet i revoliutsiia: O tvorchestve B. Pasternaka" ["The Poet and Revolution: On the Art of B. Pasternak"]. *Literaturnaia Gazeta* [*Literary Gazette*], December 5, 1932.

———. "Poeziia opasna?" ["Is Poetry Dangerous?"], *Literaturnaia gazeta* [*Literary Gazette*], August 15, 1931.

Shcheglov, Mark. "Studencheskie tetradi" ["Student Notebooks"], entry for February 23, 1948. *Novyi mir* [*New World*], June, 1963, p. 135.

Siniavskii, Andrei D. "Odin den s Pasternakom" ["One Day Spent with Pasternak"]. *Boris Pasternak, 1890–1960: Colloque de Cerisy-la-Salle (11–14 septembre 1975)*. Edited by Michel Aucouturier. Paris: Institut d'études slaves, 1979.

———. "Poeziia Pasternaka" ["Pasternak's Poetry"]. In Boris Pasternak. *Stikhotvoreniia i poemy*. Edited by L. A. Ozerov. Moscow: Sovetskii pisatel, Biblioteka poeta, bolshaia seriia, 1965, pp. 9–62.

Skorbina, Nina. "Boris Pasternak: Vstrechi i pisma" ["Boris Pasternak: Meetings and Letters"]. *Novoe russkoe slovo* [*New Russian Word*], February 18, 1973.

Slonim, M. "Roman Pasternaka" ["The Novel of Pasternak"]. *Novyi Zhurnal* [*New Review*] 52 (1958): 94–108.

Snezhnitskii, L. "Poslednii god" ["The Final Year"]. *Vstrechi s Meierkholdom: Sbornik vospominanii* [*Meetings with Meierhold: A Collection of Reminiscences*]. Edited by M. A. Valentei et al. Moscow: Vserossiiskoe teatralnoe obshchestvo, 1967.

Stepun, F. A. "B. L. Pasternak." *Novyi zhurnal* [*New Review*] 56 (1959): 187–206.

Struve, Gleb. "Dva pisma Borisa Pasternaka" ["Two Letters of Boris Pasternak"]. *Novoe russkoe slovo* [*New Russian Word*], November 9, 1975.

———. "Iz zametok o masterstve Borisa Pasternaka; koe-chto o ego rifmakh" ["From Notes on the Craft of Boris Pasternak: Something About His Rhyme"]. *Vozdushnye puti* [*Aerial Ways*] 1 (1960): 88–117.

Superfin, G. G. "B. L. Pasternak, Critic of the 'Formalist Method.'" *Trudy po znakovym sistemam* [*Studies on Semiological Systems*] 5 (1971). Translated by Nancy Beveridge in *Russian Literature Triquarterly* 6 (1973): 607–609.

Surkov, A. "O poezii B. Pasternaka" ["On the Poetry of B. Pasternak"]. *Kultura i zhizn* [*Culture and Life*] 8 (March 21, 1947).

Sviatopolk-Mirskii, Kn.D. "B. Pasternak: Rasskazy, Krug, M.-L., 1925" ["B. Pasternak. *Stories. Krug*, M(oscow)-L(eningrad), 1925"]. *Sovremmennye zapiski* [*Contemporary Annals*] 25 (1925): 544–45.

Tarasenkov, A. "Boris Pasternak." *Zvezda* [*Star*] 5 (1931): 228–35.

———. "O gruzinskikh perevodakh Pasternaka" ["On Pasternak's Georgian Translations"]. *Znamia* [*Banner*], September, 1935, pp. 201–209.

———. "Zametki kritika (B. Pasternak)" ["Notes of a Critic (B. Pasternak)"]. *Znamia* [*Banner*], October, 1949.

Tregub, Semen. "Tri stikhotvoreniia Borisa Pasternaka" ["Three Poems of Boris Pasternak"]. *Literaturnaia Rossiia* [*Literary Russia*] 9 (February 23, 1968): 22–23.

Tsvetaeva, M. "Epos i lirika sovremennoi Rossii: Vladimir Maiakovskii i Boris Pasternak" ["Epic and Lyric Poetry in Contemporary Russia: Vladimir Maiakovskii and Boris Pasternak"]. *Novyi grad* [*New City*] 6 (1933): 28–41.

———. "Svetovoi liven: Poeziia vechnoi muzhestvennosti" ["The Luminous Downpour: The Poetry of Eternal Manhood"]. *Epopeia* 2 (1922): 10–33. Reprinted in M. Tsvetaeva. *Proza* [*Prose*]. New York: Chekov Publishing House, 1953.

Tynianov, B. "Pasternak." In *Arkhaisty i novatory* [*Archaizers and Innovators*]. Leningrad: Priboi, 1929.

Viliam-Vilmont, N. "'Gamlet' v perevode Borisa Pasternaka" ["*Hamlet* in Boris Pasternak's Translation"]. *Internatsionalnaia literatura* [*International Literature*], nos. 7–8 (1940), pp. 288–91.

Voznesenskii, Andrei. "Listia i korni" ["Leaves and Roots"]. *Literatura i zhizn* [*Literature and Life*], November 20, 1960.

———. "Molodye—o sebe" ["Young People—About Themselves"]. *Voprosy literatury* [*Questions of Literature*], September, 1962, p. 123.

———. "Nebo Borisa Pasternaka" ["The Sky of Boris Pasternak"]. *Inostrannaia literatura* [*Foreign Literature*], February, 1969. Reprinted in *Novoe Russkoe Slovo* [*New Russian Word*], May 11, 1969.

Weidle, V. "Stikhi i proza Pasternaka" ["The Poetry and Prose of Pasternak"]. *Sovremennye zapiski* [*Contemporary Annals*] 36 (1928): 459–70.

Wright-Kovaleva, Rita. "Mayakovsky and Pasternak: Fragments of Reminiscence." *Oxford Slavonic Papers* 13 (1967): 107–32. In Russian.

Zaidenshnur, E. "R.-M. Rilke u Tolstogo" ["R.-M. Rilke at Tolstoy's"]. *Literaturnoe nasledstvo* [*Literary Heritage*] 37–38 (1939): 708–12.

Zander, L. A. "Filosofskie temy v romane Pasternaka Doktor Zhivago" ["Philosophical Themes in Pasternak's Novel Doctor Zhivago"]. *Vestnik russkogo studencheskogo khristianskogo dvizheniia* [*Herald of the Russian Christian Students' Movement*] 52 (1959): 36–44; 53 (1959): 37–48.

Zaslavskii, D. "Shumikha reaktsionnoi propagandy vokrug literaturnogo sorniaka" ["Sensation of Reactionary Propaganda Around a Literary Weed"]. *Pravda* [*Truth*], October 26, 1958. Translated in Robert Conquest. *Courage of Genius: The Pasternak Affair*. London: Collins and Harvill, 1961.

Zhurov, P. A. "Dve vstrechi s molodym Klychkovym" ["Two Meetings with the Young Klychkov"]. *Russkaia literatura* [*Russian Literature*] 2 (1971): 149–54.

BOOKS AND ARTICLES
IN OTHER LANGUAGES

Barton, Paul. "L'épopée de Boris Pasternak." *Pensée française*, May, 1959, pp. 19–25.

Ben-Ishaj, M. Z. "With Pasternak in Moscow." *Ha-doar*, December 12, 1958. In Hebrew.

Conquest, Robert. "Le Sort d'Olga Ivinskaia." *Preuves* 126 (December, 1961).

Dinfreville, Jacques. "La Guerre des partisans dans le *Docteur Jivago*." *Revue de défense nationale*, January, 1960, pp. 4–50.

Duvignaud, Jean. "Le Don Quichotte de notre temps." *Arguments*, December, 1958.

D'Angelo, Sergio. "Der Fall Pasternak—Zehn Jahre danach." *Osteuropa*, July, 1968, pp. 489–501.

Ebbinghaus, Julius. "Hermann Cohen als Philosoph und Publizist." *Archiv für Philosophie* 6 (1956): 109–22.

Jastrun, Mieczysław. "O wierszach Borysa Pasternaka." In *Wizerunki: Szkice literackie*. Warsaw: Państwowy Instytut Wydawniczy, 1956, pp. 195–203.

Levitsky, Serge. "Rose Koffman-Pasternak: la mère

du poète." *Slavic and East-European Studies* 8 (1963): 73–80.

Marinetti, Filippo Tommaso. "Manifeste futuriste." *Figaro*, February 20, 1909.

Marx, Karl. "Verhandlungen des 6. rheinischen Landtags: Erster Artikel, Debatten über Pressfreiheit und Publikation der Ländstandischen Verhandlungen." *Rheinische Zeitung*, May 5, 1842.

Mehnert, Klaus. "Pasternaks Enkel." *Ost-Europa*, July, 1968, pp. 502–505.

Nilsson, Nils Åke. "Boris Pasternak och Doktor Zjivago." *Bonniers litterära magasin* 27 (1958): 2.

———. "Hos Boris Pasternak." *Bonniers litterära magasin* 27 : 8 (1958).

———. "Ovädret förbi, Pasternak inte tabu," *Stockholm Expressen*, May 25, 1959. Discusses some of the political background of the award of the prize; based on an interview with Surkov.

Pasternak, L. O. "Vier Fragmente aus meiner Selbstbiographie." In Max Osborn. *Leonid Pasternak*. Warsaw: Stybel, 1932.

Pasternak, Josephine. "Neunzehnhundert-Zwölf." *Alma Mater Philippina*, Winter, 1971–72.

Peltier, Hélène. "Ma rencontre avec l'auteur du 'Docteur Jivago.'" *Figaro littéraire*, November 1, 1958.

Peltier-Zamoyska, Helene. "Pasternak, homme du passé?" *Esprit*, January, 1963, pp. 16–29.

Proyart, Jacqueline de. "La nature et l'actualité dans l'oeuvre de Boris Pasternak (Réflexions sur la structure du cycle 'Kogda razguljaetsja' ['When Skies Clear'])." *Boris Pasternak, 1890–1960: Colloque de Cerisy-la-Salle (11–14 septembre 1975)*. Edited by Michel Aucouturier. Paris: Institut d'études slaves, 1979.

———. "Une amitié d'enfance." *Boris Pasternak, 1890–1960: Colloque de Cerisy-la-Salle (11–14 septembre 1975)*. Edited by Michel Aucouturier. Paris: Institut d'études slaves, 1979.

Rammelmeyer, Alfred. "Die Philipps-Universität zu Marburg in der russischen Geistesgeschichte und schönen Literatur." *Mitteilungen Universitätsbund*, 1957.

Ripellino, Angelo Maria. "Una Visita a Pasternak." *Corriere della Sera*, April 21, 1963.

Schwarz, Lotte. "Rencontres." *Esprit*, September, 1976.

Slater, Lydia Pasternak. "La Poésie de Boris Pasternak." In *Die Familie Pasternak*. Edited by Paul J. Mark. Geneva: Poésie Vivante, 1975.

———. "Prix Nobel de littérature 1958." In *Die Familie Pasternak*. Edited by Paul J. Mark. Geneva: Poésie Vivante, 1975.

Zamoyska, Hélène. "L'art et la vie chez Boris Pasternak." *Revue des études slaves* 38 (1961): 231–39.

SELECTED DISSERTATIONS

Barnes, Christopher J. "The Poetry of Boris Pasternak with Special Reference to the Period 1913–1917." Cambridge University, 1969.

Comings, Andrew Gordon. "From Lyricism to History: The Longer Poetic Form in Blok and Pasternak." Yale University, 1973.

Feinberg, Lawrence Edward. "Boris Pasternak's 'Gamlet': A Study in Grammatical Symmetry and Antisymmetry." Harvard University, 1969.

Gaigalas, Rimgaila E. Salys. "Boris Pasternak's 'Temy i variacii' ['Themes and Variations']: A Commentary." Harvard University, 1978.

Goldman, Howard Allen. "Shakespeare's *Hamlet* in the Work of Boris Pasternak and Other Modern Russian Poets (Aleksandr Blok, Anna Akhmatova, and Marina Cvetaeva)." Indiana University, 1975.

Hamilton, Tatiana Nicolaevna. "Osnovnaia tematika proizvedenii Borisa Pasternak" ["The Principal Thematics of Boris Pasternak's Works"]. Georgetown University, 1979.

Hedin, Anne Miller. "The Self as History: Studies in Adams, Faulkner, Ellison, Belyj, Pasternak." University of Virginia, 1975.

Iakobson, Anatolii. "Sootnesennost realno-istoricheskogo i karnavalno-misteriinogo nachal v russkoi poeme XX veka (Blok, Pasternak)" ["The Interrelatedness of the Real-Historical and the Mystery-Carnavalistic Elements of the Russian Long Poem of the Twentieth Century (Blok, Pasternak)"]. Hebrew University of Jerusalem, 1978.

Jackson, Carol Ann. "Teleological Coincidence and Eternity in Pasternak's Prose." New York University, 1978.

Magidoff, Robert. "Imagery in the Prose of Boris Pasternak's *Dr. Zhivago*." University of Michigan, 1963.

Mossman, Elliott Dunbar. "The Prose of the Poet Pasternak." Princeton University, 1968.

Odabashian, Petros. "An Onomastic Study of 'Doktor Zhivago,' a Novel by B. Pasternak." University of Pennsylvania, 1970.

O'Connor, Katherine Tiernan. "Boris Pasternak's 'Sestra moja zizn' [*My Sister, Life*]: An Explication." Harvard University, 1972.

Sheikholeslami, Erika A. Freiberger. "Der Deutsche Einfluss im Werke von Boris Pasternak." University of Pennsylvania, 1973.

Sulick, Michael John. "'Hamlet' in Translation: André Gide and Boris Pasternak." City University of New York, 1977.

Toomre, Joyce Stetson. "The Narrative Structure of Pasternak's *Doctor Zhivago*." Brown University, 1977.

Vorobiov. Alex. "Pasternak's Lyrical Creativity: The Formative Years, 1912–1922." University of Illinois at Champaign-Urbana, 1976.

Walter, Ronald F. "The Prose Fiction of Veniamin Kaverin: An Interpretive Study." Indiana University, 1974.

SELECTED ICONOGRAPHY

Drawings and Portraits
of Pasternak
by Leonid Osipovich Pasternak

Leonid Pasternak, 1862–1945. Catalog of exhibition of works by Leonid Pasternak held at Crawford Centre for the Arts, University of Saint Andrews, January 28–February 25, 1978. In chronological order.

Rosalia Pasternak Sewing with the Little Boris at Her Feet (1891–92). Canvas, oil. Cat. no. 4.

Portrait of Boris as a Boy of Eight (July 20, 1898). Black chalk. Cat. no. 14.

Family on a Terrace in Odessa: Rosalia with Her Two Sons Cleaning a Fruit (replica of pastel from 1890s painted in 1920s). Pastel over black chalk. Cat. no. 21.

Portrait of Boris Pasternak Reading a Book (n.d., ca. 1910–15). Canvas, oil. Cat. no. 39.

Portrait of Boris Pasternak with Baltic Sea in the Background (1910). Canvas, oil. Cat. no. 40.

Silver Wedding (1914). Canvas, oil (fragment). Cat. no. 45.

Boris Pasternak Writing with a Cigarette in His Right Hand (1919). Black, red, and white chalk. Cat. no. 72.

Portrait of Boris Pasternak in Profile (March 12, 1923). Black chalk and charcoal. Cat. no. 81.

Leonid Pasternak, 1862–1945. Catalogue of exhibition of works by Leonid Pasternak organized by Oxford University Press, London, March 20–May 30, 1969.

Boris, Reading (n.d.). Oil. Cat. no. 12.

The Brothers (n.d.). Oil. Cat. no. 20.

Boris Pasternak (n.d.). Charcoal. Cat. no. 79.

Memorial Exhibition of Paintings and Drawings by Leonid Pasternak, 1862–1945. Catalogue of exhibition held in the Ashmolean Museum, Oxford, April, 1958. In chronological order.

Portrait of Boris Pasternak as a Boy (July 20, 1898). Canvas, oil. Cat. no. 1.

The Artist's Sons, Boris and Alexander (April 30, 1902). Canvas, oil. Cat. no. 3.

The Artist's Sons (1904). Canvas, oil. Cat. no. 4.

Portrait of Boris Pasternak (1923). Canvas, oil. Cat. no. 43.

Portrait of Boris Pasternak (March 12, 1923). Canvas, oil. Cat. no. 44.

Portrait of Boris Pasternak (n.d.). Canvas, oil. Cat. no. 99.

Pasternak, L[eonid] O[sipovich]. *Zapisi raznykh let* [*Notes of Various Years*]. Moscow: Sovetskii khudozhnik, 1975. In chronological order.

B. L. Pasternak: Album Sketch (1916). Italian pencil, sanguine, paper. P. 142.

Study for a Portrait of B. L. Pasternak (1923). Canvas, oil. P. 135.

Portrait of B. L. Pasternak (1924). Autolithograph. P. 103.

Other Depictions

Annenkov, Iurii. Portrait of Pasternak, 1921. In *Dnevnik moikh vstrech: Tsikl tragedii.* New York: Inter-Language Literary Associates, 1966, 2:151. (Reproduced from: Georges Annenkoff, *Portraits*, Paris, 1922.)

Anonymous, Portrait of Pasternak. Plate no. 38. In Boris Pasternak. *Autobiografia e nuovi versi.* Milan: Feltrinelli, 1958.

Anonymous. Portrait of Pasternak in E. Evtushenko's Moscow apartment. Reproduced in Russian Language Specialties Catalogue, 1966.

Bagritskii, Eduard. Portrait of Pasternak inscribed "Kuntsevo, 1930." Moscow: Bagritskii Graphic Archive, Institute of World Literature. Discussed in N. D. Efros. "Grafika Bagritskogo. Pervyi opyt izucheniia." *Literaturnoe nasledstvo* 74 (1965):410–14.

Barsov, Vasilii [Wasilii Barsoff]. Portrait of Pasternak. Frontispiece. In Boris Pasternak. *Poeziia. Izbrannoe.* Frankfort on the Main: Posev, 1960.

Cherne, Leo. Bronze bust of Pasternak. Reproduced in "Pasternak in Bronze." *Life*, August 10, 1959, p. 99. Pasternak wrote the artist: "I should like to be like it always, without interruption."

Jacob, Max. Portrait of Pasternak, July, 1939. Based on photograph brought to France from the Soviet Union by Louis Guilloux. Reproduced in *Le Figaro littéraire*, July 26, 1958.

Korolev, Boris Daniilovich. Bust of Pasternak. In a conversation of September, 1962, the artist (noted for his famous 1931 monument to Bauman, in Bauman Square, Moscow) confirmed to the author that he had completed the work.

Kukriniksy. Caricature of Pasternak as Sphinx, 1924.

Lebedev, Sara. Bas-relief on Pasternak funeral monument, Peredelkino Cemetery.

Lembeck, Portrait of Pasternak. Frontispiece. In Boris Pasternak. *Bescheidenheit und Kuhnheit*. Edited by Robert E. Meister. Zurich: Die Arche, 1959.

Maslennikova, Zoia. Bronze bust of Pasternak (for which the poet sat). In Pasternak's study in his dacha in Peredelkino (See Iurii Krotkov, "Pasternaki," *Grani* 63 (1967): 77–78).

Nachshen, Donia. Portrait of Pasternak. In Boris Pasternak. *Bescheidenheit und Kuhnheit*. Edited by Robert E. Meister. Zurich: Die Arche, 1959, p. 33.

Shultz, Carole. Bronze bust of Pasternak (edition of six). Los Angeles, 1976.

Note: The list above does not include certain other portraits of Pasternak that are reproduced in this book (cf. List of Illustrations).

ADDENDUM

CHAPTERS AND ARTICLES

The following items became accessible to the author while the book was in press.

Aucouturier, Michel. "Pasternak témoin de l'actualité de Tolstoï." *Tolstoï aujourd'hui: Colloque international Tolstoï tenu à Paris du 10 au 13 octobre 1978*. Paris: Institut d'études slaves, 1980. Pp. 277–84.

Berlin, Isaiah. "Meetings with Russian Writers in 1945 and 1956." In *Personal Impressions*. London: Hogarth Press, 1980. Pp. 156–210.

Cheron, George. "B. Pasternak and M. Kuzmin (An Inscription)." *Wiener Slawistischer Almanach* 5 (1980); pp. 67–69.

Maslenikova, Z. "Portret poeta," *Literaturnaia Gruziia {Literary Georgia}* 10–11 (1978); 2 (1979); 3 (1979); 4 (1979).

Solzhenitsyn, Aleksandr I. "Noveliana." *New Republic*, March 22, 1980, pp. 23–25.

Voznesenskii, Andrei. "Mne chetyrnadtsat let . . . ." *Novyi mir {New World}*, September 1980, pp. 155–74.

Index of Pasternak's works

Above the Barriers: 168
"Aerial Ways": 94
"After the Storm" ("Posle viugi"): 344
Antony and Cleopatra (translation): 178, 194
"Apelles' Mark": 94
"Artist, The": 173
"August": 196, 258, 271
Autobiographical Sketch, An: see Sketch for an Autobiography

"Bacchanalia": 196, 214
"Bad Dream": 87
"Black Goblet, The" (*Second Centrifuge Miscellany*): 83, 339
Blind Beauty, The (*Slepaia krasavitsa*): 138, 262–64, 272
Breadth of the Earth, The: 178
"Break, The": 107

Carrousel, The: 108
"Change, The": 259
"Childhood of Liuvers, The": 77, 95, 117, 130
"Chopin": 228
Collected Poetry (1965 Soviet edition): 161n.

"Dawn": 172, 333, 348
"Death of a Poet": 131
"Death of a Sapper": 176
"Diary of Zhivult, The" ("Zapiski Zhivulta"): 139
"District Behind the Lines, A": 77
Doctor Zhivago: 55n., 109, 135, 173, 177, 179, 186, 192, 204–206, 251, 252, 256, 260, 262, 264, 272, 276, 279, 280; Scriabin's views in, 36–37; Blok's influence in, 51–52; attitudes toward sexuality in, 67; creative self-renewal in, 70; continuity of art in, 72n.; and inspiration for Lara, 76–77, 195–96; Rilke's influence on poems of, 80; concept of immortal subjectivity in, 81; precursors of, 92–95, 139–41; antecedents of Lara-Komarovskii relationship in, 127n.; attitudes toward Siberian construction in, 128&n.; "reign of the lie" in, 154, 164; attitude toward war with Germany in, 165, 168; character of Hamlet in, 170, 182; poem "Dawn" in, 172; composition of, begun, 181–82, 184; passages read from, to friends, 194; Ivinskaia's role in shaping, 195; contents of, 196–98; effect of Ivinskaia's arrest on, 201; Pasternak's attitude toward art in, 203; and initial efforts to publish, 209–19; Italian edition of, 211; Soviet and world reactions to, 221–50; Nobel Prize awarded for, 221–50; foreign editions of, 242; royalties from, 273, 276; Ehrenburg's comments on, 277; fate of, in Soviet Union, 278; Serbo-Croatian edition of, 278; as hymn to life, 287; life as self-renewal in, 288, 335, 338; philosophy of natural authenticity in, 289–94; conception of history in, 296–309, 356; attitude toward individual human life in, 310–17; image of Stalin in, 320; as summation of Pasternak's work, 327; role of religion in, 327–37; characterization of "reality as such" in, 344; stress on importance of content in, 346; role of coincidence in, 347–48; prose as medium of, 348; expansive form of, 349; power of language described in, 352; technical economy of, 355
Duineser Elegien (translation): 98

Early Trains: 173–74, 178
"English Lessons": 138n.

Fifty Poems: 19n.
"Fulfillment": 312

"Garden of Gethsemane": 316, 327
Georgian Lyric Poets: 138
Georgian Poets: 248
"Georgian Poets, The": 184

"Hamlet" (poem): 134, 182, 194, 211, 239, 271, 279, 334
"Haughty Pauper, The": 316
Henry IV (translation): 182
High Malady: 98n., 108
"History of a Counter-Octave": 92n.
"Holy Week": 194

"Illness": 107
"In Hospital": 213, 250, 326, 337, 342
In the Interlude: 241; *see also When Skies Clear*

Last Summer, The: see Tale, A
"Letters from Tula": 94

Lieutenant Schmidt: 142n., 178, 276
"Lyrical Expanse": 82

"Marburg": 69
"March": 194
"Mary Magdelene": 199, 334, 342
"May Day": 114
"May It Be": 301
Menagerie, The: 108
"Miracle": 194
"Mirror, The": 97
My Sister, Life: 70, 77, 82, 85, 89, 90, 92, 98, 102, 107, 112, 115, 122, 250, 297, 301, 355

"New Verses" (collection in *Znamia*, September, 1956): 211
"Night": 312
"Nightglow" ("Zarevo"): 174, 179, 181
"Nobel Prize, The": 242, 244
"Notes on Translations from Shakespeare": 184

"Old Park, The": 173
"On Early Trains": 318
Over the Barriers: 77, 85, 168

"Parting": 201
"Peredelkino": 173
Poems About Georgia: 221, 224, 248
Poems and Long Poems (Stikhotvoreniia i poemy): 278
"Poems of Iurii Zhivago, The": 182, 195–96, 282, 316, 335, 348
Poetry in One Volume: 142n.
Prince of Homburg, The (translation): 277

"Railway Station, The": 75
Robert Guiscard (translation): 277
Romeo and Juliet (translation): 173
"Round the Turning": 312

Safe-Conduct, A: 10, 12, 32–34, 61, 68, 71, 79, 87, 117, 118, 121, 124, 129, 131–33, 252, 255–56, 279, 315, 334, 340–41, 345, 349, 351, 355
"Sailing Away": 100
Second Birth: 70, 117, 124, 129–31, 133, 142n., 174, 203
Selected Translations: 168
Selected Verse (1933): 142n.
Selected Verse (1947): 188, 192
"Separation": 196
"Shakespeare": 138n.

Sketch for an Autobiography: 2, 3&n., 5, 34, 42, 80, 121, 132, 147, 172, 204n., 212, 214, 223, 252–56, 315; Italian edition of (*Autobiografia e nuovi versi*), 252
Slepaia krasavitsa: *see* Blind Beauty, The
Small Book of Poetry for Children (Knizhka dlia detei): 142n.
"Some Tenets": 354
Sonnette an Orpheus (translation): 98
"Soul": 312
Spektorskii: 92, 98, 119–20, 142n., 333
"Star of the Nativity": 189, 194
Starry Skies (collected volume of translations): 279
Stories: 94–95
"Summer": 301
"Summer Notes": 173

Tale, A (The Last Summer): 11, 75, 120, 135, 139, 141, 333
"Terrible Tale, A": 165
Themes and Variations: 89, 92, 102, 107
Three Georgian Poets: 198
"To Marina Tsvetaeva": *see* "To the Memory of Marina Tsvetaeva"
"To the Memory of Marina Tsvetaeva": 98, 174
"Train to the Urals": 299
"Translator's Notes, A": 178, 184
"Truth": 173
Twin in the Clouds: 75, 82

"Venice": 75
"Vesna" ("Spring"): 2
"Visit to the Army": 177

"War Months, The": 173–74
"Wasserman Test, The": 83
"Waves": 223, 303
"Wedding": 318, 342
When Skies Clear (Kogda razguliaetsia): 214, 241, 250–52, 256, 259, 265, 312
"Winterlight": 265
"Winter Night": 194, 282
"Without Love": 94
"Women in My Childhood": 11

Year 1905, The: 39, 80, 110, 112–13, 117, 130, 138n., 142n., 178, 276, 299

"Zametki Pasternaka o Shekspire": 138
"Zarevo": *see* "Nightglow"
Zvezdnoe nebo: *see* Starry Skies

General Index

Note: Life dates are given for Pasternak's
contemporaries.

Abakumov, Viktor Semënovich (1897–1954): 199
Abramov, Anatolii Mikhailovich (1917–): 173
Abravanel (Abrabanel or Abarbanella), Don Isaac ben-
 Iuda: 19
Academy, Royal Swedish: 221, 225, 226, 239, 241
Academy of Arts, St. Petersburg: 4n., 20
Academy of Sciences of the Soviet Union: 128, 275
Acmeism: 54&n., 168
Adam, Antoine (1899–): 342, 343
Adamovich, Georgii (1894–1972): 142
A.D. 1921 (Akhmatova): 168
Adventures of Julio Jurenito, The (Ehrenburg): 102
Adzhubei, Aleksei Ivanovich (1924–): 249
Afinogenov, Aleksandr Nikolaevich (1904–41): 153,
 154, 161, 240
Aftonbladet: 238
Agafonov (character in *The Blind Beauty*): 262
Agens: 352
Aikhenvald, Iulii Isaevich: 104
Akhmadulina, Bella (Izabella) Akhatovna (1937–):
 279
Akhmatova, Anna (pseudonym of Anna Andreevna
 Gorenko, 1889–1966): 198, 212, 215n., 221,
 278n., 280; first poems by, 41; dialogue of, with
 Pasternak, 54; fate of first husband of, 95; on
 Spektorskii, 120; on Maiakovskii's activity,
 122–23; on *Second Birth*, 130–31; and Paster-
 nak's intercession on behalf of husband of, 155;
 Pasternak's manner of conversing with, 157; con-
 tribution of, to welfare of Mandelstams, 158;
 Pasternak on work of, 168–69; treatment of, in
 Zhdanov era, 184; on Pasternak's marriage, 186;
 parts of *Doctor Zhivago* read to, by Pasternak,
 194; publication of "Hail Peace" by, 203; work
 of, in *Literary Moscow*, 209; Pasternak's gener-
 osity toward, 265; on *Doctor Zhivago*, 304
Akulina Gavrilovna (Pasternak's nanny): 3, 7, 9, 39,
 43, 331
Alain (Emile-Auguste Chartier, 1868–1951): 149
"Albatros, L'" (Baudelaire): 15n.
Alberti, Rafael (1902–): 135
Alekseeva-Meshieva, Valentina Sergeevna: 97
Alexander I, Tsar: 304, 320

Alexander III, Tsar: 10
Alfonso V, king of Portugal: 19
Alicata, Mario (1918–66): 215
Allilueva, Nadezhda Sergeevna (1901–32): 129
All-Union Soviet Convention of Translators: 136
Alps: 149
Amari, A.: *see* Tsetlin, Mikhail Osipovich
Anagkē (Greek concept): 304, 347
Andreas-Salomé, Louise (1861–1937): 11
Andreeva (real name Iurkovskaia), Mariia Fedorovna
 (1868–1953): 41
Andreev, Leonid Nikolaevich: 41, 67
Angelo, Sergio D' (1922–): 209–12, 273
Anima naturaliter Christiana: 335–36
Anisimov, Iulian Pavlovich (1889–1940): 42, 43n.,
 80, 82
Anna (character in *A Tale*): *see* Tornskjold, Anna Arild
Annenkov, Iurii Pavlovich (Georges Annenkoff,
 1889–1974): 74, 87, 103, 151
Annenskii, Innokentii Fëdorovich: 41, 51
An-Ski (real name Rappoport), Salomon: 26n.
Anthology of Soviet Russian Poetry in Two Volumes: 218
Anti-Fascist Congress: *see* International Congress of
 Writers for the Defense of Culture
Antipov-Strelnikov (character in *Doctor Zhivago*): 297;
 see also Strelnikov
Anti-Semitism: 323
Anti-Zionism: 330
Antokolskii, Pavel Grigorevich (1896–): 103n., 174
Antony and Cleopatra (Shakespeare, translated by Pas-
 ternak): 167, 178, 194
Apollinaire, Guillaume: 33
Apollon: 43&n., 95
Aragon, Louis (1897–): 143, 148
Arenskii, Antonii Stepanovich: 20
Arguments: 302
Arild (character in *A Tale*): *see* Tornskjold, Anna Arild
Arina Rodionovna (Pushkin's nanny): 9
Aristotle: 354
Arkhipenko, Aleksandr Porfirievich (1887–1964):
 103n.
Arnold, Matthew: 336
Aron, Raymond (1905–): 298, 301n., 303, 305
Arsenev, Nikolai Sergeevich (1888–): 104
Article 58 of Soviet Criminal Code: 200, 201
Article 133 of Stalin's Constitution: 159

Artist: 20
Artsybashev, Mikhail Petrovich (1878–1927): 67
Arvatov, Boris (1896–1940): 113n.
Arzamas period of Pushkin's evolution: 355
Arzhak, Nikolai (pseud. of Iulii Markovich Daniel): 267
Aseev, Nikolai Nikolaevich (1889–1963): 82&n.–83&n.; on Pasternak, 50; relationship of, with Pasternak, 82&n.–83&n.; filiation of, with Khlebnikov, 84; on Pasternak's *Themes and Variations*, 107; publication in *Russian Contemporary* by, 109; publication of *The Twenty-six* by, 110; as member of LEF, 113n., 114; at Chistopol, 166, 167, 171; and Tsvetaeva's suicide, 171; early poetry of, praised by Pasternak, 253; absence of, from Pasternak's funeral, 272; limited role of, in rehabilitation of Pasternak, 278; death of, 278n.
Asmus, Irina Sergeevna: 119, 141, 178
Asmus, Valentin Ferdinandovich (1894–1975): 119, 178, 266, 269, 271
Assisi, Italy: 72n., 89
Associationism: 289
Association for the Defense of Culture: 148, 151
Association of Swedish Authors: 237
Astapovo, Russia: 53
Atheism: 329, 337
At the Top of My Voice (Maiakovskii): 123
Aucouturier, Michel (1933–): 79, 120, 212
Averkevich, Liberius (Liveri; character in *Doctor Zhivago*): 290
Azarch, Raisa Moiseevna (1897–): 175
Azhaiev, Vasilii Nikolaevich (1915–68): 215

Babel, Isaak Emannuilovich (1894–1941): 16, 146–49, 154, 158, 216
Bach, Johann Sebastian: 343, 355
Bachelard, Gaston (1884–1962): 316
Backbone Flute, The (Maiakovskii): 122
"Bad Spring" (Akhmadulina): 280
Bagritskii, Eduard (1895–1934): 16, 110, 149
Bakh, Aleksei Nikolaevich (1857–1946): 128
Bakhtin, Mikhail Mikhailovich (1895–): 297
Baku, USSR: 223
Balashov, Russia: 89
Balmont, Konstantin Dmitrievich (1867–1943): 15–16, 33, 75, 96
Balthazar (Durrell): 250
Baltrušaitis, Jurgis Kazimirovich (1873–1944): 75&n., 85, 96
Balzac, Honoré de: 92, 347
Bancarella Prize: 241
Bannikov, Nikolai Vasilevich (1914–): 211, 214, 252
Baratashvili, Nikoloz Melitonovich: 138, 182
Baratynskii, Ekaterina Ivanovna: 14
Barbusse, Henri (1873–1935): 148
Barnes, Christopher J. (1942–): 48–49&n., 79–80, 85
Barron, John (1930–): 187

Bathhouse, The (Maiakovskii): 121, 205
Batiushkov, Konstantin Nikolaevich: 90
Baudelaire, (Pierre) Charles: 15n., 65, 81
Bauman, Nikolai Ernestovich: 5n., 39
Beardsley, Aubrey Vincent: 24
Becher, Johannes Robert (1891–1958): 135, 149
Beckett, Samuel (1906–): 40
Bednyi, Demian (pseud. of Efim Alekseevich Pridvorov, 1883–1945): 157, 161, 183, 184
Beethoven, Ludwig van: 21
Belinkov, Arkadii Viktorovich (1921–70): 269
Belinskii, Vissarion Grigorevich: 290, 340
Belomorsko-baltiiskii kanal imeni Stalina (ed. Gorky et al.): 144
Belorussian Railway Station, Moscow: 267
Belyi, Andrei (pseud. of Boris Nikolaevich Bugaev, 1880–1934): 126n.; Pasternak's early enthusiasm for, 33, 37, 38, 51; on Hermann Cohen, 64; investigation of Russian poetics by, 81; acceptance of Revolution by, 96; in Berlin, 1920s, 104–105; return of, to Russia, 106–107; Pasternak on, 253; widow of, supported by Pasternak, 265; and attempt to rehabilitate him in 1960s, 278; Roman Jakobson on, 348
Benda, Julien (1867–1956): 148
Benedettis (friends of Sergio D'Angelo): 273
Ben-Gurion, David (1886–1973): 242, 330
Ben-Ishaj, M. Z.: 330
Berdiaev, Nikolai Aleksandrovich (1874–1948): 104, 306, 332
Berger, Gaston (1896–1960): 71
Berger, Yves (1931–): 300
Berggolts, Olga Fëdorovna (1910–75): 198
Bergson, Henri (1859–1941): 55, 65, 290, 339, 341, 342, 353; *see also* Bergsonism
Bergsonism: 38, 289, 292, 339, 353; *see also* Bergson, Henri
Beriia, Lavrentii Pavlovich (1899–1953): 186
Berlin, Germany: 40, 69n., 89, 96, 99–103&n., 104–105, 107, 128, 147–48, 210, 264; *see also* East Berlin; Germany; West Germany
Bernstein, Leonard (1918–): 48, 249
Bezlichie ("facelessness"): 308
Bezymenskii, Aleksandr Ilich (1898–1973): 144, 146
Bialik Chaim Nachman (1873–1934): 26n.
Bible: 329, 331
Biblioteka poeta (Poet's Library): 142
Birnbaum, Henrik (1925–): 224
Blake, Patricia (1933–): 187, 248
Bloch, Jean-Richard (1884–1947): 148
Blok, Aleksandr Aleksandrovich (1880–1921): 41, 51–53, 72, 119, 168, 345n., 355; Pasternak on, 33; Pasternak's fascination with poetry of, 51–52, 253; meeting of, with Pasternak, 52; significance of 1905–1908 poetry of, for Pasternak, 52–53; *The Twelve* by, 95; on Pasternak's first translation of Goethe, 135; personification of

Russia by, 181; influence of, in *Doctor Zhivago*, 184, 194, 196; religious inspiration of, 335
Board of Union of Writers: *see* Writers' Union
Bobrov, Sergei Pavlovich (1889–1971): 43&n., 82–83, 95, 278
Boehm (Bem), A.: 130
Boevoe Znamia (*Battle Standard*): 175
Bogatyrëv, Konstantin Petrovich (1925–76): 103n., 113
Bogatyrëv, Nikolai Petrovich: 202, 240
Bogaryëv, Pëtr Grigorevich (1893–1973): 103n.
Bolsheviks: 305, 306
Bolshevism: 297, 298, 300, 305
Bolshevo rest home, USSR: 205
Book of Hours, The (*Das Stunden-Buch*, Rilke): 13, 43, 80
Book of Pictures, The (*Das Buch der Bilder*, Rilke): 80
Borges, Jorge Luis (1899–): 174
"Boris Pasternak's *The Year 1905*" (Sviatopolk-Mirskii): 110
Bowers, Faubion (1917–): 49
Bowra, Sir (Cecil) Maurice (1898–1971): 24, 26, 183, 225, 236, 300, 301
Brandukov, Anatolii Andreevich (1856–1930): 9
Braziller, George: 240n.
Brecht, Bertolt (1898–1956): 149, 208
Brik, Liliia (Lili) Iurevna (1892–): 104, 112, 121n., 122–23, 146, 198
Brik, Osip Maksimovich (1888–1945): 113n., 121n., 146, 352
British House of Lords: 244
British Society of Authors: 236
British Parliament: 248n.
Briusov, Valerii Iakovlevich (1873–1924): 16, 96–97, 136, 348
Brodskii, Iosif Aleksandrovich (1940–): 279
Broken Jug, The (Kleist): 75, 82, 172, 277
"Brothers, The" (Polonskii): 119
Brothers Ershov, The (Kochetov): 221
Brothers Karamazov, The (Dostoevsky): 332, 335
Brown, Anthony: 243, 244
Brown, Clarence (1929–): 134
Brown, Edward James (1909–): 114
Brussels, Belgium: 226
Buck, Pearl S. (1892–1973): 291
Budberg, Baroness Mariia (Marie, "Moura") Ignatevna, née Zakrevskaia, (1892–1976): 95&n.
Bugaev, Boris Nikolaevich: *see* Belyi, Andrei
Bukharin, Nikolai Ivanovich (1888–1938): 117, 145, 146, 148, 157, 159, 160, 308
Bukhteev, Olga (character in *Spektorskii*): 119
Bulgakov, Mikhail Afanasevich (1891–1940): 109, 216
Bulgarin, Faddei Venediktovich (Tadeusz Bułharyn, 1789–1859): 190
Bunin, Ivan Alekseevich (1870–1953): 209, 277, 280
Burgess, Antony (1917–): 341n., 349

Burliuk, David Davidovich (1882–1967): 83, 96
Burliuk, Nikolai Davidovich (1890–1920): 83
Burliuk, Vladimir Davidovich (1886–1917): 83, 96
Butyrki Transit Prison: 201
Byron, George Gordon, Lord: 89, 135

Café la Rotonde, Paris: 151
Caligula: 307, 320
Cambridge: 68; *see also* England
Campagne Première, rue (Paris): 151
Camus, Albert (1913–60): 223, 227, 302
Canguilhelm, Georges (1904–): 314
Capa, Cornell: 285
Capitalism: 144, 209n., 235
Captive of Time, A (Ivinskaia): 164, 282
Carr, Edward Hallett (1892–): 319, 320
Cassirer, Ernst (1874–1945): 63
Caucasian Chalk Circle, The (Brecht): 208
Caucasus: 126, 130
Central Committee, Cultural Department of: 233
Centrifuge (Futurist group): 80, 83, 89, 340
Centrifuge (journal): 76
Cervantes Saavedra, Miguel de: 136, 299
Chagall, Marc (1887–): 100, 103n.
Chaliapin, Fëdor Ivanovich (1873–1938): 22
Chambers, Whittaker (1901–61): 242
Champs-Elysées, Paris: 151; *see also* Paris
"Chapters from a Poem: Pasternak" (Akhmadulina): 280
Chardin, Pierre Teilhard de, *see* Teilhard de Chardin, Pierre
Cheka (Soviet political police): 128
Chekhov, Anton Pavlovich: 38, 112, 141, 178, 279, 355
Cheliabinsk Region, USSR: 166
Cherenkov, Pavel Alekseevich (1904–): 232
Chern, USSR: 177
Chernichovsky, Saul Gutmanovich (1875–1943): 26n.
Chernyshevskii, Nikolai Gavrilovich (1828–89): 290, 340
Chikovani, Simon Ivanovich (1902–66): 138, 182, 204
Chistopol, Tatar Region, USSR: 93, 165–68, 171–74, 252; *see also* Urals
Choboty (near Peeredelkino), USSR: 259
Chopin, Frédéric François (1810–49): 21, 48, 267, 339, 343–45, 355
Christ: *see* Jesus Christ
Christianity: 9, 11, 51, 104, 128, 308–309, 315, 327–32, 334–36, 339
Christians: 289
Christology: 334
Chukovskii (real name Korneichukov), Kornei Ivanovich (1882–1969): 109, 135, 136, 231, 233, 260, 267, 275
Chukovskii, Nikolai Korneevich (1904–65): 233
Church of Christ the Savior, Moscow: 55
Church of Saint Euplos, Moscow: 9

Chuzhak, N. (pseud. of Aleksandr Fëdorovich Nasimovich, 1880–1947): 113n.
Cicero, Marcus Tullius: 293
Cities and Years (Fedin): 109
Čiurlionis, Mikolajus Konstantinas (1875–1911): 33
Civil Defense Unit (Vsevobuch): 172
Civiltà Cattolica: 327
Civilization and Ethics (Albert Schweitzer): 265, 336
Claudel, Paul (Louis Charles, 1868–1955): 40, 250
Cloud in Trousers, The (Maiakovskii): 85
Cohen, Hermann (1842–1918): 55, 57, 61–65, 71; Pasternak in class of, 61; personality of, 63–64; philosophy of, 62–65, 330; influence of, on Pasternak, 65, 336; concept of Judaism of, 65n.; Pasternak's break with, 68–70; at Academy of Judaic Studies, Berlin, 69n.; role of, as apostle of Judaism, 69n., 330; as answer to Pasternak's quest for hero, 133; on Kant, 317; attitude of, toward religion, 336
Coleridge, Samuel Taylor (1772–1834): 353, 354
Collinet, Michel (1904–): 322
Collins, William (1929–): 215, 242
Communism: 91, 94, 114n., 130, 148, 158, 209n., 233, 294, 302, 305, 308, 313, 327
Communist Party of the Soviet Union: 109, 114n., 144, 154, 185, 305
Comte, Auguste: 290
Congress, Anti-Fascist: *see* International Congress of Writers for the Defense of Culture
Congress of the Communist Party of the Soviet Union, Twenty-Second: 277
Congress of Slavists, Fourth International (September, 1958): 224
Congress of Soviets, Ninth: 108
Congress of Soviet Writers (1936): *see* Plenary Session of Board of Union of Writers, Minsk
Congress of Soviet Writers, First All-Union (1934): 130, 135, 143–46, 152
Congress of Soviet Writers, Second All-Union (1954): 206
Congress of Soviet Writers, Third All-Union (1959): 248
Conservatory of Music, Moscow: 21, 36n., 45
Constituent Assembly (January, 1918): 300
Constitution, Stalin's (1936): 159, 161
Constructivism: 96, 101n., 113n.
Contemporary (ed. Gorky): 82
Corinth, Lovis (1858–1925): 26&n.
Craig, Edward Gordon (1872–1966): 26n., 75n.
Creative Intelligentsia (group): 216
Critique de la raison dialectique (Sartre): 305–306
Critique of Judgment (Kant): 351
Critique of Pure Reason (Kant): 64, 317, 349–50
Croce, Benedetto (1866–1952): 316
Cromwell, Thomas: 322
Crossman, Richard Howard Stafford (1907–74): 248
Crusoe, Robinson: 293

Crystallography Institute of the Academy of Sciences: 275
Cubism: 26
Cubofuturism: 83, 340
Culture and Life (*Kultura i zhizn*): 190
Czechoslovakian delegation to First Congress of Union of Writers: 143

Daily Express (London): 224
Daily Mail (London): 243
Daily Telegraph (London): 242, 276
D'Angelo, Sergio: *see* Angelo, Sergio D'
Daniel, Iulii Markovich (pseud. Nikolai Arzhak: 1925–): 267
Daniélou, Cardinal Jean (1905–74): 250
Dante Alighieri: 52
Darkness at Noon (Koestler): 200, 242, 308
Days and Nights (Simonov): 178
Debussy, Claude Achille: 33
Degas (Hilaire Germain) Edgar: 29
Deili Vral (*Daily Blat*, or *Rag*): 234, 240
Dejean, Maurice (1899–): 187
Delacroix, (Ferdinand Victor) Eugène: 24
Dementev, Nikolai Ivanovich (1907–35): 117
Descartes, René: 289, 293
Determinism: 289, 305, 346
Deutscher, Isaac (1907–67): 298, 300, 304, 305, 308
Deutschtum und Judentum (Cohen): 330
Dickens, Charles: 106, 296, 346
Diderot, Denis: 290
Dinfreville, Col. Jacques: 300
Diogenes: 241
Disintegration of Form in the Arts, The (Kahler): 240
Divine Poem (Scriabin): 35
Dobroliubov, Nikolai Aleksandrovich: 340
Doctor Faustus (Mann): 349
"*Doctor Zhivago* and the Search for God in the USSR" (Konstantinov): 328
"Don Quichotte de notre temps, Le" (Dinfreville): 299
Don Quixote: 334
Don Quixote (Cervantes): 136
Dostoevsky, Fëdor Mikhailovich: 38, 345, 355; Maiakovskii as character from, 84; Shigaliovism of, compared with Stalinism, 204&n.; "underground man" of, 290; Zhivago opposed to Prince Myshkin of, 327; influenced by Nikolai Fëdorov, 332; mysticism of, and Pasternak's, 335; as representative of doctrine of causality, 346
"Doubt" (Chikovani): 182
"Downpour of Light, A" (Tsvetaeva): 90, 98
Dualism, of body and soul: 331
Du Bolchévisme (Collinet): 322
Dudintsev, Vladimir Dmitrievich (1918–): 209, 216
Dudorov, Innokentii (Nika, character in *Doctor Zhivago*): 182
Dukhobors: 11
Dulles, John Foster (1888–1959): 225

Durrell, Lawrence (1912–): 250
Durylin, Sergei Nikolaevich (pseud. Raevskii, 1881–1954): 43
Duvignaud (real name d'Auger), Jean Octave Auguste (1921–): 299
Dybbuk, The (An-Ski): 26n.
Dynamism: 339–40, 342, 356

Early Poems (*Mir zur Feier*, Rilke): 43, 80
East Berlin: 246; *see also* Berlin
Eastern bloc: 208
East Germany: 218; *see also* Germany, West Germany
Economic-Philosophic Manuscripts of the Year 1844 (Marx): 305
Efron, Ariadna (1912?–): 172, 202, 240
Egoism, biological: 311, 315
Egypt: 309
Ehrenburg, Ilia Grigorevich (1891–1967): 16, 126n., 130, 160, 340; in exile, 40–41; relationship of, with Pasternak, 96, 105; Pasternak introduced to Tsvetaeva by, 96, 97; early publications of, 102; on café life in Berlin, 103–104; on Pasternak's role in Soviet literature, 117, 118, 258; on Pasternak's relationship with Maiakovskii, 121–22; defense of Pasternak by, at First Congress of Union of Soviet Writers, 146; role of, at International Congress of Writers for the Defense of Culture, 148–51; *The Thaw* by, 205, 208; censured by Khrushchev, 216; censured at the Third Writers' Congress, 248; on *Doctor Zhivago*, 277–78; on Pasternak's Christianity, 331
Ehrenburg, Liubov: 267, 275
Eichner, Hans (1921–): 345n.
Eighth Symphony (Shostakovich): 48
Einstein, Albert (1879–1955): 26n., 326
Eisenstein, Sergei Mikhailovich (1898–1948): 112
Elabuga-on-the-Kama, USSR: 171
Élan vital: 290
Eliot, T. S. (1888–1965): 40, 236
Elizabeth of Hungary, Saint: 133
Elizavetgrad, Ukraine: 127
Ellis-Kobylinskii, Lev Lvovich (1874–1947): 81
Emelianov, Ivan Vasilevich: 185, 186
Emelianova, Irina Ivanovna (Mme Vadim Kosovoi, 1938–): 186, 200, 206, 245, 249n., 257; Pasternak given nickname by, 187; at Pasternak's death, 266; imprisonment of, after Pasternak's death, 274
Emotionalism: 282
Encounter: 222
Engel, Iulii Dmitrievich (1868–1927): 36, 41
England: 20, 29, 151, 165, 183, 199, 215n., 224–25, 241–42, 246, 248, 276; *see also* Oxford; Cambridge; London; Great Britain
Envy (Olesha): 109, 131
"Epic and Lyrical Poetry of Contemporary Russia" (Tsvetaeva): 150n.
Epicureanism: 355

Epishkin: *see* Nikiforov, Sergei Nikolaevich
Erfahrungsinhalt: 346
Erlich, Victor (1914–): 352
Ermilov, Vladimir Vladimirovich (1904–65): 233
Escapism: 313
Esenin, Sergei Aleksandrovich (1895–1925): 16, 104, 126n., 131, 157, 184, 196, 255, 280, 335
Espresso, L': 217
Ethic of Pure Will (Cohen): 62
Etkind, Efim Grigorevich (1918–): 135
Eugene Onegin (Pushkin): 119, 324, 334
Europe: 319
Evelike role, woman's: 250
Evolution Créatrice, L' (Bergson): 55
Evtushenko, Evgenii Aleksandrovich (1933–): 209, 216, 217, 248, 279, 280
Expressionism: 26

Fadeev, Aleksandr Aleksandrovich (1901–56): 129, 171, 179; *The Rout* by, 109–10; on Pasternak's election to board of Writers' Union, 147; relationship of, with Pasternak, 159, 160; at Chistopol, 166; proposal of, with Pasternak, of Akhmatova for a Stalin Prize, 168; intercession of, for Pasternak in the Zhdanov era, 184; vilification of Pasternak by, 190; attitude of, toward Pasternak, after Zhdanov's death, 195; position of, after Stalin's death, 205; replaced as secretary of Writers' Union, 206; Pasternak's reaction to suicide of, 209
Fair Booth, The (Blok): 41
"False Friend" (Patricia Blake): 187
Fatum: 320
Faulkner, William H. (1897–1962): 348
Faure, Élie (1873–1937): 149n.
Faust (Goethe): 135–37, 193, 198–99, 202, 203, 205, 218, 254, 256, 276, 277
Federation of Associations of Soviet Writers: 119
Fedin, Konstantin Aleksandrovich (1892–1977): 16, 212; as member of Serapion Brotherhood, 96; *Cities and Years* by, 109; at Chistopol, 166, 167, 171; during World War II, 175, 176; Pasternak on, 203; relation of, to *Doctor Zhivago*, 208; advice of, sought by Ivinskaia, 233; avoidance of Pasternak by, 240, 272; as secretary of Writers' Union, 248; attitude of, toward Pasternak's funeral, 272
Fëdorov, Nikolai Fëdorovich: 332–33
Feldzer, Emmanuel: 70
Feldzer, Ida Davidovna: *see* Vysotskaia-Feldzer, Ida Davidovna
Feltrinelli, Giangiacomo (1926–72): rights to publish *Doctor Zhivago* received by, 209&n.–211; role of, in publication of *Doctor Zhivago*, 214&n.–217, 327; and Russian-language edition of *Doctor Zhivago*, 226, 242; Italian edition of *Sketch for an Autobiography* published by, 252; promise of, not to publish *The Blind Beauty* without Ivinskaia's

permission, 272; relation of, to Pasternak's Western royalties, 273; and Yugoslavian edition of *Doctor Zhivago*, 278

"Fence, The" (Evtushenko): 280

Ferdinand II, King of Aragon (Ferdinand V of Castile): 19

Ferrero, Guglielmo (1871–1942): 301

Fet, Afanasii Afanasevich (1820–92): 280

Fichte, Johann Gottfried: 324, 350

Fifth Gymnasium: *see* Moscow Fifth Gymnasium

Fifth Symphony (Beethoven): 21

Figaro, Le: 54

First All-Union Soviet Convention of Translators (1936): 136

First Congress of Soviet Writers: *see* Congress of Soviet Writers, First

Fischer, Kuno: 215

Fischer Publishing House, Germany: 224

Flaubert, Gustave: 178, 346–48

Fleishman, Lazar (1944–): 81&n.

Fleischmann, Ivo (1921–): 162

Fleurs du Mal, Les (Baudelaire): 15n.

Florence, Italy: 72&n.

Floridi, Ulisse Alessio (1920–): 327

Formalism: 84, 184

Forster, E. M. (1879–1970): 148

Fortin, René Ernest (1934–): 318

France: 29, 148n., 183, 212, 214, 215n., 223, 225, 274–75, 342; *see also* Paris, France

Francis of Assisi, Saint: 89

Frank, Ilia Mikhailovich (1908–): 232

Frank, Semën Ludvigovich (1877–1950): 104

Frank, Victor Semënovich (?–1972): 296, 304

Frank, Waldo (1889–1967): 148

Frankfurter Allgemeine Zeitung: 226

Free Philosophical Association (Berlin): 104

Free Philosophical Association (Petrograd): 104

Freidenberg, Anna (Asia) Osipovna (née Pasternak; Pasternak's aunt): 30, 151

Freidenberg, Olga Mikhailovna (1890–1955): 30

Freud, Sigmund (1856–1939): 11

Frischman (Frischmann), David (1859–1922): 330

From Six Volumes (Akhmatova): 168

Führer: 319

Futurism: 42, 54–55, 79–80, 82–84, 86–87, 96–97, 105, 114, 115, 121–22, 124, 133, 300, 339–40, 346, 350–51, 353, 355; *see also* Futurists

Futurists: 300, 339, 351, 353; *see also* Futurism

Futurists, Italian: 339

Gabo, Naum (1890–1978): 103n.

Gagarin Lane, Moscow: 90

Galich, Aleksandr Arkadevich (1918–76):

Galileo: 289

Gallimard, Gaston (1881–1975): 212, 213, 215, 223, 250, 252

Gallis, Arne (1908–): 224

Galliula (character in "Without Love" and *Doctor Zhivago*): 93

Gapon, Georgii Apollonovich (1870–1906): 38

Gaprindashvili, Valerian Ivanovich (1889–1941): 138

Gavrilovna: *see* Akulina Gavrilovna

Ge (Gay or Gué), Nikolai Nikolaevich: 10&n., 14

Gebhardie, Fräulein (Pasternak's landlady in Berlin): 41

Gendrikov Lane, Moscow: 122

Geneva, Switzerland: 36; *see also* Switzerland

Georgia, USSR: 126, 135–36&n., 137–38, 142, 182, 246, 248, 250

Georgian Writers, Union of: 248

Germany: 29, 31, 40–41, 50, 56, 68, 71–72, 81, 99–101, 103, 105, 107, 150, 153n., 165, 215n., 223–25; *see also* Berlin; East Berlin; East Germany; Munich; West Germany

Gerschenkron, Alexander (1904–): 316, 317

Ghirlandaio, Domenico: 99

Gide, André (1869–1951): 148, 154, 155, 158, 162

Giessen, Germany: 60

Gifford, Henry (1913–): 137

Gimazetdin (character in "Without Love" and *Doctor Zhivago*): 93

Ginzburg, Moisei Iakovlevich (1892–1946): 101

Gladkov, Aleksandr Konstantinovich (1912–76): 124, 166, 167, 174, 180, 181, 192, 195, 215, 252, 272, 279, 281, 308

Glahn, Lieutenant (character in Hamsun's *Pan*): 291

Glière (Glier), Reinhold Moritsevich (1875–1956): 36&n.

God: 302, 304, 328, 39, 337; related to individual human life in *Doctor Zhivago*, 310, 316, 334; Pasternak's faith in, 327; Pasternak's attitude toward, 330, 337, 342; *see also* Jesus Christ

Goethe, Johann Wolfgang von: 81, 95, 169, 198, 202, 203, 218, 264

Gofman, Iosif Kazimir (1876–1957): 22

Gogebashvili Street, Tbilisi: 246

Gogol, Nikolai Vasilevich: 72, 180, 345, 355

Gogolevskii Boulevard, Moscow: 178

Gold, Michael (1894–1967): 148

Golden Fleece, The: 29n., 37

Golos Rossii: 101

Goltsev (character in "Without Love"): 93

Gomułka, Władysław (1905–): 226

Goncharov, Ivan Aleksandrovich (1812–91): 119

Goncharova, Nataliia Sergeevna (1881–1962): 54

Goncourt, Edmond de: 34–35

Goncourt, Jules de: 34–35

Good Earth, The (Buck): 291

Gordon, Misha (character in *Doctor Zhivago*): 182, 329, 330

Goriély, Benjamin: 299

Gorky, Maxim (pseud. of Aleksei Maksimovich Peshkov, 1868–1936): upbringing of, and Pasternak's, compared, 9; portrait of, by Leonid Pasternak, 26n., 41; Pasternak writes to journal of,

82; on *The Childhood of Liuvers*, 95; correspondence of, with Pasternak about Tsvetaeva, 98&n.; in Berlin, 103n.; in exile, 106; collaboration of, in editing of *The Russian Contemporary*, 109; news about Pasternak's literary success learned by, 111–12; on Pasternak's poetic achievement, 117; Pasternak asked to help edit *Biblioteka poeta* by, 142; at first Congress of Union of Soviet Writers, 144

Gorky Institute of World Literature: 249n.

Gorky Literary Institute: *see* Gorky Institute of World Literature

Gosbank: *see* State Bank

Goslitizdat (State Publishing House for Literature): 163, 171, 208, 211, 213–14, 221

Gospels: 309, 337; *see also* New Testament

Gozzi, Carlo: 344

Graf, Oskar Maria (1894–1967): 143

Grand Duke Sergei Aleksandrovich: *see* Sergei Aleksandrovich

Great Britain: 246, 276, 323, 340; *see also* England

"Great Purge" (1930s): 154–62

"Great Terror": *see* "Great Purge"

Greece: 289, 309

Griboedov, Aleksandr Sergeevich: 161

Griboedov Street, Tbilisi, Georgia: 125

Grimm brothers: 57, 69

Gromeko, Aleksandr Aleksandrovich (character in Pasternak's prose draft of 1930s): 140

Gromeko, Anna Ivanovna (character in *Doctor Zhivago*): 81, 315, 331

Gromeko, Antonina: *see* Zhivago, Antonina

Gromeko family (characters in prose draft of 1930s and *Doctor Zhivago*): 140, 303

Gromyko, Andrei Andreevich (1909–): 225

Growth of the Soil (Hamsun): 293

Gründgens, Gustaf (1899–1963): 256

Grzhebin, Zinovii Isaevich (1869–1929): 102

Grzhimali, Ivan Voitekhovich: 9

Guardini, Romano (1885–1968): 329

Gué, Nikolai: *see* Ge, Nikolai Nikolaevich

Guerney, Bernard Guilbert (1894–1979): 258

Guichard, Katenka (character in *Doctor Zhivago*): 195

Guichard, Larisa (Lara) Feodorovna (character in *Doctor Zhivago*): 139, 195–97, 201, 273, 297, 303

Gulag Archipelago, The (Solzhenitsyn): 144, 221

Gumilëv, Nikolai Stepanovich (1886–1921): 43n., 95

Gupta, Nolini Kanta (1889–): 336

Gurev, Arkadii: 42–43

"Hail Peace" ("Hail the World," Akhmatova): 203

Hall of Columns, Moscow: 143, 184, 209

Hamburg Theater Company: 254, 256

Hamlet (character): 87, 170, 180

Hamlet (Shakespeare, translated by Pasternak): 137, 163, 169, 170, 173

Hammarskjöld, Dag (1905–61): 225

Hamsun, Knut (1859–1952): 37–38, 291, 293

Harper's: 266

Harari, Manya (1906–69): 224

Hartmann, Nicolai (1882–1950): 61, 63

Hauptmann, Gerhart (1863–1946): 26n.

Hayward, Max (1925–79): 94, 224, 281, 327

Hegel, Georg Wilhelm Friedrich: 55, 311, 316, 322, 350, 352

Hegelianism: 306, 311, 316, 328

Heidegger, Martin (1889–1976): 57

Heifetz, Jascha (1901–): 22

Heine, Heinrich: 355

Helikon Publishing House: 102

Henry IV (Shakespeare, translated by Pasternak): 182

Herder, Johann Gottfried von: 169, 324, 352

Herterich, Ludwig (1845–1932): 20

Hertzen Street, Moscow: 169

Herzen, Aleksandr Ivanovich: 91

Hesse, Hermann (1877–1962): 40, 291

Heymans, Gerardus (1857–1930): 71

"Hippodrome of Life, The" (Struve): 347

Historical symbolism: 334

Historicism: 56

History, poetics of, 296–309

Hoffmann, Ernst Theodor Amadeus: 96, 344

Holland: 226

Homo privatus: 308

Homo publicus: 308

Homo sovieticus: 278

Hope Against Hope (Nadezhda Mandelstam): 2

Horowitz, Giniia: 119

Horowitz, Vladimir (1904–): 119

Hostel Istria, Paris: 151

Hotel Continental, Milan: 217

House of Lords, British: 240

House of Writers (Dom pisatelei), Lavrushinskii Lane, Moscow: 153; *see also* Pasternak's apartment

Hughes, Olga Raevsky: 72n.

Hugo, Victor: 137, 167, 313

Humanism: 4n., 299, 304, 306, 309, 328, 340

Humboldt, Wilhelm von: 352

Hume, David: 64

Hungary: 183, 214, 248

Hunger (*Sult*, Hamsun): 38

Husserl, Edmund (1859–1938): 81

Husserlianism: 55, 81

Huxley, Aldous (1894–1963): 108, 148, 236

Hylozoism: 289n.

Iar-Kravchenko, A.: 140

Iashin, Aleksandr Iakovlevich (pseud. of Popov, 1913–68): 209, 233

Iashvili, Paolo (Pavel) Dzhibraelovich (1894–1937): 137&n., 161, 204n.; welcomed by Pasternak in Moscow, 125; hospitality of, toward Pasternak, 137–38; suicide of, 154, 159; support from Pasternak to, 155; "avenged" by *Doctor Zhivago*, 195; discussed in *Sketch for an Autobiography*,

252, 255–56; mourned by Pasternak in "Soul," 312

Iasnaia Poliana (Lev Tolstoy's estate): 180

Ibsen, Henrik: 75n.

Idealism: 50, 221

Idiot, The (Dostoevsky): 327

I Fioretti (Saint Francis of Assisi): 89

Igor-Severianin (pseud. of Igor Vasilevich Lotarev, 1887–1942): 87, 104

Ilin, Ivan Aleksandrovich (1882–1956): 104

Ilina, Mariia (character in *Spektorskii*): 98, 119

Imagism (*imaginizm*): 96&n.

Impressionism: 24, 26, 28–29, 31, 33, 37, 79, 84, 168, 339–40, 342–43

India: 246

Individualism: 313, 314, 319, 322, 343

Ingres, Jean Auguste Dominique: 24

In Search of a Hero (Tikhonov): 117

Intériorité: 311, 316; *see also* "Intimism"

International Association for the Defense of Culture: *see* Association for the Defense of Culture

International Congress of Writers for the Defense of Culture (1935): 147–48&n., 152&n.

International PEN Club: *see* PEN Club

"Intimism": 131; *see also Intériorité*

Ion (Plato): 352

Irpen, near Kiev, USSR: 118, 125, 127, 130

Isabella, Queen of Castile and Aragon: 19

Israel: 242, 330, 337

Istomina, Evgeniia (*née* Liuvers, character in "The Diary of Zhivult"): 140

Istomina, Evgeniia (Zhenia, character in "A District Behind the Lines"): 77

Italian Communist party: 209, 211, 215–16

Italy: 31, 72, 210–11, 214, 215&n., 217, 225, 238, 241, 252

Itinerants (Peredvizhniki): 3, 24, 339–40

Iudina, Mariia Veniaminovna (1899–1970): 48, 267

Iuon, Konstantin Fedorovich (1875–1958): 29

Iuriatin (town in *Doctor Zhivago*): 140, 297

Ivanov, Viacheslav Ivanovich (1866–1949): 51, 75, 82, 95–96, 212, 240

Ivanov, Viacheslav Vsevolodovich ("Koma," 1929–): 240

Ivanov, Vsevolod Viacheslavovich (1895–1963): 51, 75, 82, 95–96, 148, 175, 176, 212, 240

Ivan the Terrible (Eisenstein): 169

Ivinskaia, Irina (daughter of Olga Ivinskaia): *see* Emelianova, Irina Ivanovna

Ivinskaia, Mariia Nikolaevna (mother of Olga Ivinskaia): 186

Ivinskaia, Olga Vsevolodovna (1912–): 157n., 165, 190, 194, 211–15, 224, 233, 239, 246, 249n., 256, 257, 265, 266, 308, 332n.; on Pasternak's relationship with Tsvetaeva, 172; meeting and early contacts of, with Pasternak, 184–88, 195; role of, in shaping *Doctor Zhivago*, 195–96; imprisonment of, 199–202; release of, 205; rela-

tionship of, with Pasternak in mid-1950s, 206–207; on publication of *Doctor Zhivago*, 236–37; quarrel of, with Pasternak, 244; and manuscript of *The Blind Beauty*, 264; fate of, after Pasternak's death, 272–74; memoirs of, 281–82; on Pasternak's religious feelings, 326

Izbrannyi Maiakovskii (*The Selected Maiakovskii*): 103

Izmalkovo, Lake (near Peredelkino): 153–54, 207, 250, 259

Izvestiia: 148, 149, 157, 161, 235, 249

Jakobson, Roman Osipovich (1896–): 96, 212, 224, 294, 348, 352

James, Henry: 344–46, 349

Jena, East Germany: 259

Jesus Christ: 139, 170, 309, 317, 327–29, 331, 334, 335, 337

Jewish nationalism: 330

Jewish origin, Pasternak's: 329–30

Jewry, Russian: 329

Johannes (character in Hamsun's *Victoria*): 291

John, a Soldier of Peace (Krotkov): 187n.

Johnson, Priscilla Mary Post (1928–): 226

Jonson, Ben: 135

"Journey from Petersburg to Siberia in January, 1920, A" (Levinson): 299–300

Joyce, James (1882–1941): 40, 218, 346

Judaism: 64–65&n., 124, 329–31

Julius Caesar (Shakespeare, translated by Pasternak): 178

Jung, Carl Gustav (1875–1961): 71

Justine (Durrell): 250

Kahler, Erich Gabriel (1885–1970): 240

Kama River, Urals, USSR: 167

Kamenev, Lev Borisovich (real name Rosenfeld) (1883–1936): 108

Kamenskii, Vasilii Vasilevich (1884–1961): 96, 113n., 114

Kandinskii (Kandinsky), Vasilii Vasilevich (1866–1944): 26, 100

Kant, Immanuel: 353–54; Scriabin's references to, 36; influence of, on Pasternak, 50, 287, 317, 349–51, 353; Hermann Cohen's revision of, 62, 64–65&n.

Kantianism: 50, 62, 65, 287, 289, 349, 351, 355–56; *see also* Neo-Kantianism

Karamazov, Ivan (character in *The Brothers Karamazov*): 302

Karavaeva, Anna Aleksandrovna (1893–): 148

Karsavin, Lev Platonovich (1882–1952): 104

Kashirin (Gorky's grandmother): 9

Kataev, Valentin Petrovich (1897–): 130, 215, 233

Katkov, George (Georgii Mikhailovich, 1903–): 333n.

Kaufmann (Kaufman, Pasternak's maternal grandfather): 21

Kaufmann (Kaufman), Berta (Pasternak's maternal grandmother): 21

Kaufmann (Kaufman), Joseph (Pasternak's maternal uncle): 30

Kaufmann (Kaufman), Klavdiia Isidorovna (Pasternak's maternal aunt): 37&n.

Kaufmann (Kaufman), Rosa Isidorovna: *see* Pasternak, Rosa Isidorovna

Kautsky, Karl (1854–1938): 322

Kaverin, Veniamin Aleksandrovich (1902–): 96, 130, 267

Kayden, Eugene (1886–1977): 223

Keats, John: 135, 354

Kepler, Johannes: 289

Kerenskii, Aleksandr Fedorovich (1881–1970): 300

KGB (Soviet Security Agency): 186, 187, 199, 239, 271, 273, 283

Kharabarov, Ivan Mitrofanovich (1938–69): 249

Kharkov, USSR: 83

Khimki River Port, Moscow: 171

Khlebnikov, Viktor (Velemir) Vladimirovich (1885–1922): 54, 82n., 83, 84&n., 276, 300, 340, 348, 353; and Italian Futurism, 54; influence of, on Aseev, 82; Pasternak's poetic filiation with, 83, 84, 300, 353; exercise in versification of, 97; Maiakovskii on, 122; assessment of, in 1960s, 276; Jakobson on, 348; assessed by Pasternak, 351; theory of "self-sufficient word" of, 353

Khodasevich, Vladislav Felitsianovich (1886–1934): 95, 104, 105, 107

"Khorosho!" (Maiakovskii): 110

Khrapchenko, Mikhail Borisovich (1904–): 280

Khrushchev, Nikita Sergeevich (1894–1971): 209; Pasternak's attitude toward, 205, 308; policy of, on literary matters, 216, 248; role of in *Doctor Zhivago* affair, 221, 235–37, 249, 280; and financial help for to Pasternak's family, 275–76

Kiev, USSR: 21, 70, 118–19

Kiev Railroad Station, Moscow: 266

Kipling, Rudyard: 89

Kirov, Sergei Mironovich: 5, 154

Kirsanov, Semën Isaakovich (1906–72): 208

Kirshon, Vladimir Mikhailovich (1902–38): 148

Kivshenko, Aleksei Danilovich: 3

Klavdiia Isidorovna: *see* Kaufmann, Klavdiia Isidorovna

Klee, Paul (1879–1940): 341

Kleist, Heinrich von: 75, 82, 135, 168, 172, 277

Kliuchevskii, Vasilii Osipovich: 55

Kliuev, Nikolai Alekseevich (1887–1937): 154

Kniga chasov (translation of *The Book of Hours*, by Anisimov): 80

Kochetov, Vsevolod Anisimovich (1912–73): 221, 240

Koestler, Arthur (1905–): 199, 242, 308

Koffman, Rosa Isidorovna: *see* Kaufmann, Rosa Isidorovna

Kolas, Iakub (1882–1956): 148

Kologrivov, Lavrentii Mikhailovich (character in *Doctor Zhivago*): 297

Koltsov, Mikhail Efimovich (1898–1942): 148, 154, 160

Komarovskii (character in *Doctor Zhivago*): 297

Kominform: 190

Komissarzhevskaia, Vera Fëdorovna (1864–1910): 33, 37–38, 54, 75n.; theater of, in Saint Petersburg, 37

Kommunist: 216

Komsomol (Communist Youth Organization): 97&n., 109, 118, 235–36, 249

Konstantinov, Dmitrii Vasilevich (1908–): 327, 328

Kopelev, Lev Zinovevich (1912–): 267

Kornakov, Koka (character in *Doctor Zhivago*): 55n.

Kornilov, Gen. Lavr Georgievich: 300

Kornilov, Vladimir Nikolaevich (1928–): 280

Korolëv, Boris Daniilovich (1884–1963): 5n.

Korovin, Konstantin Aleksandrovich (1861–1939): 26, 29

Korsinkino, Russia: 78

Kostko, Dmitrii Ivanovich (stepfather of Olga Ivinskaia, ?–1952): 186

Kostko, Mariia Nikolaevna (née Ivinskaia, mother of Olga Ivinskaia): 186

Kotov, Anatolii Konstantinovich (1909–56): 211

Koussevitzky, Serge (1874–1951): 22–23, 44

Kozhebatkin, Aleksandr Melentevich (1884–1942): 43

Kozhevnikov, Vadim Mikhailovich (1909–): 208

Krakht, Konstantin Fëdorovich: 81

Krasnaia gazeta: 111

Kremlin, Moscow: 147, 150, 155, 213, 266

Krivitskii (member of *Novyi mir* editorial board): 212

Krokodil: 234, 240n.

Kronstadt, Russia: 40

Kropotkin, Prince Pëtr Alekseevich: 26n., 91, 335

Krotkov, Iurii: 127n., 186, 187

Kruchënykh, Aleksei Eliseevich (1886–1970): 83–84&n., 113n., 114, 181

Kukriniksy (artistic team): 109

Kurlov, G.: 14, 42, 55&n.

Kursk, USSR: 196

Kushner, Boris (1888–1937): 113n.

Kushnerev (head of Cooperative Publishing House): 3

Kutuzov, Mikhail Illarionovich: 304

Kuzmich, Sergei: 207

Kuzmin, Mikhail Alekseevich (1875–1936): 43n., 95

Kuznetskii Bridge, Moscow: 242

Lagerkvist, Pär Fabian (1891–1974): 250

Lakhuti, Abolgasem Akhmedzade (1887–1957): 148

Lampedusa, Prince Giuseppe Tomasi di (1896–1957): 209

Langer, Susanne Knauth (1895–): 344

Lara (Larisa, character in *Doctor Zhivago*): 139, 195–97, 201, 273, 297, 303

Larionov, Mikhail Fëdorovich (1881–1964): 29, 54

Lavrushinskii Lane: 153, 172, 177
Lawrence, D. H. (1885–1930): 250
Laxness, Halldór (1902–): 237
Lay of Opanas, The (Bagritskii): 110
Lebedev, Sarra (1892–1967): 270, 272
Lebiazhii Lane, Moscow: 90
Le Corbusier (pseud. of Charles-Edouard Jeanneret, 1887–1965): 101n.
LEF (Neofuturist group): 113&n., 114–15, 122, 124
Left Front of Art: *see* LEF
Le Gall, André (1904–): 71
Leibnitz, Gottfried Wilhelm von: 61, 290
Lenau, Nikolaus (pseud. of Niembsch von Strehlenau): 355
Lenin, Vladimir Ilich: 26n., 30, 78n., 92, 100, 108, 161, 319, 321, 322
Leningrad, USSR: 121, 151, 155, 168, 178, 184, 198, 205, 232; *see also* Saint Petersburg; Petrograd
Lenin Prize: 227
Leonidze, Georgii Nikolaevich (1899–1966): 138, 248, 280
Leonidze, Peputsa: 186
Leonov, Leonid Maximovich (1899–): 109, 166, 167, 294
Leopard, The (Lampedusa): 209n.
Le Play, Pierre-Guillaume-Frédéric: 324
Lermontov, Mikhail Iurievich: 3, 24, 89, 126, 248
Leschetizky, Theodor: 21
"Lesende, Der" (Rilke): 333
Le Senne, René (1882–1954): 71
Levin (director of Sovetskii pisatel Publishing House): 190
Levin, Iurii Davydovich (1920–): 135
Levitan, Isaak Ilich: 29, 31
Lewis, Sinclair (1885–1951): 148
Lezhnev, Abram (pseud. of Abram Zelikovich Gorelik, 1893–1938): 111, 114, 124
"Liberal conservatism": 294, 322–23
Liberalism: 206, 216, 303
Liberty of Labor (newspaper): 93
Library of the Historical Museum, Moscow: 185
Lichnost: *see* personality, cult of
Liebermann, Max (1847–1935): 26n.
Life of Man (Andreev): 41
Light and the Color Symphony of Scriabin (Balmont): 33
Lipps, Theodor: 55
Lirika (journal): 78
Lirika (literary group): 80, 82–83
Lisitskii, Lazar Markovich (El Lissitzky, 1890–1941): 103n.
Liszt, Franz: 21–22
Literary Encyclopedia: 142
Literary Fund of the USSR: 267, 275, 276
Literary Moscow: 209, 252
Literatura i iskusstvo (*Literature and Art*): 178
Literature and Life: 267

Literaturnaia gazeta: 129, 138, 142, 152n., 159, 178, 208, 212, 231, 237, 267, 278, 304
Literaturnaia Moskva: see Literary Moscow
Liuvers, Evgeniia (Zhenia, character in "The Childhood of Liuvers"): 77, 95
Liuvers, Evgeniia (character in "The Diary of Zhivult"): 140
Livanov, Boris Nikolaevich (1904–72): 31, 169
Livingstone, Angela (1934–): 79
Livshits, Benedikt Konstantinovich (1886–1939): 83, 87
Logical Investigations (Husserl): 81
Logical pyschologism: 55
Logic of Pure Knowledge (Cohen): 62
Loks, Konstantin Grigorevich: 51, 114&n.
Lomonosov, Mikhail Vasilevich: 56–57, 133
London: 29, 248; *see also* England
Lourié, Evgeniia Vladimirovna: *see* Pasternak, Evgeniia Vladimirovna
Lozinskii, Mikhail Leonidovich (1886–1955): 135–37, 170
Lubianka Prison, Moscow: 199–201
Lugovskoi, Vladimir Aleksandrovich (1901–57): 280
Lunacharskii, Anatolii Vasilevich (1875–1933): 31, 91, 100, 109, 114
Lundkvist, Arthur (1906–): 227
Lusha (character in *The Blind Beauty*): 262
Luther, Martin: 57, 69
Luxemburg, Rosa: 322
Lvov (Lwoff), Prince Aleksei Evgenevich: 4, 40n.
Lvov (Lwoff), Princess Vera Alekseevna (?–1980): 40n.
Lyric and Epic Poetry of the Great Patriotic War (Abramov): 173
Lyricism: 38, 41, 119, 340, 350–51, 356
Łysohorský, Óndra (real name Ervín Goj, 1905–): 135

Macbeth (Shakespeare): 169
McBride, Robert Medill (1879–1965): 95n.
Macmillan, Harold (1894–): 246
Madison Hotel, Paris: 150
Maiakovskii, Vladimir Vladimirovich (1893–1930): 14, 16, 42, 43, 82n., 86, 113–15, 118, 121–24, 126n., 132, 151, 255, 291, 332, 348; early revolutionary activities of, 42n., 54; early activities of, as Futurist, 54ff.; early poetic filiation of, with Pasternak, 69, 70, 76, 81n., 83–85; similarity of poetry of, to Pasternak's, 81n., 300–301; Pasternak's admiration of, 83, 84, 85; first meeting of, with Pasternak, 84; enthusiasm of, for World War I, 86; acceptance of Revolution by, 96; manner of performance of, 97; in Berlin, 103, 105; response of, to Lenin's death, 108; response of to tenth anniversary of Revolution, 110; on Pasternak's achievement (1926), 111; as member of LEF, 113–15; suicide of, 121; break of, with Pasternak, 122–23; effect

of death of, on Pasternak, 124, 129, 131, 133;
posthumous role of, 146, 149; meeting of, with
Stalin, 157n.; relation of, to *Doctor Zhivago*, 184,
196, 312; role of, in Thaw, 205

Maklakov, Vasilii Alekseevich (1870–1957): 26n.

Makovskii, Sergei Konstantinovich (1878–1962):
43&n., 95

Makovskii, Vladimir Egorevich: 8

Malevich, Kazimir Severinovich (1878–1935): 29,
100

Mallarmé, Stéphane: 33, 89, 311

Malraux, André (1901–76): 144, 148–50

Malyi Theater, Moscow: 239

"Man" (Maiakovskii): 96

Manchester Guardian: 246, 274

Mandelstam, Nadezhda Iakovlevna (1899–): 14,
89–90, 157, 158, 184, 239, 262, 276, 278,
301, 329

Mandelstam, Osip Emilevich (1891–1938): 14, 16,
43n., 132, 135, 141; dialogue of, with Pasternak, 54; inspiration of, from Italy, 72; children's
literature of, 108n.; on Maiakovskii, 122; inspiration of, from Georgia, 126n.; official disgrace of, 142; imprisonment and death of,
154–55; Pasternak's talk with Stalin about, 157;
Pasternak's financial assistance to, 158, 265;
"Ode to Stalin" by, 161; attitude of, toward
translation, 168

Manet, Édouard: 29

"Manifeste futuriste" (Marinetti): 339

Mann, Heinrich (1871–1950): 148n., 149n.

Mann, Klaus (1906–49): 143, 218

Mann, Thomas (1875–1955): 218, 349

Mannerism: 355

Mansurov (classmate of Pasternak): 73

Marburg, Germany: 55–61, 65, 68–72, 87, 105,
133, 306, 317, 330, 350, 361; *see also* Marburg
philosophical school; University of Marburg

Marburg philosophical school: 50, 55–57, 61–65,
306; *see also* Neo-Kantianism; Cohen, Hermann

Marcel, Gabriel (1889–1973): 314

"Marche Funèbre" (Chopin): 267

Margueritte, Victor (1866–1942): 149

Margvelashvili, Georgii Georgievich (1923–): 280

Maria Stuart (Schiller): 135, 213, 221, 249

Maria Stuart (Słowacki): 238, 241

Marien-Leben, Das (Rilke): 80

Marina: *see* Shchapov, Marina

Marinetti, Filippo Tommaso (1876–1944): 54, 86,
339, 340

Markel: *see* Shchapov, Markel

Marks, Adolf Fëdorovich: 11

Marshak, Samuil Iakovlevich (1887–1964): 108n.,
135–37

Martynov, Leonid Nikolaevich (1905–): 236

Marx, Karl: 220, 292, 305, 316, 323

Marxism: 62, 209n., 214, 232, 298, 301–302,
304–306, 311, 319, 322

Marxism-Leninism: 305

Marxists: *see* Marxism

Mase (Mazeh), Jacob (1859–1924): 26n.

Mashkov, Ilia Ivanovich (1881–1944): 29

Maskarad (Lermontov): 24

Maslenikov, Zoia Afanasevna: 240

Masterstvo perevoda: Sbornik shestoi: 135, 138n.

Materialism: 290

Matlaw, Ralph (1927–): 347

Maugham, W. Somerset (1874–1965): 236

Maupassant, Guy de: 345, 346

Mauriac, François (1885–1970): 227

Mechanism: 290

Meditations (Ehrenburg): 96

Meetings with Pasternak (Gladkov): 272, 279, 281

Meierkhold, Vsevolod Emilevich (1874–1940): 75n.,
144, 154, 159, 216

Mekhanosin (character in "Without Love" and *Doctor
Zhivago*): 93

Melitinskii (cousin of Zinaida Pasternak): 127

Mensheviks: 322

Mereküla, Estonia: 33n.

Merezhkovskii, Dmitrii Sergeevich (1865–1941): 15,
72

Merton, Thomas (1915–68): 327, 335

Meshchanstvo: 308

Metchenko, Aleksei Ivanovich (1907–): 280

Meudon, France: 150

Miasnitskaia Street, Moscow: 5, 65

Miasoedov, Grigorii Grigorevich (1893–1911): 8

Michelangelo: 24

Mikhailov, Nikolai Aleksandrovich (1906–): 228

Mikhalkov, Sergei Vladimirovich (1913–): 240

Mikhailovskoe, Russia: 167

Mikitenko, Ivan Kondratevich (1897–1937): 148

Milan, Italy: 72, 209&n., 211, 216–17

Miłosz, Czesław (1911–): 131, 180, 282

Minsk, USSR: 151, 152

Mirsky, D. S.: *see* Sviatopolk-Mirskii, Prince Dmitrii
Petrovich

Mitsishvili, Nikoloz Iosifovich (real name Sirbiladze,
1894–1937): 138

Mochulskii, Konstantin Vasilevich (1892–1948):
43n.

Modernism: 29, 33, 38, 40, 54, 97, 174, 216, 240,
348

Moglin, Sasha: 199

Moira: 328

Moiseiwitsch, Benno (1890–1963): 21

Mokhovaia Street, Moscow: 54n.

Molodi, Russia: 75, 78

Monarchism: 101

Monet, Claude (1840–1926): 29

Monolog (Novalis): 353

Morath, Inge: 156

Moravia, Alberto (real name Pincherle, 1907–): 226

Mordovian Republic: 201

Morozov, Mikhail Mikhailovich (1897–1952): 170

Moscow, USSR: 3–6, 8–12, 20–26, 36, 38, 44, 48, 52, 60, 65, 69, 70, 75, 77–78, 83, 85–87, 90–92, 95n., 96, 99, 101n., 117, 128, 135, 138, 143, 146–48, 151–54&n., 155, 157, 158, 184–86&n., 189, 190, 194, 195, 197, 198, 200, 201n., 204–209, 212–14, 216, 218, 224, 226, 227, 229, 232, 236, 241, 242, 244–46, 248&n., 249&n., 252, 254, 256, 264–66, 272, 274, 277, 282, 283, 300, 302, 315, 323, 330, 332, 333, 339; Pasternak's relationship to, 2, 90–91, 291–92; Pasternak's childhood in, 3–6, 8–12, 14, 36, 111; Pasternak's parents in, 20–26, 33&n., 34, 41–42, 54–55, 75, 78, 100; plan of Pasternak's parents to return to, 29–30; during uprising of 1905, 40; Pasternak's student days in, 42, 54–58, 72; return of Pasternaks to, early 1920s, 107–108; during World War II, 165–74, 177–79; described in *Doctor Zhivago*, 291–92; Pasternak's treatment of, in *Doctor Zhivago*, 299
Moscow Art Theater: 87, 169, 213, 239, 271
Moscow Association of Futurists (MAF): 113–14
Moscow Association of Proletarian Writers: 109, 114
Moscow Central Children's Theater, Sverdlov Square: 256
Moscow Fifth Gymnasium: 14, 42&n., 73, 84
Moscow Professional Union of Writers: 92, 109
Moscow Satire Theater: 205
Moscow School of Painting, Sculpture, and Architecture: 4&n., 5, 7–8, 20, 25–26, 30, 39–40, 54, 99–100
Moscow School of Fine Arts: *see* Moscow School of Painting, Sculpture, and Architecture
Moscow State Bank: 273
Moscow State University (MGU): *see* University of Moscow
Mother (Gorky): 41
Mother Volga (Panfërov): 205
Motyleva, Tamara Lazarevna (1910–): 202
Mozart, Wolfgang Amadeus: 272
Muffled Voices (ed. Vladimir Markov): 204
Munich, Germany: 147
Muratov, Pavel Pavlovich (1881–1950): 103n., 107
Musagetes (journal): 43&n.
Musagetes (literary group): 80–82, 104
Muscovites: 166, 283
Mutualité, Palais de la, Paris: 149, 150
Myshkin, Prince (character in *The Idiot*): 327
Mysteries (Hamsun): 38, 291
"Mysteries, The" ("Die Geheimnisse," Goethe): 135
Mysticism: 2, 33, 37, 52, 54, 65, 335

Nabokov, Vladimir Vladimirovich (1899–1977): 52n., 84n.
Nadal, Octave (1904–): 343
Nagibin, Iurii Markovich (1920–): 209
Nakanune Publishing House, Berlin: 103

Naked Year, The (Pilniak): 297
Napoleon I: 304, 320–22
Nashchokinskii Lane, Moscow: 154, 155
Nasimovich, N.: *see* Chuzhak, N.
NATO: 194
Nationalism: 17, 330
Natorp, Paul (1845–1924): 55, 57, 61–62, 64
Naturalism: 38, 287, 289
Nature (as pole in Pasternak's thought): 287, 289, 293, 307, 317
Navrozov, Lev (1928–): 161
Nazi army: 165
Nazism: 29
Nehru, Jawaharlal (1889–1964): 246
Neigauz, Andrian (Adik, 1925–45): 125, 166, 179
Neigauz (Neuhaus), Genrikh Gustavovich (1888–1964): 119, 124, 127, 198, 212, 266, 267
Neigauz, Stanislav (Stasik; Pasternak's stepson): 167, 266–68, 275
Neiman, Iuliia Moiseevna (1907–): 165
Neofuturism: 113, 114; *see also* Futurism
Neo-Kantianism: 57, 62, 81, 330, 349–50, 353; *see also* Kantianism
Neoromanticism: 355
NEP (New Economic Policy): 101
Neuen Gedichte, Die (Rilke): 80
Neuvecelle, Jean ("Dyma," 1912–): 212
Neva River: 128
News Chronicle (London): 244
New Statesman: 274
New Testament: 329, 331
Newton, Sir Isaac: 290
New York City, N.Y.: 204, 240
New York Herald Tribune: 276
New York Philharmonic Orchestra: 249
Nezval, Vítezslav (1900–58): 135, 141, 143
Nicolas II, Tsar: 10, 16, 39, 85
Nietzsche, Friedrich Wilhelm: 11, 33, 68, 250
Nietzscheanism: 35, 49
Nihilism: 47
Nikiforov, Sergei Nikolaevich (pseud. Epishkin): 200
Nikisch, Artur: 22
Nilsson, Nils Åke (1917–): 224, 226
1984 (Orwell): 242
"1941" (Iuliia Neiman): 165
Nivat, Georges (1935–): 245, 274
Nizhnii Ufalei, Cheliabinsk Region, USSR: 166
Nobel Foundation: 235
Nobel Prize for Literature: 221, 226, 230, 232, 233, 238, 239, 241, 257, 277
Norway, writers of: 237
Not by Bread Alone (Dudintsev): 209
Notebooks of Malte Laurids Brigge (Rilke): 79
Notre Dame, Cathedral of, Paris: 151
Novalis (pseud. of Friedrich Leopold von Hardenberg): 351
Novosibirsk, USSR: 174

Novosibirsk Theater: 174
Novyi mir (*New World*): 109, 114, 184, 187, 198,
  202, 205, 206, 208, 209, 212, 216, 231, 238,
  252, 280, 300
Nuit de feu (Pascalian term): 333

"Objectivism": 184
Objectivization: 311, 314
Oblomov, Ilia (character in Goncharov's *Oblomov*):
  119, 334
Obolenskoe: 33&n., 35–36
Obscurantism: *see* philistinism, of Stalin era
Observer, 282
October, 1917, Revolution: 141, 145, 238, 300, 303
Odessa, Russia: 11, 20–22, 33n., 54
"Ode to Autumn" (Keats): 168n.
"Ode to Stalin" (Mandelstam): 161
"Ode to the West Wind" (Shelley): 277
Odoevo rest home, USSR: 147, 366
Odoevskii, Prince Vladimir Fedorovich (1803–69):
  344
Odyssey (Homer, translated by Zhukovskii): 135
Oktiabr: 205, 280
Old Testament: 309, 329
Olesha, Iurii Karlovich (1899–1960): 109, 130, 131,
  146, 154, 159, 209
One Day in the Life of Ivan Denisovich (Solzhenitsyn):
  277
150,000,000 (Maiakovskii): 122
Onegin, Eugene (character in *Eugene Onegin*): 119,
  324, 334
On Guard (*Na postu*): 109
On Shakespeare (Hugo): 167
"On Sincerity in Literature" (Pomerantsev): 205
"On the Cause of the Decline and on the New Trends
  in Russian Literature" (Merezhkovskii): 15
Opinie: 216
Orbeli, Leon Abgarovich (1882–1958): 232
Orel, USSR: 175–77
Ort, Elise: 61, 71
Ort, Fräulein (daughter of Elise Ort): 61, 71
Ortega y Gasset, José (1883–1955): 63&n.
Orthodox church: *see* Russian Orthodox church
Orthodox Seminary, Oruzheinyi Lane, Moscow: 3
Orthodoxy: 206, 331; *see also* Russian Orthodox church
Orwell, George (1903–50): 109, 242
Osborn, Max (1870–1946): 29
Oshanin, Lev Ivanovich (1912–): 236
Østerling, Anders Johan (1884–): 226, 228, 230,
  233, 235, 241
Ostrovskaia, Raisa Porfirevna (?–1963): 175–76
Otsup, Nikolai Avdeevich (1894–1958): 103n., 112
Otto, Rudolf (1869–1937): 57
Oxford, England: 30, 183, 272
Ozerov, Lev (1914–): 138, 278

Paderewski, Ignace Jan (1860–1941): 21
Palais de la Mutualité: *see* Mutualité

Pan (Hamsun): 38, 291
Panfërov, Fëdor Ivanovich (1896–1960): 148, 149,
  205, 221, 223
Pankratov, Iurii Ivanovich (1935–): 249
Panova, Vera Fëdorovna (1905–73): 221, 233
Pantheism: 57, 287, 289, 315
Pantheon Books: 229
"Panther, Der" (Rilke): 108
Paris, France: 70, 95–96, 106n., 147–51, 152&n.,
  158, 170, 212, 246, 279
Parliament, British: 248n.
"Partisan War in *Doctor Zhivago*, The" (Dinfreville):
  300
Pasha (Pavel, character in *A Tale*): 139
Pasternak, Aleksandr Leonidovich (brother of Boris
  Pasternak, 1893–): 54, 100–101&n.; birth of,
  3n.; at gymnasium, 14, 42; on early life with
  brother, 34; in Berlin, 41; on Scriabin, 44; as
  violinist, 48&n.; marriage and career of,
  100–101&n., 169n.; at brother's death, 266
Pasternak, Anna (Asia) Osipovna: *see* Freidenberg,
  Anna Osipovna
Pasternak, Boris Leonidovich (1890–1960):
  birth of, 3
  family origins of, 3, 19ff.
  and father's artistic career, 3–5, 11–12, 20–29,
    65, 75, 86&n., 99, 100, 107, 165
  influence of nanny Akulina Gavrilovna on, 3, 9,
    331
  childhood of, 4–15
  feelings of, toward parents, 9, 31, 56, 165
  relationship of, with father, 11, 19, 30–31
  and career of mother, 21–24
  influence of Rilke on, 30, 70, 78–80, 108, 132,
    253, 332–33, 355
  relationship of, with Blok, 33, 51–53, 135, 184,
    194, 196, 335
  influence of Belyi on, 33, 37, 38, 51, 81,
    104–105, 253, 265
  relationship of, with Scriabin, 33–37, 44–49,
    132, 252–53, 297, 355
  musical studies of, 36–37, 42–49
  and political upheaval of 1905, 38–40
  stay of, in Germany, 1905–1907, 40–41
  association of, with Futurism, 42, 54, 80–85,
    96–97, 105, 113–15, 121–24, 133, 300,
    339–40, 346, 350–51, 353, 355; *see also* Cen-
    trifuge; Khlebnikov; LEF
  in Serdarda group, 42–44
  early literary pursuits of, 48–49, 51–52, 69–70,
    75–83
  dialogue of, with Akhmatova, 54, 120, 130–31,
    155, 157, 168–69, 186, 194, 265
  at University of Moscow, 55–56, 72–73; *see also*
    Bergson; Bergsonism
  at University of Marburg, 56–59, 62–65, 68–69,
    253–55; *see also* Cohen, Hermann
  love of, for Vysotskaia, 65–70

relationship of, with Maiakovskii, 69–76, 81n.,
    83–85, 111, 121–24, 129–33, 300–301
friendship of, with Tsvetaeva, 71–72, 83, 88–90,
    97–99, 105, 111–12, 126, 150, 170–72, 195
as translator, 75, 82, 134–39, 160–61, 163,
    168–70, 172–74, 178, 182, 184, 192–94,
    198, 202–205, 213, 221, 277
in Urals, 1915–17, 76–78, 82, 87
and first wife, Evgeniia Vladimirovna, née Lourié,
    77, 99–101, 124–27, 130, 266, 331
dialogue of, with Aseev, 82–83, 171, 253
dialogue of, with Gorky, 82, 95, 98&n., 111–12,
    117, 142
and World War I, 85–87
and appearance of *My Sister, Life*, 89–90, 92
and *Themes and Variations*, 89, 92, 102, 107
beginnings of, as prose writer, 94–95
dialogue of, with Ehrenburg, 96–97, 105,
    117–18, 146
in Germany, 1922–23, 99–107
and *Second Birth*, 117, 119, 124, 129–31
and *A Safe-Conduct*, 119, 121, 129, 131–33
relationship of, with second wife, Zinaida
    Nikolaevna, née Eremeev, 124–28, 130–31,
    141–42, 151, 154n., 158&n., 166, 177,
    186–87, 196, 206, 331
in Paris, 1935, 147–51
in Peredelkino, 153, 167–68, 177
during "Great Purge," 154–63
in World War II, 164–82
in Chistopol, 165–68, 171–74, 252
wartime literary endeavors of, 173–79
after World War II, 180–84
and writing of *Doctor Zhivago*, 181–82, 184,
    194–203
during Zhdanov era, 184, 188–95
liaison of, with Ivinskaia, 184–88, 195–96,
    199–202, 205–207, 233, 236–37, 244, 264
first efforts of, to publish *Doctor Zhivago*, 208–19
after publication of *Doctor Zhivago* and award of
    Nobel Prize, 221–50
in Georgia, 1959, 246–47
and *When Skies Clear*, 250–52
and *Sketch for an Autobiography*, 252–56
daily life of, in 1950s, 259–62
and *The Blind Beauty*, 262–64
final days and death of, 264–67
funeral of, 267–72
legacy and rehabilitation of, 275–83
aesthetic-philosophical system of, 287
philosophy of natural authenticity of, 289–94
philosophy of history of, 296ff.
philosophy of, in relation to socialism and Marx-
    ism, 298–304
personalist philosophy of, 310–17
subjectivity and "interiority" in work of, 311–12,
    316
views of, on community values, 318–25

love of, for Russia, 323–25
religious dimension of thought of, 327–37
Judaic values in religious philosophy of, 329–31
and Christianity, 327–29, 331, 334–37
"mystical" experience of, 333, 336–37
concept of realism and aesthetics of, 337, 339,
    342–44&n., 345–46, 348–49, 355–56
concept of dynamism and aesthetics of, 339–43,
    354
concept of romanticism of, 343–45&n., 355–56
content in relation to form in aesthetics of,
    345–46, 348–49, 354–55
Pasternak, Elena (Pasternak's daughter-in-law): 275
Pasternak, Evgeniia Vladimirovna (*née* Lourié, Paster-
    nak's first wife): 128; and characters in Paster-
    nak's works, 77; marriage of, to Pasternak,
    99–100; in Berlin with Pasternak, 101; birth of
    son of, 108; divorce of, from Pasternak, 124–27;
    poem in "Second Birth" dedicated to, 130; at
    Pasternak's deathbed, 266; role of, in Pasternak's
    religious development, 331
Pasternak, Evgenii Borisovich (Pasternak's older son,
    1923–): 108, 128, 266, 268, 275
Pasternak, Josephine (Zhozefina) Leonidovna (Paster-
    nak's sister, married to Frederick Pasternak,
    1900–): 30, 33n., 141, 165, 327; birth of, 3n.;
    on music in household, 22–23; drawings of, by
    father, 27–28; on Pasternak's first verses, 49;
    career of, 100&n.; on Pasternak's health in
    mid-1930s, 147–48
Pasternak, Karl Evgenevich (Leonid Pasternak's first
    cousin): 30
Pasternak, Lea (Pasternak's grandmother): 19
Pasternak, Leonid (Lënia) Borisovich (Pasternak's
    younger son, 1937–76): 126, 128, 145&n.,
    167, 175, 177, 186–87, 268, 275
Pasternak, Leonid Osipovich (Pasternak's father,
    1862–1945): 3–5&n., 7–10&n., 11–15,
    19&n., 20–31, 33&n., 35, 38–40&n., 41,
    43–45, 48&n., 54, 72&n., 73, 78, 91,
    100–101; early commissions and appointments
    of, 3–5; friendship of, with Tolstoy, 4, 11, 27,
    30, 53; on religious issues and Judaism, 5, 69,
    329–30; closeness of, to Tolstoy's principles, 9,
    30, 329; as illustrator of Tolstoy's *Resurrection*,
    11–12; origins and genealogy of, 19; early life,
    studies, and marriage of, 19–21, 33; on himself
    as painter, 24–29; last years and death of, in
    England, 30, 165; influence of, on his son Boris,
    30–31; relationship of, with Scriabin, 33, 35,
    44; during demonstrations of 1905, 39–40,
    40n.; further artistic pursuits of, 65, 75, 86&n.,
    99, 100, 107, 165; on vacation in Italy, 72&n.;
    and Anatolii Lunacharskii, 92; financial diffi-
    culties of, early 1920s, 99–100; in Berlin, 100;
    attitude of, toward Soviet government, 100
Pasternak, Osip (Pasternak's grandfather): 19
Pasternak, Petia (Pasternak's grandson): 275

Pasternak, Rozaliia (Rosa) Isidorovna (*née* Kaufman, Pasternak's mother, 1867–1939): 21n., 30, 48n., 54, 73, 100; and Pasternak's birth, 3; religion of, 9; career of, 21–24; in Germany, 29; Pasternak's temperamental closeness to, 31; gift of, to Pasternak, 56; death of, 165; *see also* Pasternak, Leonid Osipovich

Pasternak, Zinaida Nikolaevna (*née* Eremeev, married to Genrikh Neigauz until 1934, Pasternak's second wife, 1898–1966): 119, 148, 159, 160, 171, 172, 174, 200, 204, 205, 210, 246, 248, 256, 259, 260, 264; early relationship of, with Pasternak, 124–25; background and youth of, 127&n.; marriage of, to Pasternak, 126–28, 331; poems in *Second Birth* addressed to, 130–31; Pasternak's intended book about, 141; attitude of, toward Pasternak's work, 142; role of, during Pasternak's periods of depression, 151; and birth of Leonid, 154n.; attitude of, toward Mandelstams, 158&n.; attitude of, toward Stalin regime, 161; family earnings supplemented by, 163, 167; Pasternak's awareness of nature of, 166, 186–87; after World War II, 177; attitude of, toward Pasternak and Ivinskaia, 187, 206; as partial prototype for Lara, 196; financial difficulties of, after Pasternak's death, 275–76; death of, 276; Ivinskaia's attitude toward, 282

Pasternak's apartment, Lavrushinskii Lane, Moscow: 153, 172, 177

"Pasternak's Children" (Strachey): 282

Pasternak-Slater, Lidiia (Lydia, Pasternak's sister, 1902–): 3n., 15, 27, 30, 39–40, 43, 91, 100&n., 165

Pasternak's Lyric (Plank): 352

Paustovskii, Konstantin Georgevich (1892–1968): 87, 244, 266, 275

Pavel (Pasha, character in *A Tale*): 139

Pavlenko Street, Peredelkino: 154

Peasants (Reymont): 291

Péguy, Charles: 336

Peltier-Zamoyska, Hélène: 212

PEN Club: 235

"Peredelkino" (Akhmadulina): 280

Peredelkino, USSR: 169, 203, 210; Pasternak's dacha in, 52, 135, 188, 216, 244, 246, 331; Pasternak's neighbors in, 96, 110, 160, 208, 240; Pasternak assigned dacha in, 153; visitors to, 158n., 210, 217, 218, 224, 228, 237, 249, 250, 256, 264, 266, 279, 280, 333n.; as partial prototype for Varykino, 167–68; Tsvetaeva's anticipation of invitation to, 171; Ivinskaia's move near, 207; Pasternak's life in, 259–60, 293, 331; Pasternak's death and funeral in, 266–72; burial of Pasternak's wife in, 276; and "Peredelkino," by Akhmadulina, 280; as place of pilgrimage, 283

Peredvizhniki: *see* Itinerants

Pergolesi, Giovanni Battista (1710–36): 21

Perlin (Kiev critic): 119

Perm, USSR: 140

Perovskaia, Sofiia: 299

Personalism: 316–17, 319, 322

Personality, cult of: 308

Pertsov, Viktor Osipovich (1898–): 118, 236

Perugia, Italy: 72n.

Peter the Great, Tsar (1672–1725): 131

Petofi, Sándor: 135, 221, 355

Petrograd: 78, 99; *see also* Saint Petersburg; Leningrad

Petropavlovsk Grammar School, Moscow: 14

Petrov, Dr. Nikolai: 266

Petrovskii, Dmitrii Vasilevich (1892–1955): 145

Petrov-Vodkin, Kuzma Sergeevich (1878–1939): 29

Pevsner, Anton (real name Noton Pevzner, 1886–1962): 100

Phénomène humain, Le (Teilhard de Chardin): 250

Philipp, Moritz: 75, 85–86

Philipp, Walter: 85

Philipp the Magnanimous, Laudgraf (1504–1567): 57

Philistinism, of Stalin era (*meshchanstvo*): 308

Piatakov, Grigorii Leonidovich (1890–1937): 160

Picasso, Pablo (1881–1977): 26

"Pied Piper, The" (Tsvetaeva): 98

Pieper, Josef (1904–): 294

Pierrette's Veil (Schnitzler): 105

Pilniak, Boris Andreevich (1894–1937): 104, 129, 130, 154, 216, 287, 297

Pisa, Italy: 72n.

Pissarro, Camille: 29

Plank, Dale Lewin (1931–): 352

Plato: 55, 350, 352

Plato's Theory of Ideas (Natorp): 62

Pleve, Viacheslav Konstantinovich (Wenzel von Plehwe, 1846–1904): 38

Plumed Serpent, The (D. H. Lawrence): 250

Podvig: 309, 332–34

Poe, Edgar Allan: 89

Poedavshev, Lieut. Col.: 176

"Poem of a Mountain" (Tsvetaeva): 98

Poem of Ecstasy, The (Scriabin): 44–45

"Poem of the End" (Tsvetaeva): 98

"Poems About the Beautiful Lady" (Blok): 52

Poetics (Aristotle): 354

Poet's Library (Biblioteka poeta): 278

"Poet's Second Life, The" (Rylenkov): 280

Poggioli, Renato (1907–63): 302

Pogodin, Nikolai Fëdorovich (1900–62): 186

Poland: 21, 118, 216, 226, 241, 250

Polenov, Vasilii Dmitrievich: 3, 8

Polevoi, Boris Nikolaevich (pseud. of Kampov, 1908–): 233, 236

Polikarpov, Dmitrii Alekseevich (1904–65): 211, 233, 236, 238, 244, 246, 273, 276

Polish Writers' Union: 228, 238, 241

Politburo: 154, 237

Polityka: 241

Polivanov (character in "Aerial Ways"): 94

Polonskii, Iakov Petrovich (1820–98): 119

Polonskii, Viacheslav (pseud. of Viacheslav Pavlovich Gusin, 1886–1932): 114–15
Poltava, Ukraine, USSR: 21
Poltoratskii (Poltoratskii-Pogostin), Viktor Vasilevich (1907–): 208
Polytechnic Museum, Moscow: 97, 111, 194, 277
Pomerantsev, Vladimir Mikhailovich (1907–): 205
Populism: 119n., 128
Portraits of Russian Poets (Ehrenburg): 96, 102
Poshlost: 161
Positivism: 15, 38, 289, 291
Possessed, The (Dostoevsky): 204n.
Post-Modernism: 348
Potapov Street, Moscow: 186n., 207
Potemkin (battleship): 299
Potma hard-labor camp: 201
Pougny, Jean: *see* Puni, Ivan
Pound, Ezra L. (1885–1972): 40
Poznanie: 353
Prague, Czechoslovakia: 107, 130
Pravda: 111, 120, 129, 148, 179, 232, 238, 240, 241, 304
Precocious Autobiography (Evtushenko): 280
Prelude in G-sharp minor (1906) (Pasternak): 49&n.
Prince of Homburg, The (Kleist, translated by Pasternak): 168n., 277
Problems of Dostoevsky's Poetics (Bakhtin): 297n.
Prokofiev, Sergei Sergeevich (1891–1953): 33, 36n.
Prologue (Kaverin): 130
Prometheus: 288, 293
Propaganda, Department of (at Zhizdra): 176
Proust, Marcel: 92, 218
Proyart de Baillescourt, Jacqueline de: 212–15, 241, 243, 250
Przybyszewski, Stanisław: 37–38
Pshavela: *see* Vazha-Pshavela
Pugachëv rebellion: 167
Puni, Ivan Albertovich (Jean Pougny, 1894–1956): 103n.
Punin, Nikolai Nikolaevich (1888–1953): 155
Pushkin, Aleksandr Sergeevich: 185, 201, 248, 272n.; upbringing of, compared with Pasternak's, 9; Pasternak's origins traced to, 31; Blok's on anniversary of death of, 95; allusions to, in *Themes and Variations*, 107; effect of Georgia on, 126; Pasternak and poetry of, 141; and Pasternak's comparison of Chistopol with Mikhailovskoe, 167; and Pasternak's praise of Akhmatova, 168; and *Doctor Zhivago*, 180, 324; and Surkov-Pasternak, Bulgarin-Pushkin relationships, 190; in disgrace, 248; Pasternak compared with, 279, 313, 348; Pasternak's interpretation of "realism" of, 339, 355
Puzikov, A. I.: 213

Quesnay, François: 322

R., D. M. (journalist): 91
Rabota: *see podvig*
Rachmaninoff, Sergei Vasilievich (1873–1943): 26n.
Radio Moscow: 209, 214, 228, 232, 236, 274, 276, 277
Radio Warsaw: 223, 226, 228
Radishchev, Aleksandr Nikolaevich: 201
Radlova, Anna Dmitrievna (1891–1949): 136
Raiki, near Moscow: 33n.
Raleigh, Sir Walter: 135
Raphael (Arenskii): 20
Rationalism: 311, 327, 345n.
Rationalists: 345
Rayonnism: 54
Reader's Digest: 187
Realism: 4n., 16, 31, 94, 114, 168, 298, 337, 339, 342–44&n., 345–46, 348–49, 355–56
Reavey, George (1907–): 116
Rebikov, Vladimir Ivanovich: 41
Red Virgin Soil (*Krasnaia nov*): 109, 111
Regler, Gustav (1898–1963): 143–49
Religion: 8–9, 37; *see also* Christianity; Judaism; mysticism
Religion der Vernunft aus den Quellen des Judentums, Die (Cohen): 330
Religious symbolism: 222, 332n.
Remarque, Erich Maria (1898–1970): 92
Rembrandt van Rijn: 24, 30, 329
Remizov, Aleksei Mikhailovich (1877–1957): 26n., 104
Renaissance: 289
Renan, Ernest: 327
Repin, Ilia Efimovich: 3, 8, 11, 20, 339
"Requiem für eine Freundin" ("Requiem for a Lady Friend," Rilke): 153
Resurrection (Tolstoy): 11, 24
Retribution (Blok): 196
Return from the USSR (*Retour de l'URSS*, Gide): 158
"Revisionists," literary: 248
Revolution: 298, 300, 301, 304, 316, 332; *see also* Revolution of 1905; Revolution of 1917; Revolution of February, 1917; Revolution of October, 1917
Revolution of February, 1917: 300
Revolution of 1905: 253, 299, 303
Revolution of 1917: 299
Revolution of October, 1917: 141, 145, 238, 300, 303
Revue de défense nationale: 300
Reymont, Wladyslaw Stanislaw: 291
Ribot, Théodule Armand: 289–90
Richter (Rikhter), Sviatoslav Teofilovich (1914–): 48, 212, 267
Rickert, Heinrich (1863–1936): 81, 349
Ricks, Christopher: 282
Riesman, David (1909–): 314
Rilke, Rainer Maria (1875–1926): 26n., 38, 78–81,

132–33, 151, 218, 253, 332–33; Pasternaks visited by, 11–14; influence of, on Pasternak, 30, 70, 78–80, 108, 132, 253, 332–33; poetry of, introduced by Pasternak to Serdarda, 43, 80; poetry of, introduced by Pasternak to Russian public, 80; poetry of, translated by Pasternak, 80, 135, 253; and dialogue with Tsvetaeva, 98; Pasternak on, 355

Ripellino, Angelo Maria (1923–): 217

Robert Guiscard (Kleist, translated by Pasternak): 277

Robespierre, Maximilien François: 319, 321

Rodchenko, Aleksandr Mikhailovich (1891–1956): 113n.

Rolland, Romain (1866–1944): 148

Romanovka, Russia: 89

Romanticism: 72, 90, 104, 135, 137, 290, 343–45&n., 355–56

Romanticizing primitivism: 291

Romantics: 354

Rome, Italy: 72, 307, 308, 310; *see also* Italy

Romeo and Juliet (Shakespeare, translated by Pasternak): 173

Roncalli, Cardinal Angelo Giuseppe (Pope John XXIII, 1881–1963): 232

Rouge et le Noir, Le (Stendahl): 296

Rousseau, Jean-Jacques: 290

Rout, The (Fadeev): 110

Royal Swedish Academy: *see* Academy, Royal Swedish

Rozhdestvenskii, Robert Ivanovich (1932–): 209

Rozhdestvenskii, Vsevolod Aleksandrovich (1895–): 145

Rozhdestvenskii, Zinovii: 216

Rubinstein, Anton Grigorevich (1829–94): 21–22, 30, 97

Rubinstein, Sofiia Grigorevna: 21

Rudenko, Roman Andreevich (1907–): 246

Rudin (character in Turgenev's *Rudin*): 119

Ruge, Gerd (1928–): 218, 222

Rumiantsev Museum: 332

Russell, Bertrand (1872–1970): 236

Russia: 19, 21, 29, 30, 38, 41, 54, 96n., 97, 126, 165, 173, 181, 219, 220, 225, 246, 258, 259, 267, 300, 301, 318, 319, 334, 346; Pasternak introduces Rilke to, 79–80; Futurists' role in, 85; Change of Landmarks movement in, 106n.; depicted in *The Year 1905*, 111; translation in, 134ff.; Pasternak's depiction of history of, 141, 256, 262, 292, 298; political and social conditions in, 87, 107, 130, 178, 180, 182, 248, 282, 290; war losses of, 179; personified by Pasternak, 181; role of, in *Doctor Zhivago*, 51–52, 182, 290–94, 297, 298, 302, 308, 324; Pasternak's attitude toward, 236, 246, 293, 323

Russian Association of Proletarian Writers (RAPP): 117

Russian Contemporary: 109

Russian Futurists: *see* Futurists

Russian Orthodox church: 5, 9, 197, 269, 326, 331, 332n.; *see also* Orthodoxy

Russian Orthodox Patriarchal Church of the Transfiguration: 331

Russian Religious-Philosophical Academy (Berlin): 104

Russians, The (Smith): 282

Russkie novosti: 91

Rykov, Aleksei Ivanovich (1881–1938): 108

Rylenkov, Nikolai Ivanovich (1909–69): 280

Sachs, Hans: 135, 168

Saint-Gilles-sur-Vie, France: 150

Saint John: 332

Saint Paul: 334

Saint Petersburg, Russia: 21, 36–37, 44, 52, 81, 87, 128, 345; *see also* Petrograd; Leningrad

Saint Petersburg (Belyi): 51

Salieri, Antonio: 272

Samarin, Dmitrii: 56&n., 58, 67, 73

Samarin, Iurii: 73, 173–74

Samarin, Iurii Fëdorovich: 56n.

Samarin, Ivan Ivanovich: 56n.

Samdeviatov (character in *Doctor Zhivago*): 298

Samizdat: 278

Samovitoe slovo (Futurist concept): 353

Sanna, Giovanni (1877–): 215

Sarasate, Pablo de: 21

Saratov, Russia: 89

Sartre, Jean-Paul (1905–80): 305, 306, 314

Sashka (character in *A Tale*): 139

Satirical Verses (Vasilev): 216

Saturday Review: 224

Savitskii, Konstantin Apollonovich: 24

Savitskii, Pëtr Nikolaevich (1895–?): 117n.

Scandinavia: 225

Scarlatti, Alessandro: 21

Scheler, Max (1874–1928): 319

Schelling, Friedrich Wilhelm Joseph von: 353

Schewe, Heinz (1921–): 254, 266, 268, 272

Schiller, Johann Christoph Friedrich von: 135, 213, 221, 249

Schlegel, Friedrich von: 345n., 352

Schmidt, Lieut. Pëtr Petrovich: 41, 111, 142, 178, 276

Schnabel, Artur (1882–1951): 21

Schnitzler, Arthur (1862–1931): 105

Schönberg, Arnold (1874–1951): 33

School of Painting, Sculpture, and Architecture, Moscow: *see* Moscow School of Painting, Sculpture, and Architecture

Schopenhauer, Arthur: 33, 344, 350

Schweitzer, Albert (1875–1965): 265, 294, 336

Schweitzer, Renate: 222, 223, 225, 226, 249, 256, 264–66

Scientific socialism: 305

Scriabin, Aleksandr Nikolaevich (1872–1915): 22, 23, 30, 33–38, 44–45, 47–49&n., 55, 132, 133, 252–53, 297, 343, 355; Pasternak's early infatuation with, 32–37; and Pasternak's break with music, 44–48; role of, in Pasternak's development, 49&n., 252–53; influence of, on Pasternak, 132–33; Pasternak on, 343–44, 355
Sebastopol, Russia: 40
Secessionists: 24
Second All-Union Congress of Soviet Writers: *see* Congress of Soviet Writers, Second All-Union
Seghers, Anna (1900–): 149
Selected Works (Petöfi): 221
"Selected Works by Soviet Writers": 188
Selivanovskii, Aleksei Pavlovich (1900–37): 120, 142
Sellanraa, Isak of (character in *Growth of the Soil*): 293
Selvinskii, Ilia Lvovich (1899–1968): 186
"Semën Proskakov" (Aseev): 110
Semichastnyi, Vladimir Efimovich (1924–): 235–36, 249, 282
Semionov, Anatolii Sergeevich: 199
Serafimovich, Aleksandr (pseud. of Aleksandr Serafimovich Popov, 1863–1949): 175, 176
Serapion Brothers: 96
Serëzha (character in *A Tale*): 139, 333
Sergei Aleksandrovich (Romanov), Grand Duke: 5
Sermon on the Mount: 331
Serov, Valentin Aleksandrovich (1865–1911): 3, 8, 20, 26, 27, 29
Setun River, Peredelkino: 153, 250, 259
"Seven Days of the Week" (Kirsanov): 208
Severianin, Igor: *see* Igor-Severianin
Shakespeare, William: 69, 137, 142, 194, 205, 218, 221, 252, 264; volume of, given to Pasternak, 68; translated by Pasternak, 135–37; significance of, for Pasternak, 138; Hugo's views on, 167; *Hamlet* of, translated by Pasternak, 169–70; *Antony and Cleopatra* and *Julius Caesar* of, translated by Pasternak, 178
Shartash, Lake, Urals, USSR: 128&n., 130, 152; *see also* Urals
Shchapov, Marina (character in *Doctor Zhivago*): 303, 304
Shchapov, Markel (character in *Doctor Zhivago*): 303
Shcherbakov, Aleksandr Sergeevich (1901–45): 151
Shcherbatov, Prince Sergei Aleksandrovich (?–1962): 26
Shchukin, Sergei Ivanovich (1854–1936?): 28
Shelley, Percy Bysshe: 135, 277
Shestov, Lev (pseud. of Lev Isaakovich Shvartsman, 1866–1938): 26n., 87, 332
Shevchenko, Taras Grigorevich: 135, 182
Shigaliov (character in Dostoevsky's *The Possessed*): 204
"Shigaliovism": 204&n.
Shklovskii, Viktor Borisovich (1893–): 84, 102, 103n., 104–107, 117, 129, 166
Sholokhov, Mikhail Aleksandrovich (1905–): 209, 225, 238, 248

Shorter Soviet Encyclopedia: 137n.
Shostakovich, Dmitrii Dmitrievich (1906–75): 48, 193
Shpet, Gustav Gustavovich: 55, 82
Shultz, Carole: 281
Siberia: 110, 128n., 154, 160, 197, 221, 274, 299
Sidorov, Aleksei Alekseevich (1891–): 24
Sieburg, Friedrich (1893–1964): 226
Siege of Leningrad: 151
Siena, Italy: 72n.
Silver Dove, The (Belyi): 51
Simonov, Konstantin Mikhailovich (1915–79): 175, 178, 179, 184, 206, 208, 213, 216, 248
Simple as Mooing (Maiakovskii): 76, 84
Siniakov, Kseniia (Oksana): 83
Siniakov, Mariia: 83
Siniakov-Mamontov, Zinaida: 83, 85
Siniavskii, Andrei Donatovich (pseud. Abram Terts, 1925–): 220, 267, 278, 289
Sivtsev Vrazhek (Moscow): 90
Skalozub (character in *Woe from Wit*): 161
Skorbina, Nina: 134, 194, 196, 198, 199
Slater, Nicolas: 249
Slavinskii, V.: 328
Słonimski, Antoni (1895–1976): 241
Słowacki, Juliusz: 135, 238
Slutskii, Boris Abramovich (1919–): 236
"Small Town on the Kama, The" (Aseev): 167
Smirnov, Sergei Sergeevich (1915–76): 233, 236
Smith, Hedrick (1933–): 282
Snake Eater, The (Vazha-Pshavela): 138
Snow, Sir Charles (Percy) (1905–): 236
"Snowstorm" (Akhmadulina): 280
Sobolev, Leonid Sergeevich (1898–1971): 215, 233
Socialism: 101n., 130–31, 141, 148, 161, 209n., 232–33, 280, 297–99, 302–303, 305, 322, 333
Socialist realism: 132, 137n., 143, 149, 221, 298
Society of Itinerant Exhibitions: *see* Itinerants
Sofrino, USSR: 282
Sofronov, Anatolii Vladimirovich (1911–): 236
Sokolov, Boris Matveevich (1889–1930): 294
Soloukhin, Vladimir Alekseevich (1924–): 236
Solovëv (Soloviev), Vladimir Sergeevich: 26n., 329
Solzhenitsyn, Aleksandr Isaevich (1918–): 144, 221, 238, 239, 277, 280
Somov, Konstantin Andreevich (1869–1939): 24
Sonnets (Shakespeare, translated by Pasternak): 168
Sonnet 66 (Shakespeare): 194
Sonnet 73 (Shakespeare): 137
Sophocles: 336
Sorbonne (University of Paris): 151
Sorrento, Italy: 95
"Sound Repetitions" (Brik): 352
Sovetskii pisatel Publishing House: 190, 198
Soviet criminal code: 200, 201
Soviet era: 289, 293
Sovietism: 319

Soviet Union: 155, 158, 159, 165, 172, 182, 192, 209–11, 214–16, 221, 225, 231, 233, 237, 244, 249, 252, 264, 276, 278, 279, 281, 282

Soviet Writer Publishing House: *see* Sovetskii pisatel Publishing House

Spasskii, Sergei Dmitrievich (1898–1956): 194

Spektorskii, Sergei (protagonist of *Spektorskii*): 119–20

Spender, Stephen (1909–): 236, 346, 347

Spengler, Oswald (1880–1936): 307

Spets (military specialists): 300

Spinoza, Baruch: 65n.

Stahle, Anders Nils Oscar Kase (1901–): 234

Stalin, Iosif Vissarionovich (real name Dzhugashvili, 1879–1953): 108, 136n., 150, 192, 195, 199, 200n., 204, 209, 216, 240, 312; Pasternak's response to death of wife of, 129; Soviet writers convened by, 143; slogan of, for First Congress of the Union of Soviet Writers, 144; attitude of, toward Maiakovskii, 146; Pasternak ordered by, to attend International Congress of Writers for the Defense of Culture, 147; during the "Great Purge," 154–62; conversation of, with Pasternak about Mandelstam, 157–58; attitude of, toward *Hamlet*, 169; Pasternak's attitude toward, 200, 204, 308, 320; death of, and its effects, 204–205

Stalinism: 160, 178, 181, 204–205, 209, 239, 294, 302, 308–309

Stalin Prize for Literature: 204, 208

Stammler, Rudolf (1856–1938): 57

Starostin, Anatolii: 211, 215

State Bank (Gosbank): 249, 273

State Literature Publishing House: *see* Goslitizdat

State Publishing House of Artistic Literature (Moscow): 206, 208, 218

State Publishing House of Belles-Lettres (Goslitizdat): 138

Stendahl (pseud. of Henri Beyle): 296, 347

Stepun, Fëdor Avgustovich (1885–1965): 81, 104, 349, 350

Stockholm, Sweden: 220, 224–25, 227, 230–31, 235, 267, 285

Stolypin, Pëtr Arkadievich (1862–1911): 41

Stora, Judith: 331

Strachey, John (1901–63): 241, 282

Strangled Cry, The (Strachey): 241

Stravinsky, Igor Fëdorovich (1882–1971): 33

Streatham Hill (near London): 29

Strelnikov (character in *Doctor Zhivago*): 95, 124, 297, 305, 319–21

Stresemann, Chancellor Gustav (1878–1929): 26n.

Strindberg, Johan August: 75n.

Stroganov Art School, Moscow: 54

Struve, Gleb Petrovich (1898–): 347

Stybel, A.: 78, 91

Subjectivism: 311, 313, 345, 356

Sukhinichi, USSR: 207

Sunday Times (London): 241

Sunday Times Weekly Review (London): 273n.

Surikov, Vasilii Ivanovich: 8, 339

Surkov, Aleksei Aleksandrovich (1899–): 190; on Pasternak's poetry, 142, 144–45, 190, 276; ideological stance of, 206; role of, in efforts to prevent publication of *Doctor Zhivago*, 214–16; on award of Nobel Prize to Pasternak, 225, 228; Ivinskaia accused by, 273

Surrealists: 135, 143

Suslov, Mikhail Andreevich (1902–): 237

Sverdlovsk, USSR: 128

Sviatopolk-Mirskii, Prince Dmitrii Petrovich (D. S. Mirsky, 1890–1939): 51&n., 90, 95, 107, 117&n., 138, 142

Swain, The (Tsvetaeva): 98

Sweden: 224–25

Swedish Academy: *see* Academy, Royal Swedish

Switzerland: 36, 44

Symbolism, Russian: 15–16, 26n., 29n., 33, 37–38, 41, 51–52, 54n., 64, 75, 80–82, 87, 95, 105, 332, 334, 339–40, 350, 353

Symbolist "cosmologists": 37

Symbolists: 340, 350, 353

Symphonies in Prose (Belyi): 51

Symphony no. 8 (Shostakovich): 48

Symphony no. 5 (Beethoven): 21

Syncretism, religious: 307

System of Philosophy (Cohen): 62, 64

Tabidze, Nina Aleksandrovna: 177, 186&n.; Pasternak welcomed to Georgia by, 125–26; Pasternak's support of, 159, 205; on Pasternak's temporary admiration for Stalin, 161; as Pasternak's confidante, 171, 178, 182; as partial inspiration for Lara, 196; visited by Pasternak and his wife in Tbilisi, 246, 248; on Pasternak as poet in disgrace, 248; during Pasternak's final illness, 266

Tabidze, Nitochka: 248

Tabidze, Titian Justinovich (1895–1937): hospitality of, toward Pasternak, 125–26, 137–38; arrested, tortured, and executed, 154, 159; Pasternak's support of, 155; impact on Pasternak of fate of, 159, 161; "avenged" by *Doctor Zhivago*, 195; date of death of, 205; discussed in *Sketch for an Autobiography*, 252, 255; mourned by Pasternak in poem "Soul," 312

Tagore, Sir Rabindranath (1861–1941): 87, 249

Tale of Two Cities, A (Dickens): 296

Tambov, USSR: 184

Tamm, Igor Evgenevich (1895–1971): 232

Tarasenkov, Anatolii Kuzmich (1909–56): 192, 202

Tarasova, Alla Konstantinovna (1898–): 213

Tarusa, USSR: 244

Tass: 237

Tatar Region, USSR: 171

Tatlin, Vladimir Evgrafovich (1885–1953): 100

Tbilisi, Georgia, USSR: 125, 135, 138, 182, 184, 186n., 246, 248; *see also* Georgia
Tchaikovsky, Pëtr Ilich: 23, 26n., 47
Teachers' Center, Chistopol: 167
Tedesco, Ignaz: 21
Teilhard de Chardin, Pierre (1881–1955): 250, 311, 336
Tendriakov, Vladimir Fëdorovich (1923–): 209
Terras, Victor (1921–): 344, 355
Tertz, Abram: *see* Siniavskii, Andrei
Thaw, The (Ehrenburg): 205, 208, 269, 277
"Thaw, The" (literary-political phenomenon of the mid-1950s): 205–209
Théorie de l'art moderne (Klee): 341
Thibon, Gustave (1903–): 324
Third Antinomy of *Critique of Pure Reason* (Kant): 317
Third Congress of Soviet Writers: *see* Congress of Soviet Writers, Third
Tikhonov, Nikolai Semënovich (1896–): 96, 117, 138, 148, 149
Time: 187, 290
Times (London): 224, 246, 272, 274
Tiutchev, Fëdor Ivanovich (1803–73): 75, 153
Tiverzin (character in *Doctor Zhivago*): 297
Tobik (Pasternak's dog): 188
Togliatti, Palmiro (1893–1964): 211
Toller, Ernst (1893–1939): 143, 149
Tolstoy, Count Aleksei Nikolaevich (1883–1945): 96, 104, 106–108&n., 109, 148, 162, 203
Tolstoy, Countess Tatiana Lvovna (later Mme Sukhotin, 1864–1950): 11, 21–22, 53
Tolstoy, Count Lev Nikolaevich (1828–1910): 14, 30, 54, 56, 81n., 139n., 279, 307, 347, 354; Leonid Pasternak's introduction to, 3; and interaction of Pasternak and Tolstoy families, 4; religious influence of, on Pasternaks, 9, 326, 329; Pasternak's first sight of, 10; Leonid Pasternak's illustration of *Resurrection* by, 11, 24; visited by Rilke, 12; musical evenings at the Pasternaks' attended by, 22; portraits of, by Leonid Pasternak, 26n., 27; Leonid Pasternak's friendship with, 30&n.; death of, 53, 253; prose of, and affinities of Pasternak's, 94, 95, 141, 178, 180, 226, 252, 253, 296, 304, 319–22, 346, 355; influence of, on Pasternak's character, 252, 265, 297; philosophy of, 297, 329; philosophy of history of, 320–22
Tolstoyan philosophy and principles: *see* Tolstoy, Lev Nikolaevich
Tolstoy Museum, Paris: 212
Tonia (character in *Doctor Zhivago*): *see* Zhivago, Antonina
Tornskjold, Anna Arild (character in *A Tale*): 75, 139
Transcendental Analytic of *Critique of Pure Reason*: 350
Transcendental Esthetic of *Critique of Pure Reason*: 350
Tregub, Semën Adolfovich (1907–): 175, 176
Trenev, Konstantin Andreevich (1876–1945): 171

Trenev, Mme (widow of Konstantin Andreevich Trenev): 186
Tretiakov, Pavel Mikhailovich: 20
Triolet, Elsa (1896–1970): 104
Trotsky, Lev Davidovich (1879–1940): 108–109, 199, 322
Truba, Moscow: 3
Trubetskoi, Prince Nikolai Sergeevich: 73, 117n.
Trubetskoi, Prince Pavel (Paolo) Petrovich (1867–1938): 5
Trubetskoi, Prince Sergei Nikolaevich: 55, 213
Tsetlin, Mikhail Osipovich (pseud., A. Amari, 1882–1945): 96, 362
Tsvetaeva, Anastasiia Ivanovna (1894–): 98n.
Tsvetaeva, Marina Ivanovna (1892–1941): 19&n., 41, 91, 92, 96–99, 98n., 111–12, 119, 150, 170–72, 174, 184, 195, 209, 216, 218, 253, 255–56, 276, 289; on true greatness, 18–19; life of, in exile, 41, 100, 104, 106; German roots of, in common with Pasternak's, 71–72; Pasternak on, 83, 97–98, 253, 255; on Pasternak, 88–90, 105, 111–12, 126, 150, 172, 289; Pasternak's poetry dedicated or devoted to, 98, 174; in Paris, 150; suicide of, 170–72; posthumous recognition of, 172, 209, 216, 255–56, 312; "avenged" by *Doctor Zhivago*, 195
Tukhachevskii, Mikhail Nikolaevich (1893–1937): 145, 155, 158, 162
Tuntseva, Sima (character in *Doctor Zhivago*): 297, 306, 327, 331
Turgenev, Ivan Sergeevich (1818–83): 119, 342, 344–46
Tvardovskii, Aleksandr Trifonovich (1910–71): 179, 206, 215, 275
Tverskie-Yamskie streets, Moscow: 3
Twelve, The (Blok): 52, 95
Twenty-second Congress of the Communist Party of the Soviet Union: *see* Congress of the Communist Party of the Soviet Union, Twenty-second
Twenty-Six, The (Aseev): 110
Twórczość: 223
"Twosome" (Tsvetaeva): 98

Ukraine, USSR: 127–28
UNESCO: 241
Union of Georgian Writers: *see* Georgian Writers, Union of
Union of Writers: *see* Writers' Union
Unità: 216
United Nations: 225
United States: 208, 224–25, 241, 246, 276
Universalism: 330
University of Marburg: 56–59, 62–65, 68–69, 253, 255; *see also* Marburg
University of Michigan Press: 242
University of Moscow: 38, 42, 54n., 55–57, 72–73, 82, 154n., 169, 291

"Untimely Thoughts" (Gorky): 95

Urals, USSR: Pasternak's first stays in, 76, 77, 82, 87; depiction of, in "Without Love," 93–94; Pasternak's visit to, 1932, 128; Pasternak's stay in, during World War II, 135, 165, 168; depicted in *A Tale*, 139–40; depicted in *Doctor Zhivago*, 197, 293, 302

Urbanism: 291

Ushakov, Nikolai Nikolaevich (1899–1973): 117

USSR: *see* Soviet Union

Utilitarianism: 96

Uzkoe, USSR: 213–14, 266

Uzkoe Resthouse: 214

Vagabondages: 162

Vagabonds (Hamsun): 291

Valéry, Paul (1871–1945): 320, 353

Vannovskii, Pëtr Semënovich: 14&n.

Varykino, Urals, USSR: 168, 291, 355

Vasilev, Sergei Aleksandrovich (1911–): 216

"Vasilii Tërkin" (Tvardovskii): 179

Vavilovs (Pasternak's landlords in Chistopol): 167

Vazha-Pshavela (pseud. of Luka Pavlovich Razikashvili, 1861–1915): 138

V boiakh za Orel (*In the Fighting for Orel*): 175–76

Vedeniapin, Nikolai Nikolaevich (character in *Doctor Zhivago*): 37, 297, 306, 327

Venice, Italy: 72

Vereshchagin, Vasilii Vasilevich (1842–1904): 3

Verhaeren, Émile: 26n.

Verlaine, Paul: 135, 168n., 339, 342, 343, 355

Vernadskii, George (1887–1973): 117n.

Versts (Tsvetaeva): 98

Viazemskii, Prince Pëtr Andreevich: 72

Victoria (Hamsun): 291

Vienna, Austria: 21

Viliam-Vilmont, Irina Nikolaevna: 100

Viliam-Vilmont, Nikolai Nikolaevich (1901–): 101, 169, 266, 276

Villalonga, José-Luis de (1920–): 246

Villalonga, Priscilla de: 246

Vincent, Sir Edgar (Baron d'Abernon of Esher, 1857–1941): 20

Vinogradov, Aleksandr Petrovich: 186

Vinogradov, Dmitrii Aleksandrovich (1942–): 186

Vitalism: 287, 289, 291, 314

Vitebsk Art School: 100

Vladimir Ilich Lenin (Maiakovskii): 108

Vladimir Maiakovskii (Maiakovskii): 85

Vogt (Fokht), Boris Aleksandrovich (1875–1946): 57

"Voice of the Image, The" (Plank): 352

Volga River: 128, 223

Volkhonka Street, Moscow: 54–55, 91, 125, 128, 153

Volkonskii, Andrei Mikhailovich (1933–): 267

Volksgeist: 324

Volksgesinnung: 319

Volodarskii Street, Chistopol: 167

Voloshin, Maksimilian Aleksandrovich (1877–1932): 96

Voltaire: 137

Vorbild: 319

Voskresensk, Russia: 33n.

Vossler, Karl: 352

Voznesenskii, Andrei (1933–): 279, 280

Vrubel, Mikhail Aleksandrovich (1856–1910): 3, 8–10, 54, 297

Vsevobuch: *see* Civil Defense Unit

Vstrechi s Pasternakom (*Meetings with Pasternak*, Gladkov): 272, 279, 281

Vysotskaia-Feldzer, Ida Davidovna (*née* Vysotskaia, later Mme Feldzer): 37, 55n., 75, 133, 329; relationship of, to Pasternak, 65–68; and rejection of Pasternak's marriage proposal, 68–70; marriage of, 70; visited by Pasternak in Berlin, 105; visited by Pasternak in Paris, 150–51

Vysotskii, David Vasilevich: 65–66, 75

Wagner, Richard: 33, 41, 47, 81, 344

"Wagnerians" (poets): 146

War and Peace (Tolstoy): 3, 224, 296, 304, 307, 320, 321

War and the Universe (Maiakovskii): 122

Warsaw, Poland: 40, 241; *see also* Poland

We (Zamiatin): 109, 221

"We Buried the Old Man . . ." (Kornilov): 280

Weigel, Helene (1900–71): 208

Wells, H. G. (1866–1946): 109

Weltschmerz (Lenau): 355

West Germany: 223, 272; *see also* Germany

What Is Art? (Tolstoy): 354

White Guard, The (Bulgakov): 109

White Sea Canal (Gorky): 144

Wiersma, Enno Dirk (1858–1940): 71

Wilde, Oscar: 75n.

Wilson, Edmund (1895–1972): 224, 332

"Winter Day" (Akhmadulina): 279

Witness (Chambers): 242

Woe from Wit (Griboedov): 161n.

Wolff, Christian von: 57

Wolff, Kurt (1887–1963): 229, 230, 241

Woolf, Virginia (1882–1941): 250

World's Fair, Brussels: 226

Wordsworth, William: 354

World War I: 255, 299, 304

World War II: 168, 206, 252, 262, 308, 355

Writers' Club, Vorovskii Street, Moscow: 158, 166, 169, 173

Writers' Union: 148, 167, 171, 206, 209, 221, 228, 244, 246, 248, 249, 276, 315; Pasternak's relation with, 129, 158–60, 184, 231, 233; First Congress of (1934), 143–47; Pasternak at the Third Plenary Session of the Board of, 151–53; during the Zhdanov era, 184, 190; relation of, to

Doctor Zhivago, 211, 214–15, 231; Pasternak expelled from, 233, 267; reaction of, to Pasternak's Nobel Prize, 235–38; relation of, to Pasternak's funeral, 269, 271, 272

Y3 (*Igrek 3*, character in *A Tale*): 139
Young Guard, The (*Molodaia guardiia*, Fadeev): 111n., 209
Yugoslavia: 278

Zabolotskii, Nikolai Alekseevich (1903–58): 154, 209, 221
Zadonsk, USSR: 158
Zaitsev, Boris Konstantinovich (1881–1972): 103n., 105
Zamiatin, Evgenii Ivanovich (1884–1937): 109, 221
Zamoyska, Countess Hélène: *see* Peltier-Zamoyska, Hélène
Zander, Leon Alexander (1893–): 328
Zarathustra (in Nietzsche's *Thus Spoke Zarathustra*): 68
Zaslavskii, David Iosifovich (1880–1965): 232
Zbarskii, Boris Ilich: 78&n.
Zeit, Die (German newspaper): 222
Zelinskii, Kornelii Liutsianovich (1896–1970): 117, 129–31, 161, 213, 214, 223, 236
Zeller, Eduard: 57
Zhdanov, Andrei Aleksandrovich (1896–1948): 144, 184, 188–90, 193, 195, 203
Zhdanov era (*zhdanovshchina*): 184
Zhivago, Antonina (Tonia) Aleksandrovna (née Gromeko, character in *Doctor Zhivago*): 67, 139, 140, 196

Zhivago, Evgraf (character in *Doctor Zhivago*): 160, 179
Zhivago, Iurii Andreevich (character in *Doctor Zhivago*): 52, 174, 196–97, 280, 298–308, 318; attitude of, toward Nicholas II, 17; attitude of, toward 1905 revolution, 52; attitude of, toward sex, 67; idea of immortality of, 81; prototypes of, 93, 196; antithesis of, 124; benefactor of, 160; artistic refuge of, 168; poems of, 182, 196, 206, 211, 324, 334; as spokesman for Pasternak's viewpoint, 232; funeral of, 271; "vitalism" of, 289–94; as spokesman for the intelligentsia, 298–308; personalism of, 314–17; sense of man in history of, 321–25; religion of, 327, 331, 332, 334, 336; aesthetic attitudes of, 352, 355, 356
Zhivago, Mariia (character in *Doctor Zhivago*): 332
Zhivago, Tania (character in *Doctor Zhivago*): 303, 304
Zhivult (character in "The Diary of Zhivult"): 139–40
Zhizdra, USSR: 176
Zhukovskii, Vasilii Andreevich: 72, 134–36, 170
Zinoviev, Grigorii Evseevich (1883–1936): 108, 160n.
Zionism: 331
Znamia (*Banner*): 138, 174, 178, 183, 202, 205–206, 208, 211, 214, 278
Zoo; or Letters Not About Love (Shklovskii): 102, 105
Zoshchenko, Mikhail Mikhailovich (1895–1958): 96, 108n., 184, 215, 221
Zossima, Starets (character in *The Brothers Karamazov*): 335
Zvezda (*Star*): 135, 184, 190